FREE SPEECH,

"THE PEOPLE'S DARLING PRIVILEGE"

Constitutional Conflicts

A Series with the Institute of

Bill of Rights Law at the

College of William and Mary

Davison M. Douglas, Director

Neal Devins, Series Editor

FREE SPEECH,

"THE PEOPLE'S DARLING PRIVILEGE"

Struggles for Freedom of

Expression in American History

Michael Kent Curtis

DUKE UNIVERSITY PRESS   *Durham and London 2000*

© 2000 Michael Kent Curtis
All rights reserved
Printed in the United States of America on acid-free paper ∞
Typeset in Minion by Wilsted & Taylor Publishing Services
Library of Congress Cataloging-in-Publication Data appear
on the last printed page of this book.

*This book is dedicated to the
teachers, mentors, and colleagues whose
wisdom, friendship, support, and encouragement
have enriched my life, and especially to my parents,
Kent Adams Curtis (1917–1994) and
Thomas Lisle Curtis (1905–1974).*

CONTENTS

CONTENTS

ACKNOWLEDGMENTS

Many people have helped me to improve this book. If I had had the wisdom to follow all their suggestions, the final product would have been better. Still, it is far better than it would have been without the help and suggestions of many readers. Readers of the entire manuscript made many suggestions that substantially improved the final product. They include Richard Aynes, David Rabban, David Shores, William VanAlstyne, and Ronald Wright. Akhil Amar, Paul Escott, Daniel Farber, Paul Finkelman, Miles Foy, Jonathan Harkavy, Stephen Heyman, John Jeffries Jr., Michael Klarman, David Logan, William Mayton, Alan Palmiter, Robert Post, Robert Reinstein, Charles Rose, Suzanna Sherry, Avaim Soifer, David Underdown, Eugene Volokh, and James G. Wilson read selected chapters or earlier articles I wrote on the subject and made many valuable suggestions. My brother, Tom A. Curtis, a gifted writer and editor, read (and reread) and edited the entire book and improved its style. Research assistants have helped me with this project for many years. They include Paul Goodson, Jeffrey Scott Tracy, Owen Lewis, R. Bruce Thompson, Edwin G. Wilson, Kelly Patterson, Steven McCallister, Andrew Sheffer, Ryan Shuriman, Abby Wood, Andrew Hlasbe, Caroline Knox, Maryann Carlson, Edward Timberlake, Sung Choi, Christopher Jennings, William Ray, Jason Newman, and Robert Wearing. Without their help and the help of librarians John Perkins, Martha Thomas, Miriam Murphy, Haiben Hu, Maureen Eggert, and Thomas Steele, and clerical assistance from Peggy Brookshire, Anne Church, Carolyn Marshburn, Mickie Speas, and Beverly Marshall, this book would not have been possible.

I also owe a huge debt to those scholars whose work is cited in the notes and an apology to those whose works have been ignored because of my ignorance.

Special thanks also go to Valerie Millholland of Duke University Press for her guidance and encouragement.

The *Chicago Kent, Northwestern University, University of California–Los Angeles, William and Mary Bill of Rights, George Washington*, and *Constitutional Commentary Law Reviews* published earlier versions of some of the ideas set out here. I am grateful for the assistance they provided for this project. The earlier articles are "The Curious History of Attempts to Suppress Antislavery Speech, Press, and Petition in 1835–37," 89 *Nw. U. L. Rev.* 785 (1995); "The 1837 Killing of Elijah Lovejoy by an Anti-Abolition Mob: Free Speech, Mobs, and the Privileges of American Citizens," 44 *U.C.L.A. L. Rev.* 1109 (1997); "The 1859 Crisis over Hinton Helper's Book, *The Impending Crisis*: Free Speech, Slavery, and Some Light on the Meaning of the First Section of the Fourteenth Amendment," 68 *Chi.-Kent L. Rev.* 1113 (1993), a version of which also appeared in *Slavery and the Law* (Paul Finkelman ed., 1997); "Lincoln, Vallandigham, and Anti-War Speech During the Civil War," 7 *Wm. & Mary Bill of Rts. J.* 105 (1998); "The Critics of Free Speech and the Uses of the Past," 12 *Const. Comm.* 29 (1995); and "Two Textual Adventures, Thoughts on Reading Jeffrey Rosen's Paper," 66 *Geo. Wash. L. Rev.* 1269 (1998).

Last but by no means least, The Wake Forest School of Law and Deans Robert Walsh, Miles Foy and Ralph Peeples, provided invaluable assistance.

FREE SPEECH,

"THE PEOPLE'S DARLING PRIVILEGE"

In 1857 North Carolinian Hinton Helper published a searing indictment of slavery entitled *The Impending Crisis of the South: How to Meet It*. In his book, Helper insisted that slavery blighted the South, produced its economic backwardness, and undermined the freedom and economic security of nonslaveholding whites. His solution was political action in the Southern states to emancipate the slaves. According to Helper's plan, slave owners—the "lords of the lash" in Helper's rhetoric—would not be compensated for loss of their slaves. Instead they would be taxed to pay the costs for those former slaves who chose to leave for African colonies or to settle in the United States.[1]

In a state where almost three-fourths of the whites did not own slaves, widespread circulation of Helper's book and the political action it advocated might have posed a serious political threat to the slaveholding elite. It might have, but it did not. For years, violence and repressive laws had silenced antislavery speech. Helper's book became a bestseller in the North. But in his native North Carolina it was hazardous to circulate the book.

Helper advocated peaceful democratic action. "Give us fair-play," Helper implored, "secure to us the right of discussion, the freedom of speech, and we will settle the difficulty at the ballot box, not on the battleground—by force of reason, not force of arms."[2] But if slaveholders and their "cringing lickspittles" opposed democratic action with force, Helper recommended fighting back and recruiting the slaves. "In nine cases out of ten," he said, they "would be delighted to cut their masters throats."[3]

Leaders of the newly formed Republican Party were delighted with Helper's book. Here was a Southerner and a white man who dramatically pointed out the evils of the institution of slavery the Republican

Party had been founded to contain. Enthusiastic Republican politicians underwrote a plan to publish an abridgment of Helper's book as a Republican campaign document.[4]

Back in North Carolina, a few hardy souls sold and circulated Helper's book. One of these was the antislavery minister Daniel Worth. Worth preached against slavery in Guilford and Randolph Counties, sold copies of Helper's book and the Republican *New York Tribune*, and worked to convert people to the antislavery cause. The state prosecuted Worth under a statute that made it a crime to disseminate items that tended to cause free Negroes or slaves to be discontent with their lot. The fear was that this discontent, in turn, might lead to slave revolts. In 1859, North Carolina juries convicted the minister for distributing Helper's antislavery book to white citizens, and in 1860 the North Carolina supreme court upheld the conviction.[5]

The North Carolina supreme court did not mention the First Amendment (or even state constitutional protections for freedom of the press). But, if pressed, the judges probably would have explained that the First Amendment was beside the point because the Bill of Rights limited only the federal government, as the United States Supreme Court had said in 1833 in the case of *Barron v. Baltimore*.[6] Criticism of slavery was not protected speech or press under the state constitution, the judges might have continued, because criticism of slavery could have the "bad tendency" to foment discontent among free blacks and slaves, and this discontent could lead, in turn, to slave revolts. The judges might well have gone farther and explained that freedom of the press only kept government from requiring its prior approval before a book or newspaper was published (prior restraint) and did not block punishment after publication. At any rate, and for whatever reason, in the trial and later appeal of the antislavery minister, the North Carolina court did not address the issue of whether the state statute violated the right to freedom of the press.

The struggle over Helper's book highlights recurrent free speech issues. Would free speech be a national right of all Americans or would it be a matter left to state and local governments? Could fear that speech —even political speech advocating peaceful change—had a "bad tendency" to cause serious harm justify suppressing it? What, after all, was the meaning of the right to free speech, free press, and freedom of religion? Modern free speech doctrine has repudiated legal theories like those used to punish distributors of Helper's book. But the Supreme

Court came to its current protective view of free speech only very gradually and only in the twentieth century.

This book is not a survey of free speech history—obscenity cases, libel cases, labor cases, and the rest. Instead, it is the story of a few struggles for free speech in American history. The struggles recounted here occurred in major American political battles that erupted from 1798 to 1866: the struggle between Federalists and Jeffersonian Republicans over the 1798 Sedition Act, the fight over slavery and the attempts to suppress antislavery speech, and the attempts to suppress antiwar speech during the Civil War. These were the most significant national free speech controversies between 1791 and 1868. The dates mark the ratification of the first Bill of Rights (which limited only the national government) and the ratification of the Fourteenth Amendment, which eventually provided a "second" Bill of Rights—a truly national one that limited the states.[7] (Free speech ideas in the twentieth century are reviewed in chapter 17.)

These free speech struggles were not only about free speech. Fundamentally they were also struggles for democratic government. In these struggles, Americans had widely divergent ideas about the meaning of freedom of speech and about how literally to take the creed that in the United States "we the people" rule.

The struggle for representative government had roots in England, and the English history of free speech and press was one factor that shaped American free speech debates. In seventeenth- and eighteenth-century England, there were strikingly different approaches to freedom of discussion—to free speech, free press, and freedom to express religious beliefs. (For the sake of brevity I will often refer to these freedoms collectively as freedom of speech.) The orthodox legal view developed in the king's courts and in a parliament composed of an oligarchic House of Commons and a hereditary House of Lords. It emphasized broad government power to suppress criticism of those in power and to suppress expression of unorthodox ideas. The opposing view was espoused by those who sought a more representative parliament and greater freedom of religion. These dissenters sought to limit government power over speech and to provide greater protection for freedom of discussion.

By the time of the American Revolution, there were two American approaches to free speech—an orthodox legal view and a more popular free speech tradition. There was a chasm between the orthodox understanding of the right many judges would apply and the popular right many citizens exercised and thought they had. But the popular view of free speech had real-world effects—in elections, in legislatures, for at least some judges, and in actions by government officials. Between the ratification of the Bill of Rights in 1791 and ratification of the Fourteenth Amendment in 1868, American citizens—activists, newspaper editors, ministers, lawyers, and politicians—developed and expanded a protective, popular free speech tradition. Their ideas, struggles, and their legacy are the subject of this book. The free speech tradition was popular in two senses: it grew up outside the courts (and often contradicted judicial doctrine), and it had significant popular appeal.

Free Speech Battles from the Bill of Rights Through the Civil War: A Preview

The framers and ratifiers who supported the federal Constitution proposed in 1787 (without the Bill of Rights) generally said that the Constitution gave Congress no power over speech and press.[8] The First Amendment seemed to make things doubly secure. This "no federal power" consensus was soon challenged by the Federalists, who passed the Sedition Act of 1798.

The Sedition Act made it criminal to make false and malicious criticisms of the government, the Federalist president, or Congress—but not of the Republican vice president, the president's likely opponent in the next election. (At that time, before the Twelfth Amendment, the person who got the second highest vote total in the electoral college became the vice president.) The act had a sunset provision: it would expire with the end of the term of the Federalist president. As the Federalists who passed the Sedition Act made clear, the act punished assertion of false political ideas, arguments, and conclusions, as well as false facts. Jeffersonian Republicans made two attacks on the act. First, they insisted that the federal government had no power to pass it—it was simply without a delegated power over speech or press. Many Republicans appealed to states' rights. But this was often a states' rights appeal of a special sort: states' rights to protect the right of free speech from national legislation. Second, they contended that the act violated freedom of speech and press protected from federal action by the First Amendment.

In 1798 freedom of the press was already the people's "darling privilege," as Federalist congressman Harrison Gray Otis of Massachusetts put it during the Sedition Act debate. Otis said Jeffersonian Republicans were misleading the people into believing that their "darling privilege" was threatened by the act. He insisted that this was not so. Freedom of the press meant only what William Blackstone's treatise on English law said it meant: one could publish a newspaper without first getting a license to do so from a government censor. But the government could punish those whose publications had a tendency to cause harm. By such an understanding there was less to free press than met the popular eye.[9] Otis quoted a host of legal authorities to show that protection for freedom of speech was far less sweeping than people might think. Implicit in Otis's words is the suggestion that Jeffersonian Republicans were appealing to a broader, popular misunderstanding of free speech.

The Sedition Act debate and later free speech struggles implicate three issues that run through the story of free speech in the United States: (1) Does the federal government have any power to punish speech? (2) What sort of speech will be protected under freedom of speech? and (3) Are state governments, as well as the federal government, prohibited from suppressing the freedom of speech and press referred to in the First Amendment?

The Sedition Act passed both houses of Congress, was signed by President Adams, and was upheld by Justices of the United States Supreme Court sitting as trial judges. But it produced substantial public opposition and was repudiated in the election of 1800. Thomas Jefferson, whose party had been the target of the act, was elected president, the act expired, and Jefferson pardoned those convicted under it.[10] From 1800 to 1860, most politicians treated the act as unconstitutional: it had been repudiated in the court of public opinion. The national government had little or no power over speech or press.

But that view of national power did not settle the matter of the scope of the "darling privilege." Instead, it raised the question of state power. After the Sedition Act, a major battle over the scope of free speech erupted over antislavery speech and the demand of the Southern elite that criticism of slavery be suppressed. Northern states refused to pass laws to silence abolitionists. Many in the North argued that such laws would violate free speech. Meanwhile, Southern states increasingly made criticisms of slavery a crime. That was the case, for example, for Hinton Helper's antislavery book, *The Impending Crisis of the South: How to Meet It.*

In the North, the federalism-based theory, by which the national government lacked power to suppress speech, protected antislavery speech.

Power to suppress—if any existed—had to be exercised by the states, and Northern states refused to suppress antislavery speech. In the South, that same federalism undermined free speech because it made freedom of speech or suppression a matter of local option. The South chose suppression.[11]

Finally, there was a major battle over the meaning of free speech during the Civil War. Then the earlier pre– and post–Sedition Act consensus—that the federal government (or the Congress) lacked power over speech confronted the Constitution's war power—and the "no federal power" over speech claim went up in smoke. A general, acting under a Republican administration that had been elected as the party of free speech, arrested a prominent Democratic politician for making an antiwar speech and tried and convicted him before a military commission.[12] But military arrests of antiwar speakers provoked massive public protests that such arrests violated free speech. The public uproar caused the Lincoln administration to moderate its course.

There is a common theme in the outcome of each story. The public reaction to the Sedition Act ensured that it would not be reenacted. In the Northern states, serious legal incursions on abolitionist speech, press, or petition were checked, not by courts, but by citizens urging a broadly protective understanding of free speech. The uproar over suppression of free speech during the Civil War also limited repression. In each case, attempts to keep criticism of the Federalists, of slavery, and of the war out of the public domain produced a strong public protest. Whether the popular tradition had more public support at any given time and place than the tradition of repression is open to question, but it is one beyond our power to answer with certainty. It is clear that it often had substantial support. Of course, free speech suffered defeats as well. Still, in response to the Sedition Act, the attack on antislavery speech, and the assault on antiwar speech during the Civil War, people espoused ideas that have since become central parts of free speech legal doctrine.

Response to attacks on antislavery speech played a prominent role in the movement to a national view of free speech. These struggles for free speech helped shape the Fourteenth Amendment, our "second Bill of Rights." Today, the Fourteenth Amendment is the legal mechanism by which the states are required to respect freedoms of speech, press, religion, and assembly articulated in the First Amendment. (The Fourteenth Amendment provides that persons born in the nation are citizens of the United States and that "no state shall . . . abridge the privileges or immunities of citizens of the United States; nor shall any state deprive any person of life, liberty, or property without due process of law.") Since the states have frequently suppressed free speech, the Fourteenth Amendment is a crucial contemporary protector of free speech.

HISTORY AND FREE SPEECH LAW

Understanding these free speech struggles, and the popular free speech tradition they illuminate, is important today for citizens, lawyers, and judges. Because free speech disputes from 1791 to 1868 are a crucial part of the background of the Fourteenth Amendment, they are significant for those who adhere to the view that the Constitution should be interpreted in accordance with the original intent of its framers or ratifiers. Similarly, they are important for those who think a constitutional provision should be understood based on the original meaning of the words in the constitutional text (such as "privileges or immunities of citizens of the United States"), and also for those who believe that history is simply one factor to be consulted in the search for constitutional meaning.

One method of legal analysis is to use a clear or paradigm case as a way to understand other problematic cases. Most Republicans concluded that the effort to suppress advocacy of peaceful abolition of slavery violated the central meaning of free speech, and today most of us would agree with them. So free speech struggles over slavery help us to evaluate other suppression theories. Finally, these free speech struggles are relevant because history provides vicarious experience, and experience is necessary for wise judgment.

The popular free speech tradition is also significant as a precursor of key modern free speech ideas. These ideas stand in vivid contrast to the theories that justified suppression of antislavery speech, theories used in the controversy over slavery and that survived the demise of slavery.

FREE SPEECH IDEAS TODAY

Since the 1930s, courts usually have protected speech about public affairs from government suppression.[13] Current free speech doctrine embraces the idea of a public domain where government typically may not suppress discussion on matters of public concern because of the ideas advanced. The public domain is bounded by the line that separates protected from forbidden expression and by another line that describes those places or situations in which speech receives its highest protection.[14]

Those who have benefited from the Court's tough rules to protect speech in the public domain have included students protesting segregation in South Carolina,[15] critics of the actions of Alabama officials during the struggle for integration,[16] a Klansman who said blacks should go back to Africa and Jews should return to Israel and who suggested violence might be necessary at some point,[17] school children who refused to salute the flag,[18] a state legislator who endorsed the claim that the war in Vietnam was genocide and who expressed sympathy for those who refused to serve,[19] a young man who burned the American flag as a protest,[20] and another who wore the slogan "Fuck the Draft" on his jacket.[21] Within broad limits, free speech doctrine denies the government the power to say which ideas are orthodox and acceptable and which ideas are beyond the pale. The rules apply generally to a wide range of points of view. A case protecting the rights of African Americans to protest segregation cited a case protecting a man who gave a racist speech.[22] Some critics charge that the Court has taken its broad and general rule against suppressing ideas on public affairs too far. But when freedom of speech is attacked, many think of the courts as the first line of defense.

The Courts as Protectors of Free Speech

Our contemporary emphasis on the role of the courts as protectors of free speech is altogether proper. One of the main objects of the Bill of Rights was to empower the courts to check abuses of liberty. When he introduced the Bill of Rights in the first Congress, James Madison optimistically suggested that "independent tribunals of justice will consider themselves in peculiar manner the guardians of those rights; they will be an impenetrable bulwark against every assumption of power in the legislative or executive; they will be naturally led to resist every encroachment upon rights expressly stipulated for in the Constitution."[23] For much of American history things often did not work out that way. From the Sedition Act through the Civil War and continuing through the first quarter of the twentieth century, courts were too often hostile to dissenting speech when it was under attack. Often when free speech battles were fought and won in the political arena, courts were simply not involved.

We tend to forget how recent robust national judicial protection is. Today, most Americans associate our free speech "rights," "liberties," "immunities," or "privileges" (as they were commonly called in the eighteenth and nineteenth centuries) with the First Amendment to the Constitution. (Such rights are typically protected by state constitutions as well.) Americans generally believe that they have a federal constitutional right to free speech and freedom of religion that belongs to them wherever they go in the United States. They understand free speech to be a national right and one that is enforceable in the courts. Many think—too simply, as most lawyers see it—that the government lacks power to deny free speech.

While Americans may disagree about the precise boundaries and content of free speech and free press, the freedom to discuss and advocate political, economic, scientific, and religious ideas is central to our idea of free speech. So is the right to criticize the conduct of government officials and private citizens who wield extraordinary power. Many would insist that there are limits even to these ideas of free speech. But some proposed limits would be flatly rejected by most Americans. For example, few would accept the notion that one is free to speak or write on political topics without prior permission from government but that the government could broadly punish such speech after it was expressed. Many would be skeptical of the claim that speech that expressed bad ideas about politics or religion should be suppressed because in the long run it would have a tendency to lead to unfortunate consequences. Probably most Americans would flatly reject the idea that while the federal government lacks power to abridge freedom of speech or of the press, state governments should be able to punish any political or religious speech if their constitutions and laws permitted. Today, the courts typically protect free speech in all these situations. But it was not always so.

Strong judicial protection of speech is a worthy tradition. It is also a comparatively recent one. For much of American history, as the case of the North Carolina antislavery minister Daniel Worth shows, many judges have been less protective of free speech. Indeed, there is an older judicial doctrine that was far more receptive to suppressing free speech. The older doctrine is a stark contrast to our modern ideas of free speech.

THE OLD VIEW FROM THE BENCH AND ELSEWHERE:
A CRABBED AND STUNTED FREE SPEECH

In 1833 in *Barron v. Baltimore*, the Supreme Court ruled that the guarantees of the federal Bill of Rights limited only the national government, not state or local governments.[24] (As a matter of original understanding, the decision probably was correct.) The *Barron* decision protected statutes that Southern states used against antislavery speech from Supreme Court review.

Most Southerners did not own slaves, and some opposed slavery. The restriction of antislavery speech by Southern statutes tended to keep slavery off the political agenda in those states. Legal and extralegal suppression of antislavery speech protected an entrenched economic elite from the democratic process and silenced those who wanted to speak against the horrors of slavery and for the humanity of the slave.

In 1856, the newly created Republican Party made a strong run for the presidency. The party had been founded to oppose the spread of slavery to the national territories, and many Republicans hoped local political opposition would end slavery in the states where it existed. But in 1856 and 1860 Southern laws and mobs kept supporters of Republican presidential candidates from campaigning in Southern states. Unhappily, the Southern approach to free speech was not unique.

The Bad Tendency Doctrine

From the Sedition Act through the Civil War, a number of scholars, judges, politicians, and legislators thought speech that had a tendency to produce harmful results was not protected speech. The "bad tendency" rationale, inherited from England, was a major theory justifying suppression. By this approach, speech that *might* cause harm in the long run could be suppressed. The bad tendency theory relieved the government of any need to prove imminent or even probable danger. Courts often said the truth of the statement that had a "bad tendency" was no defense.[25] Because of the uncertainty of causation in human affairs, the sweep of the bad tendency theory is vast. The North Carolina statute under which Daniel Worth was prosecuted was written in terms of bad tendency. Some Southerners thought the Declaration of Independence could lead slaves to revolt. Many Southerners were sure that the political ideas of Abraham Lincoln's Republican party should be suppressed in the South because of their bad tendency.[26]

The bad tendency theory was not limited to the South or the period before the Civil War. In a 1914 case from Massachusetts,[27] the state court upheld the conviction of a man charged with carrying a red flag in a political parade. It was emblazoned in gold letters with the words "Finnish Socialist Branch, Fitchburg, Mass." The court found parading with the flag was a violation of a state statute that forbade parading with a red or black flag or with an inscription opposed to organized government. The rationale was that the legislature might reasonably conclude that the red flag might tend to produce "turbulence." A "rational connection with the preservation of public safety" was all that was required.[28]

No proof was needed that any turbulence occurred. No proof was necessary that disorder was likely. All that was required was that a rational person might believe that the flag had a tendency to cause turbulence— as all truly controversial ideas do. Today, a law that targeted carrying a flag because of its political message would violate the guarantees of the First Amendment, and simple concern about possible disturbance would not be enough to justify suppression.[29]

Modern commentators are rightly critical of the idea of a heckler's veto—that an arrest of a speaker can be justified because a hostile observer threatens violence.[30] They suggest that, whenever possible, the police should protect the speaker and restrain those who threaten violence. The Massachusetts court decision meant that the heckler did not need to cast his veto or even threaten to. A rational possibility that he would was enough.

The United States Supreme Court also too often embraced crabbed conceptions of free speech. In *Patterson v. Colorado,*[31] decided in 1907, the Supreme Court expressed doubt that the First Amendment limited the states. Even if it did, the Court continued, the amendment was limited to banning prior restraints (having to get a government license before publication) and did not preclude punishment even for true statements about public affairs. The Court upheld the contempt conviction of a newspaper editor who had criticized a disgraceful Colorado state supreme court decision. He had done so while a petition for rehearing was pending. The Court said the editorials had the bad tendency to interfere with the administration of justice. The truth of the criticisms was irrelevant.[32] (The Court did suggest that criticism might be protected after the state court's decision was final.) With reference to criticism of other branches of government, the Supreme Court was more protective of free speech values.[33] State court decisions split on the right to criticize state officials, including judges;[34] some early cases were protective of free speech.[35]

According to free speech historian David Rabban, from 1870 through the First World War most courts tended to be hostile to free speech concerns and to justify suppression based on bad tendency. During and after World War I, courts used the bad tendency theory to uphold punishment of dissenters who criticized World War I, including some who confined their criticism to urging lawful means to oppose the war.[36]

Lawyers, judges, and law students are trained to look for constitutional law precedents in decided cases. After reading the bad tendency cases, they might conclude that the narrow, suppressive older judicial doctrine was how free speech was generally understood in the United States before the 1930s. But there was another approach, a robust and protective popular tradition that grew and gathered strength in the years before the Civil War. The "popular" free speech tradition grew up outside of the courts and was directed to the sovereign people and their representatives. It came primarily from activists, not from the Supreme Court of the United States or state supreme courts. The tradition was "popular" in another sense—it had significant popular appeal and it affected the behavior of politicians.[37]

A Popular Tradition for Protecting Free Speech

The idea of a broadly protective free speech guarantee welled up from American citizens—newspaper editors, ministers, politicians, antislavery activists, lawyers, and others who were responding to attacks on free speech. There had been seeds of such a protective tradition among dissenters in England. The popular free speech tradition compares well with the stunted and crabbed view of free speech and press articulated by some judges and some commentators from the founding until the 1930s. (There were, of course, also activists on the other side.)

The Nature of Free Speech

Those who espoused the popular pro–free speech tradition wanted broad protection for speech and press. They extended protection to unpopular speakers who asserted ideas that they thought were wrong or even evil. They denied that the government had legitimate power to establish orthodoxy. By this view, free speech was a basic and inherent right of all Americans, and it broadly protected the right to speak and write about political, religious, and scientific topics. Government lacked the power to ban such speech. This view implicitly, and often explicitly, rejected the claim that speech with a bad tendency should be suppressed.

Many of those who adhered to the popular free speech tradition rejected suppression of unpopular dissenters because they feared that suppressing their ideas required delegating discretion, a discretion that was likely to be abused. They also seem to have believed that certain types of speech were simply protected by freedom of speech, and that was that. These citizens espoused the idea that protection of free speech must be general. Incursions on the rights of those engaging in dangerous speech —the abolitionists, for example—involved dangers for all. A broad reading of free speech was one part of the popular tradition. The other insisted that free speech must be protected in every state by a national constitutional guarantee.

The Nationalization of Free Speech

In the mid-1830s, Congress rejected even very limited national legislation against abolitionist speech. But in this case, arguments were often based on the division of powers between the nation and the states. A number of congressmen explained that the federal government lacked any power over speech and that the states themselves could provide any necessary remedies.

In contrast, many citizens, ministers, editors, lawyers, and politicians developed the idea of free speech as national instead of state-centered. Particularly after 1837, these free speech advocates began to proclaim that free speech was a national right or immunity, enshrined in the federal Constitution. They believed citizens had a right to exercise free speech in South Carolina and Massachusetts and anywhere else in the nation: state laws that abridged freedom of speech violated the federal Constitution. Activists, politicians, editors, ministers, and others developed the idea of a strongly protective national free speech guarantee enshrined in the federal Constitution *before* ratification of the Fourteenth Amendment in 1868 and long before 1925 when the United States Supreme Court finally assumed that states could not abridge the national free speech right protected by the First and Fourteenth Amendments.

Opponents of slavery and leaders of Lincoln's Republican Party sought freedom for criticism of slavery, even in the South. Some worked out a protective legal theory to explain why the Constitution's First Amendment (*"Congress* shall make no law ... abridging freedom of speech or of the press") protected free speech from state abridgment. By this view the Bill of Rights added new rights or immunities to the catalogue of national privileges protected by Article IV, Section 2, of the Constitution or by the guarantee of republican government.[38] In 1866 Republicans in Congress proposed the Fourteenth Amendment, which provided that no state should abridge the privileges or immunities of citizens of the United States or deny to any person life, liberty, or property without due process or deny equal protection to any person. Two of the three leading Republicans on the committee that framed the amendment explained that "privileges" of citizens of the United States included Bill of Rights liberties such as free speech and press. Free speech was often invoked by Republicans who defended their approach to Reconstruction (of which the Fourteenth Amendment was the centerpiece) in the congressional campaign of 1866.[39]

By the 1930s, the Supreme Court began squarely to reject the bad tendency theory and to hold that the First Amendment protected the people against state laws abridging their right to free speech.[40] In the 1960s, the Court embraced strong protections for free speech.[41] As these dates suggest, the Supreme Court was slow to extend strong protection for free speech.

THE USES OF THE PAST

Is the Crabbed View the Original View?
Is Current Doctrine Legitimate?

Law students, including those who eventually become judges, first learn the law from casebooks. Later in their careers, lawyers search for and find constitutional law in cases. In these sources, they rarely see detailed stories about the free speech battles over sedition, abolition, antiwar speech, and Reconstruction.[42] The omission is entirely understandable—casebooks are too big already, and cases deal with specific and current problems. It is also quite unfortunate. Stories such as those in this book illuminate the central importance of free speech and the protection of dissent for individual liberty and American democracy. They show the long existence of a vibrant popular free speech tradition outside of the courts as well as the power of demands for suppression.

To the extent that a popular free speech tradition helped to prevent repressive legislation, it left no court decisions or statutes. As a result, it is invisible to the eyes of some law teachers, lawyers, and judges. What remains visible are court decisions that illustrate the development of robust Supreme Court protection for free speech after 1925.

Court decisions are the result of certain vectors. These vectors include the text of the constitutional provision; the structure of the Constitution or how the document is to function as a whole; prior judicial decisions; the history surrounding the provision; major political events, such as the Great Depression and the victory by the North in the Civil War; the ethical aspirations the provision reflects; and sound public policy.[43] The problem, of course, is that there is no consistent understanding of the weight to be given to the various vectors. One possible response to this problem is to follow a single method, the teaching of history.

The theory of original meaning focuses on the common public understanding of the words of a constitutional provision at the time of enactment. (The closely related idea of original intent typically focuses on the intent of those who framed or ratified the constitutional provision.) According to these ideas, now much in vogue, the words and legal concepts in the Constitution should be given the "common" meaning the words had at the time the constitutional provision was ratified or the particular meaning that their drafters or ratifiers intended. The unstated assumption is that the original understanding was crisp, clear, and generally shared. To many critics, free speech doctrines that the Court arrived at after 1925 seem unconnected to common understanding in 1868 or to the intentions of the framers and ratifiers of the First and Fourteenth Amendments, ratified respectively in 1791 and 1868. Of course, there are alternatives. For example, the Court may simply have been tardy in attending to the original meaning of the constitutional text.

The theory of original meaning is supported by ideas of popular sovereignty—the idea that the people ultimately rule. Since constitutional provisions were ratified by representatives of the sovereign people (the argument goes), the common understanding of these provisions at the time of enactment should control and limit judicial decisions.

Some scholars and judges have emphasized the intent of the framers of a constitutional provision or the intent of delegates elected to ratify it. Others have emphasized the original meaning of the words in the text of the Constitution. Since both framers and ratifiers are, by democratic theory, merely representatives of the sovereign people, advocates of these approaches should go further: the popular understanding of citizens should control. As Justice Frankfurter argued, "[A]n amendment to the Constitution should be read in a 'sense most obvious to the common understanding at the time of its adoption. . . . For it was for public adoption that it was proposed.'"[44] Justice Scalia insists that we should look, not only at the statements of the framers and ratifiers, but also and equally at "those of other intelligent and informed people of the time" to "display how the text of the Constitution was originally understood."[45] The problem, of course, is that with so many people involved, there will inevitably be many views.

While some seek the contemporary meaning of freedom of speech in the understanding of the constitutional text in 1791, when the First Amendment was ratified, those committed to such methods also need to examine the public understanding of the "privileges or immunities of citizens of the United States" guaranteed by the Fourteenth Amendment in 1868. By 1866, most citizens seem to have repudiated the Sedition Act and the idea of freedom of speech as limited to a protection against prior restraint. Many had repudiated the bad tendency approach. Similarly, by 1866 there was a widespread belief that freedom of speech was a privilege or immunity of American citizenship that limited, or should limit, state governments.

All methods for reaching judicial decisions are problematic, and original meaning is no exception. It seeks to use history to see that judges are faithful to the decisions of "the people" embodied in the Constitution. But what history means now and how it should be used are intensely controversial subjects. Political factions constantly strive to gain control of history.[46] Historian C. Vann Woodward cites the Commissar from George Orwell's novel *1984*: "Who controls the past controls the future; who controls the present controls the past."[47]

There is a paradox involved in the search for the true historical intent or meaning. We owe much progress in the history of liberty to seventeenth-century and later generations of English people who mis-read the original meaning of the Magna Carta, transforming it from a triumph by feudal barons into a charter of liberty for all the English. Colin Rhys Lovell, the historian of English constitutional history, considers this "manifesto of feudalism" to be "one of the most notoriously misrepresented documents in English history, largely because succeeding generations of Englishmen read into its provisions meanings relevant to their own times."[48] Other landmark decisions that most of us revere are not easily explained based simply on a narrow interpretation of original understanding. As Charles Miller has noted, we make inconsistent demands on judges. "No other nation possesses a written constitution (still in use) as old as America's and no other nation worships its constitution with such reverence. Yet we expect the judiciary to be both contemporary and rational when expounding constitutional law."[49]

History and Constitutional Law

Still, history does play a significant role in judicial decisions. Communities naturally appeal to historic common values, and battles over history are one aspect of our struggle to define ourselves as a community. How we define ourselves is important, and history is an important part of that endeavor.

History can help to limit judicial discretion and to reinforce the view that government officials (including judges) are limited by the fundamental decisions that "we the people" reach.[50] But if we seek historical understanding, we should pursue not just the congressional history from the year or so in which a provision is proposed and ratified. We must not limit ourselves to congressional debates, legal texts, and the decisions of courts. For deeper understanding, we need history with a wider focus. People understand the world in light of their experience, and the free speech battles recounted here were part of the experience of those who framed and ratified the Fourteenth Amendment. They had witnessed more than thirty years of suppression of free speech and other civil liberties to protect slavery.

We also need to widen our focus in another way. We should remember that those who gave us the Constitution are not just framers assembled in Philadelphia in 1787. They include all the people who supported the document and its many amendments—the Republicans and antislavery activists (women as well as men, black as well as white) whose transformation of public opinion helped give us the Thirteenth and Fourteenth Amendments; the women and men, citizens, politicians, and feminists who gave us the Nineteenth Amendment; the Progressives and Populists who gave us the income tax amendment and direct election of senators, and so on. The framers are not simply James Madison, Alexander Hamilton, James Wilson, and the rest, but include, for example, John Bingham and Jacob Howard, leaders in the Thirty-ninth Congress that framed the Fourteenth Amendment.

In the largest and truest sense, the creators of the Thirteenth and Fourteenth Amendments include those who helped to transform national understanding on the issues involved—the abolitionist women who circulated and signed antislavery petitions and began to make women an active political force; the Grimke sisters, from Charleston, South Carolina, who fought against slavery, racism, and for free speech rights for women; Frederick Douglass, the former slave and famous orator; Harriet Beecher Stowe, who wrote *Uncle Tom's Cabin,* a best-selling novel that highlighted the cruelties of slavery; and the newly freed African Americans who petitioned the Congress that proposed the Fourteenth Amendment, asking Congress to protect them in their rights to free speech, free press, and free assembly and to keep arms.[51] The creators include William Lloyd Garrison, who fought against slavery and for racial equality and braved mob violence designed to suppress his ideas,[52] and Elijah Lovejoy, who died defending his press from an antiabolitionist mob determined to silence antislavery speech.[53] Another creator was Hinton Helper, the Southerner whose book indicting slavery became a Republican campaign document that it was a crime to circulate in his home state. The creators of constitutional provisions, of course, also include those who were opposed to moving too far and too fast. All these people helped define the privileges and immunities of free speech, press, and religion under the Fourteenth Amendment.

THE USES OF FREE SPEECH

Free speech has many functions. Its role as a centerpiece of democracy is only one. For example, it is a key aspect of individual freedom and it is important to scientific understanding. Those who espoused the popular tradition of free speech from the Sedition Act to the Civil War clearly thought of freedom of speech as more extensive than merely speech about politics.[54] The tradition emphasized that free speech is crucial for individual transformation and progressive social change. Abolitionists claimed free speech even though many of them thought of themselves as discussing slavery as a matter of religion and morals, not as a political question.

Still, the popular tradition especially emphasized free speech in relation to democracy, as well as free speech as an inherent human right. How well the democratic system is performing today—or has ever performed—is open to question. Without some broad protection of the right to dissent, democracy and intellectual enquiry cannot work.[55] Free speech protects the right to dissent, and dissent is crucial if the sovereign people are to have a chance to be part of the decision-making process and to be given full information and alternatives. Information and the opportunity to participate are, of course, required for intelligent and widely accepted decision making.

Democracy is a system in which the sovereign people have a continuing right to consider alternatives and to seek to shape their collective fate. By democratic theory, all citizens have a right to raise issues and to seek to put issues on the agenda as subjects for collective action. Democracy provides a framework for decision, not a result. An essential part of democracy is the idea that existing institutions, practices, ideas, leaders, and theories are subject to criticism and to revision or replacement. But at crucial times in American history the nation has failed to live up to its free speech and democratic ideals.

The absence of robust national protection for free speech has had heavy costs. Since slavery was insulated from free speech and democratic change, the issue was settled in the awful carnage of the American Civil War. Political violence drove Americans of African descent and their Republican allies from political power during Reconstruction, another rejection of free speech and democracy. The nation had fought one bloody war to preserve the Union and (as it turned out) to free the slaves. It lacked the will to fight a long guerrilla war to protect the political and constitutional rights of the newly free slaves and their Republican allies in the South.

Although leading Republicans had intended that the Fourteenth Amendment's privileges or immunities of citizens of the United States, which no state could abridge, would include the right to free speech, press, religion, and the right to petition, the United States Supreme Court essentially read the privileges-or-immunities clause out of the Constitution.[56] Not until 1925 did the Court suggest that the right to free speech and press was protected against state action by the due process clause of the Fourteenth Amendment,[57] and not until the 1930s, 1940s, and 1960s did a broadly protective reading of First Amendment freedoms take shape in the Supreme Court. (There had, however, been some notably protective state court decisions under state constitutions.)

In the 1960s, advocates of integration and voting rights renewed the struggle, and this time the nation entered the battle for political and civil rights. Those who struggled for civil rights were protected by a First Amendment now squarely held to prohibit state denials of free speech and free press.

By the 1990s, however, some on the left (like some on the right) began to see broad free speech protection for dangerous ideas as a problem. Suggestions for action include selectively reviving the bad tendency test, enacting group libel laws (treating some racist or sexist speech as libel), expanding antipornography laws to reach hitherto protected expression, making flag burning a crime, prosecuting administration officials who criticize a special prosecutor, enacting laws designed to make it easier to recover damages from critics of food safety, and many more. All of these proposals focus on punishing speech because of its message. These suggestions are in serious tension with the popular free speech tradition recounted here and with current Supreme Court doctrine.

Focusing on our free speech tradition can provide wisdom and perspective. But while the past is like the present in some ways, it is different in others. Though the central ideas of the free speech tradition are necessary for free speech and democracy, it does not follow that they are sufficient. Still, because many free speech problems tend to recur, the ideas of the past are not so alien from present concerns as they might seem at first.

Before embracing broad and vague exceptions to free speech, critics might consider how theoretical justifications for suppression have been invoked in the past.[58] In the nineteenth century, many claimed that because the Constitution recognized and legitimized the concept of slavery, criticism of the institution was impermissible—in essence abolitionism was "unconstitutional" speech. Such ideas were essentially attacks on the democratic process. It was far from clear to many at the time that banning abolitionist speech advocating peaceful change was an attack on democracy. They probably saw the elimination of abolitionist speech as a narrow, discrete, and easily contained exception to free speech. As slavery became a central political issue, and as suppression extended to almost all antislavery speech, the fallacy of seeing a ban on antislavery speech as a limited and narrow exception became clearer.

The battle for democracy and free speech recounted in the following chapters was largely a popular battle. The idea of popular protection for free speech might sound strange to modern ears. Today, quite properly, many think of courts as protecting free speech against popular majorities. Without free speech for those who are in the minority today (but who, with free speech, might become a majority tomorrow), popular government is an illusion. Ironically, protecting minority speech needs popular support for its long-term survival. The idea of appealing to public opinion to protect basic liberties has a long heritage.

Judicial protection for freedom of speech and of the press is essential, and deeper understanding of the popular free speech tradition is important for judges and lawyers. But the free speech tradition ultimately belongs to the American people and derives strength from their commitment to it. A deeper general understanding of the meaning of free speech is crucial. Like the *Titanic* or a supertanker, liberty requires redundant safety devices—lifeboats as well as a double hull.[59] It needs courts, juries, public support, a system for broad access to the debate, and understanding by politicians. Politicians, lawyers, and judges have a special duty to protect free speech. But free speech is too important to leave exclusively to judges, lawyers, and politicians. It belongs to the American people.

1

The English and Colonial Background

American colonists brought English law, or rather some of it, with them to the new world. English law provided Americans with ready-made rationales for the suppression of speech: freedom of the press was no more than protection against prior restraint, truth did not justify criticisms of government or its officials, and the law punished circulation of ideas with a tendency to cause harm. (A major harm was bringing government or its officers into disrepute; the harm did not have to be imminent or even likely.) These ideas were initially developed for a monarchy in which the king was sovereign. They continued to serve a mixed government of king and Parliament, in which a very oligarchic Parliament was supreme. These English justifications for suppression appear again and again in the struggle for representative government and free speech in early American history.

Still, this legal orthodoxy was hotly contested. A radical seventeenth-century critique insisted that the people (not Parliament) were sovereign and that government was the agent or trustee of the people. In this view, free speech was an essential mechanism to ensure representative government and to see that governmental officials did not abuse the people's trust. The radical critique also rejected the orthodox legal view of the role of the jury—which held that the judge, not the jury, should decide, for example, if a book was seditious.

Seventeenth-Century Origins

American revolutionaries saw the history of seventeenth-century England as a guide to the meaning of liberty. As one scholar has noted, they "argued their case against Parliament and the King largely in the language of Whig history and the supposedly ancient Anglo-Saxon rights of Englishmen."[1] This tradition of dissent, which developed in England in the seventeenth and eighteenth centuries, shaped the later American story of free speech.

The interrelated struggles of the seventeenth century were struggles between contending groups for political power and the right to define the nature of the nation: a contest between king and Parliament over the power of Parliament, struggles over freedom of debate in Parliament and over basic legal liberties—including the power of the king to imprison without trial. There were also major conflicts over religion. One important figure in the political conflicts was Edward Coke, a former judge and distinguished legal writer and champion of the view that the king was limited by the law. Coke and others led Parliament to adopt the Petition of Right of 1628. The petition proclaimed several rights, including rights against taxation without the consent of Parliament, against imprisonment without cause shown, against denial of due process of law, and against quartering troops in private homes.[2]

Seventeenth-century opponents of the king were routinely prosecuted. The crown arrested and punished printers and publishers of unorthodox political and religious tracts. Religious dissenters, including many whose idea of religious freedom was the freedom to suppress those with different views, were also victims of the king's courts. Like many of those facing arrest and punishment, the critics of the king and, later, of Parliament developed an intense interest in the law and looked to legal procedures for protection. Although they appealed to history for justification, they were also innovators. Many sought the future in their vision of the past.[3]

The Levellers and Constitutional Limitations

In England in the 1640s, religious ideas about the equality of all souls and the accessibility of religious truths to all people led some to a secular egalitarianism that threatened existing hierarchies. These dissenters held that government, like religion, was something ordinary people could understand, and that ordinary people should enjoy free speech about government. Free speech and press implies the right of anyone to investigate (and challenge) existing political, economic, social, or religious hierarchies. In that respect it is profoundly egalitarian.

During the English Civil War of the 1640s, one group of English dissenters (eventually known as the Levellers) developed a theory of popular sovereignty that was similar to the American revolutionary view. Popular sovereignty became, in turn, a primary justification for broad protection of speech related to public affairs. The Levellers were also suspicious that those with governmental power might abuse that power for personal ends. This suspicion became a second rationale for broader protection of speech. Levellers appealed to the jury as a shield against oppressive governmental power. (Their arguments for a broad role for the jury also reappear in later English and American arguments over governmental power and free speech.) The Levellers also developed the idea of a constitution that expressed the wishes of the sovereign people and limited governmental power.[4]

As understood by some present-day historians, the English Civil War that produced the Levellers was a conflict between a powerful landed gentry represented in Parliament and the king and his supporters. The opponents of the king appealed to the "people" to support their cause and to man the armies that confronted the king.[5] With the defeat of the king, the broad parliamentary coalition fractured. Some more middling supporters of the parliamentary cause, members of the army, merchants and artisans, and members of dissenting religious sects, demanded greater religious toleration and a greater share of power—including the right to vote for members of Parliament. They looked for meaning in the bloody struggle of the Civil War and found that meaning in a rebirth of freedom—electoral, political, and religious. They thought they were pursuing a "rebirth" of freedom because they believed in a golden age of Anglo-Saxon liberty that had been destroyed by the Norman Conquest.

By the mid-1640s, a persistent and courageous group of Leveller dissenters coalesced around John Lilburne, an extraordinary and charismatic crusader for what he termed "the rights of freeborn Englishmen." Lilburne had remarkable abilities to mobilize, express, personify, and focus discontent. Under King Charles I, he had been whipped, pilloried, and imprisoned by the bishops presiding over the royal court of the Star Chamber for refusing to answer incriminating questions about his role in importing Protestant religious books. From the pillory Lilburne made a speech attacking his prosecution as illegal and unjust. When the authorities gagged him, he reached under his shirt, where he had concealed some of his outlawed tracts, and threw copies to the crowd. During the Civil War, Parliament freed him and declared his imprisonment illegal. Lilburne joined the parliamentary army and rose to the rank of lieutenant colonel, but he eventually resigned rather than take an oath to support a Presbyterian religious establishment.[6]

Lilburne and his supporters sought a unicameral Parliament that reflected the population and that was elected by broader suffrage. They also sought the abolition of the hereditary House of Lords, protection of basic liberties against the power of Parliament, and greater freedom of religion. When Lilburne and his followers appealed to Parliament to enact broader suffrage and religious toleration, they soon found themselves at odds with their former parliamentary allies. Lilburne's group was branded as "Levellers" by their opponents, who claimed that general adult male suffrage would lead to economic leveling.

Leaders in Parliament and in Cromwell's government attempted to force Levellers to answer self-incriminating questions. They targeted them with searches for incriminating papers and pamphlets, with attempts to keep their tracts from the public by requiring a government license before publication, with search-and-destroy missions aimed at their hidden printing presses, and with charges of sedition and treason. In the face of these attacks, Lilburne and other Leveller leaders appealed to the rights of freeborn Englishmen, set out, as they thought, in the Magna Carta, in the Petition of Right, in the common law, in parliamentary declarations, and in the writings of Sir Edward Coke. They also appealed to natural law.

In many of their appeals to what they considered historic liberties, they put parliamentary declarations against the king to new uses. Lilburne and other Leveller leaders insisted that Magna Carta limited Parliament as well as the king. But Leveller William Walwyn, a merchant and prolific pamphleteer, insisted that Magna Carta itself represented only a part of the liberties of the people. "MAGNA CARTA (you must observe)," Walwyn wrote, "is but a part of the peoples rights and liberties, being no more but what with much striving and fighting, was by the blood of our Ancestors, wrested out the pawes of those Kings, who by force had conquered the Nation, changed the lawes and by strong hand held them in bondage."[7]

When the letter of the law did not provide protection, embattled Leveller leaders turned elsewhere. They appealed to the *spirit* of the law over its letter. They made innovative legal claims. In 1649, Lilburne was tried for treason by Cromwell's government for political and (as Cromwell saw it) essentially revolutionary activity. Lilburne demanded procedural rights for which no precedent existed, such as the right to counsel (unavailable in cases of treason) and to see a copy of the indictment. He objected to questions calling for self incrimination. In his various trials, Lilburne asserted a host of rights that later appeared in American bills of rights: the rights to counsel, to public trial, to have a copy of the indictment, and against self-incrimination.[8] Tried by judges he believed to be bent on his conviction, Lilburne insisted that his jury was the judge of law as well as fact. The jury in Lilburne's 1649 treason trial acquitted him, in spite of a hanging charge from the bench.[9] In addition to purely legal claims, Lilburne and other Leveller leaders appealed to natural rights.

The Levellers proposed that their written constitution should become law by an agreement of the people, or at least the "well affected" part of them. As the Leveller leaders saw it, the people were the principal; Parliament and, indeed, any officers of the government were merely their agents. Levellers feared that the governmental agents might seek to increase their power at the expense of the people. To respond to what they saw as the aggressive nature of power, the Leveller constitution, the Agreement of the People, protected basic liberties—freedom of religion, a right against self-incrimination, and a right to counsel, to jury trial, and against ex post facto laws. It decreed that government was without power to infringe these enumerated liberties.

On the issue of freedom of religion, the Leveller Agreement of 1649 provided: "[W]e do not impower or entrust our said representatives to continue in force or to make any Lawes, Oaths, or Covenants, whereby to compell by penalties or otherwise any person to anything in or about matters of faith, Religion or Gods worship or to restrain any person from the profession of his faith, or exercise of Religion according to his Conscience."[10] Leveller William Walwyn made psychological arguments against compulsion in religious matters. "[C]onscience being subject only to reason (either that which is indeed, or seems to him which hears it to be so) can only be convinced . . . thereby, force makes it runne backe, and struggle."[11] Walwyn argued against forced worship on spiritual grounds: compelling a person against conscience was compelling him or her "to doe that which is sinfull: for though the thing may be in it selfe good, yet if it doe not apeare to be so to my conscience, the practice thereof in me is sinful."[12] Finally, as one Leveller pamphlet argued, there was a sphere of a person's nature beyond the power of the state. People owned themselves: "[A]ll just humaine powers are but betrusted, confer'd and conveyed by joint and common consent, *for to every individuall in nature, is given an individuall propriety by nature, not to be invaded or usurped by any . . .* and by naturall birth, all men *are equal and alike borne to like propriety and freedome.*"[13] Some rights were beyond the power of the people to delegate to their government. The principal could not give his agent powers the principal did not possess. So as to worship "compell, yee cannot justly; for ye have no Power from Us so to doe, nor could you have; for we could not conferre a Power that was not in our selves, there being none of us, that can without wilfull sinne binde ourselves to worship God after any other way, then what (to a tittle,) in our owne particular understandings, wee approve to be just."[14]

The Levellers insisted that guarantees of liberty had to be general, to apply to all. Factions that denied liberty to others ultimately endangered it for themselves. In this view they expressed a theme of equality of liberty that became a powerful tradition. As Walwyn wrote: "I wish you would be but as carefull to preserve intirely, the due and formall course of Law to every man, without exception, friend, or foe, as we have been: and though at present you may please your selves with the sufferings of your adversaries (as you fancy them) yet you therein but treat down your own hedges, and pluck up that Bank that lets in the sea of will, and power, overwhelming your own liberties."[15] As John Lilburne put it, "[F]or what is done to any one, may be done to every one." Since all were "members of one body, that is, the English Commonwealth, one man should not suffer wrongfully, but all should be sensible, and endeavor his preservation; otherwise they give way to an inlet of the sea of will and power, upon all their laws and liberties, which are the boundaries to keep out tyranny and oppression." The person who failed to assist in such cases, Lilburne insisted, "betrays his own rights, and is over-run, and of a free man made a slave when he thinks not of it . . . and incurs the guilt of treachery to the present and future generations."[16]

Government Control of the Press in the Seventeenth and Eighteenth Centuries

The Levellers claimed and exercised a freedom to criticize government, but precedent was squarely against them. Initially and in the early seventeenth century, the crown had punished the crime of sedition or seditious libel in a special court—the Court of the Star Chamber.[17] The jury was no problem for government prosecutors because the Court of the Star Chamber operated without a jury. The court required defendants to answer questions about their activities under oath; failure to answer was treated as a confession. Though the Court of the Star Chamber was swept away in the Civil War of the 1640s, seditious libel and many of its repressive legal rules survived in the common law courts.[18] For critics, the doctrine of seditious libel was tainted by its origin in an oppressive court.

Even by the orthodox *eighteenth*-century view, freedom of the press did not limit seditious libel prosecutions, because of the doctrine that freedom of the press consisted only of freedom from prior restraint. The claim that "no prior restraint" is the full definition of free press will make a number of appearances in the free speech stories that follow, as will the claim for a broader role for the jury in free speech cases. So it is useful to explain these ideas here before resuming the story of the Levellers.

Prior Restraint

In seventeenth-century England, the government required a license from a government censor before a book, pamphlet, or newspaper was published. The censor's task was to make sure published books were acceptable to the government. Unacceptable books were denied a license. Publishing a book without a license was a crime, much as driving a car without a license is a crime today. Requiring a license was a "prior restraint."

The use of prior restraints gave government a powerful way of controlling the press and thus suppressing dissent. To punish the crime of publishing without a license, the government did not need to prove that the book, pamphlet, or newspaper was treasonous or seditious. It needed only to prove that the defendant had published the book and that he lacked a license, just as a person may be punished for driving without a license although her driving might otherwise be perfect.

Initially, this censorship system was enforced by the Stationers Company, which was given both a monopoly on printing and powers to search out law violators, seize presses, and arrest sellers of unlicensed books. The licensing system expired in 1694. By the time of the American Revolution, the licensing system had long been defunct.[19]

The Role of the Jury

The seventeenth-century device of prior restraint kept from the jury and in the hands of the government the larger question of whether the contents of the book were unlawful—whether the book or newspaper was one people should be permitted to read. A major theme in the early history of free speech is the role of the jury, which ideally represented a body of lay people beyond government control.

The demise of the licensing requirement could increase the role and power of the jury. The expansion of the jury's power was potentially very significant because the jury could refuse to follow the judge's instructions, and the judge typically represented the ruling hierarchy. In seditious libel cases, however, English law had another device to reduce the influence of the jury. This was the doctrine that in those cases (basically cases of antigovernment speech), the *only* issue for the jury was whether the defendant had published the book. The question of whether the contents of the book were unlawful was for the judge, appointed of course by the government. (Until 1701 in England, and in the American colonies until the Revolution, judges held their offices at the pleasure of the monarch, so a ruling that displeased the monarch and his or her ministers might mean the imminent loss of a judge's job. After 1701 judges in England could be removed only by a joint address of both Houses of Parliament, but in the colonies they continued to serve at the pleasure of the crown.)[20]

In several landmark cases of the trials of political dissenters, the defendants argued that the jury was the judge of law as well as fact, which meant, at least, that the jury should decide if the defendant's conduct was criminal and if a book or newspaper was in fact treasonous or seditious. Lilburne made the argument for a broad role for the jury in his 1649 treason case and in a later case where he was prosecuted for violating a decree banishing him. In 1670, William Penn, founder of Pennsylvania, made the claim when he was prosecuted for holding a religious meeting in the street after the law forbade Quakers to meet in their meeting houses. In the 1680s, the "seven bishops" made the claim. They had petitioned the king not to be compelled to read a royal decree annulling an act of Parliament from their pulpits, and, as a result, they were charged with sedition. In each of these cases, juries acquitted, disobeying contrary instructions from the court.[21]

By the eve of the American Revolution, the question of the scope of the jury's decision in cases of libel and seditious libel was hotly contested, with English judges divided on the issue. Lord Mansfield continued to insist that the jury could only decide the issue of publication, while the judge should decide whether the publication was libelous. In a case involving an alleged newspaper libel on the king, Lord Mansfield had instructed the jury that it was to decide only publication, not whether the article was libelous. The jury rebelled. As judge and legal scholar Thomas Cooley noted, "[T]he jury, dissatisfied with these instructions, and unwilling to make their verdict cover matters upon which they were not at liberty to exercise their judgement, returned a verdict of 'guilty of printing and publishing only.'" (It was a tactic similar to that initially used by the jury unwilling to convict William Penn.) Lord Mansfield considered the verdict inadequate and felt constrained to order a new trial. Lord Camden and other English judges supported a broad role for the jury. Not until 1792, did Parliament provide that the jury in cases of criminal libel should give a general verdict and would no longer be limited to the issue of publication. At that time Parliament announced the act was declaratory of what the law had always been.[22]

The Levellers on Press Freedom

The royal machinery of censorship, including the Court of the Star Chamber, was swept away in the early years of the English Civil War. In 1649, confronted with broad unrest, Parliament ordered the military to strictly enforce laws against unlicensed publications. The law provided for the destruction of printing presses, whipping the peddler of unlicensed pamphlets, and forty days' imprisonment or a forty-shilling fine for the author.[23]

The Levellers strenuously objected to Parliament's decision to reinstitute the licensing system for books and pamphlets. In 1644, Leveller William Walwyn called for full toleration of religious opinion but suggested that writing dangerous or scandalous to the state could be prohibited.[24] By 1649, after their writing was branded scandalous or seditious, Levellers claimed a broader scope for freedom of the press. Liberty of speech and of the press, they insisted, was essential to freedom. It allowed the people to exercise their sovereign power. "[F]or what may not be done to that people who may not speak or write, but at the pleasure of Licensers?" Censorship, a Leveller pamphlet insisted, "hath ever ushered in a tyrannie; mens mouth being to be kept from making noise, whilst they are robd of their liberties." In the evil days of royal prerogative "upon pretense of care of the publike, Licensers were set over the Press, Truth was suppressed," and the people were kept ignorant. Ignorant people were "fitted only to serve the unjust ends of Tyrants and Oppressors."[25]

While attacking the system of licensing books, a Leveller pamphlet argued that counterspeech was the answer to the danger of press abuse. Significantly, it did not suggest the alternative of subsequent punishment.

> As for any prejudice to Government thereby, if Government be just in its Constitution, and equal in its distributions, it will be good, if not absolutely necessary for them, to hear all voices and judgments, which they can never do, but by giving freedom to the Press; and in case any abuse their authority by scandalous Pamphlets, they will never want able Advocates to vindicate their innocency. And therefore . . . to refer all Books and Pamphlets to the judgment, discretion or affection of Licensers, or to put the least restraint upon the Press, seems altogether inconsistent with the good of the Commonwealth, and expressly opposite and dangerous to the liberties of the people.[26]

The Levellers had a distinguished predecessor in their complaints against Parliament's revival of the licensing system. In 1644 John Milton wrote *Areopagitica*, his famous pamphlet against licensing. Milton did not argue against prosecutions after publication. Indeed, unlike the Levellers, he suggested that possibility as one remedy for evil books, and he exempted "papists" from his plea for religious toleration. Still, many of Milton's arguments—the partial and scattered nature of truth, the ability of truth to win in a fair fight, clashing opinions as producing truth, the inferiority of "cloistered virtues," and his call for "liberty to know, to utter, and to argue freely according to conscience"—exceeded his limited goal of arguing against licensing.[27]

In addition to attacking licensing, Levellers also invoked a limited definition of treason. In his treason trial for harsh criticisms of Cromwell and the government, Lilburne insisted that mere words could not be treasonous.[28]

As a result of their agitation for fundamental change, Leveller leaders were accused of a number of crimes, including sedition—lessening the affection of the people for the government or inciting discontent against government—and treason. Labeling criticism of government as a crime because it caused discontent was in conflict with Levellers' ideas of popular sovereignty. So it is not surprising that the Levellers specifically criticized the crime of sedition.

In 1647 the Levellers had circulated an earlier version of their "Agreement of the People" in the army. When the army commanders suppressed Leveller agitation, the Levellers again petitioned Parliament for the adoption of their Agreement. Parliament responded by imprisoning the petitioners—Thomas Prince, a cheesemonger, and Samuel Chidley, a printer who served as treasurer for the Levellers. They were alleged to be guilty of "seditious and contemptuous avowing and prosecuting of a former Petition . . . stiled an agreement of the people, formerly adjudged by this house, to be destructive to the being of Parliaments." The Levellers strenuously objected to treating a petition as seditious, and they denied that sedition was a crime: "for no man knows what is sedition."[29]

As their complaint about the crime of sedition shows, it is quite unlikely that the Leveller view of freedom of the press merely allowed the citizen the right to publish without a license but then gave the state broad power to punish after publication. Proponents of fundamental change who were being imprisoned for critical writing needed a broader protection than that. But, of course, modern ideas of press freedom were not fully developed in the seventeenth century. Although Levellers demanded freedom of press and petition in their pamphlets, they failed fully to elaborate these rights or to include these freedoms in their Agreement of the People.

The Levellers' Agreement

The rights that were enshrined in the Levellers' Agreement would be protected from later parliaments because the Agreement, unlike an act of Parliament, was to be "unalterable." Furthermore, the Levellers warned, later parliaments might be "corrupted; and besides Parliaments are to receive the extent of their power and trust from those that betrust them; and therefore the people are to declare what their power and trust is, which is the intent of this Agreement."[30] This was a very early use of the argument that a constitution that came from the people was a supreme authority that could limit the legislature and all aspects of government.

Although Leveller leaders like Lilburne saw the Parliament as representing the people, still they considered Parliament clearly distinct from the people. So it was appropriate to organize the people to assert their interests to Parliament, by petitions and in other ways. Defenders of parliamentary prerogative, on the other hand, saw Parliament as the embodiment of the people, not as their representative. Petition and other campaigns that were directed not simply at informing Parliament but at organizing popular will were improper because they appealed to a center of power beyond Parliament. There was a wide gap between ideas of popular and parliamentary sovereignty.

From the Restoration of the Monarchy to the American Revolution

The Levellers were eventually suppressed and had little influence on the ruling elite in England. Still, some scholars insist that their influence did persist, transmuted through English radicals to American revolutionaries.[31] At any rate, a group of English Radical Whigs in the later seventeenth and early eighteenth century embraced some similar ideas. But the Levellers also rejected monarchy and the hereditary House of Lords. Before 1776, many English radicals did not directly challenge these institutions, and some saw the balance between king, lords, and commons as a unique safeguard of liberty.

In the years that followed the Civil War, the monarchy was restored, but Parliament, not the monarch, became dominant. During its seventeenth-century struggles with the monarch, Parliament enacted important guarantees of English liberty that limited the power of the crown. There were no effective limits on the power of Parliament, however. With the restoration of the monarchy in 1661, Parliament passed harsh statutes aimed at religious dissenters, persecuting Quakers and other Protestant dissenters. Many Levellers had, in fact, become Quakers, and some Quakers repeated Leveller themes.[32]

In 1677, Quakers, including William Penn, established the colony of West Jersey. The Charter or Fundamental Laws of West Jersey contained provisions for representative government, protection for liberty of conscience, and guarantees, including jury trial and public trial, for those accused of crimes. The charter provided that it was a fundamental law, not alterable by the legislature. The constitution was signed by 150 persons, making it a sort of Agreement of the People. The first name of the list was Edward Billing, a Quaker who had suffered savage persecution and who was much influenced by the Levellers; the fourth was William Penn.[33]

Radical Whigs in the Seventeenth and Early Eighteenth Centuries

Between the accession of Charles II in 1661 and the "abdication" of James II in 1688, radical Whigs were engaged in antigovernment and revolutionary activity. Men like John Locke and Algernon Sidney wrote republican tracts that were enormously influential in eighteenth-century America. Both Locke and Sydney were proponents of the idea that government rested on the consent of a free people, of the principle of wider religious toleration, of the right of those who were "independent" to a share of political power, of the fiduciary nature of governmental power, of equal subjection of everyone to the law, and of the right of revolution.[34] Sidney supported religious toleration because true faith required "a rational and natural right of disputing what is uncertain, and of not receiving it till convinced that its a certain truth."[35] Like Levellers and other Whig pamphleteers of the 1680s, Sidney believed that juries should have the power to judge law as well as fact.[36]

After Parliament deposed one king in 1688 and replaced him with another, England remained a highly stratified oligarchical class society with a hereditary House of Lords and a House of Commons that was far from popularly elected. Though the power of the king waned and that of Parliament waxed, the ruling faction continued to take advantage of legal rules like seditious libel that had been developed to protect the crown's power.

While many were apparently pleased with the new status quo, one group of Whigs thought change had not gone far enough. This small group existed from the Glorious Revolution of 1688 to about 1727 and considered themselves the heirs of Civil War republicanism. These radical Whigs described themselves as Real Whigs. They generally believed in separation of powers, reform of Parliament, more frequent elections, and more equitable distribution of parliamentary seats. They championed religious liberty, including tolerance for Jews, atheists, Unitarians, Muslims and, by the eighteenth century, "even 'well behaved Catholics.'" Englishmen, even Englishmen in the colonies, were entitled to be ruled by laws to which they had consented. In spite of references to popular sovereignty, aristocratic "radicals" of the seventeenth and early eighteenth centuries were not necessarily advocates of adult male suffrage or even of a greatly expanded electorate. While they spoke of sovereignty of the people, some limited the term to the "better" sort, that is, those who were economically independent.[37]

The Eighteenth Century: Radical Whig Ideas Before the Revolution

Later in the eighteenth century, manhood suffrage—or at least a much expanded franchise—gained increasing support among radicals. At one time or another, later radicals also argued for distribution of parliamentary seats based on population, alterations in the law of seditious libel to permit greater press freedom to criticize government, and total withdrawal of government control of religious practice.[38]

James Burgh in his *Political Disquisitions*, insisted that "every man has a life, a personal liberty, a character, a right to his earnings, a right to a religious profession and worship according to his conscience, &c." So, Burgh continued, "the poor are in danger of being injured by the government in a variety of ways." Still, he noted "the commonly received doctrine" was "that servants, and those who receive alms, have no right to vote for members of parliament." As a result, "an immense multitude of the people are utterly deprived of all power in determining who shall be the protectors of their lives, their personal liberty, their little property . . . and the chastity of their wives and daughters &c."

Burgh noted that in the aggregate the little property of the poor amounted to "a very great object." While the poor were given "no share in determining who shall be the law givers," they bore "a very heavy share" of the tax burden, since taxes on malt, beer, leather, soap, and candles were paid chiefly by the poor. "The landed interest," Burgh observed, "would complain grievously, if they had no power of electing representatives." It was "an established maxim in free states" that those who contributed to the government should "have a share in electing those who spend their tax money."[39]

The Radical Whigs transmitted radical ideas from the English Civil War era to colonial America.[40] They were fearful of corruption and suspicious of abuse of power. Like the Levellers, Radical Whig thinkers saw the people as the principal and government as the people's agent.[41] The theory of popular sovereignty has important implications for freedom of speech because speech is a mechanism by which popular sovereignty is effected. Americans had no House of Lords, no hereditary aristocracy, and after the Revolution, no king. The right to vote was broader than in England. In postrevolutionary America, ideas of popular sovereignty began to be transformed in a more literal and eventually more democratic direction. The "people" began to include more and more people. Since people understand words and ideas in light of their experience, the ideas of the Radical Whigs would begin to have a somewhat different meaning to Americans.

English and American thinkers of the eighteenth century, influenced by the Radical Whig tradition, did not at first totally reject the crime of seditious libel. Still, some recognized a broad right to criticize government and public officials that significantly departed from English law.[42] Two particularly influential writers were John Trenchard and William Gordon, who wrote *Cato's Letters: Essays on Liberty, Civil and Religious.* Trenchard and Gordon had graduated from universities in Ireland and Scotland, had been trained as lawyers, and devoted much of their lives to writing political essays.

In 1720 *Cato's Letters* appeared in England as newspaper essays. First published as a book in 1723, the *Letters* consisted of short essays on a wide variety of subjects: "The Fatal effects of the South-Sea Scheme and the Necessity of punishing the Directors; Of Freedom of Speech; That the same is inseparable from publick Liberty; Considerations on the destructive Spirit of arbitrary power; The sad Effects of general corruption, quoted from Algernon Sidney, Esq; the Right and Capacity of the People to judge of Government; Against standing Armies;" and so on.[43] *Cato's Letters* were the most popular and esteemed source of political ideas in colonial America. According to historian Leonard Levy, they were reprinted in "every colonial newspaper from Boston to Savannah." "Cato's" rhetoric—referring to free speech or press as a "bulwark of liberty" and "essential to the security of a free state"—was repeated in state bills of rights and in Madison's proposed bill of rights in the first Congress under the new federal Constitution.[44]

Cato's theory of free speech was "daring and well-developed."[45] Freedom of speech, Cato insisted, is a "sacred privilege" that was, like private property, "essential to free Government." "Without Freedom of Thought," Cato declared, "there can be no such Thing as Wisdom; and no such Thing as publick Liberty, without Freedom of Speech."[46] Cato insisted on broad freedom to discuss public measures. In part, this conclusion came from Cato's understanding of the nature of government. "The Administration of Government is nothing else, but the Attendance of the Trustees of the People upon the Interest and Affairs of the People. And as it is the Part and Business of the people, for whose Sake alone all publick Matters are, or ought to be, transacted, to see whether they be well or ill transacted."[47] While recognizing that public measures could be misrepresented, Cato often seems to endorse the remedy of counter-speech.

> Misrepresentation of publick Measures is easily overthrown, by representing publick Measures truly: When they are honest, they ought to be publickly known, that they may be publickly commended; but if they be knavish or pernicious, they ought to be publickly exposed, in order to be publickly detested.
>
> To assert, that King James was a Papist and a Tyrant was only so far hurtful to him, as it was true of him. . . .
>
> . . .
>
> All Ministers, therefore, who were Oppressors, or intended to be Oppressors, have been loud in their Complaints against Freedom of Speech, and the License of the Press; and always restrained, and endeavoured to restrain, both.[48]

Although the law had typically not treated truth as a defense in the cases of libel (including seditious libel), Cato insisted that the doctrine "only holds true as to private and personal Failings; and it is quite otherwise when the Crimes of Men come to affect the Publick. Nothing ought to be so dear to us as our Country, and nothing ought to come in Competition with its Interests. Every crime against the publick is a great Crime."[49]

In response to complaints about libel on government, Cato noted the tendency of those in power to libel the people. "[T]he People often Judge better than their Superiors, and have not so many Biasses to Judge wrong, and Politicians often rail at the People, chiefly because they have given the People occasion to rail."[50]

Cato did not endorse absolute freedom to criticize either people or government, and sometimes Cato seems to indulge in studied ambiguity. Libels against government, Cato said, were always "base and unlawful, and often mischievous; especially when Governments are impudently charged with Actions and Designs of which they are not guilty,"[51] but Cato disapproved of prosecuting people for libel in connection with matters affecting the welfare of the public. In such cases, Cato insisted truth was a defense, and he proposed other safeguards as well.[52] Although recognizing a distinction between the liberty and the licentiousness of the press, Cato clearly had a much narrower view of what counted as licentiousness.

Cato admitted that words libelous in their natural and genuine meaning ought not to escape punishment. Still, he warned against abuses of doctrines that construed seemingly innocent language as criminal. He suggested a presumption that would substantially protect freedom of expression:

> There are so many Equivoques in language, so many Sneers in Expression, which naturally carry one Meaning, and yet may intend another, that it is impossible by any fixed and stated Rules to determine the Intention, and punish all who deserve to be punished. But to get rid of this Inconvenience at the Expense of giving any Man, or Number of Men, a discretionary Power to judge another's Intentions to be criminal, when his Words do not plainly denote them to be so, is subverting all Liberty, and subjecting all Men to the Caprices, to the arbitrary and wild Will, of those in Power. A Text in Scripture can not be quoted, without being said to reflect on those who break it.[53]

Cato therefore insisted on a presumption of innocence for challenged speech.

> It is a Maxim of Politicks in despotick Government, That Twenty innocent Persons ought to be punished, rather than One guilty Man escape; but the Reverse of this is true in free States. . . . And therefore when an innocent or criminal Sense can be put upon Words or Actions, the meaning of which is not fully determined by other Words or Actions, the most beneficent Construction ought to be made in favour of the Person accused. . . .
>
> This Truth every man acknowledges, when it becomes his own Case, or the Case of his Friends or Party; and almost every Man complains of it when he suffers by it: So great is the Difference of Mens having Power in their Hands or upon their Shoulders![54]

Cato had no illusions about the consistency with which people argued for free speech.

> This Liberty has been approved or condemned by all Men, and all Parties, in proportion as they were advantaged, or annoy'd by it: When they were in Power, they were unwilling to have their Actions scanned and censured, and cried out, that such Licence ought not to be borne and tolerated in any well constituted commonwealth; and when they suffered under the Weight of Power, they thought it very hard not to have been allowed the Liberty to utter their Groans, and to alleviate their Pain, by venting some Part of it in Complaints; and it is certain, that there are Benefits and Mischiefs on both Sides of the Question.[55]

Cato struck the balance in favor of freedom of speech. "I must own, that I would rather many Libels should Escape, than the Liberty of the Press should be infringed; yet no Man in England thinks worse of Libels than I do." A law vigorous enough to reach all libel would also deter speech and press that should be protected, he warned. To punish "by a general Law any Libel so much as it deserves," Cato warned, was too dangerous, "since such a Law, . . . being of such vast Latitude, would make all Writing whatsoever, how innocent soever, and even all Speaking, unsafe." Leonard Levy suggests that Cato made "genuflections toward the law" to keep on the safe side, but favored a much restricted law of libel.[56]

According to Cato, libels rarely caused baseless discontent with government; freedom of speech and press, with their abuses, were less dangerous than the alternative. Cato seemed to recognize the tension between the law of libel and freedom of the press. He took a long view: "As long as there is such Things as Printing and Writing, there will be Libels: It is an evil Arising out of a much greater good."[57]

In contrast to the popular tradition to which Cato contributed, the orthodox English view made criticism of rulers the crime of sedition. Truth was no defense. As an English judge put it in 1704, "If a man attempts to sap the confidence of the people in their officers, their supreme magistrate, and their legislature, he effectually saps the government. If people should not be called to account for possessing the people with an ill opinion of government, no government can subsist. For it is very necessary for all governments that the people should have a good opinion of it."[58] By this theory, true criticisms of government were regarded as worse than false ones.

Cato in America

In the early eighteenth century, Radical Whig ideas began to surface in America. In 1735, John Peter Zenger, printer of the *New York Weekly Journal*, published criticisms of William Cosby, the royal governor of New York, and was tried for sedition. Zenger's trial was "clearly the most significant political trial of the pre-revolutionary period." The record of the trial was widely reprinted in the colonies and in England.[59]

The *Weekly Journal* was controlled by a political faction hostile to Cosby. It reprinted Cato's letters on free speech and press. In its criticism of Cosby, the *Journal* had said the "LIBERTIES AND PROPERTIES" of the people of New York were "precarious, and . . . SLAVERY is like to be entailed on them and their posterity if some past things be not amended." Furthermore men's deeds to real property were destroyed, "JUDGES ARBITRARILY DISPLACED, NEW COURTS ERECTED WITHOUT THE CONSENT OF THE LEGISLATURE . . . BY WHICH, IT SEEMS TO ME, TRIALS BY JURIES ARE TAKEN AWAY WHEN A GOVERNOR PLEASES."[60] After unsuccessful efforts to get a grand jury to indict Zenger, Cosby had him charged by a procedure known as information, in which the prosecutor proceeds against the defendant on the basis of a document signed only by the prosecutor.

The trial came before a judge who was appointed by Cosby and who could be removed by him. Not only did Cosby have a willing henchman on the bench, he also had repressive English precedents on the law of seditious libel on his side. These precedents tended to support the view that the only question for the jury to decide was whether the defendant had published the item, while the issue of whether the content of the paper was seditious was for the judge to decide. Truth was no defense.

So when Zenger's attorney admitted that his client had published the items in question, his admission produced some astonishment. He went on to assert that the publication of such complaints was "the right of every free-born subject to make when the matters so published can be supported by truth." He attacked English precedent relied on by the prosecutor as the product of the Star Chamber and the repressive policies of King Charles I, who (after all) had been beheaded. Though the court denied that truth was a defense or that the question of sedition was for the jury, Zenger's attorney argued to the jury (as had the Leveller John Lilburne) that it was the judge of law as well as fact. In rhetoric reminiscent of the Levellers, he insisted that the right to make truthful criticisms of government was one of the rights of "freeborn Englishmen." The jury agreed, disobeyed the judge's instructions, and acquitted.[61]

Technically, the decision to acquit Zenger was not a legal precedent because jury verdicts are not considered authoritative statements of the law. But in the popular tradition of free speech and press, Zenger's case set a very important precedent indeed. It stood for the proposition that truthful statements on matters of public concern were protected speech. It was also part of a tradition that insisted that juries should decide (in the first instance) not only if the defendant had published the paper but also whether it was libelous or otherwise unprotected.

However, views of the Levellers, Cato, Zenger's jury, and the Radical Whigs were not the law or the orthodox legal view in England. If radicals insisted the people were sovereign, the English establishment view was that Parliament (or the monarch in Parliament) was sovereign. If radicals insisted on fundamental rights written into a basic constitution, William Blackstone expressed the prevailing view of the English leadership in his influential *Commentaries on the Laws of England*: parliamentary power was unlimited.[62] If radicals insisted on the right of the sovereign people to criticize their "agents" or "trustees," whom they had temporarily empowered to handle public affairs, English law treated such criticism as impermissible. Still, even in England, by the eighteenth century, actual exercise and tolerance of press freedom was ahead of the law.

The idea of a loyal opposition was slow to develop in England, as the case of John Wilkes demonstrates. Wilkes was born in 1727, the second son of a wealthy malt distributor. He was given a classical education and devoted most of his life to politics. Wilkes was elected to Parliament in 1761 and soon began to edit a paper critical of government policy, *The North Briton*. In issue number 45 he criticized the king's speech (written by the leaders of the party in power) on peace with Spain. He lamented that the king "whom England truly reveres, can be brought to give the sanction of his sacred name to the most odious measures." The government, unsure of the identity of all involved, issued a "general warrant" for the arrest of the authors, printers, and publishers of *The North Briton*. (A general warrant commands seizure of all persons or things involved in an alleged crime and does not particularly describe the persons or things to be seized. American colonists had already protested against general warrants. According to John Adams, James Otis's argument against them in the Writs of Assistance case was one of the origins of the American Revolution.)[63]

In due time the trail led to Wilkes, who was arrested at his home. Government agents, acting under the general warrant, ransacked his house and papers. Wilkes lectured his captors on the illegality of general warrants and finally agreed to accompany the officers only if they transported him in a sedan chair. After being carried in style to his interrogators, Wilkes refused to answer incriminating questions. Wilkes was confined, but later released on the ground of parliamentary privilege. In London he became a popular hero, greeted with shouts of "Wilkes and Liberty."

Wilkes and other targets brought legal actions against those who searched for evidence in The North Briton case under the assumed authority of a general warrant. Chief Justice Charles Pratt decided the warrants in the Wilkes case were illegal,[64] a decision subsequently confirmed by a resolution of Parliament. But Wilkes's troubles were far from over.

The House of Commons ordered The North Briton, no. 45, burned by the common hangman, but a mob rescued it. In the meantime an obscene poem written by Wilkes was discovered by the government; officials were appropriately outraged. Wilkes was expelled from Parliament and indicted for the poem and for The North Briton, no. 45. He fled to France, where, on being asked how far free press extended in England, he replied that he did not know but was trying to find out. He was convicted in absentia.

On his return, the government at first decided to ignore him, but Wilkes ran for Parliament and was elected. At this point, he was ordered arrested and sentenced to prison. On his trip to prison he was rescued by a mob. Wilkes escaped from the mob and dutifully went to prison. Parliament refused to seat him, but his constituents repeatedly reelected him.

Though in prison, Wilkes remained a hero on both sides of the Atlantic. Americans identified strongly with Wilkes: his fate was theirs. They saw the refusal to seat Wilkes, like the attacks on American colonial assemblies, as attacks on representative government. Americans named towns and counties for Wilkes. English and American supporters contributed 17,000 pounds sterling on his behalf. After several reelections that Parliament refused to recognize, he finally took his seat without opposition in 1775.[65]

The Wilkes affair suggests that, while the British government and law regarded criticism of government policy as unlawful, many of Wilkes's supporters, who elected and reelected the convict to Parliament, did not. The struggle between Wilkes's constituents and a Parliament that announced it would not seat him also suggests that many believed in a popular sovereignty superior to Parliament. Wilkes's immense support among the people is evidence of strong popular rejection of the use of seditious libel against him. Wilkes "symbolized opposition to traditional controls on political expression," as Norman Rosenberg has noted in his classic history of the law of libel.[66]

Through much of English history, up to and including the late eighteenth century, political dissent had been treated as treason. In 1663, for example, John Twyn was charged with printing "a seditious, poisonous and scandalous book." The book asserted that the king should be accountable to his subjects. The court held "printing and publishing such wicked" ideas, was an overt act of treason—"compassing and imagining the king's death." Twyn was executed.[67] The Treason Act of 1696 sought to limit such political prosecutions and to mitigate the "savage political warfare of the Restoration" which "had seen Whigs and Tories hustling each other's leaders off to block and gallows after treason trials which had been travesties of justice." The statute required two witnesses to the same overt act of treason.[68] Since treason was one of the chief weapons against antigovernment speech and press, attempts to limit it are important chapters in free speech history.

In late-eighteenth-century England, around the time of the American Sedition Act trials, a politically motivated government stretched the requirement of the 1696 act of an overt act for treason. It brought constructive treason prosecutions against members of the London Constitutional Society and the London Corresponding Society, both of which had been agitating for democratic change. The evidence supporting the convictions consisted of proof that the

> two societies . . . which had branches all over the country, carried on an agitation for the establishment of universal suffrage and annual parliaments, in the course of which they called a Convention, consisting of representatives from a number of branch societies. Members of the societies wrote letters, and made speeches, and cir-

culated books and pamphlets, and the Convention held meetings and passed resolutions, ostensibly and avowedly in order to further their political objects by constitutional means.[69]

Treason was not the only theory supporting suppression. Sir William Blackstone invoked other criteria in explaining the English meaning of freedom of the press, in volume 4 of his *Commentaries on the Laws of England*, published in 1769. According to Blackstone, freedom of the press was only the freedom not to submit proposed books and pamphlets to prior approval by government censors:

> In this, and the other instances which we have lately considered, where blasphemous, immoral, treasonable, schismatical, seditious, or scandalous libels are punished by the English law, some with a greater, others with a less degree of severity; the *liberty of the press*, properly understood, is by no means infringed or violated. The liberty of the press is indeed essential to the nature of a free state: but this consists in laying no *previous* restraints upon publications, and not in freedom from censure for criminal matter when published. Every freeman has an undoubted right to lay what sentiments he pleases before the public: to forbid this, is to destroy the freedom of the press: but if he publishes what is improper, mischievous, or illegal, he must take the consequence of his own temerity.

Blackstone explained that in "their largest and most extensive sense," libels were any writings or pictures with "an immoral or illegal tendency." He focused on "malicious defamations of any person, and especially a magistrate" that would expose him to public hatred or contempt. The "direct tendency" of such libels was to provoke a breach of the peace by stirring people up to violent revenge. Whether "the matters of it be true or false" was therefore "immaterial."[70]

James Burgh made a radical departure from the English law in his book *Political Disquisitions*, published in 1774. According to free speech scholar Stephen Smith, people in the founding generation, including members of the Continental Congress, admired Burgh's work. John Adams said every American should read it. Thomas Jefferson put Burgh on his list of recommended reading for a legal education.[71] Burgh insisted on the right and duty of "every subject's having a watchful eye on the conduct of Kings, Ministers, and Parliament." A subject not only should be "secured, but encouraged in alarming his fellow-subjects on occasion of every attempt upon public liberty."[72] If it were "dangerous and penal to inquire into their conduct," Burgh warned, "the state may be ruined by their blunders, or by their villainies, beyond the possibility of redress."[73] The subjects' "betters" were more likely "to conceal than detect the abuses committed by those in power."

Burgh believed that truth was not a sufficient defense, and he anticipated and went beyond our own current limits on the law of defamation in the interest of protecting comment on public affairs: "No man ought to be hindered saying or writing what he please on the conduct of those who undertake the management of national affairs, in which all are concerned, and therefore have a right to inquire, and to publish their suspicions concerning them. For if you punish the slanderer, you deter the fair inquirer."[74]

From the American Revolution to the American Bill of Rights

Both in the later colonial period and immediately after the Revolution, the press in America exercised a very broad actual freedom. For those who framed the Constitution and the Bill of Rights, criminal court prosecutions for seditious libel were rare events. There were no successful prosecutions during the colonial period after Zenger's 1735 acquittal. Grand juries refused to indict; and petit juries refused to convict. Public pressure limited the legislators' practice of punishing those who criticized them. As historian Leonard Levy has noted, a "nearly epidemic degree of [unpunished] seditious libel infected American newspapers" during the later colonial period and after independence.[75]

In 1774, the American Continental Congress made a significant declaration about free speech in its Address to the Inhabitants of Quebec. The address was an effort to gain support for the American cause in Canada. Since the inhabitants of Quebec had been "educated under another form of government," the American Congress sought to explain the essentials of free government. The address began with a suspicious view of power and praised freedom of the press as one of the essential guarantees of freedom. Press freedom was expected to produce unity, and it was not limited to political expression: "The importance of [freedom of the press] consists, besides the advancement of truth, science, morality, and arts in general, in its diffusion of liberal sentiments on the administration of Government, its ready communication of thoughts between subjects, and its consequential promotion of union among them, whereby oppressive officers are shamed or intimidated, into more honourable and just modes of conducting affairs."[76]

During the Revolution, however, American revolutionaries engaged in many practices that clearly violate our current understanding of freedom of speech and press: rebellious colonists suppressed Loyalist opinions, often by extra legal means; American revolutionaries also exiled loyalists.[77] Nor was repression limited to the press. With the landing of a large British army on the Chesapeake, Pennsylvania authorities arrested Quakers thought to be "inimical to the American cause" and searched them based on a general warrant of the sort that colonists had condemned and that the Fourth Amendment subsequently forbade. All their papers of a political nature were seized. All of this was done on the advice of the Continental Congress.[78] During the Revolution, Congress provided that people could be summoned before a magistrate to take the oath of allegiance to the American cause. Those who refused to take the oath could be exiled.[79] All these facts might lead one to conclude that the early American idea of freedom of the press was quite limited.

What shall we make of the paradox of revolutionary patriots hailing freedom of the press while silencing Tories? A new nation was being formed by revolution against the old. Perhaps at such times it is inevitable that adherents to the new nation separate from the adherents to the old and that general conceptions of liberty are disregarded. As Thomas Paine noted in an essay republished in the newspaper, the New York *Time Piece*, in 1797, "[I]n the commencement of a revolution, the revolutionary party permit to themselves a *discretionary exercise of power* regulated more by circumstances than by principle, which were the practice to continue, liberty would never be established, or if established would soon be overthrown."[80]

The searches and seizures of the Quakers in America during the Revolution occurred in the face of actual invasion. At any rate, it was after acts like the suppression of the Tory press, loyalty oaths, the searches of Quakers, and a Massachusetts legislative declaration finding certain persons guilty of treason, that Madison noted that one objection to a bill of rights was that state bills of rights had been repeatedly violated. This fact, he said, led some to think that bills of rights were useless.[81]

During the Revolution and after, Americans added state and federal constitutional guarantees that seem to have restricted some repressive revolutionary practices. Sometimes the implication that a prior law or practice could be inconsistent with liberty was explicit. Article VI, chapter 6 of the Massachusetts constitution of 1780, for example, provided that the prior laws of the province would continue in force, "such parts only excepted as are repugnant to the rights and liberties contained in this constitution."[82] The Massachusetts constitution forbade legislative declarations of treason, a practice Massachusetts had engaged in during the Revolution just eighteen months before.[83]

During the Revolution, states adopted constitutions that contained protections for (or at least recognition of) individual rights. Most listed freedom of the press and freedom of religion. Pennsylvania's constitution of 1776 had *two* provisions for freedom of the press:

> XII. That the people have a right to freedom of speech, and of writing, and publishing their sentiments: therefore freedom of the press ought not to be restrained.
>
> . . .
>
> Sect. 35. The printing presses shall be free to every person who undertakes to examine the proceedings of the legislature or any part of government.[84]

In addition, Pennsylvania attempted to guarantee impartial selection of juries. Pennsylvania also protected the "natural and unalienable right" of people to worship God "according to the dictates of their own consciences and understanding." None who acknowledged the being of God could be denied any civil right. No authority existed to "interfere with, or in any manner controul, the right of conscience in the free exercise of religious worship."[85]

Did the English common law of seditious libel survive these state constitutions and the First Amendment? As Leonard Levy has demonstrated, there were a few prosecutions for seditious libel in the American states after the Revolution and adoption of the Bill of Rights, despite state constitutional protection for free speech and press, but there were also claims that such prosecutions for seditious libel violated the guarantees of free speech and press.[86]

Courts were slow to repudiate orthodox English legal doctrine. In a 1788 decision, the supreme court of Pennsylvania convicted a printer of contempt of court for commenting on a pending libel action against him. The printer had suggested that his case involved "the rights of the press and of all freemen." He argued that the judges were prejudiced and that the law of libels was incompatible with liberty and "destructive of the privileges of a free country." Chief Justice McKean held that comment on a pending case interfered with the administration of justice. While every citizen had a right under the state constitution to "examine the proceedings of government" that right did not extend to "anticipations of the acts of the legislature, or the judgements of the court." This proviso seems to prohibit criticism of pending legislation. Press freedom, the chief justice explained, protected publication motivated by the public good, not items intended to delude or defame. By criticizing his opponent and the fairness of the judges, Chief Justice McKean said, the printer was guilty of acts that had a tendency to "corrupt the administration of justice." He was fined and imprisoned.[87]

Some followed Blackstone and insisted that freedom of the press was limited to protection against prior censorship, but did not preclude criminal punishment after publication. Others rejected this view of the English law. In America, freedom of the press and of speech are linked in the First Amendment and in many state bills of rights. A mere protection against a requirement of a license before speaking could hardly have been the understanding of freedom of speech. Governments have never attempted to require people to get prior approval before they spoke. As Thomas Cooley recognized in his 1868 book, *Constitutional Limitations*, such a requirement is utterly impractical and had never been attempted—in England, in the colonies, or in the United States up to the time he wrote. From that fact Cooley concluded that the freedom of the press must also be more than simply a protection against prior restraint.[88]

Many insisted that truthful discussion of public affairs was protected and that the people had a right to criticize their public officials. Attack on private reputation, according to this view was a different matter. On matters of public affairs, however, truth was a defense. The extent of protection for mistaken criticisms on matters of public affairs was less clear, though some, like Burgh, demanded broad protection here also.

There were two traditions in great tension with each other: a more protective tradition associated with the Radical Whig heritage and the popular practice of press freedom, and an older more repressive legal tradition from England. Broad power to punish all speech and press critical of government or public officials was inconsistent with the protection for free speech advocated in the Radical Whig tradition and by Cato, Zenger, and American colonists in one revolutionary declaration. But it was fully consistent with English common law. Typically, American states received only so much of the common law as was consistent with their constitutions and applicable to America's different circumstances.[89] These provisions recognized that some English law was simply not appropriate in America.

Although the Tory press had been silenced in the Revolution, after the Revolution, the major justification for suppression was removed. There was wide practical freedom for the press. The idea of a unified people was gradually abandoned. In addition, leaders like James Madison increasingly recognized the danger that the majority posed to free speech and press.[90]

There was a strong popular free speech tradition that rejected the limited Blackstonian view. In Pennsylvania, for example, people contended that the state constitution's free press guarantees barred any prosecutions for political libels. There were also defenders of a more restrictive view. Political libel prosecutions had almost disappeared in the 1780s and early 1790s.[91] The First Amendment was ratified in this context.

By the end of the American Revolution, the basic rights of Englishmen, including habeas corpus, protection against ex post facto laws and unreasonable searches, jury trial, right to counsel, and other procedural rights, and rights such as freedom of press, speech, and religion appeared in bills of rights in many state constitutions. Like state constitutions, the American Constitution contained some crucial protections of liberty. The treason clause protected free speech and press by severely limiting the crime of treason: "Treason against the United States, shall consist only in levying War against them, or adhering to their Enemies, giving them Aid and Comfort. No person shall be convicted to Treason unless on the Testimony of two Witnesses to the same overt Act, or on Confession in open Court."[92] The Constitution also prohibited ex post facto laws and bills of attainder.

Still, the omission of many other basic rights from the new American Constitution was one of the major arguments against its adoption. Among the missing items were protection for speech, press, petition, and religious conscience. Antifederalists demanded rejection because the Constitution lacked a bill of rights and protections for speech, press, and religion. Critics also objected to the Constitution because it made the government less reflective of "the people." At the same time, some framers of the American Constitution valued devices like having the senate elected by state legislatures and the president elected by an electoral college and other provisions as ways to protect wealth from "levelling." Some, like John Adams, suggested that even more undemocratic measures might be required.[93]

The absence of a bill of rights from the Constitution, the explanation for the absence, and finally the addition of the First Amendment all became arguments in a major controversy over political liberty and free speech and press in the new American nation—the debate over the Sedition Act. The Sedition Act is not simply an artifact from a bygone era of American constitutional law. The issues raised by the act go to the very heart of freedom of speech in a democracy. These issues reappeared, again and again, in nineteenth- and twentieth-century battles over free speech.

2

The Debate over the Sedition

Act of 1798

In 1964 law professor Harry Kalven wrote a celebrated article on the case of *New York Times v. Sullivan*. Sullivan, a Montgomery, Alabama, city police commissioner, had sued the *Times* because of statements that civil rights leaders had made in a paid *New York Times* advertisement. That advertisement harshly criticized "Southern violators," citing the arrest of Martin Luther King, the bombing of his house, and the police department's handling of the battle for integration. Some allegations about police behavior were not correct. Sullivan recovered a substantial verdict from an Alabama jury, but the Supreme Court reversed. It held that a public official had to show either intentional falsity or reckless disregard of the truth to collect a libel judgment based on criticism of how he performed his public duties. Professor Kalven was an enthusiastic supporter of the decision. He wrote: "The concept of seditious libel strikes at the very heart of democracy. Political freedom ends when government can use its powers and its courts to silence it critics. My point is not the tepid one that there should be leeway for criticism of the government. It is rather that defamation of the government is an impossible notion in a democracy. In brief, I suggest that the presence or absence in the law of the concept of seditious libel defines the society."[1]

In another publication, Kalven suggested that seditious libel was a paradigm case of what is impermissible in democratic society.[2] The paradigm case illuminates the rule that should be applied in deciding other, more doubtful, cases. The more a new case resembles the clear paradigm case—the more it implicates the same policies and purposes of the law—the stronger the argument for deciding the new case in the same way.

SEDITION, ABOLITIONIST SPEECH, AND ANTIWAR SPEECH: SEDITION AS A PARADIGM CASE

The Sedition Act of 1798, which is the subject of this and the next two chapters, is a paradigm case. It raised the question of whether criticism of the government, advocating public policy, and criticizing the way public officials perform their job should be crimes in the American republic. In the controversy over the Sedition Act, its opponents emphasized the need for free speech in democratic government. They noted that the Sedition Act prevented or greatly impeded discussion of appropriate public policy. They said it undermined popular sovereignty because it deprived the people of basic information necessary for intelligent exercise of the vote. Critics also highlighted the partisan political purposes of the act, which tried to silence one political party and to protect the power of the other. Finally, they argued that the national government simply lacked power to pass such an act because the First Amendment clearly deprived the national government of power over speech or press. Critics of the act appealed to states' rights as well as to the right of free speech. In the case of the Sedition Act, the arguments reinforced each other.

After the Sedition Act controversy, the major free speech struggles recounted in this book involve the attempts to silence antislavery speech and antiwar speech during the Civil War. The story of the Sedition Act helps us understand these struggles. The rejection of national power over speech *and* the place of free speech in democratic government that emerged from the struggle against the Sedition Act shaped the debate over antislavery speech. The role of free speech in a democracy shaped the debate on antiwar speech. Following the consensus that developed against the Sedition Act, Congress refused to pass even a comparatively mild national limit on antislavery speech. The "no federal power over speech" consensus also led some people to argue that the matter was for the states, an echo of one strand of the Sedition Act debate.

The Sedition Act experience is also central to our understanding in a more fundamental way. It taught that the power to suppress criticism of either public officials or government and the power to suppress advocacy of public policy must be tightly confined if democracy is to survive. The reason, of course, is that wide-open debate on public policy is central to democratic government. "Robust and wide-open" debate both allows the people to participate in their government and to consider alternative courses of action.

Although antislavery speech was aimed at the institution of slavery and the behavior of slave owners as well as at governmental action, the lesson of the Sedition Act was relevant. The experience of the act suggests that people must be free to criticize government and debate public policy. Must they not also be free to criticize major social institutions such as slavery that shape government and society? Where slavery was dominant, it shaped law, government, economics, and even religion. Criticism of the exercise of private power often stimulates and accompanies a call for government action. Criticisms of slavery—like any criticism of the use and abuse of private power—also involved implicit and often explicit calls for government action. Opponents of slavery suggested that the nation should ban the interstate slave trade and prohibit slavery in the territories and in the nation's capital. They criticized the fugitive slave law. Eventually, many also argued for political action at the state level to end slavery in all the Southern states. Advocating political change was one of the types of speech that opponents of the Sedition Act saw as essential to republican government.

The attempts to silence antislavery speech echo the Sedition Act experience. Laws against antislavery expression silenced Lincoln's Republican Party in half of the nation while allowing freedom of discussion for their opponents. In this respect, the rules against antislavery speech were simply much more effective versions of what the Sedition Act had attempted. Finally, as in the case of the Sedition Act, the popular free speech tradition helped to defeat national action against abolitionist speech and attempts to suppress antislavery speech in the North.

In short, the case of the Sedition Act brilliantly illuminates the essentially antidemocratic nature of the effort to protect the institution of slavery from criticism. It does the same, of course, for the effort to silence critics of the government's policy during the Civil War.

The Sedition Act is central to the free speech struggles recounted in this book in still another way. The attack on the act emphasized two themes—freedom of speech and protection of states' rights. Many critics of the act appealed to states' rights in an effort to protect free speech, much as today consumer advocate Ralph Nader appeals to states' rights against federal laws that restrict state common law or statutory rights to sue makers of defective products. As slavery became the main political issue agitating the nation, the tension between the idea of free speech as (potentially, at least) merely a limit on the national government and the idea that free speech was essential to representative government became increasingly clear. Both the Sedition Act and the battle for free speech about slavery are chapters in the growth of the idea that democratic government for the United States required national constitutional protection for free speech: a protection that limited the states as well as the national government and that allowed broad protection for discussion of public affairs.

For all these reasons, the Sedition Act, to which I now turn, is an important part of our free speech story. This chapter discusses the legislative struggles over the framing of the act and the public debate the act engendered. Chapter 3 will explore the act's enforcement and theories of free speech that followed it.

From the Revolution to the Bill of Rights

In the Sedition Act debate, in the debate over antislavery speech, and in the debate over antiwar speech, ideas of popular sovereignty were crucial. Such ideas were not new: arguments from popular sovereignty had simmered in England at the time of the Levellers, grew during the American Revolution, and were mobilized in the fight over the ratification of the Constitution.

The Articles of Confederation, the first constitution for the nation, had provided that they should be perpetual. They also provided that any amendments must be approved by all states. Under a mandate to propose amendments to the Articles, the assembly that became the Constitutional Convention instead wrote an entirely new constitution—one that provided it would be effective on ratification by only nine states. The procedure was irregular, if not unconstitutional. Supporters of the new Constitution used the theory of popular sovereignty to justify the departure from the procedure for constitutional change authorized by the Articles. By this theory, the states were not sovereign, nor was the Congress that existed under the Articles. The sovereign was the people of the United States. If the agents of the people in the Constitutional Convention had exceeded their authority, the people, as their principal, could ratify their acts. And that, the theory goes, is what the people did. In the *Federalist Papers*, Alexander Hamilton also used the theory of popular sovereignty to justify judicial review.[3] If one objection to the new Constitution was the irregular way in which it was proposed, a second major objection was the lack of a bill of rights.

The framers left a bill of rights out of the Constitution. When challenged on that score in the ratification process, they responded with a collection of arguments. They insisted that the Constitution already contained guarantees of liberty (a sort of virtual bill of rights) and that the federal government lacked the power to perform the feared invasions of liberty. (It had no delegated power to interfere with the liberty of speech and press, for example.)[4] Somewhat inconsistently, they warned that guarantees of liberty were dangerous because a limitation on power implied the existence of the power that was limited, much as the provision that the government cannot take property for public use without paying for it suggests that it can take property if it does pay for it. And they argued that listing rights was dangerous because it would imply that those rights not listed did not exist, an argument at odds both with the idea that the Constitution already contained a virtual bill of rights and with the notion that the Constitution did not abrogate the unenumerated rights of mankind.[5]

The final argument against a bill of rights was based on popular sovereignty. Bills of rights were devices needed to limit the power of the king in favor of popular rights. In the United States, the people were sovereign, and since the people would not invade their own rights, a bill of rights was superfluous.[6] This argument is extraordinarily hollow, as the Levellers had understood many years before. The agents to whom the people periodically delegate the management of their affairs are not identical to the people. As in any agency relation, there was the danger that the agents would use the delegated power for their own purposes, not for those of the principal. The argument also ignored another reason for a bill of rights—protection of the minority against the majority. Fortunately, this popular sovereignty argument against a bill of rights did not prevail.

The failure to include a bill of rights in the new federal Constitution had been one of the arguments against its adoption. A number of state ratifying conventions proposed amendments, including amendments securing freedom of the press. A Maryland proposal was defended by its drafting committee on the ground that "preservation of this great fundamental right" may "prove invaluable" in "prosecutions in federal court for libels." Whatever else this committee understood by freedom of the press, it clearly thought it would affect seditious libel prosecutions and was more than a protection against prior restraint.[7]

In the face of mounting opposition, some Federalists relented and suggested a bill of rights should be added as an amendment to the new Constitution. In the first Congress under the new Constitution, James Madison sought to fulfill that pledge. Most of Madison's proposed amendments passed Congress, were ratified by the states, and became the Bill of Rights.

Madison apparently conceived of most of his provisions as limits only on federal power. He proposed to put them in Article I, Section 9, with other limitations on the power of Congress. However, he also insisted that some federal limits should be set on state powers: "[N]o State shall violate the equal right of conscience, freedom of the press, or trial by jury in criminal cases." Madison described freedom of the press, the right to trial by jury, and the right of conscience interchangeably as "rights" and as "privileges." He used the "no state shall" form specifically to limit states in reference to these rights. While most state constitutions secured these rights, Madison favored a "double security on those points." "State governments," Madison warned, "are as liable to attack the invaluable privileges as the General Government is." Madison rejected a suggestion to leave the matter to the states; he said the limitation on state power was "the most valuable amendment in the whole list."[8] The select committee, to which Madison's draft had been referred, expanded Madison's limit on the states to prevent states from infringing "the freedom of speech or of the press." In this form, Madison's proposal passed the House of Representatives.[9] Though Madison persuaded the House, the Senate did not concur. It rejected Madison's "most valuable" amendment.

Rather than creating rights, Madison and other framers saw the Bill of Rights as primarily declaratory and "prohibitory." The Bill of Rights simply declared and affirmed the existence of natural or inherited rights of "freeborn Englishmen," and it secured them from federal denial. Madison sometimes distinguished between the right and legal protection for it.[10] This view would become important again when the framers of the Fourteenth Amendment sought to protect basic rights such as free speech, not by creating such rights explicitly, but by assuming their existence (recognized in the Bill of Rights) and providing that no state should abridge the privileges or immunities of citizens of the United States.

A bill of rights, Madison said, would give legitimacy to principles of liberty, help the people to internalize these values, and provide a basis for rallying against abuses of power. It would also give new power to the courts. Madison announced, with excessive optimism as it turned out, that "courts of justice" would form "impenetrable barriers" against violations of the liberties in the Bill of Rights. Madison also saw a role for the states, anticipating a later controversy over the role of state legislatures in the Sedition Act debate. State legislatures, Madison announced, "will jealously and closely watch operations of this Government, and be able to resist with more effect every assumption of power." The legislatures were "sure guardians of the people's liberty."[11] Alexander Hamilton had made a similar argument in *The Federalist*, before the addition of the Bill of Rights. He assured the doubtful that "state governments will, in all possible contingencies, afford complete security against invasions of the public liberty by the national authority." They could "discover the danger at a distance" and "at once adopt a regular plan of opposition" including communicating with other states to "unite their common forces for the protection of their common liberty."[12]

The Background of the Sedition Act

In 1791, the Bill of Rights became part of the Constitution. By 1798 it faced its first, crucial test.

George Washington had been elected president unanimously. Though Federalists had supported the Constitution, and Antifederalists had opposed it, there were at first no national political parties in the new nation.

The unanimity was short-lived. During Washington's administration, political groupings began to coalesce around Alexander Hamilton, on one side, and James Madison and Thomas Jefferson, on the other. The Madison-Jefferson group began to call themselves Republicans, while the other group called itself Federalists. (The Republicans tended to call the Federalists monarchists or Tories; the Federalists called the Republicans Jacobins and disorganizers.) According to one explanation, the Federalists were a national political party that represented mercantile, shipping, and financial interests. As David Anderson puts it, they believed that "those who owned the country had a duty to preserve it from . . . democracy, immigration, and licentiousness."[13]

Republicans suspected that Hamilton and some other leading Federalists were crypto-monarchists who wanted to move the nation in a less democratic direction. In the Constitutional Convention, Hamilton had advocated an executive with an unlimited tenure—a sort of elected king, and a senate elected for life.[14] By 1790, John Adams, too, believed that a hereditary president and senate would eventually be required to save the nation from corruption. Adams hoped it would not come to that, but he believed it would. As one student of his thought explains, Adams "now betrayed a disturbing lack of confidence in . . . the long term future of republican government." Both Adams and Hamilton had been concerned with maintaining "balance" between factions in order to ensure stable government, and both had suggested these antidemocratic devices in the service of balance. Still, both Adams and Hamilton denied any present designs to change the form of government. They said they were willing to give the experiment a fair chance.[15] Republicans were not reassured.

In contrast to those who thought the government excessively democratic and insufficiently balanced, many Republicans suggested that the Senate, which was chosen by state legislatures, was insufficiently democratic. Republicans generally favored expanding the suffrage by letting free men (or at least free white men) vote. Federalists typically opposed expanded suffrage.[16]

Thomas Cooper, a Republican publicist, attempted a balanced description of the differences between the parties: Federalists, he suggested, wished to increase the power of the executive; Republicans to diminish it. Federalists thought that the people had too much power; Republicans thought there was too little democracy. Federalists favored a standing army, thinking it was necessary to protect against foreign aggression and domestic commotions; Republicans thought a militia sufficient. Federalists thought the liberties of the country were endangered by licentiousness of the press. Republicans thought liberty was endangered "by the restrictions of the press."[17]

Federalists tended to deny the legitimacy of political opposition. Like many others, they were suspicious of an opposition party, or faction, as it was called. "The idea of a legitimate opposition—recognized opposition, organized and free enough in its activities to be able to displace an existing government by peaceful means—is an immensely sophisticated idea," as Richard Hofstadter has noted.[18] In 1798 many Americans had not reached this level of sophistication. But Madison and some other Republicans had. As early as January 1792, James Madison announced that in "every political society, parties are unavoidable." Madison thought the evils of parties could be mitigated. One way to do that was to establish "political equality among all," to avoid a group's exerting political influence out of proportion to its numbers. In pursuit of this goal, Madison now favored "withholding unnecessary opportunities from a few, to increase the inequality of property, by immoderate, and especially unmerited, accumulation of riches." He supported "the silent operation of laws, which, without violating the rights of property, reduce extreme wealth towards a state of mediocrity, and raise extreme indigence towards a state of comfort."[19]

Finally, Republicans tended to be supportive of the French Revolution after Federalists had become hostile to it. As French revolutionary armies overran many nations of Europe, Adams and others worried about France's unprecedented domination of the continent.[20] While Republicans still detested Britain, Hamilton and some Federalists tended to favor closer ties with this old enemy.

In 1798, the French were affronted by a treaty between the United States, their formal ally since the Revolutionary War, and the British. The French began to attack American shipping, ostensibly to deny supplies to Great Britain. President Adams sent a mission to France in an effort to resolve the impasse peacefully. Representatives of the French foreign minister Talleyrand demanded a bribe, a disavowal of portions of a speech by President Adams, and a loan to France before the Directory would deal with the American envoys. When news of these demands was published in the United States, there was a backlash against the French. From April 1798 to March 1799, some three hundred addresses supporting the government's stand against France poured in from popular meetings throughout the nation. Men formed voluntary militia companies. Some arch-Federalists pressed for war. Congress passed appropriations to build a navy (as President Adams had requested) and also for a substantial army that the president had not requested. An undeclared naval war began between the United States and France.[21]

This development left the formerly pro-French Republicans in a difficult spot. They objected to the use of the crisis for domestic partisan purposes, and they criticized the French and proclaimed their own loyalty and their readiness to defend the nation in case of war.[22] But they favored peace and criticized the military build-up as a standing army. The army, they feared, might be used to involve the nation in an unnecessary war or against the Federalists' political opponents. Republicans favored reliance on a militia instead. The Federalist belief that organized political opposition was illegitimate was intensified by the threat of war and suggestions (all too common in wartime) that dissent was disloyal.

The political advantages of this crisis were not lost on the Federalists. Referring to the French threats, demand for a bribe and refusal to deal with the American peace mission, Federalist senator Theodore Sedgwick wrote, "It will afford a glorious opportunity to destroy faction."[23]

Against this background, Congress soon considered a bill against "sedition." The *Massachusetts Mercury*, a Federalist paper, said a bill against "seditious practices" was essential to national defense and would be "highly gratifying to every good Citizens [sic]." The nation was plagued by "parracidal miscreants ... preying on the vitals of the country ... by the propagation of the most infamous falsehoods." These "[w]retches ... who call themselves Americans, Patriots, and Republicans" had done more than our enemies "to render our Government and our rulers infamous and contemptible in the eyes of the world." It was "high time that a stop should be put to their career."[24] The *Albany Centinel* noted with pleasure that the press was "almost unanimously devoted to the good of their country." Still, "two or three in our populous towns" were "prostituted to the designs of intriguing foreigners." But there was "another class of printers deserving censure:—the dangerous neutrals" acting under "the deceptive cloak of impartiality." Nothing should be published that would "suppress just indignation" at the French, the *Centinel* announced. "It is traitorous to be doubtful."[25]

To many Federalists, whose sagging political fortunes had been revived, the actions of the French seemed heaven-sent. In the midst of crisis with France, President John Adams received a number of supportive patriotic addresses from citizens, legislatures, and grand juries. In his response to an address from the inhabitants of his home town, Adams explained that the "tongues and pens of slander" were "instruments with which our enemies expect to subdue our country." But a "signal interposition of Providence" had "for once detected frauds and calumnies which from inexecution of the laws and indifference of the people were too long permitted to prevail."[26]

The town of Weston told the president that they had "no disorganizers" and that their votes had proved their "federalism." In response, Adams congratulated the town on "their signal felicity, in having no disorganizers. Two or three of this description ... are sufficient to destroy the good neighborhood. . . . A town that is free of them," Adams continued, "will ever prove their federalism in elections."[27]

The Federalist press explained that criticism of the elected government was improper, disloyal, and traitorous. In a column published in October 1798, after the passage of the Sedition Act in July, Federalist papers branded the critics of the government as traitors: "Whatever American is a friend to the present Administration of the American Government, is undoubtedly a true Republican, a true Patriot: For the Administration is, of necessity, elected by a *majority* of the people. . . . Whatever American *opposes* the Administration is an Anarchist, a Jacobin, and a Traitor. If men *dislike* the present Officers of our Government, let them vote for others at the next election. . . . It is *Patriotism* to write in favor of our Government—it is Sedition to write against it."[28] Scholar James P. Martin argues that Federalists simply had a different view of representative government. By this view, representatives, not ordinary people, were to debate public policy.[29] If that was their view, it mirrored parliamentary criticism of the Levellers. But it was a view more preached than practiced by the Federalist press.

There were ugly scenes, with Federalist mobs or militias menacing Republican congressmen and threatening physical attacks on Republican editors. Armed Federalist militias roamed cities and attacked dissidents. Republicans organized their own militia groups, and the nation seemed to face the prospect of armed clashes between rival factions.[30] The *Gazette of the United States*, a paper supported by Alexander Hamilton, suggested a physical attack on Benjamin Franklin Bache, Benjamin Franklin's grandson and the editor of the *Aurora*.[31] The *Aurora* reported that a plan to demolish the house of a Republican congressman was foiled by an armed group of Republican resisters. Troops attacked and beat or whipped editors and cut down liberty poles (poles containing slogans in favor of "liberty" and against the Sedition Act and Federalists). No doubt, as the Federalist press suggested, there were also incidents of Republican-initiated violence.[32]

John Adams had wisely suggested appointing both Republicans and Federalists to the officer corps of the new army, but George Washington, commander of the provisional army, excluded Republicans. Washington wrote Secretary of War James McHenry warning against commissions for professed "democrats" in the New Army. (In those days "democrat" was a term of abuse that Federalists hurled at Republicans). "[Y]ou could as soon," Washington observed, "scrub the blackamore white as to change the principles of a profest Democrat and . . . he will leave nothing unattempted to overturn the Government of this Country."[33] Federalists denied Republicans employment and expelled them from voluntary societies.[34]

CONGRESS DEBATES THE SEDITION ACT

In this highly emotional political climate, Congress passed the Sedition Act and the Federalists enforced it. As finally passed, the Sedition Act made it a crime to "write, print, utter, or publish . . . any false, scandalous, and malicious writing or writings, against the government of the United States, or either house of the congress of the United States, or the president of the United States, with intent to defame . . . or to bring them, or either of them, into contempt or disrepute; or to excite against . . . any of them, the hatred of the good people of the United States."[35] The Republican vice president was not covered, and the act had a sunset provision by which it would expire at the end of President Adams's term.

To reach its final form, the Sedition Act underwent considerable refinement. On June 26, 1798, Senator Lloyd had introduced an act to define treason and punish sedition. It declared the people and government of France to be enemies of the United States and made Americans guilty of aiding, abetting, or comforting France or Frenchmen guilty of treason. The act also made it sedition to attempt to weaken the confidence of the people of the United States in their government, or defame the administrators thereof, or defend the present hostile conduct of France.[36] A House version punished anyone who should "traduce or defame the Legislature of the United States, by seditious or inflammatory declarations . . . with intent to create a belief . . . that the . . . Legislature in enacting any law, was induced thereto by motives hostile to the Constitution, or liberties, and happiness of the people." It also prohibited traducing or defaming the president, and any court or judge, "by declarations tending to criminate their motives in any official transaction."[37]

Representative John Allen of Connecticut argued that if any nation needed such a law it was the United States. If any doubted the need, he said, let "gentlemen look at certain papers printed in this city and elsewhere" that demonstrated a "dangerous combination" designed "to overturn and ruin the Government by publishing the most shameless falsehoods against the Representatives of the people . . . [suggesting] that they are hostile to free Governments and genuine liberty."[38] For example, he noted, "in the Aurora, of last Friday, we read the following: 'The period is now at hand when it will be a question difficult to determine, whether there is more safety and liberty to be enjoyed at Constantinople or Philadelphia?'" As this and other examples make clear, the falsity that Federalists were attacking by the Sedition Act went beyond factual matters and encompassed "false" opinions or criticism directed to public policy and the political conduct of elected officials.

Allen was sure that the nation was in peril. "A conspiracy against the Constitution, the Government, the peace and safety of this country, is formed, and is in full operation. It embraces members of all classes; the Representative of the people on this floor, the wild and visionary theorist in the bloody philosophy of the day, the learned and ignorant."[39] Allen read again from the *Aurora*, a leading Republican paper: "'Where a law shall have been passed in violation of the Constitution, making it criminal to expose the crimes, the official vices or abuses, or the attempts of men in power to usurp a despotic authority, is there any alternative between an abandonment of the Constitution and resistance?'" The editor, Allen fumed, declares what is unconstitutional, and then invites the people to "resistance." "This," he said, "is an awful, horrible example of 'the liberty of opinion and freedom of the press.' Can gentlemen hear these things and lie quietly on their pillows? Are we to see all these acts practiced against the repose of our country, and remain passive? Are we bound hand and foot that we must be witnesses of these deadly thrusts at our liberty?"[40] Allen's other examples included hostile comments on the policy of the government toward France and letters by congressmen to their constituents. Allen insisted the bill did not interfere with freedom of the press. People were always "answerable for malicious publication of falsehood; and what more does this bill require?"[41]

Representative Robert Goodloe Harper of South Carolina "knew that liberty of the press had been carried to a very considerable extent in this country." But he rejected "harangues on the liberty of the press, as if it were to swallow up all other liberties." Now that a congressman on the floor was "pronouncing invective against the Government, and calling upon the people to rise against the law" and congressmen were sending letters imputing vile motives to others, it was time to sound the alarm.[42]

Federalist Harrison Gray Otis of Massachusetts defended the bill in a deeply researched speech. He argued that Congress had power to punish insurrections and efforts to intimidate their officers. If these could be made criminal, "it follows that all means calculated to produce these effects, whether by speaking writing, or printing, were also criminal. From the nature of things, therefore, the National Government is invested with a power to protect itself . . . or it must be indebted to and dependent on an individual State for its protection, which is absurd."[43] Otis contended that freedom of speech and of the press were not infringed by the act. This was so because the words "freedom of speech" or "freedom of the press" had a "certain and technical meaning" borrowed from England: "This freedom . . . is nothing more than the liberty of writing, publishing, and speaking one's thoughts, under the condition of being answerable to the injured party, whether it be the Government or an individual, for false, malicious, and seditious expressions, whether spoken or written; and the liberty of the press is merely an exemption from all previous restraints."[44] In support of this doctrine, Otis quoted Blackstone's *Commentaries* to prove that in England, formerly, the press had been subject to a licenser. "This restraint," he continued, "was afterward removed, by which means the freedom of the press was established."[45]

Otis reviewed judicial decisions and statutes of the various states, showing a restrictive view of freedom of the press. For example, the Massachusetts constitution contained a free press provision: "[Y]et in the law establishing the Supreme Court of that State, cognizance is given to it, among other things, over all offences and misdemeanors of a public nature 'tending to a breach of the peace, oppression of the subject, raising of faction, controversy or debate, to any manner of misgovernment.'" Otis recited a long litany of examples from many states. While Republicans were attempting to "deceive the people and alarm their fears, that they were threatened with the deprivation of a darling privilege," in fact these were "idle terrors" since "no innovation was attempted."[46] For Otis, freedom of the press was defined by its historic application by courts and English text writers.

A common Federalist refrain was that rights are limited by other rights. Federalist congressman Robert Goodloe Harper asked and then answered a series of rhetorical questions:

> Did this liberty of the press include sedition and licentiousness? Did it authorize persons to throw, with impunity, the most violent abuse upon the President and both Houses of Congress? . . . As well might it be said that the liberty of action implied the liberty of assault, trespass, or assassination. Every man possessed the liberty of

action; but if he used this liberty to the detriment of others, by attacking their persons or destroying their property, he became liable to punishment for this licentious abuse of his liberty. The liberty of the press stood on precisely the same footing. Every man might publish what he pleased; but if he abused this liberty so as to publish slanders against his neighbor, or false, scandalous, and malicious libels against the magistrates, or the Government, he became liable to punishment.[47]

Representative James Bayard of Delaware, a Federalist, proposed an amendment allowing the defendant to prove truth, and Representative William Claiborne, a Republican from Tennessee, proposed one allowing the jury to be judges of law as well as fact—that is to decide not only whether the defendant had published the item but whether it was seditious. Both amendments were accepted and became part of the act.[48]

The Federalists hammered away at the theme that Republicans were seeking to protect malicious liars. "Let it be remembered," Representative Francis Dana of Massachusetts intoned "that the uttering of malicious falsehoods, to the injury of the Government, is the offence which it is now intended to restrain; for, if what is uttered can be proved true, it will not, according to this bill, be punished as libelous." Dana insisted that "the rational, the honest, the Constitutional idea of freedom of language or of conduct" involved the "limitation of doing no injury to the rights of others."[49] Dana asked a series of questions, designed to put Republicans on the spot. "Why is the gentleman from Pennsylvania so very anxious on the subject? Or is [liberty of the press] abridged by a law to restrain lying? Could the framers of the Constitution intend to guarantee, as a sacred principle, the liberty of lying against the Government? What do gentlemen understand by 'the freedom of speech and of the press?' Is it a license to injure others or the Government, by calumnies, with impunity?"[50] Truth, Dana noted, would not be punished. The "rational and honest" constitutional idea of freedom of language was "doing what is not injurious to others."[51]

Republicans made a number of replies. First, they insisted that under the original Constitution Congress lacked any power over the press. They read the First Amendment as reinforcing this understanding and specifically denying Congress power over the press. (Federalists replied that this reading ignored the fact that the prohibition limited only abridging "*the freedom of* the press.") Congressman Nathaniel Macon of

North Carolina examined the opinions expressed at state conventions called to ratify the Constitution. The "best way," he said, "of coming at the truth of the construction of any part of the Constitution, [is] by examining the opinions that were held respecting it when it was under discussion in the different States." By quoting statements from that time Macon sought to prove that "it was never understood that prosecutions for libels could take place under the General Government; but that they must be carried on in the State courts, as the Constitution gave no power to Congress to pass laws on this subject. Not a single member in any of the conventions gave an opinion to the contrary." The states, Macon insisted, had complete power over the press. Macon's claim, that proponents of the Constitution had denied that the congress (or sometimes the federal government) had power over the press, was correct.[52]

The Republican argument based on the division of power between the federal and state governments raised the possibility that the issue was merely jurisdictional. If so, the question would not be whether the suppression contemplated by the Sedition Act was a violation of freedom of the press, but which government had the power to engage in suppression. Some Republicans seem to have framed the issue mainly in this way.

Republicans had very practical reasons for making a jurisdictional claim. The Sedition Act would be used against critics of President Adams. Defendants would be charged by United States attorneys appointed by Adams. And as Representative Nicholas noted, in a point Republicans made again and again in the following years, the trials would be before judges appointed by the president and juries selected by a marshal who held his office at the pleasure of the president.[53]

Representative Albert Gallatin of Pennsylvania was a leader of Republicans in the House. Gallatin had come to America from Switzerland as a young man. He settled in western Pennsylvania and was elected to the state legislature in 1790. There he worked for a statewide system of public education, modernization of the laws of the state, and the abolition of slavery. In 1794 Gallatin was elected to the federal House of Representatives, and by 1797, he was a leader of Republicans in the House. He particularly distinguished himself by his expertise on financial matters. Gallatin served in the House until 1801, when President Jefferson appointed him secretary of the treasury.[54]

In the Sedition Act debate, Gallatin said that in his own state of Pennsylvania, state court sheriffs selected jurors; in federal court, they were selected by the marshal, "the creature of the Executive." The difference, he insisted, was crucial for political offenses, such as the Sedition Act.[55] (Gallatin was right to be concerned. In prosecutions that followed the passage of the Act, Federalists would use their power to eliminate Republicans from Sedition Act juries. For example, several years later a lawyer witness at Justice Chase's impeachment trial testified that Justice Chase had instructed the federal marshal to eliminate any democrats from the jury panel in the sedition trial of James Callander in Virginia.)[56]

While Republicans denied any federal power over the press and insisted that power to deal with libels was exclusively for state courts, they also made practical and functional arguments against the Sedition Act. Logically, these were equally applicable to state governments as well as the national government. So when a Republican defendant faced a Massachusetts state law sedition trial in 1799, he employed a number of Republican anti–Sedition Act arguments.

In answer to the argument that the Sedition Act could do no harm because it reached only malicious lies, Republicans in Congress pointed to the realities of the situation. In fact, Representative John Nicholas of Virginia argued, the law would do far more than suppress falsehood. He recognized the chilling effect such statutes had on speech, a concept that much later, in the 1960s, was often invoked by the Supreme Court. "If this bill be passed into a law," Nicholas said,

> the people will be deprived of that information on public measures, which they have a right to receive, and which is the life and support of a free Government; for, if printers are to be subject to prosecution for every paragraph which appears in their papers, that the eye of a jealous Government can torture into an offence against this law, and to the heavy penalties here provided, it cannot be expected that they will exercise that freedom and spirit which it is desirable should actuate them; especially when they would have to be tried by judges appointed by the President, and by juries selected by the Marshal, who also receives his appointment from the President, all whose feelings would, of course, be inclined to commit the offender if possible. Under such circumstances, it must be seen that the printers of papers would be deterred from printing anything which should be in the least offensive to a power which might so greatly harass them. They would not only refrain from

publishing anything of the least questionable nature, but they would be afraid of publishing the truth, as though true, it might not always be in their power to establish the truth to the satisfaction of a court of justice. This bill would, therefore, go to the suppression of every printing press in the country, which is not obsequious to the will of Government.[57]

Nicholas argued from the "nature of our Government." He noted that "all its officers are elective, and that the people have no other means of examining their conduct but by means of the press" and its "unrestrained investigation" of the "conduct of the Government." A free press was "the heart and life of a free Government." If the press was to be shackled, one "might as well say to the people, we, your Representatives, are faithful servants, you need not look into our conduct." To restrict the press, Nicholas said, "would be to destroy the elective principle, by taking away the information necessary to election, and there would be no difference between it and a total denial of the right of election, but in the degree of usurpation."[58] Albert Gallatin announced that the principles of the law of political libels were to be found in the edicts "of the worst Emperors of Rome" and in "the decisions of the Star Chamber."[59]

Republicans often noted that a remedy for libel existed at state law. Representative Edward Livingston of New York said, "Every man's character is protected by [state] law, and every man who shall publish a libel on any part of government is liable to punishment" by state governments. Curiously, Livingston also said he knew of no such thing as slanders against the government. When charged with "passing an unconstitutional act—with violating our oaths" congressmen should attempt to disprove the facts and let the public judge. To instead prosecute the man who makes the charge may "establish error as soon as truth" and would "crush them by force or arms, not by the force of reason." It was "the same system which . . . lighted the fires of Smithfield [where Protestants were burned at the stake], and which has produced so much bloodshed and ruin amongst mankind."[60]

Congressmen are protected by the Constitution's speech-and-debate clause from criminal or civil liability for anything they say during debate. While some Federalist congressmen lamented what Republicans were saying on the floor of the House, all recognized that they were immune from civil or criminal liability. Congressman Nathaniel Macon of North Carolina, who also noted the availability of state law libel prosecutions, suggested that a privilege like the one that congressmen enjoyed under the speech-and-debate clause should also extend to the people in a representative government: "The people might be as safely trusted with free discussion, as they whom they have chosen to do their business."[61]

Congressman Nicholas rejected the claim that the Congress could and should distinguish liberty from the licentiousness of the press. First Nicholas pointed out the "express" prohibition of the First Amendment. Second, he insisted that the proposed exception to free speech lacked any clear meaning and would open the door to abuse. Licentiousness "was so indefinite a thing, that what was deemed licentiousness today by one set of men, might, by another set, tomorrow, be enlarged, and thus the . . . information to be given to the public would be arbitrarily controlled."[62] The understanding of the people would check false charges, Nicholas optimistically observed, and members of the legislature were in a good position to refute false charges made against them. For Federalist advocates of the act, at least, there was considerable truth to what he said. Most of the press—90 percent according to Albert Gallatin—supported the Federalists.[63]

Republicans noted again and again that the act was conceived for partisan purposes, and would be applied in partisan battles. Indeed, Albert Gallatin suggested it was designed as a party weapon, to "enable one party to oppress the other." For the Federalists would "have the power to punish printers who may publish against them, whilst their opponents will remain alone, and without redress, exposed to the abuse of Ministerial prints." The Federalists, he suggested, sought to "suppress all presses which they consider as contrary to their views; to prevent a free circulation of opinion; to suffer the people at large to hear only partial accounts, and but one side of the question; to delude and deceive them by partial information, and, through those means, to perpetuate themselves in power."[64]

The bill, Gallatin and others warned, was aimed not simply at false facts, but at political opinions. He asked how the truth of opinions could be proved. The issues would be decided not by disinterested philosophers, but by people motivated by political predilections. What would happen, Gallatin wondered, if the administration chose to prosecute an "individual thinking, as [Gallatin himself] did, that the present bill was unconstitutional, and that it had been intended, not for the public good, but solely for party purposes?" He asked, "[W]ould a jury, composed of the friends of that Administration, hesitate much in declaring the opinion ungrounded, or, in other words, false and scandalous, and its publication malicious," in the then prevailing atmosphere of party animosity?[65]

Republicans also rejected the argument that freedom of the press was limited to a protection against prior restraint. The idea that Congress could impose a prior restraint, Gallatin said, had never been hinted even by the most violent opponents of the adoption of the Constitution. The First Amendment, he implied, would not have been directed at a problem none thought existed. Instead, according to Gallatin, the First Amendment had been understood to mean that "Congress could not pass any law to punish any real or supposed abuse of the press." He ridiculed the claim that "[s]o long as we do not prevent but only punish your writings, it is no abridgment of your liberty of writing and printing." Both previous restraint and subsequent punishment were precluded, Gallatin said.[66]

Furthermore, he noted, the First Amendment precluded Congress from abridging liberty of *speech* or press. A sound construction of the Constitution, he insisted, "must . . . be applicable to both" the free speech and free press clauses. But the idea that the First Amendment only prohibited prior restraint "was absurd, so far as it related to speech; for it pre-supposed that Congress, by the Constitution, as it originally stood, might have passed laws laying such restraints upon speech." What, Gallatin wondered, could these possibly have been, "unless gentlemen chose to assert that the Constitution had given Congress a power to seal the mouths or to cut the tongues of the citizens of the Union; and these, however, were the only means by which previous restraints could be laid on the freedom of speech."[67]

The Sedition Act passed the House by a vote of forty-four to forty-one and became law on July 14, 1798. As noted above, the act made it a crime to write, utter, or publish "any false, scandalous, and malicious, writing . . . against the government of the United States, or either house of the congress of the United States, or the president of the United States with intent to defame [them]."[68]

Compared to the English common law, the act was a considerable improvement. Truth *was* a defense and a jury, not the judge, would decide if the item was seditious. Nevertheless, John Adams said he expected the act to produce a "hurricane" of protest, and, he ruefully noted later, the response was even worse than he expected.[69]

The Republican Protest

Republicans attacked the Sedition Act in resolutions adopted by public meetings and in the press. The Republican press suggested that the Sedition Act was despotic. According to the *Aurora*, the nation's leading Republican paper, "the present agitation in the U. States is said to arise from the shock of a diversity of opinions, promoted by the liberty of *talking* and *writing*." Fortunately, the *Aurora* sarcastically noted, the problem would soon be cured. "By influence of *Sedition* and *Alien Bills* all Americans will be on one side, and a tranquility will prevail all over the United States, similar to that so happily enjoyed in *Constantinople*."[70]

The *Aurora* reprinted an address by Thomas Cooper, who had edited another paper in Pennsylvania. Cooper explained that he did not question the good motives of federal officials, but he insisted their acts tended toward despotism. What, he asked, would he do if he were in power and wished to install a despotism? The first blow would be aimed at the liberty of speech and press. "For the free discussion of public characters is too dangerous for despotism to contemplate. Hence I would multiply laws against libel and sedition, and fence round the characters of the officers of government by well contrived legal obstacles.—Whatsoever should tend to bring them into contempt should be sedition."[71]

Republicans attacked the Sedition Act as a flagrant violation of the First Amendment and as a violation of the right to freedom of speech and press possessed by Americans. They also attacked it as a violation of rights reserved to the states and to the people. The states' rights argument was often explicitly linked to protecting free speech. For example, resolutions from a meeting in Philadelphia insisted that power to abridge the freedom of press was not delegated to Congress. Instead "power of restricting the freedom of speech and the press [was] reserved to the states and the people." Despite the implication that the states could restrict speech, the resolution then immediately quoted the Pennsylvania Constitution: "[F]ree communication of thoughts and opinions, is one of the invaluable rights of man."[72]

Republicans repeatedly asserted the lack of federal power over the press. But the typical Republican complaint went beyond a jurisdictional objection—beyond, that is, a suggestion that the only problem with Sedition Act prosecutions was that the suppression occurred on the federal rather than the state level. While the lack of federal power was regularly asserted, Republicans also insisted that a basic right or "privilege" of free speech was imperiled by the Sedition Act. A meeting of citizens of Mifflin County, Pennsylvania, resolved that "the free communication of thoughts and opinions is one of the most valuable rights of man, and cannot be abridged or restrained without an infraction of the liberties of the people and the law of nature; therefore all laws restraining the freedom of speech and of the press, are nugatory and void." The citizens insisted that the right was secured to citizens of Pennsylvania by their constitution prior to the adoption of the federal Constitution; "therefore any act of the general government abridging those rights, cannot be a constitutional act."[73]

A resolution from inhabitants of Woodford, Kentucky, also attacked the Sedition Act as a "direct" violation of the Constitution and an outrage "against our most valuable rights: that to speak, write, and censure freely are privileges of which freemen cannot divest themselves, much less be abridged in them by others." For "servants of the people to tell those who created them, that they shall not, at their peril, examine into the conduct of, nor censure those servants, for the abuse of power committed to them, is tyranny more insufferable than Asiatic slavery." Free speech, press, and jury trial were "among the inseparable rights of freemen."[74] A meeting of citizens of Fayette and adjoining Kentucky counties resolved that "the privilege of speaking and publishing our sentiments on all public questions" was "unequivocally acknowledged and secured to us by the constitution of this state as well as that of the United States," and laws to impair these rights were void.[75] The Boston *Independent Chronicle* printed a piece written in Newark, New Jersey, warning that force was resorted to against "the dreadful ORDEAL of free discussion. But can a law," the writer asked, "founded on a violated Constitution, repress a sacred right vested in every freeman by the immutable law of nature?" The writer noted the attacks on the Republican Philadelphia *Aurora* had increased its circulation. The increased support was caused by "freemen indignant at the . . . attempt to abridge a right solemnly guaranteed by the Constitution." Even friends of the government, the writer continued were revolted "at being compelled to resign their dear bought privileges."[76]

The *Aurora* published an address on the upcoming presidential election. Part of the writer's objection was based on states' rights. But a second objection was based on the restriction of the freedom of speech, and the two objections were linked together. The Sedition Act had taken the matter from state courts where, the writer optimistically announced, independent and upright judges and juries would recognize that criticism of public officials was not criminal but a public duty and that truth could never be a libel.[77] The essay suggested the Sedition Act was "not only a breach of the constitution, but an open attack of party, on the liberty of speech and of the press, and of the dearest rights of the people." It undermined "that free investigation of our public measures which we supposed the constitution had secured to all our citizens."[78] People understood that the Bill of Rights meant that "the rights of religion, of the press and of jury, are sacredly preserved to us; the people have by their constitution prevented congress or the general government from ever altering them; no authority inferior to that of the people can now touch them—such as they are, with all their privileges at the adoption of their amendment, such are they to remain."[79]

Critics outside of Congress also noted the inevitably political character of the law and its enforcement. A public meeting at Suffolk County, New York, resolved that the act interfered with the right that "every citizen of a free republic ought to enjoy of publishing his opinions respecting the propriety or impropriety of the measures adopted by his government." The resolution insisted that the claim that the defense of truth cured problems with the act was illusory. Most alleged seditious libels would involve matters of opinion that would "admit of no other proof than the arguments by which they are supported. These will make different impression on the minds of others, according to their habits of thinking, their prejudices, or their passions." Political trials would produce political judgments. "The political sentiments and prejudices of the judges and juries will, in that case, be the only standard of truth; and a public opposition to any measure of the government, however unconstitutional or pernicious to the true interest of the nation it may be, will be silenced by the force of law, and the people consequently deprived to the right, which they ought ever to enjoy, of communicating their political opinions to each other, respecting the conduct of their civil rulers, through the medium of the press."[80]

Republicans feared that government power would be used to punish critics of the administration, while leaving Federalists free to attack their opponents. A petition from twelve hundred citizens of Northampton County, Pennsylvania, asked about the effect on representative government: "If the press is to be open only to those men, in power, and the door shut against their political opponents; if the censure of the former may be construed into a design to bring government into disrepute, and the vilest calumnies against the latter are left without notice, . . . is it not an advance towards the establishment of that lengthy continuance in office so inimical to the genius of a republican government?"[81]

The *Aurora* found the claim that liberty of the press was merely protection against prior restraint a "very *comical* argument." Similarly, it announced, even without a constitutional guarantee, any man had the liberty of kicking congressmen out of their seats, "being only answerable for his conduct!!!" "There is to be no previous restraint imposed upon a man," the paper continued, "he is neither to have his eyes *poked out*, his *fingers cut off*, nor to be *debarred the use of pen and paper*." But "if he makes use of his eyes, his fingers, and pen ink and paper in such a way as may be deemed improper by the administration, why to be sure he shall have another liberty, that of *lying down or standing erect in a cell, of paying* 1000 *dollars fine*." The New York *Time Piece* declared the "sedition bill" an "excellent harmonizer of parties" since "they must all sing to the same tune."[82]

The New York *Time Piece*, the *Aurora*, and other Republican papers reprinted copious extracts about freedom of speech and press from *Cato's Letters*, the influential eighteenth-century English essays on government. The *Time Piece* also reprinted the Bill of Rights.[83] "A True American" writing in the Boston *Independent Chronicle* insisted that freedom of the press was "the only rational security" for enjoyment of all other rights. It required "the most unlimited disquisition as to the conduct of public men in their official characters." Free government "presupposes a continued appeal to public understanding," which required a free press. The True American suggested that the line between protected and unprotected speech be drawn between opinion and action—overt acts of resistance.[84]

A resolution attacking the Sedition Act passed the Virginia legislature in December of 1798. It had a strong flavor of states' rights. According to the resolution, the Federal Constitution was a compact between the states that limited the federal government to enumerated powers. When the federal government exceeded its powers, "the States who are parties [to the compact], have the right and are in duty bound to interpose for arresting the progress of the evil, and for maintaining within their respective limits the authorities, rights and liberties appertaining to them." The Virginia resolutions and those of Kentucky, which nullified the Sedition Act, raised the specter of a direct clash between the states and the federal government.

The Virginia resolution also addressed the free press issue. It insisted that the Constitution delegated no power over the press to the federal government and that the First Amendment expressly prohibited such exercise of power. The Virginia resolution also made a more fundamental criticism: the Sedition Act should "produce universal alarm, because it is levelled against that right of freely examining public characters and measures, and of free communication among the people thereon, which has ever been justly deemed the only effectual guardian of every other right."[85] The only other state to pass a critical resolution was Kentucky. Other state legislatures either ignored the Virginia and Kentucky resolutions or condemned them.

In the 1798 debate on the Sedition Act in the Virginia legislature, critics of the act emphasized both that it exceeded federal power *and* that it violated the right of free speech. For example, John Taylor attacked the act not only as exceeding federal power but also as violating the principle of free speech. He rejected the claim that the law was "not to restrain the freedom, but the licentiousness of speech." Taylor said that "men find no difficulty, in pronouncing opinions to be both false and licentious, which differ from their own."[86] According to Taylor, Blackstone's definition of liberty of the press "wholly quibbles away the liberty of the press."[87]

Taylor found the Sedition Act a violation of "the right of opinion" which "should be held sacred."[88] The act did not merely punish publication of false facts. Instead, Taylor said, supporters of the act said all "falsehood" was punishable by it:

> The great error in this doctrine arose from dropping the word "fact," and taking that of "falsehood," which includes "opinion," as well as fact. To say that such laws as the alien and sedition existed, would be to assert a fact and if he (Mr. Taylor) was prosecuted for it, it might be proved. But to assert that these laws were unconstitutional and oppressive, and productive of monarchy, would be an opinion, constituting a degree of criminality under the sedition-law, subjecting a man to punishment, and yet it was not a fact capable of being proved.[89]

William Daniel Jr., a member of the Virginia House of Delegates from Cumberland County, also opposed the act. He saw in it an attempt to shield the president from criticism much as the king in England was shielded. Daniel rejected the claim that freedom of the press was limited to protection against prior restraint. He also insisted that the act was not primarily aimed at false facts. Instead it was aimed at political inferences from accepted facts. It was a fact that the Congress had passed the Sedition Act and that the First Amendment prohibited Congress from abridging the freedom of speech or of the press. His conclusion, "that Congress, in enacting the said laws, had violated the Constitution, assumed powers not delegated to them, and usurped the rights and liberties of the people," was, he said, just the sort of political opinion reached by the Sedition Act.[90]

The Defense of the Sedition Act

The press reported defenses of the Sedition Act made by leading judges. Supreme Court Justice Iredell's defense of the Sedition Act—given in a charge to a grand jury—was published by the Republican *Aurora*. Justice Iredell began by explaining that in the United States no oppression was permitted with impunity. Citizens, who were governed by laws made by persons they had chosen, had no grievance to complain of. "But in the midst of this envied situation we have heard the government as grossly abused as if it had been guilty of the vilest tyranny, as if common sense or common virtue had fled from our country, and those principals of republicanism, which have so strongly characterized its counsils, could only be found in the happy soil of France." Since the Sedition Act had been grossly misrepresented, Justice Iredell continued, he would show it was constitutional.[91]

The First Amendment provided that Congress could make no law respecting an establishment of religion. By comparison, Iredell suggested, Congress could make a law respecting the press, but it could not abridge its freedom.[92] "What might be deemed the freedom of the press, if it had been a new subject, and never before in discussion might indeed admit of some controversy. But so far as precedent, habit, laws, and practices are concerned, there can scarcely be a more definite meaning."[93] The true definition was in Blackstone's *Commentaries*: No license could be required to publish. But if the press published "any dangerous or offensive writings" that were of a "pernicious tendency," then the writer or publisher could be punished. Actually, Iredell continued, the law passed by Congress was less severe than the common law. Truth was a defense.

As a result, "any thing short of a wilful falsehood" was protected.[94] Justice Iredell explained that the press was capable of producing great good or great evil. In wicked hands it could seduce weak minds into seriously criminal acts. Control over abuses of the press was just as necessary in a republic as in a monarchy. "Take away from a Republic the confidence of the people," he warned, "and the whole fabric crumbles into dust."[95]

The Federalist *Massachusetts Mercury* published a charge to a grand jury by Chief Justice Dana of the Massachusetts Supreme Court. Even though he discussed the common law crime of sedition, not the Sedition Act, he seemed to define sedition narrowly. It was, Chief Justice Dana explained, "the offense of endeavoring by advised and deliberate speaking, or by writing, or printing and publishing, to spread abroad, false, groundless, and scandalous rumours and reports, touching the constitution, laws, or administration of the government, with an intent to excite, and stir up a forcible and open opposition against them." If, however, the intent can be gathered from the tendency of the words, much of the apparent narrowness disappears. Sedition, he continued, was a crime at common law, and prohibition of sedition was necessary to preserve any government. All governments had a right of self-preservation, so the national government did also. An explicitly delegated power was not required.

Chief Justice Dana also explained that sedition laws did not abridge the liberty of the press. He distinguished between "*liberty* and the *licentiousness*, the rational *exercise* and the *abuse* of the press, between a fair and candid examination of public men, and public measures, and that false and malicious misrepresentation and calumny of men and things which tended to weaken the confidence of the people in their best friends and in the wisest measures." The rights of free speech and press were like any other right, "maintainable so long as they are kept within due bounds, but restrainable, and punishable whenever they interfere with the rights of others, or with the welfare of Society."[96]

The Massachusetts legislature, in its response to the Virginia Resolutions, made a similar point. "The genuine liberty of Speech and Press," the legislators announced, "is the liberty to utter and publish the truth; but the Constitutional right of the citizen, to utter and publish the truth, is not to be confounded with a licentiousness . . . that is only employed in propagating falsehood and slander."[97] During the debate, Mr. Lowell denounced "the monstrous, the absurd idea, that this right is more sacred than any other." Rights were limited by other rights. "I have a right to walk the street, but I must not run down my neighbour.—I may brandish my cane, but not on my friend's head."[98]

Nor did the Massachusetts legislature accept Virginia's claim of lack of federal power over the press. The Supreme Court of the United States, without explicit constitutional authority, could protect itself against conduct that would disturb its proceedings. The United States government had a similar inherent right.[99]

In evaluating the Sedition Act, one might merely weigh the arguments of the Federalists and of the Republicans on the scale of theory. In fact, however, Federalists put their conceptions into practice, so it is possible to see how a law defended on the plausible ground that it only reached deliberate and malicious lies worked out in practice.

3

Sedition in the Courts: Enforcement

and Its Aftermath

MATTHEW LYON

Matthew Lyon, the Republican congressman from Vermont, was the first person indicted under the Sedition Act. Lyon was born in Ireland in 1750, forty-eight years before the Sedition Act was passed. He emigrated to America in 1765, paying for his passage by an indenture to work for three years after his arrival. In 1774 he moved to Vermont, and he served as an officer during the American Revolution. Lyon was cashiered for "indiscipline in his command," according to the account in the *Dictionary of American Biography* (men under his command had withdrawn from an exposed position), or for cowardice, according to Professors Stanley Elkins and Eric McKitrick, authors of a massive recent study of the Federalist era. He was reinstated and served (according to the favorable account) with distinction.

In 1783 Lyon moved to Fair Haven and became a leading businessman, opening an iron works, manufacturing paper, and selling ship timber. He started a newspaper devoted to republicanism and the interests of the poor and middling people. According to Elkins and McKitrick, Lyon was involved in a French plan to induce Canadians to revolt against the British, and he was accused of various corrupt schemes.

In 1797, Lyon was narrowly elected to the federal House of Representatives. As both a Republican from Federalist New England and a native of Ireland, he was subjected to derisive remarks by Federalists almost from the moment he took his seat. (Professors Elkins and McKitrick attribute much of his problem to being a freshman who talked too much. They describe him as engaging in "populist bombast.")

In Congress, Lyon was soon involved in controversy. He objected to the custom of the House waiting on the president as unrepublican. Federalist representative John Allen responded to Lyon by appealing to Americans of better blood, provoking Lyon to reply that he was not "descended from the bastards of Oliver Cromwell, or his courtiers, or from the puritans who punished their horses for breaking the Sabbath, or from those who persecuted the Quakers or hanged the witches."

The Federalist press harshly attacked and lampooned Lyon. On the floor of Congress, Lyon was insulted by Representative Roger Griswold of Connecticut by a reference to a wooden sword Lyon allegedly had been required to wear for cowardice during the Revolution. Lyon spat in Griswold's face. Griswold returned to the House and beat him with a cane. An effort in February of 1798 to expel Lyon from Congress failed to get the necessary two-thirds vote.[1] (No effort, apparently, was made to discipline Griswold.)

Like other Republicans, Lyon had opposed the Federalists' military measures. A harsh Federalist press attack charging him with criminal disloyalty was republished in *Spooner's Vermont Journal.* Lyon wrote a reply to the editor on June 20, 1798, well before the July 14 passage of the Sedition Act. One of the three counts of the indictment against Lyon was based on this letter to the editor, which the *Journal* published on July 31, 1798, after the passage of the Sedition Act. The second and third counts were, at least, based on speeches that Lyon made after passage of the act. In these he quoted a letter from Joel Barlow, an American poet and speculator then living in France. The Barlow letter was about the confrontation between the United States and France.

In his letter to *Spooner's Journal*, Lyon rejected the idea that the president was entitled to unquestioning obedience. The portion of Lyon's letter to the editor cited in the indictment said that when Lyon saw the efforts of the executive devoted to the happiness of the people, the executive would have his "zealous and uniform support." But, "whenever I shall, on the part of the Executive, see every consideration of public welfare swallowed up in a continual grasp for power, in an unbounded thirst for ridiculous pomp, foolish adulation, and selfish avarice . . . when I shall see the sacred name of religion employed as a state engine to make mankind hate and persecute one another, I shall not be their humble advocate."[2]

The offending part of the Barlow letter said that the misunderstanding between the two governments (France and the United States), has become extremely alarming; . . . and a disposition to a wrong attribution of motives, are so apparent as to require the utmost caution in every word . . . from your Executive. I mean, if your object is to avoid hostilities. . . .

But when we found [President Adams] . . . telling the world that, although he should succeed in treating with the French, there was no dependence to be placed on any of their engagements, that their religion and morality were at an end, that they would turn pirates . . . , and it would be necessary to be perpetually armed against them, though you were at peace; we wondered that the answer of both Houses had not been an order to send him to a mad house.[3]

At his trial, Lyon represented himself. He unsuccessfully challenged the constitutionality of the Sedition Act and argued that the statements he made were true. Justice Patterson charged the jury that it had two issues to consider: whether Lyon published the pieces and whether they were seditious. The constitutionality of the act was, he said, for the court, not for the jury. He said that Lyon conceded publication of "a large part of the libelous matter." On the second issue, Justice Patterson told the jury: "[Y]ou will have to consider whether language such as that here complained of could have been uttered with any other intent than that of making odious or contemptible the President and government, and bringing them both into disrepute. If you find such is the case, the offence is made out, and you must render a verdict of guilty." Lyon, in his account of the trial, wrote that the charge dwelled on the "intention and wickedness" of his conduct "in a most elaborate manner" and that it insinuated that the Barlow letter was a forgery.[4]

The jury convicted, and the judge sentenced Lyon to four months in prison and a fine of one thousand dollars, with Lyon to remain in prison until the fine and costs were paid. The federal marshal imprisoned Lyon in a primitive jail without heat, far from his home and family, and at first denied him the use of pen and paper. That edict was soon revoked, and Lyon sent a long letter describing his version of the trial and his confinement to Senator Mason of Virginia.[5]

On November 1, 1798, the *Aurora* commented on Lyon's conviction: "Matthew Lyon of Vermont has had the honour of being the first victim of a law framed directly in the teeth of the Constitution of this federal republic—the ancients were wont to bestow particular honour on the first citizen who suffered in resisting tyranny." On November 9, the *Aurora* reprinted long excerpts from Lyon's letter to Senator Mason of Virginia.[6]

While historians differ in their evaluation of Lyon, they agree that Federalists had converted him into a martyr for liberty. Francis Wharton, a lawyer who edited a collection of American state trials, reports that a mass of Lyon's constituents, enraged by the harshness of his imprisonment, planned to demolish the jail and liberate Lyon, a plan he "succeeded in suppressing." Lyon refused to seek a pardon.[7] Highly placed Republicans raised a subscription to pay his fine.

Meanwhile Lyon campaigned for reelection to Congress from his jail cell, aided by his new newspaper, *The Scourge of Aristocracy*. He won reelection in a crowded field with a vote almost double that of his Federalist opponent. Writing to his constituents from "Verginnes jail," Lyon noted that though "2 judges and thirty jurymen have been found to declare [him] guilty of evil intentions, more than three thousand five hundred enlightened freemen have declared him NOT GUILTY, and by their re-election have plainly announced . . . their confidence in him."[8] On the day set for his release, Senator Mason came in person to pay his fine in gold with funds collected from leading Republicans. Lyon, who feared new plans to arrest him, proclaimed he was on his way to Congress, and immediately set out. His declaration was designed to bring him within the immunity from arrest that congressmen enjoy when traveling to Congress. He was met with huge welcoming crowds, dinners, and parades.[9]

In Congress, in February of 1799, Lyon faced still another resolution to expel him, this one because he had "been convicted of being a notorious and seditious person, and of a depraved mind, and wicked and diabolical disposition."[10] Representative Bayard insisted that Lyon's crime tended to subvert the government. Federalists claimed Lyon had been found guilty of intentionally broadcasting false statements designed to bring the government into disrepute. Republicans countered that Lyon had been convicted for political opinions. They denied that opinions could be false if they did not contain false facts and pointed out that Lyon had been reelected by constituents who knew of his conviction. Finally, Republicans insisted on the unconstitutionality of the law.[11] Albert Gallatin, a Republican leader in the House, said Lyon's crime was political "and it will always be determined according to the situation of the parties at the time. . . . We may say what we please," Gallatin continued, "about the purity of our courts and juries . . . ; decisions on political questions will always be influenced by party spirit." The vote in favor of expulsion was forty-nine to forty-five, less than the constitutionally required two-thirds vote.[12]

After his Sedition Act conviction, Lyon served the term in Congress to which he had been reelected. Then, in 1801, he migrated to Kentucky and represented that state in Congress from 1803 to 1811. During this time (according to the *Dictionary of Biography*) he emerged as a vigorous speaker and debater who "displayed elements of statesmanship sufficient to refute the earlier slanders." In Congress he fought for democracy as he understood it—denouncing the tyranny of House rules, the appointment of committees by the Speaker, the congressional caucus, and arbitrary government of the western territories. He opposed Madison's embargo and suffered heavy business losses in the War of 1812.

In 1810, Lyon was defeated for reelection to Congress. His friend President James Monroe appointed him factor to the Cherokee Nation in Arkansas. At the age of seventy-three he made a lengthy round trip by flat boat to New Orleans. He was elected a territorial delegate to Congress in the second Arkansas territorial election, but died before taking his seat.[13]

In 1840, forty years after the Sedition Act expired, Congress considered a bill to repay Lyon's fine. The committee report in favor of the bill said that the Sedition Act was passed under "a mistaken exercise of undelegated power" and was "null and void." The issue had excited "universal and intense interest," was acutely investigated, and "conclusively settled." The committee recommended repaying the fine so as to place beyond question the mandate of the Constitution against abridging the liberty of the press. The bill was supported by representatives as diverse as Waddy Thompson, a strong supporter of slavery from South Carolina, and Representative Slade, an antislavery congressman from Lyon's district in Vermont. Slade recalled that a great assembly had met at the jail to celebrate Lyon's release and that a cavalcade half a mile long followed Lyon as he began his journey to Congress. The group had stopped at Slade's house for cake and hard cider. The bill to refund the fine to Lyon's heirs passed the House by a vote of 124 to 15.[14]

A COMMON LAW PROSECUTION

Most of the targets of the Sedition Act were Republican newspaper editors. Occasionally, however, Federalists prosecuted their Republican targets under state law. That was the case in President Adams's home state of Massachusetts. Though Massachusetts had no sedition act, Thomas Adams, the editor of the *Independent Chronicle,* and his brother Abijah were indicted in February 1799, under the Massachusetts common law. The allegedly seditious article criticized the Massachusetts legislature for its failure to join Virginia's attack on the Sedition Act and for its resolution denying the legislature's "right to decide on the constitutionality of the act." The article had said it was difficult "for common capacities to conceive of a *sovereignty* so situated that the *Sovereign shall have no right to decide on any invasions of his constitutional powers.*" It expressed the hope that "for the convenience of those tender consciences who may hereafter be called upon to swear allegiance to the State, that some gentleman skilled in federal logic will shew how the oath of allegiance is to be understood." To Chief Justice Dana this amounted to charging the members of the legislature with violating their oaths. As he explained in the course of sentencing Abijah Adams, "[M]embers of the Legislature who voted for those proceedings are charged in effect, with having violated the Oath of Allegiance to the Commonwealth, and [with having] invited the Deity to witness a falsehood—are compared to the rebellious and fallen Angels." This "indecent and outrageous calumny is spouted forth upon them" simply because they had rejected the Virginia heresy and denied that states could declare the Sedition Act unconstitutional.[15]

The Suffolk county grand jury indicted the Adams brothers after it received Chief Justice Francis Dana's charge. Dana announced that all printing and publishing was unlawful that had a direct and manifest tendency to stir up "uneasiness, jealousy, distrust, and sedition" or to turn the allegiance of citizens from the commonwealth.

The editor of the *Chronicle* was too ill for trial, but the trial proceeded against his brother Abijah Adams, the bookkeeper, who had also handed out copies of the paper to purchasers. Chief Justice Dana, who presided over Adams's trial, had no patience with Republicans. He had earlier branded them as a French faction filled with advocates of atheism, anarchy, and bloodshed.[16]

At trial, the prosecutor argued that the common law crime of sedition was fully in force in Massachusetts: truth was irrelevant. The defense, as related (and elaborated) in a later account in the *Independent Chronicle*, denied that the common law of seditious libel "in its full extent could be considered as consonant to the genius and spirit of a Republican Government." So the defense denied that "the American people ever intended to adopt it at large in this country." Only those provisions of the common law "applicable to the circumstances of our people and government" had been adopted in Massachusetts. A law "which may be fit and proper for a monarchy, aristocracy and despotism must necessarily be unsuitable to the circumstances of a people in a republican government." The British government, "founded originally on usurpation," needed such measures. Government based on the consent of the governed did not.[17]

The defense argued that sedition prosecutions violated the free press provision of the Massachusetts constitution. It rejected the claim that freedom of the press was limited to protection against prior restraint. Under that rule freedom of writing and publishing could be considered free "in the most arbitrary and despotic countries." By the prior restraint definition of a free press, a Turk could criticize his government, though of course, "this boasted privilege terminates with the loss of his head."[18]

Though "private character" was protected from wanton, malicious invective, the defense insisted that "with respect to public men and public measures, the case was considered essentially different." As to such matters considerable latitude was required. In America, "the principal utility to be expected from *a free press* was supposed to be derived from its application to men in office and measures of government." A "degree of licentiousness" was "inseparable from its genuine, actual freedom, and the nicest operation of *mental chemistry*" could not "dissipate the one without losing in the process some valuable portion of the other." These contentions particularly enraged Justice Dana who found the defense even more objectionable than the original crime.[19]

Finally, the defense targeted the claim that the statement for which Adams was indicted was libelous. It had implied that the oath that legislators took to support the state's sovereignty required legislative protest against the Sedition Act. To make this mild statement into a charge of perjury against members of the legislature required "forced unnatural *inuendoes*" and punishment for "mere errors of opinion." The premises for the opinion were clearly stated, and the defense insisted that a critical opinion based on fully disclosed premises could not be libelous. By the alchemy of the common law "the most lifeless incongruous materials" assumed "the visible aspect of *murders, treasons* and *rebellions*."

Where, the *Independent Chronicle* demanded, were the "seditious consequences, so figuratively displayed" by the prosecution? These properties of the offense "are only discoverable in the vagaries of imagination." The *Chronicle* quoted a British barrister and insisted the whole case against Adams amounted to this: "That a certain newspaper was published, containing *certain paragraphs* which *might have been read*, and which if construed in a *certain way*, might be considered a reflection on the character of our legislature, in consequence of which *certain false opinions might* have been formed, from all of which something terrible might have happened."[20]

According to a very limited report in the *Massachusetts Mercury*, the jury found Abijah Adams "guilty of publishing only." This verdict had been used in 1770 by an English jury that was, as Thomas Cooley wrote in his 1868 legal treatise *Constitutional Limitations*, "unwilling to make their verdict cover matters upon which they were not at liberty to exercise their judgment." The English court had found the verdict ambiguous and ordered a new trial. The Boston verdict was also similar to the verdict in William Penn's 1670 case, when the jury refused to convict him for a religious meeting held in the street. Nevertheless, Chief Justice Dana apparently found this verdict sufficient to impose judgment. Without the benefit of a jury verdict on the point or a general verdict of guilty as charged, he decided that the article was seditious and the defendant was guilty.[21] The rule that the jury could only consider publication and that a finding of publication justified a verdict of guilty had been the orthodox English common law rule, although the British Parliament had changed the rule seven years earlier by Fox's Libel Act of 1792.

In sentencing Abijah Adams, Chief Justice Dana again explained the nature of freedom of the press. He endorsed the analysis of the Massachusetts legislature when it rejected the Virginia Resolution. Freedom of the press secured "the constitutional right of the citizen to utter and publish the truth, . . . not to be confounded with a licentiousness in speaking and writing [by] . . . propagating falsehood." The "freedom of the press" was "a security for the *rational* use, and not the *abuse* of the Press." The constitutional guarantee merely protected against having to get approval of a licenser before publishing. "A citizen may print what he pleases," the Chief Justice explained, "but if it be afterwards found false or libelous he must take the consequence."

Still, the sentence—thirty days imprisonment—was comparatively mild. According to the *Independent Chronicle*, the fact that the court allowed evidence of truth, the lightness of the sentence, and the jury verdict—guilty of publishing only—all showed that the principles of the common law of seditious libel were not being fully accepted, even as the court purported to rely on them.[22]

SEDITION ACT PROSECUTIONS

In contrast to common law, the federal Sedition Act let the jury pass on the issue of sedition and made truth a defense. These theoretical improvements, however, made little difference in practice.

Prosecutions in Massachusetts

In 1799, several defendants were indicted in Massachusetts for violating the Sedition Act by the erection of a "liberty pole." The pole had an inscription attached: "No Stamp Act; no Sedition, no Alien-Bill; no Land Tax; Downfall to the Tyrants of America; Peace and Retirement to the President." A wealthy and well-connected defendant charged only with assisting in the erection of the pole pled guilty and received a small fine plus six hours imprisonment. Another defendant, David Brown, a local radical, had been a leader in setting up the pole. According to the *Massachusetts Mercury*, his indictment was based both on his part in erecting the pole and on his writings, which represented the government as a tyrannical association to benefit the wealthy at the expense of ordinary people. Brown also pled guilty. He expressed sorrow for expressing his political sentiments, especially in the manner he had done. But he refused to deliver the names of those who had subscribed to his writings, saying he would lose all his friends. Since he was unable to pay a fine, he asked for a sentence of imprisonment only.[23]

For his writings and his much more active role in the "sedition pole," Justice Samuel Chase sentenced Brown to eighteen months in jail and a fine of four hundred dollars. Since Brown lacked the resources to pay the fine, he seemed to be condemned to perpetual imprisonment.[24] His was the most severe sentence handed out under the Sedition Act.

In his study of the Sedition Act, James Morton Smith reports that Brown's "real offense was his partisan political remarks to the less well-to-do people in Massachusetts," which were limited to "legitimate at-tempts to stir up discontent with the Adams administration." Brown's petitions to John Adams for a pardon were rejected, but he was released in 1801 when the newly elected president Thomas Jefferson pardoned all violators.[25]

Thomas Cooper

Thomas Cooper, another Sedition Act defendant, was born in 1759 in Westminister, England, to a wealthy family. He received a classical edu-cation and attended Oxford University. He studied medical subjects and chemistry and was also trained, rather inadequately according to one writer, in the law. In England, Cooper became a radical, advocating the abolition of both slavery and restrictive religious tests. Cooper also criti-cized the "privileged orders" and urged political reform. In response to the wave of political repression that swept England during the French Revolution, he emigrated to America in 1794 and settled in Pennsylva-nia, where he practiced law and medicine.[26]

Cooper unsuccessfully sought a position with the Adams administra-tion shortly after Adams's election. When he subsequently became dis-illusioned with the administration, Cooper became a Jeffersonian and a Republican publicist. In response to criticisms from Cooper, Adams published Cooper's application for employment, and Federalists pic-tured him as a disappointed office seeker. The statements in Cooper's reply to this charge became the basis of the Sedition Act prosecution against him.

In his reply, published in October 1799, Cooper explained that when he applied for office, Adams was "hardly in the infancy of political mis-take. Even those who doubted his capacity thought well of his inten-tions." Cooper wrote that his job application had been made before the Adams administration saddled the public with a permanent navy and standing army. It was also before Adams had "interfered to influence the decision of a court of justice" to send Jonathan Robbins, whom Cooper alleged to be an American citizen impressed into the British navy, back to the British for a court-martial for his part in a mutiny and massacre of the officers of the British ship.[27] Each of these statements was alleged to be a violation of the Sedition Act.

In his address to the jury, Cooper pointed out the unequal contest in which he was involved. In effect, he was pitted against the president. "Who nominates the judges who are to preside . . . , the marshal who has the summoning of the jury? The president."[28]

If, Cooper said, he had falsely and maliciously libeled the president's character, punishment would follow under the statute. But he insisted he had done no such thing. His comments dealt with the president's public acts. "I say nothing of his private character," Cooper insisted, "and I attack only the tendency of measures notorious to the world."[29]

Cooper argued that confidence in the president could not be instilled by the methods the government was attempting. "It cannot be exacted by the guarded provisions of sedition laws, by attacks on the freedom of the press, by prosecutions, . . . on those who boldly express the truth, or who may honestly and innocently err in their political sentiments." Cooper insisted that the prosecution was inconsistent with republican government. "[I]n the present state of affairs, the press is open to those who will praise, while the threats of the law hang over those who blame the conduct of men in power." The people could not "exercise on rational grounds their elective franchise, if perfect freedom of discussion of public characters be not allowed."[30]

Cooper also defended his statements. For example, he noted that presidents were human beings and not infallible. It could not be seditious to suggest they make political mistakes or lack capacity. The existence of the army and the navy were "notorious" facts.

Justice Chase told the jury that all civilized countries punished sedition. Because ours was a government founded on the opinions and confidence of the people, protection against sedition was especially necessary: "If a man attempts to destroy the confidence of the people in their officers, their supreme magistrate, and their legislature, he effectually saps the foundation of the government."[31]

Chase told the jury that the prosecution was required to prove two things: publication (which was not denied) and that Cooper published with an intent to defame. Bad motive was established, Chase suggested, because Cooper had implied that the president was unfit for the office to which he had been elected.[32] Justice Chase indicated that Cooper had made outrageous charges—a standing army, a permanent navy, borrowing money at 8 percent. "What!" Justice Chase replied indignantly, "the president . . . saddle us with a permanent navy, encourage a standing army, and borrow money at a large premium? And . . . that this is in time of peace?" If this were true, Chase intoned, what opinion must the jury form of the president? But, Chase continued, these charges were false. The army was *provisional*, funded every two years, not a *standing* army. "There is no standing army," Chase announced. Nor was the nation at peace, as Cooper's article suggested. There was an undeclared naval war with France. "I cannot suppress," Chase told the jury, "my feelings at this gross attack upon the president."[33]

As to the charge of influencing the judiciary in the Robbins case, Chase told the jury that Robbins's real name was Nash, that he was a British citizen, not an American, and that his extradition was properly sought by the British under a treaty for the crime of murder on a British ship.[34] A recent study has found that Cooper was indeed mistaken in asserting that Robbins was an American citizen,[35] but it is far from clear that Cooper deliberately falsified Robbins's nationality.

The jury found Cooper guilty. He was fined and imprisoned.

After Republicans triumphed in the election of 1800, Cooper was made a judge in Pennsylvania and served from 1804 to 1811. As a judge, Cooper came in conflict with his former allies in the democratic faction, and he was removed from office by the governor on application of the legislature. Charges against him included imprisoning a Quaker for not removing his hat in court; putting questions to a prisoner charged with a crime that asked the prisoner to incriminate himself; sending private notes to criminal juries during trials, and browbeating counsel, witnesses, and parties. After being removed from the bench, Cooper became a professor of chemistry at Carlisle (now Dickinson) College in Pennsylvania and then at the University of Pennsylvania. In 1820 he took a job as professor of chemistry at South Carolina College.[36]

During the South Carolina period of his life, Cooper repudiated the natural rights philosophy of Thomas Jefferson; rejected the claim of the Declaration of Independence that all men are created equal and entitled to inalienable rights; opposed universal suffrage; repudiated his earlier antislavery opinions and became a staunch supporter of slavery. He insisted that slaves were better treated than free workingmen in England and denied that Negroes would work except in slavery. In his South Carolina phase, Cooper also advocated laissez-faire economics, nullification (the idea that states could declare acts of Congress void, subject only to being revived by a constitutional amendment), and secession.[37]

Among Cooper's extensive writings about political and economic questions was a treatise entitled *The Right of Free Discussion*, published in 1829 while he was in South Carolina. In it he supported very broad rights of free speech and press.

> I intend . . . to maintain the RIGHT OF FREE DISCUSSION, in its fullest extent; as applied to any and every question, opinion, tenet or doctrine, political, theological, moral, metaphysical, or philosophical within the widest range of human inquiry; and I trust I shall shew, that the cause of truth, and the interest of the public, require free and full exercise of the right now claimed; and that in all times and places, those who have been so anxious to throw fetters around the human intellect, have had no other motive for so doing, than to keep the persons and the property of their fellow men, more completely within their own management and control.[38]

Cooper rejected the claim that ideas should be suppressed because of their bad tendency. According to Cooper, actions, and not opinions, were the proper objects of control. As to bad tendency, it had been invoked by the holy alliance against the British "latitude of discussion," by the British monarchist against the American republican, and "the various parties in our own republic make the same outcry against each other." Cooper suggested that the "laws regulate our *actions* which are within the powers of regulation, and leave our *opinions* alone." He insisted that "quiet, unmolested, continued discussion, is ultimately the most effective peace maker." This had been proved among "our own innumerable sects and parties."[39]

But in spite of his apparently unequivocal defense of free speech, in 1836 Cooper wrote Representative James Hammond of South Carolina, his former student, advocating concerted Southern action to prevent any congressional discussion of abolition petitions. Any discussion, Cooper warned, would concede the right to legislate on the subject. "If the northern members claim the right of discussion, it implies *a claim to act on the question*; for why discuss a subject that you are prohibited from acting on?"[40] The position is a curious one for the man who wrote, "[T]hose who have been so anxious to throw fetters around the human intellect, have had no other motive for so doing, than to keep the persons and the property of their fellow men, more completely within their own management and control."[41]

*Attacks on the Republican Press and
on the Right to Petition*

The advocates of the Sedition Act had quoted from Republican papers to show its necessity. After it was passed, Secretary of State Timothy Pickering pored through Republican papers and wrote to United States attorneys urging them to consider prosecution. Federalists initiated prosecutions against four of the five leading Republican papers and against a number of minor papers in a systematic attack on the Republican press. At least four papers folded under the pressure of prosecution. The Boston *Independent Chronicle* succumbed after a common law prosecution and the death of its editor.[42] James Morton Smith counts at least seventeen indictments for sedition against Republican newspaper editors and politicians, fourteen under the Sedition Act, and three for the common law crime of sedition.[43] One of the few major Republican papers to survive the assault was the *Aurora*.

In their efforts to suppress opposition, Federalists had prosecuted William Duane, the editor of the *Aurora*, in 1798 in state court, for an affray. The affray was a scuffle that occurred when Federalists objected to Duane and his colleagues circulating a petition against the Alien and Sedition acts in a churchyard. Opponents of the petition had apparently begun a brawl. The jury acquitted Duane.[44]

After this failure, Federalists tried again in the summer of 1799. They prosecuted Duane for sedition for charging improper British influence on the State Department. This prosecution was hastily abandoned when Duane announced that he had a letter from John Adams in which Adams had made the charge. Then in 1800, the Federalist Senate sought to punish Duane in a proceeding it instituted for breach of its privileges. Duane was accused of violating the privileges of the Senate because he published the text of a bill to set up a special Federalist dominated electoral commission to decide who had won contested states in the presidential election of 1800. (Duane had mistakenly asserted that the bill had passed the Senate, a mistake he subsequently corrected.) The Senate first found Duane guilty and then gave him a chance to offer evidence in mitigation of his offense. When the Senate refused to let Duane's counsel question its jurisdiction to try him, his counsel withdrew, and Duane went into hiding and continued to edit his paper. Jefferson was elected president before the Federalists found him.[45]

The Federalists also indicted Jedidiah Peck, a member of the New

York state legislature, for circulating a petition demanding repeal of the Alien and Sedition Acts and criticizing the Adams administration's foreign policy. A Republican paper reported that Peck had been arrested at midnight, "manacled and dragged from his home." His journey from his home to New York City "manacled," as the Republican press reported it, took five days. At each stop he was met by "throngs of indignant citizens" who supported Peck and opposed the arrest. Because the arrest was for a petition to Congress, Peck had two First Amendment claims—a free speech–free press claim and one based on the right to petition. Federalists had second thoughts, however, and never brought him to trial. In the meantime Peck was resoundingly reelected.[46]

Turn of the Tide

To the great dismay of Alexander Hamilton and other arch-Federalists, John Adams, on learning that the French would be receptive, sent peace commissioners to France. The prospect of war with France diminished, and so did national hysteria. In May of 1800 Congress authorized the president to disband the army, a step he promptly took. Hamilton, deprived of his army and dreams of military glory, printed and circulated among his intimates a letter attacking John Adams. Excerpts soon appeared in the press, and Hamilton copyrighted it (so he could control its use) and published it as a pamphlet. Thomas Cooper, who had been jailed for criticisms of Adams, asked if Hamilton's harsh attack was immune from punishment: was "*Republicanism* to be the victim of a law, which *Aristocracy* can break through with impunity?" The Republican press gleefully reported Cooper's demand that Hamilton be prosecuted. The Federalists were badly split; they lost the election of 1800.[47]

The Sedition Act and Free Speech Theory

James Madison

Periods of crisis spawn political and legal theory, and that was the case with the crisis of civil liberty produced by the Sedition Act. In December 1799, James Madison wrote a lengthy report on the Sedition Act for the Virginia legislature. He had been a state legislator in Virginia, a leader in passage of the Virginia statute on religious freedom, a leading framer of the federal Constitution, and a prime author and prime mover in the adoption of the federal Bill of Rights. In the new government under the Constitution, Madison served in Congress and became a leader of the Republicans in the House.

Madison's report insisted that the federal government was one of enumerated powers; the power over the press, he said, was simply not a power the federal government possessed. In support of this point, Madison noted the virtually universal Federalist claim during ratification that a free press guarantee was unnecessary because the national government lacked power over the press. Madison rejected the Federalist claim of power under the necessary-and-proper clause and the delegated power to suppress insurrections because he found the relation between criticism and revolt too weak. He also rejected the assertion that federal courts had a common law criminal jurisdiction that included seditious libel, as well as the claim that this jurisdiction provided power to pass the act.[48]

Madison also relied on the First Amendment, which he regarded as a second security device that reiterated the immunity of the press and of speech from federal regulation. The Federalist response had been that freedom of speech and press must be measured by the understanding of those terms at English common law—with the protection being limited to one against prior restraint. By this view, publications with bad tendencies could be punished. Madison denied that this could be the American idea of freedom of the press. He took a functional instead of a formalistic approach, noting that both prior restraint and subsequent punishment would have a similar effect. "It would seem a mockery to say, that no law should be passed, preventing publications from being made, but that laws might be passed for punishing them in case they should be made."[49]

To further support his argument that the English understanding of press freedom could not prevail in America, Madison noted the difference between the two systems of government. In England, Parliament was sovereign and its powers were unlimited. Guarantees of rights in the British system merely limited the king. "Under such a government as this, an exemption of the press from previous restraint by licensers appointed by the king, is all the freedom that can be secured to it." But in the United States, the people were sovereign and guarantees of liberty limited all branches of government "by constitutions paramount to laws." As a result, "security of the freedom of the press requires, that it should be exempt, not only from previous restraint by the executive, as in Great Britain, but from legislative restraint also; and this exemption, to be effectual must be an exemption not only from the previous inspection of licensers, but from the subsequent penalty of laws."[50]

The nature of the American republic also required a different interpretation. The elective system of the United States required "a greater freedom of animadversion than might be tolerated by the genius of such a government as that of Great Britain." There, the hereditary king could do no wrong and the House of Lords was also hereditary and therefore "not responsible" and could "do what it pleases."[51]

The American idea of freedom of the press, Madison insisted, must be understood in light of American practice and public understanding. "In every state, probably, in the Union," Madison noted, "the press has exerted a freedom in canvassing the merits and measures of public men, of every description, which has not been confined to the strict limits of the common law. On this footing, the freedom of the press has stood."[52] Madison's claim for a strong tradition of practical press freedom has received powerful scholarly support in recent years. In the years after the Revolution, the press acted as if the law of seditious libel did not exist. It is reasonable to conclude that ordinary Americans would have understood the guarantee of the First Amendment in light of the practice of press freedom.[53]

Madison noted that Federalists had been "in the habit of . . . unrestrained animadversion on the proceedings and functionaries of state governments." But, Madison hastened to add, he was not claiming "for the state governments an immunity greater than they have hitherto enjoyed. Some degree of abuse is inseparable from the proper use of everything." It was better to let "noxious branches" flourish "than by pruning them away, to injure the vigour of those yielding the proper fruits."[54]

Madison emphasized that free speech and press were central values in representative government. The Constitution made government responsible to the people: it "supposes it may happen, that the President, the Congress, and each of its houses may not discharge their trusts, either from defect of judgment or other causes. Hence, they are all made responsible to their constituents, at the returning periods of election; and the President . . . is . . . subjected to an intermediate impeachment." If government officials fail to live up to their trusts as anticipated, they should be brought into contempt or disrepute. But whether circumstances justify bringing them into contempt" can only be determined by a free examination thereof, and a free communication among the people thereon."[55]

The idea that the Sedition Act did no harm because it was only aimed at falsity was specious, Madison said. Even when the question was purely factual, full and formal proof was difficult and vexatious. But in sedition cases, most of the questions were not purely factual. It must be "obvious to the plainest minds," Madison continued, "that opinions, and inferences, and conjectural observations, are not only in many cases inseparable from the facts, but may often be more the objects of the prosecution than the facts themselves . . . and that opinions and inferences, and conjectural observations, cannot be subjects of that kind of proof which appertains to facts, before a court of law."[56]

Representative government, Madison noted, involves competition for election. But under the Sedition Act the competition was inherently unequal. Supporters of incumbents were permitted to criticize challengers; supporters of challengers faced jail for criticism of those in power.[57]

A minority report was apparently written for dissenting members of the Virginia legislature by John Marshall, later the most famous Chief Justice of the United States. Almost alone among Federalists, Marshall had opposed the Sedition Act and voted for its repeal in Congress. Still, his report defended it against a charge of unconstitutionality. The minority report sounded familiar Federalist themes: freedom of the press was simply a protection against prior restraint, and government could punish speech with a bad tendency. The minority report also justified a broad reading of national powers and judicial review of acts of Congress. Like the majority of the Massachusetts legislature, the Virginia minority report also insisted that the constitutionality of the Sedition Act was a matter for the federal courts.[58]

Tunis Wortman

Tunis Wortman published his *Treatise Concerning Political Enquiry, and the Liberty of the Press* in 1800. He was a New York lawyer, an author of political tracts, and prominent in Tammany politics. According to Wortman, the powers of government were delegated by society. Therefore, society had a right to dissolve its constitution and replace it with another "whenever the voice of public opinion has declared such dissolution to be essential to the general welfare. Society must, therefore, necessarily posses the unlimited right to examine and investigate" to determine if its "purposes have been realized; or how far they have been departed from." Just as society had that right, so did every individual in it. "The position which maintains the general right of a commonwealth to exercise the freedom of political discussion, intends that such is a common privilege appurtenant to each of its members," he wrote.[59] "There is no natural right," Wortman announced, "more perfect or more absolute, than that of investigating every subject which concerns us."[60]

Wortman insisted that free inquiry would lead to progress and social improvement. Government had no special expertise in the search for truth. "Government does not possess any extraordinary or peculiar powers of logic: its distinguishing property is Force." Instead, Wortman had faith in the understanding of ordinary people. He rejected the claim that the ignorant masses should not decide questions of government because "every intellectual Being is possessed of the attribute of judgment ... [and] the common medium of such discriminating faculty, is abundantly sufficient to decide upon the customary detail of human affairs."[61]

Furthermore, Wortman said, free inquiry was essential to human happiness. "[M]uch of the happiness of intelligent and social Beings consists in the pleasures of unrestrained conversation, the charms of security, and the sublime delight of communicating their ideas with a confidence unmingled with terror. Deprived of this invaluable privilege, Society loses all its charms."[62]

Wortman's analysis was "exclusively confined to a consideration of the effects of Misrepresentation in public or political transactions." His proposed safeguards were limited because "[p]ersonal transactions are not the subject of general concern." Injuries to private character could be redressed in a civil action. In human affairs, Wortman noted, we must often choose between evils. As to public concerns, evils of licentiousness were less than those of criminal prosecution for opinion.[63] "Freedom of Investigation" was "pre-eminently requisite to guard against the abuses of Authority."[64] Wortman rejected criminal libel prosecutions, and, logically applied, his view seems to permit civil defamation actions only for attacks on private character.

According to Wortman, the problem with government control of free discussion was the danger of abuse of power. Criminal law, Wortman said, "is invariably liable to be exerted as an engine of Power," and it provided a handy tool to "an administration for the purpose of crushing those individuals whose sentiments are viewed as obnoxious." After having seen Sedition Act prosecutions, he asked, with studied understatement, "Can we always be secure in the independence and impartiality of the tribunal by whom it is administered? Will judges never lean in favor of those constituted authorities which are the fountains of patronage and preferment?"[65]

Governments, Wortman insisted, were "not so zealous to punish Falsehood from an enlightened and disinterested attachment to Justice, as they are ready to smother opinions that are unfavorable to their designs."[66] Indeed, Wortman asked, "why should we examine only one side of the picture? Why this extreme solicitude to shield a Government from Licentiousness, and yet this lethargic inattention to the poison which lurks in Flattery?"[67]

Wortman rejected the bad tendency argument as a justification for suppression of speech. To support his conclusion he cited the Virginia statute on religious liberty and argued that its reasons were equally persuasive in general support of free inquiry. He quoted the act:

> To suffer the Civil Magistrate to intrude his powers into the field of Opinion and to restrain the profession or propagation of principles on supposition of their ill tendency, is a dangerous fallacy, which at once destroys all (religious) liberty: because he being, of course, judge of this tendency, will make his opinions the rule of judgment and approve or condemn the sentiments of others, only as they shall square with or differ from his own. It is time enough for the rightful purposes of Civil government for its officers to interfere when principles break out into overt acts against Peace and Good order. And, finally, that Truth is great, and will prevail, if left to herself.[68]

Wortman rejected motivation as well as truth as a test. "Nothing can be more difficult," he insisted, "than to pronounce with certainty upon the sincerity of the man who may have misstated the transactions of Government." He doubted those in authority would accurately distinguish "Malevolence" from "mistaken Zeal."[69]

Wortman noted both the tendency of sedition prosecutions to chill protected speech and that this tendency was aggravated by the vagueness of the definition of sedition. It would "be the continual tendency of such system to damp the ardour of Political Enquiry, and to inspire the mind with terror. The investigation of public measures will incessantly be associated with the dread of prosecutions and penalties. . . . In vain shall we attempt to estimate the precise extent of prohibition, or ascertain what we are permitted to speak, and at what point we are compelled to silence."[70]

John Thomson—Free Speech and the Speech-and-Debate Clause

An obscure lawyer essayist named John Thomson wrote about liberty of the press in 1801. One of his remarkable contributions was to emphasize that the freedom of the people to discuss public matters should be as broad as that enjoyed by legislators. Free discussion, he insisted, is "an inherent right, and of a nature not to be delegated; it must of course always continue with the people. It will also appear, that this right is guarantee'd to them by the Constitution of their Government."[71]

The speech-and-debate clause of the federal Constitution protected legislators from civil or criminal actions for things said in debate in Congress. "Why," Thomson demanded, "should they who are the *servants* or *agents* of the people . . . impose restrictions upon the thoughts, words, or writings of their sovereign?" The speech-and-debate clause was needed so that Congress could exercise the "functions of a Legislative body." Similarly, a very broad guarantee of free speech and press was necessary so the people could exercise their democratic function. "If free discussion be advantageous to them, it must be equally so to the people." It was absurd, Thomson wrote, to suppose the people divested of that which their public agents enjoy.[72]

While Federalists and others had distinguished between the liberty and license of the press, Thomson denied that "license" was a useful or meaningful concept. Attempts to define it "have uniformly proceeded from men who evidently wished nobody to enjoy the Liberty of the Press but such as were of their opinion."[73] He rejected the power of the government to establish orthodox opinion.[74]

Thomson recognized that free debate would produce many errors, but argued that even errors were useful. "When detected by accurate reasoning, the truth will appear with increased lustre." Thomson concluded with a plea for broad freedom of discussion. "Let the whig and tory, the royalist and aristocrate, the republican and democrat [and all other partisans] . . . be allowd to express their opinions . . . with the same unconstrained freedom with which men of science discuss their subjects of investigation." Freedom of religious opinion had been recognized in the United States and "superstitious enmity" and "uncharitable fanaticism of one denomination against another" had practically disappeared. Thomson expected the same effects from giving all political opinions the same freedom.[75]

The Ambiguous Legacy of Thomas Jefferson

In his first inaugural address, Jefferson said that if there were any who wished to dissolve the Union or change its republican form, "[l]et them stand undisturbed as monuments of the safety with which error of opinion may be tolerated, where reason is left free to combat it."[76] Nevertheless, Jefferson believed printers could be liable for false facts. As he put it in a 1789 letter to James Madison, the people should not be "deprived or abridged of their right to speak to write or otherwise to publish any thing but false facts affecting injuriously the life, liberty, property, or reputation of others or affecting the peace of the confederacy with foreign nations."[77] (Much of the criticism for which Jeffersonians had been prosecuted under the Sedition Act struck them as matters of opinion, not fact. But Republicans also warned of the chilling effect of a rule that reached all false facts bearing on public measures and the reputation of political leaders.)

At any rate, Jefferson's statements on free speech are far from consistently libertarian. In 1803, he wrote Thomas McKean, governor of Pennsylvania, that the "federalists having failed in destroying the freedom of the press by their gag-law, seem to have attacked it in an opposite form, that is by pushing its licentiousness & its lying to such a degree of prostitution as to deprive it of all credit." He advocated action to deal with this "dangerous state of things" by efforts to restore the "credibility" of the press. To accomplish this objective, Jefferson urged utilizing "restraints provided by the laws of the states." He advocated only selected prosecutions, since "a general prosecution . . . would look like persecution."[78] In 1804 he wrote Abigail Adams that his view of the unconstitutionality of the Sedition Act did not "remove all restraint from the overwhelming torrent of slander, which is confounding all vice and virtue, all truth & falsehood, in the U.S. The power to do that is fully possessed by the State

Legislatures." In 1807 he lamented that "suppression of the press could not more completely deprive the nation of its benefits than is done by its abandoned prostitution to falsehood."[79]

But when a bookseller was prosecuted for blasphemy in state court for sale of a book on the creation of the world, Jefferson reacted with horror. "I am really mortified to be told that, in the United States of America, a fact like this can become a subject of inquiry, and of criminal inquiry too, as an offence against religion. . . . Is this then our freedom of religion . . . ?" And in 1823 Jefferson said all state constitutions provided for freedom of the press "subject only to liability for personal injuries. This formidable censor of the public functionaries, by arraigning them at the tribunal of public opinion, produces reform peaceably, which must otherwise be done by revolution."[80]

St. George Tucker: Blackstone for Americans

If there was a strongly libertarian defense of freedom among popular writers, the judicial and scholarly tradition was often a different matter. St. George Tucker occupies a middle ground. Tucker was a Jeffersonian and a Virginia judge and law teacher. He wrote a searing attack on the institution of slavery in 1796, in which he lamented that Americans had imposed "on our fellow men, who differ in complexion from us, a *slavery*, ten thousand times more cruel" than the grievances that gave rise to the Revolution.[81]

William Blackstone's *Commentaries* had been a prime authority for those who supported the Sedition Act. In his edition of the *Commentaries*, St. George Tucker added an appendix to adapt Blackstone to republican America. Tucker recited the arguments against the Sedition Act and concluded that the federal government lacked power over speech and press. As he explained:

> The danger justly apprehended by those states which insisted that the federal government should possess no power, directly or indirectly, over the subject, was, that those who were entrusted with the administration might be forward in considering every thing as a crime against the government, which might operate to their own personal disadvantage; it was therefore made a fundamental article of the federal compact, that no such power should be exercised, or

claimed by the federal government; leaving it to the state governments to exercise such jurisdiction and control over the subject, as their several constitutions and laws permit.[82]

While noting that regulation of free speech and press was left to the states, subject to their constitutions, Tucker also noted the need for broad protection for free speech in republican government. He found liberty of speech and of discussion in all speculative matters to consist of "the absolute and uncontrollable right of speaking, writing, and publishing our opinions concerning any subject, whether religious, philosophical, or political . . . ; the expedience or inexpediency of all public measures, with their tendency and probable effect; the conduct of public men and generally every other subject, without restraint, except as to the injury of any other individual, in his person, property, or good name."[83]

Right to protection of a person's character was not forfeited by accepting public employment. Though the federal government lacked power to punish libel, redress could be had under state law. Like other Republicans, Tucker seems to have distinguished between criticism of the public function and criticism of the private person. At any rate, he notes that "for injuries done the reputation of any person, *as an individual*, the state courts are always open."[84] Still, Tucker noted that the nature of republican government requires broader protection of freedom of speech and press than that permitted in England, and he rejected the doctrine that freedom of the press was limited to protection against prior restraint.

Joseph Story: Blackstone Revisited

Joseph Story was a Supreme Court justice, a law teacher at Harvard, and an author of several legal treatises. Story espoused the judicial and scholarly (as opposed to the popular) consensus. He denounced "loose reasoning on the subject of the liberty of the press," as if the press, "like the king of England . . . could do no wrong." He quoted Blackstone with approval. The liberty of the press was freedom from prior restraint, but "dangerous or offensive" writings with a "pernicious tendency" could still be made criminal.[85]

Story considered state constitutional guarantees for free speech and press, such as those of Massachusetts. He asked a series of rhetorical questions: "Does it prohibit the legislature from passing any laws which shall control the licentiousness of the press . . . ? Does it stop the legislature from passing any laws to punish libels and inflammatory publications, the object of which is to excite sedition against the government, to stir up resistance to it laws . . . ?" Would Virginia's guarantee prevent the legislature from passing laws to punish those who publish or circulate writings "the design of which avowedly is to excite the slaves to general insurrection"? It was important to be able to canvass boldly public measures and the acts of public men. But one must exercise rights so as not to interfere with the rights of others or the public safety.[86]

Blackstone's views were the law of the states on the question, Story insisted. Still, Story went beyond Blackstone when he said the truth uttered with good motives and justifiable purposes was a defense, a defense that seems less protective than the Sedition Act. Story reserved judgment on whether the federal government had any power over speech or press.[87]

As I read the history of the Sedition Act, the dispute was about both free speech and democracy *and* about limits on federal power and states' rights. There is another view of the Sedition Act, however, that suggests that the quarrel was really about slavery and states' rights. That question is the subject of the next chapter. The chapters that follow the next will examine the debates about free speech for opponents of slavery.

4

Sedition: Reflections and Transitions

Many commentators have understood the battle over the Sedition Act as a crisis of free speech, civil liberty, and democratic government. A revisionist view insists that Jeffersonian Republicans were contending not for liberty, but for slavery and states' rights.[1] According to the revisionist view, Jeffersonians "were responsible for the most flagrant denials of free speech and press ever perpetrated in this country, and they did this on behalf of the institution of slavery."[2]

Jeffersonian critics of the Sedition Act invoked both states' rights *and* a broadly protective idea of free speech for Americans. Between 1798 and 1800, many Republicans who invoked states' rights often optimistically assumed broad protection for free speech under state constitutions. They were invoking states' rights to protect free speech from oppressive national legislation. To see the attack on the Sedition Act as simply about states' rights leaves out at least half of the picture.

A REVISIONIST VIEW

The revisionist view identifies Federalists Alexander Hamilton and Judge James Kent as the true free speech heroes. The accolades are based on their roles (as defense counsel and judge) in a seditious libel case brought against a Federalist by Jeffersonians. In that case, Hamilton and Kent did contribute a test for libel that was widely adopted in the states, though, as I will show later in this section, it was hardly a "liberal" free speech test. According to the revised account, Federalists could develop "a liberal law of free speech and press" because, unlike Republican leaders, "they were not inhibited by an attachment to the institution of slavery."[3] By the revisionist account, in the years 1798–1800, Jeffersonians were contending for the exclusive right of states to punish seditious libel because for them the United States "existed as a form of words, but not as a sovereign nation."[4]

In spite of its genuine contributions, the attempt to revise the standard history of the Sedition Act is seriously mistaken in most of its major contentions. It correctly notes the strong no-federal-power states' rights argument that was used against the Sedition Act. That argument is hardly surprising, nor is the institution of slavery needed to explain its use in the case of the Sedition Act. The jurisdictional argument—that only the states had the power to prosecute speech—was a natural one for people facing prosecution in federal court. In federal courts, all the prosecutors were Federalists appointed by President Adams—the man the prosecutions sought to protect from criticism; all the marshals who would pick the juries were also appointed by President Adams; and the judges were typically Federalists, and many of them had been appointed by President Adams.

Except for emphasizing the states' rights argument against the Sedition Act, however, major claims made by the revised account are mistaken. It is anachronistic: it reads events of 1798–1800 in light of the controversy of the 1830s. The revisionist argument correctly notes that by the 1830s, and increasingly in the years that followed, Southern states were banning abolitionist and antislavery speech. They *were* flagrantly denying free speech. Slavery, states' rights, and free speech for critics of slavery were central issues in the 1830s. That was hardly so in the period 1798–1800. The issues then were free speech and states' rights. The no-federal-power and states' rights argument was deployed between 1798 and 1800 to protect free speech; in the South in the 1830s, it justified suppression.

After the Revolution, Southern states experienced a period of comparative liberalism influenced by the philosophy of the Declaration of Independence. The Virginia legislature took tentative steps against slavery by allowing masters to emancipate their slaves without a special act of the legislature. In these early years, its courts construed the act broadly, indulging in a presumption in favor of liberty. And St. George Tucker, Virginia law professor and judge, wrote his attack on slavery. Sometime after the expiration of the Sedition Act, however, and particularly during and after the 1830s, the South increasingly became a closed society on the subject of slavery. Southerners began to explicitly repudiate the ideas of the Declaration.[5]

The states' rights–slavery explanation fails to account for much of the evidence. Denunciations of the Sedition Act by Gallatin, Madison, by the Boston *Independent Chronicle*, and by public meetings, complained that the act was a violation of the basic right or privilege of Americans to freedom of speech and was incompatible with representative government. When Massachusetts prosecuted Jeffersonian newspapermen for common law seditious libel under state law, a claim of states' rights was irrelevant. The defense and the Republican *Independent Chronicle* mobilized arguments similar to the free speech and popular sovereignty arguments used by Republicans in Congress against the federal Sedition Act.

To explain Republican arguments against the Sedition Act as the product of Republican commitment to slavery (and to see Federalism as free of that commitment) is far too simple. The Republican commitment to slavery (and Federalist freedom from that commitment) is not nearly as uniform as the revised account suggests. Virginia Republican St. George Tucker's attack on slavery, for example, was the sort of criticism Southern states would later treat as criminal; it had been part of his law lectures at the College of William and Mary. Albert Gallatin, who led Republicans in the House, and the Philadelphia *Aurora,* the leading Republican paper, were also critics of the Sedition Act and of slavery. Thomas Paine was pro-Republican—and a strong critic of slavery.[6] Consider the following entry from the *Aurora*, the leading Republican paper. The *Aurora* noted that Jefferson tried to insert criticism of slavery in the Declaration of Independence. It then considers news of a slave revolt in Virginia:

> In Wayne's Gazette [a Federalist paper] yesterday evening, the insurrection of the Negroes in Virginia and Carolina is thus treated —"The Insurrection of the Negroes in the southern states, which appears to be organized on the French plan, must be decisive with every reflecting man in those states of the election of Mr. Adams . . . "
>
> We augur better things from this unhappy, but thank God, partial revolt.—We augur from it the effectual stoppage of the African trade. We augur from it measures for a gradual emancipation of the offspring of those who now exist in slavery upon the same plan long since suggested by Dr. Franklin and which Mr. Jefferson endeavored without effect to accomplish.[7]

The revised view also suffers from internal inconsistency. The South can be faulted, according to this view, for failure to get rid of slavery. But, somewhat inconsistently, this view maintains that so long as slavery was to be retained, the choice of suppression of antislavery speech was not "unreasonable" because abolitionist literature "was indeed incendiary in the South" and threatened the existence of slavery. It would be unreasonable to expect Southerners to remain indifferent to dangers to the regime, and speech "can endanger a regime."[8] From this perspective, the real problem was a narrow Jeffersonian construction of federal authority that left the nation powerless to take steps against slavery.

This all-or-nothing view is unrealistic. Great and entrenched social institutions can be changed only after substantial effort, discussion, and controversy. Both Federalists and Republicans and, later, Whigs and Democrats believed slavery in the states was an issue only for each slave state. By this view, only the slave states had the power to end slavery in their states; the federal government had none at all. If you cannot even talk in Southern states about getting rid of slavery, abolition is quite unlikely. Since slavery could not be abolished without discussion and controversy, the conclusion that the Southern ban on discussion was not unreasonable is hardly conducive to change.

Furthermore, if the nation were to act against slavery in any way, national discussion would be required. But many Federalists were hardly favorable to discussion of the issue. Not only were many Federalists not actively antislavery in the years 1798–1800, they even deprecated discussion of liberty and equality because of its tendency to cause slave discontent.[9] Attacking discussions of liberty and equality as too dangerous to slavery is not a promising beginning for either free speech or abolition.

When slavery was involved, many Federalists (as well as many Republicans) took a narrow view both of the right to petition and the role of the national government. In 1800, a group of free blacks from Philadelphia presented a petition to Congress. They asked Congress to ban the slave trade and to revise the Fugitive Slave Act, and they sought measures that would in due course lead to emancipation. They complained that Pennsylvania free blacks were being kidnapped and carried into Maryland and Delaware.[10]

Some of the strongest Federalists came from South Carolina, and that state's representatives in Congress were vigilant in protecting slavery. South Carolina representative John Rutledge was a leading Federalist. He demanded that the petition should be tabled and not discussed. With an obvious jab at Jefferson, he noted that already "new-fangled French philosophy of liberty and equality" had made too much headway among "*gentlemen* in the Southern States by which nothing would do but their liberty."[11]

Harrison Gray Otis, an arch-Federalist from Massachusetts and a strong supporter of the Sedition Act, hoped that, contrary to the usual practice, the petition would not be sent to a committee. He had never seen one with a "more dangerous and unpleasant aspect." To encourage the petition, by paying any attention to it, "would have an irritating tendency." To treat the petition in the usual way "would teach [these free blacks] the art of assembling together, debating and the like, and would soon, if encouraged, extend from one end of the Union to the other." The "subject ought not to be meddled with by the General Government."[12]

John Randolph, Republican of Virginia, concurred. He wanted the House to act so "as to deter the petitioners, or any persons acting for them, from ever presenting one of a similar nature." The House, Randolph exclaimed, should be indignant and not deign to discuss the matter. Randolph apparently thought the Constitution had settled the security of slavery. The Constitution had "put it out of the power of the House to do anything [about] it" so the petition should not be referred to a committee or discussed.[13]

Robert Goodloe Harper of South Carolina, another strong Federalist advocate of the Sedition Act, said that agitating the question would "create discontent" and a "temper of revolt."[14] The motion to refer was amended, but the bill was sent to a committee. As amended, the motion announced that the parts of the petition that asked Congress to act on subjects about which the general government was precluded from legislating by the Constitution (seemingly including any federal plans for emancipation, no matter how gradual) tended to excite disquiet and jealousy and should receive no encouragement from the House. It passed eighty-five to one, with the brave and eloquent Federalist representative George Thatcher of Massachusetts voting no.[15]

Nor were former Federalists supportive of raising the issue of abolition in the 1830s. At the best, leading former Federalists such as Otis and James Kent supported the right of Southern states to suppress antislavery speech within their borders, and they criticized Northerners for discussing abolition. Harrison Gray Otis, a former arch-Federalist and strong supporter of the Sedition Act, spoke in August 1835 to an antiabolition meeting in Boston's Faneuil Hall. He said that for a meeting in Boston to consider "the expediency of taking measures for the abolition of slavery, I should regard . . . as identical with the question of the expediency of dissolving the union." The question "ought never to be entertained" as a public question, though individuals would remain free to express private sentiments. Attempts to develop public opinion in favor of immediate abolition had a "ruinous tendency." Forming abolitionist associations was conduct hostile to the "spirit and letter of the constitution."[16]

Otis supported the compact theory of the federal Constitution, by which slavery in the South and the right to discuss it there were matters exclusively for the slave states. Any interference by Northerners was improper. This view left the South free to suppress all antislavery speech within its borders. Nor did Otis favor discussion in the North. For a citizen of Massachusetts to seek to raise the question of abolition in the South, Otis said, was intrinsically wrong—just as it would be wrong to have an association to foment revolution in Russia. "The right of freedom of thought, and of speech, and of the freedom of the press, is one thing," Otis explained, and "that of combining to spread disaffection in other states . . . is a different thing."[17] Abolition would change the civil polity, he warned, and would give political power to those (the slaves) who had none.[18] Otis also disapproved discussing the subject of abolition of slavery in the nation's capital.[19]

Chancellor Kent also apparently justified the Southern blockade against free speech about slavery. In the summer of 1835, Kent wrote the committee for the New York meeting called to protest the activities of the abolitionists. "I am entirely in opinion," Kent wrote, "with all that portion of my fellow citizens who are decidedly opposed to the interference of abolitionists with the question and practice of slavery in the Southern states." Kent expressed agreement with resolutions passed in Boston and Portland.[20] These resolutions did not protest the suppression of free speech in the South. Instead, they attacked the abolitionists for raising the slavery issue. The Portland resolutions insisted that, under the compact that formed the federal Constitution, the national government was denied all power to interfere "in any respect" with "the condition of slaves in any other state." The matter was exclusively for the slave states. The meeting viewed agitation of the slavery question "in this [free] state" with "deep concern" because the state had "no direct interest in the question." While slavery was an evil, the initial fault lay with

Britain, and the remedy must be left to the South. Agitation of the issue would excite the passions of slaves against their masters and would make "free people of color" unhappy and discontent with the social condition in which "the established order of society" had placed them. Abolitionists, the resolution continued, were preparing the way for "all the horrors of servile insurrection and civil war."[21]

James Kent, like most at the time, denied that Congress had any constitutional power to deal with slavery in the states. His view of the federal compact seems to have made it impossible for him to endorse a liberal view of the right to engage in free speech about slavery in the South. And the South, Kent and others insisted, was the only place where discussion was appropriate. If the South chose to suppress free speech on the issue, that, apparently, was that. (Some former Federalists, nevertheless, like some members of Jefferson's party, were supporters of free speech.)

Kent and Hamilton are hardly free speech heroes. Hamilton had wanted to prosecute petitioners for criticizing the Federal whisky tax, and he wanted to extend the scope of the Sedition Act to protect more government officials including himself.[22] Kent thought the Sedition Act was too liberal. The best that can be said is that when a Federalist editor was under attack, Hamilton and Kent rallied to his defense, with a theory of free speech that borrowed heavily from the Republicans and that was more liberal than the common law, though less protective than the Sedition Act. The test was widely adopted in the states. But the repudiation of the common law by a popular and broader view of free speech was well under way, as even the Sedition Act itself shows. From that perspective, Hamilton and Kent provided a fall-back position that restrained and limited the repudiation of the common law while at the same time protecting a beleaguered Federalist. Though the formula was adopted by a number of states, its potential mischief was limited by the popular tradition. Whatever the legal formula, prosecutions for sedition—prosecutions based on criticism of public policy or the public acts of officials—were becoming more and more rare.

The attempt to ban antislavery speech from the 1830s to the Civil War raised the issue of sedition once again—but on the state as well as the national level. This time the scope of free speech in the states was directly implicated. I will turn to these controversies about antislavery speech in the chapters that follow. When I do, we will see that a broad view of freedom of discussion, like that embraced by some leading critics of the Sedition Act, was a central argument of those seeking to preserve freedom of speech on the slavery issue. These included some of those Jeffersonians who favored a plan to end slavery in Virginia, abolitionists, and members of Lincoln's Republican Party. Free speech views like those of the Federalists of 1798–1800 were espoused in an effort to justify suppression of antislavery speech. Ironically, the idea that the federal government lacked power to suppress speech and press also protected abolitionists in the North from hostile federal legislation.

The Sedition Act debate was both about the scope of free speech in a democracy and about the scope of national power. The great tension between a broad right of all Americans to free speech and states' rights would become increasingly apparent as the nation approached the Civil War. It was not yet apparent in the years from 1798 to 1800.

The opposition to the Sedition Act made a major contribution. It helped to further establish a central part of the free speech tradition: free speech was a privilege of Americans and was essential to representative government.

After the Sedition Act

Free speech history has its share of ironies. Federalists soon found themselves defending sedition cases brought by Jeffersonian Republicans. As a result, Federalists invoked a more liberal vision of the law of sedition than the common law.

James Kent and a Federalist Vision of Free Speech

James Kent was born in 1763. According to Kent's own account, he read *Blackstone's Commentaries* at age fifteen and decided to become a lawyer. He attended Yale College and apprenticed for three years in a law office. He was admitted to the bar at age twenty-one, but his legal practice did not prosper, and he found himself in financial difficulty. Kent was a Federalist and an admirer of Alexander Hamilton. His Federalist friends arranged for him to be appointed professor of law at Columbia College. His courses, after his first one, did not, however, attract students, and he resigned. Thanks again to his political friends, he received a lucrative appointment as a master in chancery, and later became a judge of the New York supreme court. In 1814 Kent was appointed chancellor of the New York court of chancery. He attended the New York Constitutional Convention of 1821 where he unsuccessfully opposed the abolition of property qualification for voting. After reaching age sixty, in accordance with New York law, he was forced to retire from the bench, and he briefly returned to teaching law. At the urging of his son, he published his lectures as *Commentaries on American Law*, one of the classics in American legal literature.[23]

One case that came before Kent was *People v. Croswell*,[24] a libel case against a Federalist editor. Harry Croswell had published an attack on President Jefferson, saying that he had paid James Callender to call Washington a traitor, a robber, and a perjurer. Croswell sought to subpoena Callender to prove the truth of the charge. This, the judge before whom he appeared refused to allow. Instead, the judge took the position that truth was no defense and that the only issue for the jury was publication. The judges who considered the editor's motion for a new trial divided equally on partisan lines and the prosecution was dropped. Alexander Hamilton was Croswell's lawyer and James Kent was one of the judges hearing a motion for a new trial in the case. In *Croswell*, both Kent and Hamilton advocated the principle that truth for good motives and justifiable ends was protected expression. Although the judges were equally divided, Kent's opinion nonetheless proved influential and was embraced in many states in the nineteenth century.[25]

Norman Rosenberg, a leading historian of libel law, has noted that in arguing for the defense of truth for good motives and justifiable ends, Hamilton and Kent rejected the Blackstonian position as too restrictive and the Sedition Act as too liberal. Rosenberg suggests that Hamilton's argument was designed to leave the law of libel robust enough to protect truly virtuous public servants while allowing attacks on those who merely pretended to have republican virtue.

In his 1804 opinion in *People v. Croswell*, Kent insisted that the crime of libel required intent and intent was for the jury. Truth for good motives and justifiable ends was, Kent insisted, evidence of good intention and essential to the liberty of the press. He quoted American declarations on freedom of the press, including the Address to the Inhabitants of Quebec and state and federal constitutional provisions. It was "impossible that [the authors of these documents] could have spoken with so much explicitness and energy, if they had intended nothing more than that restricted and slavish press, which may not publish anything, true or false, that reflects on the character and administration of public men." Advocacy of the American Revolution and the federal Constitution—"libels founded in truth and dictated by worthy motives"—would have failed to pass such a test.[26]

Nevertheless, Kent rejected Madison's report on the Virginia Resolution, which he interpreted as advocating "a press totally unshackled," as well as its suggestion "that the baneful tendency of the Sedition Act was but little diminished by the privilege of giving in evidence the truth of the matter contained in political writings." This doctrine, Kent warned, would make the press "a pest, and destroy public morals."[27] Kent summed up his view of free speech: "The founders of our government were too wise and just, ever to have intended, by the freedom of the press, a right to circulate falsehood as well as truth, or that the press should be . . . an engine for evil and designing men, to cherish, for mischievous purposes, sedition, irreligion, and impurity."[28]

In *Croswell* some Jeffersonian Republicans argued for the restrictive common law rule, which Republicans had rejected in Sedition Act debates, while Federalists Hamilton and Kent argued for a rejection of the Blackstone rule, which Federalists had quoted as the true definition of press freedom during the Sedition Act debates. The authors of *Cato's Letters* would not have been surprised: "So great is the Difference of Mens having Power in their Hands or upon their Shoulders!"[29]

Although Kent's standard—truth for good motives and justifiable ends—was on its face less protective than the Sedition Act that made truth a defense, it was a considerable advance over common law rules of seditious libel, which held truth to be no defense and publication the only issue for the jury.[30] Kent's defense of the role of the jury was important and impressive. Still, Kent's biographer asked whether "politics had not lent zest to [Kent's] legal researches." He notes that Kent had denounced the erectors of liberty poles and failed ever to express—publicly or privately—even a peep of protest against the attack on liberty involved in the enforcement of the Sedition Act.[31]

Sedition as a Federal Common Law Crime

In 1812 in *United States v. Hudson and Goodwin*, the United States Supreme Court considered a federal common law seditious libel prosecution against Federalist newspaper editors. The Court rejected federal criminal jurisdiction based on common law. Although the Court found no precedent on the issue, it said the matter had "been long since settled in public opinion."[32] The decision ended the prospect of federal prosecutions for the common law crime of seditious libel. State seditious libel prosecutions became less and less frequent, and eventually essentially ceased.[33]

As noted above, legal scholar Harry Kalven suggested that the Sedition Act was a paradigm case that highlights the central meaning of free speech in a democracy. As Kalven saw it, a sedition act is the antithesis of meaningful protection for free speech. Reasoning from this premise, he believed, helps us to understand the central meaning of the First Amendment. Free speech and political freedom, he argued, are incompatible with the principle of the crime of sedition.[34] He was right.

The essence of the crime of sedition was the claim that advocacy and criticism of public policy and criticisms of the conduct of public officials could be punished as a crime. The crime of sedition contradicts the idea that "we the people" ultimately govern, because it seeks to protect public policies, government officials, and major social institutions from public debate and criticism. As it was applied, the Sedition Act had treated political criticism and opinion as sedition. The crimes it punished included suggestions that the president lacked the capacity for the job, was given to ridiculous pomp, pursued antirepublican policies, had a standing (rather than provisional) army, or that his policies would lead to an unnecessary war with France.

Political libel actions did not end with the demise of the Sedition Act. Still, treating political criticism of the sort indulged in by Adams's opponents as sedition was disappearing in the years between the Sedition Act and the Civil War. In these years, political libel trials tended to involve charges against politicians that would have been libel if directed at a purely private person—for example, that the official was a thief or was mentally ill. The *Croswell* case itself did not involve an attack on Jefferson's policies or his capacity to be president. Instead it involved a charge that he had hired James Callender to write deliberate lies about George Washington.

In these years, political parties had their own presses, so political leaders could and did respond to alleged libels with a counterattack in their own papers. By the middle of the nineteenth century, popular sovereignty and press freedom were widely revered in theory and to a considerable extent in practice.[35] If the evolution of the law of libel in a more speech-protective direction was slow before the Civil War, the practical effect of precedent was limited by public attitudes and political practice.

But the story is not simply one of increasing protection for free speech and democracy. At times of real and imagined crisis, elites and members of the general public continued to treat some subjects as too important to be trusted to the democratic process. The idea that matters of public concern should be kept off the agenda that "we the people" would consider—the essence of the Sedition Act—reappeared in later struggles for free speech and democracy: in battles over antislavery speech and antiwar speech, and in the question of whether a multiracial democracy would operate in the South after the Civil War.

Free speech and democracy were not simply won in the battle over the Sedition Act. They had to be struggled for again and again and again. Not all the struggles were successful.

5

The Declaration, the Constitution, Slavery,

and Abolition

After the Sedition Act, the nation's next major free speech controversy was driven by slavery, and it included efforts to silence antislavery speech in the 1830s and again on the eve of the Civil War. The controversy over free speech for critics of slavery was shaped by the nation's conflicting commitments—to liberty and to the protection of slavery, to individual rights and states' rights. By the conventional wisdom of the time, shared at first even by abolitionists, the Constitution left the issue of slavery in each state to that state. So how the Southern states dealt with free speech on the subject was crucially important. By the 1830s, however, abolitionists began to demand immediate abolition. At the same time much of the South was banning antislavery speech and demanding that the North follow suit. The initial reaction in the North to the abolitionists was intensely negative. In the long run, however, the North refused to pass any laws to suppress speech against slavery. In time, more and more Northerners also criticized Southern laws suppressing antislavery speech as a violation of the American right to free speech enshrined in the federal Constitution.

The Revolution, the Constitution, and Slavery

This chapter will look at the constitutional commitments that shaped the debate, at a major debate in Virginia on ending slavery in the state, and finally at the Southern blockade against free speech about slavery. It will also look briefly at the abolitionist challenge and the initial Northern response. Several chapters that follow will focus on efforts to silence abolitionists in the North and on the defense of free speech those efforts produced.

The American revolutionaries understood their cause as a battle for liberty against a government threatening to enslave them. The slavery consisted of threats to their systems of representative government, threats to the basic rights of Englishmen, and threats to other basic rights. These rights American revolutionaries later enshrined in early state constitutions and bills of rights and still later in the Federal Bill of Rights.[1] The Declaration of Independence made broad claims for self-evident human rights: "[T]hat all men are created equal; that they are endowed, by their creator with certain unalienable rights; that among these are life, liberty, and the pursuit of happiness. That to secure these rights, governments are instituted among men, deriving their just powers from the consent of the governed."[2]

Of course, reality fell short of rhetoric, most notably in the case of slavery. Slaves were unprotected by bills of rights and had no voice in their government or in basic aspects of their lives.[3] The tension between American professions and practice was one that abolitionists pointed out again and again.[4]

It was also one repeatedly noted by Americans of the founding generation. St. George Tucker, the Virginia law teacher and judge, lamented that while America had been "the land of promise to Europeans and their descendants, it hath been the vale of death to millions of the wretched sons of Africa." While American revolutionaries had asked God "to witness our resolution to live free, or die . . . , we were imposing upon our fellow men, who differ in complexion from us, a slavery, ten thousand times more cruel than the utmost extremity of those grievances and oppressions, of which we complained."[5]

The original American Constitution of 1787 said that it was designed to secure the blessings of liberty. It contained some important guarantees of liberty such as the provision against ex post facto laws, for habeas corpus,[6] and the clause limiting treason so that simple political opposition to those in power could not be prosecuted as treason.[7] It divided power between federal and state governments and within the federal government. Divisions of power are an important mechanism for limiting its abuses.

But the document of 1787 contained basic imperfections. It lacked a bill of rights. It recognized the existence of slavery,[8] failed to prohibit it anywhere, and gave slavery enhanced political power through the clause that counted slaves as three-fifths of a person for purposes of representation in the federal House of Representatives. (At least that is so if one assumes slaves should not have been counted at all in the basis of representation.) The three-fifths provision also increased the power of the slave states in the electoral college. The Constitution protected the traffic in kidnapped and enslaved human beings until 1808, required Northern states to return escaped slaves, and committed the federal government to help to put down domestic violence in the states.[9] In the nineteenth century many Americans understood this to be a commitment to put down slave rebellions.

The framers of the Constitution of 1787, like most of us, had inconsistent goals. They wanted liberty and union, protection for liberty and protection for the institution of slavery. Time would prove these to be impossible combinations.

But the Constitution contained other provisions potentially threatening to slavery. It announced that its object was to secure "the Blessings of Liberty to ourselves and our Posterity."[10] It recognized freedom of speech, press, religion, and petition, and it provided that Congress make no law abridging them.[11] It defined treason in a way that did not cover political speech or press. The Constitution protected congressional debate from criminal or civil sanctions. It guaranteed a host of rights to those accused of crimes, though by conventional understanding these federal guarantees applied only in federal courts. It guaranteed to each state a republican form of government. It allowed Congress to regulate commerce among the states and to establish post offices and post roads. It provided for the supremacy of federal law. Finally, it gave Congress the power "to exercise exclusive Legislation in all cases whatsoever" over the seat of government and at places "purchased by the Consent of the Legislature of the State" for federal forts, arsenals, dockyards, and "other needful Buildings." It provided power to "make all needful Rules and Regulations respecting the Territory or other Property belonging to the United States."[12]

The power over territories seemed to give Congress power to contain slavery by limiting it to the states where it existed. Indeed, in the final year of the Articles of Confederation and in the first Congress under the new Constitution, Congress banned slavery from territory then under the control of Congress and provided for certain "perpetual" guarantees of civil liberties.[13] But in the face of rising Southern demands, the national government repeatedly compromised its policy of excluding slavery from new territories. The issue was crucial to the Southern political elite. If all new states were free states, the peculiar interests and institutions of the South might eventually lose the protection of the constitutional "compact." With the necessary majority, free states might amend or reinterpret the Constitution and insist on some form of emancipation.

The issue of new slave states reached a crisis over the proposed admission of Missouri. In 1819, James Tallmadge Jr., a New York member of Jefferson and Madison's Republican Party, proposed requiring gradual emancipation as a condition of the admission of Missouri. Initially, the House divided along sectional lines: Northerners voted for the amendment and Southerners voted against it. Eventually Congress embraced the Missouri Compromise: states from Louisiana Purchase territory above the latitude of 36°30' would be admitted as free states and states from below 36°30' could be slave states.[14]

The aged Thomas Jefferson, from the vantage point of Monticello, saw the sectional division over slavery as a prologue to disunion. He called the controversy a "fire bell in the night." A "geographical line, coinciding with a marked principle, moral and political, once conceived and held up to the angry passions of men, will never be obliterated; and every new irritation will mark it deeper and deeper," he wrote.[15] In the institution of slavery, Jefferson lamented, the South had "the wolf by the ears." It could neither safely hold it or let it go. Jefferson grimly foretold the destruction of the Union and the wreck of the work of 1776.[16]

ABOLITION, SLAVE REVOLTS, AND A SOUTHERN QUARANTINE

Radical Attacks on Slavery

By the 1830s, the tide of history seemed to be running against slavery. By 1804, Northern states had either abolished slavery or adopted programs of gradual emancipation. In Haiti, black revolutionaries had abolished slavery by force. In 1813 and 1814, Argentina and Columbia abolished slavery. Chile followed in 1823, Central America in 1824, Mexico in 1829, and Bolivia in 1831. By the autumn of 1833, news reached the United States that Britain had abolished slavery in the West Indies.[17] In the crisis of 1859–60, a Southern congressman compared the institution of slavery to sand castles and suggested slavery needed to be moved out of the Union to protect it from the inexorable tide of antislavery sentiment.[18] Similar, though less desperate, feelings of insecurity seized much of the Southern elite in the 1830s.

The insecurity was heightened by rumors of slave uprisings, and news of real incitements, plots, and rebellions. Denmark Vesey, handsome and intelligent, had for twenty years sailed as the slave of a sea captain engaged in the slave trade. Vesey won fifteen hundred dollars in a lottery and purchased his freedom for six hundred dollars. He became a carpenter and accumulated a considerable amount of property. He was literate and familiar with the Bible, and identified the slaves and free blacks with the Israelites. Having learned of the slave revolt in Santo Domingo and after allegedly reading newspaper stories of Northern congressmen urging abolition during the Missouri controversy, he plotted a slave insurrection in Charleston, South Carolina, in 1822, traveling to plantations to seek converts. One of these betrayed him, and his rebellion was crushed before it began.[19]

In 1829, David Walker, a free Negro, sent pamphlets south urging a slave rebellion. Walker had been born in Wilmington, North Carolina, of a free mother and a slave father. Since his status followed that of his mother, he was free. He was deeply sympathetic with the slaves and read widely in the history of slavery in the ancient world. Around 1827, he moved to Boston and established a second-hand clothing store. In 1829 he composed his *Appeal*, a "closely reasoned and eloquent" argument against slavery that urged a slave uprising. It also urged slaveholders to repent their sin before the wrath of God struck them down. The pamphlet produced panic in the South. The authorities discovered some of Walker's pamphlets in the port city of Wilmington, North Carolina, and elsewhere in the South. On discovering one in Georgia, the legislature rushed through a statute that imposed the death penalty for "circulation of pamphlets of evil tendency among our domestics." The mayor of Savannah wrote Harrison Gray Otis, the mayor of Boston seeking punishment of Walker. Otis condemned the pamphlet, but said that Walker had not violated any Massachusetts law. A price was put on Walker's head in the South, and he died in 1830, a death many thought was the result of poison.[20]

In 1831, William Lloyd Garrison launched the *Liberator*, a paper filled with harsh denunciations of slavery and slaveholders. Although he advocated nonviolence, Garrison republished Walker's appeal.[21] Some Southern papers began to inform their readers of what the *Liberator* was saying. When Nat Turner led a slave revolt in Virginia in 1831, killing sixty whites before his rebellion was suppressed,[22] Governor Floyd of Virginia attributed Nat Turner's rebellion to abolitionist papers.[23]

In Virginia, after the Nat Turner rebellion, the legislature also considered repressive measures. Remarkably, however, the rebellion also led to a legislative attempt gradually to end slavery in Virginia and to provide for colonization of emancipated slaves. Jefferson's grandson was a leader of the effort.

The Virginia Emancipation Debates of 1832: A Dress Rehearsal for an 1859 National Debate on Slavery and Free Speech

There are some remarkable similarities between the controversy over emancipation in Virginia and the later controversy that swirled around slavery between 1859 and 1860. Just as the national debate on slavery became increasingly sectional, the divisions in Virginia were also largely, though not entirely, sectional. Delegates from west of the Blue Ridge Mountains tended to favor emancipation and colonization (deportation); those from the heavily slaveholding counties of the East tended to oppose it. Slave counties in Virginia were overrepresented in the Virginia legislature, if representation were to be based on their white population.[24] Slaveholding areas were also overrepresented, by virtue of the three-fifths clause, in the federal House of Representatives.[25] So, locally and nationally, slaveholders came to controversies over slavery with added political power.

Republicans supported banning slavery from the territories. In 1832 a delegate from western Virginia suggested the desirability of banning slavery from that part of the state.[26] Like the North Carolina abolitionist author Hinton Helper in the late 1850s, supporters of gradual emancipation in the Virginia legislature based their argument more on the safety and economic well-being of the white community than on concern for the rights of the slave. Slavery, the Virginians argued, endangered whites, threatening them with slave revolts. It discouraged white artisans and mechanics from working in the state and produced white flight and economic backwardness.[27] The Virginia emancipationists suggested that abolition of slavery was justified by the power of government to abate nuisances. Indeed, analogies to slavery ranged from mad dogs to diseased cargoes on ships.[28] The list of practical dangers was capped with the prescient claim that slavery was producing sectional parties and was contributing to the future dismemberment of the Union.[29] For Virginia's supporters of emancipation, quarantining blacks on ships and prohibiting teaching slaves to read would not cure the problem. The South was trying to cure cancer with a bandage.

In addition to practical arguments against slavery, one Virginia delegate questioned whether slavery was not "the most striking [instance] upon record, of a people resolutely violating towards others, that principle of absolute freedom on which they erected their own independence."[30] Finally some Virginia emancipationists appealed to the humanity of the slave.[31] One major difference between the Virginia debate of 1832 and the congressional debate of 1859 is the increased expression of humanitarian concern for the slaves in Congress in 1859. Still, in 1859 some leading Republicans saw colonization as the next step after emancipation, and supported it for free blacks as well as slaves.[32]

While in 1832 an important segment of the political elite and establishment press in Virginia had called for an end to slavery in the state, by 1859 the press and political elite in Virginia and North Carolina treated similar appeals as criminal. Though the Virginia rhetoric was at times radical, the proposals of the 1832 Virginia emancipationists were more moderate: one resolution provided that emancipation of all slaves born after 1840 be submitted to the voters. The proposal for gradual emancipation did not necessarily assure freedom for all slaves, though it would free Virginia from slavery. Gradual emancipation left open the possibility that slaves could be sold to the deep South before the date for emancipation arrived.[33]

The Virginia emancipationist-colonizationist attack was answered with an appeal to the rights of private property, including an invocation of the Fifth Amendment guarantee against taking private property for public use without just compensation. Emancipationists answered that the right to private property was limited. It did not include the right to compensation when property endangered the community or was a nuisance.[34] John Chandler, delegate from Norfolk County, suggested that slaveowners had a questionable title to their slaves. Since liberty "rightfully, cannot be converted into slavery, may I not question whether the title of the master to the slave is absolute . . . ?" The original American owners of the slaves were receivers of stolen goods; passage of time did not improve the title of their descendants. In spite of legislative enactments, Chandler thought title to slaves remained dubious.[35]

The proposals and, to a far greater degree, the philosophy of the emancipationists seemed to threaten powerful economic interests of slaveholders. A pamphlet by "Appomattox" came to the defense of the institution of slavery. Appomattox cited, with a mixture of horror and sarcasm, some statements by proponents of abolition: "The gentleman who opened the debate . . . was very, very moderate: he only referred to the declaration in the bill of rights that *all men are by nature free and equal,* and applying it to our slaves, said, 'It was a truth held sacred by every American and by every republican throughout the world.'" And he presumed it could not be denied in that hall, as a general principle, that it is an *act of injustice, tyranny and oppression, to hold any part of the human race* in bondage against their consent."[36]

The speeches, Appomattox angrily announced, had been published in Richmond where they were likely to influence the blacks and to spread. If insurrection by the blacks did break out, it would be due "not to the hallucinations or imposture of another Nat Turner, nor to the seditious practices of negro preachers . . . nor to the dissemination of the incendiary writings of *The Liberator,* or *The African Sentinel,* or *The Genius of Universal Emancipation*—but to measures proposed, and to speeches delivered, in our own legislature, published and disseminated by our own public journals."[37] Appomattox urged his readers to "pay no regard" to claims of independence of the press. Slaveholders and their allies should take action to silence opponents of slavery including a boycott of the presses that published these "inflammatory, dangerous, mischievous" writings. He urged private action instead of "sedition laws."[38]

Free speech on slavery can be seen from two perspectives. First, it may be viewed from the perspective of formal legal reactions to it: statutes and jury and court decisions. Second, it may be viewed from the perspective of the broader social reaction to dissent. Obviously the two systems influence each other. To the extent that Appomattox convinced Virginians that criticism of slavery was illegitimate and tended to produce violence, the effect of his efforts in the long run would be to produce both legal and extralegal suppression. To the extent that the community sees dissent on a subject as not only wrong, but illegitimate, free discussion of that topic is likely to disappear.

Proponents of emancipation in Virginia refuted the claim that public discussion of the issue was a grave wrong. They made a structural argument about the role of free speech in republican government, echoing arguments that stretched back through Virginia's resolution rejecting the Sedition Act to the Radical Whig heritage. Secrecy on the issue was "unsuited to the genius of this government, which is based on the right of the people, to a free and full examination of whatever concerns their interest and happiness."[39] The Richmond *Constitutional Whig* suggested that those who sought to silence debate on the question were reviving the principles of the Sedition Act. Appomattox's letter, as "A Subscriber" wrote to a Richmond paper, "is better suited to the arrogance of a Dictator than to the equality of a republican citizen." Another writer, signing himself "Jefferson," accused Appomattox of upholding the "aristocratic principle" that discussion of the issue of slavery was to be reserved to rich slaveholders. On the contrary, the writer insisted, "this is a republic," and not "an oligarchy."[40] One of the delegates to the Virginia Assembly insisted that there was no resemblance "between the free and manly discussion of a subject, by freemen, the representatives of freemen . . . and the under-handed attempts of incendiary cut-throats [like Garrison or Lloyd], to sharpen the dagger in the hand of the midnight assassin." Feeling, he said, could no longer be repressed; lips of critics would not remain sealed. "[The] golden rule and slavery are hard to reconcile."[41]

In the end, the debate had been free and opponents of slavery had had their say. But they lost on the substantive issue: a resolution supporting legislative action for the abolition of slavery failed by a vote of seventy-three to fifty-eight.[42] Some supporters of emancipation were defeated at the next election. A major effort to end slavery in a Southern state had failed. In the years that followed efforts to protect slavery from political attack intensified.

THE SOUTHERN QUARANTINE

Faced with threats to slavery, Southern legislatures began to construct a legal Maginot Line to insulate themselves against abolitionist ideas. In 1830, for example, North Carolina prohibited dissemination of publications, "the evident tendency whereof would be to excite insurrection, conspiracy or resistence in the slaves, free negroes, and persons of colour within the State."[43] Time would show that the list of items Southerners thought had such a tendency was quite large. By 1854, the North Carolina legislature did not leave a broad construction to inference. It explicitly expanded the definition of proscribed subjects. The legislature now made it a crime to publish or circulate items, "the evident tendency whereof is to cause slaves to become discontented with the bondage in which they are held by their masters and the laws regulating the same, and free negroes to be dissatisfied with their social condition and the denial to them of political privileges, and thereby to excite among the said slaves and free negroes a disposition to make conspiracies, insurrections, or resistance."[44]

Precautions in 1830 were not limited to speech, pamphlets, and books. Since free blacks on ships were a suspected source of "incendiary" publications, North Carolina, like South Carolina and some other Southern states, provided for temporary imprisonment of free black sailors who came into Southern ports.[45] A case concerning the constitutionality of a Negro Seaman Act came before Justice Marshall on circuit, but he avoided deciding the main issue. He wrote that he was not fond of butting his head against a stone wall in sport.[46]

Today, laws suppressing antislavery expression would raise serious federal constitutional issues under the Fourteenth Amendment, ratified in 1868. The Fourteenth Amendment is now understood to require states to obey principles of free speech and free press recognized in the First Amendment. But in *Barron v. Baltimore*, in 1833, the Supreme Court ruled that guarantees of the Bill of Rights did not limit the states. Had the framers intended such a result, Chief Justice Marshall said, they would have used the "no state shall" words before the general prohibitions.[47] So it seemed that the security of the rights of American citizens had a twofold aspect. They were protected against federal action by the federal Bill of Rights; but, to the extent they were protected against state action, it was by state constitutions and bills of rights. By the time Chief Justice Marshall wrote in 1833, the right to criticize slavery had suffered serious erosion in the South. There was no federal constitutional limit (as the Court seemed to see it) against state statutes banning antislavery expression. The decision in *Barron* meant that Chief Justice Marshall could avoid butting his head against another part of the Southern stone wall.

CALL BY ABOLITIONISTS FOR "IMMEDIATE ABOLITION"

The framers of the Constitution had feared that slavery would destroy chances for union. Their solution had been compromises that offered security to slavery. With the debate over admitting Missouri as a slave state, the issue reignited. The solution of 1820 had been to compromise the issue of slavery in the territories and remove slavery from the political agenda. But in 1835, abolitionists threatened to put the divisive issue back on the agenda. The events of the 1830s involved not only slavery but a further issue as well—the meaning of guarantees for free speech, press, petition, and religion. Did these guarantees mean that abolitionists had a right to "agitate" the issue of slavery—to try to put it back on the national agenda or to place it squarely before the conscience of slave-holders?

In 1833, abolitionists began to organize societies, including a national one, and to engage in a publicity campaign aimed at ending slavery. They proclaimed their sentiments to the world: slavery was a sin and slaveholders should immediately renounce it. Still, the American Anti-Slavery Society recognized that states had control over slavery within their boundaries. The society acknowledged that Congress had no power to abolish slavery in the slave states. The abolitionists believed, however, that Congress did have power to prohibit slavery in the District of Columbia and in the national territories, and they suggested that Congress should exercise its power to ban slavery in those places. The society also thought that Congress should ban the interstate slave trade. Finally, the society renounced the use of violence by its members or by the slaves.[48]

In these respects, the practical and political aspects of the American Anti-Slavery Society's program clearly resemble the platform that the Republican Party would adopt twenty-six years later. The Republican platform of 1860 also recognized the legal right of Southern states to control their "domestic institutions," but it favored a ban on slavery in the territories.[49] Republicans also hoped that free speech would spell the end of Southern slavery.

In addition to its attack on slavery in federal territories, the American Anti-Slavery Society advocated immediate and uncompensated emancipation and incorporation of the newly freed slaves into American society as citizens, though there was some equivocation on the last point.[50] In this respect, its position was not reached by the Republican Party until after the revolutionary experience of the Civil War and the passage of the Thirteenth, Fourteenth, and Fifteenth Amendments.

There was less to immediate emancipation than met the eye, however. Abolitionists sought to persuade Americans and slaveholders that slavery was a sin; they argued that slaveholders should voluntarily and immediately relinquish their slaves, just as other sins should be immediately abjured. Abolitionists expected emancipation through change in public opinion. Eventually, as Southerners were persuaded, slavery would be abolished by individual action or by state legislation. Abolitionist leaders were influenced by the great religious awakening of their time, and they used similar techniques to seek converts from the sin of slavery.[51] Abolitionist denunciations were blunt and often bitter—slave owners were wilful sinners: "[E]very American citizen, who retains a human being in involuntary bondage as his property, is, (according to scripture) a manstealer."[52]

In 1860—with the election of Republican Abraham Lincoln, a president who was committed to containment of slavery and who hoped for its ultimate extinction—the South seceded. Leaders of the secessionist movement announced that they were threatened by abolition. Republican plans to nurture a local political opposition to slavery and the similarity of some practical aspects of the abolitionist and Republican programs helps explain why the secessionist leaders thought this was so.

Abolitionists sent paid agents throughout the North to proselytize the new antislavery gospel; they took advantage of cheap printing and the wealth of their supporters to flood the country with abolitionist literature; and finally, they aimed their efforts not just at men, but at women and children. As a result, their opponents found them sinister and threatening. The abolitionists were tireless organizers. Starting with a few societies in the early 1830s, they had increased to 1,006 groups by 1837.[53] In 1835, they engaged in a mass mailing (sending abolition literature south), the petition campaign (sending massive petitions to Congress to abolish slavery in the District of Columbia), and held public meetings, and organized new antislavery societies. In response, their critics called for suppressing abolitionism, thereby raising questions about the meaning of free speech, free press, and freedom to petition.

When the American Anti-Slavery Society announced its goal of immediate abolition, the conventional national wisdom was that slavery was an evil, one imposed by the legacy of the past, and one that was so difficult to change that little could be done. Those who opposed both slavery and the abolitionists often suggested leaving reform of the slave system to providence.[54] Moderate reformist efforts were channeled into the American Colonization Society. It proposed to colonize free blacks in Africa or in some equally distant location. But the growth of the slave population far exceeded the number of free blacks colonized, as the abolitionists demonstrated. Indeed, abolitionists charged that the South used colonization as a scheme to strengthen slavery by ridding the South of its "anomalous" free black population.[55]

THE NATION'S RESPONSE TO THE ABOLITIONISTS

Formation of antislavery societies in the North and calls for immediate abolition produced a harsh and violent reaction in the North as well as in the South. Indeed, antiabolition incidents were probably more numerous in the North than in the South; the North, after all, was where the abolitionists usually were located. From 1833 to 1837, mobs organized to prevent or disrupt abolition meetings in Utica, New York, in Boston, Massachusetts, and throughout the North. In October 1835, William Lloyd Garrison, a leader of the Massachusetts Anti-Slavery Society, was captured by a Boston mob that invaded an abolitionist meeting. The mob led Garrison around the streets of Boston with a rope around his neck.[56] In 1834, a mob broke into the home of Lewis Tappan, a leader and financial angel of the abolitionists, and destroyed his belongings. Tappan wrote that he would leave his despoiled house throughout the summer as a silent monument to the corrupting effect of slavery on the American republic.[57]

The *Boston Atlas* blamed Boston violence on the provocative position taken by the abolitionists. It branded "free discussion on the subject of slavery" as "the mischief . . . in a nut shell" and hoped that new efforts by abolitionists to renew excitement on the subject of slavery would be met with "universal scorn and indignation, that they may be indicted before the Grand Jury as PUBLIC NUISANCES, and if t[h]is fail, that they may be provided at the public expense with a wholesome . . . coat of Tar and Feathers."[58] Mobs organized to suppress abolitionist expression were typically led by community leaders, by "gentlemen of property and standing." Antiabolition furor reached a climax in 1835, as the presidential election approached.[59] The American Anti-Slavery Society had sent antislavery publications to the South in the mails, a new technique in its antislavery proselytizing. The South responded furiously. In July 1835, a group of men in Charleston, South Carolina, entered the post office, removed abolition literature and publicly burned it.[60] Southern states already had laws against publications tending to cause discontent among slaves, and Southern leaders interpreted the abolitionist literature as a violation of their statutes. Southern governors and state legislatures demanded that the North suppress abolitionists in the North and stop their "interference" with the South's peculiar institution.[61]

These events came at a sensitive time for the then dominant national

Democratic Party. Andrew Jackson's presidency was drawing to a close, and Martin Van Buren of New York was his hand-picked successor. The slavery issue threatened to disrupt the national Democratic coalition by driving a wedge between its Northern and Southern wings. Some in the South were beginning to talk of secession. At the same time, less extreme South Carolinians, such as Senator John C. Calhoun, contended that state legislatures could nullify federal laws which would then be void, unless revived by enactment of a constitutional amendment. Because of the very large majorities required for a constitutional amendment, this theory protected the South—and slavery—from national legislative action.

Martin Van Buren, the first Northern candidate of Jefferson's party, particularly needed to reassure his Southern supporters.[62] The Van Buren press accused Southern proslavery "nullifiers" and Northern Whigs of exacerbating the issue in order to disrupt the Democratic North-South coalition and to throw the election into the House of Representatives.[63] They also accused Southern "nullifiers" of acting in implicit concert with abolitionists to agitate the slavery issue in order to produce a united Southern party. This in turn would lead to disunion and civil war.[64] In this context the nation debated sensitive issues of the meaning and limits of free speech, free press, and the right to petition.

6

Shall Abolitionists Be Silenced?

A central political question racked the United States from 1835 to 1837: Would government prohibit abolitionists from criticizing the institution of slavery and from calling for its abolition? The question was perplexing. It directly pitted cherished, though poorly defined, ideas of free expression against perceived needs to protect public safety and preserve the Union.

Those who sought to silence abolitionists pursued various approaches. In the South, legislatures passed laws that could be used against abolitionist expression, and vigilantes punished them. In the North, legislatures considered laws to muzzle abolitionists, and in some cases Northern mobs took to the streets to silence abolitionists. Congress muzzled its own debates on abolition petitions. It also considered censoring the mails by banning abolitionist publications directed at the South. Each of these controversies raised again a basic question: was it legitimate to eliminate antislavery ideas and arguments from public debate—at least in the South and perhaps throughout the nation?

The years 1835 to 1837 were a defining moment for American ideas about freedom of expression. Would some topics be eliminated from the political debate?

Whether to ban abolitionist expression was a hard question as a matter of judicial precedent because there was no precedent directly on that issue. Some thought what precedent existed could, by analogy, justify state laws outlawing at least some antislavery speech and press.[1] Blackstone's views of free speech and the Sedition Act, for example, seem to provide support for suppression. But the debate did not merely focus on the musty precedents of the law. Legislative and community notions of free expression defined the limits of government suppression. Public and legislative debates focused on constitutional provisions, on the function of free speech, on federalism, and on the teachings of history. One debate focused on federal power over the press. Most who discussed that subject implicitly rejected judicial decisions upholding the Sedition Act.[2]

This story of abolition and free expression is mainly about Northern and national laws that did not pass, about suppression considered and rejected. Southern states passed laws suppressing antislavery speech and press; the national administration censored the U.S. mails; and Congress set severe limits on its discussion of abolition petitions. But these measures did not spread to form a comprehensive system of suppression. The repression of antislavery petitions and debate in Congress was a victory for suppression. But suppressing discussion of antislavery petitions in Congress proved to be a Pyrrhic victory for slavery, precisely because it violated a broad public consensus about the meaning of the right to petition.

At first, many in the North accepted Southern repression as legitimate. But as the controversy intensified between 1835 and 1837, abolitionists and others reframed the issue from one limited to slavery in the South to one embracing liberty in the North. More and more Northerners began to see the slave system not as a limited (and even useful) Southern domestic institution, but as a system whose demands for security threatened the liberty of the North. Just as Northerners eventually demanded that slavery be contained within its present boundaries, they also eventually rejected even its claim to local immunity from criticism.

The story of how the North rejected suppression has some important lessons. First, the story shows that inchoate public ideas of free speech and press are of crucial importance in protecting freedom of expression. Two of the most crucial decisions about free expression in American history—the demise of the Sedition Act and the North's refusal to suppress antislavery speech—were not based on court decisions or recondite doctrine.[3] Preserving the right of Northerners to criticize slavery and to call for its abolition turned, in part, on broad, simple, and widely held ideas of free speech and press.

Second, this story illustrates how divisions of power limited power. The federal system and the pre–Civil War idea that the federal government had no broad power to suppress abolitionist ideas meant that the issue of suppression was decided state by state. Southern states generally chose legislative suppression. Northern states rejected it. For the nation at large, piecemeal suppression meant that discussion of the legitimacy of slavery continued.

Though at first almost all abolitionists explicitly disavowed violence, they did denounce slavery as a crime against humanity. They warned of the undeniable danger of slave rebellions. Many saw these ideas as implicit calls for violence. Today, before speech on matters of public concern can be silenced on the ground of its tendency to cause rebellion or violation of the law, the law seems to require that the government must show that the speech is directed to inciting or producing imminent law violation and is likely to incite or produce such action.[4] Except where the threat is imminent, the ordinary remedy even for advocacy of rebellion is counterspeech. But the South found cold comfort in the ideas of counterspeech.

Slaves were not citizens, not part of the political community. As slaveholders and many others saw it, they could not be trusted to draw the "correct" conclusion if confronted with discussions of the evils of slavery. Furthermore, a general discussion of the evils of slavery would, many thought, eventually reach slaves. The solution advocated by the Southern elite was to eliminate the discussion. This solution had the additional advantage of making slavery safe from democracy. If democracy means that "the people" may participate in setting the political agenda and that any person has the right to advocate fundamental change through the democratic process, then refusing to allow abolition to become part of the political agenda was profoundly anti-democratic.

Most Americans at the time accepted the lawfulness of slavery; they accepted the general assumption that slaves were not to be parties to the discussion of the wisdom of slavery; and they accepted the idea that directly urging slaves to rebel could be punished. Still, even if one accepts all these ideas, harsh criticisms of slavery that were directed to peaceful action by whites should have been protected. The alternative was to reduce white citizens to hearing only that discussion of slavery that slave masters thought was suitable for slaves. Suppressing all discussion denied that slavery was a subject for democratic action.

The Case for Suppression

Advocates of suppression made two basic points to justify outlawing abolition societies and publications. First, abolition threatened to ignite slave rebellion in the South. Second, it threatened the survival of the

Union. Closely tied to both concerns was a view of the constitutional compact that made abolitionism illegitimate.

In 1831, Governor John Floyd of Virginia, then a supporter of a gradual plan to rid Virginia of slavery, attributed the Nat Turner slave revolt to abolitionist agitation reaching slaves through free Negroes and malign whites.[5] In 1831, the governor of North Carolina accused reckless Northerners of spreading sedition among the slaves and claimed that free blacks transmitted the message.[6] In 1831, a Raleigh, North Carolina, grand jury indicted the publisher of the Massachusetts-based *Liberator* for circulating the newspaper in Wake County.[7]

Of course, to incite slave rebellions abolition publications had to reach the South. In the summer of 1835, abolitionists mailed their publications to the South in large quantities. Though they sent most to the Southern elite, by 1835 the assumption that abolitionist publications would lead to slave rebellions seemed so obvious to many Northerners and Southerners that it needed no demonstration. Chancellor Kent said that the "great principle of self-preservation doubtless demands, on the part of the white population dwelling in the midst of such combustible materials, unceasing vigilance and firmness."[8]

The abolitionist postal campaign of 1835 was greeted by howls of outrage from the South and by antiabolition protest meetings throughout the North. On the issue of slave revolts, an antiabolition mass meeting in Portland, Maine, was typical. Its resolutions insisted that abolitionist agitation would excite the passion of slaves against their masters, produce slave discontent, and produce discontent among free blacks. As a result, abolitionist agitation was preparing the way for the horrors of servile insurrection.[9] Harrison Gray Otis, a former Federalist supporter of the Sedition Act and a leading citizen of Boston, warned against "immense numbers of books, pamphlets, tracts, and newspapers of the most inflammatory character." Some contained pictures and all featured harsh strictures against slave owners. Otis said the message would reach the slaves: although few slaves could read, all slaves could understand the pictures.[10] Even John Quincy Adams, soon to be seen by Southerners as an antislavery congressman, saw the abolitionists as "making every possible exertion to kindle the flame of insurrection among the slaves."[11]

Only rarely did the opponents of abolition explain in detail why the abolitionists of the American Anti-Slavery Society—who disavowed violence, sent their publications to leading Southerners, and never explicitly advocated slave resistance or revolt—were nonetheless threatening slave revolts. While critics denounced abolitionists as fanatical incendiaries, they rarely quoted them directly. Critics insisted that, whoever their immediate audience, the publications would eventually reach slaves and free blacks. Writing to the *New York Post*, a citizen who signed his letter "Plain Truth," in a rare departure from standard denunciations, actually quoted *Human Rights*, an abolition publication, for the propositions that laws sustaining the right of slavery were null and void in the sight of God, that man could not hold property in man, and that slavery was a crime. To Plain Truth, the conclusion from such sentiments was obvious:

> The unavoidable consequences of their sentiments is to stir up discontent, hatred, and sedition among the slaves. Interpreted into monitory language, they would read thus, Slaves! you are an injured race—plundered of your unalienable rights by wicked men, who falsely claim a property in you, and who are guilty of a deliberate plot, under the form of law, against your lives and happiness. Their treatment absolves you from all the ties of humanity—desertion, fire, robbery and massacre are not crimes in you; therefore we "exhort you to a quiet and peaceful demeanour." It is hard to believe the sincerity of such advice.[12]

The more sophisticated critics recognized that abolitionists were not sending their publications to slaves, since slaves could not read, but the critics insisted that wide circulation meant that the publications would fall into the hands of literate free Negroes or of malevolent white men or women inclined to pass abolitionist ideas on to slaves.[13] Logically applied, as it never entirely was, the argument reduced the free population to reading only ideas acceptable for circulation among slaves. One notable result was that discussion of the legitimacy of slavery itself became illegitimate in the South. Virginia newspapers had published the state legislative debates on abolition. Soon much of the South treated publication of the debates as unacceptable. For example, an 1836 Virginia statute criminalized statements similar to those its legislators had expressed in the Virginia debate over slavery.[14]

The danger of slave revolts was not the main argument for suppression. The Cassandras of the North warned of desolation if the Trojan horse of antislavery agitation was allowed within the citadel of political dialogue. Abolition would become a political issue; political parties would become sectional; and when the antislavery party achieved a majority, the result would be disunion and civil war. To Harrison Gray Otis of Boston and countless others, this was a "still stronger" objection to abolition.[15] "The work of destruction is more than commenced," warned the *Boston Atlas* in 1834. "The train is laid, and a single spark may blow our Constitution into atoms, and scatter its blackened fragments to the winds. Unless measures are adopted to meet and repel the efforts of the abolitionists, this country is inevitably doomed to be theatre of a civil . . . war."[16] But if slave revolts and civil war were the consequence of agitation for abolition, what was the remedy? If the remedy was to suppress abolition expression, what theory justified suppression?

Types of Suppression

Abolitionists organized associations; they held public meetings seeking new societies and converts to abolition; they printed and published a vast number of books, periodicals, and pamphlets; and they mailed some of their publications to the slaveholding states. Most of their activities were directed to converting the people of the North. But some, like their great 1835 mass mailing, were directed to reaching people in the South.

Northern Approval of the Southern Quarantine

Slave revolts were a risk only if abolitionist publications and activities reached the South. As to their activities in the South, abolitionists faced broad condemnation, North as well as South. Except for the abolitionists themselves and a few others, Northerners and Southerners alike castigated abolitionists for attempting to proselytize against slavery in the South. In the South, Southern leaders insisted, there was no dissent on the need to suppress the inflammatory publications of the abolitionists.[17]

As many contemporaries saw it, disseminating abolition literature in the South was simply a crime. Even before the abolitionist postal campaign of 1835, legislation was in place that could be used to suppress abolitionist expression in most Southern states. In 1830, North Carolina, like other Southern states, passed a law punishing disseminators of publications with a "tendency" to excite insurrection or resistance among slaves or free blacks.[18] Alabama's statute provided the death penalty for any person who distributed or published "any seditious papers . . . tending to produce conspiracy or insurrection . . . among the slaves or colored population."[19] In 1836, after the postal campaign, Virginia passed a statute providing for imprisonment of any antislavery society member who entered the state and advocated abolition or maintained that masters had no property in their slaves. The statute also banned circulating books with the intent of "persuading persons of colour within this commonwealth . . . to rebel or denying the master the right of property in their slaves and inculcating the duty of resistance to such right."[20]

Many Southerners read their laws as covering very general denunciations of slavery. The governor of Alabama and a grand jury at Tuscaloosa, Alabama, interpreted the Alabama act to outlaw a statement in *The Emancipator* that "God commands, and all nature cries out, that man should not be held as property. The system of making men property, has plunged 2,250,000 of our fellow countrymen into the deepest physical and moral degradation, and they are every moment sinking deeper."[21] On the basis of those words, the Tuscaloosa grand jury indicted the New York publisher of *The Emancipator*, and the governor of Alabama requested his extradition.

Offenses against the Southern rule of silence about slavery might be punished by law or by private action. A South Carolina newspaper insisted that slavery "shall not be open to discussion." The moment an individual "attempts to lecture us upon [the] evils and immorality" of slavery, the paper said, "IN THE SAME MOMENT HIS TONGUE SHALL BE CUT OUT AND CAST UPON THE DUNGHILL."[22] A Charleston, South Carolina, meeting called to protest the abolitionists' postal campaign did not defend slavery in its resolutions. This reticence, the meeting explained, came not from any inability to defend the institution, but rather from "a deep conviction of the fixed resolutions of the people of this state, to permit no discussion within her limits of RIGHTS, which she deems inherent."[23] Southern governors and legislatures echoed the demand that antislavery discussion must cease, in the North as well as in the South.

Support for, or at least tolerance of, Southern laws that punished abolitionist expression in the South was, at first, quite common in the North. In August 1835, a Philadelphia, Pennsylvania, mass meeting strongly protested abolitionist activity aimed at the South: "[W]e regard the dissemination of incendiary publications throughout the slaveholding States with indignation and horror." It advocated efficient, "but legal and moderate measures" to suppress this "evil."[24]

The broad national support for Southern states' suppression of abolitionist expression was based on an understanding of the Constitution by which states retained substantial sovereignty. By this view, the Constitution reserved slavery to the states. It recognized and protected slavery by constitutional provisions such as the fugitive slave clause and the three-fifths clause. Amos Kendall, President Jackson's postmaster general, said that as to slavery, the states were "as independent of each other as they were before the Constitution was formed." The slave states could "fence and protect their interest in slaves by such laws and regulations as, in their sovereign will, they may deem expedient." To ensure the safety of their people, Kendall said, Southern states had exercised their reserved rights by "prohibiting, under heavy penalties, the printing or circulation of papers" like those the abolitionists had sent South. "It has never been alleged," Kendall continued, "that these laws are incompatible with the Constitution and laws of the United States." Nor could there be such a claim, because it was a subject over which the United States "cannot rightfully assume any control." The provision of Article IV, Section 2, that the "Citizens of each State shall be entitled to all Privileges and Immunities of Citizens of the several States" was, Kendall insisted, of no aid to abolitionists. It simply gave them the same right to advocate abolition that citizens of the Southern states enjoyed—none.[25]

Kendall was postmaster general in a Democratic administration determined to conciliate the South. On this point, however, his views were shared by most mainstream politicians, regardless of party or section.[26] Accepting the premise of state sovereignty, the conclusion was inevitable. As Kendall and many others saw it, by attempting to spread abolition in the South, abolitionists were violating or circumventing valid state laws. According to most Northern opinion leaders and politicians, Southerners were perfectly within their rights in suppressing abolition in the South.

Northern Action on Abolition: Efforts at Persuasion

As the issue moved from Southern laws suppressing abolition in the South to Northern laws suppressing abolition in the North, broad support for suppression fractured. Those who wanted to silence abolitionists might seek national or Northern actions to suppress abolitionist activities in the North simply by mobilizing public disapproval of abolitionists, by physical and extralegal actions designed to suppress abolition agitation, or by national or Northern laws. Alternatives were not always clearly separated in the uproar and mass public meetings that followed the abolitionist postal campaign of 1835. When in the 1830s Northern opponents of abolition repeatedly expressed faith in the power of "public opinion,"[27] it was sometimes unclear exactly how—violently or peacefully—that "public opinion" was to be expressed.

Many seemed to believe that abolition could be neutralized by organized public expressions of disapproval (which presumably would lead abolitionists to repent), or at least that public condemnation would so isolate them as to render them powerless. This course was the least coercive and the most consistent with libertarian ideas of free speech. Still, to the extent that abolitionists were branded as criminals and traitors, as they often were, speech denouncing them might lead to lawless conduct aimed at their suppression.

Often, "public opinion" on the subject was manufactured and expressed by mass meetings that passed resolutions in most Northern cities. These in turn were reprinted virtually verbatim in much of the press.[28] The pro–Van Buren papers were particularly assiduous in publishing such items in a transparent effort to hold the South for the first Northern nominee of the Democratic Republicans. A resolution approved by a Philadelphia, Pennsylvania, mass meeting viewed the actions of the abolitionists "in organizing societies, maintaining agents, and disseminating publications intended to operate upon the institutions of the South, as unwise, dangerous, and deserving emphatic reprehension and zealous opposition." That meeting also expressed "indignation and horror" at the "dangerous and disgraceful" practice of disseminating "incendiary publications throughout the slaveholding states."[29]

In Albany, New York, the Democratic governor presided over an antiabolitionist meeting. He was supported by an all-star cast of politicians. The meeting resolved that the subject of slavery belonged "exclusively to the people of each State"; any attempt by those from other states to interfere with it would "violate the spirit" of the constitutional compact. The meeting denounced those who attempted to coerce other states into abolition as "disturbers of the public peace" and called on abolitionists to prove the purity of their motives by "discontinuing a course of conduct, which they cannot now but see must lead to disorders and crimes of the darkest dye." Those who "with full knowledge of their pernicious tendency" persisted in carrying on abolitionist discussions were branded as "disloyal to the Union."[30]

Almost every sizable Northern community held antiabolition mass meetings in the summer or fall of 1835. These meetings, like the Democratic and Whig press, typically referred to abolitionists as "fanatics" and "incendiaries."[31] Meanwhile the major political factions of the day traded charges that the other was soft on abolitionism.[32]

Typically, abolitionists were stigmatized by their critics in the leading partisan newspapers and not quoted directly.[33] To the extent that abolitionists were heard at all in the national political debate, it was mainly because wealthy backers and dedicated activists provided their own channels of communication through pamphlets, periodicals, and agents who traveled the North in search of converts. Ironically, Southern nationalists or "nullifiers" sometimes disseminated some abolition statements to show the danger and reality of the abolition threat. Later, as the national focus shifted from freedom for the slave to the freedom of Northerners to espouse the cause of the slave, abolitionists' pronouncements on abolition and freedom of expression got more attention from at least some segments of the Northern press.[34]

Northern Action Against Abolition: Coercion

In the early years of the antislavery crusade, Northern mobs often dispersed abolitionists by force. In 1835, New York abolitionists announced an organizational meeting for a New York antislavery society set in Oneida County, New York. Oneida County Democrats resolved that the meeting of "incendiary individuals" should not be "permitted to assemble within its corporate bounds" and demanded that all courtrooms, schools, and churches should close their doors against "these wicked and deluded men."[35] Initially, the abolitionists obtained permission from the local government to meet in a courtroom, but as a result of protests the local government withdrew permission. The abolitionists then assembled in a local church, but a mob forced them to vacate it. The mob also invaded the office of a local paper that had supported both Van Buren and the abolitionists and threw the paper's type into the street.[36] Finally, the abolitionist convention was able to reassemble at the nearby estate of Gerrit Smith, a wealthy sympathizer.

Leaders of the effort to suppress the New York abolitionist convention received implicit and explicit approval from other political leaders. The proceedings were reported in the *Washington Globe* (which had refused to publish the call for the abolition convention) under the chortling headline ABOLITION MEETING ABOLISHED. The *Globe* reported that the "citizens of Utica would not suffer their town to be disgraced with a meeting meditating treason against the compromises of the Constitution."[37] The *Globe* reflected the views of the administration. Indeed, Southern Democratic Party leaders may have asked their Northern counterparts to instigate mob action against abolitionists. In August 1835, Secretary of State Forsyth wrote to Vice President Van Buren, known as the little magician: "Instead of mobbing poor blacks, a little more mob discipline of the white incendiaries would be wholesome. . . . A portion of the magician's skill is required in this matter . . . the sooner you set the imps to work the better."[38] The *Utica Observer* described the suppression of abolitionists as "peaceful illegality."[39] Abolitionists did not resist physically. The leaders controlled the mob so that it achieved its objective without serious personal injury. The *Globe* noted that there had been a simultaneous disruption of an abolition meeting in Boston.[40] In 1836, in Cincinnati, Ohio, a mob representing leading citizens raided James Birney's abolitionist newspaper and threw its press in the river. Mobs destroyed abolitionist pamphlets and disrupted meetings in Philadelphia and elsewhere in the North as well.[41]

In early 1836, Senator Thomas Hart Benton of Missouri praised the action of the mobs in subduing abolitionists. As reported in the *Congressional Globe*, his fear that dissolution of the Union had begun was "quickly dispelled" by

> the great body of the people in all the non-slaveholding States. . . . Their conduct was above all praise. . . . They had chased off the foreign emissaries, silenced the gabbling tongues of female dupes, and dispersed the assemblages whether fanatical, visionary, or incendiary. . . . They had acted with a noble spirit. They had exerted a vigor beyond all law. They had obeyed the enactments not of the statutebook, but of the heart; and while the spirit was in the heart, he cared nothing for laws written in a book. He would rely upon that spirit to complete the good work it had begun—to dry up these societies . . . and put an end to publications and petitions.[42]

Senator Silas Wright of New York was equally celebratory of the work of "public opinion" in suppressing abolition. He recited the details of the disruption of the Utica (Oneida County) Convention. Specifically, Wright mentioned throwing the type of the proabolition newspaper in the streets, the refusal of the grand jury to indict those who disrupted the convention, and the subsequent election of one member of the committee of twenty-five involved in the disruption to the state senate and election of another, by the legislature, as attorney general of the state. Senator Wright "mentioned these facts . . . to show that the determined feeling of resistance to the dangerous and wicked agitators in the North had already reached a point above and beyond the law."[43]

Closing public and private places to abolitionists and using mobs to disperse them when they were able to gather were two parts of a systematic effort designed to eliminate abolition from public debate. Alvan Stewart, the New York antislavery lawyer, put it this way:

> Anti-abolitionists at the North say they believe in free discussion, in the abstract, and will not allow it to be drawn into question; but this means, as we find it interpreted and translated in the dictionary of daily experience, that each man may discuss slavery, or any thing else, in the silent chambers of his own heart, but must not discuss it in public, as it may then provoke a syllogism of feathers, or a deduction of *tar*. An abolitionist may have the abstract right of discussion, but it must be disconnected with time, or place, if a majority of his neighbors differ with him there is no place *where* or time *when* he may discuss. This abstract discussion requires an abstract place, and abstract time . . . the solitude of the wilderness, or loneliness of the ocean.[44]

While some senators celebrated conduct above the law, a number of other citizens were less sanguine. Many public meetings called to condemn abolitionists also implicitly or explicitly condemned use of lawless measures to suppress free discussion.[45] These meetings deprecated lawless action, an apparent reference to mob actions against abolitionists.[46] Some editors, even some Democratic ones, criticized extralegal suppression. In August 1835, the *Utica Observer* announced that the people of the North stood ready to "oppose all [abolitionist] *illegal* acts. To silence them is impossible; however foolish and absurd may be their opinions they have a *right* to promulgate them." Attempts at forcible suppression would merely increase their support. The *Observer* advocated "letting 'the fanatics' alone. All will see the absurdity of their preaching against *slavery, where slavery does not exist*."[47] In July, the *New York Evening Post*, a Van Buren paper with such a strong devotion to free speech that it soon got into verbal battles with the *Globe*, attributed the increase in abolition strength to "the wholly unjustifiable species of opposition which has been arrayed against them. Fanaticism was never yet put down by persecution, and mobs and riots are not very successful enlighteners of the understanding."[48]

Meanwhile, abolitionists working in the field were coming, somewhat uncertainly, to the conclusion that persecution *was* helping their cause. Abolitionist activist and editor James Birney thought that earlier New York riots would have a good effect by showing to the uncommitted the dangers slavery posed to republican government.[49]

A leader of the group of abolitionist evangelists who sought to convert the North was Theodore Dwight Weld, who faced down repeated mobs. Weld was born in 1803, the son of a Congregational minister, and grew up in western New York. He became extremely close friends with Charles Stuart, a retired British officer, who was principal of the Utica Academy. When Charles Finney, a renowned Presbyterian revivalist, came to Utica, Stuart and Weld joined his band of evangelists and preached for two years throughout western New York. Weld then entered the Oneida Institute to prepare for the ministry, together with scores of young men converted by him. Charles Stuart went to England, to preach against slavery that still existed in the West Indies, and became a lecturer for the British antislavery society. It was he who converted Weld to the cause of abolition. According to historian Gilbert Barnes, Weld's contributions to the cause of abolition were immense. Weld, who had extraordinary persuasive powers, converted the Tappans (wealthy New York merchants who had helped finance Finney's crusade) and James Birney to abolition. Weld also converted the faculty of Western Reserve College, including Elizur Wright and others who would become antislavery leaders. He enrolled at Lane Seminary in Cincinnati, where he converted the student body and the children of the president, including Harriet Beecher, the future author of *Uncle Tom's Cabin*.

The American Anti-Slavery Society had adopted the motto of immediate emancipation, and that had proved a public relations disaster. Weld, however, and the students he had trained as antislavery evangelists turned the tide in much of the North against slavery.

In March 1835, Weld, then an antislavery evangelist for the American Anti-Slavery Society, reported that at first threats, missiles, and personal violence met his lectures in Ohio and elsewhere in the North. Nevertheless, he persisted, and violence generally disappeared after later lectures in his series; at the end of the last lecture, he often reported, the entire house "rose up and pledged themselves to the principles of immediate abolition."[50]

An example illustrates Weld's technique. In the fall of 1835, Weld arrived in Painesville, Ohio, and encountered a "mob" that had passed antiabolition resolutions, including one requesting him to leave the city. The mob stoned the building where he spoke. As Weld began to speak the fifth time, the leader of the opposition interrupted, accused Weld of treason and violating the Constitution, and announced no further abolition lectures would be permitted. Weld responded that he "assumed he was speaking to the FREE PEOPLE of Painesville. [Is the gentleman who intruded] your master? Ladies are you the wives of slaves?" He set a lecture for the next day. "Do you acknowledge subjection to this man who assumes to dictate?" He told the crowd to attend if they wished to vote "no" on that proposition. The next day, Weld spoke to a large crowd.[51] Having injured his voice, Weld turned to written publicity and compiled important antislavery literature. In May of 1838, he married Angelina Grimké, the daughter of a prominent South Carolina family, who had become an antislavery activist and, with her sister, a crusader for the rights of women.

Others also agreed that violence was redounding to the benefit of abolitionists. A letter to James G. Birney concluded that in its first years the abolition society had faced public apathy. "From that difficulty your enemies have relieved you by their persecutions."[52] From a very different perspective, Duff Greene, the editor of the *Washington Telegraph*, a pronullification paper affiliated with John C. Calhoun, refused to find consolation in antiabolition meetings and mobs. Green distrusted mobs[53] and insisted that the true test of Northern intentions was not mobs or resolutions but laws aimed at suppression of abolition in the North.[54]

Abolitionists saw hopes for a radical transformation of public opinion in mob attacks on them. They reframed the issue from one of abolition to one of civil liberty for all Americans. The case of James G. Birney and his abolition newspaper is a case in point.

James G. Birney (1792–1857) was the son of a wealthy slaveholding Kentuckian. Despite owning slaves, however, Birney's father also advocated emancipation and a free state constitution for Kentucky. The younger Birney was trained as a lawyer. He settled in Alabama, where for a time he owned a plantation and slaves and practiced law. He was instrumental in including in the Alabama constitution provisions permitting the legislature to emancipate slaves. Gradually, Birney became increasingly antislavery. He became convinced that slavery was injurious not only to slaves but also to whites in slave states. Over time, he migrated politically from espousing colonization, to abolition, to a separate antislavery political party. As the South became increasingly hostile to abolition, Birney also migrated geographically, from Alabama, to Kentucky, to Ohio, and then farther north.

At his father's death, James Birney emancipated his father's slaves, paying a coheir about twenty thousand dollars so he could do so. He broke with Garrisonian abolitionists over their rejection of political activity and their rejection of the Constitution as a proslavery document. In 1840 and 1844, he was the candidate for president of the newly formed antislavery Liberty Party, polling first 6,797 votes in 1840 (0.28 percent of the popular vote) and then 62,103 in 1844 (2.3 percent of the popular vote).[55] (The winners received 1,275,390 votes in 1840 and 1,339,494 votes in 1844.)[56] Birney fell from a horse in 1845, suffered partial paralysis, withdrew from public activity, and died in 1857.[57] But in the mid-1830s, when his newspaper became a cause célèbre, most of Birney's long antislavery career was still before him.

Faced with mob opposition in Kentucky to his publication there of an antislavery weekly, Birney moved in January 1836 to New Richmond, near Cincinnati, where he began to publish the *Philanthropist*.[58] Birney wrote an account of the fate of the *Philanthropist* in a pamphlet published under the name of the executive committee of the Ohio Anti-Slavery Society.[59] The description that follows is taken mainly from the pamphlet, often in its own words.[60] Birney recounts that in the summer of 1835, there was a "REIGN OF TERROR" in the South. This spirit of lawless violence, Birney said, was not confined to the South: Northerners had encouraged it. Cincinnati's "principal daily newspapers, with, it is believed, but a single exception, sympathized with the flagellators and tormenters, and murderers of the South, and by their loud shouts cheered them on to further deeds of cruelty and blood."[61] James G. Birney, meanwhile, had been "compelled by . . . persecutions [of neighboring slaveholders]" to remove his family and antislavery newspaper from Kentucky. "Looking at the *Constitution* of Ohio, he there saw the fullest, the most honorable, and at the same time, the most solemn condemnation . . . upon slavery—and that to every one was secured the right—pronounced '*indisputable*'—*of speaking, writing,* or *printing on any subject.*" But when the Cincinnati papers learned of his project, many substantial citizens—"merchants, who have commercial connexions with Southern slave-holders—and artizans, who are mostly employed in manufacturing household furniture . . . or other heavy machinery, for the South"—actively opposed it and incited popular fury.

Birney had decided to begin publication in the town of New Richmond near Cincinnati and to conduct the paper in "a fair, and impartial, and generous" way, both because it was right to do so and because abolitionists were often criticized for their "fierce and uncharitable spirit."[62]

Still, civic leaders in Cincinnati called a public meeting to protest Birney's paper. The mayor presided, assisted by a distinguished cast of vice presidents, including a minister and a former U.S. senator and Ohio supreme court justice. Those assembled passed resolutions. One objected to "any paper which might be established for the purpose of discussing slavery."[63] Nevertheless, the *Philanthropist* continued to publish, and in April 1836, the executive committee of the Ohio Anti-Slavery Society decided to move the paper, which now had seventeen hundred subscribers, from New Richmond to Cincinnati.

Abolitionists saw a silver lining in the cloud of suppression. Birney wrote to Lewis Tappan, one of the New York financial angels of the anti-slavery movement: "You see, I am going to try Cin'i with my Press. . . . But let them mob it—as sure as they do, it will instantly make throughout this State Five Abolitionists to one that we now have."[64]

On the night of July 12, 1836, a group of men broke into the offices of the paper's printer and destroyed parts of the press. The next night placards appeared in the city proclaiming:

ABOLITIONISTS BEWARE

The Citizens of Cincinnati, embracing every class, interested in the prosperity of the City, satisfied that the business of the place is receiving a vital stab from the wicked and misguided operations of the abolitionists, are resolved to arrest their course. The destruction of their Press on the night of the 12th instant, may be taken as a warning.[65]

The *Cincinnati Evening Post* lamented its unrealized hope for peace and quiet. It had hoped "that the Abolitionists would desist from publishing their paper here, and that those who had undertaken to prevent them would be satisfied." The paper went on to predict "that unless the arm of the law is strong enough to protect the Abolitionists, some act disgraceful to our city will be performed, if they attempt the reestablishment of their press."[66]

The executive committee of the Ohio Anti-Slavery Society then published a public address recounting the destruction of the press, the threats that had been made if it were reestablished, and threats of personal violence against individual members of the executive committee. It cited provisions of the Ohio Constitution securing free speech and free press. "A band of lawless men," the address insisted, "array themselves against the Constitution, declaring that *their* will and not that of the *People* is paramount. . . . Ought we basely to surrender a right pronounced by the highest law of the land to be 'INDISPUTABLE,' to a band of men who have entered into a treasonable combination to overthrow *all* law?" No, the address concluded, "we have embraced, with a full determination, by the help of God to maintain unimpaired the freedom of speech and the liberty of the press—the PALLADIUM OF OUR RIGHTS."[67]

An article signed "Public Sentiment" then appeared in the *Cincinnati Whig*. Public Sentiment celebrated the Boston Tea Party, the lynching of Tories, and tarring and feathering. The founding fathers, Public Sentiment noted, revered and respected the laws "so long as they were productive of the public good" but did not "deem themselves slaves of the law." Public Sentiment suggested a crisis faced the nation with "the Government menaced and the union tottering upon the verge of dissolution." Other cities had suppressed abolition meetings and papers. Only Cincinnati had countenanced them. Commenting on this column, the *Whig* tersely announced its opposition both to abolitionists and mobs.[68]

On July 23, 1836, the *Cincinnati Gazette* announced an open public meeting "to decide whether [the people of Cincinnati] will permit the publication or distribution of Abolition papers in this city."[69] The *Whig* proclaimed its loathing of abolitionists and its belief in the pernicious tendencies of mobs. Still it suggested "there may be *ex necessitate rei* exception[s] to every general rule."[70]

On July 23, a public meeting issued various resolutions, beginning with this one: "[A]lthough we deprecate the existence of slavery [as an evil], . . . yet we hold it to be one for which the present generation is not responsible; and . . . we regard the conduct of the abolitionists as justly calculated to excite unfriendly disposition on [the part of the Southern states], and thus to effect injuriously our own business and prosperity." The meeting also called for the "absolute discontinuance of the publication of the said abolition paper" as the only way to "prevent a resort to violence."[71] A final resolution promised to follow in the footsteps of the patriots at the Boston Tea Party who acted "without the sanction of law." The abolitionist newspapers, the meeting sorrowfully noted, were "shielded from legal enactment according to the usual practice of our laws so as to leave us but one channel through which we can rid our fair land of its withering influence."[72]

On July 26, the *Whig* asked with evident exasperation: "Will Birney and his Abolition associates still persist in the publication of their villainously misnamed *Philanthropist*, in despite of the public voice so *significantly* expressed at the immense meeting on Saturday? If they do they are to all "intents and purposes" *mobocrats*. . . . If a mob, however, be excited by their pugnacity and violence, let them not after this have the effrontery to say that they were not the offenders."[73] Birney and his associates, the *Whig* continued, could not expect to destroy the trade of Cincinnati and the Union and be counted as "peaceable citizens." Meanwhile the *Cincinnati Republican* warned the abolitionists that "[t]here are points beyond which public sentiment, even in a free government, may not be trifled with impunity." The clear implication was that the abolitionists had crossed that line.[74]

A conference between the representatives of the Ohio Anti-Slavery Society—the publishers of the *Philanthropist*—and a committee appointed by the antiabolition meeting was held, but the abolitionists refused to desist from publishing their paper.[75] The press had been repaired, and publication would continue. At the meeting, the abolitionists proposed holding a public meeting to discuss all sides of the slavery issue, but, according to Birney, members of the antiabolition committee responded that "the people would hear no public discussion on slavery." The antiabolition committee made clear that it opposed any abolition paper. The issue was not the manner in which the ideas were discussed. "[I]t was the *discussion of slavery here*, that was thought to be injuring the business of the city."

In refusing to suspend publication, the Ohio Anti-Slavery Society argued that the *Philanthropist* was the only journal in the area discussing the slavery question and that public questions must be discussed. "We decline complying," the Executive Committee of the Ohio Anti-Slavery Society responded, "because the demand is virtually the demand of slave-holders, who, having broken down all the safe-guards of liberty in their own States, in order that slavery may be perpetuated, are now . . . making the demand of us to follow their example." After the abolitionists refused to desist, the antiabolition committee conferred again, but adjourned, advising citizens against violence.[76]

The *Cincinnati Whig* wrote, "Lay on M'Duff" and published the name and address of Achilles Pugh, the *Philanthropist*'s printer. The antiabolition group held another meeting at which it resolved that the press should be destroyed completely in a peaceable, orderly, and quiet manner. A mob then destroyed the press and Pugh's printing office, and searched unsuccessfully for Pugh and Birney. The mayor met the crowd and urged them to disperse, saying that for the mob to continue might endanger the innocent. "We have done enough for one night," he declared. Later, some mob members made an "attack . . . [upon] the residence of some blacks." Riots continued for several nights.[77]

A group of Cincinnati citizens calling themselves "the friends of Order, of Law, and the Constitution, having no connection with the Anti-Slavery Society," called for a meeting to protest the mob violence. Leonard Richards says the group included prominent lawyers and merchants but, by and large, compared to members of the antiabolition committee or the mob they had more lowly jobs (hatters, saddlers, bricklayers, and booksellers). Among the signers of the call for the meeting were S. P. Chase, later antislavery governor of Ohio, U.S. senator, Lincoln cabinet member, and Chief Justice of the U.S. Supreme Court. The Friends of Order, of Law, and the Constitution prepared a statement and a series of resolutions for consideration. One insisted on a right that was the bulwark of all others, "the right of every citizen to write, speak, and print, upon every subject, as he may think proper, being responsible to the laws and the laws ONLY, for the abuse of that liberty." If the right was abused, a judicial remedy was available. If necessary, the legislature could consider new laws.[78]

When the Friends of Order, of Law, and the Constitution assembled, they found their meeting place already occupied by a large group of those who had held previous antiabolition meetings. The Friends sat by helplessly as the antiabolitionists resolved that the "establishment of an Abolition Press in this city has been the cause of all our recent difficulties."[79] The abolitionists persisted, however, and an abolition press continued to publish in Cincinnati.

Infuriated public opposition would lead many to rethink, to doubt, and to retreat. Many leading abolitionists, however, saw themselves as part of a historical tradition, and that view gave them strength and courage. Christ, after all, had been persecuted and killed, but he ultimately triumphed. Puritan martyrs had been burned in England, but their fame had been preserved in Foxe's *Book of Martyrs*, and the cause of Protestantism had triumphed. Later, some activists in the English revolution of the 1640s, like Algernon Sidney, had remained true to republicanism after the Restoration and had been executed for their republican faith. Yet they were heroes to American revolutionaries. Like Birney, many abolitionists (and nonabolitionists) believed that persecution would only aid the abolitionist cause.

In 1834, as we have seen, the American Anti-Slavery Society had fielded a number of abolition missionaries who traveled through Ohio and other Northern states to convert Northerners to abolition. They faced much hostility but they also enjoyed considerable success. In September 1836, two Cincinnati papers had recommended that the antislavery activists be lynched.[80]

One of the missionaries wrote Weld from the field. He had been asked to leave abolition for a more purely religious revival activity. He decided to stick with abolition. "My convictions have been greatly strengthened by the news we have just received from Cincinnati. You have probably heard that mob law is triumphant there—the press torn down and thrown into the river—the abolitionists hunted by blood thirsty men—mayor and chief men at their head. My brethren are in bonds, not only the blacks, but the abolitionists.... I have helped to raise the storm. Shall I now avoid its fury by going into a less dangerous field? God forbid."[81]

Mob violence led abolitionists to redoubled efforts. They published pamphlets to warn Americans that their own liberty was at stake: the persecution of abolitionists endangered the liberties of all. They increased their proselytizing. They sent more petitions to Congress to abolish slavery in the District of Columbia.

The basic abolitionist belief was that slavery threatened American liberty. In August 1835, after some experience with mobs in Kentucky, Birney had written to Gerrit Smith, a wealthy New York leader in the abolition cause: "The contest is becoming—has become—one, not alone of freedom for the *black*, but of freedom for the *white*. It has now become absolutely necessary, that Slavery should cease in order that freedom may be preserved to any portion of our land. The antagonistic principles of liberty and slavery have been roused into action and one or the other must be victorious. There will be no cessation of the strife, until Slavery shall be exterminated, or liberty destroyed."[82]

Events were to prove that mob action could not always be trusted to work its will through "peaceful illegality." Discomfort with rising mob violence in 1835–36, as well as its inefficiency, led some antiabolitionists to explore legal methods of suppression.

An Uncertain Trumpet:
Calls for Legal Action Against Abolitionists

The 1835 postal campaign of the abolitionists produced immediate Southern demands for protection of their "peculiar institution" from outside interference.[83] A Charleston, South Carolina, mass meeting asked the nonslaveholding states to "promptly adopt the necessary measures to punish any vile incendiaries within their limits, who, not daring to appear in person among us, where the gallows and the stake await them, discharge their missiles of mischief in the security of distance."[84] Soon, however, the South demanded suppression of the abolition movement in the North as well.

The problem was complex. Slavery was virtually nonexistent in the North and many Northerners saw freedom to criticize the institution as inherent in free speech, free press, and popular sovereignty. In the South, criticism of slavery, certainly the type that abolitionists engaged in, was widely seen as unacceptable. The North and South had separate systems with different assumptions and needs. But they were part of one country. Newspapers from the North circulated in the South, and so did speeches in Congress. The nation was increasingly connected by roads, canals, shipping, and the postal system. All of these were holes in the Southern quarantine through which abolition propaganda could enter. In the real world of an increasingly interconnected nation, the demand for security by slaveholding states required exporting at least some slave state laws to the North.

While the Northern antiabolitionist meetings were unanimous in their condemnation of abolitionists, in other respects they were deeply ambivalent. When they recommended legislation (and a number did not),[85] the meetings typically limited their recommendations to forbidding attempts by citizens of their states to circulate abolition publications in the South.[86]

General Dix, a speaker at the Albany, New York, meeting cited the maxim that "nothing is to be feared from discussion, when reason is left free to combat error." But he asked if this proposition "may not be subject to exceptions. Is it not, under the peculiar circumstances of this case, unsafe in practice, so far as it is carried on by the circulation of abolition publications in the South?" The arguments in such publications would inevitably find their way to the slave. "He becomes discontented with his condition, is sometimes stimulated to acts of violence." General Dix suggested a dual standard of freedom of discussion congruent with the difference between the slave and free states: "In communities of freemen, unrestrained discussion is indispensable as a safeguard against error and abuse. But who does not see that in dealing with an unenlightened population, placed by the force of circumstances in a peculiar relation to others, the effect of discussion may be to awaken them to a knowledge of their condition without enlightening them as to the necessity which has produced it."[87]

Still, General Dix continued, "I am not contending against the abstract right of discussion, nor do I concede that any restraint can be imposed on it, so long as it is guided by moderation and truth, excepting that which arises out of the sense of moral obligation and duty." But abolitionists had abandoned moderation and resorted to "abuse and insult" against the master and, as to the slave, "an incentive to . . . insurrection and bloodshed." The authors and supporters of these publications, "morally at least," were accessories before the fact to the crime that "may grow out of their circulation."[88] Comments like those of General Dix showed deep ambivalence and militated against broad suppression of Northern antislavery expression.

The least intrusive suggestion was passing laws in the North to punish those who participated in sending publications to the South. A second alluring possibility was extraditing abolitionists who had sent publications to the South or participated in a larger plan with that object. The latter group would include virtually the entire abolitionist leadership. But basically, the elite in slaveholding states thought security for the South required an end to antislavery agitation in the North.

So it is not surprising that some Southerners soon called for legislation to suppress abolitionists in the North. Indeed some suggested that abolition was more dangerous in the North than in the South.[89] "Let it be admitted," declared a resolution of the South Carolina legislature,

> that, by reason of an efficient police and judicious internal legislation, we may render abortive the designs of the fanatic and incendiary within our own limits, and that the torrent of pamphlets and tracts which the abolition presses of the north are pouring forth with an inexhaustible copiousness, is arrested the moment it reaches our frontier. Are we to wait until our enemies have built up, by the grossest misrepresentations and falsehoods, a body of public opinion against us, which it would be almost impossible to resist, without separating ourselves from the social system of the rest of the civilized world?[90]

Some Northerners joined Southerners in the explicit call for legal action to suppress abolition in the North. Once the issue turned from denunciation and mobs to legislation, the nation faced the practical problem of how to define impermissible acts and expression on the subject of slavery and whether such laws were constitutionally permissible. Many in the North, as we shall see, were dubious about legal suppression of abolition in the free states.

Others in the North and South took a different view of abolitionist agitation. These people believed abolition could and should be suppressed. Generally, the argument followed the usual form: "we favor free speech but . . . ."

"We are told of the freedom of speech and of the press, liberty of conscience, &c," wrote the *Wilmington, Delaware Watchman*. "[T]his is all very plausible and we are the last individuals, who would in the slightest degree abridge these invaluable and sacred rights. But moral treason or the aiding and abetting of domestic insurrection is quite a different thing, and calls for the infliction of the severest punishment."[91] A Virginia mass meeting in 1835 insisted that Virginians placed the highest value on free speech and press, and "none are willing to give a wider range to free discussion where discussion ought to be tolerated; but they cannot and will not discuss their right to existence with any one."[92]

Public meetings had condemned abolitionists and mobs had mobbed them. A major question was what the nation's political institutions would do about abolitionists. As to governmental action, in the mid-

1830s the controversy over abolitionist speech and press focused on basic and very practical issues. These included abolitionist use of the Post Office, their petitions to Congress, the demand for antiabolition laws in the North, and the issue of extradition of abolitionists for trial in the southern states. The next two chapters will focus on the response to demands for legal action against abolitionism.

7

Congress Confronts the Abolitionists:

The Post Office and Petitions

In July 1835, the leaders of the American Anti-Slavery Society sent abolition publications to the South, mainly to members of the Southern elite.
The abolitionist literature included illustrations, a recognition by abolitionists of the power of "visual impressions."[1] As noted earlier, Southern
communities erupted in protest. In Charleston, South Carolina, the
publications were seized and burned. A number of other Southern cities
held mass protest meetings and organized vigilance committees to prevent the spread of abolition doctrines.

The Postal Campaign
and the Jackson Administration's Response

The postal campaign presented the administration of Andrew Jackson
with a crisis. His postmaster general, Amos Kendall, advised the Richmond postmaster to limit delivery of abolitionist papers to actual
subscribers.[2] On August 4, 1835, Kendall answered the request of the
Charleston, South Carolina, postmaster, who had detained abolitionist
publications and asked for instructions. Postmaster General Kendall
concluded he had neither "legal authority to exclude newspapers from
the mail, nor prohibit their carriage or delivery on account of their character or tendency." Still, he said, the Post Office was to serve the states. It
should not produce their destruction. While Kendall had not seen the
papers, he understood they were "incendiary, and insurrectionary in the
highest degree." He would not order their delivery. "We owe an obligation to the laws, but a higher one to the communities in which we live."
In this situation, he said, it was "patriotism to disregard [the laws]."[3]

Meanwhile, the postmaster in New York asked the abolitionists to agree to suspend transmission of their publications until he had received the views of the postmaster general. The American Anti-Slavery Society refused to surrender any of their "rights and privileges . . . in regard to the use of the United States Mail," and the postmaster at New York embargoed their papers aimed at the South. The New York postmaster pointedly told the antislavery society that his actions could be challenged in the courts.[4] So the postal campaign was stopped in the city where it began, and the embargo was accomplished with the general approval of the Jackson administration.[5]

On August 7, 1835, Kendall wrote the president for his advice, and on August 9, President Jackson responded. Himself a slaveholder, Jackson regretted the existence of men "willing to stir up servile war." If they could "be reached," he added ominously, "they ought to be made to atone for this wicked attempt with their lives." He also regretted the spirit of mob law. Until Congress could pass a law on the subject, Jackson suggested that "those inflammatory papers be delivered to none but who will demand them as subscribers; and in every instance the postmaster ought to take the names down, and have them exposed thro the publik journals as subscribers to this wicked plan of exciting the negroes to . . . massacre." They would then be compelled to desist or "move from the country."[6]

On August 22, 1835, Postmaster General Kendall wrote a long letter, soon published in the press, specifically approving the action of the New York postmaster. He had now seen some of the papers with their "revolting pictures and fervid appeals" and was convinced that they "tend directly" to produce "evils surpassing those usually resulting from insurrection." By a series of rhetorical questions, Kendall suggested that the legal right of the abolitionists to use the mails "in distributing their insurrectionary papers throughout the Southern states, is not so clear as they seem to imagine." Did the abolitionists have the right to force postmasters to do acts that, if done by the abolitionists themselves, would brand them as felons? Was it certain that postmasters would not themselves be subject to the penalties of the law if they distributed the forbidden documents? "Can the United States furnish agents for conspirators against the states and clothe them with impunity?"[7]

Resolutions throughout the North condemned abolitionists for sending their publications to the slaveholding South.[8] By September 11, 1835, the *Washington Globe*, an organ of the Democratic Party and of Jackson's heir apparent, Martin Van Buren, thought the problem could be solved by applying Southern state laws to all offenders. This solution took Northern Democrats off the hook. Postmasters, the *Globe* announced, were "as amenable to State laws as other citizens for all acts committed in violation of their provisions" provided the laws did not violate the federal Constitution. "Let the Southern States, therefore, consult their own rights and power. Let them enforce their constitutional laws against Postmasters and everyone else. We have little doubt they will be sustained even by the Supreme Court."[9] Someone writing in the *Charleston Courier* as "Vindex" agreed. States had a right to prohibit the introduction of seditious pamphlets into their territory. "It is a law," Vindex insisted, "which the State has a right to pass, as fully as she has a right to retain her slaves—for the one is essential to the other."[10]

According to Vindex, the only possible defense for the postmaster who knowingly distributed abolitionist pamphlets would be lack of intent. But the defense would fail. Vindex said the clear and inevitable tendency of the abolition publications justified finding intent. "A man who should throw a lighted torch into your house at midnight, might as well allege that he had no intent to wrap it in flames."[11]

Vindex noted that the postmaster faced far more severe penalties for circulation than for suppression. He suggested a balancing test for any conflict between the duties involved. "What are the consequences to the community on the one hand and the other? On one side they are light as gossamer, while on the other they are of the most fearful magnitude."[12]

The abolitionists brought no legal challenge to the actions of the Post Office. The Southern quarantine reinforced by federal administrative action survived the postal campaign and was strengthened by it. Postmasters in the South faced a postmaster general in favor of suppression and faced harsh state penalties for circulation. They generally took the safest course.

Much of the national press praised the postmaster general for his stand against abolition. The Democratic press, in particular, was enthusiastic. But there were dissenters. The *Weekly Register*, a Whig-leaning paper, found "a most fearful surveillance over the post office . . . that is approved by the federal authorities at Washington!"[13] The *Evening Post*, though a pro–Van Buren paper, was severely critical. It commented on Kendall's letter to the Charleston postmaster in which he simultaneously denied he had power to prevent the circulation of any newspaper and announced that he would not assist in the circulation of incendiary papers. "Who gives him the right to judge," demanded the *Post*, "of what is incendiary and inflammatory?"[14] The *Post* insisted that the federal government lacked power to establish orthodoxy:

> Neither the General Post Office, nor the General Government itself, possess any power to prohibit the transportation by mail of abolition tracts. On the contrary it is the bounden duty of the Government to protect the abolitionists in their constitutional right of free discussion; and opposed sincerely and zealously as we are, to their doctrines and practice, we should be still more opposed to any infringement of their political or civil rights. If the Government once begins to discriminate as to what is orthodox and what heterodox in opinion, what is safe and unsafe in its tendency, farewell, a long farewell to our freedom.[15]

On December 1, 1835, Postmaster General Amos Kendall presented his report to Congress. He insisted that slavery was a subject over which the states retained sovereign power. Kendall also said that citizens of Northern states had no right to discuss Southern institutions in the South, "whatever claim" Northerners might maintain to a right of free discussion of Southern slavery "within their own [Northern state] borders." According to Kendall, Southern statutes prohibiting publications like those the abolitionists had attempted to send to the South were an "exercise of their reserved [states'] rights." Finally, he concluded that these laws did not violate the Federal Constitution and that the Constitution could not require the circulation of papers that incited domestic violence.[16]

THE PRESIDENT'S RECOMMENDATION AND THE ABOLITIONIST RESPONSE

President Jackson followed a few days later with his seventh annual message to Congress. Jackson referred to "the painful excitement produced in the South by attempts to circulate through the mails inflammatory appeals addressed to the passions of the slaves, in prints and various sorts of publications, calculated to stimulate them to insurrection and to produce all the horrors of servile war." Jackson celebrated the "strong and impressive" demonstrations of Northern disapproval of the misguided abolitionists and their "unconstitutional and wicked" efforts.

Still, recognizing that public opinion alone might not be sufficient to solve the problem, Jackson recommended a law to "prohibit, under severe penalties, the circulation in the Southern States, through the mail, of incendiary publications intended to instigate the slaves to insurrection."[17]

The executive committee of the American Anti-Slavery Society published a lengthy protest against the president's message. The society argued that Jackson's message to Congress violated basic principles of civil liberty. It measured the president's attack against abolitionists by the standards of the legal system. President Jackson had passed judgment on them though that was "a power not belonging to [his] office." He had given publicity to charges that they were engaged in "wicked and unconstitutional" efforts and that they harbored "the most execrable intentions." He had condemned them without the opportunity to be heard. They had had no notice of the charge or opportunity to meet their accusers face to face. He had made vague charges: "[Y]ou omit stating when, where, and by whom these wicked attempts were made; you give no specification of the inflammatory appeals, which you assert have been addressed to the passions of the slaves."[18] The committee said that the moral influence of the charges affected thousands of persons of good character who faced mobs and violence, but the vagueness of the charges made it impossible for them to prove their innocence.

As to the claim that their publications had a tendency to produce insurrection, the executive committee noted the wide range of ideas that the Southern elite had concluded were calculated to produce slave revolts. They cited a Southern minister of the gospel who warned against allowing slaves to hear the Declaration of Independence. Certain anti-slavery writings of President Jefferson would "expose to popular violence whoever should presume to circulate them."[19] The Committee noted that charges similar to those made by President Jackson against abolitionists had been made by those who directed violence at them. Now Jackson had "sanctioned and disseminated" their charges.[20] The committee also invited a congressional investigation and promised to produce all publications they had issued and all their books and accounts.[21] Congress ignored the invitation.

Finally, the committee said that Jackson had made false charges: that they had *attempted to circulate through the mails appeals addressed to the passions of the slaves calculated to stimulate them to insurrection, and with the intention of producing a servile war.* The committee noted that the charge was only circulation of publications. They had not been accused of putting their appeals into the hands of a single slave. The circulation was not "by secret agents, traversing the slave country in disguise" but by the mails. "And are the Southern slaves, sir, accustomed to receive periodicals by mails!" Not one publication had been alleged to be addressed to a slave; instead they had been sent to the Southern elite. The executive committee called on Jackson to lay before Congress the papers to which he referred. "This is more necessary, as the various publick journals and meetings which have denounced us for entertaining insurrectionary and murderous designs, have in no instance been able to quote from our publications a single exhortation to the slaves to break their fetters, or the expression of a solitary wish for servile war."[22]

William Jay made a similar complaint published later in 1835. Jay was a New York judge, member of the executive committee of the American Anti-Slavery Society, and the son of John Jay, the first Chief Justice of the United States. William Jay graduated from Yale College and then studied law. He was appointed judge of the court of Westchester County in 1818, a post he held until proslavery Democrats removed him in 1843. The *New York Post* described Jay's work as a jurist: his jury charges were a full exposition of the law without the slightest concession to popular opinion. Jay was a founder of the New York Anti-Slavery Society. He agitated for emancipation in the District of Columbia and opposed plans to colonize emancipated slaves as based on prejudice. He advocated settlement of international disputes by arbitration. Jay wrote extensively against slavery, and he wrote well, in a simple, vigorous, and lucid style.

In his response to criticisms of abolitionists, Jay first noted the catalogue of crimes attributed to the abolitionists, and then he asked, "When—where—how were these crimes attempted? What proof is offered? Nothing, absolutely nothing, is offered but naked assertion."[23] The Alabama indictment of R. G. Williams, the publishing agent for the *Emancipator,* provided the specific charges abolitionists had demanded, and Jay made the most of it. Alabama had selected Williams instead of a top leader of the abolitionists. The indictment contained a statement of the offending words Williams was accused of circulating:

A grand jury in Alabama conceived the bright idea that the publication of tracts at the North against slavery might be arrested by indicting the publishers as felons, and then demanding them . . . as fugitives from southern justice. It was necessary, however, to specify in the indictment, the precise crime of which they had been guilty; a necessity which the President regarded as not applicable to his message. We may well suppose, therefore, that the grand jury would endeavor to secure the success of this, their first experiment, by selecting from the various publications alluded to by the President and Mr. Kendall, as sent to the South for the purpose of exciting insurrection, the most insurrectionary, cut-throat passages they could find. Behold the result.[24]

Jay quoted the offending sentences from the indictment: "God commands, and all nature cries out, that man should not be held as property. The system of making men property, has plunged 2,250,000 of our fellow countrymen into the deepest physical and moral degradation, and they are every moment sinking deeper."[25] The indictment gave dramatic proof of the breadth of expression Alabama sought to suppress.

The Senate and the Calhoun Committee

The Twenty-fourth Congress spent much of its first few months wrangling over the reception of antislavery petitions, mainly those petitions demanding abolition in the District of Columbia. In December 1835, the Senate agreed to refer the portion of the president's message dealing with incendiary publications to a select committee including senators Calhoun of South Carolina, King of Georgia, Mangum of North Carolina, Davis of Massachusetts, and Linn of Missouri. Four of the five represented slave states.

Senator Calhoun served as chairman of the committee. He was born in upland South Carolina in 1782 to a prosperous family that owned a number of slaves. Calhoun graduated from Yale in 1804 and studied law. He opened practice near Abbeville and was quite successful, but soon turned to public affairs. He served in the South Carolina legislature and in 1810 was elected to Congress. There he advocated war with Britain and, after peace, supported a strong permanent army, an effective navy, a national bank, national roads, support for manufactures, and a system of internal taxes that would provide reliable revenue in time of war. James Monroe appointed him secretary of war. He was elected vice president in 1824 by a large majority. Calhoun hoped to become president. He allied himself with Andrew Jackson and was again elected vice president in 1828, although eventually a breach occurred between Calhoun and Jackson, as a result of personal and political conflict.

In the meantime, South Carolina had become insistently antitariff, and Calhoun adjusted his policies to this political reality. Back in South Carolina, Calhoun penned the South Carolina Exposition with its doctrine of nullification—which asserted the power of the state to declare national law void and block its enforcement—subject only to being overridden by a constitutional amendment. The theory would later prove handy in an effort to protect slaveholders against the growing power of the North. Calhoun resigned the vice presidency and returned to Washington as a senator from South Carolina.

Calhoun initially sought sectional compromise, and he hoped to be a national leader. His hopes were destroyed by the reemergence of the slavery issue. By 1835 Calhoun had become a champion of states' rights and an early spokesman for slavery as a positive good. He insisted that in all societies the few lived off the labor of the many. He believed the Northern manufacturing system was gradually reducing working men to bare subsistence. Calhoun hoped for an alliance of Northern capitalists, who he believed faced a revolt from *their* exploited workers and Southern slaveholders—a united front against common working-class enemies. Professor Richard Hofstadter, writing in 1948, dubbed Calhoun the Karl Marx of the master class.[26]

Clement Eaton in his classic study of the struggle for freedom of thought in the old South credits Calhoun with creating stereotypes of Northerners as supporters of incendiary abolitionist fanatics, stereotypes that produced intolerance. He suggests that political motivation contributed to Calhoun's decision to increase alarm over the issue of abolitionist publications. Calhoun wanted to split the Democratic Party in the South and injure New Yorker Martin Van Buren, Andrew Jackson's chosen heir. He also hoped to produce a united Southern party under his own leadership.[27]

Even before the Senate committee appointed to consider the postal bill reported, there were indications that it would not give the president what he wanted. Senators said they doubted the existence of general federal power over the press and therefore doubted any broad federal power to deal with "incendiary" publications. Many saw the issue as one of federalism and assumed broad state power over speech. For them the problem was not whether legislation to suppress abolition publications would violate the right of Americans to free speech or free press. Instead, the problem was whether the federal government had any power at all to deal with the subject. Senator Grundy of Tennessee, a loyal supporter of the president, said, "the general Government could do very little, [about abolition publications] except it should be through the regulation of the Post Office, and by aiding to give efficiency to the operation of the State laws."[28] Senator Mangum of North Carolina expressed similar views. He thought "there was in the [federal] Government no power over [the] general circulation [of 'incendiary publications']."[29] Senator Ewing, a Northerner, had supported appointment of a special committee dominated by Southerners: if Congress lacked power to act on the subject, it would be best for the South to learn that from its own senators.[30]

On February 4, 1836, Senator Calhoun reported a bill from the Select Committee on Incendiary Publications. Section 1 of the bill prohibited any deputy postmaster from knowingly receiving and mailing or delivering "any pamphlet, newspaper, handbill or other printed, written, or pictorial representation touching the subject of slavery, directed to any person or post office, where, by the laws thereof, their circulation is prohibited." The broad language of the bill seemed to cover private correspondence as well as newspapers and pamphlets. The postmaster general was to furnish deputies with the laws of the states prohibiting circulation of such items. Persons depositing items were given an opportunity to withdraw them; if not withdrawn within a month, they were to be burned.[31]

The bill had not followed President Jackson's recommendation. Jackson recommended establishing a federal standard of prohibited conduct. His proposal prohibited circulation through the mail of items calculated to cause slave revolts. Instead, the statute enforced state legislative standards.

The bill was accompanied by a report, written by Senator Calhoun, but not fully joined by a majority of the committee. The report agreed with the president as to the character and tendency of abolition papers, but did not agree with his plan for Congress to pass a law "prohibiting, under severe penalty, the transmission of incendiary publications through the mail, intended to incite slave insurrection." According to Calhoun's report, the First Amendment, animated by "the jealous spirit of liberty which characterized our ancestors . . . forever closed the door" against federal restrictions on the press. It "left that important barrier against power under the exclusive authority . . . of the States." The report cited Madison's report for the Virginia legislature against the Sedition Act, "which conclusively settled the principle that Congress has no right, in any form or in any manner, to interfere with the freedom of the press."[32] This, the report suggested, was approved by the verdict of history. The federal government simply lacked the power to regulate the press.

Indeed, the report insisted that "no one now doubts" the unconstitutionality of the Sedition Act. But surely, it insisted, the act would have been equally unconstitutional if it had inflicted punishment only for circulating seditious libel through the mail. "The object of publishing is circulation; and to prohibit circulation is, in effect, to prohibit publication. They both have a common object—the communication of sentiments and opinions to the public."[33]

The principle behind the president's proposal, the report insisted, "would subject the freedom of the press on all subjects, political, moral, and religious" completely to the will of Congress. The Sedition Act was condemned "not because it prohibited publications against the government, but because it interfered at all with the press."[34]

Calhoun objected to the president's recommendation because he claimed its logic implicitly conceded the power of the federal government to *require* as well as *prohibit* circulation. For, once its plenary power over the post was conceded, a later Congress could overcome state laws and open the floodgates to incendiary publications, punishing all who resisted as criminals. Calhoun was apparently convinced that the power to circulate antislavery publications in the South would spell the end of slavery. If Congress had the power called for by the president to control postal circulation it would also have "power to abolish slavery, by giving it the means of breaking down all the barriers which the slaveholding states have erected for the protection of their lives and property."[35]

Calhoun's somewhat paradoxical solution to this dilemma was that Congress could only reinforce state prohibitions by punishing federal officials who violated state law. The report closed by calling for unity among the propertied classes; slavery was a form of ordinary exploitation similar to capitalism and it behooved capitalists to join slaveholders in defense of their advantages.[36]

The Postal Bill in a House Committee

In the House, legislation on abolitionist publications was referred to the Post Office Committee, where it sat, awaiting the action of the Senate. On March 25, 1836, Representative Hiland Hall of Vermont announced that three minority members of the House Post Office Committee had concluded that Congress lacked power to act on incendiary publications. The majority of the committee split, some preferring to wait for Senate action and some unable to agree on the report that should be made to the House.[37] Printing of Hall's minority report was blocked in Congress, in part because of the absence of a majority report.[38] But a copy appeared in the *National Intelligencer* and exists among Hall's papers.[39] In the end, no further action was taken by the House on the incendiary publications bill.

The minority report denied that Congress could constitutionally enforce state laws restricting the press. It noted that the proposed bill would require Congress to enforce what might be myriad state statutes restricting the press. "[A]lthough the Constitution of the United States prohibits *Congress* from making any law 'abridging the freedom of speech, or of the press,' yet it contains no such prohibition on the *States*."[40] State constitutions contained some limits on state powers over the press "but without such restrictions the [state] power would be full and complete, even to the establishment of a censorship." State constitutions could be "remodelled to answer an object which the People of any State may, for the time being, desire to accomplish."[41] As a result, one state might make it unlawful to circulate publications inciting slaves to insurrection; another might prohibit any discussion of slavery. One state might prohibit discussion of Protestant doctrine; another of Catholic. Logically applied, the principle supporting the federal suppression of matters relating to slavery that were prohibited by a state meant that the federal government would be enforcing a potentially vast series of laws abridging the freedom of the press. This, the minority insisted, the Constitution did not permit:

> The meaning of the term abridge is not qualified in the Constitution by the specification of any particular degree beyond which the liberty of the press is not permitted to be diminished. Any, the slightest contraction or lessening of that liberty is forbidden. Nor does the Constitution point out any particular mode by which the freedom of the press may not be abridged. All *modes* of abridgement whatever are excluded, whether by the establishment of a censorship, the imposition of punishments, a tax on the promulgation of obnoxious opinions, or by any other means which can be devised

to give a legislative preference, either in publication or circulation, to one sentiment emanating from the press, over that of another. . . . It was . . . to secure the *substance* of the freedom of the press, that the clause was made part of the Constitution.[42]

The minority agreed with Madison that the Sedition Act had been unconstitutional because the First Amendment was "a clear prohibition of all [congressional] power over the subject of the press." As a result, Congress could "express no legislative opinion of the character and tendency of its productions." Madison's doctrine, Hall's report asserted, had obtained the almost universal assent of the American people. But even the universally repudiated Sedition Act furnished no precedent for the proposed legislation. "In the legislation now in contemplation, the prohibitory clause of the Constitution is not even sought to be evaded, by allowing the truth to be given in evidence in justification of the publication. Whether true or false, the offense will be equally criminal."[43]

Finally, the minority concluded with a ringing statement of the meaning of the First Amendment: "The People of the United States never intended that the Government of the Union should exercise over the press the power of discriminating between true and erroneous opinions, of determining that this sentiment was patriotic, that seditious and incendiary, and therefore wisely prohibited Congress all power over the subject."[44]

Criticism of the Calhoun Proposal: Two Divergent Objections

If Hiland Hall thought Calhoun's report did not follow its no-federal-power premise to its logical conclusion, others simply denied the premise. "A Virginian" writing in the *Washington Globe* attacked the Calhoun report from a different direction. The postal power included the power not to establish post offices and post roads. If Congress was not required to set up the Post Office, then it had the lesser power of determining what the mail should contain. Nor was refusal to carry items suppression of free press. "[T]here was [a] wide . . . difference between refusing to assist in circulation, and prohibiting publication."[45] Calhoun had misunderstood Madison, and, as a result, Calhoun's doctrine

not only denies to this Government the power of preventing any one from writing, printing, or publishing political libels, but [also] of writing, printing and publishing exhortations to rob, ravish, burn, and murder, and not only so, but imposes upon the Government the obligation to circulate and distribute them. . . . In all parts of the report when [Madison] speaks of the absolute freedom of discussion, he refers, not to the right of injuring individuals or communities in their persons, property or character, and instigating them to the horrors of rebellion and insurrection; but to the discussion of religious, philosophical, or political subjects; inquiring into and examining the nature of truth, moral or metaphysical, the expediency or inexpediency of public measures; and the conduct of public men.[46]

"A Virginian" did not pause to explain why abolitionist expression did not fit within the absolute protection accorded to religious, philosophical, or political discussion. If Calhoun were right about his theory of the total absence of congressional power over the press, then, "A Virginian" insisted, no power to suppress abolition publications existed anywhere: "But suppose with Mr. Calhoun, that Congress cannot interfere at all with the press; in any form or shape, or prohibit, or *refuse to circulate*, any publication, on the ground of its being intended to excite our slaves to insurrection; *because*, by the constitution of the United States, Congress can make no law 'abridging the freedom of the press.' I would like to inquire of him, what right the States have to pass such a law . . . ?"[47] "[S]tate *Legislatures*," A Virginian continued, "are under further restrictions, . . . imposed by their bill of rights and constitutions; and in such cases they can no more exercise a prohibited power, than Congress can exercise the same power." Every state bill of rights or constitution provided for the "unrestrained liberty of the press in nearly the words of the constitution of the United States." For example, Virginia provided that liberty of the press "shall forever be inviolably preserved." Yet the Southern states had passed laws that reached abolitionist publications. "How then can [Mr. Calhoun] argue from the want of power on the part of the General Government to pass a sedition law, to the want of power to prohibit the mail from circulating incendiary writings, without . . . denying that [the states] can interfere with incendiary publications?"[48]

In response to Calhoun's bill and report, "Cincinnatus" published *Freedom's Defense*, a pamphlet attacking the Calhoun bill and defending freedom of speech and of the press. Cincinnatus struck at inconsistencies in Calhoun's argument. Having proved "that Congress has no right, in ANY FORM or in ANY MANNER to interfere with THE FREEDOM OF THE PRESS," Calhoun had claimed to discover "ONE 'FORM,' ONE 'MANNER,'" in which Congress could constitutionally interfere with the freedom of the press:[49] "Here it is. The Legislature of any one State may prohibit by law the introduction within her borders of any publication which she may be disposed to prohibit, and then call on Congress to enact a law prohibiting the transmission through the mail of such publication, and may also 'demand' of every other State in the Union the passage of laws in concurrence, i.e. prohibiting discussion and publication; and Congress and the Legislatures of the States are 'bound' to yield to the 'demand' of that one State."[50]

Cincinnatus noted that slaveholding states had already demanded that Northern states adopt laws that punish their citizens for publishing abolitionist sentiments. The extreme Southern demands would create a mechanism for broad suppression of speech and of the press. Perhaps nonslaveholding states might have the duty, Cincinnatus opined, "speedily to pass conservative laws for their own 'peace and security.'" They could then "require the aid of the General and State Governments to protect them against the introduction within these States" of proslavery propaganda. The targets could include the messages of slaveholding state governors and proslavery newspapers. Such publications threatened the peace as "has already been evinced in mobs and riots which they have tended to create."[51] After raising the idea of suppressing Southern propaganda, Cincinnatus dismissed his own suggestion. Such demands, he observed, violated both federal and state constitutional guarantees.

Cincinnatus noted Calhoun's appeal for a united front of capital against labor. "Reduced to plain English," Cincinnatus noted, "it is to say that, because, in other countries, and in former times, the men in power have 'universally' abused that power, THEREFORE, they who have the power in this country have an undoubted RIGHT to abuse that power; and, lest the oppressed classes, should, by using the freedom of the press, assert their rights, those powerful men, who have already so much control over the press, ought to seize on more power that they may be more secure in holding what . . . has been unjustly obtained."[52]

Freedom of speech and of the press, Cincinnatus insisted, "is not a right reserved from Congress and vested in a State Legislature, but is reserved both from Congress and all State Legislatures, by the United States Constitution and the Constitutions of the States, to the PEOPLE."

These rights "eternally" belong to the people. They never had been and never would be "surrendered into the hands of their Rulers. The day they should do that, would number the days of their freedom." The Southern press and foreign despots should be free to pour out their "most violent and incendiary publications" so long as "we may be free to repel the attack by truth and manly argument through the press and the mail."[53]

Calhoun's Bill on the Floor of the Senate

In April 1836, the Senate debated Calhoun's bill. Senator John Davis of Massachusetts spoke first for its opponents. Davis had graduated from Yale with high honors, studied law, and was admitted to the bar. He became a forceful and successful court room advocate. He served four terms in Congress, was elected governor, and in 1835 was appointed to the Senate as a Whig. Davis favored protectionism and would later oppose any further spread of slavery to the territories. He would subsequently oppose the Mexican war. He was considered as Henry Clay's running mate in 1844, but his antislavery convictions ruled him out.

In the 1836 debate on the postal bill, Davis objected to the transfer of the regulation of the Post Office from the United States to the states. Davis noted that the committee's report concluded that Congress lacked power over the press and that the report likened the president's proposal to the Sedition Act. The committee's bill led to the same result. "The one proposes suppression of certain papers by the agency of the postmasters, and so does the other; not only the end, therefore but the means, are the same." The only difference was that in the Calhoun bill the test of criminality came from state rather than federal law. "[B]ut if Congress, by its acts, so far adopts the law of a State as to make it a rule of conduct for public officers, requiring them, under penalties, to obey it, is not such a law in fact a law of Congress by adoption?" If so, why didn't restrictions on federal power over the press apply?[54]

Davis insisted the bill covered letters as well as printed matter. Postmasters would be required to investigate the content of the mail.[55] They would confront "the great difficulty in determining what were, and what were not incendiary papers." As proof of the great difficulty in accurately identifying incendiary items, Davis cited the Alabama grand jury indictment against Williams, the publisher of the *Emancipator*. He read the offending words to the Senate: "God commanded, and all nature cries out, that human beings should not be held in bondage." According to Davis, the words would never be thought criminal by residents of the North:

> Whatever may be the views entertained in the States where slavery is lawful, . . . this language will be read with surprise . . . out of them. It will be esteemed a mere expression of opinion, a mere truism, by nine tenths of the people; and they will find it difficult to understand how, in a land where freedom of speech and the press are secured by the constitution, it can be in law criminal. If, sir, such declarations are to be denied the privilege of the mail, the constitution of Massachusetts would be excluded as libellous, because it declares all men are born free and equal. This statement is manifestly as much at war with slavery as that contained in the indictment.[56]

Davis presciently warned that Calhoun's bill would mean that speeches made in Congress could not pass through the mail.[57] Indeed, in the years to come just such items fell under the ban of slave-state censorship.[58] One state, Davis warned, could follow Alabama and make antislavery opinion criminal; another could ban certain religious sentiments as heretical; and another might ban "all political discussion, except what is agreeable to the views of its own majority. Each demands the aid of Congress to enforce its laws, because they have, under their several constitutions, a right to make such laws." What principle, he asked, would justify admitting one claim and denying the others?[59]

Who would decide, Davis demanded, and "in what manner," if the Declaration of Independence and the Massachusetts constitution "touch the subject of slavery or are incendiary?" "Who is to decide whether the people shall see the debates in Congress, and know what their agents are doing and saying here?"[60] Postmasters and their clerks would determine great rights "by an inquisitorial power as odious and offensive as that of . . . the inquisition of Spain."[61] But Davis, unlike Cincinnatus and the abolitionists, did not make a broad claim to a national right to free speech. Instead, Davis suggested that the Southern states should deal with the problem. "Why does not South Carolina, if she has not done it, make it penal for persons who take from the post offices incendiary papers, to circulate them?"[62]

Davis insisted that the First Amendment meant that Congress "shall not diminish the freedom of the press. . . . The right is reserved and we are forbidden to touch it." Grants of power were made on the condition that "this privilege was to remain unimpaired." He took a functional view, both of the post office and of the press. "The naked right to print, without the right to publish would be a humble privilege." Printing and publishing were united. Since the time of framing the Constitution, a major mode of publishing was by transmission of periodicals through the mail.[63] The press was essential to republican government.

> The press is the great organ of a free people. It is the medium through which their thoughts are communicated, through which they act upon one another, and by which they reason with, instruct, and move each other. It rouses us to vigilance, warns us of danger, rebukes the aspiring, encourages the modest, and, like the sun in the heavens, radiates its influence over the whole country. The people viewed it as vital to a republic, and gave it the mail as an auxiliary; and you might as well expect the blood to flow through the system without the heart, as to have the press exert its influence in a salutary manner through the country without the aid of the mail.[64]

Davis said that the reasons supporting the incendiary publication bill were the same as those always given for abridging the liberty of the press: because the press "sends forth incendiary, inflammable publications, disturbing the public peace, and corrupting the public mind. All censorships are established under the plausible pretense of arresting evils. . . . Great principles, fundamental in their character, are thus assailed on proof of abuses which no doubt at all times exist; and when once, through such pretenses, a breach is made, the citadel falls."[65] For this reason, the Constitution prohibited abridging the liberty of the press "come what might."[66]

Senator Daniel Webster also spoke against the bill. Webster had served in the House and been elected to the Senate in 1827. Before that, Webster had become one of the nation's top (and most financially successful) lawyers and had argued a number of landmark cases before the Supreme Court of the United States. In Congress and in the Court he was typically an advocate of strong national power. Webster increased his national fame in his famous debate with Senator Robert Hayne of South Carolina, in which Webster opposed states' rights and nullification.

On the issue of the postal bill, Daniel Webster, the nationalist, found no national power. Freedom of the press, Webster insisted, included publishing as well as printing and circulating papers through the mail.[67] Senator Webster thought the Constitution denied Congress power over the press. "Whatever laws the State Legislatures might pass on the subject, Congress was restrained from legislating in any manner whatever, with regard to the press."[68] Webster particularly objected to deciding "what should be transmitted by their ordinary channel of intelligence" based on "the character of the writing or publication." Such a doctrine was a "direct" and shocking "abridgement of the freedom of the press."[69]

Senator Henry Clay of Kentucky, another leader of the Whig Party, believed the president's call for federal legislation had met "general disapprobation." After the "most extraordinary and dangerous power had been assumed by the head of the Post office, and . . . sustained by [the president's message]," he had given the question extensive thought. Clay concluded that Congress "could not pass any law interfering with the subject in any shape or form whatever." States could apply the necessary remedy "[t]he instant that a prohibited paper was handed out."[70]

Senator Thomas Morris of Ohio objected that the bill deprived citizens of the right to be secure in their "persons, houses, papers, and effects against unreasonable searches and seizures."[71] It subjected the laws of Congress to the different policies of twenty-four states. In rejecting the postal bill, Morris also seemed to be reacting to Southern demands that Northern states suppress abolition. "[W]e, the free states . . . are called on to put the gag into the mouths of our citizens, to declare that they have no right to talk, to preach, or to pray, on the subject of slavery; that we must put down societies who meet for such purposes; that we shall not be permitted to send abroad our thoughts or our opinions upon the abstract question of slavery; that the very liberty of thought, of speech, and of the press shall be so embarrassed as to be in many instances denied to us."[72]

Morris also concluded that states "have ample . . . power to punish any person in their jurisdiction who may read or distribute any publication which their laws may prohibit." Morris, however, denied that postmasters were subject to state law: "[T]hey cannot reach the post office or the postmaster for delivery [of items prohibited by its law] as directed, because such act is under paramount authority."[73]

Other opponents objected to the vagueness of the bill and also warned of the danger of postmasters, who were political functionaries, using their power against their political opponents: "The papers of the party in power would find despatch as orthodox, while all others would be found filled with offensive matter."[74]

Several pointed out the immense burden of sifting through the mail in search of statements about slavery that might be prohibited by the various laws of different states. Senator Niles of Connecticut noted that fifty or more periodicals were issued from New York City alone. Many of them were issued daily and many were composed of items taken from other papers. "[E]ach paper must be carefully examined in its entire contents, to see if it contains anything touching the subject of slavery. This would be utterly impracticable."[75] Then if something touching slavery was found, it would be necessary to decide if it was incendiary under the law of the receiving state. "To decide what is incendiary matter would be similar to deciding what is a libel, what constitutes blasphemy or heresy. Of all cases ever tried before judicial tribunals, these are the most difficult and uncertain."[76]

Senators King of Georgia and James Buchanan of Pennsylvania supported the bill. Unlike Senator Calhoun, they found power to pass it under the postal power. Senator Buchanan agreed with critics of the bill that the First Amendment deprived Congress of power over the press. It meant that "Congress [had] no power . . . to pass any law to prevent or to punish any publication whatever." But it did not follow from this that Congress was required to distribute publications inciting insurrection. The freedom to print and to publish was unimpaired; but government could not be compelled to act as the agent of the publisher.[77]

Senator King of Georgia denied that a prohibition on sending "incendiary" publications to states that proscribed them violated the freedom of the press. The First Amendment was intended to be "a restriction on the national Legislature, intended to prevent any active interference with that right, as it existed in the States at the time the constitution was adopted." Freedom of the press "consisted in the right to print and publish whatever might be permitted by the laws of the State." The laws of the slave states prohibited delivery of incendiary items. So no one, including postmasters, had a right to deliver "incendiary" publications in those states. There was no "freedom" for the proposed congressional statute to abridge. A freedom might exist to circulate such items in free states, but no attempt was made to abridge printing or circulating the items in states that acknowledged the right to do so.[78]

While other senators analyzed the problem in terms of power, Senator King analyzed it in terms of rights. Constitutional and other rights must be reconciled. State constitutions secured the right to free speech and free press, yet states punished libelers. The right to free speech was limited by the private right to reputation. Similarly, the right to free speech and press was limited by the property right to own slaves.[79]

Early debate on the Calhoun bill showed that passage was doubtful. Supporters of the administration,[80] as well as Whigs, opposed it. Even Senator Benton, who had celebrated the achievements of antiabolition mobs and who was unwilling to make the Post Office a "pack-horse for abolitionists," thought that investing powers of censorship in ten thousand postmasters "would lead to things they might all regret."[81] Supporters of the measure postponed it and, subsequently, submitted a revised bill.[82] Because of constitutional scruples, even the original bill was limited to reinforcing the Southern quarantine. It did not seek to ban publications within any Northern states or even to ban interstate transportation of abolitionist literature. It did not even seek to punish abolitionists for mailing their publications to the South. It fell far short, for example, of contemporary antiobscenity statutes. It simply prohibited postmasters from mailing publications about slavery to states that prohibited them or from delivering the publications in violation of state law.

The revised bill also eliminated the prohibition on postmasters mailing the publications from the North to the South. It simply forbade postmasters from delivering publications about slavery that offended state laws.[83] As a result, Senator Buchanan noted that the bill "did not affect, in the slightest degree, any of the non-slaveholding States."[84] Senator Grundy noted that the revised bill did not even forbid transmission of "certain publications, no matter how incendiary." The whole effect of the bill was merely to prevent a postmaster who violated the law of the state in which he resided "from sheltering himself under the post office law."[85] The bill did no more, Senator Calhoun noted, than what the postmaster general had done without it, and, he acidly noted, without any objection by Northern Democrats who were deserting the Calhoun bill.[86]

The defense proved unsuccessful. The incendiary publications bill was defeated by a Senate vote of nineteen to twenty-five. The margin of defeat was provided by Northern Democrats and Southern Whigs who refused to support the bill. If either of these groups had supported it, and Martin Van Buren had, as expected, broken a tie in its favor, the bill would have passed the Senate.

The Post Office Act of 1836 was a general act regulating the post office.

It made it criminal for a postmaster unlawfully to detain the mail.[87] But *unlawful* detention was the key concept. "[I]t cannot be unlawful to detain that which it is unlawful to deliver," concluded Attorney General Caleb Cushing in an 1858 opinion about delivery of the *Cincinnati Gazette*.[88] In effect, states could make delivery of some political mail a crime, and the post office could refuse to deliver such mail.

The thrust of the Senate discussion of the incendiary publications bill was clear. First, Congress lacked power to punish or restrain the press. (Some denied that postal censorship of abolition publications as provided by the bill was doing either of these things.) Second, Southern states had the constitutional power to punish those who circulated abolitionist publications in the South. (At least one Senator denied that this power could reach postmasters.)[89] In practice, that meant that if abolition were to be eliminated from the political agenda, the legislatures of the Northern states would have to do it.

PETITIONS

While the Congress and the nation debated the postal controversy and the suppression of abolitionist publications in the states, Congress also debated whether to receive petitions calling for abolition of slavery in the District of Columbia, in the territories, and the abolition of the interstate slave trade. Some congressmen from the South pointed out that petitions demanding the abolition of slavery were the very sort of incendiary documents Southern states had made criminal.[90] They sought to silence antislavery petitions and agitation in Congress.

The freedom of members of Parliament (and later of members of American legislatures) to debate and the right to petition were important chapters in the history of liberty. So long as the king could arrest members of Parliament for what they said in debate, the power of Parliament as a deliberative body was seriously impaired. So long as petitioners could be arrested for their petitions, representative government was thwarted.

Freedom of debate in legislative assemblies was an important source of the right of the people to free speech and press. Once sovereignty was located not in Parliament but in the people, it was natural that the people must be free (as their representatives were) to discuss political questions. In theory the people had a right to set the agenda and through their representatives to decide all political questions. A political question in turn was one on which political action was sought. Limiting the right of Congress to consider and debate political questions raised by petitions was a twofold attack on representative government. It limited both the ability of Congress to debate the questions raised by petitions and the ability of citizens to have Congress consider their requests. The demand to reject or ignore abolition petitions ran counter to basic ideas of representative government and popular sovereignty.

For Southerners, however, discussion of slavery in Congress was deeply threatening. Once abolition in the District, for example, became part of the political agenda, it would be discussed in newspapers and throughout the land. The people would need to be informed about the subject, in both the South and the North, so they could express their views to their agents in Washington. For this reason, Senator Calhoun of South Carolina announced that discussion of abolition in Congress was more dangerous than abolitionist pamphlets in the South. Southerners could suppress those pamphlets. "It was agitation here that they feared, because it would compel the Southern press to discuss the question in the very presence of the slaves, who were induced to believe that there was a powerful party at the North ready to assist them."[91] Calhoun demanded that the petitions cease.

Calhoun's solution and that of the more extreme Southerners was that Congress should refuse to receive abolitionist petitions. Senator Preston of South Carolina insisted that Congress must recognize that antislavery petitions were, after all, abolitionist activity. Discussion of the subject must cease; Congress should take "such action . . . as would close the doors of this Hall against the agitation of this subject."[92]

One common justification for suppression was that the petitions, in denouncing slavery, libeled the South and inflicted emotional injury. "They contained reflections," said Senator Calhoun, "injurious to the feelings of himself, and those with whom he was connected."[93] The language was "highly reprehensible." One petition, Calhoun complained, spoke of dealing in human flesh and piracy. "Strange language! Piracy and butchery! We must not . . . permit those we represent to be thus insulted on that floor."[94]

The effort to silence antislavery discussion in Congress confronted three main constitutional obstacles. The First Amendment prohibited Congress from making any law abridging the right of the people to assemble and petition for redress of grievances.[95] (Of course, internal congressional procedures might not be viewed as a "law" forbidden by the First Amendment.) Second, Article I, Section 6, of the Constitution contained a provision designed to protect free speech by representatives and senators in Congress: "for any speech or Debate in either House, they shall not be questioned in any other Place."[96] Third, the right to petition was central to representative government. Many Northern and some Southern congressmen rebelled at the idea of refusing to receive abolitionist petitions. To refuse to receive abolitionist petitions, many insisted, abridged the right of petition.[97] They warned that abolitionists would turn refusal to receive petitions to their advantage. Senator Wright of New York, a Van Buren Democrat and an antiabolitionist, put it this way: "[E]very Senator would concede that a general impression prevailed among our whole people, of every portion of the Union, that the right to petition Congress in respectful terms . . . was one of the broadest rights secured by the Constitution. Refuse it upon the broad principle, as relating to this subject, and these malignant agitators will seize upon the act to draw to themselves and their cause public sympathy."[98]

The battle over abolitionist petitions in Congress involved the basic issues that surrounded the national debate on freedom of speech for abolitionists—the right to engage in antislavery political speech. Congressman John Quincy Adams emerged as the leader of opposition to congressional efforts to stifle antislavery petitions. At this point, Adams had held many government posts, including minister to Russia, secretary of state, and president of the United States. He insisted that "the true course [was] to let error be tolerated, [and] to grant freedom of speech, and freedom of the press, and apply reason to put it down." Adams hoped "that the sacred right of petition would remain unimpaired."[99] But in the end, the House voted to take abolition off the political agenda. It agreed by a vote of 117 to 68 to the following resolution on the subject:

> [W]hereas it is extremely important and desirable that the agitation of this subject should be finally arrested, for the purpose of restoring tranquility to the public mind, your committee respectfully recommend the adoption of the following . . . resolution, viz:
> *Resolved*, That all petitions, memorials, resolutions, propositions, or papers, relating in any way, or to any extent whatever, to

the subject of slavery, or the abolition of slavery, shall, without being either printed or referred, be laid upon the table, and that no further action whatever shall be had thereon.[100]

This resolution (in various forms) became the rule of the House for the next seven stormy years. To many congressmen, as Adams put it, the resolution was "a direct violation of the constitution of the United States . . . and the rights of my constituents."[101] As predicted by many, both in and out of Congress, the gag rule became a cause célèbre, and the abolitionists made the most of it. By 1837 abolitionists decided to step up the petition drive and an increasing torrent of petitions descended on Congress. These urged Congress not only to abolish slavery in the District of Columbia, but also to abolish the gag rule. The call went out from the New York staff of the Anti-Slavery Society. "Let petitions be circulated wherever signers can be got. Neglect no one." The abolitionists were enjoined to follow "the farmer to his field, the wood-chopper to the forest. Hail the shop-keeper behind his counter; call the clerk from his desk; stop the waggoner with his team; forget not the matron, ask for her daughter. . . . Explain, discuss, argue, persuade."[102]

Adams conducted brilliant guerrilla warfare against the gag rule, and the margin in support of the gag steadily declined. The story is too long to be told here. The reader can pursue the subject in Gilbert H. Barnes's classic, *The Anti-Slavery Impulse*, and in a recent gripping and powerful account by William Lee Miller, *Arguing About Slavery*. Still one battle from the guerrilla war should be mentioned. On February 6, 1837, Adams asked for direction from the Speaker. He had in his hand "a petition from twenty-two persons, declaring themselves to be slaves." Though the "paper purported to come from slaves," Adams said he was dubious. At any rate, was the gag rule (tabling the petition) the course to be followed, Adams asked, suggesting that the petition be sent to the chair for a ruling.

Southerners exploded. Petitions from slaves! One Southern representative demanded that it not be sent to the chair. Others demanded that Adams be severely punished for violation of the decorum of the House. Calls "Expel him" and "No! No!" filled the air. Representative Julius Alford of Georgia suggested, in a move reminiscent of Parliament's response to Leveller petitions, that the House order the petition burned. A resolution was quickly concocted to censure Adams for attempting to introduce a petition for abolition of slavery from slaves. Adams had sat quietly during the uproar. But finally he rose to correct a few factual mistakes. He said he had not offered the petition. He had simply asked for a ruling from the chair. Nor was the petition for abolition, but "the very reverse of this." (It apparently asked for Adams's expulsion.) Embarrassed representatives now added a new count—creating a false impression and trifling with the House. Adams was also charged with giving color to the idea that slaves had the right to petition. Representative Claiborne of Mississippi denounced his behavior as "disgraceful." Adams was like "the midnight incendiary who fires the dwelling of his enemy, and listens with pleasure to the screams of his burning victims."[103]

Regional antagonisms flared. Representative Waddy Thompson of South Carolina recalled the sins of New England, including opposition to the War of 1812 and the Alien and Sedition Acts. This latter charge provoked a response from Representative Caleb Cushing of Massachusetts: "And are they [the Alien and Sedition Acts] not precisely the things which South Carolina herself, in common with other States of the South, has recently called on the States of the North to do? That is, to extend the law of seditious libel . . . ?"[104] Only now papers were to be suppressed for "incendiary" ideas instead of subversive ones.

A Southern representative suggested that Adams might be indicted by a grand jury in the District and brought to trial. To this Adams responded with contempt: "[T]he gentleman has threatened me with an indictment before the grand jury of the District of Columbia as a felon and an incendiary, for words spoken in this House! . . . Yes, sir, he would make a member of this House amenable to a grand jury! . . . I would beg to invite that gentleman, when he goes home, to study a little the first principles of civil liberty."[105] Finally, Adams defended the right to petition, even for slaves. The right to petition was a natural right, given by God. He refuted suggestions made during the debate that the right did not belong to all, to people of bad character, to free blacks, or even to slaves:

> When you establish the doctrine that a slave shall not petition because he is a slave, that he shall not be permitted to raise the cry for mercy, you let in a principle subversive of every foundation of liberty, and you cannot tell where it will stop. . . .
>
> . . .
>
> Here then is another limitation to the right of petition. First is it denied to slaves, then to free persons of color, and then to persons of

notorious bad character. . . . There is but one step more, and that is to inquire into the political faith of petitioners. Each side will represent their opponents as being infamous, and what becomes of the right of petition?[106]

The effort to expel or censure Adams ended with a whimper: passage of a resolution saying that the petition in question could not be received by the House and another denying that slaves had the right to petition. As Adams showed, in this case and again and again, the effort to suppress discussion of antislavery petitions was increasing, not reducing, the discussion of slavery in Congress. And as Adams and others made the issue one of civil liberty, the support for the gag rule declined.

Finally, at age seventy-six on December 3, 1844, Adams made a final motion to rescind the gag rule. His motion passed by a vote of 108 to 80. The *New York Tribune* celebrated in a lead editorial: "Let every lover of freedom rejoice! The absurd and tyrannical XXVth (formerly the XXIst) Rule of the House which required the rejection of all petitions relating to slavery has been *repealed* by a decisive vote! The Sage of Quincy [John Quincy Adams] has won a proud victory for the Rights of Humanity. May he long live to rejoice over it! Here is a motion which will not go backward. There will be no more Gag-Rules."[107]

The gag rule had repressed abolitionist petitions, but it also attempted to silence congressional discussion. It gagged congressmen as well as abolitionists, underlining the abolitionists' warning that the suppression of their rights implicated the rights of others as well. The gag rule suppressed discussion based on its content—slavery. It seems to have been applied neutrally to proslavery and antislavery petitions and resolutions. Superficially at least, the gag rule was not based on point of view.[108] Of course, in reality, removing an issue from the agenda benefits the status quo. Southern states' suppression of abolitionist speech and press, in contrast, was aimed at one side of the debate. Southern nullifiers and nationalists remained free to agitate the slavery issue.

Still, Congress's action against petitions had been limited to restricting congressional discussion of them. The constitutional guarantee of the right to petition had discouraged any direct federal attempt to punish petitioners for abolitionist ideas expressed in their petitions. In Virginia, however, the state prosecuted a man in 1839 for circulating an abolitionist petition to Congress.[109] The Virginia court construed its antiabolition statute narrowly and did not decide if the petition itself was protected by the state or federal constitution.

While Congress had done its best to silence its own discussion of abolition, it did not do much more. It failed even to ban the sending of abolitionist publications to the South. Mobs also had failed to silence abolitionists. So Southerners looked to the Northern states to pass laws against abolitionist agitation. It is to that question that I now turn.

8

The Demand for Northern Legal Action

Against Abolitionists

The Southern nullifier and Southern secessionist factions were not content with compromises like the gag rule. They argued that the crux of the abolition problem was abolitionist expression in the North. Much of the South agreed. Southern reaction to abolition was becoming more unified and more extreme. But some Southerners of more national orientation saw nullifier political machinations behind the exacerbation of the slavery issue. "The tariff had failed them—the Indian question had failed them," wrote the *Georgia Courier*. "People could think differently on those points—but if they could only get the lead with the slavery card, their end was accomplished—they knew every body must follow suit." Nullifiers, the paper complained, were reading or trying to read "these inflammatory publications" at public meetings.[1] To the extent that abolitionist ideas reached the South at all it was mainly through Southern "extremists" who quoted abolition tracts to alert the South to the menace. The extremists hoped to use the crisis to forge a political re-alignment, a Southern party, and, for some, an independent Southern nation.

The Southern Demand

To many Southerners the Union would not be tolerable if abolitionists prevailed in the North. Furthermore, as long as abolition publications were abundant in the North there was danger some might reach the South. Supporters of suppression compared abolitionist publications to fire, gunpowder, and explosions. Implicit in such metaphors was the idea that the South was living on a powder keg or tinder box, and one spark could be enough to trigger an explosion or conflagration. In his

Commentaries, Chancellor James Kent noted sympathetically that self-preservation demanded "unceasing vigilance and firmness, as well as uniform kindness and humanity" from whites "dwelling in the midst of such combustible materials."[2]

Even without the aid of national or Northern legislation, the Southern quarantine had substantially suppressed the abolition movement in the South. But Southerners demanded more. Often they specifically demanded the suppression of abolition publications and societies in the North. For example, in 1835 the Virginia legislature "earnestly requested" other states "promptly to adopt penal enactments" or other measures to "effectively suppress all [abolitionist societies] within their limits."[3] The North Carolina legislature "[r]esolved, That our sister States are respectfully requested to enact penal laws prohibiting the printing within their respective limits, all such publications as may have a tendency to make our slaves discontented with their present condition, or incite them to insurrection."[4]

The North Carolina legislature did not even specify that the publications to be prohibited must be sent South. It wanted total prohibition to ensure that no abolitionist documents reached Southerners or anybody else. Likewise, the Alabama legislature called on other states "to enact such penal laws, as will finally put an end to the malignant deeds of the abolitionists."[5] That legislature also asked its sister states to "make it highly penal to print, publish, or distribute newspapers, pamphlets, or other publications, calculated or having a tendency to excite the slaves of the Southern states to insurrection and revolt."[6] South Carolina made a similar request.[7]

Sometimes Southern leaders challenged the claim that Northern state constitutional guarantees of freedom of speech and of the press made it impossible to suppress abolitionist publications. The Committee of Twenty-six of the North Carolina legislature drafted its resolutions and prefaced them with a report. That report insisted that even if state constitutional provisions protected expression of abolitionist ideas, this was no excuse for permitting abolitionists to continue. Northern states had a duty to their Southern sisters, and "they have no right to disable themselves from its performance by an organic law." Moreover, the committee concluded that the constitutional objections were based on "a total misconception of what is meant by the liberty of the press; which means not the right to publish without responsibility, but to publish without previous permission." The committee explained the "correct" view:

"Where every man has a right to publish what he pleases, but is responsible for the nature and tendency of his publication, the press is free. If he has a right to publish without such responsibility, the press is licentious."[8]

So the committee implicitly endorsed Blackstone's cramped definition of freedom of the press, revived a key argument for the Sedition Act, and implicitly rejected Madison's suggestion that speech about public men and measures was essential to republican government and should be protected.

At the least, Southern legislatures that referred to the issues of free speech and press insisted that abolition expression was an unprotected abuse of those "sacred and inviolable rights."[9] The South Carolina legislature distinguished "freedom of discussion" from "the liberty to deluge a friendly . . . state with seditious and incendiary tracts." The legislature was quite willing that "[t]he whole circumstances of the case, and the *quo animo* of the offender might be left to a jury."[10]

Crafting Tests for Suppression

But if legislation was required, how should the exception to free speech be crafted? Southern states typically had prohibited expression tending to cause slave revolts or disaffection. The legislation made the truth or the political nature of the attack on slavery irrelevant. Northern states conceivably could apply that bad tendency model to abolitionist publications intended to be sent South. But, as to slave revolts at least, this standard would not work to suppress abolitionist expression in the North because the North, generally, had no slaves.

The least restrictive law would be one prohibiting citizens of a Northern state from sending "incendiary" documents to the South with the specific intent of exciting a slave rebellion. Laws crafted in that fashion, as critics noted, allowed for the suppression of publications regardless of truth.

In fact, several Northern governors did suggest laws against abolitionists. Governor Marcy of New York noted that the avowed object of abolitionists was to abolish slavery in the Southern and Southwestern states. "[T]heir means thus far have been confined to the organization of societies among us, and to publications of various kinds on the subject of slavery." Southerners, he noted, regarded these as libels on their citizens and provocation to insurrection among their slaves. Since there were no slaves in New York and all regarded the institution as an evil, he asked, what could the abolitionists hope to accomplish in New York? New York had no power over Southern slavery. Congress had no power on the subject either, and the effort to change slavery by Northern or national legislation would violate the "compact" between North and South that made the Constitution possible. Abolitionist efforts at persuasion had been rejected indignantly in the South. Furthermore, Marcy warned, the presence of abolition presses in New York founded by wealthy New York businessmen had led to threats of a Southern boycott and "injurious consequences to our commerce."[11]

So what was the solution? Governor Marcy proposed, equivocally, that if public opinion were insufficient to solve the problem, then Northern states might provide, "by their own laws for the trial and punishment by their own judicatories, of residents within their limits, guilty of acts therein, which are calculated and intended to excite insurrection and rebellion in a sister State."[12]

THE ABOLITIONIST REJOINDER

In February of 1836, Alvan Stewart of New York—an antislavery legal thinker and leader of the New York Anti-slavery Society—excoriated Governor Marcy's call for suppression of antislavery expression. He ridiculed the idea that abolition was a monster so powerful that its extermination required the "loss of liberty of the press, of conscience, discussion, and of the inviolability of the mail." Marcy had argued that because the power to suppress abolition publications was not delegated to the federal government, it was retained by the states. "There is a class of rights," Stewart responded, "of the most personal and sacred character to the citizen, which are a portion of individual sovereignty, never surrendered by the citizen . . . either to the State or General Government, and the Constitutions of the State and Union have told the world, after enumerating them, that there is a class of unsurrendered rights." The legislatures of the states and of the Union, Stewart insisted, "are forbidden by the constitutions of the States and Union from touching those unsurrendered rights." This was so "no matter in what distress or exigency a State may find itself." To support his conclusion Stewart cited the New York constitution.[13]

Stewart also made a shrewd analysis, showing that guarantees of free expression were central to republican government. If those in power could use the criminal justice system to silence their political critics, he observed, then the people would be deprived of democratic choice. Stewart feared a replay of what the Sedition Act had attempted. "Oh, what scenes of abuse would have been played off before this world, if licensed presses, gagged discussion, and mail inquisitors had been tolerated! And we should have seen such laws passed in this State by a party who had the ascendancy, if the constitution had not forbidden it, by which one half of the community could neither speak, write, nor publish anything of their adversaries, under pain of indictments, fine and imprisonment."[14] The citizens of New York, Stewart concluded, had the right to discuss, print and circulate "their sentiments on any moral problem, or any question of right and wrong, of liberty and slavery."[15]

Stewart relied primarily on his state constitution as a protection against state action suppressing antislavery ideas. He suggested that some areas of discussion were simply beyond legislative power, however compelling the legislature's reasons for action. While Stewart related free speech to natural rights, as the slavery controversy intensified Southerners began to repudiate the natural rights philosophy. While Stewart relied on the right of the individual to discuss political and moral questions, by 1859 Southerners in Congress relied instead on the community's right to suppress dangerous doctrine. By 1859–60 the rejection of individual rights arguments and invocation of the rights of the community were well developed by Southern congressmen.[16]

SOUTHERN REACTION TO NORTHERN INACTION

The U.S. Telegraph, a pronullification paper, was mildly pleased with Governor Marcy's message. But it complained that the proposed statute extended to a "very narrow class of cases," those involving actions "calculated and *intended* to excite insurrection."[17] "Under the plea of not 'intended' to excite insurrection," groused the Telegraph, "laws passed would be a mere dead letter."[18] Furthermore, the law probably would not reach publications intended exclusively for Northern audiences. Publications not meant for the South would hardly be calculated and intended to excite slave uprisings.

The Telegraph and other Southern organs and spokesmen gloomily predicted that even such limited measures would not be enacted.[19] "[O]ur just hopes," lamented Senator John C. Calhoun in April 1836, "have not been realized. The Legislatures of the South . . . have called upon the non-slaveholding States to repress the movements made within the jurisdiction of those States against their peace and security. Not a step has been taken; not a law has been passed."[20] The Kentucky legislature came to a similar conclusion: "Enough has transpired to convince us [the legislature] that under the miserably perverted name of free discussion, these incendiaries will be permitted to scatter their firebrands throughout the country, with no check but that which may be imposed by the feeble operation of public opinion."[21]

And so in fact it was to be.

Rationales for Free Discussion and Rationalizations for Northern Inaction

The first reactions to Southern demands for suppression of abolitionists in the North came from the press. The first problem was that the federal and state constitutions contained guarantees for free speech, press, religion, and petition. While detailed discussion of the meaning of these provisions was rare, many Northerners thought that suppression of antislavery speech and press would violate these provisions. *Niles' Weekly Register* complained that many in the South "declare that it is the *duty* of the people of the Northern states to prohibit *discussions* on the 'slave question,' though it enters so largely into the construction of the government under which we live."[22] Under the heading "FREEDOM OF SPEECH AND OF THE PRESS, Guaranteed by the Constitution of the United States and of the several states," the *Weekly Register* reprinted (from the *Richmond Compiler*) federal and state guarantees for free speech and press. The *Compiler* said that the extracts from federal and state constitutions showed "that no law can constitutionally be passed for the purpose of restraining the fanatics of the North in their crusade against our rights."[23]

Because of guarantees of free speech in state constitutions and of the reverence with which they were treated, it is sometimes hard to figure out exactly what steps antiabolition meetings were actually recommending. At a "great meeting" in Connecticut, antiabolitionists pledged "to use all legal and proper means not incompatible with our rights and those great principles of liberty, freedom of speech and the press, to repress" interference in the relations in other states of master and slave.[24] At any rate, Southern demands for suppression in the North provoked a reaction. The *New York Herald* had supported the South and opposed the abolitionists. But, as reported in the *Weekly Register*, the *Herald* criticized both Southern demands that the North "pass laws infringing the liberty of the press" and Southern offers of rewards for the kidnapping of Arthur Tappan, a leader and financial angel of the abolitionists. These, the paper held, were cases of fanaticism equivalent to that of the abolitionists.[25] The *Washington Globe* reprinted a piece from the *Louisville* (Kentucky) *Advertiser* that attributed demands for Northern censorship to the machinations of the extreme Southern nullifier camp against Van Buren. Although the postmaster general had approved Southern post office action embargoing abolitionist publications, and city after city in the North had passed resolutions harshly condemning the abolitionists, "yet we are told the South is not content—will not be satisfied, until the East and North, by legislative enactments shall suppress the publication of articles adverse to slavery. . . . The *Whig* and *Telegraph* concur . . . that the circulation of abolition tracts in the North is more injurious to the country than their circulation at the South. . . . Why are they making demands of the North which cannot constitutionally be complied with, and asserting, should the North prove disobedient, war and disunion will be the consequence?"[26]

Northern legislatures responded to the Southern resolutions. The committee of the New York legislature assigned to consider the issue produced a remarkably equivocal report. It referred to the massive outpouring of public sentiment against the abolitionists and agreed with the governor that it was beyond belief that such "manifestations of public sentiment" would be disregarded.[27] But the committee also spoke respectfully of freedom of the press. It said "all errors and differences of opinion" on political rights or "measures of public policy" may safely be referred to the "tribunal" of public opinion. A free press, the committee continued, was essential to a just and enlightened public opinion. Free speech and a free press were guaranteed by the state and federal constitutions: "[I]t is a most delicate and difficult task of discrimination for legislators to determine at what point this rational and constitutional liberty terminates, and venality and licentiousness begin. It is indeed more safe to tolerate the licentiousness of the press than to abridge its freedom; for a corrective of the evil will be generally found in the force of truth."[28]

Still, the legislature insisted that it had the power to pass criminal laws to reach those "actually employed in exciting insurrection and sedition in a sister State." But the resolution concluded that the "unexampled unanimity" of public disapproval of those discussions of slavery "calculated to produce an exciting, an improper, and a pernicious influence within the limits of other States, [has] given to the Union stronger guarantees than law could furnish."[29]

Governor Edward Everett of Massachusetts rejected laws against the abolitionists, saying that laws "impairing the liberty of speech and of the press, even for the sake of repressing its abuses" were contrary to "the genius of our institutions." Instead, he seems to have insisted that at least direct incitements to slave rebellion could be reached by the common law of crimes. He appealed to the constitutional compact that left slavery to the Southern states. "Every thing that tends to disturb the relations created by this compact is at war with its spirit; and whatever by direct and necessary operation, is calculated to excite an insurrection among the slaves, has been held ... an offense against the peace of this Commonwealth" and a common law crime.[30] In spite of Everett's suggestion, Massachusetts launched no prosecutions.

The Massachusetts legislature, like all the others of the North, passed no antiabolitionist legislation. A legislative committee did recommend some weakly worded resolutions on the subject. Elizur Wright wrote to fellow abolitionist Theodore Weld in delight. The proposed resolutions seemed to him to be conclusive proof of the "progress of things." The committee had condemned the doctrines avowed and measures pursued "by whom? By the Antislavery Societies? Not at all—but, by 'such as *agitate the question*.' And what is to be done against these agitators? Why the legislature 'does earnestly *recommend* to them carefully to abstain from all such discussion, etc.' If the slaveholders are satisfied with this, they will be satisfied with 'great cry and little wool.' But even this they have not yet, and perhaps may not. The resolutions, too, condemn *mobs!*"[31]

Governor Wolf of Pennsylvania had no sympathy for the abolitionists. He thought that their "crusade against slavery is the offspring of fanaticism of the most dangerous and alarming character; which if not speedily checked may kindle a fire which it may require the best blood of the country to quench." But he said that the matter must be left to public opinion. "Legislation cannot be brought to bear upon it without endangering other rights and privileges ... The freedom of speech and of the press, which after all is the safeguard to free discussion, and the best expositor of public opinion, must not be infringed upon or controlled by enactments intended to remedy some temporary mischief only." The governor nevertheless suggested that a temperate, firm, and decided resolution of the legislature might "give tone and expression to public sentiment" and check the progress of abolition.[32]

His successor, Governor Joseph Ritner, spoke unequivocally against slavery in his 1836 message. Slavery was an evil. Pennsylvania had abolished it and had always stood against its expansion. "Above all," Governor Ritner implored, "let us never yield up the right of the free discussion of any evil which may arise in the land or any part of it."[33]

In Pennsylvania, proposals for antiabolition legislation were referred to the House Judiciary Committee chaired by Thaddeus Stevens. The committee rejected Southern demands as a violation of the rights of free speech and a free press. It announced that "[e]very citizen of the non-slaveholding states has a right freely to think and publish his thoughts on any subject of national or state policy." Without regard to residence, the Northern citizen had a right to attack the usury laws of New York or the slave laws of Mississippi as immoral and unjust. However weak, foolish, or false the arguments, it would be "tyranny to prohibit their promulgation." To accept such restrictions would reduce the Northern citizen to "a vassalage but little less degrading than that of the slaves whose condition we assert the right to discuss."[34] The report also upheld the power of Congress to ban slavery in the District of Columbia. The legislature approved neither the report nor legislation against abolitionists.

Some other Northern state legislatures and legislative committees also saw abolitionist ideas as opinion protected by free speech and press. The Vermont legislature resolved that "neither Congress nor the State Governments have any constitutional right to abridge the free expression of opinion, or the transmission of them through the medium of the public mails."[35] The report of the Ohio legislature suggested that the Southern resolutions were as dangerous as abolitionist publications. "If the slave has capacity to understand [abolitionist] publications, he can equally understand the proceedings of legislatures which so publicly and repeatedly declare their pernicious tendency." The Ohio committee's report announced that "the states have no power to restrain the publication of private opinion on any subject whatever, and the principle, if admitted, involves much greater evils to the peace of the states, than the toleration of errors and the excitements they cause can ever produce." The Ohio legislature resolved that "no law can be passed to impair the freedom of speech or the freedom of the press, except to provide remedy for the redress of private injury, or the breach of the peace resulting from abuse of either."[36]

The struggle over state legislation to suppress abolition was one crucial battle of the years 1835–37. In the end, no free state enacted repressive legislation, and several came to the defense of protection for political opinion. Some, like the New York legislature, suggested that public opinion would repress abolition, making legislation unnecessary. That argument is hard to credit. In the Southern states, public opinion, though far from uniform, was more monolithic and repressive than in the North. There, those suspected of abolition faced a clear threat of summary punishment. Still, virtually all Southern states passed laws aimed at "incendiary" antislavery agitation.

The heritage of the Sedition Act controversy—and the defense of free speech and press it spawned—shaped popular and political attitudes on the question for a critical mass of people. For these people suppressing abolition opinion, hateful as that opinion was to some of them, violated principles of freedom of political expression. Significantly, those who held these views denied that abolition could be treated as a special case—an exception because the evil feared was so significant.

Proposed antiabolition legislation was basically a more extreme version of the Sedition Act. After all, abolitionists criticized a major social and economic institution that had a huge effect on the political system. In 1835 and 1836, at least, they did not advocate crime or urge slaves to revolt. The danger of their speech came from its tendency—the tendency of criticism of the institution of slavery to produce (as abolitionist critics saw it) catastrophic results. That, of course, was how supporters of the Sedition Act saw the tendency of criticism of government officials. Of course, in each case more was involved. The Sedition Act had been aimed at suppressing political opposition. In the South, laws suppressing antislavery expression had similar political purposes. "The poor white men of the South will be tampered with," warned the *Telegraph*. "[T]he cry of 'democracy' and 'working men' will be raised. They will be told how much better will be their condition when the negro shall be transported to Africa."[37] But, in one respect at least, the Southern laws were worse than the Sedition Act. Unlike the Sedition Act, none of the Southern laws or proposed Northern laws made the truth of abolitionist criticisms of slavery a defense.

In the Senate, Daniel Webster, the nationalist Whig leader, suggested that the conduct punished by the Sedition Act was criminal by laws of all of the states at the time.[38] The implication was that the Southern states could still pass sedition acts and therefore, of course, antiabolitionist acts. For him the principle was only that the federal government lacked the power conferred on it by the now expired Sedition Act. But from 1835 to 1837, when state legislation was demanded to suppress abolitionist ideas, many people rejected the demand as a violation of free speech and a free press. The aspect of the Sedition Act controversy they relied on was not simply the federalism/states' rights distinctions of the Virginia and Kentucky resolutions, distinctions revived again in the congressional debate over post office censorship. Instead, they recalled the functional and structural argument of the Virginia resolutions: for republican government to work, free speech was essential on all issues of governmental policy. They applied these arguments to state constitutional guarantees. And they recalled Jefferson's rhetoric that truth and counterargument were the antidote for error—a principle from which Jefferson, incidentally, sometimes deviated.[39]

The result was a limited, but more nearly absolute, protection for political opinion—opinion that did not fall into some other free speech exception, such as the prohibition on libel of a person's private character or treason accomplished by words. The lines were fuzzy, and the concept was developing. Several advocates of repression mentioned an exception for conduct that caused breaches of the peace.[40] In response to calls to prosecute abolitionists for breach of the peace, the *Evening Post* suggested that such prosecutions should be aimed at those who used force to silence speakers, not at the speaker.[41] (It was an early response to the idea of a heckler's veto over exercise of First Amendment rights.) In any case, the central decisions in the years from 1835 to 1837 were clear: the attempt to have free states pass statutes suppressing abolitionist ideas failed. Nor would Congress pass laws suppressing abolitionist publications.

In other respects, however, the advocates of suppression were more successful. The gag rule continued in Congress until 1844. The post office had censored and continued to censor abolitionist publications aimed at the South, though some got through in plain brown wrappers. Although the North refused to enact suppression laws, Southern states had passed them. Vocal domestic Southern opposition to slavery reached a brief high water mark in the 1830s and thereinafter began to recede in much of the South. Southern laws and vigilance committees silenced abolition expression and did their best to take opposition to slavery off the Southern political agenda. As a result, the institution could only be dislodged by violence. "If you fear discussion, if you maintain that the South cannot afford it," Professor Francis Lieber wrote to John C. Calhoun, "then you admit at the same time that the whole institution is to be kept up by violence only, and is against the spirit of the times and unameliorable, which means, in other words, that violence supports it, and violence will be its end."[42]

9

Legal Theories of Suppression and the

Defense of Free Speech

Those demanding suppression of abolitionist expression had all assumed that abolitionist speech and press were not the sort of thing the federal and state constitutions were meant to protect. If abolition expression was not protected speech or press, what was it? It fell, supporters of suppression insisted, into one or more unprotected categories of expression.

Suppression Theories

Treason

Some denounced abolitionist views as treason. But this argument was deeply flawed for most Americans. The framers of the federal Constitution were familiar with how the English law of treason had been politically abused.[1] Hence, the *Federalist Papers* defended the Constitution's severely limited definition of treason (waging war against the United States and giving aid and comfort to their enemies) as a crucial guarantee of civil liberty.[2] The treason clause was an important guarantee protecting political speech and press.[3] Abolitionists pointed to the federal guarantee to refute the claim that their actions constituted treason.[4] State constitutions were typically equally restrictive.[5]

In the conflict over antiabolition petitions, some congressmen suggested that John Quincy Adams's actions, in presenting petitions allegedly from slaves or those advocating disunion, were treason or indictable as a violation of the law of the District of Columbia. Adams's withering reply suggested that such congressmen needed to review the first principles of civil liberty. Because of the treason and speech-and-debate clauses, claims that Adams had committed treason were isolated suggestions that other Southern congressmen refused to join.[6]

Seditious Libel

Seditious libel, or sedition, was a more promising theory to exclude abolition from the protections of free speech and press. By 1835, a broad consensus emerged that the federal government lacked power to pass sedition laws or even laws directly restraining the press.[7] However, several senators said state sedition laws were another matter.

After the Sedition Act, commentators, courts, and legislatures struggled to reconcile the English and American models for free speech and press. Limitations on public debate and prosecutions for criticism of public officials were recognized in English law. In England, parliament was sovereign. In contrast, in the American system, the *people* were sovereign. As a result, James Madison had insisted that popular sovereignty required popular freedom of debate on political issues.[8] Similarly, John Thompson, a New York lawyer, argued that just as parliamentary sovereignty required freedom of debate in parliament that could not be controlled by the king, so in America popular sovereignty required a similar immunity for the sovereign American electorate.[9]

Though state judicial law evolved in the direction of broader liberty in the years after the Sedition Act expired, some states were more restrictive than the Sedition Act itself and refused to recognize falsity as an element of the crime of libel or truth as a defense. Legislatures tended to respond by broadening the protections for free speech and press.[10] James Kent, in his *Commentaries*, insisted the English common law doctrine—that truth was not admissible—prevailed except where changed by statute or constitutional provision. Kent believed the trend to make truth alone a sufficient justification was pernicious. It should only justify the alleged libel where the publication was for good motives and justifiable ends. This was the New York doctrine.[11]

By 1835, little if any judicial authority held that state sedition laws violated state free press guarantees. Still, the defense of truth or truth for good motives and justifiable ends began to limit the rigor of the common law.[12] In his *Commentaries on Criminal Law*, Joel Bishop cited a definition of libel that included alienating men's minds "from the established constitution of the state" and further suggested that any publication "which tends to excite any crime whatever, may be treated as a libel." Still, Bishop insisted that publications apparently coming within these broad definitions would not be libels "if a suppression of it would be a restraint upon that open discussion of proper subjects which is essential to the liberty of the people." Bishop deduced "this doctrine . . . from the cases generally, and the reasons of the law" rather than from "any express decision."[13]

In 1835, at the height of the controversy over abolition agitation, William Sullivan, LL.D., insisted that Massachusetts could and should ban abolitionism as sedition. Rights, he insisted, were limited by the rights of others. Abolitionist meetings and publications tended to "destroy the peace, commerce, amity, and friendly intercourse" of Massachusetts citizens with citizens of the South. Abolitionists had perverted the constitutional "privilege of public meetings" into a public evil that the legislature could forbid by criminal statutes. The state legislature could declare meetings "[held] in non-slave-holding States" and designed "to promote immediate and general emancipation" to be "unlawful, disorderly, seditious, and against the peace . . . of this Commonwealth; and punish those who appear at such meetings."[14]

Sullivan "hoped and expected" Massachusetts to "enact laws declaring the printing, publishing, and circulating papers and pamphlets on slavery; and also the holding of meetings to discuss slavery and Abolition, *to be public and indictable offenses.*" Failure to suppress abolition, he accurately (if prematurely) warned, would lead to integrated schools, "colored men" admitted to all the occupations of life, colored army commanders, colored jurymen, and colored legislators.[15]

The *Evening Post* carried a debate between two correspondents, "Plain Truth" and "Veto," on legal justification for suppression of abolition. For Plain Truth, libel was not protected expression. A publication that had the "direct tendency . . . to excite *rebellion against the laws* is libelous."[16] Abolitionist expression had the plain and natural tendency to excite slave insurrections. Therefore, "these firebrands of sedition—these fanatical disturbers of the publick peace" should be surrendered to "the indignant justice of their country." Nor would the defense of truth be sufficient to provide constitutional protection. Plain Truth insisted that truth was only a defense when published for good motives and justifiable ends.[17]

Writing in the same paper, Veto criticized Plain Truth's analysis. Veto had no sympathy for abolitionists, who he believed were guilty of "virtual though unintentional urging of insurrection and massacre." Still, Veto opposed the demand that Northern states suppress abolitionist publications and protested "in the name of freedom and free discussion." He wrote, "I deny totally that the Northern Legislatures have the power to prevent the publication of any document whatever."[18] So far, Veto's remarks could be read as only condemnation of prior restraint. But Veto went further. He cited the New York constitution: "Every citizen may freely speak, write and publish, his sentiments *on all subjects* being responsible for the abuse of that right, and no law shall be passed to restrain or abridge the liberty of speech or the press. What can our legislature, were it ever so well disposed, do in the teeth of this provision?"[19]

Veto insisted that Northerners had abolished slavery because they were determined not to permit the "odious" institution to "endanger the right of free discussion." Remarkably, Southern demands contained "the distinct admission" that slavery "will not bear discussion. They say expressly that they cannot permit any examination of it." The North, Veto announced, would not cooperate in the "Southern plan of abridging private right. We have nothing here that will not bear the broad light of truth."[20]

In September 1835, Veto responded directly to Plain Truth's plan to ban discussion of abolition as libel. He insisted that a person accused of criminal libel could defend himself by establishing the truth of the assertions, a good motive in publishing them, and a justifiable end in view at the time of publication. He cited Chancellor Kent for the proposition that the state constitution guaranteed the accused the right to present facts to the jury to establish good motives and justifiable ends.[21]

Veto envisioned a very interesting political trial. If Mr. Tappan or the editor of the *Emancipator* were indicted for a libel tending to stir up slave revolt by saying that "slavery is a cruel institution, that it originated in robbery, that it leads to oppression on the part of the master, and misery on the party of the slave . . . &c. &c." then "Mr. Tappan or the Editor would have a right to produce evidence to prove the truth of the facts so alleged by him and that no judge would dare shut it out." He could then proceed to prove a good motive—a humane desire to "free the Africans from bondage." He could show that his action was justified by showing that slavery "is a serious evil to those states in which it exists." He added that "under our present Constitution no law can be passed which shall make the course to be pursued on an indictment for libel any different from what I have now described it to be, and . . . the *'tendency'* of the writing has nothing to do with the matter."[22]

Finally, Veto quoted the argument of Justice Smith Thompson in *People v. Croswell*.[23] If English law were the standard, then "all those enlightened and manly discussions which prepared and matured the great events of our Revolution, or which, in a more recent period pointed out the recklessness and folly of the confederation and roused the nation to throw it aside and to erect a better government on its ruins" would be suppressible. These were libels on the existing establishments, because they tended to defame them. "THEY WERE, HOWEVER, LIBELS FOUNDED IN TRUTH AND DICTATED BY WORTHY MOTIVES."[24]

Veto's conception of free speech was more protective of political expression than the conception he criticized. But, ultimately, it left protection for freedom of speech in the hands of juries and limited political speech to "truth" spoken for justifiable ends. Its most libertarian feature was that it rejected the idea that bad tendencies justify punishment. Other Northern writers suggested that protection for abolitionist speech was broader. Under state constitutions, they insisted, no law could be passed to punish political opinion.[25]

In 1836, there was a common law trial involving sedition in the District of Columbia. Reuben Crandall was tried for circulating incendiary (abolitionist) papers in the District. The indictment cited the tract's argument that emancipation was in the best interest of the slaveholders. This was so because "[t]he slave will become conscious, sooner or later of his strength. . . . His torch will be at the threshold, and his knife at the throat of the planter."[26] The prosecution was based not on a statute, but on the common law of sedition. Indeed, the prosecutor, Francis ("Oh, say can you see") Scott Key, insisted that "[t]he repeal of the sedition law left the common law, by which these offenses always were punishable, in full force."[27] Although Crandall possessed a number of copies of the abolitionist tract and had allowed one critic of abolitionism to take a copy away and read it, proof that he had been circulating the tracts in Washington to propagate abolitionist ideas was thin. The jury acquitted.

Group Libel

Southern representatives argued that abolitionist petitions and pamphlets were like ordinary libel of an individual except that an entire class was libeled—slaveholders. Senator John C. Calhoun complained of references made to slaveholders as dealers in human flesh and pirates. Libel of individuals was unprotected expression, so libel of the group of slaveholders was also unprotected, and therefore justified refusing to receive petitions for abolition.[28] By implication the argument also justified Northern action to suppress abolition as criminal libel. Representative Henry Hammond clearly thought libel of Southerners (or slaveholders) as a group should be treated like individual libel: "Did freedom of speech or freedom of the press allow of licentiousness? If a man in New York were to say of his neighbor what those papers say of the Southern people, would he not be indicted as a slanderer? And if he wrote the slanders would he not be indicted as a libeler? Then are not the people of the South entitled to the same protection?"[29]

In spite of this creative theory, there seem to have been no Northern group libel prosecutions for criticizing slaveholders. Bishop suggested that petitions, like court proceedings, received very broad protection against libel actions.[30] Today, at common law, libel is typically not applicable to members of very large groups.[31] But if group libel and seditious libel were not effective tools of suppression, an individual libel action occasionally was successful.

Libel of a Private Person

In 1830 William Lloyd Garrison was indicted for criminal libel. Garrison was coeditor (with the Quaker Benjamin Lundy) of the newspaper, *The Genius of Universal Emancipation* published in Baltimore, Maryland. Garrison had published an article noting (correctly) that Francis Todd of Newburyport, Massachusetts, owned a ship that had transported a cargo of slaves from Maryland to New Orleans. (While the foreign slave trade was criminal, domestic trade was not.) Garrison asserted, incidentally, that the slaves were chained and kept between decks and that commerce in slaves could account for Todd's extraordinary wealth. Although this part of Garrison's article was not mentioned in the indictment against him, evidence for the prosecution indicated that it was false. In fact, prosecution witnesses said, the slaves were allowed to walk on the deck and were not chained. Furthermore, this was Todd's first venture into the domestic slave trade.[32] Garrison's article appeared under the headline "The Ship Francis." Garrison wrote:

> I do not repeat the fact because it is a rare instance of domestic piracy, or because the case was attended with extraordinary circum-

stances; for the horrible traffic is briskly carried on, and the transportation was effected in the ordinary manner. I wish merely to
illustrate New-England humanity and morality. I am resolved to
cover with thick infamy all who were concerned in this nefarious
business. . . . It is no worse . . . to engage in the foreign slave trade,
than to pursue a similar trade along our own coasts; and the men
who have the wickedness to participate therein, for the purpose
of heaping up wealth, should be SENTENCED TO SOLITARY CON-
FINEMENT FOR LIFE; they are the enemies of their own species
—highway robbers and murderers; and their final doom will be,
unless they speedily repent, to occupy the lowest depths of per-
dition.[33]

Though the Maryland law recognized truth as a defense, the jury convicted Garrison. He was sentenced to a fine of fifty dollars or prison for
six months. Since he could not pay the fine, Garrison was imprisoned.
He was freed after forty-nine days in jail when New York philanthropist
Arthur Tappan paid his fine. Shipowner Todd later sued Garrison civilly.
The case was brought to trial while Garrison was out of town, and Todd
recovered a verdict of one thousand dollars, which, however, he made no
effort to collect.[34]

Garrison devoted his time in jail to writing an account of his trial, an
account he expanded and republished in 1834. He said he republished the
account because his enemies used his libel conviction to defame him.[35]
Garrison's pamphlets about the trial noted that libel prosecutions tested
"how far [freedom of the press] has been restricted by power . . . or perverted by licentiousness." In his case, he thought the answer was clear. He
condemned his trial as "a burlesque upon the constitution."[36]

Garrison insisted that it was his "right—and no body of men can legally deprive me of it—to interrogate the moral aspect and public utility
of every pursuit or traffic. . . . Free inquiry is the essence, the life blood
of liberty."[37] The 1834 version of his account of the trial republished editorials expressing astonishment at the libel verdict against him, along
with a resolution of the Manumission Society of North Carolina. The
society denounced the "illegal and unconstitutional decision in Garrison's case" and insisted that he "did not surpass that liberty which is
guaranteed to the press by the constitution of the United States."[38] In
his biography of Garrison, Henry Mayer suggests that the prosecution

against Garrison was politically inspired. Mayer chronicles the later use Garrison's enemies made of libel law and of his criminal conviction.[39]

In his account of his trial, Garrison noted that prosecutions of editors were rare, a fact he attributed to "the republican nature of our government, the equity of our laws, and the rights secured to the press by the constitution." Still, he thought he saw a growing tendency of courts to stifle free inquiry.[40] William H. Seward, the Whig and later Republican politician who became governor of New York and later Lincoln's secretary of state, had an additional explanation for the lack of prosecutions—the reliance on counterspeech. He cited the proliferation of presses, books, and newspapers. The political press, he noted, was "divided between contending parties, and again subdivided with nice adaptation to the tempers and tastes, the passions and prejudices of the community," and it conducted party warfare with "energy, zeal, and . . . unsparing severity." The press, Seward reported, "no longer fears the . . . frowns of power." Instead, it "not infrequently forms public opinion which controls everything." Still, it was not despotic. The multiplicity of presses and its "divisions distract its conduct and prevent a concentration of its powers upon any one object." It was often "capricious and often licentious." Yet "if it assails, it arms the party assaulted with equal weapons of defence, and yields redress for the injuries it inflicts."[41]

Prosecution Under the Common Law

In his message to the Massachusetts legislature, Governor Edward Everett invoked the constitutional "compact" that recognized slavery and conceded to the Southern states "important rights and privileges connected with it. Every thing that tends to disturb the relations created by this compact is at war with its spirit; and whatever, by direct and necessary operation, is calculated to excite an insurrection among the slaves, has been held . . . an offense against the peace of this Commonwealth, which may be prosecuted as a misdemeanor at common law."[42]

In spite of Southern requests to suppress abolitionist expression in Massachusetts and his suggestion of common law prosecutions for publications with a direct tendency to lead to slave revolts, Everett was unwilling to endorse general statutes for the suppression of abolitionist publications. This was because "the genius of our institutions and the character of our people are entirely repugnant to laws impairing the liberty of speech and of the press, even for the sake of repressing its abuses."[43] Everett called on patriotic citizens to abstain from discussion.[44] If a direct tendency to cause slave revolts required transmission to the South, Everett's theory was limited to publications sent South. Some critics, however, assumed that Everett's theory justified the suppression of abolitionist publications aimed only at Northerners.[45]

There seem to have been no Northern prosecutions based on the common law breach of the peace theory or any other common law theory. In the District of Columbia, as noted above, Reuben Crandall was prosecuted for the common law crime of sedition. There were calls for such prosecutions in New York State, as the *Washington Globe* reported: "[G]rand jurors of Oneida county . . . presented the abolition publications as incendiary and call on the people to 'destroy all such publications, wherever and whenever they can be found.'" The *Globe* expressed its approval, and the newspaper and the grand jury did not seem to limit their strictures to papers sent South. The *Globe* embraced the bad tendency test: papers "tending to excite insurrection and to break up the peace and harmony of States, are certainly as indictable as libels leading to breaches of the peace between individuals."[46]

The theories discussed above all turned on the issue of whether abolitionist expression was constitutionally protected. The issue of extradition was somewhat different. It focused on one mechanism of suppression.

Extradition—Prosecution of Northerners Under Southern Laws

Yet another legal theory to suppress abolitionists for publications reaching the South was to punish Northern disseminators under Southern laws in Southern courts. This "bright idea,"[47] as abolitionist legal theorist William Jay ironically called it, had obvious advantages. Virtually the entire abolitionist leadership could be prosecuted. The prosecutions would take place in a venue where juries would be most sympathetic to slavery and most hostile to abolitionists. The claim was not entirely implausible. Southerners argued by analogy that a culprit who fired a mortar across state lines from a Northern to a Southern state should be extradited. Why should the rule be different for abolitionists launching their incendiary verbal missiles from the North to the South?[48]

Southerners advanced two theories to justify extradition, one based on comity and one that might be called "constructive flight." Comity originated as a doctrine between independent nations. In international law, one nation could, and sometimes did, extradite its citizens who offended the law of another. Southerners insisted that comity was even more appropriate between sister states. As for the second theory, the federal Constitution provided for delivery of persons "charged in any State with Treason, Felony, or other Crime, who shall flee from Justice, and be found in another State."[49] In this case some Southerners insisted on a liberal construction of the Constitution to prevent abolitionists from escaping justice.

Northerners disagreed with both theories. "Novus Anglus," writing for the *New Haven Herald*, insisted that abolitionists had never been in the South and therefore had not fled from it as the Constitution contemplated. As to comity, extradition was "conceded only in extreme cases, where the offenses charged are of the deepest dye, & equally criminal by the laws of every State." A slight offense in one state might be punishable by death in another. Some states would grant a fair trial, but in others the trial would be a mockery. South Carolina, Novus Anglus noted, nullified the tariff of 1828 and made attempted enforcement a crime. If the state had attempted to enforce the law of treason, would the Northern editor who urged enforcement and sent his paper to Charleston be extradited?[50]

Novus Anglus believed extradition would undermine the freedom of the press in the North. Connecticut made truth a defense to libel, but "in some of our sister states, proof of the truth of the libel would be no justification at all." In fact, Southern laws typically were written in terms of the bad tendency of the expression or directly forbade certain types of expression. Truth, apparently, was irrelevant. Extradition would provide a power over the press "which would prove absolutely fatal to the liberties of the country. A publication innocent in Connecticut, because true, might subject the writer to be whipped in one state, branded in another, imprisoned in a third, and finally perhaps, to be hung under the . . . laws or usages of a fourth." Such a power would destroy freedom.[51]

The extradition theories were tested, at least in the political arena. Governor John Gayle of Alabama demanded the extradition of Robert Williams for publication of the *Emancipator*, the "seditious" paper that had said "'God commands, and all nature cries out, that man should not be held as property.'" Governor Gayle insisted that the constitutional provision for delivery of fugitives should be liberally construed because "it is in favour of the rights of the states, and because, without such construction, they will be deprived of the power of self protection." The word "flee" he insisted was synonymous with the word "evade." Even independent states under the doctrine of comity should surrender serious offenders against the laws of other states. The problem with comity, as Gayle recognized, was that it left "too much in the power of the applied to, to judge of the nature of the crime."[52]

Governor William Marcy of New York refused to extradite Williams. Williams had not fled from Alabama, Marcy noted, since he had never been there. Finally, Governor Marcy lectured Governor Gayle on the dangers of loose construction. "If your construction be correct, [the fugitive-from-justice] clause has conferred the power on each state to pass laws that have an extra-territorial operation, and to prescribe rules to which the citizens of all the other states must conform."[53] This, Marcy insisted, was a serious diminution of state rights. As Southerners saw it, however, abolitionists were being sought for acts which had an effect outside of the state where they resided.

Demands for the suppression of abolitionist publications, petitions, and associations produced, in turn, both Northern resistance and defense of freedom of speech, press, and petition. In 1835, 1836, and 1837, major controversies erupted over abolitionists' use of the Post Office, over petitions, over Northern legislation to suppress abolition, and, as we have seen, over extradition. While the controversies were distinct, they involved common elements—the limits of free speech, press, and petition rights; the effort to remove the issue of slavery from the political agenda; and broadly speaking, the issue of extra-territoriality. Would aspects of the slave code be enforced in the North or would the liberties enjoyed by Northerners imperil slavery?

Southern demands for laws to suppress abolitionist speech and press in the North changed public opinion in the North—a "great reaction" *Niles' Weekly Register* called it—even among those who had been disposed to put down the abolitionists. The *Weekly Register* now saw the free speech and press issue as producing sectional divisions: "The *Missouri question* is revived in another shape, and in a highly excited manner."[54] Before demands to suppress abolition by Northern censorship laws, papers like the *Weekly Register*, the *Evening Post*, and the *Washington Globe* had largely presented the abolitionists through the words of their opponents. They portrayed abolitionists as "incendiaries" and "miserable fanatics." On the free speech issue, at least, the *Weekly Regis-*

ter and the *Post* now occasionally directly quoted what the abolitionists had to say: slavery was a threat to the liberty of the North. The *Weekly Register* republished an antislavery poem by Quaker poet and antislavery activist John Greenleaf Whittier:

> Is't not enough that this is borne?
>   And, asks our haughty neighbor more?
> Must fetters which his slaves have worn
>   Clank round the Yankee farmer's door?
> Must *he* be told, beside his plough,
>   *What* he must speak, and *when* and *how*?[55]

"The time is coming," the *Evening Post* announced in November 1835, "when the freemen of the Northern states must decide whether their legislation shall be that of their own will or dictated to them by the slaveholding sections of the Union."[56]

Many Northerners rebelled at the idea of protecting slavery from all criticism. The governor of Georgia had suggested that if abolitionists *"only have to encounter the weapon of reason and argument, have we not reason to fear*, that their untiring efforts may succeed in misleading the majority." In response, the *Evening Post* insisted it was unwilling to protect a system unable to survive reason and argument.[57] Writing about the censorship at the Charleston post office, the *Post* wrote that neither the government nor mobs should be permitted to enforce political orthodoxy.[58]

One significant effect of the effort to silence abolitionists was that it produced a defense of freedom of expression. By 1859 a broad defense of free expression on the subject of slavery was a central part of the ideology of the Republican Party. In the eyes of many, free expression became a right of American citizens. But from 1835 through much of 1837 the idea of a national right to free speech that limited state abridgments was still in its infancy.

The Defense of Free Speech

William Ellery Channing

Even before the 1837 killing of an abolitionist editor defending his press from an antiabolition mob, more and more people began to defend free speech and press and to criticize mobs. One early defender of free speech was William Ellery Channing, the great Unitarian minister. In 1835, Channing wrote his book *Slavery*, a moderate antislavery manifesto. Channing's views epitomized the nonabolitionist, antislavery, pro–free speech perspective.

While Channing was antislavery, he was no abolitionist. He found abolitionist criticism too often harsh and uncharitable. Channing opposed the typical abolitionist mode of agitating the slavery question, but he favored discussion. "There was never such an obligation to discuss slavery as at this moment," Channing wrote,

> when recent events have done much to unsettle and obscure men's minds in regard to it. This result is to be ascribed in part to the injudicious vehemence of those who have taken into their hands the care of the slave. . . . Let no man touch the great interest of humanity, who does not strive to sanctify himself for the work by cleansing his heart of all wrath and uncharitableness, who cannot hope that he is in a measure baptized unto the spirit of universal love. Even sympathy with the injured and oppressed may do harm, by being partial, exclusive, and bitterly indignant.[59]

Still, Channing defended the rights of abolitionists to engage in free speech about slavery—his was one of a number of early protests against denials of free speech—and he rejected mob rule. One problem with mob rule, as Channing and others pointed out, was that it was inconsistent with representative government. The theory of the American nation was that the people were sovereign and that their will, expressed through representative institutions, should control. This will was filtered and checked in many ways. But, in theory at least, these limits were imposed by the people themselves in their federal and state constitutions. A corollary to the idea of popular sovereignty was that the people had the right to set the agenda and that citizens had the right to raise issues for general consideration.

Mobs violated republican government in two ways. Because mobs circumvented established institutions for determining popular will, the rule imposed by the mob was not the legitimate voice of the people. Second, because mobs kept matters off the agenda, they prevented the people from considering issues and alternatives in the first place.

Channing made the first point quite clearly. "Mobs call themselves, and are called, the People, when in truth they assail immediately the sovereignty of the People. . . . [T]he People is Sovereign. But by the People we mean not an individual here and there, not a knot of twenty or a hundred or a thousand individuals in this or that spot, but the Community formed into a body politic, and expressing and executing its will through regularly appointed organs. There is but one expression of the will or Sovereignty of the People, and this is Law."[60]

The argument that the law was the only form by which the will of the people could be legitimately executed left open the possibility of silencing abolitionists through law rather than mobs. At times Channing suggested that, if changes were required, the matter should be put before the legislature or a state constitutional convention. But in the end, he implied that silencing abolitionists was not consistent with representative government because it precluded popular choice.

> Of all powers, the last to be intrusted to the multitude of men is that of determining what questions shall be discussed. The greatest truths are often the most unpopular and exasperating; and were they to be denied discussion, till the many should be ready to accept them, they would never establish themselves in the general mind. The progress of society depends on nothing more than on the exposure of time-sanctioned abuses, which cannot be touched without offending multitudes, than on the promulgation of principles which are in advance of public sentiment and practice, and which are consequently at war with the habits and prejudices, and immediate interests of large classes of the community. Of consequence, the multitude, if once allowed to dictate or proscribe subjects of discussion, would strike society with spiritual blindness and death. The world is to be carried forward by truth, which at first offends, which wins its way by degrees, which the many hate and would rejoice to crush.[61]

Suppression by law of abolitionist ideas was not consistent with Channing's free speech philosophy.

Channing believed that directly inciting slaves to rebel could and should be made criminal. But Southern defenders of slavery and their Northern allies insisted on a level of suppression that went far beyond that. They justified suppressing speech that did not directly counsel slave revolts because, they insisted, antislavery speech, simply by virtue of its denunciation of slavery, had a natural tendency to produce revolts and disunion. Channing and others squarely rejected the bad tendency rationale.

> Of all pretenses for resorting to lawless force, the most dangerous is the *tendency* of measures or opinions. Almost all men see ruinous tendencies in whatever opposes their particular interests or views. All the political parties which have convulsed our country have seen tendencies to national destruction in the principles of their opponents. So infinite are the connections and consequences of human affairs, that nothing can be done in which some dangerous tendency may not be detected. . . . There is a tendency in laying bare of deep-rooted abuses to throw a community into a storm. . . . Exclude all enterprises which *may* have evil results, and human life will stagnate. . . . The truth is, that any exposition of slavery, no matter from whom it may come, may chance to favor revolt. It may chance to fall into the hands of a fanatic. . . . A casual, innocent remark in conversation may put wild projects into the unbalanced or disordered mind of some hearer. Must we then live in perpetual silence?[62]

As Northern critics noted, the bad tendency rationale might require banning publication of the Declaration of Independence.[63]

The Abolitionist Defense

At the height of the crisis of 1835, James G. Birney, the Kentucky abolitionist editor who had moved to Ohio, wrote to Gerrit Smith. Birney referred to "the exorbitant *claims* of the South on the liberties of the free states—demanding that every thing that has heretofore been deemed precious to them should be surrendered, in order that the Slaveholder might be perfectly at ease in his iniquity."[64] Birney suggested an irrepressible conflict between principles of liberty and slavery, an idea that would later become commonplace in the Republican Party. He and many other Americans reframed the debate over slavery into a debate over the liberty of American citizens: "The contest is becoming—has become,—one, not alone of freedom for the *black*, but of freedom for the *white*. It has now become absolutely necessary, that Slavery should cease in order that freedom may be preserved to any portion of our land. The antagonistic principles of liberty and slavery have been roused into action and one or the other must be victorious. There will be no cessation of the strife, until Slavery shall be exterminated, or liberty destroyed."[65] The attacks on free expression for abolitionists shaped Birney's thinking and would shape that of a host of others.

The call for a New York antislavery society convention warned that "the privileges of the free are now doomed as a sacrifice on the altar of perpetual slavery. . . . [W]e shall speedily be all free or all slaves together."[66] The platform of the Convention resolved that "free enquiry and discussion is the corner stone of liberty; and the safeguard of truth, and is dreaded only by tyrants and the wicked: and that it is the RIGHT of American citizens to discuss the subject of slavery as well any other subject; and to express their opinions freely, and fully; privately, and openly."[67] It denounced "any attempt to control or deter this freedom" as "an assumption of illegal power, and an infringement on *rights* given us, by God, and guaranteed to us by the Constitution of the United States, and of the individual states." Free discussion was a right abolitionists would never relinquish. "This high constitutional privilege we shall assert, and exercise in all places, and at all times. . . ." The meeting resolved that "principles, opinions, institutions and usages, which cannot bear thorough examination and inquiry are unworthy of Americans, and ought to be abandoned."[68]

While some others analyzed the rights of free speech and press in light of positive law, abolitionists insisted that the rights were God-given rights that state and federal constitutions secured but did not create. "No," said Gerrit Smith, "the constitution of my nation and state create none of my rights. They do, at the most, but recognize what is not theirs to give." The abolitionist convention in Utica in 1835 resolved that "the right of free discussion" was "given to us by our God."[69]

Still, abolitionists appealed to constitutional guarantees, and from 1835 through 1837 they typically appealed to both federal and state guarantees. Federal guarantees prevented federal censorship, they suggested, and state guarantees prevented state suppression. Indeed, abolitionists suggested that their critics appealed not to the Constitution but to their understanding of the North/South bargain or compact that the critics claimed underlay it. Explicit constitutional guarantees, the American Anti-Slavery Society complained, were thus "set at naught by men, whom your favour has invested with a brief authority." These men measured liberty of conscience, of speech, and of the press not by the Constitution but by "the COMPACT by which the South engages on certain conditions to give its trade and votes to Northern men. . . . All rights not allowed by this compact, we now hold at sufferance."[70]

While abolitionists appealed to the federal Constitution and to the constitutions of the Northern and Southern states,[71] in the years 1835–36 they rarely suggested unequivocally that Southern censorship violated the federal Constitution. The paradigm of 1835–37 was that of the semi-sovereign state. In the end, the position tolerating Southern suppression was unstable: it left the rights of opponents of slavery in the South to be decided by Southern courts, from which no appeal existed.

Still abolitionists insisted that states—with their own constitutional guarantees—lacked power to suppress abolitionist expression. In the long run, a party dedicated to the ultimate extinction of slavery could not accept a decision to ban its discussion in the South. To accept such limitations left opponents of slavery preaching antislavery where slavery did not exist. So it is hardly surprising that many abolitionists, and later Republicans, soon embraced the idea that federal guarantees for free speech, free press, and freedom of religion were needed to protect Americans throughout the nation and that Southern suppression of antislavery speech violated and should be seen to violate federal constitutional principles.

Once slavery became a political issue, indeed the central political issue, the tension between ideas of republican government and slavery became apparent and unbearable. The Constitution contained guarantees drawn from the experience of the struggle for liberty in England. These guarantees were designed to protect representative government. Congress could not abridge free speech, free press, or freedom of religion. Political speech could not be treason. The people had a right to petition, and members of Congress were protected from punishment for things said in congressional debates. All of these provisions posed threats to the institution of slavery.

The Constitution also guaranteed to each state a republican form of government. But in much of the South, as the Civil War approached, one of the major political factions of the day could not advocate its ideas, nor could anyone discuss peaceful elimination of slavery. To abolitionists, and later to Republicans, this was not republican government. It was, as Republicans in 1859 saw it, despotism.

In contrast to those in Congress who insisted that states retained the power to suppress abolition though the federal government did not, representatives of the Massachusetts Anti-Slavery Society, like many nonabolitionists, suggested that both governments were equally re-stricted from suppressing political opinion. "The power of restricting freedom of speech and of the press was withheld from the Legislature of MASSACHUSETTS, *for the same reason* that it was withheld from the GENERAL GOVERNMENT, and to *the same extent.*"[72]

Abolitionists appearing before a committee of the Massachusetts leg-islature insisted that, in violation of constitutional provisions, the "slaveholding States . . . have bound the lips and pen of the *free white cit-izens*." These Southern statutes and similar proposals to limit abolition-ist speech in the North were justified with the claim that "the Legislature is invested with authority to suppress whatever discussion or publica-tion shall be deemed subversive of the public safety or peace." In short, speech that had bad tendencies could be suppressed. Such an assump-tion of power by the legislature, the Massachusetts Anti-Slavery Society insisted, "would nullify the provisions of the Constitution, and place that discretionary power in legislators, which it was the manifest intent of the Constitution to withhold from them." The object of the constitu-tional restriction was that "the legislature shall be intrusted with no such discretionary power; shall take into consideration no such sup-posed contingencies."[73]

In their rejection of the bad tendency test, Massachusetts abolitionists (like Tunis Wortman before them)[74] cited the Virginia Statute of Reli-gious Freedom. They suggested its principles were equally applicable to speech and press.

> To suffer the civil magistrate to intrude his power into the FIELD
> OF OPINION, and restrain the profession or propagation of princi-
> ples, on supposition of their ill tendency, is a dangerous fallacy,
> which at once destroys all religious liberty, because, he, being of
> course the judge of that tendency, will make his opinions the rule
> of judgement, and approve or condemn the sentiments of others,
> only as they shall square with, or differ from his own. It is time
> enough for the rightful purposes of civil government, for its offi-
> cers to interfere, when principles break forth into OVERT ACTS
> against peace and order; and finally, truth is great, and will prevail,
> if left to herself; she is the proper and sufficient antagonist of
> error.[75]

Finally, abolitionists noted the extent of the violation of their rights. They could not travel in half the states of the Union without imperiling their lives. If the sentiments of Pinckney or Jefferson on the subject of slavery were found among their papers "our Southern brethren deem us worthy of public stripes." Though they paid like other citizens for the support of the United States Postal Service, "[w]e may use it only at the discretion of our Dictators."[76] The representatives of the Massachusetts Anti-Slavery Society asked their legislature "to maintain and assert the doctrines of freedom."[77] As we have seen, a significant number of influential nonabolitionists insisted on freedom for political opinion and that truth was the appropriate antidote for error. Like Madison's report on the Sedition Act, they insisted that constitutional guarantees of free speech were designed to change the common law.[78]

Women joined the abolitionist crusade and began to circulate and sign petitions for the abolition of slavery. A few made abolitionist speeches to "promiscuous" (that is, sexually integrated) audiences, a practice many found shocking.

The Grimké sisters were abolitionist activists from an aristocratic family in slaveholding South Carolina. Frustrated by the repressive atmosphere of Charleston, they had moved to the North, and they soon joined forces with Theodore Dwight Weld. (Angelina Grimké married him in 1838.) The Grimkés' impeccable Southern credentials made them especially embarrassing to the South. They wrote and spoke extensively against slavery.

In pamphlets, the Grimkés urged Southern women and clergymen to work against slavery. Charleston's postmasters publicly burned their pamphlets. Coached in public speaking by Theodore Weld, the Grimkés made a highly successful whirlwind speaking tour of New England that added many recruits to the abolitionist cause. In February 1838, Angelina Grimké became the first woman to address a committee of the Massachusetts legislature. In her speech she movingly explained why she was there: "As a Southerner, as a repentant slaveholder, and a moral being I feel I owe it to the suffering slave, and to the deluded master, to my country and to the world to do all that I can to overturn a system of complicated crimes, built upon the broken hearts and prostrate bodies of my countrymen in chains and cemented by the blood and sweat and tears of my sisters in bonds."[79]

Grimké insisted that free discussion in the North was a key to ending slavery in the South. She made this point by quoting reasons advanced by Southerners who demanded suppression of antislavery discussion in the North. Exhibit 1 was Duff Green, the editor of the pro-Calhoun

United States Telegraph. He wrote that the abolitionists did not intend slave insurrections, nor could they produce one if they wanted to. Instead, Green insisted, "we have the most to fear from the organised action upon the consciences and fears of the slaveholders themselves" and from creation of a "morbid sensibility on the question of slavery" among Southerners. Another example came from the Charleston *Southern Patriot*. The newspaper said the discussion of slavery in Congress would mean "in the lapse of a short period, [slavery would] be undermined." Grimké also quoted the report of a South Carolina legislative committee. The committee insisted that if abolitionists were permitted to continue with their falsehoods and misrepresentation in the North, the result would be "a body of public opinion which it would be impossible to resist, without separating ourselves from the social system of the rest of the civilized world." Grimké also pointed out a number of cases in which abolitionist literature was reaching people in the South, in spite of the Southern blockade.[80]

She agreed with a critic that "the tendencies of the age are toward Emancipation," but insisted "nothing but free discussion has produced this tendency." The "agitation of the subject" was changing public opinion.[81]

Given their faith in the right to free speech, reason, and free discussion, it is hardly surprising that the Grimkés indignantly rejected suggestions that women had no right, or a lesser right, to petition or to speak. To Catherine Beecher's claim that "Heaven has appointed to one sex the superior, and to the other the subordinate station," Angelina Grimké answered bluntly: "This is an assertion without proof." The rights of men and women were the same. If a man "may act on society by the collision of intellect in public debate," women must have the same right.[82] Women, she insisted, must be permitted to fully exercise the "right of petition." It was their only political right. Women were suffering taxation without representation, just as the American revolutionaries had. Like them, they should be entitled to have a voice in the laws that affected them, and at the very least to petition.[83]

In 1838 in a debate over the gag rule, a congressman from Maryland suggested that many of the petitioners were women and suggested that "these females" should stick to their proper domestic sphere. John Quincy Adams responded in a long speech filled with citations to the political exploits of queens and other women, including one who dressed as a man and fought bravely in the American Revolution. Adams said he had the honor to present the memorials, petitions, remonstrances, of more than fifty thousand women, in this House. . . . I do believe . . . that four fifths, at least, have been obtained by the influence of two women of South Carolina, natives of that State; from their position, well acquainted with the practical operation of the system; intelligent, well educated, highly accomplished, and bearing a name South Carolina will not disown. . . . Their own names are attached to one of these petitions; and they are almost the only ones with which I have the honor to be personally acquainted. I say I have that honor; for I deem it an honor. And yet their right to petition has been openly denied.

Adams suggested the ladies would be willing to discuss these points with the gentleman from South Carolina. "And if he does enter on the discussion, all I shall say is that I wish him well out of it." At that point the reporter recorded "[A laugh]."[84] Adams denied that women should stick to domestic matters. To the argument that they should not be permitted to petition because they lacked the right to vote, John Quincy Adams, first asked if it was "so clear that they have no such right" as the right to vote. At any rate, he insisted, the argument was "adding one injustice to another."[85]

Political activity by women like the Grimkés provoked a hostile reaction from some ministers and some abolitionists. Criticism ranged from the idea that women were violating the natural order by engaging in politics to the argument that, as a matter of prudence, issues of the rights of women should be avoided. The Grimkés insisted on directly meeting the issue of the right of women to be politically active. They compared the attack on the right of women to speak to the attack on free speech rights for abolitionists, and they insisted that the denial of free speech rights to women would furnish a precedent for more sweeping invasions of freedom of speech.[86] The issue of women's rights eventually split the abolitionist movement.

So far, most defenders of free speech have seen it as a precious American right protected from the federal government under the federal constitution and from state action by state constitutions. Soon, however, a new and more national vision of free speech began to emerge.

In 1837 Elijah Lovejoy, an antislavery editor, was killed defending his press from an antiabolition mob. This event, coming after so many other attacks on free speech on the subject of slavery, galvanized a strong and public reaction supportive of freedom of speech. In reaction to attackson freedom of speech and press another potent idea gained ground: the idea that freedom of speech, press, and religion (all of which were implicated in Lovejoy's case) were national constitutional privileges belonging to all American citizens—privileges recognized and given at least moral authority by the federal Constitution.

10

Elijah Lovejoy: Mobs, Free Speech, and

the Privileges of American Citizens

All persons born or naturalized in the United States are citizens of the United States and of the State wherein they reside. No state shall make or enforce any law which shall abridge the privileges or immunities of citizens of the United States; nor shall any State deprive any person of life, liberty, or property without due process of law; nor deny to any person within its jurisdiction the equal protections of the law.—Section 1 of the Fourteenth Amendment, proposed 1866, ratified 1868

LOVEJOY'S ANTISLAVERY PRESS

On November 7, 1837, Elijah P. Lovejoy, the abolitionist editor of the *Alton Observer* and a Presbyterian minister, was killed defending his fourth printing press from an antiabolition mob. Three of his presses had already been destroyed. When Lovejoy's third press had arrived in the free state of Illinois, a mob had smashed it and dumped it into the Mississippi River.[1] The mob was adamant that no abolitionist paper should be permitted in Alton. Lovejoy was determined to continue publishing. Before the arrival of the fourth press, Lovejoy and a group of supporters appealed to the city authorities for protection, as they had done previously. Alton Mayor John Krum requested that the Common Council of Alton authorize him to appoint special constables to maintain order.[2] But the city council refused to act, except to advise Lovejoy and his friends not to reestablish a press in Alton.[3]

Lovejoy and his supporters put the new press in a warehouse and armed themselves. The mob stoned the warehouse, and the mob and the defenders exchanged shots. (Which side fired first was disputed by some papers at the time although most historians say the first shot came from the mob.)[4] One of the defenders of the press killed a member of the mob; other mob members got ladders, and one climbed up to set fire to the roof of the warehouse. As Lovejoy tried to shoot the arsonist, he was shot and killed.[5]

Lovejoy's death was the climax of his struggle for free speech and press on the subject of slavery. It was also a climactic event in the larger struggle for free speech about slavery and against northern mobs determined to silence abolitionists. The national reaction to Lovejoy's death was profound. For many, the event had symbolic importance that transcended Lovejoy and the issue of abolition: Lovejoy's death was an attack on free speech, free press, and republican government—not just for abolitionists, but for all. This was so because, as these people saw it, a principle turned against abolitionists today could be turned on other groups tomorrow. The attack on Lovejoy became a metaphor. The killing of Lovejoy was an attack on Northern liberty by the slave system of the South. The death raised questions of the nature of free speech, of the problem of private suppression of speech, and the nature and future of republican government.

The Lovejoy Story and the Free Speech Tradition

Lovejoy's struggle for free press and his death contributed to a great change in public discussion of free speech and press. It produced broad and strong condemnation of mob violence directed at antislavery expression. It also contributed to an emerging view that free speech and press were rights or "privileges" and "immunities" to which all American citizens were entitled everywhere in the United States. The "privileges or immunities of citizens of the United States" is a phrase that occurs in Section 1 of the Fourteenth Amendment (proposed twenty-nine years after Lovejoy's death). Those words have provoked legal controversy ever since. The firestorm of criticism that followed Lovejoy's death illuminates an early understanding of the "privileges" of citizens of the United States. The word "privilege" was commonly used from 1837 to 1868 to designate a national right to free speech. That understanding was shaped in part by public reaction to Lovejoy's dramatic death defending his press, an event well known to many framers and ratifiers of the Fourteenth Amendment.

Lovejoy's death raised enduring questions: Should speech be suppressed because of long-term dangers posed by the message? Should free speech principles be broadly defined to protect speech that the elite or even the majority find dangerous or evil? Since a function of free speech is to allow the people to set the political agenda, is it appropriate to put political topics off limits? Should controversial and despised speakers have access to a public forum to spread their messages? How consistently has the mainstream press supported broad free speech rights, and how much access does it provide for "radical" views that seem to threaten established interests?

The Lovejoy experience suggests that, as James Madison had expected,[6] constitutional guarantees of liberty do their work at popular levels as well as at the level of institutions such as the Supreme Court of the United States, state supreme courts, Congress, and state legislatures. Popular views limit and channel both legislation and private action, each of which can either constrain or empower speech.

Free Speech and Private Violence

Lovejoy's experience shows that free speech requires not only protection against governmental suppression, but also protection against private violence aimed at silencing speakers. Private (that is nongovernmental) attacks on free speech raise perplexing federal constitutional problems in a system where most constitutional guarantees of liberty have been interpreted merely to limit government, but not private, action. The problem of private suppression of speech, press, and association, which was so significant in the mid-1830s, surfaced again during Reconstruction. Then, Klan violence aimed at black and white Republicans helped end Republican rule in the South.[7] In many ways, the suppression of Republicans in the South after the Civil War replicated suppression of opponents of slavery before the war. Ultimately, with the development of the state action doctrine, the U.S. Supreme Court seemed to find that the federal government lacked constitutional power to punish many purely private attacks aimed at speech and press.[8] The doctrine may continue to limit federal power to power under the Fourteenth Amendment (as opposed, for example, to power under the commerce clause) to this day.[9] To the extent that public officials cooperate in the violent suppression of speech, however, federal power can reach otherwise "private" actors.[10]

In 1837, as today, politically motivated private violence raises thorny issues: What is the duty of federal, state, and local governments to protect advocates of unpopular causes? What should these governments do? Recently, people hostile to homosexuals aimed private violence at a lesbian center in Mississippi;[11] communists used violence against the Klan, and then the Klan killed communist marchers in Greensboro, North Carolina; in Pennsylvania, college students, unhappy with what they saw as a racist editorial policy, seized and destroyed copies of a school newspaper.[12] These actions are typically beyond the reach of Reconstruction-era civil rights statutes, as understood by the Court, though they usually violate state laws. So the nineteenth-century problem of private suppression resurfaces in different garb in the twentieth century.

THE ALTON TRAGEDY

Elijah P. Lovejoy, named for an Old Testament prophet, was born in Albion, Maine, in 1802. Lovejoy's father was a clergyman. After graduating from college and teaching school for a time, Elijah followed in his father's footsteps. He was licensed to preach by the Philadelphia Presbytery in 1833 and went to Saint Louis, in the slave state of Missouri, to edit the *Saint Louis Observer*.[13]

Lovejoy's writings reflected his strong, and sometimes intolerant, opinions. He insisted that he did not "wish to touch the rights belonging to any class of citizens, Catholic or Protestant, Jew or Mahometan." But he also asserted that "Popery and Freedom . . . are incompatible." He warned his countrymen "to be on their guard against . . . the hordes of ignorant, uneducated, vicious foreigners who are now flocking to our shores, and who, under the guidance of Jesuit Priests, are calculated, fitted and intended to subvert our liberties."[14]

Lovejoy became increasingly antislavery. In Missouri, he supported gradual emancipation. While generally in agreement with the ends the abolitionists espoused, he distanced himself from them by warning his readers against exciting "prejudices and bitterness."[15] As time went on, though, Lovejoy became more apocalyptic. In April 1835, he warned, "The groans, and sighs, and tears and blood of the poor slave have gone up as a memorial before the throne of Heaven. . . . [T]hey will descend in awful curses upon this land, unless averted by the speedy repentance of us all."[16] Still, Lovejoy continued to oppose the abolitionists' demand for "immediate and unconditional abolition."[17]

Lovejoy's editorial warnings of God's thunderbolts aimed at "authors of such cruel oppression" were soon followed by discussion of the upcoming state constitutional convention. Missouri faced a "crisis that calls for the exercise of all the candor, enlarged patriotism, and sound judgment of all our citizens. We have in our power to bequeath to posterity a benefit, for which all future generations shall bless us." His own candor included direct warnings of the dangers of slave revolts. To avoid such bloodshed, he advocated gradual emancipation.[18]

Lovejoy had taken other actions that shocked supporters of slavery. He had shipped some Bibles to Jefferson City and (apparently unknowingly) used a full-fledged abolition paper, the *Emancipator*, as packing paper. He had preached against slavery during a revival, denouncing it along with the sins of drinking and gambling. And, at a time when most of the nation's press suppressed any direct publication of abolitionist principles and documents, Lovejoy printed the platform of the American Anti-Slavery Society and expressed his agreement with most of the society's positions. In 1835, a public meeting, led by influential citizens of St. Louis, condemned abolitionists. The meeting

> [r]esolved, That the right of free discussion and freedom of speech exists under the constitution, but that being a conventional reservation made by the people in their sovereign capacity, does not imply a moral right on the part of the Abolitionists, to freely discuss the question of Slavery, either orally or through the medium of the press. It is the agitation of a question too nearly allied to the vital interests of the slave-holding states to admit of public disputation; and so far from the fact, that the movements of the Abolitionists are constitutional, they are in the greatest degree seditious, and calculated to incite insurrection and anarchy, and, ultimately, a disseverment of our prosperous Union.[19]

The resolutions further warned that the "infatuated Abolitionists" advanced a "doctrine of *amalgamation*," which would "reduce the high intellectual standard of the American mind to a level with the Hottentot." Finally, the resolution announced that "Slavery as it now exists . . . [is] sanctioned by the sacred Scriptures."[20]

Lovejoy printed the resolutions and responded to them in the November 5 issue of his paper. He insisted that he had not knowingly sent the *Emancipator* with the Bibles he shipped, but wrote, "I claim the *right* to send ten thousand of them if I choose, to as many of my fellow-citizens. Whether I will *exercise* that right or not, is for me, and not the *mob*, to decide."[21]

He insisted that the moral right to discuss slavery was not a matter for human legislation or resolutions. The true issue was the civil and political right to discuss slavery, and that was answered by the Missouri constitution: "That the free communication of thoughts and opinions is one of the invaluable rights of man, and every person may freely speak, write, and print ON ANY SUBJECT, being responsible for the abuse of that liberty."[22] If he abused his freedom of speech, he was amenable to the laws.

> But it is said that the right to hold slaves is a constitutional one, and therefore not to be called in question. I admit the premise, but deny the conclusion. . . . The Constitution declares that this shall be a perpetual republic, but has not any citizen the right to discuss, under that Constitution, the comparative merits of despotism and liberty? . . . Robert Dale Owen came to this city . . . openly proclaiming the doctrine that the institution of marriage was a curse to any community. . . . It was . . . an abominable doctrine, and one which, if acted out, would speedily reduce society to the level of barbarism . . . yet who thought of denying Mr. Owen . . . the perfect right of avowing such doctrines, or who thought of mobbing [him] . . . ?
>
> See the danger, and the natural and inevitable result to which the first step here will lead. To-day a public meeting declares that you shall not discuss the subject of Slavery. . . . The truth is, my fellow citizens, if you give ground a single inch, there is no stopping place.[23]

Lovejoy emphatically denied that the Bible sanctioned slavery. "What is the system of Slavery. . . ? It is a system of buying and selling immortal beings for the sake of gain; a system which forbids to man and woman the right of husband and wife . . . a system which tolerates . . . tearing husband and wife, parent and child asunder, chaining their victims together, and then driving them with a whip." Lovejoy further suggested that the real cause of opposition to the *Observer* was "its opposition to Popery."[24] "I *do*, therefore," Lovejoy insisted, "as an American citizen, and Christian patriot, and in the name of Liberty, and Law, and RELIGION, solemnly PROTEST against all these attempts . . . to frown down the liberty of the press, and forbid the expression of opinion."[25]

Lovejoy's defense of freedom of the press brought him expressions of support. But intense opposition continued, and he decided to move the press from St. Louis, Missouri, to Alton, in the free state of Illinois.

In the same issue of the *Observer* in which he announced his intention to move the paper to Illinois, Lovejoy editorialized against a "SAVAGE BARBARITY." A free black man named McIntosh had attempted to rescue a fellow sailor who was in the custody of law enforcement officers. When he in turn was arrested and told he could expect to spend five years in prison, the black man stabbed one of his captors to death. He was apprehended and jailed, but seized by a mob that tied him to a tree and burned him alive.[26] "It is not yet five years since the first mob . . . was organized in St. Louis. They commenced operations, by tearing down the brothels of the city. . . . The next achievement was to tear down a gambling-house. . . . The next and last we need not again repeat. . . . [I]t is difficult to withdraw our thoughts and feelings from the great provocation to violence. . . . [But w]e *must* stand by the constitution and laws or ALL IS GONE."[27]

More outrages followed. The local judge, aptly named Luke Lawless, charged the grand jury that if the death of the "murderer . . . was the act . . . of the multitude . . . of congregated thousands, seized upon and impelled by that mysterious, metaphysical, and almost electric frenzy . . . then, I say act not at all in the matter . . . —it is beyond the reach of human law."[28] The judge blamed the killing of one of the officers by the black man on the abolitionists, and he identified Lovejoy as one.[29] Lovejoy in turn criticized the judge as a foreigner and said that "[F]oreigners educated in the old world, never can come to a proper understanding of American constitutional law."[30] He detected in the judge's charge "the cloven foot of Jesuitism." "What is Jesuitism but another name for the doctrine that principles ought to change according to circumstances? And it is the very identical doctrine of the Charge." Finally, he answered the judge's suggestion that the office of the *Observer* was in danger because of what it had written about the McIntosh tragedy":

> To establish our institutions of civil and religious liberty, to obtain
> freedom of opinion and of the press, guaranteed by constitutional
> law, cost thousands, yea, tens of thousands of valuable lives. . . . We
> covet not the loss of property nor the honours of martyrdom; but
> better . . . that editor, printer, and publishers, should be chained to
> the same tree as M'Intosh, and share his fate, than that the doc-

trines promulgated by Judge Lawless from the bench, should become prevalent. For they are subversive of all law, and at once open the door for the perpetration, by a congregated mob, calling themselves the people, of every species of violence, and that too with perfect impunity.[31]

Though Lovejoy had announced his intention of moving to Alton, a St. Louis mob smashed the office of the *Observer*, but somehow failed to demolish the press. So the press survived, though not for long.[32]

Opposition dogged Lovejoy. On the arrival of the press in Alton, some men took it from the dock and threw it in the river.[33] Lovejoy replaced the press and continued to speak frankly against slavery and ever more favorably of abolition. On May 25, 1837, he wrote that the love of money was blunting the nation's moral sense. "The love of money is an earthborn, grovelling propensity, and it debases . . . all whom it influences." Slavery was one example: Lovejoy wrote that even Christian ministers, "reverend divines," taught that the Bible justified slavery. Future generations would find it difficult to believe. "Men were either too busy in making money . . . or too desirous to get a share of that earned by the forced labour of the poor slave, to hear his groans. His tears, mingled with his blood drawn by the whip of the merciless taskmaster, fell unheeded."[34]

On July 6, 1837, Lovejoy more formally aligned himself with abolitionists and advocated formation of an Illinois antislavery society.[35] Opposition to his paper mounted. On July 8, 1837, a handbill called for a meeting of "friends of the *Observer* dissatisfied with its course." The meeting expressed its "disapprobation of the course pursued by the Rev. E. P. Lovejoy, editor of the *Alton Observer*, in publishing and promulgating the doctrines of Abolitionism."[36] It found Lovejoy guilty of advocating abolitionist doctrines of "a most inflammatory character." Because Illinois was a free state, the meeting insisted, agitating the slavery issue in Illinois could do no good, but could do "much injury and damage" to Alton by antagonizing slave states. "[A]s we deprecate all violence of mobs," the meeting announced, "we now call on him, by our committee, and politely request a discontinuance of the publication of his incendiary doctrines."[37]

But Lovejoy did not desist. On July 20, 1837, he published an article explaining antislavery doctrines. What Lovejoy was saying is crucial to understanding the controversy. For this reason, I will set out Lovejoy's description of abolition principles at length.

FIRST PRINCIPLES

1. Abolitionists hold that "all men are born free and equal, endowed by their Creator with certain inalienable rights, among which are life, LIBERTY and the pursuit of happiness." They do not believe that these rights are abrogated, or at all modified by the color of the skin, but that they extend alike to every individual of the human family.

2. As the above mentioned rights are in their nature inalienable, it is not possible that one man can convert another into a piece of property, thus at once annihilating all his personal rights, without the most flagrant injustice and usurpation. But American slavery does this—it declares a slave to be a "THING," a "CHATTEL," an article of personal "PROPERTY," a piece of "MERCHANDISE," and now actually holds TWO AND A HALF MILLIONS of our fellowmen in this precise condition.

3. Abolitionists, therefore, hold American Slavery to be a *wrong*, a legalized system of inconceivable injustice, and a sin. That it is a sin against God, whose prerogative as the rightful owner of all human beings is usurped, and against the slave himself, who is deprived of the power to dispose of his services as conscience may dictate, or his Maker requires. And as whatever is morally wrong can never be politically right, and as the Bible teaches, and as abolitionists believe, that "righteousness exalteth a nation, while sin is a reproach to any people," they also hold that slavery is a political evil of unspeakable magnitude, and one which, if not removed, will speedily work the downfall of our free institutions, both civil and religious.

4. As the Bible inculcates upon man but one duty in respect to sin, and that is, immediate repentance, abolitionists believe that all who hold slaves, or who approve the practice in others, should *immediately* cease to do so.

5. Lastly. Abolitionists believe, that as all men are *born* free, so all who are now held as slaves in this country were BORN FREE, and that they are slaves now is the sin, not of those who introduced the race into this country, but of those, and those alone, who now hold them, and have held them in slavery from their birth. Let it be admitted, for argument's sake, that A., or B., has justly forfeited his title to freedom, and that he is now the rightful slave of C., bought with his money, how does this give C. a claim to the posterity of A.

down to the latest generation? And does not the guilt of enslaving the successive generations of A.'s posterity belong to their respective masters whoever they be? No where are the true principles of freedom and personal rights better understood than at the South, though their practice corresponds so wretchedly with their theory. Abolitionists adopt, as their own, the following sentiments expressed by Mr. Calhoun in a speech on the tariff question, delivered in the Senate of the United States in 1833: "He who *earns* the money—*who digs it out of the earth* with the sweat of his brow, has a *just-title* to it against the Universe. *No* one has a right to touch it, *without his consent*, except his government, and *it only* to the extent of its legitimate wants: to take more is *robbery*." Now, this is precisely what slaveholders do, and abolitionists do but echo back their own language when they pronounce it "*robbery*."

EMANCIPATION—WHAT IS MEANT BY IT?

Simply, that the slaves shall cease to be held as *property*, and shall, henceforth be held and treated as human beings. Simply, that we should take our feet from off their necks. Perhaps we cannot express ourselves better than to quote the language of another southerner. In reply to the question, what is meant by emancipation, the answer is—

"1. It is to reject with indignation the wild and guilty phantasy, that man can hold *property* in man. 2. To pay the laborer his hire, for he is worthy of it. 3. No longer to deny him the right to marriage, but to let every man have his own wife, as saith the apostle. 4. To let parents have their own children, for they are the gift of the Lord *to them*, and no one else has any right to them. 5. No longer to withhold the advantages of education and the privilege of reading the Bible. 6. To put the slave under the protection of law, instead of throwing him beyond its salutary influence."

Now, who is there that is opposed to slavery at all, and believes it to be wrong and a sin, but will agree to all this?

HOW AND BY WHOM IS EMANCIPATION TO BE EFFECTED?

To this question the answer is by the *masters themselves*, and by no others. No others can effect it, nor is it desirable that they should, even if they could. Emancipation, to be of any value to the slave, must be the free, voluntary act of the master, performed from a conviction of its propriety. This avowal may sound very strange to those who have been in the habit of taking the principles of the abolitionists from the misrepresentations of their opponents. Yet this is, and always has been, the cardinal principle of abolitionists. If it be asked, then, why they intermeddle in a matter where they can confessedly do nothing themselves in achieving the desired result, their reply is, that this is the very reason why they do and ought to intermeddle. It is because they cannot emancipate the slaves, that they call upon those who can to do it. Could they themselves do it, there would be no need of discussion—instead of discussing they would act, and with their present views the work would soon be accomplished.[38]

In Alton, another local meeting of persons dissatisfied with Lovejoy's *Observer* appointed a committee of five citizens who wrote Lovejoy to inform him of the meeting's action and to request a conference. Lovejoy thanked the writers for the courteous terms of the letter and expressed his respect toward them as individuals. But, he said he could not "admit that the liberty of the press and freedom of speech, were rightfully subject to other supervision and control, than those of the [law]."[39]

As opposition mounted, Lovejoy was stalked by opponents,[40] some hoping to tar and feather him. One mob invaded his home; another wrecked his newspaper office. Several public meetings followed. At one meeting, the Rev. Edward Beecher proposed a series of resolutions. (Beecher was the son of Lyman Beecher and brother to Harriet Beecher Stowe, who later would write *Uncle Tom's Cabin*, an antislavery novel that became a hugely successful bestseller.) Beecher's resolutions declared that the free communication of thoughts and opinions is one of the invaluable rights of man; and every citizen may freely write, speak, and print on any subject, being responsible for the abuse of that liberty. "[T]he question of abuse must be decided solely by a regular civil court, and in accordance with the law; and not by an irresponsible and unorganized portion of the community." Truth would triumph in free discussion. These principles, Beecher insisted, should be maintained independent of persons or sentiments and especially so in the case of unpopular sentiments. "These principles," Beecher's resolutions continued, "demand the protection of the Editor and of the press of the '*Alton Observer*,' on grounds of principle solely, and altogether disconnected with approbation of his sentiments."[41]

The resolutions were opposed by Usher Linder, attorney general of Illinois, and were referred to a committee pending a further meeting. Linder proposed his own resolution, which carried. It opposed any infraction of the peace in the interim between adjournment and reassembling. At the next meeting the committee report attempted to conciliate all sides and called for peace. It was sure citizens would "discountenance every act of violence . . . and cherish a sacred regard for the great principles contained in our Bill of Rights." But general principles did not decide this concrete case: "[W]hile there appears to be no disposition to prevent the liberty of free discussion . . . as a general thing; it is deemed a matter indispensable to the peace and harmony of this community that the labours and influence of the . . . Editor of the '*Observer*' be no longer identified with any newspaper establishment in this city."[42]

Lovejoy spoke to the resolutions:

> I, Mr. Chairman, have not desired, or asked any *compromise*. I have asked for nothing but to be protected in my rights as a citizen— rights which God has given me, and which are guaranteed to me by the constitution of my country. . . . What, sir, I ask, has been my offense? . . . If I have committed any crime, you can easily convict me. You have public sentiment in your favour. . . . But if I have been guilty of no violation of law, why am I hunted up and down continually like a partridge upon the mountains? Why am I threatened with the *tar-barrel*? Why am I waylaid every day, and from night to night, and my life in jeopardy every hour?
>
> . . . I plant myself, sir, down on my unquestionable *rights*, and the question to be decided is, whether I shall be protected in the exercise, and enjoyment of those rights.[43]

Most of the anti-Lovejoy resolutions passed. A few days later, Lovejoy was killed defending his fourth press from a mob.

REACTION TO LOVEJOY'S DEATH

For many Americans, Lovejoy's death crystallized the fear that slavery would destroy free speech and civil liberty in the North as well as the South. It produced an immense public reaction, one the abolitionists did all they could to cultivate. Earlier, in 1835, the *Washington Globe*, an organ of the national Democratic party, had noted with satisfaction, "[Abolitionists] have been hissed from the pulpit in Maine—their conventicles have been broken in upon and dispersed in New York—and recently in Ohio, one of their leaders was pelted with rotten eggs, and his incendiary attempt thus marked with the infamy it deserved."[44] But in late 1837, the reaction was quite different. After Lovejoy's death and the firestorm of criticism it evoked, fewer in the North supported suppression of abolition.

As the *Louisville Journal* of December 6, 1837, observed, "The death of Lovejoy has evidently created an excitement at the North, of tremendous depth and strength."[45] The *Emancipator*, the New York paper of the American Anti-Slavery Society, reported that to its direct knowledge more than two hundred newspapers had "fully and decidedly" condemned the "Alton outrage."[46] Former President John Quincy Adams insisted that "[t]he incidents which preceded and accompanied, and followed the catastrophe of Mr. Lovejoy's death point it out as a epocha in the annals of human liberty. They have given a shock as of an earthquake throughout this continent."[47]

Condemnation by press and pulpit was especially intense because the attack had been made on someone who was both an editor and a minister. Many in the press noted that their own interests and rights were at stake. "The press, we are rejoiced to say," commented the *Easton Pennsylvania Whig*, "utters one common sentiment of abhorrence at this bloody transaction. . . . Every man, and especially every journalist, must feel called upon to see to it that the outrage upon every thing we hold dear is redressed." The *Boston Times* commented, "We have been connected with the press too long not to know its value." "We are astonished," wrote the *Providence Courier*, "that even one journal can be found, so unmindful of its own rights" as not to fully condemn the attack on Lovejoy.[48]

Not all American newspapers read Lovejoy's death in this way, however. The *Cincinnati Whig, The National Intelligencer* (a leading Whig paper) and the *Washington Globe* (a leading Democratic paper) all suggested that Lovejoy's obstinate course had contributed to the tragedy. For example, the *Whig* wrote: "There has been another very serious riot at Alton, Illinois, caused by the indomitable abolitionism of the Rev. E. P. Lovejoy; who seems to have utterly disregarded the sentiments and feeling of a large majority of the people of that place and who, apparently, has taken no little pains to bring about the awful catastrophe, of which we are now to speak."[49] A sermon by Rev. Hubbard Winslow of Boston opined, "Mobs are an evil incidental to all but despotic governments; and it is the part of every good citizen to guard against exciting them. . . . In all republican governments where the power resides with the people, if you either do or publish any thing, right or wrong, so far in advance of, or aside from their views, as to strongly excite their indignation, a mob is the natural consequence."[50] But these criticisms of Lovejoy's actions were not typical.

In the mid-1830s, citizens frequently called public meetings and passed resolutions in an attempt to both shape and express public sentiment. In 1835, after the abolitionists first mailed their tracts to the South, a large number of local meetings had condemned abolitionist agitation. But after Lovejoy's death, many meetings condemned the attack on the freedom of the press. The *Emancipator* collected and reprinted resolutions from throughout the nation.[51]

Free Speech as a National and State Right, Liberty, or Privilege

The very general reaction in the North was to condemn the murder and to see it as part of an attack on the *rights, liberties, or privileges* (words commentators often used) *of American citizens* and of liberties protected by *state and federal constitutions.*

The *Baltimore Lutheran Observer*, like many papers, both described free press as a constitutional privilege and suggested that if Lovejoy had offended against the law (and those who considered the question typically insisted that he had not), then a legal remedy was the only appropriate one. But Southern slaveholders would find cold comfort in the suggestion. Not a single Northern legislature had acceded to the Southern demand that abolitionist expression be made a crime.

As the *Lutheran Observer* put it:

Whatever may have been the faults of Mr. Lovejoy, he should if guilty of a violation of the laws of the state, have been called to an account in a legal or constitutional form. Freedom of opinion and of the press is an inalienable privilege secured to us by our political *magna charta* as well as by the original inherent right of our nature, and it is impossible that the citizens of this free and enlightened republic should consent to surrender this inestimable privilege in the present age of liberal views. . . . We have . . . but little feeling in common with abolitionists, but we tell all anti-abolitionists that they are far from serving their cause by such acts of bloody ferocity; they are doing more by such deeds of violence and murder to aid the cause they wish to subvert than ten presses in Alton could effect.[52]

Press accounts and resolutions often described freedom of speech, press, and opinion as rights or privileges of American citizens and as rights established or guaranteed by the national constitution as well as by state constitutions. These statements are significant in evaluating the common understanding of words later used in Section 1 of the Fourteenth Amendment, which was proposed in 1866. The Fourteenth Amendment, which capped more than thirty years of antislavery efforts, provided that no state "shall abridge the privileges or immunities of citizens of the United States."

Could Americans have understood that American citizens—not just citizens of Illinois or a state that chose to secure the right—had a national right of free speech? Could the right equally well be described by the word "privilege" or "immunity"? The question is complex because today we think of a right or privilege as something the courts will enforce. Many in the eighteenth and nineteenth centuries distinguished the right itself from the question of whether state law provided security for it.

In 1836, the *New York Evening Post* had said that "[t]o entertain and express freely any opinion respecting our political institutions, is the privilege of all who live under a democratick government." An 1836 meeting in Willoughby, Ohio, in favor of free discussion of slavery proclaimed the "unquestionable right of all persons in this republic, to discuss every subject pertaining to its welfare." The "constitution of the United States," the meeting insisted, "protects us in so doing." The *Louisville Herald* asked, "Is a citizen of the United States . . . to be murdered defending the rights guaranteed him by the Constitution of his country?" Those who killed Lovejoy, the *New York Daily News* said, were "violators of the rights and privileges of American citizens." It was disgraceful, the *New Hampshire Courier* wrote, that local authorities had failed to protect Lovejoy, who was "battling to protect the freedom of speech, and of the press and of all the sacred rights secured to the citizens by the Constitution of these U.S." Lovejoy, said the *Brooklyn Gazette*, "was exercising a natural right, a right guarantied to him by the Constitution of his country. He fell a martyr to the freedom of speech and of the press." A public meeting in Weymouth, Massachusetts, resolved that "the freedom of speech and of the press, acknowledged and guarantied by the Constitution of these United States, cannot be abridged and taken away without the utter annihilation of our most essential rights and liberties."[53]

Lawyers were prominent in many of the public meetings held to protest Lovejoy's death. The meetings typically disclaimed any connection with abolitionists. A meeting of young men in New York resolved that "the liberty of the press, of speech, and the right of petition, are among the greatest blessings and proudest prerogatives of a free people, that their exercise is guaranteed to every citizen by the Federal Constitution."[54] Assailing these rights, the resolution continued, was "an encroachment upon the rights of citizens, and a direct and fatal attack" on that "sacred instrument which unites us as one people."[55]

Often the words "rights," "liberties," and "privileges" were used interchangeably. The *Newark Daily Advertiser* described "the right of free discussion" as an "inalienable privilege of a freeman." "Liberty of speech," insisted the *Berkshire Courier*, "must not be surrendered. It was one of the privileges left us by our fathers." Free speech was "a 'home-bred right,' a 'fireside privilege,'" according to a Concord, New Hampshire, public meeting. A public meeting in Susquehanna County, Pennsylvania, resolved that "freedom of the press is a right too sacred to be in the least invaded—a privilege too dear to be shackled or impaired by public enactments or lawless violence."[56]

Often the press noted that the Illinois constitution explicitly protected freedom of the press, and often state constitutions (sometimes alone, often in conjunction with the federal Constitution) were cited as protecting the rights of speech and press.[57] A public meeting in Belfast, Maine, for example, said that Lovejoy had "fallen a martyr in defence of rights which are guaranteed to every freeman by the constitution of the general and state governments."[58]

Lovejoy's Death and Free Speech: The Scope and Function of Free Speech

Papers often coupled a suggestion that if Lovejoy had offended the laws he could be legally punished with a clear implication that what Lovejoy had said was, or should be, protected speech. For example, the Nashua, New Hampshire, *Courier*, a paper friendly to the Democratic administration, said:

We are far from being abolitionists—we disapprove of their spirit, and believe them extravagant. We are still farther from being an advocate for slavery. . . . It matters not whether Lovejoy acted prudently or imprudently—morally right or wrong. He was in the exercise of a right guarantied by the laws, and under their protection. . . . If this freedom degenerates into licentiousness, correct the evil—if the laws are deficient, amend them. But while we retain the name of *freemen*, we will speak and publish our opinions boldly—we will have a government of laws, and not the despotism of a mob.

It was a noble remark of the father of democracy—Thomas Jefferson—that "error of opinion may be safely tolerated, where reason is left free to combat it." The odious "*sedition law*," which gagged the press by pretending to check its abuses, was a war with this freedom, and it was repealed.—The people will suffer no violation of this principle. If the rights of *one man* in one particular are disregarded and trampled down, no man—no principle is safe. . . . Lovejoy is now a *martyr* not to abolition solely, but to a high and important principle—the freedom of opinion, of speech, and of the press.[59]

One might insist that each legal suppression of speech is a particular event to be judged in isolation and on its own merits. By this approach, if the potential harms from abolitionist expression—such as slave revolts, disunion, or civil war—far outweighed its benefits, then abolitionism should be suppressed. By this view, suppression of abolitionist ideas need not threaten suppression of other expressions of opinion. The same logic could also apply in evaluating private acts of suppression. The idea that suppression tends to spread to more and more subjects could be rejected as the fallacy of the slippery slope.

In 1837, however, many opinion leaders implicitly rejected that view. Public reaction to Lovejoy's death was great precisely because many refused to view it as an isolated event or one that merely involved abolitionists.

That contemporaries refused to view the attempt to suppress Lovejoy's paper in isolation was crucial to the breadth and strength of the reaction against suppression. Because the issue was not just abolitionism or free speech for abolitionists but free speech and the rule of law for all, a great many people came to the aid of those who previously had been a despised few. Perception that events at Alton implicated general principles led to books, pamphlets, editorials, and resolutions. The importance of the broad principle was that it enlisted the many in the cause of a few.

As Edward Beecher wrote in his introduction to the *Narrative of Riots in Alton: In Connection with the Death of Rev. Elijah P. Lovejoy*, the events at Alton "are invested with unusual interest in consequence of their connection with principles of universal application."[60] "It is a case," wrote the *New York Evangelist*, "which brings out in full life the rights and privileges of an American all in jeopardy. They are universal rights. Every editor, every minister, every man in all the land, is personally interested in it."[61] The Greenfield, Massachusetts, *Gazette* insisted on meeting the issue on the frontier—in this case abolitionist speech was on the frontier of free speech and press:

> No matter on what subject the press is *first* prohibited to speak. Be the subject slavery, or politics, or religion, when the first prohibition is obeyed there is no security against further encroachments. Safety requires vigilance and resistance on discovery of the *earliest, slightest* danger. A small breach in the dykes of Holland, if left unrepaired, will shortly result in flooding that whole country with the waters of the ocean. If the American press is to be maintained free and unshackled, the first encroachments upon its liberty must be met and resisted. The danger must be proclaimed from every watchtower, and echoed through every valley. The voice of an indignant public must thunder rebuke into the ears of the first invaders. If we disregard warning, because our enemy is a feeble infant, we shall soon meet a *giant* in the field clad in a Philistine's armor.[62]

Many writers said that the danger was greater because a mob had suppressed the press. "If an abolition editor is murdered with impunity today," warned the Philadelphia *Commercial Herald*, "an Anti-Masonic or a Masonic editor may be murdered to-morrow—a Jackson or Van Buren or a Whig editor the next."[63] The editor of the Peoria, Illinois, *Register*—one of a very few Illinois papers to condemn the killing—made a similar point:

> It is folly to connect abolitionism with this tragedy. All our readers know that we have expressed ourself as decidedly against the doctrines and practices of the abolitionists as any press in the state. We are at this moment a slave owner. . . . But a man in a free state, in

the absence of any law to the contrary, may write and publish against slavery until his mind and fortune are exhausted, without any hinderance from us. Establish the principle that the mob is the law, and we shall have as many different enactments, and as many modes of executing them, as there are varieties of opinion in the majority. In one town, where the abolitionists are stronger, we shall have pro-slavery men murdered off, to avenge the blood of the Alton martyr; into another, where the infidels are strongest, we shall have churches demolished, and a periodical *auto da fe*; in another, where the temperance star is in the ascendant, the licensed coffee houses will be torn down, and the distillers burnt in their own fires; in another, where puritanism prevails, the theatres will be razed and the actors assassinated.[64]

Critics of the Lovejoy killing linked free speech to democratic government and to the sovereignty of the people. One aspect of free government was the right to try to persuade the people that accepted ideas or institutions should be changed. "[T]he Institutions of any country should be made the subject of free discussion by its citizens," a meeting in Washington County, New York, insisted, "so that any errors, which from ignorance or other cause, may have been incorporated in the system may be examined and exploded."[65] Freedom of speech and of the press were "essential elements in our free government," as a public meeting in Lawrence, Pennsylvania, put it.[66] "[I]f ever," said a public meeting in Belfast, Maine, "the time shall come when the supremacy of the laws cannot be maintained, and when the civil power cannot vindicate and protect every man in the undisturbed enjoyment of freedom of thought, of speech, and of the press, our great experiment in self government by the people will have failed."[67]

One of the most detailed discussions of free speech as essential to democracy appeared in the *Boston Daily Advocate*, a Democratic paper whose editor hastened to point out that he was no abolitionist. "We are advocates of the freedom of discussion," the editor of the *Advocate* wrote, "in its broadest sense. Were we otherwise, we could not consider ourselves democrats."

Democracy is a principle which recognises *mind* as superior to matter, and moral and mental power over that of wealth or physical force. . . . Democracy is also a principle of reform; consequently, it must examine, compare, and analyze, and how can it do this without freedom of inquiry and discussion. . . .

To argue that there are subjects, which ought not to be discussed, in consequence of their unpopularity with a majority of the people, is in reality to argue that the people are not capable of self-government; and the power of deciding what shall and shall not be discussed, ought to be invested in a censorship.[68]

While freedom of discussion might not produce truth, "it is reasonable," the editor said, "to suppose that a nearer approach to it will be made" than under a system of suppression.[69]

The individual must decide what should be discussed, subject to the public will as *expressed in the constitution and the laws.* The "right to discuss a subject of *exciting* character, is no less recognized by the constitution of this State, than one of a different nature." Indeed, the fact that it was exciting showed that it was one of public interest which should be discussed.[70]

Second, as the *Boston Daily Advocate* and others insisted, the sovereignty of the people could only be expressed by laws. A public meeting at Faneuil Hall in Boston resolved that "in a free country, the laws enacted according to the prescriptions of the Constitution are the voice of the people—are the only forms by which the sovereignty of the people is exercised and expressed and that, of consequence, a mob, or its combination of citizens for the purpose of suspending by force the administration of the laws, or of taking away the rights which those laws guarantied, is treason against the people, a contempt of their sovereignty, and deserves to be visited with exemplary punishment."[71] A number of resolutions insisted that in this country, popularly enacted laws were "our only sovereign and their appointed tribunals the only proper courts to administer them."[72]

Free speech and press were essential to representative government, and they were in danger. Threats, even to the "fanatical" abolitionists, were to be regarded as threats to the liberty of all. But what, exactly, was the nature of freedom of speech and of the press? Generally the press and the public meetings did not answer this question in detail and some, by simply insisting on the rule of law, avoided it altogether. Perhaps because the actions in Lovejoy's case were the actions of a mob, many did not discuss at any length what limits law could impose on free speech. Even if "in some degree," said the *Boston Christian Watchman*, Lovejoy "violated the just liberties of the press, and of the freedom of speech," that was not the issue. If there were any abuse, that was a question for a civil tribunal.[73] Still, there was some discussion of the nature of free speech.

Many insisted the right was not created by the national or state constitutions. These documents merely recognized and declared a natural right.[74] A public meeting in Concord, New Hampshire, resolved that liberty of the press "has its origin above and anterior to human codes and governments, and is neither to be alienated nor abridged by them,—and that all attempts to do this, either by the enactments of law, or the outrages of a mob, are violations of a higher law written by the finger of God in the heart of man." A meeting in Prospect, Maine, resolved that "liberty of speech is an inalienable right, derived from no human authority." Free speech, a candidate for office responded to an abolitionist query, "is a natural right, confirmed and guarantied by our constitution." "Mr. Lovejoy was exercising a natural right," explained the *Brooklyn Gazette*, "a right guarantied to him by the Constitution of his country." Another public meeting resolved "[t]hat as freedom of discussion is a *natural right* as well as a constitutional privilege, we will defend it for ourselves and support others in its exercise, whether they may hold opinions in conformity with our own or otherwise."[75] A meeting in Lynn, Massachusetts resolved:

> [T]he right of freedom of speech and of the press is not derived from human Governments, but proceeds from the Creator. . . .
>
> [T]he Constitution of the U. States recognizes this primal right as pre-existing and inherent in the people, and not as derived from any of its provisions, and declares that Congress shall pass no law to abridge it, and that the constitutions of almost all the free States, in like manner, and with like emphasis recognize the same right— that these constitutional provisions were intended to place—and do place the freedom of speech and of the press beyond the power of a majority.[76]

There were a great many statements of the same nature.[77]

The *Philadelphia Public Ledger and Daily Transcript* put it this way: "The right of opinion is one of those great natural rights which God gave to man, which man cannot justly invade, which is proclaimed in the Declaration of Independence, was asserted by our revolutionary fathers, is guaranteed by the Federal Constitution and the Constitution of every State. To secure this right, is one great end of all free institutions, is one great object of our whole system of constitutions, laws, legislatures, judiciaries, and executives."[78] "Upon this right, and under the supposed protection of constitutions and laws," Lovejoy had spoken against slavery for which he was murdered. "Is this freedom of opinion?" the *Ledger* demanded, and it answered: "Yes! Such freedom as the Roman Emperors accorded to the primitive christians, in offering them up to wild beasts." The *Ledger* seems ambiguous on free speech in slave states. It admitted the constitutional right of slaveholding states "to regulate their domestic relations. But we insist on the right of the other States to maintain the great natural and constitutional right of opinion. If the opinions of the abolitionists be wrong, reason can refute them."[79]

Many also discussed the content of the right to free speech and free press. Free speech and press were not without limits; people could be punished for their abuse—a formula that came directly from state constitutions. To the extent that abuse was defined, it was sometimes connected to libel of a private person and sometimes to treason, and only occasionally to other subjects.[80] Many noted that Lovejoy's actions had not violated any law. Just as many insisted on principles suggesting that what he said could not be lawfully restrained.

Freedom of speech and the press, many suggested, included the "right to discuss, freely and openly, by speech, by the pen, by the press, all political questions, and to examine and animadvert upon all political institutions."[81] The right was "so clear and certain, so interwoven with our other liberties, so necessary in fact, to their existence," the New York *Evening Post* asserted, "that without it we must fall at once into despotism or anarchy."[82] Many quoted Jefferson and declared that "[e]rror of opinion may safely be tolerated, while truth is left free to combat it."[83] A number insisted on a right of free "discussion of all subjects, whether of a religious, moral or political nature."[84] This right, a public meeting in Concord, New Hampshire, resolved, "'is the ancient and undoubted, prerogative of the people' of this Republic, . . . a right which 'has ever been enjoyed in every house, cottage and cabin in this nation.'"[85]

Proponents of free speech and a free press demanded that the majority respect the rights of the minority. "If Mr. Lovejoy could rightfully be called on to desist from publishing his paper because a majority of the people of Alton willed it—then," wrote the Utica, New York, *Magazine and Advocate*, "may the political papers in New York city, of the minority, be stopped by the majority—yes, and *our press* be driven from Utica, from *the state of New York*—from the UNITED STATES—*tomorrow!*"[86] Others concurred. "Let one editor be shot for attempting to print a newspaper for a minority," wrote the Elmira, New York, *Republican*, "and none are safe, for majorities are very fluctuating; and what is unpopular to-day may be popular to-morrow."[87] A number insisted that constitutional provisions guaranteeing freedom of the press were designed to protect the rights of the minority, not to secure the right to echo majority opinion.[88]

Discussion of the right of the minority moved seamlessly back to whether the issue raised by Lovejoy's death was simply a narrow one involving abolitionists, or whether a much more general principle was at stake. There were, as one writer pointed out, potentially a lot of vulnerable minorities.

> The question is not one of abolition or not—of negro freedom or slavery—of the right or wrong of emancipation—it assumes broader ground. . . . Shall the *freedom of the press* be maintained undiminished, or shall it be abridged and destroyed whenever it opposes the opinions of the majority, or an infuriated mob demands it? Shall men be forbidden 'to argue and utter freely' whatever their consciences may dictate because their sentiments are unpopular? . . . Shall the little band of Van Buren's friends in [Massachusetts], who have opposed, year after year, strenuously and unceasingly, the expressed and reiterated will of the vast majority of its citizens be proscribed, their presses destroyed, and be told to go into New Hampshire with their heretic notions? Shall the Quakers be again put under the ban, and their tongues bored through with hot irons and their bodies hung up in our public squares and at the corners of our streets? Shall the Unitarian and the Christian and a hundred other sects be no longer tolerated, but their presses be all swept away by the mob? Shall sects and parties begin to count numbers and combine for the suppression of those who differ from them? The question is common ground on which all lovers of freedom of the mind may unite, and banded as one man cast off in indignation from the press and the tongue the shackles which are gathering upon them. Every man who has an intellect and a conscience is concerned. Not only the abolitionist, but the man of sci-

ence should gird himself up for resistance. Let him remember the fate of Galileo. The philosopher, the poet, the man of letters, every independent thinker, has a high and solemn duty to perform.[89]

Protection, Equal Protection, and Free Speech

Mobs had destroyed three of Lovejoy's presses, and ultimately a mob killed him as he attempted to repel its attack on his fourth press. A mob had destroyed Birney's press. Mobs had attacked other abolitionists. These events raised the basic issue of protection and equal protection of the laws. In most cases, local authorities had done virtually nothing to protect the victims.

Lovejoy himself raised the issue plainly and prophetically in his speech to a public meeting shortly before his death:

> I have asked for nothing but to be protected in my rights as a citizen—rights which God has given me, and which are guaranteed to me by the constitution of my country. . . . I plant myself, sir, down on my unquestionable *rights*, and the question to be decided is, whether I shall be protected in the exercise, and enjoyment of those rights. . . .[90]
>
> Mr. Chairman, I do not admit that it is the business of this assembly to decide whether I shall or shall not publish a newspaper in this city. . . . I have the right to do it. I know that I have the right freely to speak and publish my sentiments, subject only to the laws of the land for the abuse of that right. This right was given me by my Maker; and is solemnly guaranteed to me by the constitution of these United States and of this state. What I wish to know of you is whether you will protect me in the exercise of this right; or whether, as heretofore, I am to be subject to personal indignity and outrage.[91]

By refusing to endorse resolutions supporting Lovejoy's right to publish and by resolving that he should not publish, the meeting implicitly answered Lovejoy's question.

In responding to Lovejoy's death, many noted the connection between individual rights and the protection of the law. To obtain protection for rights was, after all, the rationale of the social contract. As Edward Beecher put it in his account of events at Alton, people needed to acknowledge that "protection is a debt due from community to every citizen; and that he has a undoubted right to claim it; and that it is more grossly absurd and unjust for a community to talk of compromising it."[92]

Free speech, then, required protection to be a meaningful right. As a public meeting in Cleveland, Ohio, noted: "That it is the fundamental idea of the freedom of speech and of the press, that the citizen shall be protected from violence in uttering sentiments opposed to those which prevail around him, and that to put him in peril for uttering what the majority disapprove, is to assail the very foundation of this freedom and destroys its life."[93] If one could forfeit the right to protection for expressing views that offended the community, this would mean, Lovejoy's brothers noted in their memoir, that "Galileo [would have] deserved to be condemned and punished as he was, for . . . teaching that the earth is a sphere, turning on its axis, and revolving round the sun," and William Tyndale would have "deserved to be strangled and burned for offering such an insult to public sentiment, as to prepare and publish a translation of the New Testament in English."[94] States and cities had acted against free speech simply by not acting, by failing to provide protection.

Lovejoy's death was part of a great transformation that was taking place on the subject of free speech and slavery. The next chapter will look in more detail at that transformation and at some of the events that followed Lovejoy's death.

11

After Lovejoy: Transformations

The death of Lovejoy at Alton crystallized support for a broad and general view of free speech in the North and dramatically strengthened the view that mobs and the institution of slavery threatened liberty and representative government. In his autobiography, Horace Greeley, then a Whig, but later editor of the *New York Tribune* and a Republican, cited the death of Lovejoy as conclusively showing how slavery threatened the liberty of the North. "It was thenceforth plain to my apprehension that Slavery and true Freedom could not coexist on the same soil."[1]

THE IMPACT OF LOVEJOY'S DEATH

Before Lovejoy's death, John Quincy Adams, formerly the nation's president and in 1837 a member of the House of Representatives, had already begun his long and brilliant guerrilla war against the gag rule that attempted to silence discussion of slavery in the House. In his diary, Adams described the Lovejoy death as "[t]he most atrocious case of rioting which ever disgraced this country." Lovejoy, he concluded, "has fallen a martyr to the cause of human freedom."[2] In Concord, Massachusetts, Ralph Waldo Emerson wrote about Lovejoy's death in his journal. "The brave Lovejoy has given his breast to the bullet . . . and has died when it was better not to live. . . . I sternly rejoice that one was bound to die for humanity and the rights of free speech and opinion."[3] Lovejoy's death galvanized others into active abolitionism. For example, Wendell Phillips's career as an active abolition agitator really began with his stirring speech condemning the defense of the mob by Massachusetts attorney general William Austin.[4]

Before Lovejoy was killed, Edward Beecher had defended free speech for Lovejoy and other abolitionists. The killing propelled him also into full-fledged abolitionism. As his wife wrote, "The Alton murder has brought us all over to the [abolition] faith."[5] In 1885 Isaac Newton Arnold, an Illinois congressman and contemporary of Abraham Lincoln, wrote a biography of Lincoln, in which he said that Lincoln's election was a culmination of opposition to a constellation of events connected with slavery, including "the violence . . . by which freedom of speech and liberty of the press had been suppressed in portions of the slave states." Arnold identified Lovejoy's death as a key political event that had unleashed a crusade against oppression by Lovejoy's brother Owen and other abolitionists, a crusade consummated by "a President elected on the distinct ground of opposition to the extension of slavery."[6] Lovejoy was controversial, and some discreetly avoided mentioning him. In January 1838, in Illinois, young Abraham Lincoln gave a speech against mobs that were mobilized against gamblers, but even Lincoln did not directly mention Lovejoy or abolition.[7]

Still, a remarkable transformation of public opinion had occurred. A few years before, almost all political leaders had shunned the abolitionists and discussion of slavery. Now, at least with reference to issues of free speech, press, and petition, John Quincy Adams and a few others were directly and openly cooperating with them. The effect was like the effect on the anti–Vietnam War movement when J. William Fulbright, chair of the Senate Foreign Relations Committee, began to criticize the war. In 1842, Theodore Weld, the abolitionist activist, decided to go to Washington to work with Adams and antislavery congressmen. These men, he noted, in a point equally true in 1837 and 1838, could do more for the antislavery cause "by a single speech . . . than our best lecturers [could] do in a year." The speeches would be published in national newspapers and "scattered over the South as well as the North."[8]

Just three years before, the *Emancipator* noted in 1838, a citizen of Washington had been indicted (though later acquitted) on a charge of possession of abolition literature with an intent to distribute it. Now (in 1838) Representative Slade's "speech, which is as full of Anti-Slavery doctrine as possible, has been printed in a pamphlet form at Washington city, and a thousand copies sent out through the Post office, many of them into the southern States." The *National Intelligencer* had reprinted speeches by John Quincy Adams attacking slavery. There had been "a great change."[9] The *New York Evening Post* observed that the Alton incident "gave an impulse to the public feeling favorable to liberty of discussion,—an impulse which will end in making infamous all attempts to tyrannize over the free and honest expression of thought."[10]

But criticism of slavery remained controversial. Many substantial, wealthy, and conservative citizens continued to condemn abolitionism and discussion of slavery. The Unitarian minister, defender of free speech, and moderate antislavery spokesman William Ellery Channing himself had been critical of the abolitionist mode of agitating the slavery issue, of their sometimes harsh rhetoric, and of their tactic of sending antislavery publications to the South. Channing expressed sympathy for both slaves *and* slaveholders and saw the solution to the slavery problem as one of gradual moral education. Once the evil of slaveholding was better understood, it would begin to die out. When Channing criticized slavery in more moderate language than that used by some abolitionists and defended free speech on the subject (even for the hated abolitionists), he, in turn, found himself shunned by many of the wealthy and conservative citizens of Boston.[11]

Though wounded by that reaction, Channing should not have been surprised. As he had explained in 1836, unjustified opposition to abolition could be found in all classes: "Such are to be found in what is called the highest class of society, that is, *among the rich and fashionable*; and the cause is obvious. *The rich and fashionable belong to the same caste with the slaveholder*; and men are apt to sympathize with their own caste more readily than with those beneath them."[12] Among the wealthy and conservative classes were those "who, from no benevolent interest in society, but simply because they have drawn high prizes in the lottery of life, are unwilling that the most enormous abuses should be touched, lest the established order of things, so propitious to themselves, should be disturbed."[13]

Both historians and contemporaries have noted that antiabolition mobs contained gentlemen of property and standing. Indeed, both in Cincinnati and in Alton, public meetings that demanded the suppression of abolition papers pointed to the danger abolitionism posed to the prosperity of those cities. Demands to suppress Birney's and Lovejoy's papers were partly prompted by fear of economic reprisals by the South, as well as concern for the Union and fear of slave revolts. Southerners had quite explicitly warned Northerners of the possibility of economic retaliation if abolitionism were not suppressed. "The present state of feeling in the South," warned a New York paper, "as indicated in the resolutions referred to, plainly shows that all commercial intercourse with the South will be embarrassed, unless efficient measures are adopted by the northern States for gagging and pinioning our abolition leaders."[14] A St. Louis newspaper starkly warned the citizens of Alton that Southerners would refuse to have business dealings with those who tolerated abolitionists.[15]

Economic ties with the South existed throughout the nation and affected people of all social classes. In 1837, there was a conflict between trade, prosperity, and human rights—and many chose trade. "Thus is the love of money and power constantly trenching upon personal rights," lamented the Fall River, Massachusetts, *Patriot*, after Lovejoy's death, "and if not resisted will trample them in the dust."[16] But as those who would silence abolitionists saw it, they also chose Union and peace.

BOSTON AND THE QUEST FOR A PUBLIC FORUM

Meaningful free speech has a positive and negative aspect. In its negative aspect it protects citizens from government suppression. The positive aspect protects a citizen's exercise of free speech from interference by others and provides a place where ordinary citizens can express their views. Today the U.S. Supreme Court holds that streets, sidewalks, and parks are public places where citizens (most of whom do not own a newspaper or a television station) have a right to speak, meet, or hand out leaflets. In 1837 and 1838, a right to speak in public places had not yet been held to be protected by law. Access to a public forum was a problem not only for abolitionists, but, as it turned out, for advocates of a broad and protective concept of free speech and press.

After Lovejoy's death, William Ellery Channing, the Unitarian minister, requested the use of city-owned Faneuil Hall in Boston for a protest meeting. The meeting was intended to support free speech and to protest mob violence. Use of the hall had often been granted for political and other meetings. But the Boston mayor and aldermen turned down the request after receiving objections from a number of prominent citizens who said they feared a breach of the peace.

The mayor and aldermen gave three reasons for denying the request. First, many from outside the city would construe resolutions passed by the meeting as reflecting the sentiments of Boston citizens, and the city officials did not expect that to be the case. Second, "[t]he Board think it generally inexpedient to grant the use of the Hall to any party who have taken a side upon a highly exciting and warmly contested question."[17] Finally, "[a] Remonstrance has also been received against granting the prayer of the petition, signed by many persons" in whom the board members had great confidence.[18]

The editors of the *Salem Gazette* said they had intended to comment on the "flimsy, wretched, and most unsatisfactory reasoning put forth by the authorities of our sister city," but instead it printed Dr. Channing's letter of protest. The purpose of the meeting, Channing explained in his well-publicized letter, was to allow citizens of Boston to "express their utter and uncompromising reprobation of the violence which has been offered to the freedom of speech and the press. . . . To intimate that such resolutions would not express the public opinion of Boston, and would even create a mob, is to pronounce the severest libel on this city. It is to assert, that peaceful citizens cannot meet here in safety to strengthen themselves against violence, and in defence of the dearest and most sacred rights."[19] Channing urged the citizens of Boston to "demand the public meeting which has been refused, with a voice which cannot be denied." Channing thought that the fact that most in Boston disagreed with Lovejoy's views and that people of all political persuasions would join in the condemnation would make their statements in favor of free speech and the rule of law that much more impressive. "A citizen has been *murdered* in defense of the right of free discussion," Channing concluded. "I do not ask whether he was a Christian or unbeliever— whether he was abolitionist or colonizationist."[20] Editorials and resolutions from a public meeting poured in protesting the denial.[21]

A meeting at the courthouse to protest the denial of the use of Faneuil Hall insisted that the hall belonged to all citizens and was "consecrated to liberty and free discussion" and its use had been wrongfully denied.[22] The *Boston Daily Advocate* insisted that "Faneuil Hall is common property for the purposes of free meetings of the citizens, as much as the streets are common property for citizens to walk in." The common council had established a dangerous precedent: "[N]ine men will undertake to decide whether the opinions of the applicants for the Hall, are such as in their opinion, ought to be promulgated; and if not, they will refuse the application."[23] Facing a barrage of criticism, the aldermen relented and allowed a daytime meeting limited to the subject of mobs and free speech.

At the meeting, a number of resolutions were proposed: It was "the fundamental idea of the freedom of speech and the press that the citizen shall be protected from violence in uttering opinions opposed to those which prevail around him." If the liberty were confined to uttering "what none would deny, then absolute governments might insist of it as loudly as republics." The resolutions further provided that the laws enacted "according to the prescriptions of the Constitution" were the voice of the people and were "the only forms through which the sovereignty of the people is exercised."[24] Dr. Channing and others spoke for the resolutions.

James Austin, the attorney general of the state, spoke on the other side. Austin insisted that the resolutions "republish truths never contradicted and never denied . . . and which, if they are not supposed to have some particular application, it is idle and useless to republish to the world." The real reason for publication, he said, was that the resolutions were intended to apply to the Lovejoy case. But Austin denied the general principles were appropriately applicable to that case. After all, "[i]n the State of Missouri the Reverend Mr. Lovejoy established an abolition newspaper; the effect and tendency of which, in the judgment of the white people of that State, was to excite insurrection and murder, and by what is termed a *moral suasion*, to produce a terrible war of bloodshed and destruction." Lovejoy, Austin continued, was like a man who insisted on breaking open cages containing wild beasts and setting them free to prey on the populace. "The people of Missouri had as much reason to be afraid of their slaves," Austin insisted, "as we should have of the wild beast of the menagerie." So they had driven Lovejoy out. Then Lovejoy had moved on to Illinois, just across the river from a slave state. Now the issue became one for citizens of Alton. "Here was an abolition paper," Austin continued, "in their judgment, violating the principles of religion, morality and order—exciting a servile war, under the guise of freedom, and preaching murder, in the name of Christianity. The people of Alton considered this an extreme case, and they put the paper down."[25]

Austin said the citizens of Alton had behaved like the patriots who threw the tea into Boston Harbor. "Satisfy a people that their lives are in danger," Austin exclaimed, "by the instrumentality of the press, injudiciously and intemperately operating on the minds of slaves; give them reason to fear the breaking out of a servile war," and, as much as Austin said he deplored a mob, a mob was inevitable.[26]

Wendell Phillips rebuked Austin in a forceful speech.[27] Phillips denied that the Boston Tea Party justified Lovejoy's death. The Boston patriots had attacked an illegal tax imposed without their consent. The mob in Alton met to rob a citizen of his just rights under laws "we ourselves have enacted." The state of Missouri had no more right to demand Lovejoy's silence in Illinois than the czar had "to control the deliberations of Faneuil Hall." Phillips said the claim by a Boston clergyman that in a republican government, "no citizen has a right to publish opinions disagreeable to the community," and those who do invite a mob, made republican institutions worthless. At least under the despotism of the sultan, "one knows what he may publish and what he may not," whereas with a mob "we know not what we may do or say, till some fellow citizen has tried it, and paid for the lesson with his life."[28]

According to the *Emancipator*, the *Boston Times*, "an impartial paper," reported that the Boston pro–free speech and antimob resolutions passed by a large majority, a view shared by the *Boston Daily Advocate*.[29] The New York *Evening Post* reported that the meeting was one of the largest ever held and that abolitionists had not taken an active part in the meeting.[30] The Faneuil Hall vindication of the liberty of the press received a somewhat sour reception from several of the major Boston papers. The *Richmond Whig and Public Advertiser* quoted an account from the *Boston Atlas*:

> The result was entirely satisfactory. Nothing was suffered to go down which bore the slightest taint of abolitionism. The resolutions offered on the occasion were mere plagiarisms from the bill of rights in relation to the freedom of speech, the liberty of the press, and the supremacy of the laws. Not a Fourth of July oration can be produced which does not embody all they venture to assert. Their solemn reiteration of undisputed truisms was deservedly ridiculed. In fact so superfluous and supererogatory were they regarded, that when the question was put upon the final passage, a majority of the meeting could not be found to hold up their hands. The question being put in the negative, there seemed to be an equal division of those who had taken the trouble to vote.[31]

The Boston *Evening Transcript* said that abolitionists were in a minority in the meeting, but because the resolutions were "cunningly worded" and could not be opposed by lovers of liberty, they passed. However, the *Transcript* insisted, the speech of Attorney General Austin reflected the true spirit of the meeting and the citizens of Boston.[32]

PENNSYLVANIA HALL

In May 1838, Pennsylvania abolitionists and activists opened Pennsylvania Hall, an impressive structure dedicated to freedom of discussion, especially of slavery. Managers of the Hall received letters of congratulations from former president and current House member from Massachusetts, John Quincy Adams, from Senator Thomas Morris of Ohio, and from Thaddeus Stevens, a Pennsylvania state legislator and a future leader of the Republican Party in the Congresses that proposed the Thirteenth Amendment, abolishing slavery, and the Fourteenth Amendment.

John Quincy Adams wrote his "respected friends," that he had learned with pleasure that the Pennsylvania Hall Association had erected "a large building in your city, wherein liberty and equality of civil rights can be freely discussed and the evils of slavery fearlessly portrayed." This was particularly significant because "[t]he right of discussion upon slavery, and an indefinite extent of topics connected with it, is banished from one half the States of this Union. It is *suspended* in both houses of Congress."[33]

For Senator Thomas Morris of Ohio, a hall devoted to free discussion prompted "a train of solemn reflections." Surely the hall was not required because in Philadelphia "*free* discussion on all questions connected with the religion, morality, the welfare of the country, or the rights of man, cannot be had with safety to the citizen, and the peace and quiet of the community." But if Philadelphia was safe "from all attempts to put down the right of free discussion, the liberty of speech and the press, your fellow citizens have seen and felt that all parts of our beloved country are not thus highly favored."[34] He continued, "It is gratifying indeed, that while the enemy of human rights and constitutional liberty is, in our country, making rapid advances to power, endeavoring so far as in him lies, not only to silence discussion but even to muzzle the press itself, knowing that his principles cannot stand the test of examination; Philadelphia has the honor to erect a barrier which he cannot pass, and a battery which he cannot silence, but which will effectually destroy his whole power, by the consecration of a spot where all his pretensions may be fully and fairly discussed."[35]

Within days of its opening, a mob burned down the hall, outraged by the idea of abolition or, some insisted, by white men and black women and white women and black men promenading outside the hall arm in arm. By another account, no such promenades had occurred, and by a third, the promenaders had been hired by those determined to provoke a riot.[36] Once again, most of the press seems to have fully condemned the outrage. But the *Richmond Whig and Public Advertiser*, while mildly condemning the arson, found the guilt of the mob greatly mitigated by provocation.

> [I]f ever there was a case in which a community should be excused for using violence to arrest the violation, or to enforce the observance, of the canons of decency and well ordered society, that case is made out for the citizens of Philadelphia in their late proceedings.... From the time of its dedication until it was consumed, [Pennsylvania Hall] was the head-quarters for agrarians, infidels and abolitionists, from all regions, who congregated there daily and nightly to preach and practice their abominations—Negro fellows escorted white "ladies" through the streets—white "ladies" felt honoured in sitting on the same bench with black fellows—in marked contempt for decency and public opinion. Such practices, outraging the moral sense of the community, and if continued, tending inevitably to throw society into confusion, and to engender immorality and vice, it could not be expected, that any people, having respect for themselves or affection for their children, would permit to endure.[37]

Governor Joseph Ritner of Pennsylvania promptly issued a proclamation expressing deep regret and offering a reward for apprehension of the arsonists. "The torch of the incendiary," the governor lamented, "has been applied by unmasked violators of law, in the darkness of night in the heart of a crowded city, and for the avowed purpose of preventing the exercise of the constitutional and invaluable right of 'the free communication of thoughts and opinions.'" It was the duty of the magistrate "to protect all in the exercise of their constitutional rights."[38]

With the death of Lovejoy and the destruction of Pennsylvania Hall, the future of free discussion of abolitionist ideas must have seemed bleak. But some took a long view. The editor of the *Massachusetts Spy* wrote, "[W]e are not yet prepared to believe that the spirit which has thus manifested itself in the cities, is the prevailing one of the country. On the contrary, we have found it shrinking under the withering rebuke, which it has received from the less contaminated portions of the community, whenever it has manifested in such outrageous acts." In Boston, a few inoffensive women had been mobbed for speaking against slavery. "[T]he rebuke following that act has produced such a change, that large meetings of all classes of citizens are now allowed to meet and discuss the same question in the most public manner possible." In Utica, a convention had been broken up by leaders riding roughshod over constitutional rights. Now advocates of suppression were "in a meagre and contemptible minority." So it would be, the *Spy*'s editor predicted, in Philadelphia. To a great extent, the *Spy* was right. Mob efforts to silence abolitionists did not simply cease, however. For example, mobs disrupted an antislavery meeting in New York City in 1850. This time newspapers across the North defended the free speech rights of the abolitionists.[39]

<h2 style="text-align:center">REFLECTIONS</h2>

Pivotal moments seldom seem so pivotal when they occur as they do in hindsight. Change is never total. While much remained the same after Lovejoy's death, much also had changed. One thing that remained the same was federal postal policy excluding abolitionist pamphlets from mail directed to Southern states. Another was the congressional gag rule.

Lovejoy's killing accelerated and increased the popular expression of broad ideas of free speech and press as the rights of Americans. The United States Supreme Court had articulated a different view: rights in the Bill of Rights were simply limits on the federal government. U.S. senators, for example, had suggested that federal guarantees of free speech and press did not limit the states. But in response to perceived threats to liberty, popular and broad ideas of free speech and press were rising to the surface from newspapers and public meetings, and these were often more libertarian and national in scope than those held by the governing elite. Many of the papers and meetings were not abolitionist.

Free Speech as a Right of American Citizens

In the early 1830s, discussions of the right (or liberty, or privilege) of free speech and press often tied it to rights set out in state law and state constitutions. Mention of the federal Constitution, as a limit on state action, was less frequent. But after Lovejoy's death in 1837, free speech and free press were frequently referred to as rights or privileges of American citizens—not just of a citizen of a state that might or might not protect these rights—and as a federal as well as state constitutional rights. The change was to have startling implications, although these were rarely discussed by the general press or meetings in 1837. The emerging Northern consensus now implied that the suppression of antislavery speech and press in the South was illegitimate, an implication that became explicit in later years.

By 1837, many people talked about the "declaratory" nature of constitutional provisions protecting speech, press, petition, and assembly. (A declaratory provision recognizes or declares a preexisting natural or legal right but does not purport to create it.) One result of this interpretation was that free speech and press could be seen as constitutional rights or privileges of American citizens even if the First Amendment had not created these rights. The First Amendment, after all, explicitly secured them only against congressional abridgment, and it did so by a denial of congressional power. For those who accepted the declaratory nature of the First Amendment, a second consequence was that state legislatures could not rightfully pass laws abridging the free speech rights or privileges of American citizens.

But many also saw free speech as a basic human right that was protected by state constitutions. In 1838, Senator John C. Calhoun of South Carolina had proposed a series of resolutions dealing with slavery. One resolved that, "in delegating a portion of their powers to be exercised by the Federal Government, the States retained severally the exclusive and sole right over their own domestic institutions and police, . . . and that any intermeddling of any one or more States, or a combination of their citizens with the domestic institutions and police of the others, on any ground, political, moral, or religious, or under any pretext whatever, with the view to their alteration or subversion, is not warranted by the Constitution."[40] Another Calhoun resolution provided that slavery composed an important part of the domestic institutions of the slave states and that no change in public opinion in other states can justify them or their citizens in open and systematic attacks on slavery.[41] Though resolutions much like these passed by comfortable margins, they were attacked by a small group of senators. Senator Morris of Ohio "conceived the resolutions of the Senator from South Carolina liable to the strongest objections, and as warring against the dearest rights and privileges of freemen. . . . When war was made on the freedom of speech, of the press, and the right of petition, these inalienable rights must and would be defended; they were Heaven's best gift to man."[42] As to the suggestion that abolitionists could be punished by state laws, Senator Morris "regarded this and other similar doctrines . . . as subversive of all freedom and of the institutions of the country. . . . [A]ll classes of men had an imprescriptible right, above all government, to the freedom of speech and the right of petition."[43] Citizens had an indisputable right "to speak, write, print, publish," on the laws and institutions of other states.[44]

Morris proposed a set of counterresolutions. They showed that Calhoun's states' rights rhetoric could easily be turned against Calhoun's own resolutions and that Morris and others saw the Calhoun resolutions as a threat to states' rights as well as individual rights. Morris invoked, though without citing them, the Ninth and Tenth Amendments. The people of the states had reserved to the states and the people powers not delegated to the federal government. Among these were "full liberty of speech and the press to discuss the domestic institutions of any of the States, whether political, moral, or religious." The Morris resolution insisted that "it would be the exercise of unauthorized power, on the part of this Government, or of any of the States, to attempt to restrain the same, and that any endeavor to do so would be insulting to the People and the States so interfered with; for each State alone has the power to punish individuals for the abuse of this liberty within their own jurisdiction; and whenever one State shall attempt to make criminal acts, done by citizens in another State, which are lawful in the State where done, the necessary consequence would be to weaken the bonds of our Union." Morris's resolution also insisted that "this Government is bound so to exercise its power as not to interfere with the reserved right of the States over their own domestic institutions; and it is the duty of this Government to refrain from any attempt, however remote, to operate on the liberty of speech and the press, as secured to the citizens of each State by the Constitution and laws thereof." Finally, Morris borrowed more language from Calhoun's resolutions, once again turning them on their heads. "[N]o change of feeling on the part of any of the States can justify them or their citizens in open and systematic attacks on the right of petition, the freedom of speech, or the liberty of the press, with a view to silence either on any subject whatever."[45]

As a correspondent for the *Boston Daily Advocate* saw it, leading Southerners had decided "that their domestic institutions cannot be protected" unless the free states surrendered "their dearest domestic institutions, freedom of speech and the press, and the right of petition." If

Northern and Southern institutions clashed, "which neither will surrender and which cannot subsist together," the writer wondered, where would it all end?[46] With all the emerging references to rights of American citizens, the rights of states and their citizens remained a key concern for parties on all sides of the dispute.

According to Morris, the Calhoun resolution was a devious attempt to silence speech without passing a law. "Let the same thing be done by law," Morris thundered, "and then see whether the people had become so base as to permit these privileges to be taken from them."[47]

Senator Oliver Smith of Indiana proposed an amendment to the Calhoun resolutions:

> *Provided*, That nothing contained in these resolutions shall be construed or understood as expressing an opinion of this Senate adverse to these fundamental principles of this government, "That all men are created equal; that they are endowed by their Creator with certain inalienable rights; that among these are life, liberty, and the pursuit of happiness. That the freedom of speech and of the press, and the right of the people peaceably to assemble to petition the Government for redress of grievances, shall never be abridged. That error of opinion may be tolerated while reason is left free to combat it. That the Union must be preserved." But, on the contrary, all those constitutional, fundamental, and political truths, are expressly recognised by this Senate.[48]

Smith's resolution was amended by substituting a statement that the Calhoun resolution was not intended to allow Congress to interfere with freedom of speech or of the press "as secured by the constitution to the citizens of the several States, within their States respectively."[49] The substitute passed over the objection of fourteen senators, including Smith. Still, Smith made a strong plea for freedom of opinion, as he understood it. "[C]ombat error of opinion by reason, not by gag laws, not by mobs, not by inquisitions, not by establishing censorships over the press, not by abridging the freedom of speech, but by reason, holding the parties responsible for the abuse of all these privileges, or rather rights, to the party aggrieved; and then the question, what are and what are not errors of opinion, must be left to the final arbiters—the people, where they must be left in every country where liberty dwells."[50]

Southern attacks on antislavery expression generated a more vigorous defense of free speech. Smith insisted that the Calhoun resolutions implied that free speech about slavery in the North was "intermeddling" with the domestic institutions of the South. He said Calhoun's resolutions embraced the principles of the Sedition Act and should be defeated.[51]

Others also saw the Calhoun resolutions as an attack on free speech. The *Boston Daily Atlas* suggested that Calhoun was assisting abolitionists in making slavery a national issue and that his motive was the establishment of a separate Southern confederacy. For many years, the South had been predominant in the nation. Now that that predominance was threatened by the growing population and political power of the North, some Southern leaders were unwilling to continue in the nation:

> It may be supposed by some, that Mr Calhoun renders these services to the abolitionists unconsciously and unintentionally. Not at all. He knows perfectly well what he is about. His object is *agitation*; he wishes to create an agitation at the North, in order that he may employ it as a means of creating agitation at the South. With this design he makes those violent assaults upon the right of petition, the liberty of speech and the press, and even the privilege of thinking, contained in his famous resolutions. Instead of acting like oil upon the waters, he knows, and he exults, that those resolutions must and will operate like fuel to the fire.[52]

While Smith, Morris, and a handful of others were not successful in recasting Calhoun's resolutions in 1838, by 1860 a united Republican Party in the Senate voted (unsuccessfully) to amend a resolution offered by Jefferson Davis and much like the one Calhoun had proposed. The 1860 Republican amendment provided that "free discussion of the morality and expedience of slavery should never be interfered with by the laws of any State, or of the United States; and the freedom of speech and of the press, on this and every other subject of domestic and national policy, should be maintained inviolate in all the States."[53] The trail followed by Republicans in 1859–60 had been blazed by a few rugged pioneers in 1837 and 1838.

Antislavery activists increasingly shifted from heavy emphasis on rights under state constitutions to at least equally emphasizing rights under the federal Constitution. In 1838 S. B. Treadwell, an antislavery editor who was a leader in his state Liberty and Free-Soil Parties, wrote the book, *American Liberties and American Slavery: Morally and Politically Illustrated*.[54] Treadwell insisted that free speech and free press were national constitutional rights. Because of the federal constitutional guarantees, Treadwell announced that communities had no right, "by mob law, or by any other law (which of course must be unconstitutional and an abridgement of the inalienable rights of man), to forcibly suppress the discussion and constitutional promulgation" of opinions which most in the community despised.[55] As Treadwell stated it: "The most obscure, or the most unpopular individual in community, stands most in need of the lawful and constitutional protection of all his rights. History and biography have most abundantly shown us, that many new systems and new theories, which obscure and unpopular persons have introduced, and for which they have been persecuted, imprisoned, and often put to death, have subsequently proved to be of immense value to the whole world of mankind."[56] Treadwell criticized "advocates for free inquiry and investigation [who] make a kind of mental reservation in this matter, and really mean those subjects only which may happen to coincide with their own peculiar notions, interests, or convenience."[57]

The Nature of the Right to Free Speech

Northerners increasingly saw free speech as a right of all Americans not to have speech restrained except according to regularly enacted laws that comported with constitutional limitations. Some things were paradigmatic examples of free speech: the right to espouse opinions on all political, moral, religious, and scientific subjects and the right to criticize laws and institutions of one's own or another state. Many suggested that free speech, though not unlimited, was a principle of general application that must be available even to evil views. Jefferson's statement that error of opinion could be tolerated where truth was left free to combat it was reiterated again and again.

One might insist on balancing the right to criticize slavery against the great dangers it threatened—disunion, slave revolts, and civil war. Many who championed free speech in the context of the Lovejoy incident, however, viewed free speech and free press as a sanctuary not to be invaded by legislative or private power, although the reasons for curtailing it seemed quite compelling. Supporters of free speech for abolitionists sometimes cited direct incitement to violence and libel of a private person as examples of unprotected speech. A number rejected a bad tendency test. Unitarian minister William Ellery Channing, a critic both of slavery and abolitionists, for example, insisted that possible effects on susceptible people could not be the test. The other view was expressed by critics of the resolutions that connected the Lovejoy issue to free speech. These people said that speech (such as antislavery speech) that threatened such grave injuries was not within the protected freedom of speech.[58]

Channing and others noted that dominant groups frequently find prevailing evils benign and criticisms of them evil. To permit governments or mobs to ban "wicked" or "dangerous" ideas threatened progressive change. Many progressive ideas were at first rejected as wicked and only later accepted and cherished. The idea that slavery should be promptly abolished (or even limited to its then existing confines) was one example. Because radical ideas (such as the abolition of slavery or even its limitation to the slave states) threaten the economic interests of dominant groups, if those groups control the government and have the power to control the agenda then such ideas may never be raised. (Something much like that had happened in the South.)

Opponents of slavery, in particular, were confident that in a fair fight ideas of freedom would vanquish those of slavery. Lovejoy, Garrison, and Birney offered space in their papers to arguments by supporters of slavery. Birney regularly printed proslavery and antiabolition declarations.[59]

A copy of a letter to John C. Calhoun in the Elizur Wright papers gives a dramatic example of this faith. Attempts to suppress antislavery speech would fail, Wright insisted, because Americans did not trust ideas that had to be protected from argument. Wright proceeded to make a remarkable proposal. An antislavery magazine he edited would

> be enlarged to the size of our large Reviews, and will be freely opened to the ablest of our opponents to the extent of 100 pages each number. That there may be no occasion for the complaint of unfair play, the replies, when we see fit to make any, will be limited to the same space & type as the respective articles that have called them forth. Here then we offer to those who deprecate the effect of our agitation, access to the same readers—the power of sending the antidote along with the poison. It will be the fault of their courage or their arguments if they do not make our Magazine a pro-slavery instead of an Anti-slavery engine. Most cheerfully shall we welcome an article from your pen, either with or without your name. Should you prefer to write anonymously, you may depend upon the in-

cog[nito status] being . . . observed so far as we are concerned. Or, should any cause prevent your writing at all, we will admit any champion of your selecting on the same terms.[60]

Free Speech as a Political Issue

While citizens, lawyers, law teachers, and law students today generally think of free speech issues as matters decided by courts, the Lovejoy experience shows that free speech is a much broader political tradition and that crucial free speech decisions are made by citizens, by the press, by legislators, and by public officials who are not judges. In 1837, the idea of free speech as a principle that covered a very broad range of opinions and ideas was an important part of that tradition. Again and again, resolutions and statements in the press insisted that Lovejoy stood for every person, and that violation of his rights (yes, even of the rights of despised abolitionists) threatened the rights of all. Because they adhered to this tradition and saw free speech and press as protecting the arena of free discussion from invasion by government or mobs, people who disliked the abolition movement could and did defend free speech for abolitionists. Rejecting the tradition and insisting on a very particular weighing of the advantages and disadvantages of tolerating abolitionist speech (or other speech seen as obnoxious) would have been much more likely to produce legal or extralegal suppression. In 1837 and 1838, if suppression of abolitionist speech had not been seen as a threat to other speech, opponents of suppression would have been limited to supporters of abolition—a small group in 1837.

Private Suppression as a Violation of the Right to Free Speech

In 1835, some politicians who were unwilling to make antislavery speech and publications unlawful in the North nonetheless celebrated the actions of mobs in breaking up abolitionist meetings and presses. Many treated acts of private suppression as either benign or only mildly problematic. By 1837, many more opinion leaders recognized that free speech and press had a positive aspect (freedom to speak) as well as a negative one (freedom of governmental suppression). When governments were unable or unwilling to protect free speech from private violence, the "right" or "privilege" or "immunity" became meaningless. So, by 1837, the press and others regularly described attacks like those on Lovejoy as violations of the right to free speech and free press and as violations of state and federal constitutional rights.

By this view, rights to free speech and free press were more than simply a shield against state or federal laws abridging these freedoms. The rights implied a positive duty of government to protect their exercise. Typically, in 1837, when mobs suppressed speech, press, or assembly, criticism for failure to protect was directed to the local government. The role of the federal government (if any) in suppressing private violence aimed at speech was almost never discussed. One correspondent of the *Emancipator* did suggest in detail how local authorities should deal with threats of private violence aimed at speech:

> As to the city authorities, when there are indications of a mob, the course of duty is plain. The magistracy is solemnly bound to protect abolitionists in their constitutional and legal rights. Instead of asking them to waive their rights, shut up their halls, postpone their meetings, or yield an iota to the requisitions of the populace, they should at once declare their purpose to protect and defend them in the full exercise of their rights as citizens. To this end the whole power of the police should be brought immediately into action. The party threatened or assailed should promptly be assured of protection, and the whole community should be made to understand that the law will be enforced. . . .[61]

How to reconcile a federal system with protection against private attacks on federally guaranteed rights to free speech was a problem for another day. As a practical matter, a federal government that was attempting to suppress discussions of antislavery petitions was not likely to be active in protecting antislavery activists from mobs.

Access to Public Discourse

A central tenet held by many Americans who came to the defense of abolitionist expression was that truth would vanquish error. Of course, the idea that truth will vanquish error in free debate (optimistic as it is) assumes a free debate in which participants have access to listeners. To a remarkable extent, abolitionists had been denied access to most of the mainstream press. Both municipal and private buildings were closed to their meetings, and newspapers attacked them. Before 1837, most newspapers never or rarely directly reported what abolitionists had to say.

On the other hand, in public meetings held to decide whether they should be silenced, Lovejoy and Birney both had had an opportunity to speak.[62] A meeting in Ohio, for example, had listened in full to the Declaration of Sentiments of the Anti-Slavery Society. On February 1, 1838, the *Emancipator* noted that "[o]ne good effect of the Alton massacre, has been to obtain an insertion of Mr. Lovejoy's elaborate Declaration of Sentiments in a considerable number of newspapers which have never before published so full and convincing a statement of the principles of the Abolitionists."[63]

Because in those days the nation had a great many newspapers, perhaps it was difficult for a ruling elite consciously or unconsciously to manufacture an official view. Still, there were serious impediments to a truly free discussion in the press. Though advertisers did not yet wield great power over most newspapers, there was still the problem of the patrons and readers. As William Ellery Channing noted: "The newspaper press is fettered among us by its dependence on subscribers, among whom there are not a few intolerant enough to withdraw their patronage, if an editor give publicity to articles which contradict their cherished opinions, or shock their party prejudices, or seem to clash with their interests. In such a state of things, few newspapers can be expected to afford to an unpopular individual or party, however philanthropic or irreproachable, an opportunity of being heard by the public. Editors engage in their vocations like other men, for a support." As a result, "the newspaper press fails of one of its chief duties, which is to stem corrupt opinion, to stay the excesses of popular passions."[64]

Abolitionists dealt with the problem as best they could. They created their own newspapers. They developed a cadre of speakers who fanned out throughout the North and spoke against slavery. They held meetings. Lovejoy's death in 1837 brought wide acceptance to the abolitionist claim that slavery threatened the liberty of the North.

The Press as Defender of Free Speech and Free Press

Much of the press had strongly and unequivocally condemned the killing of Lovejoy. Up to that point, however, and with notable exceptions, the press, pulpit, and public officials had been timid at best in defense of free speech for abolitionists. Too many papers had fanned the flames of hostility. "We are sorry to say, too," wrote the *Portland Daily Courier*,

> that the people of Alton are not alone accountable for this cruel act. The blame must fall also in some degree, upon other parts of the country where scenes of a similar character have been played, and, if not absolutely approved, have been passed over almost in silence. True they have not elsewhere attained so eminent a degree. Let our readers reflect, and they will remember more than one even in our own New England, and in our own city, too, which were only less disgraceful because not so fatal in their results. They will have occasion to remember some scenes even among us, where peaceful and respectable men have been interrupted in the exercise of their legal and constitutional rights by the assaults of a rabble, and put in danger of personal injury, for no other reason than that they dared to express their own settled opinions.[65]

In a resolution, the executive committee of the American Anti-Slavery Society complained "that a fearful responsibility rests upon editors, who have misrepresented the doctrines and measures of abolitionists, and excited misguided individuals to interrupt their meetings, and menace their persons, property, and lives."[66] Though some like the executive committee of the Anti-Slavery Society, noted the complicity of the press in the climate of suppression, few, if any, suggested legal sanctions. Perhaps the faith that error could be checked by more discussion was one factor. As a practical matter, a dominant group—as the opponents of abolitionists were at the time—was quite unlikely to prosecute itself.

Southern Suppression

Opponents of Slavery in Virginia and North Carolina Courts from the 1830s to the 1850s

While the North moved toward a broader popular theory of free speech, much of the South was another matter. On March 23, 1836, Virginia passed a comprehensive act aimed at suppressing antislavery agitation. It was a response, the Virginia legislature claimed, to attempts by antislavery societies and "evil disposed persons to interfere with the relations existing between master and slave in this state" and to incite a spirit of insurrection and insubordination in blacks. The legislature noted the flood of "incendiary books, pamphlets, or other writings of an inflammatory and mischievous . . . tendency." Although the antislavery societies were sending their tracts to free whites, not black slaves, the Virginia legislature was in no mood for fine distinctions.

The law provided a fine and mandatory imprisonment of "any member of an abolition or anti-slavery society" who "shall come into this state, and shall here maintain, by speaking or writing, that the owners of slaves have no property in the same, or advocate or advise the abolition of slavery." That part of the statute targeted outsiders. Another section of the act made it criminal for any person to produce or circulate any book or writing "with the intent of advising, enticing, or persuading persons of colour within this commonwealth . . . to rebel, *or* denying the master the right of property in their slaves, and inculcating the duty of resistance to such right." Slaves violating this section were to be whipped, sold, and transported out of the country. Whites were to be imprisoned not less than two years.[67] A third section of the act required postmasters to notify justices of the peace if incendiary documents appeared in the mail. The justice was to burn the document and, if the recipient had willingly received the book or pamphlet knowing its tendency, he too was to be punished. Finally the act provided for punishment of postmasters who failed to comply with the act. Under this statute the *New York Tribune*, a leading Republican paper, was banned by a Virginia postmaster in 1859.[68]

Some provisions of the Virginia act clearly punished political speech that did not directly incite criminal conduct.[69] Under the Virginia act, publications of some of the speeches of emancipationists in the Virginia legislature could be found to be criminal. Virginia had taken a long step toward censoring political speech. In 1832, "Appomattox" branded emancipationist sentiments incendiary and called for private action to suppress them. Significantly he refused to call for a sedition law, a law making criticism of government and existing institutions a crime.[70] By 1836 Virginia had passed one. It dampened, but did not completely silence dissent on the slavery issue in Virginia. That continued up to and during the Civil War.

The Virginia supreme court construed the statute of 1836 narrowly. It did not, however, announce that the Virginia constitution simply prohibited such legislation. In 1839, in *Commonwealth v. Barrett*, Mr. Barrett was prosecuted for circulating an antislavery petition to Congress. The petition denounced slavery in the District of Columbia as a sin against God and a foul stain on the national character.[71] The court concluded that Barrett could not be convicted under the first section of the act without proof that he was a member of an abolition society. The prosecution under the third section of the act was a felony and could not proceed by information. The legislature later plugged the loophole in the act.[72]

In 1849 Jarvis Bacon, a minister, was indicted and convicted for words in a sermon: "If I was to go to my neighbor's crib and steal his corn, you would call me a thief, but [it is] worse to take a human being and keep him all his life, and give him nothing for his labour, except once in a while a whipping." Listeners, not surprisingly, understood him to refer to slavery. The defense attorneys suggested that the Virginia statute of 1836 reached only denial of legal right to property in slaves, not moral right. Nor could the legislature make denial of moral right to property in slaves a crime. To do so would violate the Virginia constitution's free speech and freedom of religion guarantees "which [declare] that they shall pass 'no law abridging freedom of speech.' 'Nor shall any man be enforced, restrained, molested or burthened in his body or goods, or otherwise suffer on account of his religious opinions or belief, but all men shall be free to profess, and by argument to maintain, their opinions in matters of religion.'"[73]

Justice Lomax, writing for the court, held that statutes tending to restrain freedom of speech or freedom of religion "or supposed to have that tendency," should be strictly construed. The court found the defendant's words ambiguous. After all, if one kept a slave and gave him no comforts and nourishment but only whipped him, even supporters of slavery might find this act worse than stealing corn. The defendant's statements might have referred only to spiritual concerns, not to legal title. To find the defendant guilty "[w]e must make him say, that to take and keep a human being (or say slave,) is worse than stealing corn, such taking and keeping being equally without right of property in the slave-owner, as in the thief who has stolen the corn."[74] While the court decided for the defendant, it did not announce a broad constitutional protection for free speech.

Defendants in North Carolina did not fare so well. Jesse McBride was an antislavery preacher from the antislavery Wesleyan Church. He came to North Carolina from Ohio and, with a fellow Wesleyan minister who had preceded him, preached to congregations in Guilford and surrounding counties. McBride gave a young white girl a pamphlet on the Ten Commandments; it suggested that slaveholders lived in violation of the Commandments. In 1850 he was charged with violation of an 1830 North Carolina statute that made it a crime knowingly to circulate or publish any pamphlet "the evident tendency whereof would be to excite insurrection, conspiracy or resistance in the slaves or free negroes and persons of color with the State."[75] The Declaration of Rights of the North Carolina Constitution contained no explicit free speech provision, but it provided "[t]hat the freedom of the Press is one of the great bulwarks of liberty, and therefore, ought never to be restrained" and that "all men have a natural and unalienable right to worship Almighty God according to the dictates of their own consciences."[76] At trial, these provisions did not protect McBride.

The available sources do not discuss McBride's legal arguments sufficiently to know how guarantees of free press and religious liberty were applied or even if the issues were raised. Perhaps the freedom of the press provision might have been read, in the Blackstonian tradition, as limited to prior censorship rather than prohibiting subsequent punishment. Perhaps freedom of the press was more broadly understood, but simply was not understood to include attacks on the institution of slavery. At any rate, McBride was convicted and sentenced to imprisonment for one year, to stand in the pillory for one hour, and to twenty lashes. He was released as part of an agreement that he leave the state. Though a colleague continued preaching for a time, as public pressure mounted he also fled, leaving their flock without a minister.[77]

FROM MORAL SUASION TO NATIONAL POLITICS: THE TRANSFORMATION OF ABOLITION

Concern about the right to criticize slavery became more compelling as slavery became the central political issue facing the nation. In frantic attempts to secure its "peculiar institution," the Southern elite had insisted on muzzling abolitionist petitions, on silencing abolitionists (even in the North) and, most fatally, on expanded territory for slavery so that the power of slave states could continue, roughly at least, to balance that of the free.

Paradoxically, the more the Southern elite insisted on security for slavery, the more insecure slavery became. The abolitionist observation that slavery threatened the liberty of the North became more obvious to others. In 1837, William Ellery Channing highlighted the paradoxical quest for Southern security (or perhaps for an independent Southern nation) in the demand for annexation of Texas as a slave state. The annexation of Texas, he warned, would

> endanger the Union. It will give new violence and passion to the agitation of the question of slavery. It is well known, that a majority at the North have discouraged the discussion of this topic, on the ground, that slavery was imposed on the South by necessity, that its continuance of was not of choice, and the states, in which it subsists, if left to themselves, would find a remedy in their own way. Let slavery be systematically proposed as the policy of these states, let it bind them together in efforts to establish political power, and a new feeling will burst forth through the whole North. It will be a concentration of moral, religious, political and patriotic feelings. The fire, now smothered, will blaze out, and of consequence, new jealousies and exasperation will be kindled at the South. Strange that the South should think of securing its "peculiar institutions" by violent means. Its violence necessarily increases the evils it would suppress.—for example, by denying the right of petition to those who sought the abolition of slavery within the immediate jurisdiction of the United States, it has awakened a spirit, which will overwhelm Congress with petitions, till this right be restored. The annexation of Texas would be a measure of the same injurious character, and would stir up an open uncompromising hostility to slavery, of which we have seen no example, and would produce a reaction very dangerous to the Union.[78]

If the South favors expansion of slavery, Channing warned, a separate nation will be required. "It should borrow the code of the Dictator of Paraguay, and seal itself hermetically against the infectious books, opinions, and visits of foreigners."[79]

After great controversy, Texas was annexed in 1845 and a war with Mexico followed. The victory of the United States in that war greatly expanded the territory of the nation, and exacerbated the controversy over slavery in the territories. As the controversy over Texas intensified, one group of abolitionists dramatically changed tactics. In 1843 the Liberty Party, a party based on opposition to slavery and especially to its expansion, nominated James G. Birney for president. In later years there were other antislavery parties, and they also nominated candidates for president—the Free Soil Party in 1848 and the Republican Party in 1856 and 1860. Antislavery had entered politics. In the years after the founding of the Liberty Party, as the controversy over slavery intensified, antislavery parties were increasingly successful.

Demands to expand slavery had changed the political equation. The 1820 Missouri Compromise had prohibited slavery in the remainder of the Louisiana Purchase lying north of latitude 36°30′. Although the Kansas and Nebraska territories were included in the Missouri Compromise as areas where slavery was forbidden, in 1854 Congress abrogated the compromise, bowing to Southern demands. The Kansas-Nebraska Act provided for the admission of Kansas and Nebraska with or without slavery as their constitutions might provide. Slavery was no longer an institution confined to the South. Expansion of slavery threatened Northern artisans, mechanics, and farmers with direct competition from slave labor in the territories.

The Kansas-Nebraska Act struck the political world like a giant asteroid and so changed the environment that older forms of political life gradually became extinct. Thirty-seven of the forty-four Northern Democratic House members who voted for the Kansas-Nebraska Act were defeated in the next election. The Republican Party, founded in 1854 largely on hostility to the Kansas-Nebraska Act, made a strong run for the presidency in 1856. The Whig Party began to disintegrate. In 1857, in *Dred Scott v. Sanford*, the U.S. Supreme Court ruled that Americans had a constitutional right to hold slaves in all territories, a right Congress could not deny. The Republican platforms of 1856 and 1860, on the other hand, insisted that slavery in the territories deprived slaves of their liberty without due process of law and was unconstitutional. Since the keystone of the Republican platform was exclusion of slavery from the territories, *Dred Scott* implied that the Republican party platform was itself unconstitutional.[80]

After *Dred Scott*, Republicans feared a slave power conspiracy to nationalize slavery, to spread it not only to all the territories but to the free states as well. And slavery, as many Republicans saw it, inevitably required the suppression of liberty. As Senator Charles Sumner, the proabolition senator from Massachusetts put it in 1860, denial of rights to the slave "can be sustained only by disregard of other rights, common to the whole community, whether of person, of the press, or of speech.... [S]ince slavery is endangered by liberty in any form, therefore all liberty must be restrained." Tobias Plants, a conservative Republican congressman, would make essentially the same point in 1866.[81] It was part of the common faith of the Republican Party. The progression seemed clear and grim, from enslaving blacks to limiting the free speech rights of Southerners and Northerners in the South; from censorship in the South to censorship in slave territories and demands for censorship in the North; from demands for Northern censorship to the clubbing of Senator Sumner in the Senate for making a harsh antislavery speech; from slavery in the Southern states with a ban on slavery in national territory to a constitutional requirement that slavery be tolerated in all national territory—and next, Republicans feared, in Northern states as well.[82]

THE ANTISLAVERY CONSTITUTIONAL RESPONSE

In the controversy over slavery and civil liberty, an antislavery constitutional analysis began to emerge. The analysis soon mutated and spread from abolitionists to many politically active opponents of slavery. Opponents of slavery began to object that suppression of free speech in the South violated the federal Constitution. Eventually, the vision of a national Constitution that protected citizens in their basic liberties even against state denial was embraced by mainstream members of the Republican Party. There were compelling reasons for politically active opponents of slavery to embrace such ideas. Although some Southern courts lacked enthusiasm for enforcing laws against antislavery expression,[83] the prospect was bleak that Southern laws and court decisions would offer broad protection of free speech for opponents of slavery. Without free speech in the South, political elimination of slavery seemed impossible.

Radical political abolitionists began to appeal to the federal Constitution both against slavery and for protection of civil liberties against state action.[84] Abolitionists split between those who favored political action (and a separate antislavery party) and those who rejected politics. For abolitionists allied with William Lloyd Garrison, editor of the *Liberator* (who rejected voting), constitutional theory was simple. Garrisonians agreed with extreme Southerners that the Constitution was a proslavery document, and Garrison denounced it as a "covenant with death" and an "agreement with hell."[85] Garrison's ally, Wendell Phillips, insisted on interpreting the Constitution based on original intent. Phillips contended that the Constitution did not sanction interference with slavery in the states, a view shared by most opponents of slavery before the Civil War. Phillips's claim that the Constitution protected slavery in the Southern states was rejected by a small group of radical abolitionists. But Phillips went further. He insisted that even free blacks were viewed as inferior beings at the time of the adoption of the Constitution, and it did not "concede them any of its privileges."[86] But the radical political abolitionists had a very different view. For them, the Constitution protected civil liberties of whites and blacks against both state and federal action and for the most advanced, it also outlawed slavery even in the Southern states. The more moderate political antislavery activists did not go that far. But many believed that the due process clause outlawed slavery only in federal territories (as the Republican platforms of 1856 and 1860 proclaimed) and that the Bill of Rights established national liberties that states should respect.

In his 1838 book, *American Liberties and American Slavery Morally and Politically Illustrated,*[87] the newspaper editor and free soil political activist Seymour Treadwell defended free speech and asserted that state laws abridging it violated the federal Constitution. Southerners could come North and criticize Northern institutions (and even advocate slavery, as many opponents of slavery pointed out) and none attempted "to abridge their liberty of speech, or suppress their freedom of opinion, for they are American citizens, still under the gratefully waving banner of the American constitution."[88] Treadwell rejected the claim that "the States are so many independent nations, and that they may enact laws abridging the constitutional liberties of American citizens."[89]

Joel Tiffany, author of a *Treatise on the Unconstitutionality of American Slavery,*[90] espoused a radical antislavery reading of the Constitution. Tiffany was a lawyer and reporter for the New York supreme court who grew up in a hotbed of antislavery agitation in Ohio. He believed that the guarantees of liberty in the original Constitution and in the Bill of Rights limited the states and protected all citizens of the United States from state action infringing their rights. In adopting this interpretation, Tiffany, though unorthodox, was not unique.[91] Citizens were entitled to "all the privileges and immunities . . . guaranteed in the Federal Constitution"[92] which included all its "guarantys . . . for personal security [and] . . . liberty."[93] These were protected from hostile state legislation. Some of the privileges guaranteed were listed by Tiffany: for example, the right to petition, to habeas corpus, to keep and bear arms, not to be deprived of liberty without due process of law, and against unwarrantable searches and seizures.[94]

As between one citizen and another, Tiffany thought protection of rights was left largely to the states. Although the Bill of Rights limited the states, where states fulfilled their duty of protection of citizens' rights, the Bill of Rights typically did not provide a remedy for one citizen wronged by another private citizen. As a result, Tiffany insisted that his theory charted a middle course between states' rights and consolidation into a national government with virtually unlimited jurisdiction and power.[95] Then, in a dramatic leap, Tiffany concluded that slaves, like all persons born or naturalized in the United States, were citizens.[96] Although few antislavery politicians agreed that slaves were citizens, Tiffany's other constitutional doctrines became increasingly influential. Congressman John Bingham of Ohio, later author of Section 1 of the Fourteenth Amendment, was one among many in the Republican mainstream influenced by a view of civil liberty like that espoused by Tiffany.

The Kansas Territory gave Republicans a preview of what to expect from slavery in the territories, and the controversy over "bleeding Kansas" heightened concern for civil liberty. Slaveowners and opponents of slavery poured into Kansas and the territory literally became a battleground in the sectional conflict. The proslavery government of the territory enacted a slave code. It made expressing antislavery opinions a crime; provided the death penalty for helping slaves escape; and required voters to take an oath to support these laws.[97]

Bingham was one critic of the Kansas laws suppressing antislavery speech. His bristling antipathy to the Kansas statute is clear from his 1856 speech in the House of Representatives:

Congress is to abide by this statute, which makes it a felony for a citizen to utter or publish in that Territory "any sentiment calculated to induce slaves to escape from the service of their masters." Hence it would be a felony there to utter the strong words of Algernon Sidney, "resistance to tyrants is obedience to God;" . . . a felony to read in the hearing of one of those fettered bondsmen the words of the Declaration, "All men are born free and equal, and endowed by their Creator with the inalienable rights of life and liberty;" . . . Before you hold this enactment to be law, burn our immortal Declaration and our free-written Constitution, fetter our free press, and finally penetrate the human soul and put out the light of understanding which the breath of the Almighty hath kindled.[98]

Bingham's invocation of the Declaration showed the havoc that a theory justifying suppression of speech because of "bad tendencies" could play with the protection of political speech. But Bingham underestimated the potential reach of laws suppressing antislavery expression because of its perceived bad tendencies. By 1860 the North Carolina supreme court would hold that the incendiary statements need not initially be heard by, or directed to, slaves or blacks to justify conviction of those circulating them. Suppression of distribution to whites was required because of the danger the statements could eventually reach blacks.[99]

The Kansas statute barring free speech against slavery was much like those enacted in Southern states. Since Kansas was a federal territory, Bingham insisted, the limitations of the First Amendment clearly applied to it. Under the decision in *Barron v. Baltimore*, however, the guarantees of the Bill of Rights did not prevent the states from enacting such statutes. There was significant dissent from *Barron*. Indeed a significant minority of state supreme courts held that the rights in the Bill of Rights limited state legislation, *Barron* to the contrary notwithstanding.[100]

Even before the Civil War, however, John Bingham, like a number of other Republicans, read Article IV, Section 2, as directing states to respect all constitutional guarantees of liberty. One orthodox reading of Article IV limited it to protecting temporary out-of-state visitors from discrimination in certain basic rights. The article provides: "The citizens of each State shall be entitled to all Privileges and Immunities of Citizens in the several states."[101] Bingham and others read it as containing an ellipsis, as implicitly containing the material added in brackets: "The Citizens of each State shall be entitled to all Privileges and Immunities of Citizens [of the United States] in the several States."[102] He read "privileges" as dictionaries of that time and today do: as meaning rights.[103] The result was that the privileges referred to in the First Amendment and the rest of the Bill of Rights in some sense limited the states under Article IV. The privileges of citizens of the United States included those rights listed in the Bill of Rights.

In using the word "privileges" to describe rights such as free speech and jury trial, Bingham was using it exactly as members of the revolutionary and founding generation often had used it and as James Madison used the word in the debate on the Bill of Rights.[104] Bingham believed that states were morally obligated to obey the guarantees of the Bill of Rights by the oath state officers took to support the Constitution. Still, he believed the Article IV, Section 2, obligation was not legally enforceable. Although this reading seems strange to us today, it was a federalism-based reading of Article IV that fit well with interpretations the Supreme Court had put on some *other* provisions of the article.[105] This interpretation preserved an appeal to the moral authority of the Bill of Rights, and that moral authority was one way Madison hoped the bill would function to protect liberty.[106] But if moral suasion failed, judicial protection was not available.

The range of constitutional thinking before the Civil War was quite broad. Some followed the orthodoxy of *Barron v. Baltimore*, which held that the Bill of Rights did not limit the states. Some, like Bingham, believed that in some sense states were obligated to obey the guarantees of the Bill of Rights. Others, including many Southern and Northern Democrats, believed that slaves were property and that the due process clause guaranteed the right to take them into federal territories and that antislavery legislation was unconstitutional. In 1856 and 1860 the Republican platform said that slaves were persons and that the due process clause banned slavery in federal territories, though not in the states.[107]

As Republicans saw it, the slaveholding elite was struggling to make slavery national. At the same time, Republicans began to embrace the idea that the liberties of American citizens were national. By 1859–60 the idea that free speech and press were national rights or "privileges" that no state should abridge was commonly being expressed by mainstream members of the Republican Party in debate in Congress. The collision between a state-centered vision of the scope of permissible speech and a nation-centered vision produced an uproar in Congress in 1859–1860. The centerpiece of the debate was a book by North Carolinian Hinton Rowan Helper, *The Impending Crisis of the South: How to Meet It.*

12

The Free Speech Battle over Helper's

Impending Crisis

Hinton Rowan Helper was born to a farm-owning family in Davie County, North Carolina, in 1829. Except for forays into California and South America in unsuccessful attempts to make his fortune, Helper lived in North Carolina until publication of his book, *The Impending Crisis*, in 1857.[1]

The book was an appeal for antislavery political action by non–slave owners of the South. Helper advocated forming an antislavery party, refusing to vote for slaveholders, socially ostracizing slaveholders, boycotting proslavery newspapers, and boycotting slave labor.[2] Helper's plan for emancipation would not compensate slave owners; instead they would be taxed to pay the costs of colonizing their former slaves or of resettling them in the United States. Helper sought to prove, with assistance from census data, that the South had become an economic disaster area because of slavery. He saw slavery as especially inimical to the interests of nonslaveholding whites. Much of the book consisted of charts, tables, and statistics from the census to demonstrate Southern backwardness, statements from men of the revolutionary generation to show the evils of slavery, and excerpts from the Virginia abolition debates of 1832.[3]

Helper was a self-described abolitionist (free-soilers, he said, were just abolitionists in the tadpole stage),[4] and he faced the same dilemma other abolitionists faced. He sought to speak emancipation to the South, but the South refused to listen. Abolition expression was silenced by laws and mobs.

Helper repeatedly noted that free speech was denied to opponents of slavery in the South, and he protested mobbings and tar-and-featherings. "Free speech," Helper wrote, "is considered as treason against slavery: and when people dare neither speak nor print their thoughts, free thought itself is well nigh extinguished."[5] "Give us fair-play," he demanded, "secure to us the right of discussion, the freedom of speech, and we will settle the difficulty at the ballot box, not on the battleground—by force of reason, not force of arms."[6] Critics of the book did not usually cite such statements. Instead, like the *Richmond Whig,* they quoted other parts of the book, including the following passage:

> So it seems that the total number of actual slave owners, including their entire crew of cringing lickspittles, against whom we have to contend, is but three hundred and forty-seven thousand five hundred and twenty-five. Against this army for the defense and propagation of slavery, we think it will be an easy matter—independent of the negroes, who, in nine cases out of ten, would be delighted with an opportunity to cut their masters' throats . . . —to muster one at least three times as large, and far more respectable for its utter extinction. . . . We are determined to abolish slavery at all hazards—in defiance of all opposition, of whatever nature, which it is possible for the slavocrats to bring against us.[7]

These sentiments were followed by a plea for a peaceful and political resolution of differences,[8] but the *Whig* did not reprint those statements. The most sympathetic interpretation of the violence suggested by some of Helper's rhetoric is that it was contingent and designed to demonstrate Helper's willingness to meet violence with violence to protect access to the channels of political expression for supporters of emancipation.

Even in the calmest of times, the sentiments quoted in the *Whig* would have enraged Southern supporters of slavery. In fact, however, most of the controversy about the *Impending Crisis* occurred after John Brown's raid at Harpers Ferry in 1859, a raid that was designed to free slaves by force of arms.

Helper's book was first published in 1857, on the heels of Republican John Frémont's defeat in the presidential election of 1856. Many Northern opponents of slavery praised the book, which enjoyed significant, but limited, success. Opponents of slavery and Republican politicians hit upon the idea of publishing an abridgment, a "compendium" of the work and circulating it as a campaign document.[9] This project was advertised and was well under way before Brown's October 1859 raid. Over sixty Republican members of Congress had endorsed the project.[10]

THE CONTEXT FOR CONGRESSIONAL DISCUSSION, 1859–1860

On October 18, 1859, the *New York Herald* reported, "NEGRO INSUR-RECTION AT HARPERS FERRY. STRANGE AND EXCITING INTELLI-GENCE. . . . [R]egular negro conspiracy."[11] The *Herald*'s editor saw the event as a potent means of discrediting the Republican Party. The Democratic spin doctors of the day said the raid was the natural consequence of Republican doctrine. On the following day, together with more news of the events at Harpers Ferry, Virginia, the *Herald* reprinted a speech by Senator William Seward of New York, a leading contender for the Republican presidential nomination.[12] Seward had suggested an "irrepressible conflict"[13] between slavery and freedom. "No reasoning mind," the *Herald* editorialized, "can fail to trace cause and effect between the bloody and brutal manifesto of William H. Seward . . . and the terrible scenes of violence" [at Harpers Ferry].[14] Later the *Herald* printed a list of Republican endorsers of Helper's book together with what it claimed were inflammatory passages from the book. "TEXT BOOK OF REVOLU-TION," screamed the headline, "Republican Congressmen Franking Revolutionary Appeals."[15] Here was another "Black Republican" blueprint for Harpers Ferry. In December 1859 a grand jury in Wilson County, North Carolina, added a literal indictment to the political ones: it branded *The Impending Crisis* treasonous to North Carolina and called on New York Republican governor Edwin Morgan to deliver "to indictment and punishment" Republican endorsers of the book, including the governor himself.[16] Of course, no trial followed the indictment because the defendants were beyond the reach of the North Carolina court.

Many slaveholders had always viewed any call for abolition as an incitement to slaves to revolt and any abolitionist association as a conspiracy. By 1858–60, however, their fears had a greater basis in reality. Republicans typically disavowed violence and preached obedience to the law. But after years of being forbidden to discuss abolition in the South, many abolitionists were becoming more militant. In 1850 William Lloyd Garrison urged slaves to emancipate themselves by running away. In 1854 abolitionist and former pacifist Angelina Grimké Weld confessed that she preferred bloodshed and servile war to permanent slavery.[17] But while most abolitionists merely talked, John Brown, a fifty-nine-year-old abolitionist, acted. He organized a group of blacks and whites who attacked the federal arsenal at Harpers Ferry in 1859 to seize arms for the slaves he hoped would rise in revolt. The raid failed, and Brown was captured, tried, and hanged. Some abolitionists plotted with Brown or otherwise sought to instigate slave rebellions. The group that bankrolled Brown included Massachusetts minister Theodore Parker—a prolific and powerful writer against the slave power who seems to have inspired some of Abraham Lincoln's antislavery rhetoric—and Gerrit Smith, a wealthy long-time abolitionist. In 1858, Boston attorney and abolitionist legal theorist Lysander Spooner advocated arming blacks for guerrilla warfare. After the John Brown raid, Frederick Douglass also justified violence as a means of ending slavery, and Wendell Phillips proudly proclaimed that "insurrection of thought always precedes insurrection of action." Leading Republicans, meanwhile, had maintained contact with abolitionists, though there is no evidence that they knew of or supported Brown's raid. William Herndon, Lincoln's law partner, was in touch with Theodore Parker and with William Lloyd Garrison, and Herndon subscribed to the abolitionist newspaper, *The Liberator*.[18] Lincoln and Republican politicians generally condemned the John Brown raid. (Of course, whatever one thinks of it, funding John Brown's raid was not speech or press.)

THE DEMOCRATIC ATTACK

When Congress convened in December 1859, the Democrats attempted again and again to blame John Brown's raid on the Republican Party. Democrats, particularly Southern congressmen, cast themselves in the roles of prosecutor and judge. They cast Republicans as criminal defendants—accessories before the fact to the Harpers Ferry raid. Democratic logic was simple: Helper's book tended to cause violence; the violence of John Brown's raid followed publication of Helper's book; Republicans had endorsed the book; therefore the Republicans had endorsed violence. At a minimum, Democrats insisted, violence was the natural consequence of antislavery doctrines.[19] To support this charge, Democrats offered the expert opinion of a veteran abolitionist agitator. John Brown's raid, they quoted Wendell Phillips as saying, was "the natural result of anti-slavery teaching. For one, I accept it; I expected it."[20] Although the debate on *The Impending Crisis* began in the House, it soon spilled over into the Senate.

John Sherman, Republican candidate for Speaker of the House of

Representatives, like nearly half the Republican congressional delegation, had endorsed publication of an abridged version of Helper's book. A resolution proposed by Democratic representative John Clark of Missouri announced that no endorser of Helper's book was fit to be Speaker.[21] After forty-four ballots Republicans still fell just short of electing John Sherman as Speaker. Finally, Sherman withdrew in favor of a compromise candidate.

Between ballots, Democrats in the House (and also in the Senate) discussed slavery, Senator William Seward, and most of all *The Impending Crisis*. Democrats, by placing the worst possible construction on Helper's (or Seward's) words, sought to tag their political opponents as advocates of violence. Fire was the dominant metaphor. Senator Alfred Iverson of Georgia announced that Helper's book "inculcates incendiary sentiments."[22] Republicans, said Representative Roger Pryor of Virginia, had applied "the spark, and then affect astonishment at the explosion."[23] Representative Clark of Missouri emphasized Helper's announcement that nonslaveholders should act peaceably if they could, and forcibly if they must, to strike against slavery. "Do these [Republican] gentlemen expect that they can distribute incendiary books, give incendiary advice, [and] advise rebellion . . . ?" He thundered that "[s]uch advice is treason . . . rebellion." Those knowingly giving it deserved a fate it would not be respectful to announce.[24]

Concern for such civilities did not last long. Helper's book, said Senator Iverson, returning to the attack, advised "our slaves to fire our dwellings and put their knives to our throats." We "ought to hang every man who has approved or indorsed it."[25] Senator Seward shared the billing with Helper as an incendiary. Senator Jefferson Davis of Mississippi, after noting the law of accessories before the fact, cited Seward's "irrepressible conflict" speech: "That Senator made his speech before the event; he may not have contemplated the fruit it bore—if, indeed, it bore this." But, Davis said, when Senator Lyman Trumbull of Illinois defended the speech after the Harpers Ferry raid (arguing that it was being misconstrued), he was "far more guilty" than Seward.[26] Representative Reuben Davis, also from Mississippi, later suggested that Seward "deserves, I think the gallows."[27] Representative Thomas Hindman of Arkansas announced that John Brown, "was the tool of Republicanism, doing its work; and now, that the work is done, Republican politicians cannot skulk the responsibility." The country would "gibbet them for it," and the hemp that strangled Brown would strangle the instigators.[28]

So it went, week after week, as Republicans repeatedly fell a few votes short of the majority required to make Sherman the Speaker. Congressmen came to the floor armed, and some Southerners contemplated coups and blood baths and wondered about the best way to launch secession. Slave state Democrats announced that the election of a "Black Republican President" would be a good reason for secession. One suggested that the Union could be preserved only if the essentially "criminal" Republican Party disbanded.[29]

THE REPUBLICAN RESPONSE

Most Republicans in the House concluded that discussion of substantive issues was improper before the election of a Speaker.[30] So they sat in silence. Sherman announced that he had no recollection of endorsing Helper's book and in any case had not read it. He had relied on the suggestion of a friend. He disavowed any action by the North to interfere with the domestic institutions of the South. A letter from one of the sponsors of the compendium edition indicated that the compendium was supposed to delete offensive passages.[31]

Republicans worried that the Democratic effort to link them to Harpers Ferry might work, and a few conservative Republicans rushed to dissociate themselves from *The Impending Crisis*. Several recanted their endorsements, pleading ignorance, and repudiated the book.[32] Democratic Representative Lucius Q. C. Lamar of Mississippi suggested that the effort at repair came "too late for the victims of the Harper's Ferry tragedy."[33] Republicans, he said, were guilty of the blood spilled on that occasion. Several House Republicans complained (accurately) that the Democrats had grossly misrepresented Helper's book and, after the eight-week speakership deadlock was broken, more Republicans did so.[34]

The early Republican reticence is curious. They were a few votes short of what they needed, and perhaps conciliation by conservative members and silence by the rest was intended to be reassuring. At any rate, the initial failure of Republicans to vigorously defend Helper's book disgusted the *New York Tribune* and some party activists.[35] William Herndon, Lincoln's law partner, suggested that Republicans in Congress were "grinding off the flesh from their knee caps."[36] Eventually, after a Speaker was finally selected, Republicans spoke powerfully and explicitly to the issues of the day. Then Republican after Republican roundly condemned the

South for its repression of free speech. All in all, the session was remarkable for its lengthy discussions of slavery, the territories, natural rights, the views of the founding generation, the Declaration of Independence, secession, and free speech. The debate on free speech was a centerpiece of the session.

The Debate on Free Speech: Politics and Theory

The 1859 congressional debate was conducted by politicians, not by jurists, legal theorists, or political philosophers. As a result, theories, to the extent they were discussed, were often implicit rather than explicit. Some Democrats suggested that Helper's book and Seward's "irrepressible conflict" speech,[37] had incited the Harpers Ferry raid, and that the inciters were as guilty as the perpetrators. They did not frame their analysis in terms of the limits on free speech. Still, these Democrats necessarily, though implicitly, embraced a very broad definition of incitement that included those who did not in fact advocate violence as the way to end slavery. They also implicitly embraced the theory that political speech with bad tendencies could be suppressed.[38] When they supported silencing abolitionists in Southern states, they were, at least implicitly, saying guarantees for free expression under both state and federal constitutions did not prohibit such actions.

The Democrats focused the debate on Helper and Seward, as examples of the evil tendency of Republican doctrine—a doctrine said to be capable of producing horrible acts of violence. There were curious aspects to the attack. The official justification for suppression of antislavery speech in the South was that it had the tendency to cause violence and insurrections by the slaves. The slaveholder was particularly vulnerable, Jefferson Davis noted, because "[t]he negroes, as domestics, have access at all hours through the unlocked doors of their master's houses."[39] Still, for important and "proper" political purposes, Southerners and Democrats were republishing the very statements thought to be too dangerous to tolerate. Democratic and Southern newspapers ripped parts of the "incendiary" Helper book out of context and spread the excerpts throughout the North and South. They also published at least portions of Seward's "irrepressible conflict" speech.[40] Indeed, when Republicans complained that their doctrines were not permitted to circulate in the South, Southern members of Congress pointed to Southern papers that had reprinted Seward's speech.

Senator Benjamin F. Wade of Ohio, a strong foe of slavery, thought this a curious paradox. If incendiary matter was dangerous, asked Wade, was not the "most dangerous" of all that "which went to teach the people [of the South] that a great party, controlling all the free States, were sympathizing with raids upon the South; were ready to lend themselves to any uprising that might be got up there." Still this "most dangerous of all" incendiary speech was carried into Southern states by the Democratic version of Republican ideas, without Republican antidote or explanation. This was so because Republican papers were not permitted to circulate there.[41]

The final irony was that the attack on Helper's book transformed it from a moderate success to a raging bestseller. One hundred and forty-two thousand copies of the book had been distributed by the fall of 1860.[42] In December 1860 the *New York Tribune*, which was promoting the book, cheerfully reported that Southern "Fire-eaters" and Northern "Doughfaces" had by their persistent discussion of *The Impending Crisis* generated a circulation rapidly approaching that of *Uncle Tom's Cabin*.[43]

The opponents of slavery were quick to see a political agenda in the paradoxical Democratic approach to the problem. Early in the session, Senator John P. Hale of New Hampshire suggested that Northern Democrats, decimated by their support of the Kansas-Nebraska Act, were weeping crocodile tears for the victims of the Harpers Ferry raid. He said some Northern Democrats, "whom the tender solicitude of their constituents had left in the retirement of private life, free from the corroding cares of public station . . . received the news of this outbreak in Virginia with a perfect yell of delight." They hoped to use it as "something they could catch hold of to ride into power."[44] Abraham Lincoln, in a speech at Cooper Institute, suggested that Democrats were trying to use "John Brown, [the] Helper book, and the like [to] break up the Republican organization."[45] Political implications were never far from the center of the controversy. Southern secessionists used Helper, Seward, and Harpers Ferry to show why secession was imperative if a "Black Republican" were elected president; Northern Democrats used the same events as a stick with which to beat the "sectional" Republican Party; and Republicans used the secessionist speeches to discredit Northern Democrats.

In the controversy over antislavery expression, Republicans thought they heard the jingle of gold coins. Representative John Bingham of Ohio suggested that a powerful slave-owning plutocracy sought to protect slavery in order to protect its economic interests. "These gentlemen apprehend," said Bingham, "that if free speech is tolerated and free labor protected by law, free labor might attain . . . such dignity . . . as would bring into disrepute the system of slave labor, and bring about if you please, gradual emancipation, thereby interfering with the profits of these gentlemen."[46] Abraham Lincoln warned of the "proneness of prosperity to breed tyrants." Lincoln also told the story of a dissenting minister who asked an orthodox minister to read a word in a Bible verse. Then he put a gold coin over the word and asked if the orthodox minister could still read it. Slave owners, Lincoln continued, saw slaves as property and demanded "laws and institutions and a public policy that shall increase and secure its value and make it durable, lasting, and universal." Whether they saw slavery as it was, Lincoln said, "is not for me to say, but if they do they see it through a coating of 2,000,000,000 dollars, and that is a pretty thick coating." Slave property influenced the mind of the slaveholder and led him to see slavery as right.[47]

Although one complaint about Helper's book was that it would lead the slaves to violence, another concern was clearly present. Some Democrats warned of means "other than those which John Brown resorted to."[48] Helper and Republicans, Democrats asserted, were trying to develop a local opposition among the nonslaveholding white majority of the South. Ultimately, Democratic senator George Pugh of Ohio charged, they hoped "to strike down slavery [in the South] by changing state constitutions."[49] Indeed, Republicans did hope to use nonslaveholders as a great electoral lever to democratically achieve emancipation in the South. In particular, Republicans planned to use patronage, free speech, and free access to the mails to develop this local opposition after a Republican was elected president. John Sherman wrote Lydia Child suggesting that within two years of the election of a Republican president, there would be a Republican Party in every Southern state. A Republican victory, Sherman insisted, would encourage the Southern states themselves to emancipate the slaves. In this sense the Southern fear of a Republican attack on slavery in the South was well founded. Republican postmasters would not be likely to censor Republican or antislavery literature. Democratic senator William Gwin of California suggested that Southern states would not tolerate Republican postmasters.[50] (In those days, of course, postmasters were key political operatives and organizers, not just deliverers of mail.)

Some Republican complaints about suppression of speech in the

South could be handled by constitutional doctrine that was consistent with the holding of *Barron v. Baltimore* that the guarantee of free speech did not limit the states. Some Southern laws and actions explicitly discriminated against out-of-state "agitators" or publications. Those might be answered by a conventional reading of Article IV, Section 2, of the Constitution that prohibited discrimination against out-of-staters. Democrats had long pointed out, however, that laws in the South typically did not discriminate against those from other states. Antislavery expression was equally forbidden for Southern opponents of slavery.[51] Sometimes, Southerners suppressed supporters of the national Republican party or its candidates. Such actions might be dealt with not by invoking a broad view of free speech, but by insisting that the republican nature of the national government meant that such behavior was unconstitutional.[52] These limited responses might have been the main ones made, but they were not.

Because Republicans thought free speech on the subject of slavery in the South was essential to the development of a Republican party there, Republicans did not embrace a view of free speech that limited it to "legitimate" subjects of national legislation. Slavery in the states, most Republicans conceded, was not such a subject.[53] Because they insisted on the right of people in the South to discuss slavery, Republicans did not embrace the view that the free speech rights or privileges of American citizens were limited to protection of national political speech or to protection of out-of-staters against discrimination. So the Republican demand for free speech on slavery was a seamless fabric, moving without any marked transition from complaints about suppression of free speech on national topics and complaints about suppression of speech of Northerners to complaints about the suppression of antislavery expression by Southerners on both state and national topics.

Nor was freedom of expression aimed at slavery limited to political speech, narrowly defined. It included antislavery religious expression by ministers who discussed the theological aspects of slavery and antislavery artistic expression, like the bestseller *Uncle Tom's Cabin*. Similarly, appeals to the privileges and immunities of citizens of the United States, which Republicans thought were protected by Article IV, often moved seamlessly from complaints about discrimination against citizens from other states to complaints about violation of the "absolute" rights of American citizens to free speech.[54]

The Republican Demands for Free Speech

From the beginning, Republicans had made demands for free speech a centerpiece of their political program. In 1856 Republicans nominated John C. Frémont for president, and although he lost, he won many Northern states. Their 1856 campaign slogan had been "Free Speech, Free Press, Free Men, Free Labor, Free Territory, and Frémont."[55] When Republicans embraced "free speech" in the context of the struggle over slavery, that decision also implied ideas about the role and limits of free speech. Implicitly, and sometimes explicitly, most who spoke to the issue repudiated the bad tendency test by appealing instead to a core area of speech beyond government power to suppress.[56]

Early in the 1859 congressional session, Democratic senator Albert Brown of Mississippi charged that Republican senator Henry Wilson of Massachusetts had attended an incendiary antislavery meeting. The sponsors of the meeting passed a resolution declaring the right and duty of slaves to resist their masters and of Northerners to incite them to resistance. Brown asked if Wilson had spoken against the resolution. Wilson explained that he had spoken a few days before to a large meeting where he had condemned John Brown's raid. He had been invited to the second meeting to hear from the other side, and he had attended.[57]

Senator Brown's question to Senator Wilson opened a running discussion of free speech, North and South. The debate took place in the context of a resolution passed by a meeting in Massachusetts that was a clear call to resistance by slaves. It was the very sort of advocacy the Democrats were trying, with the use of less promising material, to pin on the Republicans. "Senators should remember," Wilson said, "that the right to hold meetings and to utter opinions upon all matters of public concern is an acknowledged right in my section. . . . I wish the people of other sections of the country would thus cherish the sacred right of free discussion."[58] Senator Fessenden, later chairman of the Joint Committee on Reconstruction in the Thirty-ninth Congress (the committee that proposed the Fourteenth Amendment), made much the same point. He refuted the claim that the resolution urging resistance by slaves was proof that public opinion in the North approved the Brown raid. "[W]e allow everybody to hold a public meeting that wants one, and he may say what he pleases. . . . We are not in the habit of interfering with the expression of opinion by anybody; persons may say what they like."[59]

That freedom of speech was denied to opponents of slavery in the South struck Republicans as an outrage against the principles of liberty. Senator Lyman Trumbull, a Republican from Illinois, discussed Republican support for a ban on slavery in the territories and compared it to the chameleon-like Democratic approach to the issue. "We do not preach popular sovereignty in the North, and scout it as a humbug in the South," Trumbull announced. "You do not preach it in the South at all," interjected Senator George Pugh, Democrat of Ohio. Trumbull retorted that "the men who do not allow our principles to be proclaimed in the South talk about sectionalism. A sectionalism, so pure . . . that it will not tolerate the exposition of the principles of its opponents at all where it is in power, talks to the other party about sectionalism!"[60] (In the 1858 Lincoln-Douglas debates, Abraham Lincoln, as the Republican nominee for the Senate from Illinois, had made a similar point. Douglas had argued that the Republicans were a sectional party because they could not proclaim their doctrines in the South. Lincoln had responded that the exclusion of Republicans from the South was the result of despotism. Douglas also could not go to czarist Russia to proclaim democracy and denounce monarchy.)[61]

In the Senate debate over Helper's book, Henry Wilson of Massachusetts protested that there was not a Republican Senator who could send his frank into Southern states without subjecting "his letter to be opened, examined, and destroyed." Southern papers and some Southern legislatures had offered rewards, he noted, for the heads of opponents of slavery, including some Republican members of Congress.[62] Senator Wilson proceeded to engage in a lengthy dialogue with southern Senators on free speech in the slave states. He was not discussing, Wilson insisted, inciting slaves to rebel. Southerners held such men "amenable to their laws." But, said Wilson, "throughout a large portion of the South," men who entertain opinions on slavery like those of Washington, Jefferson, and Patrick Henry, "cannot reside, . . . cannot exist, in safety."

Senator Brown of Georgia said that Wilson could go into his state and avow "any sentiments which he has a right to entertain." He would not, however, be permitted to urge Brown's slaves to cut Brown's throat.

Wilson insisted that was not the issue. He noted that Professor Hedrick had been driven from North Carolina because he supported John C. Frémont for president and that John Underwood was compelled to leave Virginia because he had attended the Republican national convention of 1856.[63] Senator Brown replied that support for Frémont was, indeed, a far different matter: "[T]here was a great deal more involved in the . . . election of Mr. Frémont . . . beyond the mere avowal of that sentiment [that Kansas should be a free state]. . . . I would not myself tolerate any man who would go to my State and avow his preference for the election of Mr. Seward upon the program he laid down in his Rochester speech." Seward would not be permitted to teach his irrepressible conflict doctrine "because our safety, . . . our peace, the peace of our hearths, depends upon the repression of such doctrines with us."[64]

Wilson said that Brown had conceded his point. "Mr. Stanard was driven from Norfolk for simply attempting to vote for Frémont. . . . In the [South], where we have an inbred constitutional right to advocate these doctrines, it is confessed that we will not be permitted to do it." He continued: "Every American citizen" had a right "to advocate exclusion of slavery from the Territories. . . . Slavery will not tolerate free speech and a free press." Senator Wilson also defended Helper's book. It contained "the most valuable information" together with a few phrases those who had recommended it would disavow.[65]

Earlier in his remarks, Wilson had made a ringing defense of free speech: "[I]n Massachusetts we have absolute freedom of speech and of the press. We deal with all public questions, all social questions, all questions that concern the human race. We have nothing there that prevents the fullest and boldest discussion." The senator from Georgia could go there and advocate slavery, the dissolution of the Union, or reopening the slave trade and he would be "listened to in peace" and "received kindly." Wilson knew that this was hard to understand for senators who came from a section where "freedom of speech on some political, moral, and social subjects is not tolerated."[66]

Most Republicans denied that Helper's book was incendiary. After the controversy erupted over Helper's book, Senator Wade said he had studied it in detail. By rhetorical questions he suggested that nothing in the book was "dangerous to the people of any section." It contained nothing that "could not safely be entrusted to the hands of any freeman." It was simply composed of arguments addressed by a nonslaveholder to his fellow nonslaveholders. "Unless such arguments are unlawful there, I see nothing in the book but what is just, right, and proper for the consideration of all men who take an interest in these matters." Wade clearly thought the book *should* be protected expression: "[H]as it come to this, in free America, that there must be a censorship of the press instituted; that a man cannot give currency to a book containing arguments that he thinks essentially affect the rights of whole classes of the free population of this nation? I hope not, and I believe not."[67]

Senator Seward also made a defense of the principle of free speech, and he mixed references showing national action to suppress speech was inappropriate with a more general statement of principle. Southerners had complained, he said, that Republicans "sanction too unreservedly books designed to advocate emancipation. But surely you can hardly expect the Federal Government or the political parties of the nation to maintain a censorship of the press or of debate. The theory of our system is, that error of opinion may in all cases safely be tolerated where reason is left free to combat it."[68]

According to Representative Sidney Edgerton of Ohio, Republicans were being denounced as traitors for adopting the antislavery opinions of Jefferson, Washington, Madison, and Henry. There had been a complete suppression of free speech in the South. "For years, he said, in most of the slaveholding states, the most sacred provisions of the Constitution have been wantonly and persistently violated. Where is the liberty of speech and of the press in the slaveholding states? Can a northern man . . . print and speak his opinions? Not if he believes in the Declaration of Independence." Nor could preachers "discuss the moral bearings of slavery."[69]

For Edgerton, threats against opponents of slavery and arrests for selling Helper's book illustrated the denial of free speech and press. Southerners had said Reverend Beecher would be hung if he came South. "And the gentleman from South Carolina informed the House that . . . they had arrested a man for selling Helper's book" and had said they would hang him. Edgerton said he had studied Helper's book. It did not, as charged, advise "insurrection, treason, servile war, arson, and murder." Those who made such charges had "never read the book. And yet to sell this harmless book in a slave State is considered a crime. Where is your constitutional liberty?" The "liberty of South Carolina" was equivalent to the "despotism of Austria."[70] Edgerton exclaimed: "Gentlemen of the South, the North demands of you the observance of constitutional obligations. She demands that her citizens be protected by your laws in the enjoyment of their constitutional rights. She demands the freedom of speech and of the press; and if your peculiar institution cannot stand before them, let it go down."[71]

Representative Henry Waldron of Michigan reached similar conclusions:

This slave Democracy tramples [the Constitution] under foot. We have sacred guarantees in that instrument in behalf of free speech, free thought, and a free press, and yet today Democratic postmasters rifle mails and violate the sanctity of private correspondence. Today a system of espionage prevails which would disgrace the despotism and darkness of the middle ages. The newspaper which refuses to recount the blessings and sing the praises of slavery is committed to the flames. The press that refuses to vilify the memory of the fathers is taken by a ruthless mob and engulfed beneath the waters. The personal safety of the traveler depends not on his deeds, but upon his opinions. And these outrages are daily committed under the rule of the Democracy, because that party has taken under its guardian care an institution which can only exist and prosper at the sacrifice and expense of the constitutional rights of the citizen. Where slavery is there can be no free speech, no free thought, no free press, no regard for constitutions, no deference to courts.[72]

Other Republican members of Congress also complained that slavery caused suppression of free speech and press—by state, federal, or territorial governments, and by mob action.[73] They expressed concern for free speech directed to state as well as national issues. John Bingham said, "Today, it would cost a man his life to rise deliberately in the Legislature of Virginia and announce a sentiment in favor of emancipation, such as [were] announced by some of her most distinguished sons in the memorable debate of 1832."[74]

One Republican objection to permitting slavery in the territories was that slavery inevitably would bring its despotic practices with it. Slave owners would pass territorial laws that denied freedom of speech and press. "They claim the right to seal every man's lips, and stop every man's mouth, on questions of great national interest," complained Representative Cydnor Tompkins of Ohio. They would "condemn as a felon the man who dares proclaim the precepts of our holy religion." They would "strip naked and cut into gashes the back of the man who utters opinions" that did not square with those of the slaveholders.[75]

While Republicans protested the slave states' system of censorship in the interests of slavery and warned that it would inevitably spread to all slave territories, some Democrats advocated extending the suppression of antislavery sentiments to the free states. The Democratic representatives Daniel Sickles of New York and Muscoe Garnett of Virginia suggested that Governor Marcy of New York had been correct in 1836 when he advocated legislation to suppress at least some abolitionist expression designed to reach the South.[76] Sickles implied that such expression should have been "put down" by law because it "lead[s] to bad consequences." Now that the North was learning that men from their states planned to carry "discord, invasion, and danger" to the South, Sickles said, the North was going to recur to the "wise and patriotic recommendation of Governor Marcy." In February and March of 1860, Republican presidential candidate Abraham Lincoln warned that Democratic senator Stephen A. Douglas advocated a "new sedition law to be enacted and enforced, suppressing all declarations that slavery is wrong, whether made in politics, in presses, in pulpits, or in private."[77]

In June 1860, after Lincoln's nomination, the Senate considered a series of resolutions on slavery offered by Mississippi senator Jefferson Davis, former secretary of war and future president of the Confederate States of America. One resolution said that slavery, "as it exists in fifteen states of this Union, composes an important portion of their *domestic* institutions." Slavery, the resolution continued, was recognized by the Constitution as "constituting an important element in apportionment of powers among the states." Nothing could justify "open or covert attacks [on slavery] with a view to its overthrow." Such attacks, the resolution declared, were a "breach of faith" and a violation of the national "compact."[78] Senator James Harlan of Iowa proposed a free speech amendment to the resolution: "But free discussion of the morality and expediency of slavery should never be interfered with by the laws of any State, or of the United States; and the freedom of speech and of the press, on this and every other subject of *domestic* and national policy, should be maintained inviolate in all the States."[79]

The Senate defeated the amendment on a straight party vote, but the amendment received the support of every Republican in the Senate who voted on the issue.[80] The resolution is strong evidence that Republicans were calling for free speech on all issues of policy—local as well as national.

The word "domestic" in the resolution meant local to the states. Slavery, according to Jefferson Davis's resolution, was an important part of the "domestic" institutions of fifteen states. Republicans sought to amend the resolution by calling for free speech on all issues of policy, "domestic" as well as national. The word "domestic" here takes its meaning from the use of the same word earlier in the resolution to refer to the "domestic" institutions of fifteen states.[81] The meaning of the word "domestic" in the free speech resolution is also illuminated by the larger context in which it was used—the context of uproar over a book advocating political action in the Southern states themselves to end slavery.

Democrats in the Senate rejected the free speech amendment. The party of James Madison rejected a broad demand for free speech on each and every political issue, including slavery. The institution of slavery had reshaped ideas of liberty to suit its needs.

On April 5, 1860, Owen Lovejoy made a bitter denunciation of slavery. Lovejoy was a congressman from Illinois, a supporter of Lincoln, an intense critic of slavery, an outspoken proponent of assisting fugitive slaves escaping from bondage, and the brother of Elijah Lovejoy, the antislavery newspaper editor who had been killed defending his press from a proslavery mob. Lovejoy's speech excoriated slaveholding as "the sum of all villainy,"[82] and it came close to causing a riot on the floor of the House. On the issue of free speech, however, Lovejoy's position was close to that of most Republicans who spoke on the issue. He supported, he said, Helper's object: organizing a party in the slave states against slavery. Those objecting to the book were insisting that "an American citizen, address[ing] himself to his fellow-citizens, in a peaceful way, through the press . . . must be hanged."[83]

Like John Bingham, Lovejoy invoked the privileges and immunities of citizens of the United States as protecting basic rights, including free speech and press. "I do claim the right of discussing this question of slavery anywhere, on any square foot of American soil over which the stars and stripes float, to which the privileges and immunities of the Constitution extend." He said: "[T]hat Constitution, which guaranties to me free speech" protected his right to criticize slavery. Just as the invocation of Roman citizenship protected ancient Romans, so American citizenship should protect Americans in their rights. "That is my response to the question of why I recommended circulation of the Helper book." Lovejoy claimed "the privilege of going anywhere . . . as a free citizen, unmolested, and of uttering, in an orderly and legal way, any sentiment that I choose to utter." Lovejoy insisted he had a free speech right to circulate any books he chose, and he specifically mentioned Thomas Paine's *Age of Reason*, a book highly critical of much of the Bible. Among his other complaints Lovejoy protested that Southern states "imprison or exile preachers of the Gospel."[84]

Lovejoy's speech ended on a somber note. Representative Elbert Martin of Virginia rejoined, "And if you come among us we will do with you as we did with John Brown—hang you up as high as Haman." "I have no doubt of it," replied Representative Lovejoy.[85]

The lack of effective national protection for free speech in the slave states had practical consequences for those hardy souls who challenged the Southern quarantine. One of those was a minister and antislavery activist, Daniel Worth.

13

Daniel Worth:

The Struggle for Free Speech in North Carolina

on the Eve of the Civil War

On the same day that Congressman Lovejoy spoke and complained about Southern states that "imprison or exile preachers of the Gospel,"[1] the *New York Times* reported that Reverend Daniel Worth, a Wesleyan minister, was convicted in North Carolina of circulating Hinton Rowan Helper's book, *The Impending Crisis.*[2] Worth was sentenced to a year in prison.[3] Worth's arrests in two counties for circulating the Helper book had been reported earlier in the antislavery press. The *National Era* reported it wearily on January 12, 1860: "We should literally have no room for anything else if we were to publish all the details of whippings, tar-and-featherings, and hangings, for the utterance of Anti-Slavery opinions in the South." It expected that Worth would be convicted and suffer "fine, imprisonment, and whipping."[4]

Worth had been born in 1795 in Guilford County, North Carolina, to a devout Quaker family. He and his family migrated to Indiana in 1822, as many North Carolina Quakers had done. There he was active in the Indiana Antislavery Society in the 1840s and later supported the Republican Party.

In 1857 Worth, by this time a Wesleyan minister, returned to North Carolina and began to preach his antislavery version of the Gospel. The American Missionary Association, a strongly antislavery organization, supplied him with financial support and fifty copies of Helper's book. Worth sold all fifty copies and ordered more, and he secured subscriptions for the *New York Tribune*, the Republican newspaper seized from the mail and burned in Virginia in 1859.[5]

Worth was aware that his work was dangerous. "[I] can preach," he reported to his nephew with satisfaction, "and have done it, as strong and direct against slavery as ever you heard me in the north, and I believe that there is not another man that could."[6] He attributed his success to his age, Southern birth, and his influential family connections.[7]

Worth had substantial reason for concern. The intellectual quarantine in North Carolina became ever more strict. One case shows how times were changing. In 1856, Benjamin Hedrick, a talented professor of chemistry at the University of North Carolina, had publicly supported John C. Frémont, the Republican presidential candidate. For this "offense" the university discharged him. When he returned to his home in Salisbury, North Carolina, the threat of mob violence forced him to flee the state. Laws against antislavery expression were merely the tip of an iceberg, and conformity was, as in Hedrick's case, often enforced by public opinion expressed through mob action. Hedrick was "exposed" in the *Raleigh Weekly Standard*. At the end of the affair, the *Standard* exalted: "We may have aided to *magnify* him somewhat in the public eye, but that was one of the unavoidable incidents, and not the object. Our object was to rid the University and the State of an avowed Frémont man; and we succeeded. And we now say, after due consideration . . . that no man who is avowedly for John C. Frémont for President ought to be allowed to breathe the air or to tread the soil of North Carolina."[8] Hedrick soon became a close friend of another exile from North Carolina, Hinton Rowan Helper, the author of *The Impending Crisis*.

After the Harpers Ferry raid, pressure to suppress Worth increased. On November 26, 1859, the *North Carolina Presbyterian* warned that "society must be protected against cut-throats and assassins" and demanded that an unnamed fanatic abolitionist preacher be removed from the state.[9] The *Raleigh Weekly Standard* asked for the name: was he the fanatic Daniel Worth, the minister who had even been referred to in Helper's book as a Southern minister preaching against slavery?[10] On December 17, 1859, the *North Carolina Presbyterian* obligingly supplied Worth's name. "[I]t is notorious," the paper wrote, "that [Daniel Worth] has been inculcating, publicly and privately, his incendiary doctrines in Randolph and Guilford counties, and the time has come when he should be compelled to abandon this work."[11] On December 10, 1859, the North Carolina Council of State passed a resolution saying postmasters who delivered incendiary books or newspapers to the addressee should be prosecuted as circulators of the item. Another resolution enjoined all public officers to subject out-of-state merchants, book dealers, tract distributors, and lecturers to "the strictest scrutiny."[12]

On December 21, 1859, Worth wrote to the American Missionary Association forecasting "times of trial. . . . Since the unfortunate affair at Harper's Ferry, the county is in a tremendous ferment. Threatenings reach me from various quarters."[13] The North Carolina papers were filled with denunciations of Helper's book and of the sixty-eight Republican congressmen who endorsed it. The *Raleigh Register* reprinted excerpts from *The Impending Crisis* to show the enormity of the offense. It quoted a passage in which Helper demanded "as the only true means of attaining to a position worthy of sovereign States . . . an energetic, intelligent, enterprising, virtuous, and unshackled population, an untrammelled press, and the freedom of speech. For ourselves, as white people, and for the negroes and other persons of whatever color or condition, we demand all the rights, interests and prerogatives that are guaranteed to corresponding classes of mankind in the North."[14] By Christmas, Daniel Worth was under arrest.

The North Carolina press was full of reports of Worth's arrest and preliminary hearing. Raleigh and Greensboro papers of all political persuasions were unanimous in their condemnation of Worth.[15] In the *Greensboro Patriot*'s account of the preliminary hearing, the editor said he had not read Helper's book, "but from extracts which were read on the trial" it was "infamous" and should "consign to infamy" and "condign punishment" all who circulated it.[16] In politics, each party used Helper's book in an attempt to tar the other. Democrats charged that Whig congressman John Gilmer had been mailed a copy by Helper. Gilmer denied knowing possession of the book. Gilmer's supporters then claimed that Governor Ellis had received a copy of the book. Ellis responded that he had thrown the first copy he received out the window, and when a second copy of the book was sent to him, he used its incendiary pages to light his pipe.[17]

The *Raleigh Standard* noted efforts to circulate Helper's book and called for increased vigilance. "We would," it sternly lectured, "again remind Postmasters of their duties in this respect. Let every copy of Helper's book, and every copy of the *New York Tribune*, and every document franked by [Republican senator] Seward, [Republican senator] Wilson, Burlingame, [Republican representative] John Sherman, and other abolitionists which may come to their offices, *be committed to the flames*."[18]

Politicians, judges, and ordinary citizens united in their effort to suppress Worth and his associates. John T. Harriss, a farm laborer in Randolph County, wrote Governor Ellis "a fiew lines concerning Daniel Worth he has bin circulating a seditious Book . . . by the title of Helpers impending Crisis one Jacob Briles, senr has one [as did Jacob junior] . . . and it can bea proven that they got them of this same Daniel Worth."[19] The governor promptly wrote an irate letter to Judge Dick, a superior court judge. "The local magistrates," the governor protested, "have been, up to this time wholly remiss in suppressing the most flagrant violations of Law—the circulation of incendiary books & papers, and the use of language calculated to incite slaves to insurrection."[20] Upon receiving Harriss's letter from the governor, Judge Dick wrote the governor to say that he "forthwith issued a warrant for Jacob Bryles [Briles] senr," instructing the sheriff "to search for books." The judge assured the governor that all that properly could be done was being done, "and I fear that more will be done than ought to be done." Had Worth been released on bail, the Judge said, he would have been hung. No one, the judge promised, would escape against whom evidence could be obtained.[21] Following this promise, the press reported the arrest of a number of others suspected of involvement with the Helper book.[22]

At least one North Carolinian did criticize the prosecutions, but he wrote from the safety of his exile in New York City. Benjamin Hedrick, the deposed and exiled chemistry professor, wrote to his old friend Thomas Ruffin, formerly chief justice of North Carolina. He asked Ruffin to use his influence to "arrest the terrorism and fanaticism which now so much disturbs the South. . . . Some of the men recently arrested are among the best men in the state." Their persecution could only be stopped by intervention of upright citizens. Hedrick continued:

> In order that you may have an opportunity to know also what offense is laid to some of these men I send you a copy of Helper's book. You will find not a word in it is addressed to either free or slave negroes, That most of the sentiments that are current in the state and attributed to this book, are the fabrications of the New York Herald. Please examine the book and see if there is any thing in it that one free-man may not properly address to any other. For myself I am free to admit that I do not approve of every proposition advocated in the book, nor with the manner in which some good propositions are maintained. But unless we tolerate difference of opinion we must have despotism at once.[23]

Hedrick also sent Ruffin a copy of a searing indictment of slavery published in Greensboro in 1830. It argued that slaves were entitled to state constitutional protections of liberty and that they were the victims of kidnapping. Hedrick also alluded to an 1832 speech by Judge William Gaston of the North Carolina supreme court to show that "[i]t was not then treason to discuss slavery, and to print opinions adverse to the system."[24] Hedrick later engaged counsel for Worth and raised money for his defense.[25]

Meanwhile, Judge Ruffin received correspondence about Worth from Reverend George McNeil, the editor who had "exposed" Worth. McNeil passed on a letter from Jonathan Worth, Daniel's influential cousin.[26] "In addition to the horror of having a minister of the Gospel, aged 68 years whipped," Jonathan Worth warned, "[t]he abolitionists at home and abroad will turn it to account." Jonathan Worth also complained about the statute under which Worth had been convicted:

> Judge Shepherd held at Montgomery last week, that an article in the religious creed of a Society declaring that Slavery is inconsistent with Christian religion, if printed and circulated among its members, would make the person circulating it indictable under this Statute, because all religious societies admit slaves as members and such an article would have an "evident tendency to make them dissatisfied with their social condition." This reasoning seems to be clear. It follows that all Quakers are indictable under this Statute and liable to ignominious punishment. . . . Its execution, according to this interpretation would produce general horror.[27]

Jonathan Worth would have limited the statute to those intending to "produce dissatisfaction among slaves" and said his cousin, except for his age and otherwise "exemplary character," was a fit case for the execution of the statute. All things considered, he hoped the whipping would be omitted and Daniel Worth would be permitted to leave the state.[28]

THE TRIALS OF DANIEL WORTH

Daniel Worth was charged with violating section 16 of chapter 34 of the North Carolina statutes, passed originally in the 1830s and revised in 1854. Section 16 made it a crime to circulate "any written or printed pamphlet or paper . . . the evident tendency whereof is to cause slaves to become discontented with the bondage in which they are held . . . and free negroes to be dissatisfied with their social condition." For the first offense, persons violating the statute were to be whipped, put in the pillory, and imprisoned for not less than a year. For the second offense the punishment was death.[29]

At his preliminary hearing, Worth admitted selling Helper's book, but denied that his object was to stir up insurrection. His was a mission of peace.[30] Worth was bound over for trial in superior court. He remained incarcerated pending trial. Meanwhile, an additional shipment of Helper's book was seized and publicly burned.[31]

At Worth's first trial, in Randolph County, the prosecutor read the jury the indictment, containing lengthy extracts from *The Impending Crisis*. The Guilford indictment (which is probably similar) quoted Helper's argument that slavery was a nuisance and nonslaveholders were concerned with it just as they would be in the case of mad dogs; that slavery was worse than stealing; and that slave and free negro victims of crimes were not permitted to testify against white oppressors. The indictment also quoted the passage in which Helper compared, in the event of violent confrontation, the number of slaveholders who would be arrayed against nonslaveholders—not counting slaves who would often be "delighted with an opportunity to cut their masters' throats."[32] Unlike the *New York Herald*, the indictment quoted the rest of the passage: a hope and belief that the matter would be adjusted without violence; a desire for peace, not war; and finally Helper's plea to give us "freedom of speech, and we will settle this difficulty at the [ballot] box, not on the battleground by force."[33] Though the indictment went on for some eighteen pages, the passages referred to are representative.

Jury selection was difficult because so many potential jurors were already convinced of Worth's guilt.[34] At trial, the state proved that Worth sold the book. Jacob Briles, uncovered as a result of the letter from the farm laborer to Governor Ellis, became a witness for the state and testified against Worth. Counsel stipulated that the book need not be read. Worth offered no evidence. Unfortunately, the local newspaper did not report the "able and sometimes truly eloquent" arguments on both sides.[35] The court charged the jury that a book was within the reach of the statute, though the statute specifically listed only papers and pamphlets. Whether the book was incendiary was left to the jury to determine. The jury retired at 11 P.M. and returned a guilty verdict at 4 A.M. the next morning. Judge Bailey sentenced Worth to a year in prison and excused the whipping.[36]

The Guilford trial was a repeat performance with the same lawyers and judge, but this time the jury convicted in fifteen minutes.[37] Worth appealed, his bond was reduced, and he quietly slipped out of North Carolina. The authorities apparently wanted to avoid not only the provocative spectacle of an elderly minister of the gospel placed in the pillory and whipped—an outcome the judge had apparently foreclosed—but it seems they also wanted to avoid the spectacle of Worth's imprisonment. Worth went on a speaking tour of the North to raise the funds necessary to reimburse his bondsmen. If he could not raise the funds and if he lost his appeal, he said he would return to be imprisoned.

In a speech in New York, Worth insisted that Helper's book was not "addressed to the colored people" and he had never given the book to them. Worth said he had defended himself at the preliminary hearing, making what "they said was a regular abolitionist harangue." "I quoted from Mr. Helper's book the language of Thomas Jefferson" to the effect that in a contest between slave and master, God would be on the side of the slave.[38] Worth reported that his friend Hinton Helper had contributed fifty dollars to his bail fund.[39]

The North Carolina supreme court affirmed Worth's conviction.[40] It was not necessary to prove, the supreme court held, that the book was delivered to slaves or free Negroes or that it was read in their presence. "The circulation, within the State, is alike prohibited, whether it be amongst whites or blacks," Justice Charles Manly wrote. "The Legislature seems to have assumed, that if a circulation, within the State, was once established, that its corrupting influence would inevitably reach the black."[41] Guilt turned on intent. A copy could be delivered by one person to another without incurring guilt, when it was delivered to gratify curiosity, "both parties to the act being equally opposed to the design."[42] With this observation, perhaps Manly had solved the paradox of why it was lawful for North Carolina papers to publish extracts from Helper's book but criminal for the book's proponents to circulate it. Finally, Manly had no problem finding the work inflammatory. Every passage of it, "in the most inflamatory words," declared that "the slave ought to be discontented with his condition, and the master deposed from his, and that the change should be effected, even at the cost of blood."[43] If Worth's counsel explicitly raised the free press, freedom of religion, or free speech issues, the North Carolina supreme court ignored them. The North Carolina constitution had no explicit protection for free speech but asserted that "the freedom of the Press is one of the great bulwarks of liberty, and therefore ought never to be restrained."[44]

In 1860, the North Carolina legislature amended the incendiary document statute. Worth's crime, circulating an "incendiary" book on the subject of slavery, was henceforth punishable by death for the first offense.[45]

The trials of Daniel Worth dramatically show what local option on free speech meant for Republicans. Worth had been distributing a Republican campaign document, one most Republicans in the House had endorsed. Republicans hoped to develop a political opposition in the Southern states that would abolish slavery state by state. Worth's fate showed how, at its kindest, the South would treat political opposition and religious dissent about slavery. Indeed, Worth's case showed that trials, prison, whipping, and the death penalty might face congressional endorsers of Helper's book if they could be brought within the power of Southern courts. The facts are a crucial part of the background of the much disputed history of the Fourteenth Amendment.

THE FOURTEENTH AMENDMENT'S PRIVILEGE AND IMMUNITY OF FREE SPEECH

Historian James McPherson has suggested that the Civil War was a second American Revolution.[46] Democrats repeatedly insisted that the Republicans were a revolutionary party. Indeed one of the characteristics of the Helper book that critics found outrageous was his suggestion that slavery was the unfinished business of the first American revolution.[47] In 1860, Senator James Chestnut Jr. of South Carolina said the Republican Party was governed by the red Republican principles of France, though it had "changed its complexion" and "blacked its face."[48] The fundamental fallacy of the Republican Party, he continued, was that it held "that the Declaration of Independence is the basis of the Constitution."[49] When they considered the power and duties of the government with reference to the domestic affairs of the states, Republicans "string their sophistical arguments" on the "abstract opinions" of the Declaration, Chestnut said.[50] "This fatal error arises . . . out of the untenable postulate that all men, under all governments, are naturally and equally entitled to liberty, without reference to the well-being of society or to their own fitness to enjoy and preserve it."[51]

In response to charges like those of Chestnut, Republicans insisted they were the true conservatives, conserving the heritage of liberty espoused by the Declaration of Independence and the leaders of the American Revolution. In 1860, Republicans repeatedly invoked the antislavery expressions of the revolutionary fathers. They cited antislavery statements of Thomas Jefferson, James Madison, and George Washington, and early antislavery resolutions from Georgia and other colonies.[52] And they cited Luther Martin, delegate to the Constitutional Convention from Maryland, again and again: slavery was incompatible with republicanism and had the tendency to destroy those principles on which it was supported.[53]

Secession by the South was, as some historians have suggested, a preemptive counterrevolution. As Southerners saw it, Republicans would not be content with banning slavery from the territories. Republicans insisted, with Lincoln, that Americans should never forget that slavery was wrong everywhere. They hoped that the election of a Republican president and the use of patronage would establish an antislavery party in the Southern states. That party would then abolish slavery on a state-by-state basis. Senator Seward suggested that if free speech were restored in the South, the Republicans promptly would have as many supporters there as the Democrats did in the North.[54] Democrats said Southern states would never tolerate election of a Republican president who would appoint officeholders and postmasters who would be unlikely to eliminate antislavery publications from the mails.[55]

Secession by the South did inaugurate the second American revolution. Within five years, slavery had been abolished and Republicans had proposed an amendment to make blacks citizens and to secure civil liberty for all American citizens. The basis of their philosophy was, as Senator Chestnut suggested, the idea of the Declaration of Independence that government was established to secure equality and individual rights. Republicans were no longer willing to allow local denials of basic rights. The need to protect citizens against state denials of their constitutional rights was reiterated time and again by the congressional Republicans who proposed the Thirteenth and Fourteenth Amendments. They insisted on giving all citizens the "shield" of "all the guarantees of the Constitution."[56] In the same debates, Republicans referred again and again to denials of civil liberty that had characterized the pre–Civil War years.[57] The main exhibits in their litany of horrors were state denials of freedom of speech, press, and religion. The controversy surrounding the Helper book and the trial of Daniel Worth help illustrate, from a distance of many years, what Republicans were talking about.[58]

The Impending Crisis and Early Republican
Understanding of Free Speech

The controversy over Helper's book also gives some insight into early Republican understanding of the guarantees of freedom of speech, press, and religion. By the 1860s there was still scholarly support for the idea that the freedom of the press merely meant a guarantee against prior restraint.[59] Under that theory, government could not censor books in advance of publication but could punish the author after circulation.

In the cases of denial of free press complained of by Republicans, and certainly in the case of Helper's book, the problem that confronted Republicans was subsequent punishment, not prior restraint. Yet they repeatedly insisted that such subsequent punishment also violated the rights to freedom of speech and of the press.

One might see free speech as a right that protected speech on national topics but not on state topics or a guarantee that protected speech from federal but not state suppression. On balance, the debates from the Thirty-sixth Congress do not support the idea that most Republicans thought such a bifurcated reading of freedom of expression was accurate or desirable. Republican complaints about denial of free speech and press rights included matters that were directly related to the national government and those that were not. Essentially, the Helper book itself was addressed to eliminating slavery in the slave states. Most congressmen agreed that slavery, as a domestic issue in the Southern states, was peculiarly a matter of state concern, a matter over which Congress had no power. But Republicans saw the South's suppression of Helper's book, a book addressed to a matter of uniquely state concern, as a flagrant denial of free speech and free press.

Finally, in the controversy over Helper's book in 1859 and 1860, many Republicans championed a robust view of free speech. Like James Madison at the time of the Sedition Act, they suggested a hard central core to the First Amendment that included the right to discuss public measures and public questions. And they supported this right even for those who advocated conduct they considered barbarous and horrible—human slavery and reopening the African slave trade. Implicitly, at least, they rejected the idea that speech on such matters should be suppressed because of its bad tendency. Indeed, one Republican showed Democrats how easily the bad tendency test could be manipulated to make Southerners guilty of the kidnapping of free blacks in the North. He did so, however, not to embrace the bad tendency argument, but to support his rejection of it.[60]

The laws protecting slavery from criticism were sedition acts, broadly defined. They made it a crime to criticize one legal and social institution and to advocate its abolition. Legal scholar Harry Kalven has suggested that freedom cannot survive sedition acts—acts that make some political speech criminal.[61] The controversy over *The Impending Crisis* suggests that he was correct. This second controversy over seditious speech, however, was far different from the first. This time the threat came from the states, not from the national government, and for that reason arguments about the lack of federal power to suppress speech were irrelevant. What was needed to help prevent other episodes like the suppression of Helper's book and other core political speech, was a set of national privileges that no state could abridge.[62]

From the formation of the Republican Party to the Civil War, Republicans championed broad rights to free speech. The Civil War severely tested their commitment.

14

The Struggle for Free Speech in the Civil War:

Lincoln and Vallandigham

The free speech story so far has a satisfying neatness. Free speech, by and large, has appeared as the ally of progress. The critics of free speech have been critics of the democratic process (in case of the Sedition Act) and defenders of the institution of slavery. The Fourteenth Amendment was the culmination of a battle for liberty, not merely for former slaves, but for all Americans.

But a broadly protective vision of free speech protects all dissenters. While the dissenters have often been progressive, that is not always so. Many opponents of the Lincoln administration's war policy were racist opponents of the Emancipation Proclamation.

THE ARREST OF VALLANDIGHAM AND ITS MEANING

At 2:40 A.M. on May 5, 1863, 150 Union soldiers from the command of General Ambrose Burnside arrived at Clement L. Vallandigham's home in Dayton, Ohio. The soldiers' mission was to arrest Vallandigham, a prominent Democratic politician and former congressman, for an anti-war political speech he had made a few days before at a Democratic Party rally. After Vallandigham refused to submit, the soldiers attempted to break down his front door. Finally, soldiers broke several doors and captured Vallandigham. They put him on a train for Cincinnati to be tried before a military commission, appointed by the same general who had ordered his arrest.[1] Vallandigham's efforts to secure a writ of habeas corpus failed. After his conviction, President Lincoln changed Vallandigham's sentence from imprisonment to banishment to the Confederacy.

The most immediate response to the Vallandigham arrest was a riot in his hometown. A mob burned the local Republican newspaper building and cut telegraph lines. Order was restored only when General Burnside declared martial law and sent in troops.[2]

The arrest of Vallandigham produced a tidal wave of criticism. The arrest focused national attention on the meaning of free speech in time of war (especially civil war), on the relation of free speech to democratic government, and on civil liberties for critics of the Lincoln administration. Critics insisted the arrest violated Bill of Rights guarantees of free speech, free assembly, jury trial, due process, and right to grand jury indictment. Both Democrats and Republicans described such rights as "privileges" or "immunities" as well as "rights" and "liberties."

Within a month of Vallandigham's arrest and exile, General Burnside suppressed the *Chicago Times* newspaper, but this time Lincoln countermanded the order. Less than a year later Republicans in Congress introduced a resolution to expel Democratic congressman Alexander Long of Ohio for advocating (in a speech made on the floor of the House) peace and recognition of the Confederacy. Some cited the Vallandigham case as precedent to justify the proposed expulsion.

The cases raised basic civil liberties issues: the power of the military to try civilians and close newspapers in areas where no combat raged and where civil courts were functioning; the power to try and imprison or otherwise punish people for antiwar speech; and, generally, the scope of the war power. These cases involved two kinds of issues: first, the scope of national and military power during internal rebellion and second, the extent to which the First Amendment limits that power. Here I focus on the free speech–free press issue.

Before the Civil War, abolitionists and, later, Republicans had invoked protective concepts of freedom of speech, press, assembly, and religion to defend against attempts to suppress antislavery expression. They claimed the right to discuss questions of public policy fully and freely on every inch of American soil "to which the privileges and immunities of the Constitution extend," as Representative Lovejoy put it in 1860. "[T]hat Constitution," he said, "guaranties me free speech."[3] In response to an uproar over Republican endorsement of Hinton Helper's strongly antislavery book, Republicans in the United States Senate supported a resolution that asserted, "[F]reedom of speech and of the press on [the morality and expediency of slavery and on] and every other subject of domestic [state] and national policy, should be maintained inviolate."[4] Republicans, abolitionists, and others described the rights to free speech and press as constitutional privileges belonging to all American citizens, rights enjoyed by virtue of the federal constitution. Antislavery activists and Republicans had implicitly and explicitly repudiated the notion that free speech or press was limited merely to a protection against prior restraints, but that punishment after publication was permissible. Instead they insisted that, by punishing antislavery speech and press, slave states refused to tolerate freedom of speech. Similarly, they implicitly and sometimes explicitly rejected arguments that the bad tendency of antislavery speech (a tendency that outraged Southerners and that their Northern allies had insisted threatened slave revolts and disunion) justified suppression.[5] The Republican Party slogan in 1856 was "Free Speech, Free Press, Free Men, Free Labor, Free Territory, and Frémont."[6] The Civil War raised the free speech issue again, though this time critics of emancipation and the war invoked the protection of free speech.

Vallandigham's Politics

In the years before the Civil War, the Democratic Party had been an uneasy coalition between, among others, Southern planters and Northern artisans. Slavery was a wedge issue that threatened to split the Northern and Southern wings of the party and to drive Democrats from power. Some Democrats had opposed expansion of slavery and opposed restrictions on free speech on the subject of slavery. Many Democrats had supported a law to ban antislavery publications from the mails and had supported a gag law to prohibit discussion of antislavery petitions in Congress. Other Democrats had opposed the postal ban and the gag rule and contributed crucial votes to defeat the ban and, eventually, the gag rule.[7] But, as the Civil War approached, the leadership of the party made greater efforts to satisfy escalating Southern demands to protect the institution of slavery. Ultimately, the effort to satisfy the South failed, and in 1860 the Democratic Party, like the Union itself, split into Northern and Southern factions. With secession, most Northern Democrats supported the war, but many opposed the Emancipation Proclamation. Vallandigham, though, was a member of the peace wing of the Democratic Party.

At least since the 1850s, Vallandigham had supported the main Southern approach to the constitutional crisis that led to the Civil War. By the 1850s, many Southerners demanded the right to settle their slaves in any of the national territories. This demand was dramatically advanced when Congress passed the 1854 Kansas-Nebraska Act. That act repealed the Missouri Compromise, which had prohibited slavery in federal territory north of latitude 36° 30'. The Kansas-Nebraska Act had galvanized Northern sentiment against the expansion of slavery, ignited a political firestorm, and led to the formation of the Republican Party.[8]

In 1855, Vallandigham described the act as "that most just, most Constitutional, and most necessary measure."[9] He explained that abolition was the cause of the sectional crisis wracking the United States.[10] Initially, when confronted by the abolitionists, according to Vallandigham: "even the North started back aghast. . . . [Abolition] was denounced as treason and madness from the first. Its presses were destroyed, its assemblies broken up, its publications burned, and it lecturers mobbed everywhere, and more than one among them murdered in the midst of popular tumult and indignation. The churches, the school-houses, the courthouses, and the public halls were alike closed against them."[11] Gradually, Vallandigham claimed, the abolition movement had established the Free Soil antislavery parties, "disguis[ing] its odious principles and its true purposes, under the false pretence of No Extension of Slavery."[12]

Like many of his contemporaries, Vallandigham was a racist. "No negro emigrant could be naturalized," he declared in an 1858 speech in Congress. "It is not alone [the Negro's] descent from slaves . . . that degrades him in the scale of social and political being. It is his color and his blood. It is because he is the descendant of a servile and degraded race."[13] (After the Civil War, most Democrats, at first, opposed national protection for the rights of newly freed slaves.)[14]

As a Democratic congressman from Ohio, Vallandigham had been one of the most persistent critics of the Lincoln administration's war policy. Republicans and Unionists in the state legislature redrew the lines of his district and targeted Vallandigham for defeat, and, in 1862, Vallandigham did indeed lose his bid for re-election to Congress. By January 1863 he had decided to run for governor of Ohio.[15]

Vallandigham opposed the draft, but he told an 1862 mass meeting in his congressional district that "[w]hoever should be drafted, should a draft be ordered according to the Constitution and the law, is in duty bound . . . to . . . go; he has no right to resist, and none to run away."[16]

In 1863, Vallandigham also openly opposed continuing the Civil War. "But ought this war to continue?" Vallandigham asked in an 1863 speech. "I answer, no—not a day, not an hour. What then? Shall we separate? Again I answer, no . . . , no!"[17] He dismissed concerns about slavery. "Neither will I be stopped by that other cry of mingled fanaticism and hypocrisy, about the sin and barbarism of African slavery." He thought the horror of the war and the policy of the administration required a change of policy. "Sir," he said, "I see more of barbarism and sin, a thousand times, in the continuance of this war, the dissolution of the Union, the breaking up of this Government, and the enslavement of the white race, by debt and taxes and arbitrary power."[18] Opposition to the war was often extreme. The *Dayton Empire*, a newspaper heavily influenced by Vallandigham, had described Ohio governor Dennison's efforts to raise Union troops after Fort Sumter as designed to "butcher men, women, and children" of the South.[19]

In 1863, Vallandigham was a supporter of "the Union as it was"—a constitution that recognized and supported slavery in a union of slave and free states. Actually, under his plan the Union would not be exactly as it was. Under a constitutional amendment he proposed after the outbreak of the Civil War, no bill would become a law without support from a majority of senators and representatives from each of the nation's four sections (the South was one), and no one could be elected president without a majority of the electoral college votes from each section.[20] The proposal promised long-term security for slavery because it gave the South a veto on legislation and on the election of a president.[21]

Vallandigham hoped that antislavery feeling was ebbing in the West. He thought Westerners were beginning "to comprehend, that domestic slavery in the South is a question, not of morals, or religion, or humanity, but a form of labor, perfectly compatible with the dignity of free white labor in the same community, and with national vigor, power, and prosperity, and especially with military strength."[22] Indeed, part of Vallandigham's solution for the Civil War was to end abolition agitation. "In my judgment, you will never suppress the armed Secession Rebellion till you have crushed under foot the pestilent Abolition Rebellion first. . . . It must be met by reason and appeals to the people, through the press and in public assemblages, and be put down at the ballot-box."[23]

In general, Vallandigham counseled obedience to the laws. But if the freedom of the ballot was infringed, he and other Democrats suggested revolt would be appropriate. Vallandigham said: "No matter how distasteful constitutions and laws may be, they must be obeyed. I am opposed to all mobs, and opposed also . . . to all violations of constitution and law by men in authority—public servants. The danger from usurpations and violations by them is fifty-fold greater than from any other quarter, because these violations and usurpations come clothed with false semblance of authority."[24]

Before his arrest, Vallandigham also criticized the Lincoln administration for its military arrests of civilians and suspension of the writ of habeas corpus. Indeed he suggested that if the president engaged in further "arbitrary arrests," he should be impeached.[25]

ARBITRARY ARRESTS

Lincoln faced a huge rebellion, rebel sympathizers, and resistance and spies throughout the nation. The loyalty of key states like Maryland, Missouri, and Kentucky was doubtful. The president faced one of the most extreme threats in the nation's history, and his administration responded with military arrests and suspension of the writ of habeas corpus. Lincoln explained his policy in his 1861 message to Congress:

> The whole of the laws which were required to be faithfully executed were being resisted, and failing of execution, in nearly one-third of the States. Must they be allowed to finally fail of execution, even had it been perfectly clear, that by the use of the means necessary to their execution some single law, made in such tenderness of the citizens's liberty, that practically, it relieves more of the guilty, than of the innocent, should, to a very limited extent, be violated? [A]re all the laws, *but one*, to go unexecuted, and the government itself go to pieces, lest that one be violated? . . . But it was not believed that any law was violated. The provision of the Constitution that "The privilege of the writ of habeas corpus, shall not be suspended unless when, the cases of rebellion or invasion, the public safety may require it," . . . is a provision . . . that such privilege may be suspended when, in cases of rebellion, or invasion, the public safety *does* require it.[26]

Military arrests of civilians not in the immediate theater of war and suspension of the writ of habeas corpus, however, disturbed friends as well as critics of the administration. In his biography of Lincoln, David Donald reports that critics of the arrest policy included both conservative and radical Republicans. For example, Lincoln's conservative friend Orville H. Browning thought arrests ordered by the administration were "illegal and arbitrary and did more harm than good." Senator Lyman Trumbull of Illinois agreed that "all arbitrary arrests of citizens by military authority ... are unwarrantable, and are doing much injury, and that if they continue unchecked the civil tribunals will be completely subordinated to the military, and the government overthrown."[27]

But many others supported the administration and insisted that the Constitution provided sweeping powers to respond to the emergency. In time of civil war, they said, the Constitution justified tough measures.[28] Supporters of the administration, and the administration itself, cited the landmark 1849 Supreme Court case of *Luther v. Borden*[29] to justify military arrests and trials of civilians. In that case the Supreme Court had upheld the Rhode Island legislature's statewide imposition of martial law against a military and political challenge from those seeking to democratize the highly undemocratic government of the state.[30] But the dissent of Justice Woodbury, objecting to martial law where the civilian courts were functioning, resonated powerfully for many Americans.

THE VALLANDIGHAM ARREST, TRIAL, AND APPLICATION FOR HABEAS CORPUS

Vallandigham's Arrest: The Proclamation by President Lincoln

On September 24, 1862, Abraham Lincoln issued the following proclamation:

> Now, therefore, be it ordered, first, that during the existing insurrection and as a necessary measure for suppressing the same, ... all persons discouraging volunteer enlistments, resisting militia drafts, or guilty of any disloyal practice, affording aid and comfort to Rebels ... shall be subject to martial law and liable to trial and punishment by Courts Martial or Military Commission:
>
> Second. That the Writ of Habeas Corpus is suspended in respect to all persons arrested, or who are now, or hereafter during the rebellion shall be, imprisoned in any fort, camp ... or other place of confinement by any military authority or by the sentence of any Court Martial or Military Commission.[31]

After this proclamation, as well as before it, the military arrested a number of civilians. Congress was sufficiently concerned with such arrests to pass the Act of March 3, 1863. This act both authorized and limited presidential suspension of the writ of habeas corpus. It authorized "the President of the United States . . . to suspend the privilege of the writ of habeas corpus in any case throughout the United States, or any part thereof." No officer was required to produce any person detained by the authority of the president, "but on the certificate, under oath, of the officer . . . that such person is detained by him as a prisoner under authority of the President, further proceedings under the writ of habeas corpus shall be suspended."[32]

But in the 1863 act Congress also tried to put limitations on executive power. It required the secretaries of state and war to furnish the federal courts "a list of all persons, citizens of states in which administration of the laws has continued unimpaired in the said Federal courts, who are now, or may hereafter be, held as prisoners of the United States, by order or authority of the President . . . as state or political prisoners, or otherwise than as prisoners of war." If a grand jury attending such "courts having jurisdiction in the premises, after the passage of this act, and after the furnishing of said list, as aforesaid, has terminated its session without finding an indictment or presentment, or other proceeding against any such person," the act required the federal judge to bring such person before him for discharge. It required the military commanders to obey the order of the judge. However, no one was to be discharged without first taking an oath of allegiance.[33]

Lincoln did not issue another proclamation suspending the writ until after the Vallandigham arrest. The effect of the 1863 act on Lincoln's 1862 proclamation was unclear. At the time of Vallandigham's arrest many contemporaries doubted that the writ was suspended in Ohio. If the act of Congress implicitly superseded the prior suspension, a new proclamation would be required. If the suspension of September 24, 1862, continued in effect, it would seem to cover Vallandigham's case, but in that event, the Act of March 3, 1863 seemed to require either a civil trial at the end of the grand jury term or a release.

On March 16, 1863, Lincoln appointed General Ambrose Burnside, fresh from his unsuccessful engagement at Fredericksburg, to the post of commanding general of the Department of Ohio.[34] On April 13, 1863, Burnside issued General Order number 38. It warned of death for those giving active physical aid to the Confederacy—such as writers and carriers of secret letters. But it went further and specifically targeted speech. "The habit of declaring sympathies for the enemy will not be allowed in this Department. Persons committing such offenses will be at once arrested. . . . [T]reason, express or implied, will not be tolerated in this Department."[35] When the order was issued, Union armies had suffered a series of defeats in the east, antiwar sentiment was growing, and morale in the army was low.

The *Cincinnati Commercial* reported that the general was serious about Order 38 and that it covered disloyal language as well as disloyal acts: "We learn from reliable authority that General Burnside is determined to execute his Order No. 38. This order extends not only to acts in favor of rebels, but to words or expressions of sympathy in their behalf."[36]

Many applauded the order. Colonel Joseph Geiger told a Union mass meeting that he "thanked God that in the person of General Burnside we have a man who will attend to [Northern traitors] with a strong arm . . . —who, in enforcing his General Order No. 38, will squelch out the Northern traitors here."[37] The problem, one writer in the *Commercial* explained, was the bad tendency of criticism, however pure the motive behind it: "[T]o disaffect the people is to paralyze the Government. Therefore all denunciation of the President, his measures and his motives, in so far as it has any effect at all, being to destroy public confidence in the Government and to disaffect the people, is to that extent, . . . fatal in its tendencies, and affords direct countenance, aid and comfort to treason and traitors."[38]

Democrats feared that all political opposition to Lincoln administration war policy, a key political issue, was under attack. They had serious reasons for concern. For example, in Indiana, General Milo Hascall issued General Order number 9. It prohibited newspapers and public speakers from endeavoring "to bring the war policy of the Administration into disrepute," and it warned against active opposition "to the war policy of the administration." A Democratic congressman wrote the general asking just what these phrases meant. General Hascall replied in the press:

> What I mean by the expression, "or endeavor to bring the war policy of the Government into disrepute," is this: Certain measures have been determined upon by the Congress . . . and the Executive, such as the Internal Revenue and Tax Bills . . . , the Confiscation Act, the Conscription Act, the act authorizing the Executive to use negroes in every way possible to cripple the enemy . . . , the Proclamation of Emancipation . . . , and other measures having an immediate bearing on the war; and these I call the *war policy* of the Gov-

ernment or Administration. . . . The only practical effect, then, of allowing newspapers and public speakers to inveigh against these measures, is to divide and distract our own people, and thus give material "aid and comfort" to our enemies. . . .

It is a more serious thing than many are wont to suppose to divide and distract our country and prolong the war.[39]

Arrests included both politicians and ordinary citizens.[40] Criticism of arrests for antiwar speeches was not limited to Democrats. Union General Halleck complained of Union officers who assumed "powers which do not belong to them," and whose conduct was "inciting party passions and political animosities."[41] Meanwhile, Governor Morton of Indiana, faced with rising outrage over Hascall's suppression of speech and press, demanded that Hascall be replaced because he was harming the Union cause.[42]

Even prowar Democrats saw attacks on allegedly "disloyal" sentiments as a direct attack on the democratic process and on the sovereignty of the people. On April 14, 1863, the *Detroit Free Press* sounded a basic theme which would be elaborated and repeated again and again in coming months. "As a party [Democrats] have never declared against the war; but they have a right to do so. As tax-payers, as men liable to the draft, and therefore liable to be shot down, they have the right to say the struggle ought to cease or ought to go on, or ought to be conducted upon this policy or that policy, as their convictions dictate to them. The constitution and laws accord them that right."[43]

The Arrest and Trial of C. L. Vallandigham

The arrest of Clement L. Vallandigham seemed to confirm Democrats' fear that the administration was engaged in a pervasive attack on political speech.

General Burnside knew that Vallandigham, an outspoken antiwar activist, was scheduled to speak to a May 1, 1863, Knox County Democratic political rally in Mount Vernon, Ohio. Military agents in civilian clothes monitored the speech. Soldiers arrested Vallandigham in the early morning hours of May 5, and his trial by a military commission of seven officers began the next day, May 6. Vallandigham, an experienced trial lawyer, represented himself. The prosecution was represented by the judge advocate. By May 7 the court finished hearing evidence and argument. (This was a speedy trial indeed, and Vallandigham was unable in this very short time to subpoena one of his defense witnesses.)[44] He was tried on the following charge: "Publicly expressing, in violation of General Orders No. 38, from Head-quarters Department of the Ohio, sympathy for those in arms against the Government of the United States, and declaring disloyal sentiments and opinions, with the object and purpose of weakening the power of the Government in its efforts to suppress an unlawful rebellion."[45]

The charge was supported by the following specification:

In this, that the said Clement L. Vallandigham, a citizen of the State of Ohio, on or about the first day of May, 1863, at Mount Vernon, Knox County, Ohio, did publicly address a large meeting of citizens, and did utter sentiments in words, or in effect, as follows, declaring the present war "a wicked, cruel, and unnecessary war;" "a war not being waged for the preservation of the Union;" "a war for the purpose of crushing out liberty and erecting a despotism;" "a war for the freedom of the blacks and the enslavement of the whites;" stating "that if the Administration had so wished, the war could have been honorably terminated months ago;" that "peace might have been honorably obtained by listening to the proposed intermediation of France;" . . . charging that "the Government of the United States was about to appoint military marshals in every district, to restrain the people of their liberties, to deprive them of their rights and privileges;" characterizing General Orders No. 38 from Head-quarters Department of the Ohio, as a "base usurpation of arbitrary authority," inviting his hearers to resist the same, by saying, "the sooner the people inform the minions of usurped power that they will not submit to such restrictions upon their liberties, the better;" . . . [a]ll of which opinions and sentiments he well knew did aid, comfort, and encourage those in arms against the Government, and could but induce in his hearers a distrust of their own Government, sympathy for those in arms against it, and a disposition to resist the laws of the land.[46]

General Burnside ordered Vallandigham's arrest without consulting the president.[47] But the general acted in a context set by the president himself. At first, Burnside seemed to have presidential support. On May

8, 1863, having learned of the arrest from the newspapers, President Lincoln wired General Burnside: "In your determination to support the authority of the Government and suppress treason in your department, you may count on the firm support of the President."[48]

Vallandigham sought a writ of habeas corpus from the federal court. Judge Humphrey H. Leavitt, who had been appointed to the bench by President Andrew Jackson, denied Vallandigham's petition for the writ. After conceding that if the criminal procedure guarantees of the Bill of Rights were applicable then the arrest would not be legal, Leavitt pointed to other factors including "the present state of the country, and, . . . the expediency of interfering with the exercise of the military power." He said that "The Court can not shut its eyes to the grave fact that war exists, . . . threatening the subversion and destruction of the Constitution itself. In my judgment, when the life of the republic is imperiled, he mistakes his duty and obligation as a patriot who is not willing to concede to the Constitution such a capacity of adaptation to circumstances as may be necessary to meet a great emergency, and save the nation from hopeless ruin. Self-preservation is a paramount law."[49] The judge was hostile to antiwar speech. "And here, without subjecting myself to the charge of trenching upon the domain of political discussion," he announced, "I may be indulged in the remark, that there is too much of the pestilential leaven of disloyalty in the community."[50] Once the writ of habeas corpus was denied, the military trial proceeded.

At the trial, Vallandigham's May 1 speech, to what was a very large Democratic county political rally, was the basis of the charge against him. Vallandigham and other prominent Ohio Democrats, including Representatives George S. Pendleton and Samuel S. Cox had been present. The editor of the *Mount Vernon Democratic Banner* had presided at the meeting. Meeting vice presidents and secretaries were present, representing various townships in the county, and committees met during the meeting to transact party business. Because the meeting was so large, there were a number of speakers' stands, with Vallandigham speaking from the main one. A full transcript of his nearly two-hour speech does not seem to exist.[51]

According to Captain Hill, a witness for the prosecution, Vallandigham attacked Order 38, saying that

"he was a freeman;" that he "did not ask David Tod [the Governor of Ohio], or Abraham Lincoln, or Ambrose E. Burnside for his right to speak as he had done, and was doing. That his authority for so doing was higher than General Orders No. 38—it was General Orders No. 1—the Constitution. That General Orders No. 38 was a base usurpation of arbitrary power; that he had the most supreme contempt for such power. . . . That he was resolved never to submit to an order of a military dictator, prohibiting the free discussion of either civil or military authority. "The sooner that the people informed the minions of this usurped power that they would not submit to such restrictions upon their liberties, the better."[52]

Captain John A. Means, another witness for the prosecution, testified Vallandigham had said that the war was an abolition war, not one waged for the preservation of the Union.[53] Vallandigham purportedly said he would spit on Order 38 and trample it underfoot.[54]

According to Captain Means, Vallandigham also said "he would not counsel resistance to military or civil law; that was not needed." He referred to the president as "King Lincoln" and urged his listeners to come together at the ballot box and hurl the tyrant from his throne.[55]

As the testimony of Captain Means suggests, it seems quite likely that Vallandigham had advocated only peaceful political action. The Republican *Cincinnati Commercial* reported a Vallandigham speech made shortly before his arrest. According to the *Commercial*, Vallandigham told his followers that abolitionists had instigated the war to put down Democrats and bring about Negro equality; and that the war was designed to free the Negro and enslave the white man. But instead of counseling revolt, the paper reported, Vallandigham "stopped short, and talked about 'obeying the laws' and 'peaceable remedies.'" According to the correspondent, "a good many of the admirers of Vallandigham lost confidence in him. He had fallen far short of their expectations."[56] If Vallandigham had advocated violence or law-breaking, his archfoes in the *Commercial* would have been eager to report the fact.

S. S. Cox, a Democratic congressman from Ohio, testified for the defense. According to Cox, Vallandigham directed no epithet at General Burnside. Vallandigham had said nothing advocating forcible resistance of either laws or military orders. "He stated the sole remedy to be in the ballot-box, and in the courts. I remember this distinctly, for I had been pursuing the same line of remark at Chicago and Fort Wayne, and the other places where I had been speaking, and with the purpose of repressing any tendency toward violence among our Democratic people." According to Cox, "Mr. Vallandigham did not say a word about the conscription."[57]

At the close of the evidence Vallandigham entered the following protest: he said he had been "[a]rrested without due 'process of law,' without warrant from any judicial officer" and had "been served with a 'charge and specifications,' as in a Court-martial or Military Commission."

> I am not in either "the land or naval forces of the United States, nor in the militia in the actual service of the United States," and therefore am not triable for any cause, by any such Court, but am subject, by the express terms of the Constitution, to arrest only by due process of law, judicial warrant, regularly issued upon affidavit, and by some officer or Court of competent jurisdiction for the trial of citizens, and am now entitled to be tried on an indictment or presentment of a Grand Jury of such Court, to speedy and public trial by an impartial jury of the State of Ohio, to be confronted with witnesses against me, to have compulsory process for witnesses in my behalf, the assistance of counsel for my defense, and evidence and argument according to the common laws and the ways of Judicial Courts. And all these I here demand as my right as a citizen of the United States, and under the Constitution of the United States.[58]

Furthermore his "alleged 'offence' " was "not known to the Constitution of the United States" or in violation of any law.

> It is words spoken to the people of Ohio in an open and public political meeting, lawfully and peaceably assembled, under the Constitution and upon full notice. It is words of criticism of the public policy of the public servants of the people, by which policy it was alleged that the welfare of the country was not promoted. It was an appeal to the people to change that policy, not by force, but by free elections and the ballot-box. It is not pretended that I counseled disobedience to the Constitution, or resistance to laws and lawful authority. I never have. Beyond this protest, I have nothing further to submit.[59]

As noted above, the United States district court refused to release Vallandigham on a writ of habeas corpus, the military tribunal convicted, and the Supreme Court declined to review the military conviction. The denial of the writ was apparently not appealed.[60] President Lincoln changed Vallandigham's sentence from imprisonment to banishment to the Confederacy. In the Confederacy, Vallandigham boarded a blockade runner, which took him to Bermuda. From there he sailed to Canada. The Democrats of Ohio nominated him for governor, and from his remote Canadian base he proceeded to wage his campaign for governor. He was resoundingly defeated.

Events After Vallandigham's Banishment

Massive protests followed Vallandigham's arrest and trial. The Democratic press was uniformly critical. Protest meetings were held in many cities. Even many Republicans were critical. Burnside offered to resign, but Lincoln declined the offer. On May 29, 1863, however, he telegraphed Burnside (in code) that "[a]ll the cabinet regretted the necessity of arresting, for instance, Vallandigham, some perhaps doubting, that there was a real necessity for it—but being done, all were for seeing you through with it."[61]

Judging by reports in the *Cincinnati Commercial*, Vallandigham's arrest was far from the only arrest under Order 38 for disloyal sentiments. Other arrests included a Democratic newspaper editor, many people who expressed otherwise unreported "disloyal language," a critic of Vallandigham's arrest, a man expressing hope for Confederate victory, and a man allegedly advocating shooting officers who captured deserters.[62] In addition, the military closed a number of newspapers (at least temporarily) or threatened them with closure.[63]

Apparently unchastened by the Vallandigham experience, in early June 1863, General Burnside issued Order 84, suppressing publication of the *Chicago Times* newspaper. (Illinois was also in the area under Burnside's command.) Wilbur Storey, the editor of the *Times,* was a racist who wrote of the "natural and proper loathing of the negro." After the Emancipation Proclamation, he denounced the war as a "John Brown raid on an extended scale."[64] Storey had protested the Vallandigham arrest and banishment. The rights of free speech and press and assembly, Storey insisted, "existed before the Constitution, but lest they might be invaded, the Constitution forbade . . . any law circumscribing them." Still, President Lincoln and "military satraps" had "punished as crimes the exercise of these constitutional privileges."[65]

This time the case came before a judge less sympathetic to suppression. Around midnight, Federal Judge Thomas Drummond issued a temporary order forbidding the military suppression of the *Times* before a full hearing. News reports suggest that Judge Drummond had telegraphed Supreme Court Justice David Davis, a close Lincoln advisor who was critical of military arrests of civilians, to join him in hearing the case.[66] On granting the temporary order, Judge Drummond made a statement:

> [I] desire to give every aid and assistance in my power to the Government and to the Administration in restoring the Union; but I have always wished to treat the Government as a government of law and a government of the Constitution, and not as a government of mere physical force. I personally have contended, and shall always contend, for the right of free discussion, and the right of commenting, under law, and under the Constitution, upon the acts of officers of the Government.[67]

At 3:30 A.M. on June 3, soldiers disregarded the order, entered the *Times* office, and destroyed some recently printed papers. As the *New York Tribune* headline put it: "SUPPRESSION OF THE CHICAGO TIMES. The Writ of the Court Disregarded."[68] On June 3, 1863, General Burnside attempted to justify his order to the public, returning to his theme of the civilian citizen as soldier.

> [The citizen] too, has sacrifices to make; but the country's demand upon him is comparatively but small. [I]t merely asks that he shall imitate the loyal example of the soldiers in the field, so far as to abate somewhat of that freedom of speech which they give up so entirely. The citizen would be . . . unfaithful to his country, if . . . he were unwilling to give up a portion of a privilege which the soldier resigns altogether. That freedom of discussion and criticism which is proper in the politician and the journalist in time of peace, becomes rank treason when it tends to weaken the confidence of the soldier in his officers and his Government.[69]

In his diary, Gideon Welles, Lincoln's secretary of the navy, described the arrest of Vallandigham and the suppression of the *Chicago Times* as "arbitrary and injudicious" and an infringement on "the constitutional rights of the parties." Every member of the Cabinet, he thought, "regrets what has been done," but the Cabinet was divided as to what to do next.

Though Welles thought Vallandigham and the *Chicago Times* were aiding the rebellion and were traitors in their hearts, still he concluded by lamenting that military commanders should "without absolute necessity disregard those great principles on which our government and institutions rest."[70]

Massive protest followed the seizure of the *Chicago Times*. A huge public rally in Chicago protested the seizure of the paper, much of the press was critical, and local leaders sent a telegram to President Lincoln calling for revocation of the order suspending the newspaper.

Representative Isaac Arnold and Senator Lyman Trumbull (both Illinois Republicans) telegraphed the president urging him to give the citizen request urgent consideration. Yielding to intense political pressure, Arnold sent a second telegraph saying the first was not intended to express an opinion on the merits.[71] The Illinois House of Representatives passed a resolution of protest.[72] The president also received an urgent telegram urging revocation from both Supreme Court Justice David Davis and from Lincoln's law partner William Herndon: "We deem it of the highest importance," they wrote, "that you revoke the order . . . suppressing the Chicago Times."[73] Davis was Lincoln's close confidant and political advisor, his 1860 campaign manager, and Lincoln's appointee to the Supreme Court.

This time President Lincoln promptly revoked the order and the *Chicago Times* resumed publication.[74] Facing a strong backlash from some Illinois Republicans, however, Arnold and Trumbull defended the revocation and made at least one public statement explaining their telegram as simply seeking prompt attention for a request by constituents.[75] Arnold said he approved of President Lincoln's revocation order because "in my judgment the order of Gen. Burnside was unwarranted by the law and the Constitution."[76]

After the huge public meeting in Chicago to protest its suppression, the *Chicago Times* engaged in some editorial crowing: "Wednesday was a day for Chicago to be proud of. By the voice of her citizens she proclaimed to the world that the right of free speech has not yet passed away; that *immunity* of thought and discussion are yet among the inalienable *privileges* of men born to freedom. . . . Twenty thousand bold men with one acclaim decreed that speech and press shall be untrammeled, and that despotism shall not usurp the *inborn rights of the American citizen*."[77]

Leaders often tend to find a compelling necessity for suppression, when, in retrospect, the necessity looks much less compelling. General Burnside suppressed the *Chicago Times*, but when Lincoln countermanded the suppression order, the evils feared by General Burnside did not materialize. Lincoln dealt with one of the most acute crises in national history, but even he seems to have overestimated, in Vallandigham's case, the need to suppress free speech. We now know that the Lincoln administration justified the suppression of Vallandigham on the basis of "compelling necessity," even when members of the cabinet themselves doubted the wisdom or the necessity of the arrest. In the end, it was popular reaction—a reaction invoking the popular free speech tradition—that led Lincoln to be much more cautious about suppression.

The free speech tradition invoked in Vallandigham's case included core ideas: that criticism of the actions of government officials and advocacy of peaceful change in public policy were protected speech; that free speech was a basic human right; that it was central to popular government; that infringements on free speech therefore violated the ultimate sovereignty of the people; and that free speech required broad equality of treatment for opposing views. Broad belief in these ideas prevented Civil War repression of political speech from becoming more pervasive. Critics warned that suppression also posed dangers because it threatened the function of free speech as a framework for democracy. Free speech, like democracy, was a process, not a result. And without free speech, they insisted, they would not have democracy.

Supporters of the arrest marshaled counterideas. Advocates of suppression pointed out the dangers to national unity posed by dissent. (Whether suppression of Vallandigham in fact enhanced national unity is dubious.) They distinguished between liberty and license and in doing so they made arguments like those that supported the Sedition Act and the suppression of antislavery speech. The arguments were also similar to those expressed in judicial cases and in a scholarly tradition that insisted that freedom of speech and press did not encompass license.[78] In time of rebellion, they argued, free speech rights are far more limited than in peacetime (even in states not in rebellion and distant from military conflict). They insisted that in time of rebellion or war, speech that tends to produce bad results should be suppressed. They also might have invoked the Sedition Act and insisted that freedom of speech was limited to protection against prior restraint. That such arguments were not made shows the extent to which the robust popular free speech tradition had triumphed on that issue.

The chapter that follows looks in detail at arguments for these two clashing traditions. The contestants clashed over Vallandigham's arrest, over the suppression of the *Chicago Times*, and over a resolution to expel an antiwar congressman for making an antiwar speech on the floor of the House of Representatives.

15

The Free Speech Tradition Confronts

the War Power

The arrest of Vallandigham was widely reported in the nation's press. Some Republican papers greeted the Vallandigham arrest as long overdue. "The arrest of this individual by order of Gen. Burnside," the *Cincinnati Commercial* noted with apparent satisfaction, "is an act that will convince the most heedless that Order No. 38 will be enforced, and the lines definitely drawn between traitors and patriots." The writer said he did not know "[u]pon what specific charge the arrest ... has been made." Nonetheless, he was pleased with the arrest: "Those who are not the friends of the Government are its enemies. Mr. Vallandigham is one of its enemies."[1]

A few days later the *Commercial* returned to its defense of Order 38. "[T]here is nothing in the celebrated Order 38 which should disturb the feelings of any loyal man. It is not designed to abridge the liberty of the individual, where that liberty is not used to the detriment of the Government." While temperate discussion would be permitted, the paper noted, violent and incendiary language and arguments that would lead to law violation would not be allowed.[2] Most Ohio Republican papers and politicians endorsed the arrest.[3]

To justify the action against Vallandigham, the *Commercial* cited rhetoric used by the most provocative critics of the arrest. It quoted the *Dayton Empire*, a pro-Vallandigham paper, as announcing, immediately after Vallandigham's arrest, "If the spirit of the men who purchased our freedom through the fiery ordeal of the revolution, still lives in the hearts of the people, as we believe it does, then all will yet be well, for it will hurl defiance to military despotism, and rescue, through *blood and carnage*, if it must be, our now endangered liberties."[4]

THE FREE SPEECH–POPULAR SOVEREIGNTY RESPONSE
TO VALLANDIGHAM'S ARREST

For many Democrats, the Vallandigham arrest was not an isolated event, but part of a larger attack on political freedom. For that reason, many Democrats who rejected Vallandigham's peace proposals rallied to his defense. Some criticisms of the arrest were general. Others focused more particularly on free speech values. Many noted that Vallandigham was not accused of violating any specific statute.

The *Albany Argus* denounced the arrest as a "crime against the Constitution,"[5] and the *Detroit Free Press* lamented that the "arrest of Mr. Vallandigham, and his hasty trial before a secret military court is an event which arouses the indignation of all lovers of the constitution and laws."[6]

After Judge Leavitt's decision denying Vallandigham's petition for habeas corpus, the *Detroit Free Press* wrote, "With a deep sense of the responsibility of every word we put upon the printed page, we solemnly declare our conviction that the Republic is in the deepest peril which ever menaced her." The paper insisted that "[t]he right to speak, to give intelligent utterance to our wants, passions, desires, impulses, the Heaven giving privileges of man over the brute, must be exercised untrammeled by fear, unmolested by power, or there is nothing worth living for left to American citizens."[7] In another editorial the same paper said:

> We have never been champions of Mr. Vallandigham. In many particulars we have disagreed with him in opinion; but we have seen nothing in his course which he was not permitted by the constitution and laws to do; but even if he is guilty of any offense, he is entitled to a trial by a jury of his country and by the law of the land. If, in his case, a military court—the most offensive of tribunals to a free people—is allowed to usurp the office and functions of these, we will be justified in asserting that the worst apprehensions of the designs of the administration are fulfilled, and that American liberty is so dead, that even its forms are no longer observed.[8]

The *Detroit Free Press* recited the charge against Vallandigham. The charge did not allege that Vallandigham had "violated any law of the United States," but simply an order issued by a general. "There is no pretence that he transcended the privileges guaranteed to him by the constitution and laws." Indeed, there was no proof offered that he "has ever persuaded one man not to enlist, one to desert his flag, one to falter in his duty to the Union." In essence, the Vallandigham case was "an announcement that no man, in these free and loyal States, shall utter a sentiment which the hero of Fredericksburg disapproves of. . . . [I]t is monstrous to hold that men who may be taxed or drafted, shall not advocate peace whenever and wherever they please; provided they do it in accordance with the constitution and the laws."[9]

Democratic governor Horatio Seymour of New York sent a letter to a protest meeting held in Albany, New York. He wrote that the Vallandigham arrest "involved a series of offenses against our most sacred rights. It interfered with the freedom of speech; it molested our rights to be secure in our homes against unreasonable searches and seizures; it pronounced sentence without trial, save one which was a mockery, which insulted as well as wronged."[10]

Criticism by the Democratic *Cincinnati Enquirer* was muted. Burnside had visited the editors on the day of Vallandigham's arrest and warned them that they too could be imprisoned.[11]

Call for a Political Response to Suppression

After the arrest (and after the suppression of the *Chicago Times*), many Democratic speakers and papers counseled against violent action—at least unless the administration made direct efforts to interfere with the ballot. Francis Kernan was a highly regarded lawyer and Democratic member of Congress from New York who had first attained prominence as a brilliant orator for the antislavery Free Soil Party.[12] He spoke to an "immense meeting" at the state capitol in Albany called to protest the Vallandigham arrest. He expressed a common Democratic theme: obedience to law.

> We will allow none to lead us into violence, but by our firmness and calm determination to stand by our rights, we will force our opponents into respect for them. We have one remedy in the ballot box. If those in authority do not observe our rights, we can turn them out, through the ballot box. We have another remedy, if we believe the laws of our law makers unconstitutional, in the courts. And we

have still another, which is quite as good and efficacious, and that is in the voice of the people, uttered from assemblages such as this, where we are discussing our rights, peacefully but manfully—a voice terrible to those who are delinquent in their trusts.[13]

Free Speech and Representative Democracy

Other protest meetings were held throughout the North.[14] George V. N. Lothrop, a scholarly leader of the bar and former Michigan attorney general, spoke to a huge protest meeting held at the Detroit City Hall. Lothrop was a Democrat who opposed Vallandigham's views and who, by his own account, had "unreservedly" supported the government "against the insurrection."[15]

Still, Lothrop insisted on a broad and tough definition of freedom of speech. He said that soldiers had arrested Vallandigham for allegedly "expressing sympathy for rebels, declaring disloyal sentiments and opinions with a view to weaken the power of the government." Without "inquiring whether the words [Vallandigham] used will fairly bear this construction," Lothrop rejected the claim that they did or could state a legal offense. "I dwell not on the uncertainty of what is disloyal; but the point I make is whether a man can be arrested for any quality of opinions on public affairs?" Lothrop said it was a postulate that "*without free discussion there can be no free government.* . . . Hence we can readily see at what price we must lay down this right."[16]

For Lothrop, the right to free speech had a tough central core, impervious to government invasion. "What is free speech under the constitution? Clearly the right to canvass and discuss without reserve public measures and acts. Anything short of this is inadequate."[17] As a result, "Mr. Vallandigham had the full right to approve, criticize or denounce the war and all acts and measures of the administration at his pleasure. As a citizen he might form any opinion on these subjects and freely express them." All agreed on the right to "approve and applaud" administration policy. But while Vallandigham's accusers considered approval meritorious, "they object when he condemns and denounces."[18]

Lothrop responded to a friend who claimed that freedom of speech did not protect "license."

He meant that the expression of opinions regarded as unsound, unpatriotic, or of evil tendency, should be deemed not a true freedom, but a license to be restrained. But this obviously destroys all free discussion. . . . It makes, if I apply the rule, all opinions that I reject contraband to all other persons. But the very fact of a guaranty of freedom of speech implies that men will honestly differ, and that the privilege of expression is to be equal to all. The right of expression shall not depend upon . . . the quality of the opinions in the judgment of another. The guaranty means this or it means nothing.[19]

The constitutional guarantee, Lothrop insisted, was framed "to protect what you call license." After all, it was "the *unpopular* opinion of to-day that needs these guaranties." The idea of limiting free speech to ideas that were popular would mean free speech principles only applied when they were not needed. "The man who runs with the majority needs no guaranty. He is never disloyal."[20]

"[A]buses and licenses," the Republican *Evening Post* admitted "of course adhere to this unlimited freedom of public criticism; but these are apparently inseparable from the use, and without the abuse we should scarcely have the use." Who, the *Post* asked, should draw such lines outside of the courts? The question might suggest that so long as the courts drew the line, punishment for expression was permissible. The *Evening Post*'s following comments and its general editorial policy suggest that, as to criticism of government policy, it thought no one should be permitted to treat peaceful political criticism of government policy as abuse.[21]

Resolutions passed at an Albany protest meeting insisted on protection for political speech and quoted from Daniel Webster. "It is the ancient and undoubted prerogative of this people to canvass public measures and the merits of public men. It is a 'homebred right,' a fireside privilege. It had been enjoyed in every house, cottage, and cabin in the nation. It is as undoubted as the right of breathing the air or walking on the earth."[22]

With increasing emphasis, critics noted the threat to popular government posed by actions of the administration. Free speech was essential to democracy. "If freedom of speech is surrendered," the *Detroit Free Press* noted, "it will no longer be pretended, we presume, that the ballot-box can represent the views and wishes of the majority of the people. . . . Without freedom of speech, the ballot box is a farce."[23] If the president had the war power to stifle speech, then he could make elections meaningless (for elections without free speech were a mockery). By the same war power logic, the president could simply dispense with elections. As the *Detroit Free Press* glumly observed:

> [I]t is plain that if meetings may be [dispersed], speakers banished, and journals suppressed because they are opposed to the war or the conduct of it, the polls may be closed, or voters excluded from them, for the same reason. If it is disloyal to make a speech against the war, it is doubly disloyal to vote for men who are opposed to it. . . . If the president may suspend the *habeas corpus*, suppress the courts, and put the lives, liberty and property of the citizens of loyal and peaceable States into the keeping of military tribunals, we cannot see why he cannot suppress the ballot box and declare it a "military necessity" to continue the Presidency in himself . . . so long as he has an army to back him.[24]

The nexus between free speech and democracy was a theme at many Democratic conventions, including the Ohio convention that nominated Vallandigham. It resolved,

> First, that the will of the people is the foundation of all free government: that to give effect to this will, free thought, free speech and a free press are absolutely indispensable. Without free discussion there is no certainty of sound judgment[;] without sound judgment there can be no wise government. That it is an important and constitutional right of the people to discuss all measures of their Government, and to approve or disapprove, as to their best judgment seems right; that they have a like right to propose and advocate that policy which, in their judgment, is best, and to argue and vote against whatever policy seems to them to violate the Constitution, to impair their liberties, or be detrimental to their welfare; that these and all other rights guarantied to them by their Constitution are their rights in time of war as well as in times of peace, and of far more value and necessity in war than in peace, for in peace, liberty, security, and property are seldom endangered, in war, they are ever in peril.[25]

In addition, the resolutions also condemned the Emancipation Proclamation.

George Pugh, the former United States senator who served as Vallandigham's habeas corpus lawyer, was the Democratic nominee for lieutenant governor. In his speech to the convention he explained, "The question of prosecuting the war, or concluding a peace, can not be intelligently decided till we hear both sides, and all sides. Any idea of discussing such questions, under fear of military dictation, or the Order 38, [is] shame and mockery."[26]

The Principal-Agent Metaphor and the Sedition Act Analogy

The right of free speech followed from the principal-agent relation between the people and elected officials—from the basic idea of representative government. The Ohio Democratic convention resolved that administrations and government officials were merely the agents of the people "subject to their approval or condemnation, according to the merit or demerit of their acts."[27]

The *Detroit Free Press* argued that the claim that opposition to the war amounted to disloyalty was "heretical and wicked. It is only another form of saying that the people have ceased to be sovereign, and must sustain every act of their agents, right or wrong." The *Free Press* said that whether a war should be supported depended on a number of factors: was it a just war; could it be terminated by an honorable adjustment; was there a reasonable hope of success; was it practicable, constitutional, and consistent with public liberty? The *Free Press* concluded that "[i]n a free country at least, the men who are liable to fight, and who *must* be taxed to support the war, can never surrender the right to ask these questions, and to answer them according to the convictions which their consciences entertain. And no one can legally accuse them of disloyalty because he does not agree with their answer."[28]

Some Democrats suggested that the Lincoln administration was reviving the tyranny of the Sedition Act used by the John Adams administration against its political opponents. In Vallandigham's case, however, Congress had not even passed a law purporting to authorize the arrests.[29] Representative Daniel Voorhees of Indiana said the Republicans were the ideological heirs of the Federalists who enacted the Sedition Act. The Sedition Act was

a law by which, if Mr. Vallandigham, or myself, or anybody else, made a speech that the President didn't like, he would be taken up, and confined, and put in prison as a seditious person. Now a days, without any such law, they take a man up, keep him in prison as long as they like, and turn him out whenever they get tired of him, without making explanation or apology to him. . . . I, upon the other hand, dare to trust the people, and clothe them with power to regulate their own affairs. I stand by the literal meaning of the Constitution, that Congress shall pass no law abridging the freedom of speech or of the press.[30]

A writer for *Harper's Weekly* suggested that the administration's error was its distrust of the people. "Arresting seditious talkers implies a fear that the people have not sense or strength of mind enough to resist the appeal of sedition."[31]

Nor, critics insisted, were these principles of free and equal speech dissolved by calling criticism "treason." Democrats regularly highlighted the Constitution's very limited definition of treason and the historical and functional reasons for the limit. As David Seymour (formerly a Democratic congressman) explained to a meeting in Troy, New York, in America "no such offence as *implied treason*" existed. The use of bold and even severe free speech about government policy "is not and cannot be held to be '*adhering*' to our enemies, 'giving them aid and comfort.' Any different construction of this constitutional definition," he explained, "would confound all right of free speech."[32]

Republican Critics of Suppression

Opposition to the Vallandigham arrest and the suppression of the *Chicago Times* was not limited to Democrats. The New York *Evening Post*, a pro-Republican and proemancipation paper, was strongly critical. The *Evening Post* rejected General Burnside's assertion that since soldiers could not criticize the war policy of the administration, neither could civilians. It responded: "But he forgets that persons 'in the military and naval service of the United States' are subject to military law, while the ordinary citizen is subject exclusively to civil law."[33] At any rate, General Burnside's theory was subversive of democratic government. "[N]o governments and no authorities are to be held as above criticism, or even denunciation. We know of no other way of correcting their faults, spurring on their sluggishness, or restraining their tyrannies, than by open and bold discussion. How can a popular Government, most of all, know the popular will, and guide its course in the interests of the community, unless it be told from time to time what the popular convictions and wishes are?"[34]

The *New York Tribune*, a strongly antislavery Republican paper, was ambivalent. It doubted that any good would come from the episode and hoped that the president would turn Vallandigham loose. The *Tribune* wrote that Vallandigham was a "Pro-Slavery Democrat of an exceedingly coppery hue.... [I]f there were penalties for holding irrational, unpatriotic and inhuman views with regard to political questions, he would be one of the most flagrant offenders." But, the *Tribune* suggested, "our Federal and State Constitutions do not recognize perverse opinions, nor unpatriotic speeches, as grounds of infliction."[35] (Republicans often called peace Democrats "Copperheads," after the snake.)

A few days later the *Tribune* returned to the subject of Vallandigham's arrest. It suggested that Vallandigham unintentionally helped the government, and it noted the free speech problems raised by the arrest. "We reverence Freedom of Discussion—by which we mean Freedom to uphold perverse and evil theories, since nobody ever doubted the right to uphold the other sort."[36]

A German-American antislavery paper expressed shock when it learned that Vallandigham's only crime was "a public speech." It denounced the sentence as despotism because "Mr. Vallandigham ... was sentenced simply for making use of the freedom of speech guaranteed by the constitution. [W]e do not acknowledge any *misuse* of free speech, as was invented by the European police." The paper's prescription for the "so-called misuse of the freedom of speech" was that it "must be neutralized by the counteracting better use of the same."[37] The *Bedford Standard*, another Republican paper, also criticized the arrest.

> [A]t a time when we see the opinions we have so long advocated in the face of many who would gladly have silenced us, so rapidly gaining favor among the people, we think there is no need of attempting to shut the mouths of such men as Vallandigham. If we are successful all his tirades will fall unheeded. If we are unsuccessful, and continually so, no power on earth can prevent the formation of such a public opinion as will compel a change of policy on the part of the administration, or lead to the election of a new one. Let us have faith in the power of truth, and oppose those we believe to be in error with the weapon of truth.[38]

Colonel A. S. Diven spoke to a Republican meeting at Albany, New York. Diven was a strongly antislavery lawyer, soldier, and railroad promoter. He had been a Free Soil candidate for governor of New York in

1859 and from 1861 to 1863 served in Congress, where he supported emancipation in the District of Columbia and authored the first bill authorizing the use of black troops.[39] According to the *Albany Argus*, he said that he "was opposed to the abridgement of discussion. He maintained the right of the people to discuss and criticize the action of the government, whether in peace or in war, to the fullest extent!"[40]

How extensive the condemnation of the Vallandigham arrest was is difficult to determine. The *Detroit Free Press* asserted that opposition to the arrest was quite general and was not "confined to any one party."

> This is shown conclusively, by the extracts we have published from the leading editorials of such republican papers as the New York *Tribune*, The New York *Evening Post*, the New York *Commercial Advertiser*, the Albany *Statesman*, the Boston *Advertiser*, the Boston *Traveller*, the Springfield *Republican*, backed as the New York *Evening Post* truly says, by at least three-fourths of the republican party itself. But the republican press and party among those who voted for Lincoln do not stand alone, for the anti-slavery press are unanimous in condemning the course of the administration.[41]

In fact, abolitionists were divided on the issue. Ezra Heywood, a radical who had left the ministry to become a lecturer for the Massachusetts Anti-Slavery Society, introduced a resolution at the society's 1863 meeting supporting free speech and criticizing the prosecution of Vallandigham. The resolution was met with the argument that it should not be passed by an antislavery organization since it helped the South, and it was tabled.[42] In contrast to the *Detroit Free Press*, the Democratic *Albany Argus* complained that most Republican journals had failed to come out squarely for free speech.[43]

Certainly, some Republican papers like the *Cincinnati Commercial* and the *Chicago Tribune*, and many Republican orators, fully supported Burnside's suppression of critical speech. For example, the *Chicago Tribune*, mixing its metaphors, lamented that Vallandigham, the "Queen Bee of the Copperhead hive," had only been sent South "instead of being hung, as he deserved."[44] Still, there was substantial Republican opposition to General Burnside's suppressions of speech and press. A large crowd assembled to protest the general's suppression of the *Chicago Times*. "A full half of the crowd that got together in the Court house Square last evening," the *Chicago Tribune* lamented, "was, we are sorry to say, made up of Republicans." These the *Tribune* found "out of place" in an "assemblage" pretending to defend free speech, but in fact "met to assail the Government and weaken its power."[45]

Shortly afterwards, Republican senator Lyman Trumbull addressed a crowd that included a number of Republicans who were unhappy about his telegram urging President Lincoln to give urgent consideration to the request to overrule General Burnside. "Has it come to this," Trumbull asked,

> that you will deny in the free city of Chicago the right of a citizen to discuss the acts of the President? [Cries of "We won't allow it" . . .] Is there a man in this audience who has not expressed today his dissatisfaction with some act of the President? [Cries of "Yes," "Yes," "We have none of us expressed any dissatisfaction."] Ah! do all of you, then, think the President's revocation of Gen. Burnside's order suppressing the Chicago Times was *right*? [Cries of "No!" "No!" 'It was wrong!' . . .] *Then you all deserve to be taken in hand by the military power and sent beyond the lines.*[46]

Trumbull insisted that the Republican Party should not surrender its position as the advocate of liberty and free speech. He thought that incidents like the suppression of the *Chicago Times* were damaging the administration and the war effort. These acts allowed critics to charge that "we are opposed to the freedom of speech and opinion, to the freedom of the press; in favor of curtailing personal liberty, and in favor of a despotism."[47] He continued, "Now we should not allow these things. We have been the advocate of free speech for the last forty years, and should not allow the party which during the whole time has been using the gag to usurp our place. We are fighting for the restoration of the Union, and the preservation of the Constitution, and all the liberties it guarantees to every citizen."[48]

The Burnside Critics' View of the Nature of Free Speech

Many citizens believed that there was a central core of protected expression that the government could not suppress, regardless of how impressive its interest in doing so appeared. For them this core included expression of opinion on public policy—such as the wisdom of pursuing the war and the legality, tyranny, or wisdom of General Burnside's suppression of expression. For many others, the very grossness of the suppression—an arrest or prior restraint based on an edict of a general issued outside the immediate area of military conflict, unsupported by a law passed by Congress, and unreviewed by a court—meant that detailed discussion of the limits of free speech was unnecessary.

For many critics of the suppression, free speech was a basic principle that involved equal rights for the critics as well as supporters of governmental policy—including the war policy. As George V. N. Lothrop said, "[T]he very fact of a guaranty of freedom of speech implies that men will honestly differ, and that the privilege of expression is to be equal to all."[49] To deny expression to those with contrary views risked weakening the basic framework that supported liberty for all. "We freely concede," said the *Bedford Examiner*, "to any one the same right to criticize the administration which we claim for ourselves. If we disapprove of a pro-slavery policy, we expect to say so without molestation. Let those who disapprove of an anti-slavery policy do the same."[50] Former Democratic congressman David Seymour spoke to a Democratic rally in Troy, New York, and insisted that the Constitution broadly protected free expression of ideas. Protection for diverse views was implicit in a broad right of free speech. "No gag law on the press; no swords nor bayonets, nor chains, nor prisons, nor exile, can, under our Constitution, legally restrain or repress them," he said. "This is true in morals, in social life and in religion. It is true of the atheist, the mormon and the abolitionist. Even the abolitionists—the Phillipses, the Sumners, the Wades, the Garrisons, and their whole tribe—have a right to preach heretical doctrines."[51] Sanford Church was a former district attorney, state legislator, and lieutenant governor of New York who, in 1870, would be elected to sit as a judge on its highest court. At a mass meeting in Erie County, Church exclaimed, "Let Vallandigham talk! Let Anna Dickinson [a fiery abolitionist orator] talk! Let all the host of radical declaimers in petticoats or breeches talk!"[52]

Because of the broad principle of liberty, those who disagreed with Vallandigham felt free to come to his defense. "The views of Mr. Vallandigham have nothing to do with the question," the *Detroit Free Press* explained. "The same feeling would have been aroused if Mr. Greeley [editor of the *New York Tribune*] or Wendell Phillips [the abolitionist orator] had been arrested and thrown into prison for exercising the rights guaranteed to them under the constitution."[53]

A number of speakers warned Republicans against establishing a principle that could later be turned against them. Wirt Dexter, a leading Republican lawyer in Chicago,[54] spoke to the crowd that gathered to protest the suppression of the *Chicago Times.* "I don't wish to see this kind of treatment turned upon the party of which I am a member," he warned, "and I say to republicans to-night, gentlemen, be careful how you approach this abyss that opens before us."[55] Senator Trumbull made the same point, applying it to executive and military suppression of a newspaper. "Did it ever occur to you," Trumbull asked, "that the next election may put an entirely different face upon affairs? . . . The same chalice you hold to the lips of your adversaries today, to-morrow may be returned to your lips."[56] The New York *Journal of Commerce* explained the "distinction between discussion or counsel and 'treason.' It said, "the most ardent partisan can see it by reversing circumstances and imagining an administration in power which should attempt to pursue a policy contrary to his views." In that case, "he would readily perceive" his right to discuss "the policy, and . . . to endeavor by argument, by reason, by publication . . . to influence the votes of his fellow-citizens at coming elections."[57] The *Boston Pioneer* emphasized the point demanding "*a right for all.*" Otherwise those who approved the Vallandigham sentence could not complain if they were packed off to prison in Florida if *they* criticized the administration.[58]

Some, like the *National Intelligencer*, claimed that suppression was selective. According to that newspaper, Vallandigham had said that the war aim had changed from preserving the Union to freeing the slaves; these statements were at least part of the basis for his conviction. Meanwhile, Wendell Phillips, the fiery abolitionist orator, had said that the war had become a war for abolition and had advocated disunion rather than union with slave states. No one had suggested prosecuting *him*. The *National Intelligencer* suggested that proposed distinctions between the cases would not wash, and drew the following conclusion.

> We know it will be said that the difference between Mr. Vallandigham and Mr. Phillips is this: [Vallandigham's] purpose is to *weaken* the Government while the purpose of [Mr. Phillips] . . . is rather to *strengthen* the Government in its struggle with the rebellion. But who does not see that such a representation assumes that very point in dispute? At the same time it ascribes to Mr. Vallandigham a disunion purpose which he constantly disclaims, while Mr. Phillips has expressly announced that he will accept disunion on the condition of emancipation being secured. We believe that the Government might better afford to let Mr. Vallandigham and

Mr. Phillips enjoy the privilege of "free speech" according to their respective notions of propriety, than to proceed against either of them for words spoken in public discussion.[59]

A Narrow View: Free Speech as Limited to Freedom from Prior Restraint

One critic of the suppression took a narrow view of free speech. James F. Joy, a Republican lawyer who announced that he despised his clients' politics, represented the owners of the *Chicago Times*. Joy assumed that freedom of speech was limited to a protection against prior restraint, and he said that Congress could decide what speech to allow and what to proscribe. "It is fully competent," Joy sweepingly announced, "for Congress to enact a law punishing licentiousness of the press,—punishing libels upon the government, or upon public officers, or any other form of publication calculated to injure the government and bring it into disrepute, or to throw obstacles in the way of its measures, or tending to sedition and disturbance of the public peace."[60] (In fact, Madison, Jefferson, many framers of the Constitution, and many members of Congress both at the time of the Sedition Act and in the mid-1830s believed Congress had no such power.)[61] But, Joy suggested, Congress dare not pass such statutes because the popular view was that they would infringe freedom of speech and press.[62]

Many recognized some limits to the class of protected speech. Senator Trumbull suggested that if the editors of the *Chicago Times* had encouraged resistance to the draft, they could be arrested, tried in federal court, and thrown into prison.[63] He did not suggest Congress could make it criminal to make false criticisms of government. By emphasizing that he did not advocate disobedience to the law, Vallandigham and many of his supporters recognized, at least, that such advocacy was problematic.

The Defense of the Administration

The Charge of Hypocrisy

Defenders of the administration took several tacks. First, they said it was graceless for a party, many of whose members had supported suppression of antislavery speech, to criticize this suppression of free speech. "Since the arrest of the treason-shrieker, Vallandigham," the *Chicago*

Tribune noted, "his disciples fill the air with cries about the Constitutional right of 'free speech.' [W]e wish to ask those Copperhead defenders of free speech how much of this *Constitutional and sacred privilege* did their party allow to be exercised in the South before the war broke out?"[64]

The paper asked, "How much 'free speech' was tolerated in Secessia during the twenty years before the war broke out?" Opponents of slavery were "arrested, imprisoned, fined, tar and feathered, rode on a rail, whipped, ducked, and even hung for daring to exercise [their] 'Constitutional right of free speech.'"

> "Ah, but," replies a Copperhead, "that abridgment of free speech was made to prevent any discussion of the 'divine institution;'" Very true; but is slavery above the Constitution? . . . If Southern Democrats may, by mob violence, backed by Southern courts, stifle free speech in defiance of the Constitution, on the plea that slavery must not be discussed, with what consistency do Northern Democrats complain of the Generals of the army, in time of war and national peril, who forbid violent and seditious assaults upon the Government, the intention and effect of which is, to strengthen the enemy and weaken the Union?[65]

John Brough was the Union candidate for governor of Ohio, running against Vallandigham. He noted that George Pugh (the Democratic candidate for lieutenant governor) had supported a bill for the Kansas territory that contained the following section: "if any man shall print, publish, indite or give form or shape to published matter, tending to stir up a rebellion of slaves in Kansas, he shall be punished" by a fine of five hundred dollars and six months' imprisonment. Pugh said he regretted the section, but he had defended it as necessary where slavery existed. "The difference between us," Brough announced to the delight of his audience, "seems only to be that we recognize a 'military necessity,' and he a 'negro necessity.'" At that point the paper recorded "Laughter."[66]

The pro-Republican *New York Tribune* noted the effort in the 1830s to silence abolitionists by laws and violence. This effort, it suggested, had enjoyed considerable Democratic support: "Politicians, lawyers, bankers, merchants—all who considered themselves anybody or aspired to be somebody—held meetings to denounce and silence [abolitionists]; "respectable" halls and churches were sternly refused them; . . . vicious boys and rowdies rotten-egged them; . . . while Mayors, Congressmen and dry goods jobbers wrote letters to the South, proclaiming their intense disgust and abhorrence of their "treasonable" inculcations."[67] The *Tribune* noted with barely repressed glee the conversion of many Democrats to a strong view of free speech. "The times have bravely altered since then," the *Tribune* noted, "and altered, we rejoice to say, for the better. The right of free discussion—which means the right to proclaim and defend unpopular views, since the other sort have no need of protection—is now affirmed and upheld by those who for a quarter of a century persistently scouted and trampled on it." Indeed, now, in the midst of civil war, with the nation on the brink of destruction, meetings were held where determination "to resist the draft, to repudiate the public debt, and to embarrass and cripple in every way the National authorities, is proclaimed amid thunders of applause."[68] The *Tribune* concluded that free speech has limits. Still, "truth is truth, though the devil utter it, and Free Speech is one of the most precious of the Rights of Man."[69]

There were charges of inconsistency on all sides. (Republicans, after all, had campaigned in 1856 and 1860 as the party of free speech.) The *National Intelligencer* acknowledged some advocates of free speech were recent converts, but concluded that fact should not obscure the merits of the case. The paper urged its readers to strive "to separate a good cause from the infirmities of the men into whose hands it is suffered to fall."[70] It was a mistake to judge a principle by the consistency of its advocates.

War Time as Different: The Necessity Defense

Those who supported suppressing Vallandigham and the *Chicago Times* insisted that free speech did not protect license. Politicians and citizens, General Burnside had announced, "must not use license and plead that they are exercising liberty."[71] After all, the nation was at war. In times of peace, a writer in the *Chicago Tribune* announced, free speech could be tolerated as a "harmless right." But things were quite different "in times of war and revolution." Ordinarily, "even the licentiousness of speech is better than a too rigid restriction of it; but we can't afford to be quite so generous," the writer noted, "at the present time, when . . . the very existence of the nation" is at stake.[72]

"The advocates of treason," Republican congressman Jehu Baker of Illinois said, "talk of liberty of speech and the press, without once thinking of the distinction between the liberty of a man and the license of a beast." Suppose, the congressman asked, a man should gather young people together and tell them "that the principles of the Decalogue are all bosh; . . . that a graven image is as good a God as any. . . . Incomparably worse are the fruits of . . . the teaching of treason against a just and excellent government." Baker invoked the metaphor of fire to emphasize the danger.[73]

In addition to invoking the liberty-license argument and noting the inconsistency of their opponents, supporters of the administration pointed to many examples of extreme antiadministration rhetoric that had not resulted in arrest. Certainly, this fact shows that the Lincoln administration was not consistent or relentless in its effort to stamp out antiwar or antiadministration speech. The administration was primarily concerned with the negative effects of antiwar speech on the war effort. Initially at least, Lincoln remained relatively passive and left the matter to the discretion of subordinates, whom he instinctively tended to support. The commander in the field (Burnside in this case), Lincoln suggested in his reply to New York critics, is the best judge of the need to suppress speech.[74]

But public outrage over the Vallandigham and *Chicago Times* cases made Lincoln more cautious. His acute political sensitivity led him quietly to restrain subordinates.[75] "The moral of the event would be lost," the *Detroit Free Press* noted after the revocation of the order suppressing the *Chicago Times*, "if we did not emphasize the force of public opinion—the fear of the consequences which prompted it. Everyone knows that Burnside's crazy acts . . . had heated the popular mind to an ominous extent." The *Detroit Free Press* hoped for a repudiation of the policy that led to Vallandigham's arrest and the forced closure of the *Chicago Times*. "What public opinion demands from [President Lincoln] is an express disclaimer of the power to do such things in the future."[76]

In private, Lincoln reined in his generals. "I regret to hear of the arrest of the Democrat editor," Lincoln wrote General John Schofield in July of 1863, shortly after the Vallandigham and *Chicago Times* affairs. "I fear this loses you the middle position I desired you to occupy. . . . Please spare me the trouble this is likely to bring."[77] Again, in October of the same year, Lincoln wrote General Schofield who, in an effort to root out rebels, had required all inhabitants of a county to leave their homes. Lincoln specifically addressed the suppression of speech and press, and urged restraint: "Under your recent order, which I have approved, you will only arrest individuals, and suppress assemblies, or newspapers, when they may be working palpable injury to the Military in your

FREE SPEECH

charge; and in no other case will you interfere with the expression of opinion in any form, or allow it to be interfered with violently by others. In this, you have a discretion to exercise with great caution, calmness, and forbearance."[78] On the day General Burnside issued his order suppressing the *Chicago Times*, Stanton, the secretary of war, wrote General Burnside to advise him that President Lincoln disapproved General Hascall's action interfering with newspapers in Indiana. Stanton added,

> Since writing the above letter the President has been informed that you have suppressed the publication or circulation of the Chicago *Times* in your department. He directs me to say that in his judgment it would be better for you to take an early occasion to revoke that order. The irritation produced by such acts is in his opinion likely to do more harm than the publication would do.... But while military movements are left to your judgment, upon administrative questions such as the arrest of civilians and the suppression of newspapers not requiring immediate action the President desires to be previously consulted.[79]

So Lincoln finally decided that suppression of political speech outside the war zone was too important a matter to be left to generals.

The claim that when the survival of the nation was at stake all other considerations became secondary was a powerful defense of suppression and argument for a broad reading of the Constitution's war power. Supporters of suppression noted that the Constitution provided for the war power, for the power of the president as commander in chief, and suspension of habeas corpus in time of rebellion or invasion. As a result, apologists for the administration argued, the war power, the law of war, and the law of necessity trumped everything, including free speech. Administration lawyers in the Vallandigham habeas corpus case and Northern intellectuals who supported the administration invoked these arguments. Constitutional justifications of the president's power were often sweeping. As a writer for the *Chicago Tribune* explained, "The *war power* is *limited only* by the *laws and usages* of nations. This power is tremendous: *it is strictly constitutional; but it breaks down every barrier so anxiously erected for the protection of liberty, of prosperity and of life.*" The same writer noted that "one of the great evils of the war, is that it requires for its prosecution such a concentration of power in the hands of the executive, that there is a very great danger of abuse in its exercise." But a perfect choice was not available. "[W]e must never forget that in this un-

[336]

happy condition of things our choice is reduced to a choice of evils. Shall we submit to a temporary despotism now, in order that we may be saved from one ten-fold more fearful in the future?"[80]

William Whiting, solicitor for the War Department, explained that while the war power was constitutional, it was not limited. "Nothing in the Constitution or laws can define the possible extent of any military danger. Nothing therefore in either of them can fix or define the extent of power necessary to meet the emergency."[81] As a result Whiting broadly justified military power to arrest civilians far from the scene of battle: "Military crimes, or crimes of war, include all acts of hostility to the country, to the government, or to any department or officer thereof . . . *provided* that such acts of hostility have the effect of opposing, embarrassing, defeating, or even of interfering with, our military or naval operations in carrying on the war, or of aiding, encouraging, or supporting the enemy. . . . [M]ilitary arrests may be made for the punishment or prevention of military crimes."[82] "Soldiers and sailors give up much of their personal liberty," Whiting noted. Similarly, in civil war every citizen "must needs be curtailed of some of his accustomed privileges," including civil, municipal, and constitutional rights.[83]

Some were blunt. "The President of the United States has, in effect, been created Dictator," with power over liberty comparable to that of the Russian czar, wrote George William Curtis, in *Harper's Weekly*. "But," he concluded, "it is well" for it was necessary for success.[84] Ralph Waldo Emerson concluded that "absolute powers of a Dictator" were necessary during the war.[85]

President Lincoln crafted two politically potent defenses of his policy. The first came in response to a letter from a New York group critical of the Vallandigham arrest; the second responded to the Ohio Democrats' demand for Vallandigham's release. Because Lincoln's response needs to be read in the context of criticism, I will first review the critique of Lincoln's actions by the New Yorkers and others.

THE CRITICS REVISITED: THE ARGUMENTS LINCOLN WILL ANSWER

The New Yorkers had objected to Vallandigham's military arrest and trial because it took place in an area where the civilian courts were functioning; because it deprived Vallandigham of constitutional guarantees like jury trial and grand jury indictment; and because the arrest was based on a political speech.[86] A major subject of dispute was the war power of the president. If the president, as commander in chief, can dispense with civil courts and constitutional guarantees for civilians in areas that are not part of the theater of war, then freedom of speech can be suspended in war time. Indeed, the government in the Vallandigham habeas corpus case advocated a similar position.

Many rejected unlimited presidential power. They insisted that military law must be limited to the theater of war and to members of the armed services. Senator Trumbull, for example, took this position in his Chicago speech about the suppression of the *Chicago Times*:

> In certain districts the military law is supreme. Gen. Grant is in command of an army in the State of Mississippi, which is in revolt. Will any one deny his right to make arrests, his right to suppress newspapers.... No.... The great difficulty is in these districts, where rightful civil Government is in operation, where the judicial tribunals are open and the law respected—the laws which afford a remedy for every wrong. As a rule, we must remember that the civil law is superior to the military law, and the cases are rare, very rare, where the rule can be reversed. It here resolves itself into the plain naked question of whether the President and his Generals, by the simple clicking of the telegraph can cause the imprisonment of A, B, or C. If one General can do it, another can do it, and where is the end? ... [Great sensation and murmurs] Do you propose to interfere with the ballot-box? [Cries of "No! No!" "Never! Never!"] I am glad to hear you say that, and glad you are so unanimous. Did it every occur to you that the next election may put an entirely different face upon affairs?[87]

The *Evening Post* made a similar analysis, rejecting General Burnside's claim that the duty of civilians could be based on the rule for the military. "But he forgets," the *Evening Post* insisted, "that persons 'in the military and naval service of the United States' are subject to military law, while the ordinary citizen is subject exclusively to civil law." Vallandigham was not a soldier or in a place where combat raged. Martial law had not "been proclaimed to exist in the department of the Ohio," the *Evening Post* continued. But even had it been proclaimed, "we doubt whether any authority under it can be exercised against persons who are not immediately within the scope of active military operations."[88]

A reasonable reading of the act of Congress authorizing the suspension of the writ of habeas corpus is that Congress used the theater-of-war distinction. The act denied the immediate benefit of the privilege of habeas corpus to political prisoners arrested by authority of the president. But Congress required either indictment before the end of the term of the grand jury or release for those who were seized in those areas where the civil courts were functioning.

The *National Intelligencer* published a long, detailed, and scholarly article on the subject. It insisted that the March 1863 habeas act meant that Vallandigham's military trial was improper. Instead, he should have been handed over to civil authorities for trial or release. The newspaper bolstered this conclusion by asserting that charges against Vallandigham had been made an offense by Congress with jurisdiction in the federal courts.[89]

Professor James Randall in his 1951 study *Constitutional Problems Under Lincoln* also takes the view that the 1863 act should have applied to cases like that of Vallandigham. "Had this law been complied with," he says, "the effect would have been to restore the supremacy of the civil power." According to Professor Randall, "the way was laid by congressional action for the speedy release of all citizens against whom no violation of Federal law could be charged."[90] He reports, however, that the act was rarely complied with and that Judge Advocate General Holt construed the act not to apply to citizens (like Vallandigham) arrested or tried by the military.[91]

President Lincoln's Response to His Critics

President Lincoln made telling use of the necessity argument in reply to his critics. (One irony, of course, is that the arrest of Vallandigham, based on supposed military necessity, produced extensive and vehement criticism of the administration, and open discussion of the possibility that armed resistance might become necessary. These critics were generally not arrested.)

Lincoln rejected the claim that Vallandigham, as a person who was not in the military and not in a theater of war, was entitled to the criminal procedure guarantees of the Bill of Rights. Lincoln noted that the Civil War was a case of rebellion and that in such a case the Constitution authorized the suspension of the writ of habeas corpus when public safety required it. Arrests by ordinary civil process and those required in cases of rebellion were different. In the case of rebellion, "arrests are made, not so much for what has been done, as for what probably would be done. The latter is more for the preventative and less for the vindictive than the former."[92] So, in rebellions, basic Bill of Rights guarantees did not apply because it was necessary to restrain people who were guilty of no civil crime. "The man who stands by and says nothing when the peril of his Government is discussed, cannot be misunderstood," Lincoln announced. "If not hindered, he is sure to help the enemy; much more, if he talks ambiguously—talks for his country with 'buts' and 'ifs' and 'ands.'"[93]

The New Yorkers had insisted that no military arrests should be made "outside of the lines of necessary military occupation, and the scenes of insurrection." Lincoln rejected the distinction: "Inasmuch, however, as the Constitution itself makes no such distinction, I am unable to believe that there *is* any such constitutional distinction."[94]

Lincoln denied that Vallandigham was arrested for criticism of administration policy and of the edict of General Burnside.

> It is asserted, in substance, that Mr. Vallandigham was, by a military commander, seized and tried "for no other reason than words addressed to a public meeting, in criticism of the course of the Administration, and in condemnation of the Military orders of the General." Now, if there be no mistake about this; if this assertion is the truth and the whole truth; if there was no other reason for the arrest, then I concede that the arrest was wrong. But the arrest, as I understand, was made for a very different reason. Mr. Vallandigham avows his hostility to the War on the part of the Union; and his arrest was made because he was laboring, with some effect, to prevent the raising of troops; to encourage desertions from the army; and to leave the Rebellion without an adequate military force to suppress it.[95]

In his later reply to the Ohio Democrats who demanded Vallandigham's return, Lincoln admitted, "I certainly do not know that Mr. V. has specifically, and by direct language, advised against enlistments, and in favor of desertion, and resistance to drafting."[96] But that was the effect of his words: "[T]his hindrance of the military, including maiming and murder, is due to the course in which Mr. V. has been engaged" more than to any other cause, Lincoln said, and to Vallandigham personally more than to any other man.[97]

In his response to the New Yorkers, Lincoln asserted that the rebellion could only be suppressed by military force. Military force required armies. "Long experience has shown," Lincoln noted, "that armies cannot be maintained unless desertions shall be punished by the severe penalty of death. . . . Must I shoot a simple-minded soldier boy who deserts, while I must not touch a hair of a wily agitator who induces him to desert?"[98]

It was a powerful point. But, judging by Vallandigham's case, it included antiwar political speech that even *tended* to cause desertion or draft resistance—as will inevitably be the case for some who hear vigorous antiwar speech. After all, Vallandigham had repeatedly counseled obedience to the law and use of the ballot box to effect change. Acceptance of Lincoln's bad-tendency principle, in short, seems to outlaw all antiwar political speech and to put the democratic process in abeyance for the duration.

Finally, Lincoln denied that his acts would prove to be a precedent for repression in time of peace: "I can no more be persuaded that the Government can constitutionally take no strong measures in time of rebellion, because it can be shown that the same could not be lawfully taken in time of peace, than I can be persuaded that a particular drug is not good medicine for a sick man, because it can be shown not to be good food for a well one."[99]

The Rejoinder to the Lincoln Defense

The Democratic press promptly challenged Lincoln's defense of the Vallandigham banishment. The *Detroit Free Press* debunked Lincoln's claim that Vallandigham was tried and punished for encouraging desertions. "To say that [President Lincoln] is disingenuous," the paper commented tartly, "would be to use a very mild expression for a very strong fact." In fact, the paper said, Vallandigham was tried and convicted for violating Order 38 by declaring disloyal sentiments with the object of weakening the government in its effort to suppress the rebellion. "Not one word," the *Free Press* insisted, "can be found in it accusing him of encouraging desertions. That would be an offence against the laws for which Congress have provided adequate punishment through the medium of the civil courts, and for which, if he was guilty of it, he was only amenable in the loyal and peaceable State of Ohio to those courts." Why, if the offense was encouraging desertions, the *Free Press* demanded, was he not charged with it?[100]

As to the president's claim that the rebellion elsewhere allowed military trials in Ohio, the *Free Press*'s response was equally acid. "In a word, Mr. Lincoln claims that he possesses absolute power where there is no rebellion, simply because it may be necessary to exercise it where there is— that whenever his opinion of public welfare justifies it, he may strike down the laws passed by Congress in any given case, and substitute some general order 38 in their stead."[101]

A New York committee organized to protest the Vallandigham arrest published a response to the president that was also printed in much of the press and circulated as a pamphlet. The New Yorkers denied that the power to suspend habeas corpus in time of invasion or rebellion meant that all constitutional guarantees of liberty could be rightfully suspended.

> Inasmuch as this process may be suspended in time of war, you seem to think that every remedy for a false and unlawful imprisonment is abrogated; and from this postulate you reach, at a simple bound, the conclusion that there is no liberty under the constitution which does not depend on the gracious indulgence of the Executive only. This great heresy once established, and by this mode of deduction there springs at once into existence a brood of crimes or offenses undefined by any rule, and hitherto unknown to the laws of the country; and this is followed by indiscriminate arrests, midnight seizures, military commissions, unheard of modes of trial and punishment, and all the machinery of terror and despotism.[102]

The New York committee indignantly rejected the idea that such arrests were justified because they reached conduct or threats of injury not forbidden by the criminal law. They quoted Lincoln's assertion that the "arrests are made not so much for what has been done, as for what probably would be done" and his assertion of the dangerousness of the man who "says nothing when the peril of his government is discussed." They highlighted Lincoln's acknowledgment that the arrests were not for the constitutional crime of treason or "for any capital or otherwise infamous crimes," and his denial that the proceedings were "in any constitutional or legal sense criminal prosecutions."[103]

The committee insisted these statements by the president proved just how dangerous the claimed power was:

The very ground, then, of your justification is, that the victims of arbitrary arrest were obedient to every law, were guiltless of any known or defined offense, and therefore were without the protection of the constitution. The suspension of the writ of *habeas corpus* instead of being intended to prevent the enlargement of arrested criminals, until a legal trial and conviction can be had, is designed, according to your doctrine, to subject innocent men to your supreme will and pleasure. Silence itself is punishable, according to this extraordinary theory, and still more so the expression of opinions, however loyal, if attended with criticism upon the policy of the government. We must respectfully refuse our assent to this theory of constitutional law. We think that men may be rightfully silent if they choose.[104]

Finally, the committee explicitly rejected the idea that the power to suspend the writ of habeas corpus also suspended the effect of constitutional guarantees of liberty. Arrests without warrant that violated constitutional guarantees could not "become in any sense rightful, by reason of a suspension of the writ of *habeas corpus*." The "suspension of a single and peculiar remedy for such wrongs" did not bring "into existence new and unknown classes of offenses, or new causes for depriving men of their liberty."[105]

Efforts to Expel an Antiwar Congressman

Later, in 1864, Republicans in Congress moved to expel antiwar congressman Alexander Long from Ohio, who made a speech suggesting that the war could not be won without unreasonable suffering and that the North should recognize the Confederacy. Speaker Colfax explained that "I believe in the freedom of speech," but Long had "declared . . . in favor of the recognition of this so-called confederacy."[106] For Representative Godlove Orth of Indiana, the matter was simple enough. "A man is free to speak so long as he speaks *for* the nation," but he should not be permitted to speak "*against* the nation . . . on this floor."[107] Failure to expel would lead to "demoralization in our Army . . . and riots all over the land."[108]

The Long case, said Representative Rufus Spaulding of Ohio, was like that of Vallandigham. Vallandigham was "'waiting and watching over the border' because he indulged in too much license of speech. And so it must be . . . in Congress and out of Congress." No citizen "can be permitted to utter sentiments, in time of war" that would "distract and dishearten" soldiers.[109] (Earlier, on February 29, 1864, the House of Representatives had rejected, by a party line vote, a resolution denouncing Vallandigham's arrest and banishment.)[110]

Democrats often repudiated Vallandigham's views as well as those of Long. But Democrat Andrew Jackson Rogers of New Jersey nonetheless insisted that the Vallandigham arrest and banishment had "struck a deadly blow at the rights of the free people of America."[111]

Critics of the motion to expel Long insisted the issue was free speech, democracy, and representative government. For Representative Charles Eldridge of Wisconsin, the question "involves the sacred right to free speech in general, and the right of free parliamentary debate."[112] Representative Kernan, a Democrat from New York, saw the issue as "our free system of government, and that free discussion among the people, and free debate in our legislative bodies, without which our institutions and liberties cannot long be maintained." The issue of war or peace was one for Congress and the people. Long's "erroneous views should be controverted by arguments," Kernan said, not silenced by expulsion. Under the proposed course, Kernan warned, in times of excitement, the representative who advocated unpopular views "will be expelled and thus silenced. You will have no debate except that which runs in the one groove."[113]

Kernan and others relied on the Constitution's protection for free speech. Kernan said the Constitution provided "'Congress shall make no law abridging the freedom of speech or of the press.' If [Long's opinions] can be expressed . . . anywhere in the country, they certainly may be here. . . . This is the body to decide upon questions of peace or war."[114] Democrat Andrew Jackson Rogers insisted that Long could not "be expelled for the exercise of any right guarantied by the Constitution."[115] Rogers said the speech would not be unlawful, in the constitutional sense, outside of Congress, because of the guarantees of the First Amendment.[116]

"Are we to be told," demanded Representative William Finck of Ohio, "that the grave questions of peace and war cannot be discussed here? What questions . . . are of greater importance to the people than questions of peace and war?" Finck, and others, suggested partisan motivation was at work. Republicans were ordering hundreds of copies of Long's offending speech, obviously planning to circulate it. "If that speech gives aid and comfort to the enemy," Finck asked, "why do gentlemen on the other side of the House give so much aid and comfort to the speech?" Finck cited Daniel Webster's 1834 speech on the "high constitutional privilege" of free speech.[117] Representative Eldridge also cited Webster on the "ancient and undoubted prerogative of this people to canvass public measures" (a "fireside privilege"), and he cited Thomas Jefferson on the danger of political intolerance and on "the safety with which error of opinion may be tolerated where reason is left free to combat it."[118]

The power to expel, Representative Pendleton insisted, was limited to disorderly conduct. The House, he insisted, lacked the "constitutional power . . . to expel a member for the expression of any opinion upon any political question" that was pertinent to its business.[119] Opinions were for constituents who "were to decide whether they were wise and sound." To expel their representative was to "disfranchise them" and to "enact again the farce of the British House of Commons in the case of Wilkes." Pendleton noted that the speech-and-debate clause protected a member from libel actions or offenses against private rights based on a speech on the floor of the House. By much stronger reason, he concluded, "he is not to be called in question here by the House itself for the free expression of opinion in fair debate."[120]

In the 1830s and 1840s, John Quincy Adams had waged a long struggle to vindicate the right to present antislavery petitions. Pendleton recalled the attempt to censure Adams for presenting a petition from citizens in favor of dissolution of the Union: "[Adams] rose in his place all trembling with excitement, and in one of those historic speeches which will live as long as the history of the English language shall remain, vindicated the right of the people to petition for a redress of their grievances, and the right of Representatives to present their petitions. . . . And he argued the question against all comers . . . until, ashamed of the efforts they had made to repress this freedom of debate in the American Congress, the majority . . . at last laid the resolution on the table."[121]

Ultimately the motion to expel Representative Long was amended to one of censure. As amended, the motion to censure did not explicitly refer to Long's speech in the House. It cited "his open declarations in the national Capitol and publications in the city of New York [apparently of the speech in Congress] . . . in favor of a recognition of the so-called confederacy." It declared him unworthy of membership in the House.[122] In the end the motion to censure carried by a vote of eighty to sixty-nine with Republicans generally voting yes and Democrats and a number of Union representatives voting no.[123]

One factor that led Republicans to amend the expulsion resolution to one of censure may have been the strongly negative reaction from the press, including many Republican papers. (Republicans explained the change to censure as motivated by the impossibility of getting a two-thirds vote.)[124] "We are . . . glad," the *National Intelligencer* wrote, "that the leading organs of the Republican party . . . , while condemning the opinions and views of Mr. Long, propose to answer them by the force of argument and rational appeal . . . , and not by the violent proceeding of parliamentary expulsion—thereby sacrificing in the person of Mr. Long the right of free discussion which pertains to him as a Representative of the People."[125] Press criticism, like that in Congress, invoked freedom of speech as well as freedom of debate in Congress.

The New York *Evening Post* insisted that "Mr. Long's speech was a perfectly legitimate expression of opinion. He thinks that the rebels must be allowed to go in peace or be extirpated; and he stated his thought calmly and respectfully, in proper words." The *Post* strongly disagreed with him, but it was "not, however, unwilling that those who have come to other conclusions should have the full liberty to express them, whether in the newspapers or on the floors of Congress." Congressmen who simply "controvert argument by argument," and who "present only, logic, eloquence, appeal, in favor of their views," were simply "exercising the rights which belong to all freemen." The *Evening Post* insisted, rather optimistically, that truth would conquer falsehood.[126] "Our laws assume the intelligence and good sense of the people, and allow every man to be heard. They are not afraid of discussion. They demand, indeed, the fullest and freest ventilation of every subject, that the good and evil of it may be known." Those who chose the side of foul wrong could be safely left to the "contempt" of contemporaries, and to "the execration of posterity."[127]

The Constitution provides that members of Congress may not be questioned "in any other place" for speeches and debates on the floor of Congress. It allows expulsion, but does not specifically discuss expulsion of a member of Congress by the House or Senate for political opinion expressed in a *congressional* debate.[128] Critics in the press looked at the spirit of the speech-and-debate guarantee. An editorial in the *New York Times,* a strongly proadministration paper, made explicit what was at least implicit in many press comments:

> The Constitution takes care to secure the utmost freedom of debate in Congress by making special provision that "for any speech or debate in either House, members shall not be questioned in any other place." What could have been the object of this unlimited immunity but the recognized necessity that every Representative should be in a position to do completest justice to his own sentiments and those of his constituents? That is a principle which lies at the foundation of every representative Government. But why is it not as much a violation of this principle for men in the Capitol to deter a Representative from speaking his sentiments as for men outside the Capitol? It is the intimidation that is the evil, and it don't matter a particle whence the intimidation proceeds. For any power in Congress or out of Congress to exercise it is to violate one of the most sacred principles of the Constitution.[129]

"It is the duty," the *Times* insisted, "of every honest legislator, when great public concerns are at stake, to declare his honest convictions." The duty was greater "if these convictions are opposed to the dominant sentiment. It is the weakest side that has the strongest need of argument; for it is their only power." The claim that Representative Long's speech was treasonous was "preposterous," the *Times* continued. "It is not treasonable to advocate, or question, or gainsay any construction of the Constitution. It is not treasonable to look at the gigantic proportions of the rebellion and draw the conclusion that it cannot be put down."[130] In another editorial, the *Times* told "these men in Washington that passion is making them mad." How, the *Times* asked, "is it possible for true men so to misunderstand the American people as to suppose they will submit quietly to this destruction of free debate in the council halls of the nation?"[131] Other papers reached similar conclusions.[132]

The rejection of the attempt to expel Long by leading Republican papers like the *New York Times* seems implicitly to reject the Vallandigham arrest as well. The sentiments were similar; only the *location* was different. If the war power or necessity supersedes all other constitutional guarantees, or if arguing for peace is intolerable, then it is hard to see why Representative Long should have been spared by his colleagues. (Indeed such rationales explained why he was censured.) If neither of these things is so, it is hard to see why Vallandigham should be exiled.

Of course, the speech-and-debate clause explicitly protects speech in Congress, but it does not explictly protect it from actions by Congress itself. The First Amendment protects speech outside of Congress—and, critics argued, also within Congress. Free speech in Congress is essential for representative government. So is free speech in the nation at large.

Evaluating the Suppression

Recent precedent tends to support the right to oppose a war (provided the speaker does not advocate violation of the law that is likely to come about very quickly) and to reject the bad tendency test, and the idea that failing to express patriotic sentiments might be criminal.[133] The situation confronting Lincoln was a rebellion and Lincoln had a substantial constitutional argument for suspending the writ of habeas corpus. But even if holding Vallandigham without trial were justified, to convict him by a military tribunal for a political speech that urged his hearers to obey the law and seek a remedy at the ballot box, was an extreme departure from free speech norms. Shortly after the Civil War, the Court suggested that such trials by military commissions were unlawful, but this precedent did not protect Japanese Americans from relocation orders during World War II.[134]

The Vallandigham and *Chicago Times* cases pitted free speech against the power of the president as commander in chief. The most powerful argument for free speech during wartime came from the nature of the American government—from democracy. This free speech argument insisted that democracy entailed the right of the people who would be affected by government policy to attempt to persuade other citizens to change it. Because the right was a continuing one, government policy had to be open to criticism and revision. The agency metaphor captured at least part of this idea. The people were the principal, government officials were the agents, and free speech, free press, and free assembly were the only way the principal could consult in order to communicate their wishes to, or to discuss replacing, governmental agents. Free speech could not legitimately be foreclosed by government policy because that foreclosure would rob the people of their collective right to determine their fate and their individual right to try to persuade others to change course. By this understanding, individuals would retain a personal right to speak even if the majority had decided it had heard enough and wanted to shut them up. Though popular sovereignty is a metaphor (and therefore highlights one aspect of the truth while hiding others), the aspect it highlights is powerful and important.

In setting out these principles, critics of suppression of speech were essentially correct. In representative government people have a right to seek to control their fate both by deciding who should represent them and by keeping their representatives informed of their needs and desires. People liable to be conscripted, shot, maimed, or killed (and to have these things happen to friends and loved ones) should have a continuing right to consider the wisdom of the war in which such sacrifices are demanded. The alternative is to turn the lives of the many over to the unchecked and unscrutinized power of a few. Free speech is essential to preserving the structure of representative government under the Constitution and also reflects a basic right of individuals to talk about crucial issues that shape their lives.

At first blush, the idea that democracy precludes majority suppression of minority arguments may seem paradoxical. But a people deprived of a continuing right to evaluate alternatives is a people deprived of their right to chart their own course. As Friedrich von Hayek has noted, one should not confuse what the law is and what the law ought to be: "If democracy is to function, it is as important that [what the law is] can always be ascertained as that [what the law ought to be] can always be questioned. Majority decisions tell us what people want at the moment, but not what it would be in their interest to want if they were better informed; and, unless [majority decisions] could be changed by persuasion, they would be of no value. The argument for democracy presupposes that any minority opinion may become a majority one."[135]

Daniel Voorhees, a Democratic member of the House of Representatives from Indiana during the Civil War, insisted that the question involved in cases like that of Vallandigham was an old one: "It involves the old struggle for power between the governors and the governed—the rulers and those who are ruled. In a Government of kings, the theory is that all power comes from him and is derived from him. But the theory of this Government is quite different from that. It is that all power is derived from the people, and that the people are the only source of power."[136]

The problem, of course, was the Unionists' fear that it was difficult and dangerous to adhere to free speech–popular sovereignty norms in time of war. This was especially so in a civil war, a "rebellion" in which the Constitution permitted suspension of the privilege of the writ of habeas corpus. The proponents of free speech attempted to address this dilemma by distinguishing, first, between soldiers and civilians and, second, between areas where military operations were ongoing and areas in which civil courts and other civil institutions continued to function. For the free speech advocates, free speech was a fundamental right to be preserved if at all possible.

Lincoln's critics insisted that the power to suspend the privilege of the writ of habeas corpus—to suspend one remedy for unlawful arrest—should not be taken as supporting the right broadly to suspend free speech. A second argument was that suspension could be justified only when the civil courts are not in operation, as in the theater of war. Conversely, suspension was not justified outside the area of immediate conflict where the courts can function. This reading construes the limit or justification for suspension ("shall not be suspended, unless when in Cases of Rebellion . . . the public safety may require it") narrowly and limits the cases where necessity is present. The response, of course, is that the language of the clause refers to cases of rebellion when the public safety requires suspension—and does not explicitly refer to the theater of war or whether the courts can function. Lincoln insisted the military could act preventively in the interest of public safety.

There is a clear tension between Lincoln's reading of the habeas clause, and the structural idea of representative government and the guarantees of free speech, press, petition, and assembly. The amendments in the Bill of Rights came after the Constitution's habeas corpus clause and the fifth amendment provision for grand jury indictment expressly excepted cases "arising in the land or naval forces . . . when in actual service, in time of War, or public danger." No express exception was made for military trial of civilians in wartime or time of public danger. Nor was an exception made to free speech guarantees for wartime. Because of the central place of free speech in individual freedom and democratic decision making, those who sought to limit the government's power to suppress free speech during civil war were correct.

Lincoln himself recognized the tension between the war power and democracy, and this recognition plus strong public opposition to suppression of speech helped keep suppression from becoming more pervasive.

Lincoln was convinced that in cases of rebellion strong but temporary measures were permitted to save democracy. He could no more believe that military arrests in time of rebellion would lead to the loss of "Public Discussion, the Liberty of Speech and the Press" in the peaceful future than he could "believe that a man could contract so strong an appetite for emetics during temporary illness as to persist in feeding upon them during the remainder of his healthful life."[137] The limits of Lincoln's compelling metaphor appeared in the arrests of the critics of World War I.[138] Those arrests were based on statutes and the convictions were carried out by the civil courts. The World War I–era Supreme Court used a wartime-is-different analysis and misapplied metaphors about shouting fire in a crowded theater to justify suppression of speech. There was no rebellion or invasion. The danger was far less than in the Civil War. Nonetheless, the nation returned to the strong medicine of suppression of political criticism in a much less acute illness.

In any case, Lincoln was unwilling to carry his rebellion–war power logic to its ultimate conclusion—which would have justified suspension of elections. In October 1864, Lincoln responded to those who had suggested that, even if the Democrats should win, he would not accept electoral defeat. "I am struggling," Lincoln said, "to maintain the government, not to overthrow it." Therefore he would serve until the end of his term and no longer unless he was reelected. The will of the people was the ultimate law, Lincoln said: "If they should deliberately resolve to have immediate peace even at the loss of their country, and their liberty, I know not the power or the right to resist them."[139]

On November 10, 1864, Lincoln elaborated his conclusion. An election in the midst of a great civil war was dangerous, because it divided a nation that needed all its strength to put down the rebellion. But, in spite of the danger, "the election was a necessity." He added, "We can not have free government without elections; and if the rebellion could force us to forego, or postpone a national election, it might fairly claim to have already conquered and ruined us."[140] It is equally true that we cannot have free elections without free speech.

When Vallandigham was nominated for governor, the tension between his arrest and democracy became acute. The mayor of Cincinnati gave a speech to the police, insisting on equality of treatment for members of both political parties. The police must not, he warned, "permit personal feeling or prejudice to move you to arrest the members of one political party rather than those of another." He elaborated, "[I]n other words, you must not arrest a man for huzzaing for Vallandigham any more than you would if he did so for Brough [the Union candidate]. It is no offense for a citizen to give utterance to his preference for any candidate."[141] But why, if Vallandigham's speech was subject to sanction, were voters free to cheer for him and his ideas, or vote for him? If, as Lincoln suggested, silence in the face of disloyal sentiments justified military arrest, why was cheering permitted?

Lincoln failed to come to grips with the extent to which arrests like those of Vallandigham threatened the value of popular rule that he cherished. Basically, he accepted the idea that the bad tendency of speeches like Vallandigham's and the importance of other constitutional values justified suppression. That, read in the context of the Vallandigham case, was the meaning of his powerful question: "Must I shoot a simple soldier boy who deserts but not touch one hair on the head of the wily agitator who induces him to desert?"

Acceptance and full implementation of Lincoln's principle outlaws antiwar political speech and puts the democratic process in abeyance for the duration of the war. That is so because a strong criticism of war *will*, as advocates of suppression insist, increase the number of those who are unwilling to risk their lives for the cause. But silencing the antiwar politician, rather than disciplining the deserter, ends democracy in wartime. That, plus the strong negative reaction it produced, may be why such suppression never became more pervasive.

The Power of the Free Speech Tradition

The high public regard for freedom of speech and concern for the relation of free speech to popular government kept the repression from becoming more extensive. The *Detroit Free Press* was probably right in attributing Lincoln's decision to revoke the suppression of the *Chicago Times*, at least in part, to the "force of public opinion—the fear of consequences."[142] The strong negative reaction to the Vallandigham case probably led Lincoln to rein in General Burnside in the case of the *Chicago Times*. Americans' support for and use of free speech checked and limited the administration's encroachment on free speech and free press.

Important elements in the free speech tradition were concepts of a broad and general right to free speech that entailed equality of right and protection for speech that was thought to be evil, wrong, and dangerous. As a result, many Republicans and opponents of slavery stood up to protect the rights of Vallandigham and the *Chicago Times*, believing that assaults on the tradition ultimately threatened the liberty of all.

The Washington correspondent of the *National Anti-Slavery Standard* warned that administration policy imperiled the idea of free speech: "Let the Democrats ... obtain power and make a compromise with the rebels upon the basis of a pro-slavery government, it would instantly be claimed that the good of the country required that all agitation of the question of slavery must cease.... It is the good of the country which now justifies the suppression of Copperhead journals. Necessity is the plea."[143] Wirt Dexter, the Republican lawyer who spoke against the suppression of the *Chicago Times*, made the point directly: "[W]ithout any remarkable foresight, I can see that this thing may return to plague the inventors of it. ... I don't wish to see this kind of treatment turned upon the party of which I am a member."[144] Republican Senator Lyman Trumbull asked, in a speech defending his opposition to the suppression of the *Chicago Times*, "Did it ever occur to you that the next election may put an entirely different face upon affairs?" In reference to the same case, Congressman Arnold explained that he did not want to "aid in the establishment of [a] precedent which will limit my freedom of speech, nor prevent my declaring what I believe, that the cursed spirit of Human Slavery is the cause of all our troubles, and that we shall never have permanent peace and union until it has been destroyed."[145] By this view, free speech, like an election, is a framework for political choice, not a result. Suppression of political freedom of speech threatened the framework in a very basic way.

There is, of course, another way to read the evidence. One could see arguments about free speech as strategic political rhetoric employed by partisans when handy—as a weapon for political advantage, not a principle to be adhered to. Stanley Fish, in a book entitled *There's No Such Thing as Free Speech—And It's a Good Thing Too*, suggests that general free speech principles do not exist. Instead, free speech is "the name we give to verbal behavior that serves the substantive agendas we wish to advance."[146] "Contest the relevance of free speech principles fashioned by your enemy," Professor Fish advises, "but if you manage to refashion [free speech ideas] in line with your purposes, urge them with a vengeance."[147]

A cynic could read the battle over antislavery and then antiwar speech in this way. The Vallandigham case reveals some remarkable inconsistencies. The Republican Party came to power as the party of free speech. It protested state and national attempts to suppress antislavery speech. Southerners and some Democrats invoked the bad tendency test, constitutional protections provided for slavery and the danger of slave revolts and civil war to justify suppression of antislavery literature. In the Vallandigham case, Democrats demanded free speech for critics of the war policy of the administration, and Republicans (to justify suppression) pointed out its dangers, the power to suppress rebellion, and bad tendencies.

The *National Intelligencer* noted the inconsistency problem and took a thoughtful view: "It is easy to perceive that many who now raise their voice in vehement championship of "free speech" are seeking rather to subserve the interests of party than to promote the ends of justice and patriotism. It is from the midst of such mingled motives that truth nearly always emerges, for it is difficult to separate a good cause from the infirmities of the men into whose hands it is suffered to fall. But if the Administration will not do homage to the law it must be content to see its opponents profit by such suicidal recreancy."[148]

In both the Vallandigham episode and in earlier controversy over antislavery speech, however, a number of people invoked free speech principles despite inconsistency with their general political agendas. In the 1830s, dissident Northern Democrats and border state Whigs had refused to vote for a law banning antislavery publications from the mails. Antiabolition newspapers (as the New York *Evening Post* then was) and a number of Democrats stood up for free speech for abolitionists.[149] Many Republicans and Republican newspapers rejected the Vallandigham arrest and the suppression of the *Chicago Times*. Republican attorney Wirt Dexter, spoke against the military suppression of the *Chicago Times*: "A man who refuses to act in a crisis like this," he said, "because in so doing he may incidentally rescue his political opponent, is a demagogue and unworthy [of]the name of citizen."[150] In short, many believed free speech did entail basic principles more important than short-term partisan advantage, and their belief was an important factor in protecting freedom of speech from far more extensive suppression. These people and the tradition they adhered to were important protectors of free speech.

THE GREAT EMANCIPATOR AND FREE SPEECH

Finally, what are we to make of Abraham Lincoln, the president who oversaw the suppressions of free speech described here? Lincoln was a great American president. He saved the Union, though at a very great cost in human life and suffering. He led the nation to abolish slavery, moving it closer to the spirit of the Declaration of Independence. By abolishing slavery, the nation alleviated much suffering. Lincoln was also the first American president to entertain a black man—Frederick Douglass—in the White House. In doing so he began to depart from the deep racism that has scarred American life.[151]

Psychologists suggest a halo effect influences and distorts our evaluation of particular acts. "If a person has one salient (available) good trait, his other characteristics are likely to be judged by others as better than they really are."[152] (The same thing happens in reverse, of course—the horns and pitchfork effect. So the advocacy of free speech, peaceful change, and democratic decision making by many Democrats outraged over the Vallandigham arrest tends to be neglected because many of them were racists opposed to emancipation.)

Real-life heroes, unlike those of fiction, are human beings. Good people in difficult circumstances can make dreadful mistakes. Consider Franklin Roosevelt, another great president, who, listening to his generals after the bombing of Pearl Harbor, approved a military plan to incarcerate Americans of Japanese descent. The war power theory generated to support suppression of speech by the Lincoln administration would in time be used to support the constitutionality of the Japanese internment.

Lincoln's Emancipation Proclamation was also based on the war power, and if the proclamation was justified by the war power (as it was), one might ask, why was punishment of Vallandigham not justified? The Emancipation Proclamation was aimed only at parts of the nation in rebellion and where the federal government was not in control. It struck directly at the labor supply necessary to sustain the Confederate war effort and with the same bold stroke converted many of those who were working for the enemy into soldiers in the cause of freedom.[153]

The nation ultimately recognized its mistake in the Sedition Act cases.[154] It eventually recognized its mistake in the Japanese internment.[155] It would be wise to recognize now that Lincoln, too, was wrong in his justification of the Vallandigham arrest and to recognize that he departed seriously from the nation's better free speech tradition. Apologists for Lincoln's action left us a legacy of a limitless war power that supported suppressing free speech during World War I. Of course, suppression of political speech did not begin with suppression of antiwar speech by the Lincoln administration, and Lincoln confronted a grave crisis unique in American history. Still, one fact bears repeating: his administration justified the first criminal punishment of speech by the federal government since the Sedition Act.

Vallandigham's and his followers' support for free political speech would be more inspiring if so many Americans of African descent had not been omitted from their political calculus. It would be more inspiring if more of Vallandigham's partisans had supported free speech for abolitionists and opponents of slavery. But many Americans (Democrats, Republicans, and abolitionists) supported both free speech for opponents of slavery and for Vallandigham. These people helped to light the way for future generations.

16

A New Birth of Freedom? The Fourteenth

Amendment and the First Amendment

The Fourteenth Amendment was proposed in 1866 and ratified in 1868. It made all persons born in the United States and subject to its jurisdiction citizens of the United States; provided that "no state shall ... abridge the privileges or immunities of citizens of the United States"; and denied to the states power to deprive any person of life, liberty, or property without due process of law. The amendment also secured equal protection of the law to all persons. The meaning of these majestic phrases remains controversial. Increasingly, judges and scholars have attempted to find that meaning in history. Meaning is contextual: to fathom the meaning of words to people of a bygone era, we need to understand the historical context in which they were uttered.

The Fourteenth Amendment had many provisions and purposes. One purpose was to make guarantees of free speech national and to require states to respect the rights set out in the First Amendment. The determination to nationalize protection for free speech grew out of free speech struggles in the years before the Civil War. Of course, because of the number of people involved, the number who said nothing on the subject, and the fact that most attention at the time was focused on issues other than the meaning of Section 1 of the Fourteenth Amendment, the most we can hope to achieve is probability and a hypothesis that is stronger than its competitors.

THE HISTORICAL CONTEXT OF THE FOURTEENTH AMENDMENT

The Civil War was a second American revolution, and the Thirteenth, Fourteenth, and Fifteenth Amendments gave birth to a profoundly changed Constitution and Bill of Rights.[1] The most revolutionary aspect of the change was the attempted transformation of the African American population from slaves to citizens with equal civil rights. (Southern and many Northern states had subjected even free blacks to degrading discrimination—badges of slavery, as some Republicans put it in 1866.) In another sense the change was less revolutionary—amending the Constitution to reflect principles of the Declaration of Independence.

Compared to the racial revolution, proposed changes in the means of protecting basic liberties were far less revolutionary. Many Americans believed that the basic rights of freedom of speech, press, and religion belonged to all American citizens. These rights had been recognized and also "protected" by the Bill of Rights against abridgment by the federal government. State constitutions typically had similar guarantees. The Declaration of Independence indicated that government was organized to protect basic rights. The Fourteenth Amendment merely added a new enforcement mechanism—a "double security" to use Madison's phrase. The ship of liberty would henceforth have lifeboats as well as a double hull.[2] States retained broad power to structure their law, so long as they complied with the Constitution.

In the debates of 1864–66 on slavery and individual rights, Republicans recalled the events of 1835–60. For them, these events epitomized the danger of state sovereignty unrestrained by national guarantees of individual rights. Congressmen recalled mobs destroying antislavery presses and Southern laws banning antislavery speech, press, and religion.[3] In the debates over abolition between 1835 and 1837, as in earlier debates over sedition, supporters of free speech and free press referred to these freedoms alternately as rights or privileges. They emphasized the strength of the word "abridge" in the First Amendment.[4] By 1859, and even more strongly from 1864 to 1866, leading Republicans were asserting that these privileges were, or should be, protected by the federal Constitution and Bill of Rights against state interference.

The Immediate Historical Context of the Fourteenth Amendment

In 1866, President Andrew Johnson sought immediate readmission of the Southern states to Congress (once they ratified the Thirteenth Amendment), but Congress balked. No Southern states allowed African Americans to vote. With the ratification of the Thirteenth Amendment and its implicit repeal of the clause making slaves three-fifths of a person for purposes of representation in the federal House of Representatives, former slaves grew from three-fifths to whole persons for purposes of representation. As a result, if nothing more were done, the defeated Southern states would come to Congress with substantially increased representation. The South, which had lost the war, might win the peace.

Furthermore, as Republicans saw it, a renewed spirit of recalcitrance was evident in the South. Southern states had passed Black Codes that discriminated against blacks in rights to own property, to testify, and to enter into contracts and also denied them fundamental rights referred to in the Bill of Rights. For example, Southern communities had denied blacks the right to bear arms, to assemble, to address meetings, and to preach without prior permission. Congressmen complained that constitutional rights of Unionists and blacks were once again being violated. Southerners once again suppressed free speech and other constitutional rights.[5]

In this situation, in 1866, Representative John Bingham insisted that a constitutional amendment, the fourteenth, was needed to give Congress the power to enforce "all the guaranties of the Constitution."[6] Others claimed that Congress already had such power: some Republicans in Congress said they could find legislative power in the federal Bill of Rights to pass a civil rights bill.[7] That bill was passed in spite of objections that Congress lacked power to enact it. As enacted, it guaranteed blacks the same rights to own property, to contract, and to testify that whites enjoyed, and it secured to all citizens the full and equal benefit of all laws and provisions for the security of person and property as enjoyed by white citizens. Bingham, wisely, insisted on a constitutional amendment as well.

In 1866, many in Congress seemed poised to readmit the Southern states upon their ratification of the Fourteenth Amendment.[8] Resistence to black suffrage in many states of the North produced a paradox. In 1866, most Republicans were committed to equal political rights for the newly freed slaves as a matter of principle. The party needed the votes of the newly freed slaves to be competitive in the South. Yet Northern resistance to the idea of black voters was so strong that the party was not yet ready to insist on black suffrage in the South. It adopted suffrage for blacks in the South only after all the Southern states, except Tennessee, rejected the Fourteenth Amendment. Southern intransigence strengthened the position of advocates of black suffrage. Even then, African American males were at first given the vote only in the Southern states. In 1866, before these developments, Republicans knew that without the black vote, their chances of controlling governments in the Southern states were slim. That meant, in effect, that the only security for the rights of Republicans and their allies in the South might be the guarantees of the Thirteenth and the proposed Fourteenth Amendments.

Nothing heightens respect for the guarantees in the Bill of Rights so much as the recognition that one may be the subject of prosecution. In 1860 Republicans who sponsored an abridged version of Helper's book were being treated as criminals in the South. They were shielded from prosecution only because they were beyond the jurisdiction of the Southern states. Suppose John Bingham and other congressional Republicans who endorsed Helper's book had been apprehended in North Carolina and had escaped lynching. They would have been tried, convicted, and punished by whipping and imprisonment or, under the 1860 version of North Carolina's incendiary literature statute, by hanging. In February 1860, Abraham Lincoln alluded to the threats facing Republicans. He exhorted them not to be "frightened [from our duty] by menaces of destruction to the Government nor of dungeons to ourselves."[9]

The world of 1865–66 was dramatically different from that of 1859–60. The South had lost the war; slavery was abolished. Many in the North held the once-despised abolitionists in higher regard. President Lincoln had invited William Lloyd Garrison, a famous abolitionist, to meet with him, and Lincoln selected Garrison as one of the official party of dignitaries sent to witness raising the national flag once more over recaptured Fort Sumter.[10] By 1866 an endorser of the Helper book had become the Speaker of the House of Representatives. Three of the seven Republican House members of the joint committee that reported the Fourteenth Amendment had endorsed the book.[11] One of these three was John Bingham, the principal author of Section 1 of the Fourteenth Amendment.

The Views of Two Leading Framers

When John Bingham proposed the constitutional amendment in 1866, he said it was needed to require states to obey all the guarantees of the Constitution, to apply the Bill of Rights to the states, to allow Congress to pass legislation to enforce the Bill of Rights, and to reverse the decision in *Barron v. Baltimore*.[12] The words Bingham chose for this purpose included the provision that "no state shall . . . abridge the privileges or immunities of citizens of the United States."

John Bingham and the other endorsers of Helper's book had personal experience with the importance of guarantees of free speech and the other guarantees of the Bill of Rights. When he said that states would henceforth be required to respect these guarantees, it is likely that he meant what he said. To most Republicans such a "completion" of the constitutional plan was unlikely to be controversial.[13]

The late Supreme Court Justice Hugo Black championed John Bingham as the father of the application of the Bill of Rights to the states and described him as the James Madison of the Fourteenth Amendment.[14] Some scholars have reacted with incredulity. They have answered Black's comparison of Bingham with Madison with ad hominem attacks on Bingham and with suggestions that a plan to require states to obey the Bill of Rights heralded the destruction of federalism.[15]

Still, Bingham did follow Madison's plan for a double security for the basic constitutional rights in the Bill of Rights. He used the word "privileges" to describe constitutional rights, including those in the Bill of Rights. That was one of the two words Madison used in Congress in 1789 to describe free press, freedom of conscience, and jury trial. Bingham used Madison's "no state shall" formula to require states to respect basic constitutional rights such as those in the Bill of Rights.[16] He went further than Madison and included other constitutional privileges as well, such as the protections against cruel and unusual punishment and against unreasonable searches and seizures. Perhaps experience with statutes that allowed the whipping of ministers who advocated an antislavery gospel and experience with searches of the mail and of travelers for "incendiary" documents led him to conclude that double security for these privileges or immunities was required. Perhaps in 1866, when Bingham said that Section 1 of the Fourteenth Amendment was needed to prevent states from inflicting cruel or unusual punishments, he thought of the whip and the pillory, the punishments provided for outspoken opponents of slavery.[17] There is substantial evidence to support Justice Black's comparison of the roles of John Bingham and James Madison. Senator Jacob Howard, the Senate manager of the amendment, expressed views of the Fourteenth Amendment and the Bill of Rights similar to Bingham's.

Howard was a former attorney general of Michigan. Since the chairman of the committee that produced the Fourteenth Amendment was ill, Howard was selected to explain it to the Senate. He explained that "privileges or immunities" secured by the Fourteenth Amendment would include "the personal rights guarantied and secured by the first eight amendments of the constitution; such as the freedom of speech and of the press; the right of the people peaceably to assemble and petition the Government for a redress of grievances." He noted that "it is a fact well worthy of attention that the course of decision of our courts and the present settled doctrine is, that all these immunities, privileges, rights, thus guarantied by the Constitution or recognized by it, are secured to the citizen solely as a citizen of the United States. . . . They do not operate in the slightest degree as a restraint or prohibition of state legislation." States were "not restrained from violating the principles embraced in them, except by their own local constitutions, which may be altered from year to year. The great object of the first section of this amendment is, therefore, to restrain the power of the States and compel them at all times to respect these great fundamental guarantees."[18] Most framers and supporters of the Fourteenth Amendment, however, spoke in generalities. Many said the amendment would protect all the rights of citizens, all constitutional rights, and the rights accorded the citizen by the supreme law of the land.[19]

Ratification and Free Speech

The congressional campaign in 1866 was a referendum on the plan of reconstruction embodied in the Fourteenth Amendment. The great issues of 1866 were the status of the newly freed slaves, of the Southern states and of their representation and power in Congress, of the rights of American citizens in the South, of the Confederate debt, and whether the rebellious Southerners might claim compensation for their emancipated slaves. The Fourteenth Amendment addressed all these issues, and both the Republicans and their opponents campaigned on them. The amendment, which represented a proposed peace treaty between the North and South, was the centerpiece of the Republican congressional campaign. In addition to its guarantees of civil liberty, Section 2 of the amendment provided that states could no longer count disfranchised male citizens to swell their representation in Congress.

In the 1866 congressional campaign, Republican leaders referred to the amendment as securing freedom of speech, the right to bear arms, all rights of American citizens, and all constitutional rights.[20] References to "the Bill of Rights" were typically not used. Democrats did not stump the nation complaining that Republicans would require states to obey the hated commands of the federal Bill of Rights. Perhaps they were reluctant to make that argument, so recently after appearing as champions of free speech, free press, jury trial, and grand jury indictment in the Vallandigham controversy. It is true that, in Vallandigham's case, they had contended the *federal* government was violating these rights, but their rhetoric suggested these were precious rights that no government should abridge. At any rate, appeals to race hatred and vague warnings about "consolidation" were the appeals most Democrats chose.

The insistence on protecting constitutional rights to free speech, press, religion, and assembly throughout the nation was a recurring theme in the 1866 campaign. It was clearly expressed in the convention of Southern loyalists who assembled in Philadelphia in 1866. The convention was attended by a number of influential Republicans from the North, and its activities were reported in detail by the Republican press.

The call for the convention was issued in July and read again when the convention met in September. It put the question squarely: "To the loyal unionists of the South: The great issue is upon us. The majority in Congress, and its supporters, firmly declare that 'the rights of the citizen enumerated in the Constitution, and established by the supreme law, must be maintained inviolate.' . . . Rebels and Rebel sympathizers assert that 'the right of the citizens must be left to the States alone, and under such regulations as the respective States choose voluntarily to prescribe.'"[21]

A letter that accompanied the call expressed the hope that Southern loyalists would at least receive protection for "all Constitutional rights of American citizens."[22] The Southern loyalists' "Appeal of the Loyal Men of the South to their Fellow Citizens" was widely reprinted in the Republican press. It reflected their understanding that free speech rights were among the rights of citizens of the United States that states must respect. "Seeds of oligarchy," the appeal noted, were "planted in the constitution by its slavery feature" and had produced monstrous results. The recognition of slavery

> wrung from the reluctant framers of that great instrument enabled these [slave] States to entrench themselves behind the perverted doctrine of State Rights. . . . The hand of the government was stayed for eighty years. The principles of constitutional liberty lan-

guished for want of government support. Oligarchy matured its power with subtle design. . . . Statute books groaned under despotic laws against unlawful and insurrectionary assemblies aimed at the constitutional guarantees of the right to peaceably assemble and petition for redress of grievances; it proscribed democratic literature as incendiary; it nullified constitutional guarantees of freedom and free speech and a free press; it deprived citizens of other States of the privileges and immunities in the States.[23]

Andrew Jackson Hamilton had been appointed provisional governor of Texas by Abraham Lincoln. He was a former Texas congressman who had remained loyal to the Union. Before that he had been attorney general of Texas. In 1866, Hamilton, a gifted orator, campaigned for Republican congressional candidates throughout the North. In Trenton, New Jersey, speaking on the central issues of the election, Hamilton said that Republicans agreed with Andrew Johnson in wanting the Union restored. But "althoug [sic] much was said about the Union as it was and the Constitution as it is," that was not what Hamilton sought. "He wanted a Union of loyal men in which all, even the humblest, can exercise the rights of American freemen every where—not the least of which are the rights to speak, to write, and to impress their thoughts on the minds of others. . . . Any other [Union] than one which guaranteed these fundamental rights was worthless to him."[24] The need to protect constitutional rights of free speech throughout the nation was repeated by Republicans again and again during the campaign of 1866.[25]

Later Congressional History and Free Speech

History after the ratification of the Fourteenth Amendment is an even less certain guide to how it was originally understood. To the extent that the later history corroborates the earlier, however, it is especially pertinent. In 1871 John Bingham explained that the privileges or immunities of citizens of the United States were chiefly contained in the first eight amendments to the Constitution: "Sir, before the ratification of the fourteenth amendment, the State could deny to any citizen the right of trial by jury, and it was done. Before that the State could abridge the freedom of the press, and it was so done in half of the States of the Union. . . . Under the Constitution as it is . . . no State hereafter can imitate the bad example . . . of Georgia and send men to the penitentiary, as did that

State, for teaching the Indian to read the lessons of the New Testament."[26] Bingham explained that he followed Chief Justice Marshall's suggestion in *Barron v. Baltimore*. Marshall had said then that if the authors of the Bill of Rights intended to require states to obey the bill, they would have prefaced the guarantees with the words "no State shall."[27] In 1871, many agreed with Bingham: the Fourteenth Amendment would correct that deficiency and require the states to obey Bill of Rights guarantees.[28] Some, however, made remarks that scholars have seen as inconsistent with application of the Bill of Rights to the states.

In the 1866 debates in Congress over the Civil Rights Bill, most Democrats opposed both the bill and the proposed Fourteenth Amendment. Several had appealed to legal orthodoxy, denying that the guarantees of the Bill of Rights applied to the states. Consequently, they insisted that the Bill of Rights could not provide congressional power to pass a civil rights bill.[29] Congressman Bingham made a similar point when he insisted that an amendment was required to provide congressional power to enforce Bill of Rights guarantees against the states.[30] After the adoption of the Fourteenth Amendment, however, several Southern Democrats interpreted it as applying Bill of Rights guarantees to the states.[31]

Treatises

There were four constitutional law treatises written shortly after the Fourteenth Amendment was proposed. Three of these, as Richard Aynes has noted, said that the amendment was designed to require states to obey Bill of Rights guarantees. The great exception was Thomas Cooley's, the most eminent treatise of the four. His *Constitutional Limitations* (1868), was silent on the meaning of Section 1 of the Fourteenth Amendment. Subsequently he read the privileges-or-immunities clause to exclude the Bill of Rights. Cooley later suggested that free speech was protected against the states by the due process clause of the Fourteenth Amendment.[32]

Historic Usage: The Privileges of Citizens of the United States and Free Speech

What leading proponents understood the Fourteenth Amendment to mean is one way to understand its meaning. Another way is to focus on how ordinary citizens would have understood the words of the amendment. Exploring common usage of words like "privileges" and "immunities" and exploring common understanding of the rights of American citizens in the years before the amendment was proposed are ways to search for common understanding.

The second sentence of the Fourteenth Amendment says that "no state shall make or enforce any law which shall abridge the privileges or immunities of citizens of the United States; nor shall any state deprive any person of life, liberty, or property without due process of law." Freedom of speech and of the press were commonly described in the years before the 1868 ratification of the Fourteenth Amendment as "privileges." The word "privilege" was used as equivalent to "right" or "liberty." "Immunity" was sometimes used to indicate lack of governmental power. Furthermore, many described free speech and press interchangeably as rights or privileges or immunities belonging to citizens of the United States.

Examples of these usages are worth recalling. In the debate on the original Bill of Rights, James Madison described freedom of the press and the rights of conscience as "those choicest *privileges* of the people, ... unguarded in the British constitution."[33] Madison proposed that jury trial, free press, and rights of conscience should also limit state governments because states were "as liable to attack the invaluable *privileges* as the General Government is."[34] (Free speech controversies of the nineteenth century show that Madison's concern was justified.)

In the debate over the Sedition Act, both Jeffersonians and Federalists referred to free press and free speech as privileges of the American people. Republicans often insisted these rights or privileges were protected by state and federal constitutional guarantees. Critics of the killing of Elijah Lovejoy, for example, described freedom of speech and press as national constitutional privileges of American citizens.[35] Indeed, between 1837 and 1866, many Americans assumed that the Constitution already recognized such a national right that no state should abridge.

In 1860, Representative Owen Lovejoy, brother of the slain Elijah Lovejoy, invoked the privileges and immunities of citizens of the United States as protecting basic rights, including free speech and press. "I do claim the right of discussing this question of slavery anywhere, on any square foot of American soil over which the stars and stripes float, to which the privileges and immunities of the Constitution extend."

Lovejoy insisted that "that Constitution, which guaranties to me free speech" protected his right to criticize slavery. Lovejoy claimed "the privilege of going anywhere ... as a free citizen, unmolested, and of uttering, in an orderly and legal way, any sentiment that I choose to utter."[36]

Representative James Wilson was chairman of the House Judiciary Committee in the Congress that proposed the Fourteenth Amendment. In the 1864 debate on abolition of slavery he said, "[F]reedom of religious opinion, freedom of speech and of press, and the right of assemblage for the purpose of petition" were rights of American citizens that no state could constitutionally deny. Still, slavery had practically destroyed these rights. It had "persecuted religionists, denied the privilege of free discussion, prevented free elections, [and] trampled upon all of the constitutional guarantees belonging to the citizen." According to Wilson, "[T]he people were pressed to the earth and denied the inestimable privileges which by right they should have enjoyed ... by the Constitution."[37]

Democrats as well as Republicans described free speech and press as privileges of citizens of the United States. When the Democratic *Chicago Times* celebrated the meeting to protest General Burnside's 1863 suppression of the paper, it said that the protest proved that "the right of free speech has not yet passed away; that *immunity* of thought and discussion are yet among the inalienable *privileges* of men born to freedom.... Twenty thousand bold men with one acclaim decreed that speech and press shall be untrammeled, and that despotism shall not usurp the *inborn rights of the American citizen*."[38]

Much earlier, James Madison had seen the privileges of free press, of freedom of conscience, and jury trial as belonging to American citizens and recognized by his proposed Bill of Rights. He saw his proposed limits on federal and state power as security devices. As finally passed, the Bill of Rights declared the rights, but the security device was applied only to the federal government, not the states. In the Fourteenth Amendment's guarantee that "no state shall ... abridge the privileges or immunities of citizens of the United States," the nation applied a security device against the states for protection of these rights. Usage at the time shows that many would have understood it to do exactly that. Eventually, the U.S. Supreme Court found protection for free speech against state denial under the Fourteenth Amendment's due process clause.

Applying the Fourteenth Amendment

If the First Amendment protection for free speech was to be applied to the states, what was the nature of the protection applied? Did the Fourteenth Amendment absolutely deny to states the power to abridge freedom of speech of citizens of the United States, or did it give citizens a right to free speech that could be overcome whenever the governmental interest was sufficiently compelling? For many opponents of slavery, the protection was "absolute," but limited. They thought states were denied power over freedom of speech by their state constitutions and by an idea of inherent human rights to the same extent and for the same reason the national government was. For such people, the First Amendment's denial of power over speech, though addressed to Congress, represented a general principle. But these people did not find freedom to speak unlimited. For many people certain types of expression—treason, libel of a person with respect to private actions, and solicitation of a crime were simply not within the boundaries of freedom of speech. The similarity of the text of the Fourteenth Amendment ("No state shall make or enforce any law which shall abridge the privileges or immunities of citizens of the United States") and of the First Amendment ("Congress shall make no law . . . abridging the freedom of speech") may also support such a reading. In any case, judges would still face the problem of determining the dimensions of freedom of speech. While there is substantial historic support for Justice Black's view of a limited but absolute freedom for citizens, those who expect history to speak with one voice are destined to be disappointed. As the history reported here shows, some also took a different view, and some advocated different positions at different times.

AN ALTERNATIVE ANALYSIS

History is rarely entirely uniform.[39] Some scholars advocate a different reading of the historic record and of the text. I will present some of their arguments and respond to them. My response draws heavily on the free speech stories told in this book.

The language of the Fourteenth Amendment's privileges-or-immunities clause is somewhat similar to language of the privileges-and-immunities clause of Article IV, Section 2 of the Constitution, which says that "the citizens of each state shall be entitled to all privileges and im-

munities of citizens in the several states." By the orthodox judicial interpretation, the Article IV privileges-and-immunity clause protects only
temporary visitors from other states, and it means that "the citizens of
each state shall be entitled to certain privileges and immunities granted
by state law in the states they visit." (By this view, out-of-state visitors
enjoy a limited equality in certain basic rights with in-state residents;
but what the state gives, it may take away—provided it takes from residents and visitors alike.) Literally applied, reading the phrase "privileges or immunities of citizens of the United States" in the Fourteenth
Amendment as reiterating the orthodox understanding of the principles
of the privileges-and-immunities clause of Article IV won't work, because the clause would then only help temporary visitors from other
states, not in-state residents. Supporters intended the Fourteenth
Amendment to benefit former slaves and loyal whites in their own states.
It will not do to read it only to help them if they left their states and temporarily visited another.

The alternative argument deals with this problem by seeing the Fourteenth Amendment as *an adaptation* of the Article IV antidiscrimination concept. By the alternative view, the privileges-or-immunities
clause of the Fourteenth Amendment simply protects against racial discrimination (and perhaps very similar types of caste discrimination) in
certain basic rights that states have granted to citizens *within* their states.
By this view, however, what the state has granted, it could take away, provided it deprived all races of the right.

In effect, those who follow this approach read "abridge" in the Fourteenth Amendment to mean "discriminate with reference to." They read
"privileges or immunities of citizens of the United States," to mean only
"rights that citizens enjoy by virtue of state laws that are subject to repeal." While reading "privileges or immunities of citizens of the United
States" to mean "privileges enjoyed under state law" and reading
"abridge" to mean "discriminate" may seem a strained reading, some
scholars have read the words in this way, and they point to evidence from
the congressional debates on the Fourteenth Amendment.[40]

Evidence from Congressional Debate

A few congressmen did refer to equality or a protection against discrimination in connection with the privileges-or-immunities clause of the
Fourteenth Amendment. These men did not deny that the clause would

also protect rights such as free speech. They did not repudiate statements by Bingham and Howard to that effect, but their statements seem inconsistent with the principle Bingham and Howard announced.[41] Is that necessarily so? The privileges-or-immunities clause of the Fourteenth Amendment refers to rights outside of the clause. Most, but not all, privileges and immunities in the Constitution in 1866 were set out in the Bill of Rights. Others, such as the protection against bills of attainder and ex post facto laws and the limited protection from state discrimination for temporary visitors from out of state were set out in the body of the original Constitution. Some, like the right to travel from state to state, are simply inferred from the structure of the federal Union. Congressmen may well have thought some Fourteenth Amendment privileges and immunities of citizens of the United States were set out in the Bill of Rights *and* that the pre–Fourteenth Amendment Constitution also contained a privilege or immunity to equality that prohibited state racial discrimination in basic civil rights. Such people would not have seen any inconsistency between statements that the amendment's privileges-or-immunities clause protected free speech and statements that it protected against discrimination.[42]

A Textual Analysis

A different and purely textual argument claims that the First Amendment is merely a congressional disability ("*Congress* shall make no law abridging freedom of speech, or of the press"). By this view, the First Amendment creates or declares no rights or general immunity from suppression but merely declares a lack of federal power. As a result, there is no right or liberty or immunity in the First Amendment to apply to the states under the Fourteenth Amendment.[43] If that were the way most Americans in the period 1866–68 saw references to freedom of speech, press, petition, and assembly in the First Amendment, the argument would be powerful. But as we have seen, many Americans in 1866 believed that the First Amendment declared that national privileges or immunities belonged to all citizens of the United States. They saw it as a declaration of basic rights rather than as simply allocating the sole power to permit or suppress free speech to state governments.

The Civil Rights Bill and the Fourteenth Amendment

The Civil Rights Act of 1866 made all persons born in the United States citizens and provided that such citizens should have the same right to contract, testify, and hold property, as well as the full and equal benefit of all laws and provisions for security of person and property enjoyed by white citizens. Some congressmen said that the act was equivalent to the Fourteenth Amendment.[44] If the Civil Rights Act had been understood by Republicans merely to assure equality under state law, one might conclude the Fourteenth Amendment also merely secured equality under state law. Such a mere equality reading cannot account for the statements of Bingham and Howard about the amendment and the Bill of Rights or for statements by those who suggested that a national federal constitutional right to free speech would be protected by the amendment. For that matter, scholars' assumptions that the Civil Rights Act merely secured equality under state law and that it was identical to Section 1 of the Fourteenth Amendment cannot account for Section 1's guarantee of a national standard of due process.

The basic fallacy is deeper, however. The Civil Rights Act secured to all citizens "full and equal benefit of all laws and provisions for security of person and property" enjoyed by white citizens.[45] Guarantees such as those in the Bill of Rights had long been described as provisions for the security of person and property.[46] (The federal Constitution is supreme law.) Many congressional Republicans assumed that, properly construed, the Constitution already required states to obey the guarantees of the Bill of Rights, even prior to the ratification of the Fourteenth Amendment.[47] For such people the phrase "full and equal benefit of all laws and provisions for the security of person and property" would include provisions of the Bill of Rights effective against the states. For them there would be no inconsistency between an asserted general equivalence of the Civil Rights Act and the Fourteenth Amendment and the idea that the Fourteenth Amendment required states to respect free speech.

Some Republicans explicitly said that the Civil Rights Act protected the right to free speech. For example, Senator Dixon, a Republican from Connecticut who eventually broke with the party over its failure to more promptly restore the rebellious states, said, "One Congress cannot bring about the millennium. . . . For this time we have reason to be content;

for we have put down armed resistance to the laws, and Congress has given us, in the civil rights act, a guarantee for free speech in every part of the Union. It is our own fault if, having thus secured the right to argue, we do not enlighten prejudice and mere opposition, and show that equal liberty is the best for all."[48] Dixon spoke within days of the introduction of the Fourteenth Amendment for consideration by the House and Senate. The *New York Post* made similar assertions. While it rejected the claim that the Civil Rights Act granted all citizens (including women) the right to vote, in 1866 the *Post* did read the act to secure to all citizens, including women, the rights of free speech, petition, and assembly.[49]

The Southern states' abridgments of free speech to protect slavery applied equally to black and white, Southerner and Northerner. Still, before and during the Civil War, Republicans insisted these laws violated a federal constitutional right to free speech.[50]

Reconstruction, the KKK, and the Unraveling of the Fourteenth Amendment

All of the Southern states except Tennessee promptly rejected the proposed Fourteenth Amendment. Congress responded by providing for establishment of new governments in the Southern states. Before their readmission to Congress, Congress required Southern states to call constitutional conventions, elected by nearly universal manhood suffrage, and to write new state constitutions that granted suffrage to former (male) slaves. (Confederates who had taken an oath to support the Constitution and who had subsequently rebelled were excluded from voting for delegates to the state constitutional conventions, but the new state constitutions did allow such people to vote.) New legislatures, elected by whites, blacks, and former slaves, ratified the Fourteenth Amendment, and, once it was ratified, representatives and senators from the Southern states were seated in Congress. For a time, a biracial coalition of Republicans ruled the Southern states.

As historian Eric Foner noted, "Reconstruction at the state level profoundly altered traditions of southern government. Serving an expanded citizenry and embracing a new definition of public responsibility, Reconstruction governments established the South's first state-funded public school systems, adopted measures designed to strengthen the bargaining power of plantation laborers, made taxation more equitable, and outlawed racial discrimination in public transportation and accommodations."[51]

But many former leaders of the South found Reconstruction intolerable. They joined terrorist bands, such as the Ku Klux Klan, and used violence to drive white and black Republicans from power. For a time, the national government responded. Congress passed civil rights legislation designed to protect citizens in the exercise of their constitutional rights, and the federal government prosecuted Klansmen under these federal criminal statutes. The statutes were designed to protect constitutional rights from private violence as well as state action. At first, these prosecutions met with significant success. There were, however, serious constitutional challenges to the legislation.[52]

An early case involving the use of the new federal statutes against those who were terrorizing the former slaves and their white political allies was *United States v. Hall*, decided in 1871. In *Hall* the defendants were charged with conspiring to deny other citizens their rights of freedom of speech and assembly. The defendants responded that even if the charges were true, they did not charge a federal crime because Congress lacked the constitutional power to pass such a statute and because rights to free speech and assembly were not federally secured rights. Judge (and later Justice) William B. Woods rejected the defense. He held that under the Fourteenth Amendment a person born or naturalized in the United States was entitled to all the privileges and immunities secured by the Constitution of the United States to its citizens. Woods continued:

> The amendment proceeds: "No state shall make or enforce any law which shall abridge the privileges and immunities of citizens of the United States." What are the privileges and immunities of citizens of the United States here referred to? . . . Among these we are safe in including those which in the constitution are expressly secured to the people, either as against the action of federal or state governments. Included in these are the right of freedom of speech, and the right peaceably to assemble. . . . We think, therefore, that the right of freedom of speech, and the other rights enumerated in the first eight articles of amendment to the constitution of the United States, are the privileges and immunities of citizens of the United States.[53]

The statute under which the defendants were charged made it a felony to "injure, oppress, threaten, or intimidate any citizen with intent to prevent or hinder his free exercise and enjoyment of any right or privilege granted or secured to him by the Constitution or laws of the United States, or because of his having exercised the same."[54] Judge Woods held that the indictment alleged a violation of the act. He also held that Congress could constitutionally reach the acts of private individuals within the states intended to deprive citizens of First Amendment freedoms.

Judge Woods's reading of the Fourteenth Amendment to protect First Amendment rights was implicitly rejected in 1873 by the United States Supreme Court. The blow fell in the *Slaughter-House Cases*, a case whose facts seemed remote from issues of Reconstruction, free speech, and Klan terror. Still, the *Slaughter-House* rationale as interpreted in later cases undercut federal protection for basic rights.[55] According to these later cases, the protection of individual liberty remained a state concern. This holding effectively obliterated the privileges-or-immunities clause of the Fourteenth Amendment. The implications of *Slaughter-House* for Reconstruction became clear three years later in *United States v. Cruikshank*. In that case, the Court rejected each of the key holdings of *United States v. Hall*. Thanks to the Court's decisions, instead of being one of the brightest stars in the constitutional constellation, the privileges-or-immunities clause of the Fourteenth Amendment became a smouldering meteorite.

The Fourteenth Amendment in the Slaughterhouse

The Louisiana legislature had created a corporation and authorized it to establish a slaughterhouse in New Orleans and several surrounding counties. Butchers who had been slaughtering animals elsewhere could use the newly created slaughterhouse by paying a fee. But the slaughterhouse was to be the only slaughterhouse in the area. In this respect, it was granted a monopoly. No other slaughterhouses were permitted in the counties in which the monopoly had been granted. This was the statute challenged by a group of butchers in the *Slaughter-House Cases*.[56]

The statute was justified as a health measure, as an exercise of the police powers of the state. The earlier regime of multiple slaughterhouses had caused health and environmental problems, and the new facility had environmental advantages. In the nineteenth century, states had often given monopoly privileges to encourage capital investment in new enterprises.

Butchers attacking the Louisiana act claimed it violated the Thirteenth Amendment and the privileges-or-immunities, due process, and equal protection clauses of the Fourteenth Amendment. The Court rejected all their claims. This discussion will focus only on the Court's destruction of the privileges-or-immunities clause.

Justice Miller, who wrote for the Court, first discussed the history of the post–Civil War amendments. He insisted, curiously, that a very superficial investigation was all that was required. The "most cursory glance at these articles discloses a unity of purpose,"[57] he declared, and then went on to say,

> [O]n the most casual examination of the language of these amendments, no one can fail to be impressed with the one pervading purpose found in them all, lying at the foundation of each, and without which none of them would have been even suggested; we mean the freedom of the slave race, the security and firm establishment of that freedom, and the protection of the newly made freedman and citizen from the oppressions of those who had formerly exercised unlimited dominion over him. It is true that only the 15th Amendment, in terms, mentions the negro by speaking of his color and his slavery. But it is just as true that each of the other articles was addressed to the grievances of that race, and designed to remedy them as the fifteenth.[58]

Justice Miller's "most casual" and "cursory" analysis found the purposes of the Fourteenth Amendment in the abuses of the Black Codes. The newly freed slaves, he tells us, "were in some States forbidden to appear in the towns in any other character than menial servants. They were required to reside on and cultivate the soil without the right to purchase or own it. They were excluded from many occupations of gain, and were not permitted to give testimony in the courts in any case where a white man was a party."[59]

All of this is true enough, though it is radically incomplete, extremely "casual," and appallingly "cursory." Justice Miller leaves out the entire history of suppression of civil liberties of white opponents of slavery, including Republicans, in the South before the Civil War. He is silent about the suppression of free speech in the South for Republicans as well as abolitionists. (The slogan of the Republican Party in 1856 and 1860 demanded free speech, free soil, free labor, and free men.) He fails to note that Black Codes abridged privileges including free speech, the right to hold religious meetings, and the right to bear arms, and that there were complaints about such deprivations in the Thirty-ninth Congress.[60] The struggles for free speech about slavery before the Civil War show that Justice Miller's constricted reading of the privileges-or-immunities of citizens of the United States secured by the Fourteenth Amendment was seriously mistaken.

The failure to mention the history of suppression of free speech in the South is puzzling. The issue was raised in Justice Bradley's dissent:

> The mischief to be remedied was not merely slavery and its incidents and consequences; but that spirit of insubordination and disloyalty to the National government which had troubled the country for so many years in some of the States, and that intolerance of free speech and free discussion which often rendered life and property insecure, and led to much unequal legislation. The amendment was an attempt to give voice to the strong National yearning for that time and that condition of things, in which American citizenship should be a sure guaranty of safety, and in which every citizen of the United States might stand erect in every portion of its soil, in the full enjoyment of every right and privilege belonging to a freeman, without fear of violence or molestation.[61]

Having completed his historical exegesis, Justice Miller proceeded to a constitutional one. The Fourteenth Amendment, he noted, made all persons born in the country and subject to its jurisdiction both citizens of the United States and of the states in which they reside. These distinct citizenships had different characteristics and different privileges attached to each. Only privileges or immunities of citizens of the United States were placed "under the protection of the Federal Constitution."[62] So far his opinion is consistent with protecting Bill of Rights liberties against state abridgment.

But Justice Miller announced that the great mass of civil rights and civil liberties were privileges and immunities of *state* citizenship. These he identified with the fundamental rights of Article IV, Section 2.

> [The Article IV, Section 2 privileges-and-immunities clause] did not create those rights, which it called privileges and immunities of citizens of the States. It threw around them in that clause no security for the citizen of the State in which they were claimed or exercised. Nor did it profess to control the power of the State governments over the rights of its own citizens.

Its sole purpose was to declare to the several States, that whatever those rights, as you grant or establish them to your own citizens, or as you limit or qualify, or impose restrictions on their exercise, the same, neither more nor less, shall be the measure of the rights of citizens of other States within your jurisdiction.[63]

Justice Miller then asked a loaded rhetorical question: "Was it the purpose of the 14th Amendment, by the simple declaration that no State should make or enforce any law which shall abridge the privileges and immunities of citizens of the United States, to transfer the security and protection of all the civil rights which we have mentioned, from the States to the Federal government? And where it is declared that Congress shall have the power to enforce that article, was it intended to bring within the power of Congress the entire domain of civil rights heretofore belonging exclusively to the States?"[64]

The correct answer to that question is "No." Most Republicans did not intend to threaten state power with national laws that could override all state laws. However, requiring states to obey the Bill of Rights does not do that.

Having said that Republicans did not intend to nationalize all state law and all civil rights by the privileges-or-immunities clause, Justice Miller proceeded (unintentionally perhaps) to imply that in fact the clause did nothing at all. "Lest it should be said that no such privileges and immunities are to be found if those we have been considering are excluded, we venture to suggest some which owe their existence to the Federal government, its national character, its Constitution, or its laws."[65] What then were the privileges or immunities so crucial to Americans of African descent, the persons for whom Miller incorrectly suggested the amendment was exclusively fashioned? Behold the result:

All citizens could travel to Washington, D.C., to transact business with the national government.
They had free access to the seaports and to the subtreasuries.
They could demand the care and protection of the federal government when on the high seas or within the jurisdiction of a foreign government.
They had the right to use the navigable waters.
They had the right to peaceably assemble and petition government (only the national government, as it later turned out).

In short, they had exactly the same bundle of enforceable privileges they would have had without the passage of the Fourteenth Amendment or (for Americans of African descent) as they would have had if the Fourteenth Amendment consisted solely of the citizenship clause. (I assume, as Republicans did, that blacks became citizens by the passage of the Thirteenth Amendment.)[66]

These privileges have some common characteristics. All of them are implied by the very nature of the federal government and could be derived by structural arguments, even before the passage of the Fourteenth Amendment. By this reading, the Fourteenth Amendment's protection of "privileges or immunities of citizens of the United States" added nothing to the Constitution as it existed before its enactment.

These "privileges" hardly relate to pressing problems of the newly freed slaves. It is remarkable, isn't it? As the Court read the premier guarantee of Section 1, Republicans wanted to protect newly freed slaves on their transatlantic cruises to Paris and on their arrival in the French capital. As Justice Swayne noted in his dissent, the *Slaughter-House* majority performed a judicial miracle: it turned bread into a stone.[67] The miracle was performed in the name of federalism—holding "with a steady and an even hand the balance between State and Federal power."[68]

The shortcoming of Justice Miller's *Slaughter-House* decision was not that it rejected the butchers' invitation that the Court set itself up under the privileges-or-immunities clause as the supreme arbiter of the reasonableness of economic legislation, an invitation the Court later accepted under the due process clause in the 1905 *Lochner vs. New York* case. (*Lochner* struck down a law requiring a 60 hour week for bakers.)[69] The great failure of the Court was that its rationale deprived the privileges-or-immunities clause of its central core. It left protections of Bill of Rights liberties to the tender mercies of the very states that had so recently made mincemeat of them. All the struggles over free speech and slavery show how deficient Justice Miller's opinion was and undergird subsequent scholarly criticisms of his judgment.

The *Slaughter-House Cases* majority invoked the paradigm of the semisovereign state (modified to prevent denial of certain rights to blacks), insisted that almost all a citizen's basic rights were created or protected by state law, and so, implicitly at least, rejected the idea that any Bill of Rights liberties limited the states. After all, it would hardly be necessary to dredge up "privileges" such as the right to visit seaports, to seek the protection of the federal government on the high seas and in foreign nations, to visit subtreasuries, and to travel back and forth to Washington, D.C., if Bill of Rights liberties were examples of such privileges. In *United States v. Cruikshank*, decided just three years after *Slaughter-House*, the implication became explicit.

United States v. Cruikshank and the State Action Syllogism

In *United States v. Cruikshank*,[70] the defendants were indicted for conspiring to deprive Americans of African descent of privileges or immunities, including the right to assemble and to bear arms. *Cruikshank* involved two distinct problems: whether the Bill of Rights guarantees were protected at all by the Fourteenth Amendment and whether in enforcing the Fourteenth Amendment Congress could reach acts of purely private individuals that were designed to suppress free speech rights. The Court cited the *Slaughter-House* decision to establish the limited nature of rights protected by the federal government. The federal government, the Court noted, "can neither grant nor secure to its citizens any right or privilege not expressly or by implication placed under its jurisdiction." The right to assemble was not created by the Constitution. "It was not, therefore, a right granted to the people by the Constitution. The Government of the United States, when established, found it in existence, with the obligation on the part of the States to afford it protection."[71]

The Court cited the rule of *Barron v. Baltimore*[72] as settled doctrine. Eight years after the ratification of the Fourteenth Amendment, the Court said it was "now too late to question" the idea that states were free to violate liberties in the federal Bill of Rights: "The particular Amendment now under consideration assumes the existence of the right of the people to assemble for lawful purposes, and protects it against encroachment by Congress. The right was not created by the Amendment; neither was its continuance guarantied, except as against congressional interference. For their protection in its enjoyment, therefore, the people must look to the States. The power for that purpose was originally placed there, and it has never been surrendered to the United States."[73] Had the indictment alleged a conspiracy to interfere with a petition to the national government, the Court said, federal power to protect the petitioners would have existed.[74] That would have been so even if the Fourteenth Amendment never had been enacted.

Consistent with this view, the federal government also lacked power to protect African Americans in their right to bear arms. "This is one of the amendments that has no other effect than to restrict the powers of the National Government, leaving the people to look for their protection against any violation by their fellow-citizens of the rights it recognizes, to [state police powers] . . . 'not surrendered or restrained' by the Constitution of the United States."[75]

In short, contrary to much popular understanding, and the understanding of leading Republicans in the Thirty-ninth Congress, the Court held that after ratification of the Fourteenth Amendment American citizens did not possess any of the privileges, immunities, or rights set out in the Bill of Rights as a protection against action by their states. The claim to protection against individual violence was weaker still. American citizens had no right to free speech, to free press, and no general right to assemble. They simply had a protection against federal interference with such rights, and would actually enjoy the rights if they happened to exist by state law and if the state chose to protect them rather than to terminate them. The pre–Civil War paradigm of the semisovereign state, free to deprive all its citizens of fundamental rights set out in the Bill of Rights, was resurrected by the Supreme Court largely intact.

The idea that the federal government had to create a personal liberty before it could protect it is odd. By natural rights views widely held in the eighteenth and nineteenth centuries, governments did not create rights to free speech or press or the right to bear arms. Governments simply recognized them and were established to protect them. *Cruikshank* itself recognized that the federal government could protect the right to petition Congress—even though the Court said the right to petition was not created by the Constitution. This was so for structural reasons—the right was inherent in republican government.[76] The Constitution also provides that the United States shall guarantee *to each state* a republican form of government,[77] a fact not discussed in *Cruikshank*.

Attacks on Free Speech by Private Persons

In any case, the *Cruikshank* Court adhered to the state action syllogism: the Fourteenth Amendment limits the power of the states; individuals are not states; therefore the federal government lacks power under the

Fourteenth Amendment to reach private action. The Court conceded that the federal government could, however, perhaps enforce the limited equality of right implicit in due process and explicit in equal protection.[78]

Power in the federal government to protect rights in the Bill of Rights against individual invasion is complex and the evidence as to original understanding is unclear. Federal protection of free speech and other Bill of Rights liberties from private action raises the problem of a limitless federal jurisdiction that could fully absorb the powers of the states. If the federal government could enforce rights to life, liberty, and property against *all* private invasions, the separate sphere for the states (a value shared by most Republicans) would disappear. A prototype of the Fourteenth Amendment had given Congress power to secure to all persons equal protection in the rights to life, liberty, and property. It encountered substantial opposition because of the fear that it could make virtually the entire domain of state law subject to federal preemption.[79]

The framers of the Fourteenth Amendment wanted to protect individuals' fundamental rights from invasion, to establish federal power to protect American citizens, and to preserve a substantial role for the states in the federal system. Accomplishing all these objectives requires accommodation and judicial creativity, but accommodation would hardly have been beyond the power of a Supreme Court committed to the goals. For example, the Court could reasonably have held that only those private actions undertaken with the specific intent of depriving persons of constitutional rights would be within the power of Congress. Murder or burglary committed by a private person deprives a person of life or property without due process, but denying due process is not the object of the action. In contrast, lynching a prisoner before trial to punish him for an alleged crime is specifically designed to deprive a person of a constitutional right. Ordinarily, assault or murder is simply a matter of state law. But an assault in 1872 in North Carolina, for example, for the purpose of punishing a person for espousing Republican Party doctrine would be something Congress could make a federal crime. In such cases, the private party seeks to exercise what is normally within state power, and does so so for the purpose of depriving a citizen of a constitutional right.[80] At the very least, the guarantee of republican government coupled with the First and Fourteenth Amendments should be sufficient to reach all private violence aimed at political speech, press, and association.

Something like this solution seems to have been reached by Republicans in Congress who were concerned with Ku Klux Klan atrocities, constitutional limitations, and preserving the role of the states. The Act of 1870 punished those private persons who "injure, oppress, threaten, or intimidate any citizen *with intent to prevent or hinder his free exercise and enjoyment of any right or privilege granted or secured to him by the Constitution or laws of the United States* or because of his having exercised the same."[81] The Enforcement Act of 1871 punished those who "shall conspire together, or go in disguise upon the public highway or upon the premises of another *for the purpose*, either directly or indirectly, *of depriving any person* or any class of persons *of the equal protection of the laws, or of equal privileges or immunities under the laws.*"[82] By this approach, most crimes would have remained exclusively state matters. Some, those specifically designed to deprive a person of constitutional rights, would have been subject to both state and federal prosecution. Another possibility would be to find federal power to protect free speech from private attack when the Court or the Congress found that states had been unable to protect the individual's right to free speech.

A critic can point out that these suggestions are in some tension with the "no state shall" language of those parts of Section 1 of the Fourteenth Amendment that follow the citizenship clause and with some of the divergent strands of its history. The Supreme Court has often (and quite recently) failed to treat such arguments as determinative when they collide with ideas of how the Constitution as a whole must function.

Nor should one conclude that such federal power would necessarily allow preemption of state laws protecting against private violence aimed at free speech. The nature of the federal system could broadly protect such traditional state activity from federal preemption, provided the state remedy did not seek to nullify the federal one.

Although the Supreme Court had liquidated the privileges-or-immunities clause and allowed states to violate the federal Bill of Rights,[83] it eventually resurrected protection against state denial under the due process clause.[84] By the 1960s the Court had embraced broadly protective concepts of free speech and, since 1925, it has also embraced the rule that states must obey federal guarantees of free speech and press. The Court's rejection of the bad tendency test and its development of a more protective free speech doctrine are the subjects of the next chapter. During the second Reconstruction of the 1960s, the spiritual descendants of the abolitionists were protected by the federal Constitution against state efforts to suppress them—efforts similar to those Southern states had used with great success against opponents of slavery before the Civil War.

17

Where Are They Now?

A Very Quick Review of Suppression Theories

in the Twentieth Century

The attempt to suppress antislavery speech, like the attempt to suppress "sedition" though the Sedition Act, illuminates the meaning of the constitutional guarantee of free speech. Whatever else free speech should protect, it should protect such arguments as the claim that slavery is a cruel and evil institution that should be abandoned. It should protect the advocacy of peaceful political and social change. From that premise, it follows that those theories used to justify suppression of such antislavery speech should be viewed with suspicion. Opponents of abolition invoked at least eight theories to justify suppression: (1) abolitionist speech had a bad tendency, (2) antislavery speech incited crimes, (3) certain points of view on slavery were illegitimate because of the Constitution, (4) susceptible slaves should be protected from abolition tracts, (5) certain harsh forms of denunciation were unacceptable, (6) the feelings of slaveholders should be protected, (7) abolitionists committed group libel, and (8) their actions constituted sedition. In addition to attempting to suppress abolitionists, the opponents insisted that the Post Office should prevent the transmission of abolition publications.

The idea that freedom of the press was merely a freedom from prior restraint, in contrast, was rarely invoked in the debate over abolition publications. On this score, opponents of the Sedition Act seemed to have carried the day to such an extent that the limited Blackstone definition of press freedom virtually disappeared from the public debate.

How have twentieth-century courts evaluated suppression theories invoked against "sedition," antislavery speech, and anti–Civil War speech? At first, the courts largely forgot or ignored the robust free speech tradition that was mobilized against suppression of antislavery speech and that helped to mold the Fourteenth Amendment. But more recent court decisions, particularly since the 1930s, have reincarnated crucial aspects of the free speech tradition and enshrined it in constitutional law. The Supreme Court has narrowly limited the reach of theories that allow governmental suppression of speech. It did so in the interest of protecting the right to engage in robust and uninhibited speech on public questions. These decisions significantly advanced both free speech and democracy.

Earlier chapters have provided very detailed accounts of particular free speech struggles. The current chapter is different. It seeks to summarize the later career of suppression theories in almost one hundred years of free speech history and to do so primarily for the benefit of readers who are not specialists in free speech. Necessarily, this chapter and the parts of the conclusion that deal with recent developments are brief and general. Nonspecialists (including law students, lawyers, and law professors) who read drafts of this book in manuscript typically resisted my suggestions to eliminate or greatly condense this chapter. For better or worse (and with greater or less success), I have tried to write this book for nonspecialists as well. Specialists in free speech may want to skip to the conclusion.

The Bad Tendency Test

Bad Tendency in Its Ascendency

A major argument used against abolitionist speech was its tendency to cause slave revolts or disunion. The bad tendency test lived on well into the twentieth century. The Supreme Court began clearly to repudiate it only in the 1930s. The advantage of the test was that it provided a supple and effective way of dealing with dangerous speech. The disadvantage was that it was a powerful weapon for silencing dissent on public issues.

The test had wide appeal and a long history. Blackstone had invoked it. Bad tendency had been one key approach invoked by North Carolina and other Southern states in their effort to silence antislavery speech. It was invoked against antiwar speech during the Civil War and World War I. In the bad tendency approach, the assumed likelihood that the speech would lead to bad consequences in the long run was sufficient to make it criminal. The consequences did not need to be immediate. Remote bad consequences were enough. No proof was required that they had come about or even that they probably would. It did not matter that statements that had bad tendencies were true. Nor did it necessarily matter that the speaker advocated only legal political action, if the tendency of the words was to cause a serious evil.[1] At times of great stress, such as wartime, the test had particular appeal.

Lincoln appealed to bad tendency in his defense of the military arrest, trial, and conviction of Clement Vallandigham for an antiwar, antiadministration speech in Ohio. In his reply to the Ohio Democrats who demanded Vallandigham's release, Lincoln admitted, "I certainly do not *know* that Mr. V. has specifically, and by direct language, advised against enlistments, and in favor of desertion, and resistance to drafting." But that, Lincoln argued, was the effect of what he had to say.[2]

The rebellion could only be suppressed by military force, Lincoln explained in his response to New York critics of Vallandigham's arrest. Military force required armies. "Long experience has shown that armies cannot be maintained unless desertions shall be punished by the severe penalty of death. . . . Must I shoot a simple-minded soldier boy who deserts," Lincoln asked, "while I must not touch a hair of a wily agitator who induces him to desert?"[3] Lincoln's powerful question reached antiwar political speech that even *tended* to cause desertion or draft resistance. Out of the many who hear such speech, some will be persuaded, and it is reasonable to assume some of these will resist or desert. If consistently followed (as it was not), Lincoln's bad tendency view would have outlawed antiwar political speech and put the democratic process in abeyance for the duration of the war. Similar reasoning later justified suppression of dissent during World War I, including the dissenters who avoided making any explicit call to violate the law.

The bad tendency test also reached cases where the potential threat to the state was far less serious. *Patterson v. Colorado*, decided in 1907, involved a stolen election in which the state supreme court functioned as an accessory.[4] Patterson was a populist editor, battling Republicans who sought to protect the state's utility monopoly from plans for municipal electric power. In 1904, a Democratic antimonopoly candidate had defeated the Republican governor by nine thousand votes. At the same time, the voters passed a home rule constitutional amendment giving Denver the ability to establish municipal electric power. As a result of another constitutional amendment, additional seats were to be created on the state supreme court.

The apparently defeated and lame duck Republican governor appointed new members to the court before their seats were in existence or scheduled to be filled. The reconstituted court promptly proceeded to rule for the Republicans so as to defeat the claim of the Democratic candidate that he was the duly elected governor, despite his apparent election victory. The court did not stop there. It also, contrary to orthodox legal understanding, held parts of a state constitutional amendment for home rule unconstitutional under the state constitution.

In this context, Patterson published an editorial saying that the court was subservient to the Republican Party and the utility monopoly. He published his critique after the decision by the Colorado supreme court, but while a petition for rehearing was pending. As a result, Patterson was charged with contempt on the theory that criticism of the judges in a case still before them had a tendency to interfere with the impartial administration of justice.

Patterson admitted authorship and sought to defend on the grounds of truth. If he had been charged with libel, the Colorado constitution would have guaranteed Patterson the right to prove truth as a defense and the right to a jury trial. Such a trial would have raised embarrassing questions. Because he had been charged with contempt, the Colorado supreme court denied these rights to Patterson. The court Patterson had criticized convicted him of contempt, and it held that truth was no defense. Patterson appealed to the United States Supreme Court.[5]

A central issue raised by Patterson was the right to publish negative, but true, information about government.[6] The practical lesson of the cases under the Sedition Act of 1798 was that the protection for true criticisms of government did not go far enough. Justice Holmes, however, was unwilling to go even that far. According to Justice Holmes, even if the First Amendment limited the states—a point he declined to decide—and even if the charges were true, still that would afford no protection to Patterson: "In the first place, the main purpose of such constitutional provisions is 'to prevent all such *previous restraints* upon publications as had been practiced by other governments,' and they do not prevent the subsequent punishment of such as may be deemed contrary to the public welfare. *Commonwealth v. Blanding*, 3 Pick. 304, 313, 314; *Respublica v. Oswald*, 1 Dallas, 319, 325. The preliminary freedom extends as well to the false as to the true; the subsequent punishment may extend as well to the true as to the false."[7] The state supreme court had concluded that the publication tended to interfere with the administration of justice. That was enough to justify punishing Patterson for contempt.[8]

Although the prosecution was for contempt, it was a contempt closely akin to common law prosecutions for seditious libel. Like the common law of sedition, the contempt action protected government officials from criticism, restricted discussion of public affairs, and denied the defense of truth. While common law sedition greatly restricted the role of the jury, contempt eliminated it altogether. Because he seemed to limit the First Amendment to a protection against prior restraint, Holmes appeared to justify harsh common law rules of seditious libel. Although Holmes cited judicial precedent supporting his position, his analysis was superficial and ahistorical. He did not weigh the competing libertarian and Blackstonian historical traditions. He ignored the substantial popular understanding—strengthened in the debate over the Sedition Act and the crusade against slavery—that a broad right to discuss public questions was a privilege of American citizens. He paid no attention to the history of suppression of civil liberties leading up to the Fourteenth Amendment. Nor did Holmes consider the tension between his broad view of the power of the state to suppress true statements and the constitutional idea of popular sovereignty.

Some of Holmes's contemporaries had considered the conflict between sedition and popular sovereignty. Sir James Stephen, in his 1883 *History of the Criminal Law of England*, had noted the conflict between the crime of sedition and the idea of self-government, a recognition consistent with the Radical Whig view of the relation of the people to their government:

> If the ruler is regarded as the superior of the subject, as being by the nature of his position presumably wise and good, the rightful ruler and guide of the whole population, it must necessarily follow that it is wrong to censure him openly . . . and that whether mistaken or not no censure should be cast upon him likely or designed to diminish his authority.

> If on the other hand the ruler is regarded as the agent and servant, and the subject as the wise and good master who is obliged to delegate his power to the so-called ruler because being a multitude he cannot use it himself, it is obvious that this sentiment must be reversed. Every member of the public who censures the ruler for the time being exercises in his own person the right which belongs to the whole of which he forms a part. He is finding fault with his ser-

vant. If others think differently they can take the other side of the dispute, and the utmost that can happen is that the servant will be dismissed and another put in his place.[9]

Of course, protection for speech comes at a cost. Irresponsible newspaper comment on judicial proceedings can and does whip up popular passion and lead to miscarriages of justice.[10]

Patterson was judged by judges for criticizing judges. In a 1912 case involving criticism of a United States attorney and in a 1917 case in which a lawyer was cited for contempt for criticizing Congress, the Supreme Court was significantly more protective of free speech. The Court limited contempt of Congress to acts that directly interfered with the ability of Congress to perform its duties and found that criticism of Congress did not meet that test.[11] In the case involving criticism of the United States attorney, the Court said that citizens had a serious interest in the conduct of prosecutors. At least in the absence of express malice, such conduct was "a legitimate subject of statement and comment."[12]

Some state supreme courts also approved suppression of expression thought to have bad tendencies. The Massachusetts court did so in a 1914 case involving a man convicted under a state statute that prohibited parading with a red or black flag or with a sign bearing an inscription opposed to organized government. (The defendant had carried a red flag with the inscription "Finnish Socialist Branch, Fitchburg, Mass.") The court said that carrying the flag could be punished because the legislature regarded the red flag "as the symbol of ideas hostile to established order," and it had apparently concluded that carrying red flags "in parades would be likely to provoke turbulence."[13] Free speech historian David Rabban finds that from 1870 through World War I, in spite of some speech-protective decisions, most courts embraced the bad tendency test to justify suppression of a wide range of expression.[14]

From Bad Tendency to Clear and Present Danger

The courts, including the United States Supreme Court, adhered to a narrow reading of free speech in cases that arose during World War I. After war was declared, Congress passed an act making it criminal to willfully cause or attempt to cause insubordination, disloyalty, or refusal of duty in the military, or to willfully obstruct the recruiting or enlistment service of the United States.[15] By an amendment Congress passed on May 16, 1918 (and repealed in 1921), additional offenses were added: saying anything with the intent to obstruct the sale of war bonds; uttering, printing, or publishing any disloyal or abusive language intended to cause disrepute as regards the form of government of the United States or the Constitution or the flag; uttering any language intended to incite resistance to the United States; or uttering words supporting any country at war with the United States.[16] States passed similar statutes.

As Harvard law professor Zachariah Chafee noted in his influential book *Free Speech in the United States*, as applied by most federal judges, the bad tendency test allowed conviction for any words whose indirect effect was to discourage enlistment and the war spirit—provided the defendant had the intent to achieve that result. But, as Chafee notes, courts told juries that intent could be inferred from the indirect injurious effect of the words, because people intend the natural consequences of their acts. Furthermore, it was not necessary that the remarks be addressed to a soldier; it was enough that they might eventually reach one.[17] (That rule was similar to the one the North Carolina court applied to uphold a conviction for distribution of Hinton Helper's antislavery book to whites.)

Under these standards, people were tried, convicted, and sentenced to long terms in prison, for example, for telling a woman who was knitting socks for soldiers, that no soldier would ever see them; for telling women, "I am for the people and the government is for the profiteers" (that decision was reversed in 1920); for urging broader exemptions for conscientious objectors; for circulating a chain letter for peace denying that Germany had made a promise to end submarine warfare; for screening a movie about the American Revolution because one scene portrayed a massacre by British soldiers; and for circulating a pamphlet arguing that Christ's principles condemned war.[18] One man was sentenced to ten years in prison for saying, when he refused the demand of self-appointed inquisitors that he kiss the flag, that it was merely cloth, paint, and marks, and might be covered with microbes.[19] The Supreme Court did not review these cases, but it heard a number of cases arising under the World War I acts.

In 1919, Charles Schenck was convicted of violating the 1917 Espionage Act, which prohibited interference with recruiting and enlistment. He had sent a flyer to draftees. It had the Thirteenth Amendment, which outlawed slavery, printed on one side, and denunciations of the war on the other. "[I]n form at least," Justice Holmes conceded, "it confined itself to peaceful measures such as a petition for the repeal of the act."[20]

Holmes believed the flyer would tend to obstruct the draft. To the claim that it was nonetheless protected by the First Amendment, Holmes suggested that the amendment's protections shrink in time of war. (Holmes had fought for the Union in the Civil War. Perhaps the controversy over the Vallandigham case and Lincoln's reply were etched on his memory.) At any rate, Holmes used the metaphor of fire, which had seen extensive service in the effort to suppress antislavery speech.

> The most stringent protection of free speech would not protect a man from falsely shouting fire in a theater and causing a panic. [The] question in every case is whether the words used are used in such circumstances and are of such a nature as to create a clear and present danger that they will bring about the substantive evils that Congress has a right to prevent. It is a question of proximity and degree. When a nation is at war many things that might be said in time of peace are such a hindrance to its effort that their utterance will not be endured so long as men fight.[21]

As a result of the decision in *Schenck* and similar cases, legislatures could ban wartime political criticism of the war and the draft. One could, of course, make the criticism before the issue arose or after the question was no longer significant. This seemingly unpromising language from *Schenck* was later cited by Justices Holmes and Brandeis as providing a strong, "clear and present danger" protection for free speech.

In *Debs v. United States*,[22] the Court upheld a prison sentence imposed on socialist leader Eugene Debs. The government had charged Debs with violating the Espionage Act by interfering with recruiting. The alleged interference was a speech Debs had made criticizing the United States' role in World War I. In the speech Debs said that the master class declared wars and the subject class fought the battles, and he said that his listeners were fit for something better than slavery and cannon fodder. He also praised fellow socialist war and draft resisters whom he had visited in jail.

Justice Holmes upheld the conviction, relying again on the bad tendency of the speech. The evidence justified finding "that one purpose of the speech, whether incidental or not does not matter, was to oppose not only war in general but this war, and that the opposition was so expressed that its natural and intended effect would be to obstruct recruiting."[23] Constitutional objections, he said, had been answered in *Schenck*. Debs was both a labor and political leader who had run for president in 1904, 1908, and 1912. He ran for president from jail in 1920 and received nearly a million votes. As law professor Harry Kalven noted in 1973, "[I]t is somewhat as though [the 1972 antiwar Democratic presidential candidate] George McGovern had been sent to prison for his criticism of the Vietnam war."[24]

Scholarly Criticism

The World War I decisions produced substantial scholarly criticism.[25] Law professor Ernst Freund, writing in 1919, criticized the *Debs* decision. He concluded that "to know what you may do and what you may not do, and how far you may go in criticism, is the first condition of political liberty." But to "be permitted to agitate at your own peril, subject to a jury's guessing at motive, tendency, and possible effect" made free speech precarious at best. Freund noted that in wartime, when government policies are supported by a passionate majority, the checking function of the jury fails.[26]

Walter Nelles in his 1918 book, *The Espionage Act Cases*, insisted that threats, offers of bribes, direct solicitations of crime, and demonstrable falsehoods like libel and fraudulent representation were historic exceptions to the First Amendment. But no exception existed "predicated upon honest expression of belief as to matters resting upon judgment." Nelles's argument on this point tracked that made by opponents of the Sedition Act of 1798. Nelles insisted that "the substance of the constitutional guaranty is the protection of such expressions, even though persons converted by such expression may be led by their consciences to do acts which are forbidden." He concluded that some insubordination would "unnaturally and improbably" result from antiwar criticism, but in any given case such a reaction would be "a priori unlikely." If knowledge of likelihood that strong criticism of wartime policy might produce isolated acts of insubordination was sufficient to establish criminal intent, he said, then freedom of speech on the subject of the war was at an end.[27] The conservative political scientist John W. Burgess also said that Espionage Act prosecutions based on speech that advocated change by accepted constitutional processes violated the First Amendment.[28]

Judge Learned Hand was also critical of the way the courts handled the World War I cases. He construed the Espionage Act to provide protection for the speech unless it incited criminal action. But Hand believed that Debs's speech met his test, a fact that illustrates the vagueness of the incitement test.[29]

Zachariah Chafee, a Harvard Law professor, was a particularly influential scholarly critic who made very substantial contributions both to free speech doctrine and to the understanding of free speech. In his 1920 book, *Free Speech*, Chafee looked beyond judicial decisions (most of which were unhelpful) to the history of free speech and the purpose and function of free speech in a democratic society. Like Thomas Cooley and others before him, Chafee emphasized the historic and functional relation of free speech to popular sovereignty. As a result, he rejected the idea that the First Amendment simply enacted William Blackstone's crabbed view of free press and speech. In doing so, Chafee helped spark an academic controversy that has deepened and enriched our understanding of free speech history. He clearly identified (and strongly rejected) the use of the bad tendency test as a measure of constitutional protection for speech, whether in wartime or peacetime.[30] Most important, he saw enfolded in the *Schenck* opinion language that could provide support for a much more robust Supreme Court protection for speech—"whether the words are used in such circumstances and are of such a nature as to create a clear and present danger that they will bring about the substantive evils Congress has a right to prevent." Chafee's innovative and expansively protective reading of *Schenck* had considerable influence on Holmes and Brandeis and, through them, on the later course of free speech law.

According to Chafee's innovative reading, "Justice Holmes draws the boundary line very close to the test of incitement at common law and clearly makes the punishment of words for their remote bad tendency impossible." Still, Chafee criticized the Holmes test for "not requiring that the utterances in themselves satisfy an objective standard"—that they must incite violation of the law—a test suggested by Learned Hand.[31]

Finally, Chafee provided striking evidence of the harm wrought by the tendency of some Progressives and many others to see free speech simply as one interest among many, subject to regulation just as was a "freedom to contract" for child labor, or for payment of workers only in script redeemable only in the company story, or for employment in a dangerous workplace, or for employment of workers for more than sixty hours per week. All of these claimed "rights" could be regulated when the legislature found them to be deleterious to the nation, and many seemed to treat free speech in the same way. By example after example, Professor Chafee illustrated the danger of the bad tendency doctrine for the democratic function of free speech. His case histories demonstrated the extent to which plausible suppression theories had been broadly applied to stifle free speech.[32]

Chafee was a pioneer, and his work had shortcomings. Writing in the Progressive tradition, he emphasized the democratic function of free speech, and he suggested balancing individual and social interests for free speech against social interests in repression. As a result, perhaps, he gave less emphasis to free speech as an individual right.[33] Scholars charge that he slighted the libertarian radical and conservative defenses of free speech. Professor Hans Linde and others (including Justices Hugo Black and William O. Douglas) have pointed out the limits of the clear-and-present-danger test. As crafted by Chafee and confined by the *Schenck* decision in which he discovered it, the test risked protecting impotent radicals advocating revolution, while sometimes failing to protect advocacy of democratic change that created greater dangers for state policy (such as Schenk's attack on the draft). Indeed, Justice Holmes may have applied the test in just that way. Chafee did not always fully explore the historic case for the free speech rights that he sought to defend. For example, he was unaware of the substantial historical evidence that supported requiring states to obey national free speech guarantees of the Bill of Rights because of the privileges-or-immunities clause of the Fourteenth Amendment. Mark Graber has argued that, like most of our free speech discussion today, he failed fully to come to grips with the effect of wealth on democracy and free speech rights.[34]

Some suggest that Chafee's advocacy for free speech led him to read more into *Schenck*'s references to clear and present danger than was there and to obscure earlier negative precedent. In his 1920 discussion of the Sedition Act and World War I cases, Chafee suggested that bad tendency and presumed intent had disappeared in this country and had not been applied between the Sedition Act and 1917. If his contention was intended to apply beyond his discussion of sedition cases, it was mistaken and puzzling, since Chafee himself discussed and cited a number of bad tendency cases decided before World War I.[35]

As David Rabban has noted, starting in 1920 Justice Brandeis wrote a series of opinions that emphasized the central function of free speech in democratic government. In these brilliant and luminous opinions, Brandeis relied extensively on Chafee's scholarship. In 1927, in *Whitney v. California*, Brandeis created "probably the most effective judicial interpretation of the First Amendment ever written" and one that made clear and present danger a very robust protection for dissent.[36] Whatever his shortcomings, Chafee made lasting and substantial contributions to scholarship and to our understanding and protection of free speech.

REPUDIATION OF BAD TENDENCY
IN THE COURT

After World War I, the Supreme Court continued to uphold the convictions of radical speakers, including some who went beyond Debs and Schenck and directly advocated unlawful violence. Justices Holmes and Brandeis, however, began to dissent, and Brandeis gave extraordinary bite to the previously toothless clear-and-present-danger test. In *Abrams v. United States* in 1919, Justice Holmes announced that "the ultimate good desired is better reached by free trade in ideas—that the best test of truth is the power of the thought to get itself accepted in the competition of the market."[37] That, Holmes now said, was the theory of the Constitution: "It is an experiment, as all life is an experiment. . . . While that experiment is part of our system I think we should be eternally vigilant against attempts to check the expression of opinions that we loathe and believe to be fraught with death, unless they so imminently threaten immediate interference with lawful and pressing purposes of the law that an immediate check is required to save the country."[38] Justice Holmes had also changed his mind on seditious libel. "I wholly disagree with the argument of the Government that the First Amendment left the common law as to seditious libel in force," Holmes wrote. "History seems to me against the notion. I had conceived that the United States through many years had shown its repentance for the Sedition Act of 1798, by repaying the fines it imposed."[39] The Sedition Act of 1798 only punished false statements. Holmes, therefore, seems to have implied a distinction between libel of a private person in which false and defamatory statements could be actionable and criticisms of government and of public acts of public officials that might be false and defamatory but were still protected by the First Amendment.[40] Although those claiming the protection of the First Amendment often continued to lose, in 1925 in *Gitlow v. New York*,[41] the Court assumed that First Amendment freedoms were fundamental rights protected by the due process clause of the Fourteenth Amendment. These guarantees were limits on state power after all.

In 1927, a concurring opinion by Justice Brandeis in *Whitney v. California* provided a detailed analysis of his increasingly robust clear-and-present-danger test. Brandeis began his *Whitney* concurrence on an inauspicious note, doubting that the Court correctly found protection for substantive liberties under the Fourteenth Amendment's due process clause. But since the Court found such liberties in the due process clause, Brandeis insisted on protection for free speech as well. (He seems unaware of the substantial historical record that justified finding a free speech guarantee in the privileges-or-immunities clause.) After its somewhat uncertain beginning, Brandeis's opinion grew eloquent and powerful. Brandeis related free speech to self government and to individual development:

> Those who won our independence believed that the final end of the State was to make men free to develop their faculties, and that in its government the deliberative forces should prevail over the arbitrary. They valued liberty both as an end and as a means. They believed liberty to be the secret of happiness and courage to be the secret of liberty. They believed that freedom to think as you will and to speak as you think are means indispensable to the discovery and spread of political truth; that without free speech and assembly discussion would be futile; that with them, discussion affords ordinarily adequate protection against the dissemination of noxious doctrine; that the greatest menace to freedom is an inert people; that discussion is a political duty; and that this should be a fundamental principle of American government. They recognized the risks to which all human institutions are subject. But they knew that order cannot be secured merely through fear of punishment for its infraction; that it is hazardous to discourage thought, hope and imagination; that fear breeds repression; that repression breeds hate; that hate menaces stable government; that the path of safety lies in the opportunity to discuss freely supposed grievances and proposed remedies; and that the fitting remedy for evil counsels is

good ones. Believing in the power of reason as applied through public discussion, they eschewed silence coerced by law—the argument of force in its worst form. Recognizing the occasional tyrannies of governing majorities, they amended the Constitution so that free speech and assembly should be guaranteed.

Fear of serious injury cannot alone justify suppression of free speech and assembly. Men feared witches and burnt women. It is the function of speech to free men from the bondage of irrational fears. To justify suppression of free speech there must be reasonable ground to fear that serious evil will result if free speech is practiced. There must be reasonable ground to believe that the danger is imminent. There must be reasonable ground to believe that the evil to be prevented is a serious one. . . . [E]ven advocacy of [law] violation, however reprehensible morally, is not a justification for denying free speech where the advocacy falls short of incitement and there is nothing to indicate that the advocacy would be immediately acted on.

Those who won our independence by revolution were not cowards. . . . To courageous, self-reliant men, with confidence in the power of free and fearless reasoning applied through the process of popular government, no danger flowing from speech can be deemed clear and present, unless the incidence of the evil apprehended is so imminent that it may befall before there is an opportunity for full discussion."[42]

Justice Brandeis flatly rejected bad tendency and even simple incitement as insufficient to justify suppressing speech. Punishing lawbreakers and not the speaker, Brandeis suggested, is usually the way to deal with those who commit crimes after exposure to speech. As he said, "[T]he deterrents ordinarily to be applied . . . are education and punishment for violation of the law." Even advocating breaking the law did not justify denying free speech "where the advocacy falls short of incitement and there is nothing to indicate that the advocacy would be immediately acted on."[43] Here Brandeis wrote about speech on public affairs, not, for example, speech proposing commercial transactions.

The majority in *Whitney*, of course, saw things differently. It endorsed as "not open to question," the proposition that the state "may punish those who abuse [freedom of speech] by utterances inimical to the public welfare, tending to incite to crime, disturb the public peace, or endanger the foundations of organized government and threaten its overthrow by unlawful means." That was so, at least, unless the legislative act outlawing advocacy of violent overthrow was "unreasonable or arbitrary."[44]

In *Gitlow v. New York* the Supreme Court had ruled that calls for violent overthrow of the government could be punished by the legislature without specific proof of danger or imminence: "The state cannot reasonably be required to measure the danger from such utterance in the nice balance of a jeweler's scale. A single revolutionary spark may kindle a fire that, smouldering for a time, may burst into a sweeping and destructive conflagration."[45]

The Rejection of the Bad Tendency Test by the Court in the New Deal Years

Although Holmes and Brandeis did not persuade their colleagues, the Holmes-Brandeis doctrine grew from an acorn in *Schenck* to what seemed a mighty oak during the New Deal years. The effect of a much strengthened clear-and-present-danger test was to repudiate the bad tendency doctrine. The Brandeis test had the great virtue of providing very robust protection for dissent. The virtue came at the cost of making suppression of speech that was evil or dangerous more difficult.

Meanwhile, in 1931 before any Roosevelt appointments, the Court began to take on a decidedly more civil libertarian cast. By 1939, after Roosevelt appointed several justices, the Court had rejected the bad tendency test, rejected the idea that the First Amendment merely protected against prior restraint, protected the right to speak on streets and in parks, and applied the clear-and-present-danger test to strike down restrictions on speech. All in all, it was a remarkable change of course.[46]

The Supreme Court explicitly rejected the bad tendency test when it overturned the conviction in *Herndon v. Lowry*.[47] Herndon, an organizer for the Communist Party, had possessed literature calling for a separate state for Americans of African descent in the South. He was charged with violation of a Georgia statute (originally passed in response to the fear of antislavery agitation). That statute forbade attempting to induce others to join in a resistance to the lawful authority of the state with the intent to overthrow the state by violence. The United States Supreme Court explained the reach of the statute as it was construed by the Georgia court:

> If the jury conclude that the defendant should have contemplated that any act or utterance of his in opposition to the established order or advocating a change in that order, might, in the distant future, eventuate in a combination to offer forcible resistance to the state, or, as the state says, if the jury believe he should have known that his words would have "a dangerous tendency" then he may be convicted. . . . If, by the exercise of prophesy, he can forecast that, as a result of a chain of causation, following his proposed action a group may arise at some future date which will resort to force, he is bound to make the prophesy and abstain, under pain of punishment, possibly of execution. Every person who attacks existing conditions, who agitates for a change in the form of government, must take the risk that if a jury should be of opinion he ought to have foreseen that his utterances might contribute in any measure to some future forcible resistance to the existing government he may be convicted of the offense of inciting insurrection.[48]

The Court found that the Georgia statute that permitted such a conviction violated the First and Fourteenth Amendments.

In 1941 in *Bridges v. California*, the Court applied the Brandeis version of the clear-and-present-danger test to overturn contempt convictions of a labor leader and a newspaper for criticism of judges in pending cases. "What finally emerges from the 'clear and present danger' cases," Justice Hugo Black explained for a five-person majority, "is a working principle that the substantive evil must be extremely serious and the degree of imminence extremely high before utterances can be punished." Black said the clear-and-present-danger cases did not establish the outer boundaries of constitutionally protected expression; they were "a minimum compulsion of the Bill of Rights."

Justice Black wrote that "the First Amendment does not speak equivocally. It prohibits any law 'abridging the freedom of speech, or of the press.' It must be taken as a command of the broadest scope that explicit language, read in the context of a liberty-loving society will allow."[49] He found the suppression did not fit into any well-recognized category of speech that was outside the protection of freedom of speech.

The 1950s and Reduced Protection for Speech

In the late 1940s, with the deaths of Justices Murphy and Rutledge, two of the Court's most consistent supporters of broad First Amendment rights, and with the growing power of world Communism, the character of the Court's decisions began to change. At the height of the red scare of the 1950s, in a time of great fear over domestic and international Communism, the Court abandoned the strong version of the clear-and-present-danger test.

In 1951 in *Dennis v. United States*, the plurality opinion for a divided majority upheld a conviction of Communists for violation of the Smith Act. The defendants were charged with knowingly and wilfully advocating and teaching the duty of overthrowing the government of the United States by violence. The plurality held that in cases of advocacy of violence, the test was the gravity of the evil discounted by its improbability—meaning the government could punish very dangerous speech though the evil was quite unlikely to occur. Since the gravity of the evil was great, not much probability or imminence was required.[50] The test would have justified silencing abolitionists if one read their statements, as many did at the time, as implicitly advocating violence. It would, of course, also have reached Northerners who said slave revolts were justified as well as those who advocated them.

Justice Frankfurter concurred. He emphasized the distinction "between the statement of an idea which may prompt its hearers to take unlawful action, and advocacy that such action be taken." He recognized the serious difficulty of distinguishing between the two.[51] He also recognized that "[s]uppressing advocates of overthrow inevitably will also silence critics who do not advocate overthrow but fear that their criticism may be so construed." Sustaining the conviction would restrict "the interchange of ideas." But under the circumstances, Frankfurter thought the choice was one for the legislature.[52] Justices Black and Douglas dissented.

The Warren Court and Dissent

After further changes in personnel the Court shifted again. By the end of the 1960s the Court had broadly interpreted the protections of the First Amendment. At the same time it began to narrow the definition of those classes of speech, from obscenity to libel,[53] that the state could suppress.

As a result, the Court substantially expanded the scope of protection both for books and film and for discussion of matters of public concern.

The Court also gave broad protection to speech that earlier courts would have read as advocating or having a tendency to produce illegal conduct. During the Vietnam War Julian Bond was elected to the Georgia legislature, but it refused to seat him. There was no dispute about the reason. Bond, a pacifist, had endorsed a Student Nonviolent Coordinating Committee statement of "sympathy with and support" for the men unwilling to "respond to a military draft which would compel them to contribute their lives to United States aggression in Vietnam." The statement said the war was "a hypocritical mask behind which [the United States] squashes liberation movements" and that the United States was murdering Vietnamese. He also expressed "support" for young men "unwilling to respond to the military draft."[54] In his endorsement, Bond had emphasized legal alternatives to military service. He later explained that he did not advocate that people break laws.[55] The Court found that Bond's statements fell short of incitement and were protected by "central commitment" of the First Amendment to robust and wide-open debate on public issues.

The Court later made clear that such statements could not be punished unless they were directed to inciting or producing imminent lawless action and were likely to incite or produce such action.[56] At least for an antiwar speaker who does not directly incite imminent draft resistance, the facts that the speaker argues that a war is unwise or evil and that some listeners may agree and later desert as a consequence is not a sufficient basis for punishing the speaker. By this rationale, if anyone is to be punished, it must be the soldier who deserts, not the politician who publicly questions, even vigorously, the wisdom of the war. Otherwise, all political criticism could be proscribed.[57]

In 1969, the state of Ohio prosecuted a Klansman under a statute banning speech that advocated violence as a means of political reform. The Klansman had said that if the president, the Congress, and the Supreme Court continued to oppress the white race, "there might have to be some revengence taken." He advocated sending "Jews back to Israel" and urged people to "bury the niggers."[58]

In *Brandenburg v. Ohio*, the Court overturned the conviction and found the statute unconstitutional on a basis resembling Justice Brandeis's concurring opinion in *Whitney v. California*. The per curiam decision had been written by Justice Fortas and was joined by every member of the Court. The Court "explained" its robust test for speech that advocated illegal conduct. Such speech could not be punished unless "advocacy is directed to inciting or producing imminent lawless action and is likely to produce such action."[59]

In the Communist cases in the early 1950s, the Court had balanced the gravity of the evil of a Communist revolution and takeover against its improbability, to measure claims of free speech and press.[60] By the late 1960s the Court began to look at speech with bad tendencies in a different way. It asked whether the speech fit into a few narrowly defined categories of expression that could be banned. If not, absent proof of speech directed to inciting or producing imminent lawless action and plainly likely to incite or produce such action, the Court tended to find the proscription of speech invalid. Later, it also subjected many efforts to punish speech on public affairs to an apparently high level of scrutiny, both of the legitimacy of the governmental interest and of whether that interest could be achieved by less restrictive means. The governmental interest in stifling dissent on certain subjects was treated as simply impermissible.

SPEECH AND THE ESPECIALLY SUSCEPTIBLE

A key argument for banning antislavery speech directed to white citizens was the claim that it would eventually reach slaves. Even most of those who thought citizens had a right to consider and deliberate about slavery assumed the discussion was not one to which slaves should be a party. By this view, slaves who heard denunciations of the system would not understand the "weighty" reasons for it. A solution reached by many Southern states, and rejected by Northern ones, was simply to ban denunciations of slavery.

What to do about speech that is not considered suitable for some people—because most think they lack the ability to evaluate it properly—is a recurring one in constitutional law. The problem exists, for example, with reference to sexual materials that have serious value (and are therefore protected by the First Amendment for adults) but that are not suitable for young children. In general, the Supreme Court has upheld a dual standard—one for adults and one for children. Those who give a child sexual material that the Court finds constitutionally protected only for adults can be punished. But government may not broadly ban such materials for everyone in order to prevent them from falling into the hands of children. Adults, the Court holds, may not be reduced to reading material suitable only for children. To do so, it has said, would be to burn down the house to roast the pig or to reduce the level of discourse reaching the mailbox to that appropriate for the sandbox.[61]

Southern states took a different approach. They banned antislavery publications given to citizens and voters, in order to prevent them from falling into the hands of slaves. Since many Southerners interpreted such materials as inciting revolt, threatening existing rights, and violating the constitutional compact that protected slavery, they also thought such speech was simply not protected from state suppression. They evaluated antislavery speech as courts have often evaluated libel of a private person, "fighting words," and obscenity as unprotected speech.

SUPPRESSION BASED ON THE FORM OF EXPRESSION

Some of those who favored silencing abolitionists explained that the evil was not the discussion of slavery but the harsh and denunciatory way abolitionists addressed the issue. Critics were particularly incensed that abolitionists used pictures—wood block prints—depicting the cruelty of slavery. Current First Amendment law has rejected attempts to suppress public discussion because speakers—whose ideas would otherwise be protected speech—employ "unacceptable" words or symbols. An example of the approach is the case of *Cohen v. California*.[62]

During the Vietnam War, Cohen came to a California courthouse wearing a jacket emblazoned with the slogan "Fuck the Draft." He was convicted under the state's offensive-conduct statute that prohibited "behavior which has a tendency to provoke *others* to acts of violence or to in turn disturb the peace."[63] After noting that Cohen's words did not fit any existing category of unprotected speech or threaten imminent violent action, the Court concluded that to punish the way Cohen chose to express himself would violate fundamental First Amendment values. In what some might see as a "distasteful abuse of a privilege," the Court saw instead "the broader enduring values which the process of open debate permits us to achieve." It found no principled way to decide which forms of expression would be permitted and which proscribed. Finally, it noted the importance of protecting both "relatively precise, detached explication" and "inexpressible emotions."[64]

In 1989, the Court held that the First Amendment protected a young man who had burned the American flag in an act of a political protest. An effort to ban symbolic communication that was driven by concern about the message sent was simply not permissible. Nor could the legislature allow those who purported to be patriotic to use the flag in their political messages while prohibiting critics of national policy from burning it to symbolize dissent. In the facts of that case the Court found no imminent danger of breach of the peace.[65]

Such symbolic protests had a long history. On July 4, 1854, to protest the return of a fugitive slave, abolitionist William Lloyd Garrison had burned a copy of the Constitution, which he had denounced as "a covenant with death" and an "agreement with hell."[66]

PROTECTION OF FEELINGS

Senator Calhoun suggested that one reason governments should suppress abolitionist speech was its impact on the feelings of slaveholders. The tough protection for speech on public affairs crafted by the modern Supreme Court depends on a corollary without which much of the difference between the current test and the bad tendency test would disappear. At least since the 1940s, the Court has rejected suppressing speech on matters of public concern based on the anger and hurt feelings it causes.

In *Cantwell v. Connecticut*, the Supreme Court reversed the breach of the peace conviction of a Jehovah's Witness who stopped people on the street and asked permission to play a phonograph record for them. When permission was granted, Cantwell played his record, which attacked the Roman Catholic Church. His Catholic listeners were infuriated, so Cantwell packed up his record player and departed. In reversing his conviction the Supreme Court said:

> In the realm of religious faith, and in that of political belief, sharp differences arise. In both fields the tenets of one man may seem the rankest error to his neighbor. To persuade others to his own point of view, the pleader, as we know, at times, resorts to exaggeration, to vilification of men who have been, or are, prominent in church or state, and even to false statement. But the people of this nation have ordained in the light of history, that, in spite of the probability of excesses and abuses, these liberties are, in the long view, essential to enlightened opinion and right conduct on the part of the citizens of a democracy.[67]

Recently, the Court has refused to find that speech on matters of public concern that causes "hurt feelings, offense, or resentment" is sufficient to strip the speech of constitutional protection.[68] As the Supreme Court has said, it has a "longstanding refusal to allow damages to be awarded because the speech in question may have an adverse emotional impact on the audience."[69] That is so, at least, when the speech is uttered in discussing public affairs and not in an environment such as a workplace, in which First Amendment protections apply in an attenuated fashion.[70] Offensive speech on public questions confronts a paradox: community norms of civility play an important role in political discourse, but government typically lacks the power to require protected speech to be expressed with civility.

Selective Suppression

Opponents of abolition contended that abolitionist speech was illegitimate. Slavery, and the exclusive power of Southern states to regulate the institution within their boundaries, they insisted, had been established by the Constitution. The South banned abolitionist criticism, so such criticism was illegitimate. On this issue, at least, they said the Constitution had picked a side in the debate.

A central argument for protecting Jeffersonian Republicans threatened by the Sedition Act, abolitionists, and critics of the Civil War was the idea that free speech guarantees apply equally and generally to Republicans and Federalists, abolitionists and advocates of slavery, and supporters and opponents of the Civil War.

On the eve of World War II, the Supreme Court had at first upheld state power to expel Jehovah's Witness children, who refused to salute the flag, from public schools. Just a few years later, in *West Virginia Board of Education v. Barnette*, however, the Court reversed itself. In *Barnette*, the Court rejected the claim that it should leave protection of the Witnesses' First Amendment freedoms to "public opinion and . . . legislative assemblies rather than to transfer such a contest to the judicial arena" because all effective means of political change were left free: "The very purpose of a Bill of Rights was to withdraw certain subjects from the vicissitudes of political controversy, to place them beyond the reach of majorities and officials and to establish them as legal principles to be applied by the courts. One's right to life, liberty, and property, to free speech, a free press, freedom of worship and assembly, and other fundamental rights may not be submitted to vote; they depend on the outcome of no elections."[71]

While a mere rational justification would suffice for regulation of public utilities, legislation that collided with the Fourteenth Amendment because it also collided with the First Amendment was not to be "infringed on such slender grounds." Incorporation of Bill of Rights guarantees in the Fourteenth Amendment, the Court insisted, made the command of the due process clause stronger and more specific than the due process clause would be without incorporation. The Court's historic function was to dispense its judgment when "liberty is infringed."[72]

Justice Jackson concluded his opinion for the Court in *Barnette* with a ringing statement of the lack of government power to establish orthodoxy: "If there is any fixed star in our constitutional constellation, it is that no official, high or petty, can prescribe what shall be orthodox in politics, nationalism, religion or other matters of opinion or force citizens to confess by word or act their faith therein. If there are any circumstances which permit an exception, they do not now occur to us."[73] So the Court, in 1943, endorsed the claim that the government lacks power to establish political orthodoxy. Opponents of the Sedition Act and of the bill banning abolitionist publications from the mails had made the same claim more than one hundred years before.[74]

In justifying Clement Vallandigham's military trial and conviction, Abraham Lincoln had suggested that those who remain silent when disloyal sentiments are expressed were, like Vallandigham, subject to trial and punishment. To the extent that the court adheres to *Barnette*, it disposes of Lincoln's embarrassing suggestion that people could be arrested for failing to speak up to oppose those who criticize the war or the draft.

In the 1960s the Court adhered to the no-orthodoxy tradition, protecting racist speech as well as speech by advocates of integration. Free speech protected opponents as well as supporters of the Vietnam War. The rule of *West Virginia Board of Education v. Barnette* against government-imposed orthodoxy supported this approach of not punishing disapproved ideas. A decision protecting civil rights demonstrators in Columbia, South Carolina, cited a case protecting a speech by a racist in Chicago. So did a decision protecting antiwar speech during the Vietnam War.[75] A decision protecting speech by a Klansman cited a decision that protected an African American antiwar state legislator, and the case of the Klansman was, in turn, cited to protect a radical who burned the American flag as a political protest.[76] The Court's commitment to broad free speech rights occurred at the same time it was dismantling state-imposed racism and upholding congressional statutes that attacked private discrimination in employment, public accommodations, and housing.

THE POST OFFICE

Even if the government could not establish orthodox political opinions, could it at least refuse to circulate the unorthodox ones? In 1835, abolitionists sent a mass mailing of their antislavery pamphlets to leading white Southerners. President Andrew Jackson suggested a stopgap measure until legislation could be passed. Postmasters should deliver abolitionist publications only to subscribers who demanded them, and they should release the names of such subscribers to the press.[77]

Subsequently, Congress debated (and refused to pass) legislation forbidding postmasters to deliver mail dealing with slavery when the item violated the law of the receiving state. Senator Davis of Massachusetts insisted that the right to use the Post Office was part of the liberty of the press. Senator (and later president) James Buchanan of Pennsylvania denied Davis's claim. He agreed that Congress had no power to prevent any publication whatever, but, he insisted, that did not mean the government had to deliver the publication through the Post Office.[78] Still, with no statutory authorization postmasters refused to deliver abolitionist publications to the South. During World War I the postmaster banned antiwar newspapers and magazines from the mails.

In 1965, the Supreme Court considered a case involving a journal mailed from communist China. An act of Congress required destruction of unsealed mail from a foreign country that met a broad definition of "communist propaganda." The addressee could save the item from the flames by filling out a card for each item saying he wanted to receive communist propaganda. The Court ruled that the statute violated the First Amendment "because it requires an official act (viz., returning the reply card) as a limitation on the unfettered exercise of the addressee's First Amendment rights." It quoted from Justice Holmes's dissent in an earlier case: "The United States may give up the post-office when it sees fit, but while it carries on the use of the mails it is almost as much a part of free speech as the right to use our tongues." Any addressee, the Court said, "is likely to feel some inhibition in sending for literature which federal officials have condemned as 'communist political propaganda.'" The act was "at war with the 'uninhibited, robust, and wide-open' debate and discussion that are contemplated by the First Amendment."[79]

GROUP LIBEL

In the battle over slavery, members of the Southern elite suggested that antislavery speech should be prohibited because it libeled slave owners—describing them as man stealers, dealers in human flesh, and perpetrators of a cruel bondage. The suggestion seems never to have gone beyond rhetoric; no proposed laws were drafted, and no group libel cases seem to have been initiated. In modern tort law, negative comments about very large groups of people typically do not support an individual civil legal claim for damage.[80]

But in the 1950s, in *Beauharnais v. Illinois*, the Court held that a state legislature could make group libel a crime. Beauharnais objected to movement of black families into his Chicago neighborhood, so he prepared a petition to the city council, sponsored by his White Circle League. The petition called on "[o]ne million self respecting white people in Chicago to unite. . . . If persuasion and the need to prevent the white race from becoming mongrelized by the negro will not unite us, then the aggressions . . . rapes, robberies, knives, guns and marijuana of the negro surely will."[81] Beauharnais was charged and punished under a law that made it criminal to publish items that portrayed "depravity, criminality, unchastity, or lack of virtue of a class of citizens, of any race, color, creed or religion," exposing them to "contempt, derision, or obloquy or which is productive of breach of the peace or riots."[82]

Justice Frankfurter, speaking for a bare majority of the Court, upheld the statute, using a standard of great deference to the judgment of the legislature. "[I]f [a libelous] utterance directed at an individual may be the object of criminal sanctions, we cannot deny to a State power to punish the same utterance directed at a defined group, unless we can say that this is a wilful and purposeless restriction unrelated to the peace and well being of the state."[83] In short, a plausible legislative belief that such group defamation had a bad tendency to produce evil consequences was sufficient to justify legislative suppression. Because libel is not protected speech and because group libel was like ordinary libel, Frankfurter said, Justice Brandeis's tough clear-and-present-danger test was inapplicable.

The Court upheld suppression of political speech in a petition to government because it contained group libel. Frankfurter said such racist speech could undermine individual group members' standing in the community, their education, employment, and prospects in life.[84]

At trial, Beauharnais had attempted to prove that his claim of criminal propensities was true. This he was not permitted to do, based on his failure to satisfy the Court that he acted for good motives and justifiable ends.[85] Indeed there is something deeply repugnant about allowing a jury to find such generalizations about groups to be "true." By contrast, in individual libel actions, truth is now a constitutional defense.[86]

Four Justices dissented. Justice Black noted that Beauharnais's speech was in a petition to the Chicago city council, and he suggested that the right to petition was protected by the First Amendment. Black denied that the petition was like libel involved in "private feuds." It fell into no historically well-established exception, he said, and was immune from punishment. "Every expansion of the law of criminal libel so as to punish discussions of matters of public concern," Justice Black warned, "means a corresponding invasion of the area dedicated to free expression by the First Amendment."[87]

The *Beauharnais* case relied on the premise that group libel, like libel in general, was without constitutional protection. But in *New York Times Co. v. Sullivan*, the Court extended heightened free speech protection to statements about the public conduct of public officials that otherwise could have been held libelous. It suggested that debate on matters of general public concern should be robust and wide open.[88] Many argued that *Beauharnais* did not survive the *New York Times* decision.

At least as to matters of public concern, modern doctrine holds that the government typically lacks power to remove subjects from discussion because of the topic or the viewpoint of the speaker. So, for example, the government could not ban all discussions of abortion or child labor, nor could it ban anti- but not proabortion speech. In 1992, the Court, in a quite technical opinion, extended this doctrine to unprotected speech, subject to certain complex exceptions. The upshot seemed to be that use of otherwise unprotected speech such as "fighting words" or libel could not be prohibited to those who are hostile to gender or racial equality while being allowed to those whose views on these subjects were positive.[89] The decision (*RAV v. St. Paul*) overturned the conviction of a young man charged with burning a cross on the lawn of a black family. The court has recognized that symbolic expression can be protected speech. Government can prohibit open burning in times of drought. It cannot ban flag burning to suppress the message it sends.

The cross burning violated a local ordinance that prohibited placing objects on public or private property, including a burning cross or Nazi swastika, "which one knows or has reasonable ground to know arouses anger or alarm or resentment in others on the basis of race, color, creed, religion or gender." Though a narrowly drawn statute could reach such conduct, the Court found the St. Paul ordinance was unconstitutional. Basically, *RAV* interpreted the St. Paul ordinance as allowing some groups but not others to use fighting words (fighting words are generally face-to-face insults likely to provoke a fight). For that reason, the Court found that the statute was impermissible discrimination based on the point of view of the speaker—something the Court had long suggested is typically not permitted in the case of presumptively protected speech.

The decision in *RAV* seems implicitly to overrule *Beauharnais*. *RAV* may also provide a second rationale to make the Sedition Act of 1798 unconstitutional, since it banned seditious libel used against the federalist President but not if used against the Republican vice president. More broadly, the Sedition Act protected incumbents, but not challengers. The concept of sedition, by definition, does not protect challengers.

Seditious Libel

In its expansion of free speech rights, the Warren Court repudiated (or some would say severely limited) the doctrine of seditious libel, though it permitted certain libel actions by public officials. The Supreme Court confronted the tension between the law of libel and the principles of free speech in the 1964 case of *New York Times Co. v. Sullivan*.[90] That libel suit, based on criticisms of Southern officials by supporters of Martin Luther King Jr., raised the question "Could a defamation action be used to silence criticisms of Southern governments and officials?" Broad protection of the reputation of Southern officials would tend to stifle or "chill," in the Court's words, political dialogue. In some ways it was a repeat performance of the Sedition Act of 1798 and of the later suppression of antislavery speech in the South. The cases involved a common element: the use of governmental power, through civil (1964) or criminal (1798) defamation actions or through general criminal laws, to keep issues and discussions off the public agenda and out of the public domain.

The Supreme Court concluded that a defendant accused of libeling a public official in connection with his official conduct was protected from paying damages unless the statement was intentionally false or made in reckless disregard of the truth. This fact had to be proved with convincing clarity. These were matters the courts themselves could decide, and the *New York Times* Court held that the evidence before it failed to establish the required level of culpability with the convincing clarity the Court found necessary to protect free expression:

> The general proposition that freedom of expression upon public questions is secured by the First Amendment has long been settled by our decisions. The constitutional safeguard, we have said, "was fashioned to assure unfettered interchange of ideas for bringing about of political and social changes desired by the people." . . .
> . . .
> Thus we consider this case against the background of a profound national commitment to the principle that debate on public issues should be uninhibited, robust, and wide-open, and that it may well include vehement, caustic, and sometimes unpleasantly sharp attacks on government and public officials. . . .
> . . .
> The constitutional protection does not turn upon the "truth, popularity, or social utility of the ideas and beliefs which are offered." . . . As Madison said, "Some degree of abuse is inseparable from the proper use of every thing; and in no instance is this more true than in that of the press."[91]

In this case, the Court recognized a central fact. Protection for the truth requires protection for some falsehood. This is so for at least two reasons: because what is considered true often turns out to be false and because political factions tend to find their beliefs and factual assertions to be true and those of their opponents to be false.[92]

Factual error and defamatory content were not sufficient to strip criticism of official conduct of constitutional protection. "This is the lesson to be drawn from the great controversy over the Sedition Act of 1798 . . . which first crystallized a national awareness of the central meaning of the First Amendment."[93] Probably all the convictions under the 1798 Sedition Act would have failed to satisfy the Warren Court's *New York Times* standard. Although proponents often said it reached only *intentionally* false and malicious statements, the act applied, quite selectively, only to opposition statements of fact and opinion. A central lesson of the

Times case was that without strong judicial limits, libel actions could be used to silence dissenting views and to keep ideas off the public agenda.

Before the *New York Times* decision, Kansas and a minority of American states extended a privilege of fair comment to defamatory criticisms of public officials. Malice or intentional falsity could defeat the privilege. In *Coleman v. MacLennan*, the Kansas court quite broadly explained that its fair comment privilege "must apply to all officers and agents of government . . . ; to the management of all public institutions, educational, charitable, and penal; to the conduct of all corporate enterprises affected with a public interest, transportation, banking, insurance; and to innumerable other subjects involving the public welfare."[94] The Kansas court cited Judge Cooley's *1868 Treatise on Constitutional Limitations* for the proposition that "free and general discussion of public matters . . . [is] absolutely essential to prepare the people for intelligent exercise of their rights as citizens."[95] In *New York Times*, the Court cited the Kansas case with approval.[96]

Justices Black and Douglas concurred in the judgment, insisting on absolute immunity for criticisms of the way public officials do their duty and absolute immunity for discussion of public affairs.[97] In the *New York Times* case, the Court cited the national repudiation of the Sedition Act to justify its decision. It treated the Sedition Act as a paradigm of what the First Amendment forbids. The citation was apt.

In responding to Alabama's attempt to use the law of libel to punish the civil rights activists' criticism of Southern officials, the Supreme Court and the law professor who represented the *Times* could also have cited additional pertinent history: the battles for free speech on the subject of slavery, the Southern laws that made criticism of slavery a crime, the Republican criticism of these Southern laws, and the statements by leading Republicans that the Fourteenth Amendment would protect free speech from such assaults in the future. The effort to suppress antislavery speech that occurred from 1830 to 1860 illuminates a central meaning of freedom of speech protected by the Fourteenth Amendment.[98] Without the Fourteenth Amendment's limit on state power, Commissioner Sullivan probably would have won his suit against the *New York Times*.

The Court frequently applied the First and Fourteenth Amendments to protect speech advocating civil rights. Throughout the South, members of the NAACP legal staff would explain to parents and children how to initiate desegregation lawsuits, and they would invite them to authorize the lawyers to bring suit. Virginia prosecuted an NAACP staff member for violating a statute against soliciting legal business, and Virginia's highest court upheld the convictions. The United States Supreme Court reversed; it held that the First Amendment protected vigorous advocacy, including advocacy of litigation to achieve peaceful social change.[99]

When Alabama attempted to force the NAACP to disclose its membership lists, the Court held that the attempt violated freedom of association protected by the First and the Fourteenth Amendments. Past disclosures of NAACP membership had subjected the members to economic reprisal, loss of employment, and threats of physical injury. The Court found that compelled disclosure of affiliation with groups advocating controversial ideas could inhibit freedom of association and that Alabama had failed to demonstrate a sufficient state interest in obtaining the list.[100] Federal courts also protected civil rights marches protesting segregation—on streets, sidewalks, and on the grounds of the South Carolina State House.[101] In the 1950s and 1960s, the free speech guarantees of the Fourteenth Amendment provided substantial protection for those who fought for racial justice in the South and for those who reported the struggle.

Conclusion

Democracy is a principle which recognizes mind as superior to matter, and moral and intellectual power over that of wealth or physical force. . . . Democracy is also a principle of reform; consequently, it must examine, compare, and analyze, and how can it do this without freedom of discussion. . . .

To argue that there are subjects, which ought not to be discussed, in consequence of their unpopularity with a majority of the people, is in reality to argue that the people are not capable of self-government; and the power of deciding what shall and shall not be discussed, ought to be invested in a censorship.—"Freedom of Discussion," *Boston Advocate*, January 3, 1838

According to one view, contemporary American understanding of free speech was largely shaped by McCarthy-era attempts to restrict Communist speech.[1] Of course, the history of free speech is far more extensive than that of the McCarthy era. In this book I have attempted to excavate a much longer and richer history. This history shows the importance of free speech ideas in protecting the right to dissent and reveals how suppression theories have been invoked in the past in efforts to silence dissent and limit democracy. It shows how the struggles to protect the speech of Jeffersonian Republicans, of opponents of slavery, and of opponents of the Civil War illuminate the function of free speech and the dangers of broad suppression theories. It shows that theories that justify suppressing advocacy of peaceful political change are inconsistent with our best understanding of free speech. History shows why courts and ordinary citizens have embraced tough tests to protect so much speech from suppression because of its message. Not least, it shows the crucial role played by committed and active citizens in protecting freedom of discussion.

History can also help us to understand how the world has changed.

Throughout our story free speech has been basic to democracy. Robert Dahl, one of our leading democratic theorists, has defined criteria for democracy; as nations approach or depart from these ideal criteria, they are more or less democratic. A central criterion is that "each citizen ought to have adequate and equal opportunities for discovering and validating . . . the choice on the matter to be decided that would best serve the citizen's interests."[2] Citizens, he says, should also have equal opportunity to put matters on the agenda for collective decision. He recognizes that "influence is a function of resources." As a result, equality is a demanding criterion that "would require a people committed to it to institute measures well beyond those that even the most democratic states have hitherto brought about."[3] Another important protector of democracy is that political and economic power be dispersed and not concentrated in a small social or economic group—that there be many loci of private and public power.

Dahl's insight highlights the difficulty of applying nineteenth-century ideas in a twenty-first century world. Our world of ever more concentrated economic and corporate power and the extremely expensive and increasingly concentrated mass medium of television is far different from the world of the first half of the nineteenth century. This brave new world raises difficult problems for democracy. Problems of money and speech have always been with us, but they are markedly different in the age of television and vast mass media empires. New technologies may disperse power or they may simply become new centers of concentrated power.

This chapter will review the development and meaning of the free speech tradition and then look at nineteenth-century suppression theories and at how the popular free speech tradition responded to them. After briefly describing the transition from nineteenth- to twentieth-century ideas of speech and economic liberty, it will examine two out of a great many modern challenges facing free speech—one concerned with money, speech, and politics and another that would greatly relax rules against suppressing dangerous speech. These two problems directly implicate central values of the popular free speech tradition—democracy and the right to dissent. The first problem—the challenge of wealth and speech—might be addressed in ways consistent with the core values of the popular free speech tradition. For example, we could expand opportunities for free speech without suppressing speech. With regard to the second problem, by contrast, *broad* rationales to justify suppressing speech because of its dangerous message are in conflict with the free speech tradition. This chapter will consider calls for greater power to suppress dangerous speech in light of history. The chapter will consider, in turn, the popular free speech tradition, several modern challenges that it faces, and the extent to which the history of attempts to suppress sedition, antislavery, and antiwar speech illuminates modern problems.

A Popular Tradition That Protects
Free Speech and Dissent

Political activists, editors, ministers, and other Americans contributed to a popular free speech tradition that stretched from seventeenth-century England through the American Civil War and beyond. In controversies over the Sedition Act, slavery, and the Civil War, Americans argued that free speech protected discussion of moral, social, political, artistic, and scientific ideas. Their claims about free speech confronted theories that justified suppression. Some ideas developed by the popular American free speech tradition have become embedded in constitutional law, such as the idea that states must obey national guarantees of free speech, that "bad tendency" alone does not justify suppressing speech about matters of public concern, and that government may not use the criminal or civil law to establish political orthodoxy.

In the major struggles for free speech from the Sedition Act through the Civil War, the courts provided little protection for freedom of speech. In the Sedition Act cases, for example, judges sentenced political critics of President Adams to jail. Likewise, no Southern court struck down bans on antislavery speech as a violation of its state's constitution. Indeed, the North Carolina supreme court upheld the conviction of an antislavery minister for giving white men copies of an antislavery book. On the subject of slavery, the North Carolina court reduced free citizens to reading items the court found suitable for slaves.[4]

Nor did the United States Supreme Court ever void any Southern statute banning antislavery speech. Because it held that the national Bill of Rights did not limit the states, the Supreme Court did not review state free speech cases. During the Civil War, a federal court refused to issue a writ of habeas corpus to free Clement Vallandigham, who faced a military trial for making an antiwar speech in Ohio. On the other hand, another federal court was poised to enjoin General Ambrose E. Burnside's military suppression of a newspaper in Illinois, but President Lincoln himself, responding to public concern, countermanded the general's order.

In the free speech controversies over the Sedition Act, slavery, and Civil War, most victories for free speech were not won in the courts. Instead, they were won in the forum of public opinion: free speech victories were won in elections that repudiated the Sedition Act; in Northern legislatures that refused to pass laws to silence abolitionists; in Congress, when it refused to pass the postal ban on antislavery literature and when it finally repealed the gag rule that prohibited congressional discussion of the abolition of slavery; and in popular protests over suppression of antiwar speech that curtailed Lincoln administration reprisals against dissenters. The free speech tradition among the people was ahead of the courts, just as the popular effort to establish representative democracy had been ahead of existing legal structures. It was articulated in newspapers, mass meetings, and by social activists and politicians. Only very gradually did it become legal doctrine. Representative democracy is the radical idea that ordinary people must be trusted to present, hear, and evaluate very divergent approaches and to make the right choices. Belief that they can and will do so is a faith, and the battles over free speech recounted here show the faith has been powerful, but far from universal.

But if there were victories, there were also defeats—the prosecution of Jeffersonians, the suppression of antislavery speech in the South, Northern antiabolition mobs, and the punishment of antiwar speech during the Civil War and during World War I. During Reconstruction, Southern terrorists, led by some in the Southern elite, were unwilling to tolerate free speech or a multiracial democracy and the Republican Party that supported it. Reconstruction failed, and the Republican coalition was suppressed. Not until the 1960s did multiracial democracy exist in much of the South.[5]

Free speech advocates did not articulate a single rationale. Instead, they appealed to a web of justifications, including natural rights, democracy, and the advancement of truth. Abolitionists and other free speech advocates insisted free speech was a God-given right that state and federal constitutions protected but did not bestow. They contended that it was essential for making democracy work; it implemented popular sovereignty. Free speech fostered the search for truth, and it advanced social, religious, and scientific progress. Arguments for the positive social function of free speech and arguments for inherent rights reinforced one another.

Proponents of the popular free speech tradition defined the right to free speech broadly. Abolitionists and Republicans appealed to the precious right of American citizens to discuss all political, religious, moral, and scientific topics on every inch of American soil. Free speech was not simply a protection against prior restraint. It encompassed far more than the right to publish without a license and to be jailed, whipped, or hung afterward.

After the crisis of the mid-1830s, opponents of slavery increasingly claimed that state governments (and not just the federal government) must not abridge the rights of speech, press, religion, and petition. They felt that these were national rights. During the Civil War, in response to federal attacks on antiwar speech, Democrats, too, appealed to a broad free speech right belonging to all American citizens. Though some of these ideas were unorthodox, they were crucial to the democratic function of free speech.

Without a broad understanding of freedom of speech, the government, the majority, or mobs may suppress dissent and advocacy of democratic change. Without a national guarantee of free speech, the immunity or privilege would be a matter of local option—as in fact it was from the 1830s through the Civil War. During those years, many Southern states chose to repress freedom of speech about slavery, the central political issue facing the South and, indeed, the nation.

Those who appealed to free speech insisted that it embraced more than speech about politics. They said it protected poets, philosophers, literary people, scientists, moralists, and ordinary people who enjoyed the pleasure of expression.[6] As they saw it, the breadth of its protections explained why everyone should be concerned about attacks on free speech. Abolitionists, the second Republican Party, and antiwar Democrats during the Civil War appealed to a constellation of free speech values in which democracy and the right to express and appeal to conscience were the brightest stars.

According to the democratic strand of the free speech tradition, citizens possessed ultimate sovereignty. They had a very broad right to put controversial issues on the agenda, to seek to shape public discussion, and to participate in decisions. Democracy without broad protection for free speech was meaningless. The right to appeal to conscience ensured the right to raise moral questions, whether or not the speaker suggested political action.

The popular tradition insisted that truth was more likely to emerge if the government did not have broad power to suppress ideas and opinions. So the right to free speech protected ideas that were wrong as well as those that were virtuous, those that were foolish as well as those that were wise. It protected, as the *New York Tribune* put it in 1863, "irrational, unpatriotic and inhuman views with regard to political questions."[7] The tradition was particularly concerned with protecting unpopular views, recognizing that popular ones rarely needed protection.[8] Since all these ideas were a part of the background understanding of the privileges or immunities of citizens of the United States, they are one important factor in understanding the legal meaning of the Fourteenth Amendment's protection for speech.

Most abolitionists and opponents of slavery supported free speech even for horrible ideas that justified human slavery. Unlike their opponents, these abolitionists insisted on free speech for all sides of the debate. Abolitionists not only attacked slavery, they republished Southern justifications for it. Abolitionists saw calls for censorship as a confession of weakness. Members of Lincoln's Republican Party insisted that Southerners had the right to come to the North and advocate slavery and reopening the slave trade, a trade Republicans saw as a crime against humanity. Similarly, Republicans believed the right of free speech meant that *they* had the right to criticize slavery everywhere—in the South as well as in the North. Opponents of slavery believed that ideas of liberty and equality would be more likely to defeat slavery so long as persuasion and argument were the only weapons allowed in the contest.

Of course, abolitionists, Republicans before the Civil War, and Democrats during the Civil War had special reasons to support free speech. Dissenters from the status quo tend to benefit from free speech, as supporters of the status quo do not. Those already in power need not worry that their views will be suppressed. But increasingly, people demanded free speech for their political opponents. Free speech advocates who opposed abolition still insisted on protecting abolitionist speech. Many Republicans rallied to the defense of free speech rights of anti–Civil War Democrats.

In spite of their optimistic faith that truth would vanquish error, the abolitionists did not sit back and wait for the invisible hand to select the best from the marketplace of ideas. They passionately and tirelessly argued for the rights of free blacks and slaves and repeatedly confronted bigotry with the weapons of free discussion. Some of the wisest advocates of free speech also emphasized the need for charity, understanding, and kindness in expressing controversial truths. Others did not: to critics of his harsh rhetoric, William Lloyd Garrison responded that, "I have need to be *all on fire*, for I have mountains of ice about me to melt."[9]

Theories of Suppression

As we have seen, Southern slaveholders and their Northern allies made powerful arguments to justify the suppression of antislavery speech. First, advocates of suppression proclaimed that incitement to violence and revolt is not protected speech. They insisted that (whatever the text) the subtext of criticism of slavery was incitement. They also argued that criticism tended to produce slave revolts and that this fact justified suppression. Second, advocates of suppression contended that rights are limited by other rights.[10] Federalists repeatedly deployed this argument to support the Sedition Act: the right of free speech was limited by the right of government officials to be protected against false opinions and facts about their conduct of public affairs. Similarly, slaveholders argued that their property rights limited the free speech rights of antislavery critics. Third, advocates of suppression claimed that criticism of slaveholders as kidnappers, dealers in human flesh, and violators of basic human rights libeled slaveholders. Fourth, they justified suppression because such denunciations injured the feelings and social standing of slaveholders. Fifth, critics of abolitionists and Republicans argued that because slavery in the states was recognized by the Constitution, and control of it was left entirely to the slave states, which banned antislavery speech, criticism of slavery was illegitimate. Finally, they argued that antislavery speech threatened to spark a civil war, so the nation had compelling reasons to suppress it. Nothing short of suppression, they argued, would work.

One consistent thread running through all these rationales was fear of harm. Demands for suppression have always invoked the harm words can cause, including injury to the government in times of peril; injury to the property, social standing, and reputation rights of slaveholders; harms of slave revolts and civil war; harms of antiwar speech; harms to individuals; and harms to national unity when people refuse to perform patriotic acts.[11]

RESPONSES TO ARGUMENTS FOR SUPPRESSION

Supporters of broad free speech rights implicitly—and often explicitly—rejected the claim that a tendency to cause evil results, or group libel, or the emotional distress suffered by slaveholders harshly denounced by abolitionists justified suppressing speech. Some said that overt unlawful acts should be required before the government had power to intervene. Most simply insisted that these theories for suppressing speech were inconsistent with the rights of free speech on political, social, and moral questions.[12]

At first glance, the effort to silence abolitionist speech might not seem to be an attack on democracy. After all, the Constitution had accepted slavery in the South and promised it protection. By this view, the American people simply had agreed to remove one item—the legitimacy of slavery in the South—from the national agenda. Abolitionists who sought to put human slavery back on the public agenda were violating the constitutional compact that left the matter to the slave states. Setting the agenda, however, is a crucial democratic act. As Robert Post has noted, "The state ought not to be empowered to control the agenda of public discourse, or the presentation and characterization of issues within public discourse, because such control would necessarily circumscribe the potential for collective self-determination."[13]

Antislavery editor and free speech martyr Elijah Lovejoy rejected the theory that antislavery speech was impermissible because the Constitution sanctioned slavery and left full control of it to the slave states.[14] As Lovejoy pointed out, republican government was a basic constitutional value. Nevertheless, he continued, people were permitted to advocate monarchy or despotism. They could attack the institution of marriage, if they wanted to. Lovejoy and other supporters of broad free speech rights insisted that all sides had an equal right to express their views on political and social questions.

Advocates of free speech often accepted the idea that rights were limited by other rights. (Of course, free speech theories typically recognize that rights are limited by other rights. The question is which other rights should limit free speech and in what circumstances.) They did not fully explain how they reconciled their belief in broad rights to free speech with the rights of others. They insisted implicitly that the idea that rights are limited by other rights must be narrowly confined to protect the democratic and truth-declaring function of free speech. James Madison and other Jeffersonian Republicans, for example, asserted that ideas of free speech and representative government explained why the concept of seditious libel was not acceptable in republican America.

Still, rights to free speech were limited, and the dimensions of the limits were rarely explored or explained. For example, free speech advocates sometimes suggested that treason, defamation of private character, and incitement to violate the law were not protected. But, as the context makes clear, they typically defined treason, libel, and incitement much more narrowly than did their critics.

The Free Speech Tradition Under Fire

Today, we hear renewed calls to recast free speech doctrine. The free speech tradition discussed in this book grew in the eighteenth and nineteenth centuries and became enshrined in constitutional law largely in the twentieth century. A central part of the tradition was the plea to hear diverse voices and judgments, the idea that the best course could be charted after considering multiple perspectives. Free speech furthered democracy, and it was a way for people to challenge entrenched power. At least in the nineteenth century, and to a considerable degree today, the free speech tradition also reflected the view that free speech and democracy would flourish best without much government regulation of speech. In the nineteenth century, a broad reading of these ideas facilitated free speech; an economic system in which wealth and access to communication were widely distributed reenforced free speech values. Today, two opposing positions are in serious tension. On one side, there is the idea that all voices and judgments should be heard and that speech challenges entrenched power; on the other is the idea of leaving free speech to be allocated based on economic power.

Classical and Modern Liberalism and Free Speech in the Nineteenth Century

The popular free speech tradition discussed in this book matured in the first half of the nineteenth century, in a world quite different from the modern world. In major respects it was a far less democratic age. States denied the vote to all women, slaves, and to most free Americans of African descent. But in other ways, the first half of the nineteenth century was a time of robust democracy. Many people attended political speeches and rallies. Politicians courted voters through rallies and through the press. Mass politics was also mass entertainment, and politics had fewer competitors for an audience than it does today.

The press tended to be overtly partisan, so politicians could reach audiences through their party press. Newspapers reprinted their speeches and reported congressional debates, often in great detail, giving politicians more direct, substantial, and unfiltered access to the public than they enjoy in today's world of shrinking sound bites. Politicians therefore had a personal stake in preserving press freedom. The partisan press often gave speeches by opponents short shrift, yet the opposition press responded. As the nineteenth-century free speech struggles show, many people supported broad protection for free speech.

Though running a newspaper has always been an expensive endeavor, in the nineteenth century it did not involve the great concentrations of capital that today characterize newspaper chains or television empires. Newspapers reprinted comments from other papers as well as debates in Congress, so news gathering was inexpensive. Most cities of any size had a number of newspapers. Dedicated groups with sufficient resources, like the abolitionists or associations of working men, could and did have their own papers. Newspapers, moreover, were just one of several economical methods of reaching a mass audience—others included books, pamphlets, and stump speaking—and speakers needed only native ability, education, and access to those resources in order to make their views known. A spoils system that provided incentives for people to work for political parties probably allowed the development of more independent political parties for people to choose from, though at a cost. When slavery changed from being an object of moral outrage to being a basic political issue, for example, an antislavery party came into existence.

In this context, as it is today, strong protection against government suppression of free discussion was a necessary condition for political freedom. It also may have been closer to being a sufficient one.

Late eighteenth- and early-nineteenth-century free speech ideas emerged in a world with fewer government limits on the economy. Many assumed that crucial decisions could simply be left to the invisible hand of the market. By the late nineteenth and early twentieth century, some saw freedom to enter into contracts and freedom from government economic regulation as the essence of liberty. Following these theories, some courts struck down laws that, for example, limited bakers to a sixty-hour work week, or provided for a minimum wage, or required companies to pay workers in cash rather than scrip that was redeemable only in the company store. Those courts held that such laws violated a constitutionally protected liberty to contract.[15] The giant corporation and the lone worker were both treated as two equally independent persons free to enter or reject bargains.

Are the free speech ideas of the eighteenth and nineteenth centuries viable today? Should those who reject a totally unregulated market also reject a largely unregulated marketplace of ideas? Putting the question in this way is too general. It lumps government rules that enhance speech for those with limited resources—such as providing a public forum for expression in streets and parks, universal computer and Internet access, or public financing of political campaigns for those who accept it—with suppression of speech because of its message. Efforts to enrich our public dialogue by expanding free speech opportunities for those with limited resources do not abridge free speech. They expand it. Of course, by empowering other perspectives, the ability of wealth to monopolize the discourse is reduced. But the right to free speech does not carry with it a right guaranteeing great wealth virtually exclusive effective access to public discourse.

By the later years of the nineteenth century, the need for some restraints on economic freedom became clear to many, a view eventually endorsed by progressive Democrats and Republicans. As capital combined into increasingly large units, arguments against worker protections based on a supposedly neutral right to contract between the lone worker and the giant corporation struck Populists, Progressives, and many Republicans and Democrats as fraudulent. As the carpetbagger and radical Republican novelist Albion Tourgee wrote, "The power of wealth, is just as properly subject to restraint as that of the biceps and is even more liable to abuse."[16]

Many saw the problem as a reincarnation of the struggle against the "slave power." "The unholy and lawless determination to acquire wealth and personal comfort at the expense of a weaker and less fortunate race, was the underlying spirit of slavery," wrote Populist James B. Weaver. But "in the very midst of the struggle for overthrow of the slave oligarchy, our institutions were assailed by another foe mightier than the former, equally cruel, wider in its field of operation, infinitely greater in wealth, and immeasurably more difficult to control." Weaver added, "It will be readily understood that we allude to the sudden growth of corporate power."[17] Theodore Roosevelt put it this way in his 1912 presidential campaign:

> The only way in which our people can increase their power over the big corporation that does wrong, the only way in which they can protect the working man in his conditions of work and life, the only way in which the people can prevent children working in industry or secure women an eight-hour day in industry, or secure compensation for men killed or crippled in industry, is by extending, instead of limiting, the power of government. There was once a time in history when the limitation of governmental power meant increasing liberty for the people. In the present day the limitation of governmental power, of governmental action, means the enslavement of the people by the great corporations who can only be held in check through the extension of governmental power.[18]

The modern progressive view is typified by the philosopher of science Karl Popper in *The Open Society and Its Enemies*:

> Freedom ... defeats itself, if it is unlimited. Unlimited freedom means that a strong man is free to bully one who is weak and to rob him of his freedom. This is why we demand that the state should limit freedom to a certain extent, so that everyone's freedom is protected by law. Nobody should be at the *mercy* of others, but all should have a *right* to be protected by the state.
>
> Now ... these considerations, originally meant to apply to the realm of brute-force, of physical intimidation, must be applied to the economic realm also. Even if the state protects its citizens from being bullied by physical violence ... it may defeat our ends by its failure to protect them from the misuse of economic power. In such a state, the economically strong is still free to bully one who is economically weak, and to rob him of his freedom. ... [U]nlimited economic freedom can be just as self-defeating as unlimited physical freedom, and economic power may be nearly as dangerous as physical violence; for those who possess a surplus of food can force those who are starving into a "freely" accepted servitude, without

using violence. . . . [A] minority which is economically strong may in this way exploit the majority of those who are economically weak.[19]

Popper suggested that these problems had been addressed by state regulation of child labor, limitations of the hours of labor, unemployment insurance, worker safety laws, and so on.

In the early twentieth century, Progressives rejected concepts of economic liberty that severely limited state power, and they often associated appeals to individual rights with claims that economic power should be unrestrained. As David Rabban and Mark Graber have shown, the Progressive attack on the rhetoric of rights led some Progressives to skepticism about claims to an individual right to free speech.[20] But the suppression of speech and press that accompanied World War I appalled many progressives and gave them a new appreciation for the importance of First Amendment rights.

During the Great Depression, a new progressive synthesis emerged. Government regulation of economic matters would be acceptable if the regulation passed a weak test of rationality, which the government almost never failed. The New Deal Supreme Court soon rejected claims, accepted by earlier courts, of a liberty of contract that limited governmental power over economic matters. These decisions, together with a broad interpretation of the commerce clause, made possible the national minimum wage, maximum hours, worker safety, collective bargaining laws, as well as bans on child labor. Meanwhile, Bill of Rights liberties such as freedom of speech, of the press, of assembly and of religion often received a much higher level of protection. New Deal liberals embraced the views of Justice Brandeis in *Whitney v. California* and strongly protected most speech on public affairs from governmental suppression. They saw free speech as a basic American right. (There were exceptions: commercial speech got no protection from the New Deal Court, corporate participation in politics had been limited by reforms since the Progressive era, and the Supreme Court later upheld rules requiring some balance of views on radio and television.) Much free speech doctrine emerged from this synthesis.

Today the synthesis faces new challenges. Some attack the idea that economic liberties such as liberty of contract should receive minimal protection, while others criticize broad rules protecting speech from suppression.[21] There are serious reasons to fear that our system of freedom of expression is threatened by increasing concentration of wealth and power. These may leave us with a political system responsive to wealthy contributors rather than to voters and a system of mass communication that is both able and inclined to filter information provided to the American people in the interest of a corporate bottom line.[22] How to evaluate these problems and respond to them while preserving the essence of free speech and democracy is the most pressing problem facing those who wish to retain the kernel as well as the shell of free speech and democracy.

A market economy can promote both greater wealth and democracy; it does not lead to equality of wealth. But how such an economy is organized has a crucial bearing on democracy. American history suggests that a variety of economic arrangements are compatible with a successful market economy. Long ago Alexis de Tocqueville recognized that laws that affect the distribution of wealth, such as the laws of inheritance, are crucial constitutional arrangements that can silently produce either a democracy or an aristocracy.[23] James Madison had similar insights. He advocated "political equality among all," to avoid a group's exerting political influence out of proportion to its numbers. In pursuit of this goal, Madison favored "withholding unnecessary opportunities from a few to increase the inequality of property, by immoderate, and especially unmerited, accumulation of riches." He supported "the silent operation of laws, which, without violating the rights of property, reduce extreme wealth towards a state of mediocrity, and raise extreme indigence towards a state of comfort."[24]

The power of money to limit democracy was recognized early in our history. Democracy and free speech, as the *Boston Advocate* insisted, were principles that recognized "moral and mental power" as superior to wealth or physical force. Antislavery and other free speech advocates rejected claims that entrenched economic power ought to have its way. Republicans saw slavery as a dangerous "slave power" that sought to use its economic and political power to threaten democracy and free speech.[25] Abraham Lincoln recognized the tendency of concentrated wealth—in that case of slave owners—to establish laws to promote its economic interests, even when those interests collide with fundamental rights or with the interests of the public at large.[26]

All of this suggests that progressive taxation and laws limiting economic concentration—including media concentration—are devices that deserve careful exploration by those who would preserve both democracy and free speech. It further suggests that laws that increase the opportunity of all citizens, regardless of wealth, to understand and participate in public affairs (such as public finance for candidates who qualify and choose it, a broadly available free public forum for speech, and a general right of access to computers and the Internet), are crucial for democracy and free speech.

Lessons from History

Dangerous Speech in Historical Perspective

The South suppressed abolitionist speech before the Civil War, but, unhappily, the South was not unique. The Federalists also insisted on prosecuting political opinion critical of the John Adams administration. The Lincoln administration prosecuted antiwar speech during the Civil War, as did the Wilson administration during World War I.

Again and again, people in power have treated speech that advocated lawful change through the democratic process as an incitement to lawless action or as tending to produce lawlessness. This fact illuminates an important function of Justice Brandeis's clear-and-present-danger test and the speech-protective test that the Supreme Court adopted in the *Brandenburg* case.[27]

Only imminent and serious evil can justify repression, Brandeis insisted. He said even calls for violating the law should be protected if they do not threaten lawless action before discussion can take place. This conclusion followed from Brandeis's belief that the fitting remedy for bad counsels was good ones. The idea that counterspeech is the most fitting remedy for dangerous statements had roots deep in the popular free speech tradition.

The Brandeis test protects vigorous democratic political dissent in practice by overprotecting it in theory. The ease with which the critics of the Federalists, the abolitionists, the Republicans of 1856 to 1860, and critics of the Civil War and World War I were charged with advocating violence or law violation or fitted into the category of bad tendency suggests the need for a tough test to prevent suppression of dissent. From today's perspective, most of these suppressions were wrong. Bad tendency and incitement as justifications to suppress speech are like icebergs; much of their potential for silencing dissent lies below the surface. Rationales for suppression slide smoothly over less compelling cases. (Of course, in the case of abolition, of antislavery speech on the eve of the Civil War, in the Civil War itself, and in World War I, some *did* advocate violence.)

A second lesson may be drawn from this history. Tests for the suppression of speech are not applied by disinterested scientists. Instead, the rules are typically deployed by political combatants. These are the people who pass repressive legislation and decide to prosecute. Even judges are often quite political in their decisions, as the *Worth* case, the Sedition Act cases, and many World War I cases show.[28]

Suppression theories typically are not applied with an even hand. Federalists insisted on prosecuting "lies" (very broadly defined) published by Republicans but showed no interest whatever in prosecuting falsehoods by their own newspapers. Southern secessionists quoted from Hinton Helper's book, *The Impending Crisis of the South*, to show the need for secession. No one prosecuted them. But Republicans in the South could not quote Helper to argue for emancipation, or even publicly endorse their presidential candidate. Critics of the Civil War and World War I were prosecuted; supporters were not. During World War I, Joseph Gilbert, a leader of the radical Nonpartisan League, was prosecuted for an antiwar speech he allegedly made against enlisting.[29] A historian of the event concludes that the charges were manufactured as part of a political vendetta: the bad tendency test made the task of the prosecutor much easier.[30]

The history of free speech shows the need for broadly protective free speech rules applied generally and equally. A political debate in which one side is harried by prosecutions while the other is left to operate without restraint is a mockery. Criminal (or civil) libel laws and bad tendency tests must be strictly confined because they can easily be invoked for partisan purposes or to keep issues off the political agenda. Because those in power decide whether to prosecute alleged crimes, and because courts are reluctant to second-guess decisions not to prosecute, more than a rule of equality is required. When one side controls the prosecutor, a general rule against political lies or calls to unlawful action will not, in practice, be applied to both sides of the political dispute. So protection for freedom of speech requires limiting the available rationales for suppression.

Speech and Harms in American History

Free speech has its risks. Slave owners insisted that antislavery speech injured their feelings, undermined their status in the national community, and threatened slave revolts. Both Northerners and Southerners warned of the risk of slave revolts and civil war. Even as applied to speech that discountenanced slave revolts while condemning slavery, the fear of revolt was plausible. As William Ellery Channing noted, human events are so interconnected that an evil tendency is easy to hypothesize from a fundamental attack on any major social institution. Furthermore, as Channing also recognized, there are always some people likely to turn to violence in an effort to right perceived wrongs. So a strong denunciation of slavery (or a line from the Declaration of Independence) could lead to violence. As Southerners saw it, they were sitting on a powder keg, and opponents of slavery were lighting matches. Their fears were not baseless. There *had* been slave revolts. Sometimes, at least, criticism of slavery seems to have contributed to plans to rebel.[31]

Still, banning discussion of peaceful ways to end slavery was unacceptable and also had its own risks. Since slavery was increasingly excluded from the democratic process in the South, eventual violence was likely. Some of the hysteria about antislavery speech was manufactured for political purposes: slaveholders had strategic reasons for fanning fears of slave revolts and massacres of whites. The hysteria over slave revolts helped to silence democratic threats to masters' slave property and to support the cause of secession. But secession produced civil war, and, ironically, emancipation.

Judge Learned Hand faced the issue of harms squarely in the World War I Espionage Act case involving *The Masses,* a radical journal. The Espionage Act prohibited obstructing recruitment or causing insubordination in the military, and it closed the mails to publications that violated the act. Broadly interpreting the act, the postmaster of New York City excluded *The Masses* from the mails because of its antiwar articles. Hand's opinion in the case frankly recognized that such publications could in fact result in the harms the statute sought to prevent, but he construed the statute narrowly:

> Political agitation, by the passions it arouses or the convictions it engenders, may in fact stimulate men to the violation of law. Detestation of existing policies is easily transformed into forcible resistance . . . and it would be folly to disregard the causal relation be-

tween the two. Yet to assimilate agitation, legitimate as such with direct incitement to violent resistance, is to disregard the tolerance of all methods of political agitation which in normal times is a safeguard of free government. The distinction is not a scholastic subterfuge, but a hard-bought acquisition in the fight for freedom.[32]

Hand's opinion recognized both the harm caused by agitation and the harm caused by suppression and, despite the harm agitation might engender, sought to protect the democratic function of free speech.

Of course, reactionary speech, like progressive speech, also threatens harms. As some opponents of slavery recognized, press attacks on abolitionists and the misrepresentation of their views contributed to anti-abolition mobs, led by gentlemen of property and standing. Misrepresentations probably contributed to the death of Elijah Lovejoy. During Reconstruction, the press in North Carolina, for example, was overwhelmingly anti-Republican. It grossly vilified and misrepresented the Republican Party, closed its papers to corrections of its factual mistakes, and reveled in racist stereotyping. The press in the North was also quite critical of Reconstruction.[33] Press hostility to Reconstruction may have made Klan violence seem more benign to many people. These facts might lead one to conclude that the problem was insufficient control over the press—too much freedom of speech rather than too little.

Still, the problem facing abolitionists and Republicans during Reconstruction was not too much commitment to free speech (and democracy) but too little. Violence was especially tempting because so many in the South rejected the legitimacy of free speech and democratic action about either slavery or race. The weakness of the popular free speech tradition (especially in the South) encouraged violence that did not end with the Civil War. As Albion Tourgee saw it, techniques developed to silence critics of slavery (and the South's rejection of free speech) were revived during Reconstruction to silence those who supported civil and political rights for blacks.[34]

Suppression Theories in the Light of History

Today, some justify limiting speech by appealing to concepts such as group libel, adverse emotional effects resulting from some political speech, the tendency of some speech to produce harm, and the idea that core constitutional values make certain messages illegitimate. It may be tempting to dismiss advocates of revision as insignificant because their claims are not supported by current Supreme Court decisions. But the popular development of free speech ideas in America shows the importance of taking popular legal claims seriously, long before the courts embrace them. Ironically, suppression theories advocated by modern critics resemble historic rationales for limiting antislavery speech. This fact does not prove that current plans to shrink free speech protection are wrong as a matter of policy. Attempts to protect the vulnerable are not quite like protecting politically powerful slaveholders. At first blush, different free speech rules for the vulnerable and the dominant may seem to make sense.

The similarity of current suppression theories to those of the past suggests caution. Historic attempts to use these ideas to suppress democratic discussion of positive social change should make us wary of attempts to resurrect them for benevolent purposes. The past use of suppression theories also shows how dissent—both progressive and reactionary—is protected by broadly protective free speech ideas. The free speech tradition did not always succeed in protecting unpopular speech. But where it was strongly held, it often did so. Where the tradition was weakest, suppression and violence were most pervasive. The free speech tradition provided substantial protection for dissenting speech and democracy.

The proponents of restricting speech today may have a ready answer to the history of attempts to suppress antislavery speech, and its invocation of ideas of group libel, protection of the slaveholder from emotional injury, and the bad tendency test. They may argue that antislavery speech should have been protected, but not because of a broad theory of free speech. Instead, they might argue, it should have been protected because it supported the cause of the oppressed.[35] It is most unlikely that in the 1830s such an approach—protect abolitionist speech because it is good or advocates equality and the cause of the oppressed—would have worked. Dissenters by definition reject dominant values. If their only protection comes from the evaluation of the justice of their cause by judges or legislatures, they will not get much protection.

Throughout much of our history, many judges have accepted dominant values. Many judges, like many Americans, initially failed to see oppression in cases where most of us now clearly see it—slavery and discrimination against free blacks before the Civil War, the status of women in the nineteenth century, or of African Americans segregated and denied the right to vote in the South after Reconstruction. Broad ideas of free speech—when they have been accepted—have made it possible to challenge dominant values whether or not those in power found the system oppressive.

A crucial test came when Southerners and others demanded that Northern legislatures pass laws suppressing abolitionist speech and associations. In the end, the North refused to pass these laws, even though abolitionists were quite unpopular and support for equality for blacks was slim indeed. The effort failed because many in the North believed in a broad free speech right to discuss public issues. Although many conceded that abolitionist speech had bad tendencies and most seemed to think the nation would be much better off without it, they feared that the precedent of suppressing abolitionist speech would inevitably spread. In the language of today's critics, they could be dismissed as embracing the fallacy of the slippery slope—the idea that one suppression will inevitably lead to more. But there is a more sympathetic way of understanding their concerns. Northerners were unwilling to trust suppression of speech to doctrines increasing the discretion of public officials, for fear that discretion would be abused.[36]

The history of the Sedition Act, of the controversy over antislavery speech from 1830 to 1860, and the suppression of antiwar speech, all raise crucial questions: Can doctrines like group libel, broad punishment for advocacy of law violation, the idea that speech on certain topics is foreclosed by other constitutional values, and the bad tendency test be retooled for this century without at the same time providing a handy tool for suppressing dissent? Can we be sure that the politically dominant will not seize and adapt such rules to silence their critics?[37] Might a version of these doctrines have been used against progressive political movements such as the crusade against slavery, the civil rights movement, or the struggle for women's rights? (The founding declaration of the women's rights movement could have been viewed as group libel of men, since it asserted "repeated injuries and usurpations on the part of man toward woman, having in direct object the establishment of an absolute tyranny over her.")[38] Will those in power confine the operation of the rules in the ways suggested by critics of broad free speech rights? Will the new rules be used to silence valuable dissent on issues none of us can foresee? Consider the frequent failures of courts to protect free speech and democracy before the present tests were in place. How much protection would we have had for dissenting political speech if the public had broadly rejected the central ideas of the popular free speech tradition? At critical times, broad ideas of free speech have provided protection for progressive political dissidents. Departures from those ideas have provided rationales for suppression.[39]

The more deeply one understands the times, the better one can understand the plausibility of fears of serious harm that led to suppression. At the time they are expressed, these fears always look powerful and compelling. It was for this reason that Justice Brandeis was loath to justify suppression based on fear of serious injury or the simple bad tendency of speech.

The decisions of the Supreme Court from the 1930s through the 1960s increased protection for public discourse. Though these decisions may have suffered some recent erosion,[40] so far they remain largely in place. They have protected progressives and reactionaries, advocates of racial equality and racists. As a result of these decisions, we naturally tend to forget the very serious attacks on free speech, democracy, and public discourse that have characterized so much of American history. Today many tend to be aware of the real harms speech can inflict and to discount the dangers of suppression. They forget the long history that gave rise to the protective free speech ideas of Justice Brandeis and the Warren Court.

It is grossly inadequate to consider only the narrow judicial effect of the changes critics demand. Instead we must try to evaluate the effect of the changes on the consensus in favor of free speech. The effort of 1835–36 to suppress abolitionist speech failed in the North, not because of judicial decisions and certainly not because abolitionist speech was seen as worthy or on behalf of the oppressed. Instead, it failed because of a consensus that suppression of political speech with bad tendencies was too dangerous to undertake. Had the public been convinced that such scruples were foolish, the widespread distaste for abolitionists, together with the conviction that abolitionist doctrines were dangerous indeed, would probably have resulted in suppression.[41]

Free speech, like democratic elections, provides a framework, not a result. At times in American history, the powerful have used their power to subvert the democratic process by stealing votes or intimidating voters. These democratic failures have been contained by a deep belief that vote stealing and intimidation are illegitimate—by a belief in democracy. At times, the powerful have denied free speech even on political questions to those with less power. These deprivations have also been limited because of a belief in free speech. Indeed, the stronger the public commitment to democracy and free speech, the more dangerous such tactics are for those who practice them.

Those victimized by vote stealing or denials of free speech on political questions might respond, when they have the power to do so, by stealing votes or denying free speech to their opponents. Their opponents could then respond in kind when they have the opportunity. The result would be an unraveling of the democratic process. These observations do not suggest that careful, precise, and limited changes in the free speech or free election framework will destroy democracy. Indeed, wise changes could strengthen democracy. They do suggest that broadly rejecting the central principles of the free speech tradition and establishing broad and vague rules to allow suppression are far more dangerous than critics suppose.

FINAL REFLECTIONS

It would be satisfying, as this book concludes, to present the ultimate solution to free speech conundrums. Instead, the moral I draw from these free speech stories is the modest suggestion that logic and philosophy must be tempered by experience.[42] Plans for radical surgery (by amendment or otherwise) to cure the defects of free speech doctrine should be assessed in the light of the vicarious experience afforded by history. The meaning of that experience will depend on several factors, including how one interprets the history and one's view of the role of history in constitutional law.

The Legacy of the Free Speech Tradition

Many of the supporters of the popular free speech tradition saw themselves as combatants in a profoundly important constitutional struggle. They took the right to free speech seriously and discussed it extensively. When they saw free speech threatened, even by plans to suppress the speech of those with whom they passionately disagreed, they carefully considered what the incursions meant for the idea of free speech. They recognized that a free speech regime that did not protect unpopular and hated ideas was an empty concept. Even in the midst of civil war, many prowar advocates of the free speech tradition insisted on protection for antiwar speech.

Advocates of the free speech tradition also recognized the crucial function of free speech in a democracy. Because they understood democracy as providing citizens with the right to present and consider a range of choices about public affairs, they passionately resisted efforts to restrict the range of ideas to which "we the people of the United States" had access. Because they saw that a national democracy could not operate if half the nation was closed to free speech, they insisted on national protection for free speech. Finally, many supporters of the free speech tradition were conscientious students of the history of liberty. They saw history as a way to understand the reasons for guarantees of liberty and the dangers of abuses of power.

Today some seem to suggest jettisoning central parts of our free speech tradition: discarding rules against government-enforced orthodoxy, discarding rules that seek to treat competing ideas in an equal fashion, selective revival of the bad tendency test, and dismantling the strong version of the clear-and-present-danger test that Justice Brandeis did so much to craft. Some even advocate freeing states from the commands of the national Bill of Rights.

The central ideas of our free speech tradition have been crucial for democratic government and the right to dissent. They were achieved only after years of struggle by courageous people willing to brave mobs, jails, and even death. Many serious national problems can be traced to the rejection of free speech and democracy in American history—from the refusal to allow democratic discussion about peacefully ending slavery in the pre–Civil War South to the violent end of Reconstruction. Once we understand the abuses of power that prompted the free speech tradition, we can better understand the risk of abandoning it.

The battles for free speech and democracy in American history show what the free speech tradition is about. That is not to say that current ideas of free speech are perfect or that Supreme Court doctrine should be protected from criticism and revision. That is not so. For better or worse, each generation adapts and applies the rules and traditions of the past to the problems of the present. Change is necessary and inevitable. (In addition, we should explore creative solutions to more free speech dilemmas. These include teaching and practicing mediation and conflict resolution and the teaching and practice of tolerance.)[43]

But revision without an understanding of the reasons for the popular free speech tradition and the constitutional protections it produced is likely to be both shallow and dangerous. Only by understanding the recurring attempts to silence dissent in American history can we appreciate what the creators of our free speech tradition achieved. The free speech tradition is our legacy from citizen activists —men and women, black and white, Republicans and Democrats, Southerners and Northerners—who struggled and suffered to make the American ideal of free speech and democracy a reality. Preservation of their legacy for future generations will be more likely if we understand, and thoughtfully reflect on, the meaning of their struggle.

NOTES

INTRODUCTION

1   Hinton Rowan Helper, *The Impending Crisis of the South: How to Meet It* 35–39, 62–66, 116, 149, 175–79 (George M. Fredrickson ed., Harvard University Press 1968) (1857) [hereafter Helper]. For a fuller discussion of these events see chapters 11 and 12 infra.

2   Helper, supra note 1, at 149.

3   Id. at 149; quoted in "A False and Genuine Helper," *Richmond Whig*, Jan. 8, 1860, at 4.

4   David M. Potter, *The Impending Crisis, 1848–1861*, at 387 (1976); "Revolutionary Designs of the Abolitionists—New York Names Endorsing Treason," *N.Y. Herald*, Nov. 26, 1859, at 4.

5   State v. Worth, 52 N.C. 488 (1860).

6   32 U.S. 243 (1833).

7   Robert Cortner, *The Supreme Court and the Second Bill of Rights* (1981). For a discussion of free speech in the period after the Civil War and through World War I, see David Rabban, *Free Speech in Its Forgotten Years* (1997).

8   Akhil Reed Amar, *The Bill of Rights: Creation and Reconstruction* 36–37 (1998).

9   5 *Annals of Cong.* 2151 (1798).

10 See generally chapters 2 and 3.

11 See generally chapters 4–13.

12 See chapters 14 and 15.

13 See Brandenburg v. Ohio, 395 U.S. 444 (1969); Bond v. Floyd, 385 U.S. 110 (1966); Cohen v. California, 403 U.S. 15 (1971); Texas v. Johnson, 491 U.S. 397 (1989). But see Dennis v. United States, 341 U.S. 494 (1951).

14 See Robert C. Post, "The Constitutional Concept of Public Discourse: Outrageous Opinion, Democratic Deliberation, and *Hustler Magazine v. Falwell*," 103 *Harv. L. Rev.* 601 (1990). The public domain is also bounded by the line between *places* where speech is generally protected against government suppression—in newspapers, on television, on public sidewalks and in public parks—and the places where it may be prohibited.

15 Edwards v. South Carolina, 372 U.S. 229 (1963).

16   New York Times v. Sullivan, 376 U.S. 254 (1964).

17   Brandenburg v. Ohio, 395 U.S. 444 (1969).

18   West Virginia Board of Education v. Barnette, 319 U.S. 624 (1943).

19   Bond v. Floyd, 385 U.S. 110 (1966).

20   Texas v. Johnson, 491 U.S. 397 (1989).

21   Cohen v. California, 403 U.S. 15 (1971).

22   Edwards v. South Carolina, 372 U.S. 229, 237 (1963) citing Terminiello v. Chicago, 337 U.S. 1 (1949).

23   2 *The Bill of Rights: A Documentary History* 1031 (Bernard Schwartz ed., 1971).

24   Barron v. Baltimore, 32 U.S. 243 (1833). The rule was applied to the freedom of religion under the First Amendment in Permoli v. New Orleans, 44 U.S. 589 (1845).

25   See, e.g., State v. Worth, 52 N.C. 488 (1860); note 27 infra; Patterson v. Colorado, 205 U.S. 454, 462 (1907).

26   See generally chapters 12 and 13.

27   Commonwealth v. Karvonen, 106 N.E. 556, 557 (Mass. 1914). For a discussion of early cases, see David Rabban, "The First Amendment in Its Forgotten Years," 90 *Yale L.J.* 514 (1981); Michael Gibson, "Freedom of Expression from 1791 to 1917," 55 *Fordham. L. Rev.* 263 (1986) [hereafter "Freedom of Expression"].

28   106 N.E. at 557. See generally David Rabban, "The First Amendment in Its Forgotten Years," 90 *Yale L.J.* 514 (1981) (emphasizing the limited protection of free speech in the years between the Civil War and World War I); "Freedom of Expression," supra note 27 (emphasizing some speech-protective decisions).

29   See, e.g., Texas v. Johnson, 491 U.S. 397 (1989); Stromberg v. California, 283 U.S. 359 (1931); Brandenburg v. Ohio, 395 U.S. 444 (1969).

30   Harry Kalven Jr., *The Negro and the First Amendment* 140 (1965); Daniel A. Farber, *The First Amendment* 106–07 (1998).

31   205 U.S. 454 (1907).

32   205 U.S. at 462.

33   Marshall v. Gordon, 243 U.S. 521 (1917); Gandia, v. Pettingill, 222 U.S. 452, 457 (1912); "Freedom of Expression," supra note 27, at 283.

34   "Freedom of Expression," supra note 27, at 263, 285 n.41.

35   David Rabban, *Free Speech in Its Forgotten Years* 2, ch. 3 (1998); for protective decisions see, e.g., id. at 132, 156; Hamilton v. Eno, 81 N.Y. 116 (1880); Diener v. Star Chronicle Publ. Co., 132 S.W. 1143 (1910); Coleman v. MacLennan, 98 P. 281 (Kan. 1908); People v. Altman, 241 App. Div. 858; *In re* Hartman, 182 Cal. 447 (1920) (red flag cases); *In re* Campbell, 64 Cal. App. 300 (1923)(IWW); see Zachariah Chafee Jr., *Free Speech in the United States* 159–66 (1941); Chafee insisted that pre–World War I twentieth-century bad tendency decisions were inconsistent with free speech principles. E.g., id. at 164, 162 n.30, 163 n.32; 167 n.45. See also Zachariah Chafee Jr., *Freedom of Speech* 8, 9, 186–88 (1920).

36   E.g., Debs v. United States, 249 U.S. 211 (1919); Gilbert v. Minnesota, 254 U.S. 325 (1920); Schenk v. United States 249 U.S. 47 (1919). In *Schenk*, the Court noted that Schenk had sent his criticisms of the draft to recruits. For an account of Gilbert's

trial, see Carol E. Jensen, "Agrarian Reforms and the Politics of Loyalty," in *Historic U.S. Court Cases, 1690–1990*, at 498 (John W. Johnson ed., 1992).

37 Recent scholarship has done much to document the existence of protective ideas of free speech outside the court from the 1870s to World War I. See David M. Rabban, *Free Speech in Its Forgotten Years* (1997). See also Mark Graber, *Transforming Free Speech: The Ambiguous Legacy of Civil Libertarianism* (1991).

38 See, e.g., *Cong. Globe*, 35th Cong., 2d Sess. 982–84 (Rep. Bingham's reading of art. IV, sec. 2, to protect national privileges of citizens) (1859); *Cong. Globe*, 36th Cong., 1st Sess., app. 205 (Rep. Lovejoy) (1860); *Cong. Globe*, 38th Cong., 1st Sess. 1202 (Rep. James Wilson) (1864); *Cong. Globe*, 39th Cong., 1st Sess. 1072, 1075 (1866) (Sen. Nye). Joel Tiffany, *Treatise on the Unconstitutionality of American Slavery* 55–58, 97–99, 139–40 (1849); Michael Kent Curtis, *No State Shall Abridge: The Fourteenth Amendment and the Bill of Rights* 43–56, 59–61 (1986) [hereafter Curtis, *No State Shall Abridge*]. See also chapters 9–12, infra.

39 See, e.g., Curtis, *No State Shall Abridge*, supra note 38, chapters 3 and 5.

40 See, e.g., Herndon v. Lowry, 301 U.S. 242 (1937); Stromberg v. California, 283 U.S. 359 (1931); DeJonge v. Oregon, 299 U.S. 353 (1937).

41 E.g., Bond v. Floyd, 385 U.S. 110 (1966); Brandenburg v. Ohio, 395 U.S. 444 (1969).

42 But see, e.g., New York Times v. Sullivan, 376 U.S. 254 (1964). For books that pay substantial attention to free speech history, see William Cohen and Jonathan Varat, *Constitutional Law* 190–99 (1997); William W. Van Alstyne, *First Amendment Cases and Materials* 10–32 (1995).

43 See Phillip Bobbitt, *Constitutional Fate* (1982), for a pioneering discussion of styles of constitutional argument; Charles L. Black Jr., *Structure and Relationship in Constitutional Law* (1969); Akhil Amar, "The Bill of Rights and the Fourteenth Amendment," 101 *Yale L.J.* 1193 (1992) Richard H. Fallon, Jr., "A Constructivist Coherence Theory of Constitutional Interpretation," 100 *Harv. L. Rev.* 1189 (1987) [hereafter Fallon, "Coherence Theory"]; Curtis, *No State Shall Abridge*, supra note 38, at 11.

44 Adamson v. California, 332 U.S. 46, 63 (1947) (Frankfurter, J., concurring) (citing Eisner v. Macomber, 252 U.S. 189, 220 (1920) (Holmes, J., dissenting)).

45 Antonin Scalia, *A Matter of Interpretation: Federal Courts and the Law* 38 (1997). For a very different and quite impressive effort to use history to explain the meaning of the Constitution, see Bruce Ackerman, *We the People: Transformations* (1998).

46 See, e.g., Fred Arthur Bailey, "Free Speech and the Lost Cause in the Old Dominion," 103 *Va. Mag. Hist. and Bio.* 237 (1995) (Virginia conservatives' largely successful battle to present a history of the Civil War favorable to the South and to purge textbooks and teachers who questioned the wisdom of the Civil War and of the antebellum slaveholding elite). For a recent debate, see, e.g., Laurie Goodstein, "Fresh Debate on 1802 Jefferson Letter," *N.Y. Times*, Sept. 10, 1998.

47 From C. Vann Woodward, *American Attitudes Toward History* 1–20 (1968) reprinted in *Historian as Detective* 30 (1981).

48 Colin Rhys Lovell, *English Constitutional and Legal History* 112–13 (1962). For Rep-

resentative John Bingham's statement that the Magna Carta protected only free men while the due process clause protected all persons, see *Cong. Globe*, 39th Cong., 1st Sess. 1292 (1866).

49 Charles Miller, *The Supreme Court and the Uses of History* 50 (1969).

50 For a powerful argument that certain political decisions are equivalent to constitutional amendments, see, e.g., Bruce Ackerman, *We the People: Transformations* (1998).

51 *Cong. Globe*, 39th Cong., 1st Sess. 227 (1866); Curtis, *No State Shall Abridge*, supra note 38, at 56 (1986).

52 Henry Mayer, *All on Fire: William Lloyd Garrison and the Abolition of Slavery* 200–10, 402 (1998).

53 See chapters 10 and 11.

54 E.g., "Sound the Alarm," 2 *Emancipator* 133 (Dec. 28, 1837) (quoting *Herald of Freedom*); *Memoir of the Rev. Elijah P. Lovejoy* 300 (Joseph C. and Owen Lovejoy eds., New York, Arno Press, 1968) (1838); Seymour B. Treadwell, *American Liberties and American Slavery: Morally and Politically Illustrated*, at xxxvii (Negro Univ. Press 1969) (1838).

55 See generally, Steven Shiffrin, "The Politics of the Mass Media and the Free Speech Principle," 69 *Ind. L.J.* 689 (1994).

56 Slaughter-House Cases, 83 U.S. 36 (1872); United States v. Cruikshank, 92 U.S. 542 (1876); Maxwell v. Dow, 176 U.S. 581 (1900); Curtis, *No State Shall Abridge*, supra note 38, at 88, 49–56, 171–96.

57 Gitlow v. New York, 268 U.S. 652 (1925).

58 For discussion of such ideas, see Robert Post, "Recuperating First Amendment Doctrine," 47 *Stan. L. Rev.* 1249, 1276 (1995); Mark A. Graber, "Old Wine in New Bottles: The Constitutional Status of Unconstitutional Speech," 48 *Vand. L. Rev.* 349 (1995); Eugene Volokh, "The Constitutional Tension Method," 3 *U. Chi. L. Sch. Roundtable* 223 et seq. (1996); Michael Kent Curtis, "Critics of 'Free Speech' and the Uses of the Past," 12 *Const. Comm.* 29 (1995).

59 The metaphor comes from Randy E. Barnett, "Reconceiving the Ninth Amendment," 74 *Cornell L. Rev.* 1, 23–34 (1988).

1 The English and Colonial Background

1 Charles A. Miller, *The Supreme Court and the Uses of History* 173 (1969); see also Bernard Bailyn, *The Ideological Origins of the American Revolution* (1976) [hereafter Bailyn, *Ideological Origins*].

2 1 *The Bill of Rights: A Documentary History* 17–21 (Bernard Schwartz ed., 1971) [hereafter Schwartz, *Documentary History*].

3 J. R. Tanner, *English Constitutional Conflicts of the Seventeenth Century, 1603–1689*, at 36–67 (Greenwood Press 1983) (1928).

4 *An Agreement of the People* (1647), in *Leveller Manifestos of the Puritan Revolution*, at 230 (Don M. Wolfe ed., 1967) [hereafter Wolfe, *Leveller Manifestos*]; for the later version, see *Agreement of the People* (1649), in id. at 337–50.

5   Edmund S. Morgan, *Inventing the People: The Rise of Popular Sovereignty in England and America* 60–73 (1988); see *A Remonstrance of Many Thousand Citizens* (1646), in Wolfe, *Leveller Manifestos*, supra note 4, at 119.

6   For a fine biography, see Pauline Gregg, *Free-Born John: A Biography of John Lilburne* (1961); for a brief account of Lilburne and the Levellers, see Michael Kent Curtis, "In Pursuit of Liberty: The Levellers and the American Bill of Rights," 8 *Const. Comm.* 359 (1991) [hereafter Curtis, "Levellers"].

7   William Walwyn, *Englands Lamentable Slaverie*, in 3 *Tracts on Liberty in the Puritan Revolution*, at 313–14 (William Haller ed., 1979) [hereafter Haller, *Tracts on Liberty*].

8   E.g., Leonard Levy, *Origins of the Fifth Amendment* 313 (1968); 1 James Fitzgerald Stephen, *History of the Criminal Law of England* 367 (Burt Franklin 1973) (1883) [hereafter Stephen, *History of the Criminal Law*]; Henry Noel Brailsford, *The Levellers and the English Revolution* 640 (1961) [hereafter Brailsford, *The Levellers*]. For earlier accounts of the Levellers, see, e.g., Theodore C. Pease, *The Leveller Movement* (1915); Joseph Frank, *The Levellers* (1955). For the Levellers and criminal jury trial, see Thomas C. Greene, *Verdict According to Conscience: Perspectives on the English Criminal Trial Jury, 1200–1800*, at 153–99 (1985). For recent scholarship on the Fifth Amendment, see John H. Langbein, "The Historical Origins of the Privilege Against Self-Incrimination at Common Law," 92 *Mich. L. Rev.* 1047 (1994); Eben Moglen, "Taking the Fifth; Reconsidering the Origins of the Constitutional Privilege Against Self-Incrimination," 92 *Mich. L. Rev.* 1086 (1994).

9   Curtis, "Levellers," supra note 6, at 381–86.

10 *Agreement of the People*, sec. X (1649), in *The Leveller Tracts, 1647–1653*, at 323–24 (William Haller and Godfrey Davis eds., 1964) [hereafter *Leveller Tracts*]. The agreement went through several versions.

11 William Walwyn, *The Compassionate Samaritan*, in 3 Haller, *Tracts on Liberty*, supra note 7, at 61, 71.

12 Id. at 86.

13 Richard Overton, *An Appeal* (1647), in Wolfe, *Leveller Manifestos*, supra note 4, at 157, 162.

14 Richard Overton, *A Remonstrance of Many Thousand Citizens* (1646), in Wolfe, *Leveller Manifestos*, supra note 4, at 113, 122.

15 Walwyn's *Just Defense* (1649), in *Leveller Tracts*, supra note 10, at 350, 368.

16 John Lilburne, *The Just Defense of John Lilburne* (1653), in *Leveller Tracts*, supra note 10, at 450, 455.

17 Fredrick S. Siebert, *Freedom of the Press in England, 1476–1776*, at 381(1965).

18 Id. at 120–21, 166, 270.

19 Id. at 4, 141–46, 182, 260–63.

20 Colin Rhys Lovell, *English Constitutional and Legal History: A Survey* 412–13 (1962) [hereafter Lovell, *English Constitutional History*].

21 E.g., 4 *Cobbett's Collection of State Trials and Proceedings for High Treason and Other Crimes and Misdemeanors*, 1270 (1 Car. 2 (1649)) (Thomas Bayly Howell ed., London, R. Bagshaw 1809)—Lilburne trial for treason [hereafter *State Trials*]; Thomas Green, *Verdict According to Conscience: Perspectives on the English Crimi-*

nal Trial Jury, 1200–1800, at 192–99 (1985); 1 Schwartz, *Documentary History*, supra note 2, at 144–58 (trial of William Penn); The trial of the seven bishops, 12 *State Trials* 183 (4 Jam. 2 (1688)).

22 See Leonard W. Levy, *The Emergence of a Free Press* 24–25, 37–45, 128–29, 156–58, 212, 285 (1985); Akhil Reed Amar, *The Bill of Rights* 72 n.*; Thomas Cooley, *Constitutional Limitations* 460–61 (Legal Classics Library 1987) (1868); 1 *Documentary History*, supra note 2, at 152 (trial of William Penn); in Penn's case the jury's first verdict, which the court rejected as inadequate to support a conviction was "Guilty of speaking in Gracious-street." When required to find Penn guilty as charged or not guilty, it found him not guilty; Libel Act of 1792 (ch. 60).

23 Wolfe, *Leveller Manifestos*, supra note 4, at 323.

24 William Walwyn, *The Compassionate Samaritan* (1644), in Haller, *Tracts on Liberty*, supra note 7, at 63, 84.

25 *To the Right Honourable, the Supreme Authority of this Nation, the Commons of England* (1649), in Wolfe, *Leveller Manifestos*, supra note 4, at 326, 327–28.

26 Id. at 328.

27 John Milton, *"Areopagitica" and "Of Education"* 18, 42, 45, 49, 51 (George Sabine ed., 1951).

28 4 *State Trials* 1270, 1367.

29 Richard Overton, *An Appeal* (1647), in Wolfe, *Leveller Manifestos*, supra note 4, at 239–40.

30 *An Agreement of the People* (1647), in Wolfe, *Leveller Manifestos*, supra note 4, at 230. The idea of fundamental law died in England but lived on in America. See J. W. Gough, *Fundamental Law in English Constitutional History* (Fred B. Rothman 1985) (1955); Bailyn, *Ideological Origins*, supra note 1, at 180–84, 187 (early American ideas of the functions of a constitution).

31 See Richard Ashcraft, *Revolutionary Politics and Locke's Two Treatises of Government* 149, 164–65, 165 n.145, 208–09, 243–48 (1986); Brailsford, *The Levellers*, supra note 8, at 640; F. Donnelly, "The Levellers and Early Nineteenth Century Radicalism," 49 *Bull. of Soc'y for the Study of Lab. Hist.* 24 (1984); Caroline Robbins, *The Eighteenth-Century Commonwealth Man: Studies in the Transmission, Development, and Circumstance of English Liberal Thought from the Restoration of Charles II Until the War with the Thirteen Colonies* 15, 19, 240 (1959); see also Curtis, "Levellers," supra note 6, at 387–93, for examples of apparent influence.

32 1 Schwartz, *Documentary History*, supra note 2, at 144–58 (trial of William Penn and William Mead, 1670).

33 Brailsford, *The Levellers*, supra note 8, at 640; 1 Schwartz, *Documentary History*, supra note 2, at 125–29.

34 John Locke, *Second Treatise on Civil Government: An Essay Concerning the True Original, Extent, and End of Civil Government* (1690), in *Social Contract: Essays by Locke, Hume and Rousseau* 87 (Ernest Barker ed., Oxford Univ. Press 1960); see Leonard Levy, *Emergence of a Free Press* 97, 98 (1985) [hereafter Levy, *Emergence*]; Alan Houston, *Algernon Sidney and the Republican Heritage in England and America* 179, 200–01 (1991) [hereafter Houston, *Algernon Sidney*].

35 Houston, *Algernon Sidney*, supra note 34, at 125 (quoting Sidney's *Maxims*).

36 Id. at 215.

37 David Mayer, "The English Radical Whig Origins of American Constitutionalism," 70 *Washington U. L.Q.* 131, 162–63 (1991) [hereafter Mayer, "Whig Origins"]; Houston, *Algernon Sidney*, supra note 34, at 203–08; Caroline Robbins, *The Eighteenth-Century Commonwealth Man*, 9, 16, 40, 370 (1959).

38 Bailyn, *Ideological Origins*, supra note 1, at 47.

39 1 James Burgh, *Political Disquisitions* 37–38 (Da Capo Press 1971) (1774).

40 E.g., Bailyn, *Ideological Origins*, supra note 1, at 34–37; David Rabban, "The Ahistorical Historian: Leonard Levy on Freedom of Expression in Early American History," 37 *Stan. L. Rev.* 795, 823–29 (1985) [hereafter Rabban, "Ahistorical Historian"].

41 Bailyn, *Ideological Origins*, supra note 1, at 110–12.

42 Rabban, "Ahistorical Historian," supra note 40, at 806–16.

43 J. Trenchard and T. Gordon, 1 *Cato's Letters* lxii–lxxii (Da Capo Press 1971) (1755) [hereafter *Cato's Letters*].

44 Levy, *Emergence*, supra note 34, at 109–10, 113; David A. Anderson, "Origins of the Press Clause," 30 *U.C.L.A. L. Rev.* 455, 524, 527 (1983) [hereafter Anderson, "Press Clause"].

45 Levy, *Emergence*, supra note 34, at 109.

46 1 *Cato's Letters*, supra note 43, at 96 (Letter 15).

47 Id. at 97 (Letter 15); also reprinted in *N.Y. Wkly. J.*, Feb. 18, 1734, and in *Freedom of the Press from Zenger to Jefferson*, at 12 (Leonard Levy ed., 1966) [hereafter Levy, *Zenger to Jefferson*].

48 1 *Cato's Letters*, supra note 43, at 101 (Letter 15).

49 Id. at 246 (Letter 32).

50 Letter, 32, in Levy, *Zenger to Jefferson*, supra note 47, at 16; also reprinted in *N.Y. Wkly. J.*, Feb. 25 and Mar. 4, 1734.

51 1 *Cato's Letters*, supra note 43, at 250.

52 Levy, *Emergence*, supra note 34, at 112.

53 3 *Cato's Letters*, supra note 43, at 301 (Letter 101).

54 Id. at 303–04.

55 3 *Cato's Letters*, supra note 43, at 293 (Letter 100).

56 1 *Cato's Letters*, supra note 43, at 252, 253 (Letter 32); Levy, *Emergence*, supra note 34, at 112.

57 1 *Cato's Letters*, supra note 43, at 96–103, 249, 250, 252–53.

58 Rex v. Tutchin, 14 Howell's State Trials, 1095, 1128 (1704), quoted in 2 Stephen, *History of the Criminal Law*, supra note 8, at 317–18.

59 Paul Finkelman, "Politics, the Press, and the Law: The Trial of John Peter Zenger," in *American Political Trials* at 25–26 (Michael R. Belknap ed., 1994) [hereafter Finkelman, "Zenger Trial"].

60 "The Trial of John Peter Zenger," in *Law and Jurisprudence in American History* at 33–34 (Stephen Presser and Jamil Zainaldin eds., 1995) [hereafter Presser and Zainaldin].

61 For a brief edited version of the trial, see id. at 31–48; Finkelman, "Zenger Trial," supra note 59, at 31–37.

62 1 William Blackstone, *Commentaries on the Laws of England* 156–57 (1765) [hereafter Blackstone, *Commentaries*].

63 George Rude, *Wilkes and Liberty*, 22–57 (1962). "John Wilkes," 21 *Dictionary of National Biography* (1917); "The Writs of Assistance Case," in Presser and Zainaldin, supra note 60, at 55–82.

64 Wilkes v. Wood, 98 Eng. Rep. 489 (C.P. 1763), 19 Howell's State Trials 1153; see also Entick v. Carrington, 95 Eng. Rep. 807 (C.P. 1765), 19 Howell's State Trials 1029. Akhil Reed Amar, *The Bill of Rights: Creation and Reconstruction* 65–70 (1998); Presser and Zainaldin, supra note 60, at 55.

65 George Rude, *Wilkes and Liberty*, 22–57 (1962). "John Wilkes," 21 *Dictionary of National Biography* (1917); Bailyn, *Ideological Origins*, supra note 1, at 110–12.

66 Norman L. Rosenberg, *Protecting the Best Men: An Interpretive History of the Law of Libel* 46 (1986) [hereafter Rosenberg, *Best Men*].

67 Rex v. Twyn, 84 Eng. Rep. 1064 (K. B. 1663); 6 *Cobbett's Complete Collection of State Trials* 513 (1810); William Mayton, "Seditious Libel and the Lost Guarantee of Freedom of Expression," 84 *Col. L. Rev.* 91, 101 (1984) [hereafter Mayton, "Seditious Libel"].

68 Lovell, *English Constitutional History*, supra note 20, at 399. For a discussion of the influence of Whig and Radical Whig ideology on the act, see Alexander H. Shapiro, "Political Theory and the Growth of Defensive Safeguards in Criminal Procedure: The Origins of the Treason Trials Act of 1696," 11 *Law and History Review* 215 (1993).

69 2 Stephen, *History of the Criminal Law*, supra note 8, at 274–75; Mayton, "Seditious Libel," supra note 67, at 102.

70 4 Blackstone, *Commentaries*, supra note 62, at 151–52 (1769).

71 Stephen Smith, "Origins of the Free Speech Clause," in 1991 *Free Speech Yearbook* 67–68 [hereafter Smith, "Origins of the Free Speech Clause"].

72 3 James Burgh, *Political Disquisitions* 247 (Da Capo 1971) (1775) [hereafter Burgh, *Political Disquisitions*]; Smith, "Origins of the Free Speech Clause," supra note 71, at 71.

73 3 Burgh, *Political Disquisitions*, supra note 72, at 246.

74 Id. at 254; Smith, "Origins of the Free Speech Clause," supra note 71, at 71–72.

75 Anderson, "Press Clause," supra note 44, at 510; Harold L. Nelson, "Seditious Libel in Colonial America," 3 *Am. J.L. Hist.* 160, 170 (1959); Levy, *Emergence*, supra note 34, at x;

76 1 Schwartz, *Documentary History*, supra note 2, at 223.

77 Levy, *Emergence*, supra note 34, at 177–79.

78 Nelson Lasson, *The History and Development of the Fourth Amendment to the United States Constitution* 76 (1937). For the development of the rule against general warrants in England and for the cases involving John Wilkes and his allies, see id. at 43–50; for the writs of assistance cases in the colonies, see id. at 51–78.

79 G. Gardner and C. Post, "The Constitutional Questions Raised by the Flag Salute and Teachers' Oath Acts in Massachusetts," 16 *B.U.L. Rev.* 803, 812, 822 (1936). The Massachusetts constitution continued in force existing laws of the province "such parts only excepted as are repugnant to the rights and liberties continued in this

constitution." The Massachusetts Bill of Rights prohibited legislative declarations of treason although such acts had passed during the Revolution.

80 Thomas Paine, "Dissertation on First Principles of Government," *Time Piece* (N.Y.), May 12, 1797, at 1.

81 James Madison to Thomas Jefferson, Oct. 17, 1788, in 1 Schwartz, *Documentary History*, supra note 2, at 616; 2 Schwartz, *Documentary History* at 1080 (Madison advocating what became the Bill of Rights).

82 Quoted in G. Gardner and C Post, "The Constitutional Questions Raised by the Flag Salute and Teachers' Oath Acts in Massachusetts," 16 *B.U.L. Rev.* 803, 822 (1936).

83 Id.

84 1 Schwartz, *Documentary History*, supra note 2, at 231–379 (revolutionary declarations); id. at 266, Pennsylvania Declaration of Rights; (XII) see also 273 (sec. 35).

85 1 Schwartz, *Documentary History*, supra note 2, at 271 (Plan or Frame of Govt.) (sec. 25) (juries); 264 (Declaration of Rights) (II.) (religious freedom).

86 Anderson, "Press Clause," supra note 44, at 527; Levy, *Emergence*, supra note 34, at 173–219, 208.

87 Respublica v. Oswald, 1 Dall. 319 (Pa. 1788), reprinted in the 5 *The Founders Constitution* 124, 126 (Phillip B. Kurland and Ralph Lerner eds., 1987).

88 Thomas Cooley, *Constitutional Limitations* 421 (Legal Classic Library 1987) (1868).

89 See Van Ness v. Pacard, 27 U.S. 137, 145–46 (1829) (Our ancestors "brought with them and adopted only that portion [of the common law] which was applicable to their situation.")

90 Rabban, "Ahistorical Historian," supra note 40, at 842.

91 Rosenberg, *Best Men*, supra note 66, at 53–55, 60–71.

92 U.S. Const. art. III, sec. 3.

93 Houston, *Algernon Sidney*, supra note 34, at 263; John R. Howe Jr., *The Changing Political Thought of John Adams* 187–89 (1966); see Dumas Malone, *Jefferson and the Rights of Man* 452 (1951).

2   THE DEBATE OVER THE SEDITION ACT OF 1798

1 Harry Kalven Jr., "The New York Times Case: A Note on the Central Meaning of the First Amendment," 1964 *Sup. Ct. Rev.* 191, 205.

2 Harry Kalven Jr., "Group Libel, Seditious Libel, and Just Plain Libel," in *The Negro and the First Amendment* (1965).

3 Bruce Ackerman, *Inventing the People: Transformations* ch. 2, esp. 34–36, 49–53 (1998); Edmund S. Morgan, *Inventing the People: The Rise of Popular Sovereignty in England and America* 280–83 (1988); Alexander Hamilton, James Madison, and John Jay, *The Federalist Papers* No. 78, at 395–96 (Gary Wills ed., Bantam Books 1982) [hereafter *The Federalist*].

4 Akhil Reed Amar, *The Bill of Rights: Creation and Reconstruction* 36–37 (1998) [hereafter Amar, *Bill of Rights*]; Akhil Reed Amar, "Some Opinions on the Opinions Clause," 82 *Va. L. Rev.* 647, 649 nn.10–11. See, e.g., James Madison, *Notes of the Debates in the Federal Convention of 1787*, at 640 (Adrienne Koch ed., 1966) (1840)

(Sherman); *The Federalist* No. 84, supra note 3 (Alexander Hamilton); 2 *The Bill of Rights: A Documentary History* 1025, 1034 (Bernard Schwartz ed., 1971) [hereinafter 2 Schwartz, *Documentary History*] (Jackson); William Van Alstyne, Book Review, "Congressional Power and Free Speech: Levy's Legacy Revisited," 99 *Harv. L. Rev.* 1089 (1986).

5 *The Federalist* No. 84, supra note 3.

6 See id., where this argument is alluded to but not expressed in so bald a form.

7 See, e.g., James Madison, *Notes of the Debates in the Federal Convention of 1787* 640 (Adrienne Koch ed., 1966) (Sherman); *The Federalist* No. 84, supra note 3 (Alexander Hamilton); 2 Schwartz, *Documentary History*, supra note 4, at 1025, 1034 (Jackson); William Van Alstyne, Book Review, "Congressional Power and Free Speech: Levy's Legacy Revisited," 99 *Harv. L. Rev.* 1089 (1986); David A. Anderson, "The Origins of the Press Clause," 30 *U.C.L.A. L. Rev.* 455, 472 (Maryland provision) and 468–70 (lack of federal power) (1983) [hereafter Anderson, "Press Clause Origins"].

8 2 Schwartz, *Documentary History*, supra note 4, at 1028, 1033, 1113 (Madison in the first Congress).

9 Id. at 1026, 1032–33, 1112–13; Anderson, "Press Clause Origins," supra note 7, at 455, 483 (1983); on Madison's role see, e.g., Paul Finkelman, "A Reluctant Paternity: James Madison and the Bill of Rights," 1990 *Sup. Ct. Rev.* 301.

10 The Resolution of Congress March 4, 1789, transmitting the proposed amendments to the states, described them as "declaratory and restrictive clauses." *The Constitution of the United States and The Declaration of Independence* 20 (published by the Commission on the Bicentennial of the United States Constitution, Washington, D.C. 1991); Akhil Reed Amar, "The Bill of Rights and the Fourteenth Amendment," 101 *Yale L.J.* 1193, 1205–12 (1992); Curtis, *No State Shall Abridge* 24, 91 (1986); cf. Howard Jay Graham, "Our 'Declaratory' Fourteenth Amendment," 7 *Stan. L. Rev.* 3, 37 (1954–55).

11 2 Schwartz, *Documentary History*, supra note 4, at 1031–32. See generally Paul Finkelman, "James Madison and the Bill of Rights: A Reluctant Paternity," 1990 *Sup. Ct. Rev.* 301 (1990).

12 *The Federalist*, No. 28, supra note 3, at 137 (see also No. 26) (Bantam, 1982); Dumas Malone, *Jefferson and the Ordeal of Liberty* 396 (1962).

13 Dumas Malone, *Jefferson and the Rights of Man* 364–65 (1951); Anderson, "Press Clause Origins," supra note 7, at 518.

14 Stanley Elkins and Eric McKitrick, *The Age of Federalism: The Early American Republic, 1788–1800*, at 103 (1993) [hereafter *Age of Federalism*].

15 John R. Howe Jr., *The Changing Political Thought of John Adams* 187–89 (1966); see Dumas Malone, *Jefferson and the Rights of Man* 452 (1951).

16 James McGregor Burns, *The Vineyard of Liberty* 364 (1982); Samuel Chase's "Charge to the Grand Jury" in 1803, in *Law and Jurisprudence in American Legal History* 226 (Stephen B. Presser and Jamil S. Zainaldin eds., 3d ed. 1995). Thomas Jefferson to John Taylor, May 25, 1816, quoted in Richard Rosenfeld, *American Aurora* 862–63 (1997).

17 United States v. Cooper, 25 F. Cas. 631, 635 (C.C.D. Pa. 1800).

18   Richard Hofstadter, *The Idea of a Party System: The Rise of Legitimate Opposition in the United States, 1789–1840*, at 3 (1970), cited in *Age of Federalism*, supra note 14, at 264.

19   *Age of Federalism*, supra note 14, at 267.

20   "Answer [by President Adams] to the Legislature of Massachusetts," *Massachusetts Mercury*, June 22, 1798, at 3.

21   *Age of Federalism*, supra note 14, at 581–90, 643–48; Dale A. Herbeck, "*New York Times v. Sullivan*: Justice Brennan's Beautiful Lie," 28 *Free Speech Y.B.* 37, 39 (1990).

22   E.g., "Letter V, To the President of the United States," *Time Piece* (N.Y.), May 28, 1798, at 1; *Time Piece* (N.Y.), July 1, 1798, at 3.

23   James Morton Smith, *Freedom's Fetters: The Alien and Sedition Laws and American Civil Liberties* 21 (1956) [hereafter Smith, *Freedom's Fetters*].

24   "Communications," *Massachusetts Mercury*, June 12, 1798, at 2; the same article appears in "June 12," *Albany Centinel*, June 19, 1798, at 2.

25   "The Press," *Albany Centinel*, May 25, 1798, at 3.

26   "To the Inhabitants of the Town of Braintree," *Massachusetts Mercury*, July 20, 1798.

27   "The Address: The President's Answer," *Massachusetts Mercury*, Aug. 17, 1798, at 3.

28   *Massachusetts Mercury*, Oct. 5, 1798, at 2; *Albany Centinel*, Oct. 12, 1798, at 1.

29   James P. Martin, "When Representation Is Democratic and Constitutional: The Federalist Theory of Representation and the Sedition Act of 1798," 66 *U. Chic. L. Rev.* 117, 133–52 (1999).

30   E.g., Richard Rosenfeld, *American Aurora: A Democratic Republican Returns* 778–79, 204, 139 (1997).

31   Id. at 199.

32   Id. at 116, 207, 541, 620–21; Smith, *Freedom's Fetters*, supra note 23, at 257, 260, 262, 398–99. For an example of Republican violence against an editor, see Michael Durey, *Transatlantic Radicals and the Early American Republic* 254 (1997).

33   Dumas Malone, *Jefferson and the Rights of Man* 427 (1951); Richard Rosenfeld, *American Aurora* 234 (1997).

34   Smith, *Freedom's Fetters*, supra note 23, at 250; "Alexandria," May 9, *Time Piece* (N.Y.), May 16, 1798; *Time Piece* (N.Y.), July 25, 1798, at 3. See also "On Some Principles of American Republicanism," *Time Piece* (N.Y.), May 5, 1797, at 1.

35   1 Stat. 596, July 14, 1798.

36   *Massachusetts Mercury*, July 3, 1798, at 2.

37   5 *Annals of Cong.* 2093 (1798).

38   Id. at 2093–94.

39   Id. at 2096–97.

40   Id. at 2098.

41   Id. at 2097.

42   Id. at 2102, 2103.

43   Id. at 2146.

44   Id. at 2148.

45   Id. at 2148, 2151.

46   Id. at 2151.

47 Id. at 2167–68.

48 Id. at 2134, 2135, 2137.

49 Id. at 2112.

50 Id.

51 Id.

52 Id. at 2151. Amar, *Bill of Rights*, supra note 4, at 36–37 (lack of federal power over the press).

53 *5 Annals of Cong.* 2140 (Nicholas).

54 *7 Dictionary of American Biography* 103–06 (1931).

55 *5 Annals of Cong.* 2164 (Gallatin) (1798).

56 Richard N. Rosenfeld, *American Aurora* 805 (1997), citing report of the trial of Samuel Chase (1805); Gary D. Rowe, "The Sounds of Silence: *United States v. Hudson and Goodwin*, the Jeffersonian Ascendency, and the Abolition of Common Law Crimes," 101 *Yale L.J.* 919, 944 (1992).

57 *5 Annals of Cong.* 2140–41 (1798).

58 Id. at 2144.

59 Id. at 2164.

60 Id. at 2153–54.

61 Id. at 2105.

62 Id. at 2140, 2142.

63 Id. at 2143, 2145. On the proportion of Federalist to Republican presses, see id. at 2109. By one estimate there were 101 Federalist papers and 12 Republican. Anderson, "Press Clause Origins," supra note 7, at 515 n. 345.

64 *5 Annals of Cong.* 2162 (1798).

65 Id.

66 Id. at 2160.

67 Id.

68 Act for the Punishment of Certain Crimes, 1 Stat. 596 (July 14, 1798).

69 Dumas Malone, *Jefferson and the Ordeal of Liberty* 390 (1962).

70 *Aurora*, Jan 3, 1799 at 3.

71 "Mr. Cooper's Address," *Aurora*, July 12, 1799, at 3.

72 "Meeting at Philadelphia," *Aurora*, Feb. 11, 1799, at 3.

73 "Mifflin County Meeting," *Aurora*, Jan. 23, 1799, at 3.

74 "Spirit of the Times, Kentucky," *Independent Chronicle* (Boston), Sept. 24–27, 1798, at 1.

75 "Spirit of the Times, Kentucky," *Independent Chronicle* (Boston), Oct. 1–4, 1798, at 1. See "Kentucky," id., Oct. 18–22, 1798, at 1; "Virginia," id., Oct. 8–12, 1798, at 1; "Spirit of the Times, Knoxville," id., Nov. 15–19, 1798, at 1; "Spirit of the Times, Albany," id., Dec. 6–10, 1798, at 1. For a states' rights argument see, e.g., "Dr. Hill's Speech," id., Feb. 21, 1799, at 2.

76 "Newark, N.J.," *Independent Chronicle* (Boston), Sept. 24, 1798 at 3.

77 "On the Election of the President of the United States, No. IV," *Aurora*, Oct. 23, 1800, at 2.

78 "On the Election of the President of the United States, No. II (Attributed to C. Pinckney, Esq.)," *Aurora*, Oct. 20, 1800, at 3.

79 "On the Election of the President of the United States, No. III," *Aurora*, Oct. 21, 1800, at 3.

80 *Aurora*, Jan. 30, 1799, at 3.

81 "For the Aurora," *Aurora* Feb. 12, 1799, at 3.

82 "Congressional Conundrum," *Aurora*, Feb. 28, 1799, at 3; *Time Piece* (N.Y.), July 13, 1798, at 2.

83 E.g., *Time Piece* (N.Y.), July 4, 1798, at 2; "Extract," *Time Piece* (N.Y.), July 11, 1798, at 1.

84 "On the Liberty of the Press," *Independent Chronicle*, Feb 28–Mar. 5, 1799, at 3.

85 *Virginia Resolutions*, Dec. 21, 1798, reprinted in 1 *Documents of American Constitutional and Legal History* 159, 160 (Melvin I. Urofsky ed., 1989); 6 *The Writings of James Madison*, 326–31 (Gaillard Hunt ed., 1906).

86 *The Virginia Report of 1799–1800 Touching the Alien and Sedition Laws Together with the Virginia Resolutions of December 21, 1798, Including the Debate and Proceedings Thereon* . . . 26 (Da Capo 1970) (1850).

87 Id. at 119.

88 Id. at 27.

89 Id. at 119.

90 Id. at 94, 95, 159.

91 "A Charge Delivered to the Grand Jury of the U. States," *Aurora*, May 23, 1799, at 2.

92 Id. (continued), *Aurora*, May 28, 1799, at 2.

93 Id.

94 Id. (continued), *Aurora*, May 30, 1799, at 2.

95 Id. (continued), *Aurora*, May 28, 1799, at 2.

96 "Sketch of Chief Justice Dana's Charge," *Massachusetts Mercury*, Jan. 1, 1799, at 1.

97 "Answer of the Massachusetts Legislature to the Virginia Resolutions," *Mass. Mercury*, Feb. 15, 1799, at 2 [hereafter "Answer"].

98 "Sketch of the Debate in the House on the Declarations in Answer to the Virginia Resolutions," *Mass. Mercury*, Feb. 19, 1799, at 2.

99 "Answer," supra note 97, at 2.

3 SEDITION IN THE COURTS

1 11 *Dictionary of American Biography* 532–34 (1933) [hereafter *DAB*]; Stanley Elkins and Eric McKitrick, *The Age of Federalism*, 706–11 (1993) [hereafter *The Age of Federalism*] (for a much more negative account); James Morton Smith, *Freedom's Fetters: The Alien and Sedition Laws and American Civil Liberties* 221–26 (1956) [hereafter Smith, *Freedom's Fetters*].

2 Francis Wharton, *State Trials of the United States During the Administrations of Washington and Adams* 333 (Philadelphia, Carey and Hart 1849) [hereafter Wharton, *State Trials*].

3 Id. at 334.

4 Id. at 336, 340

5 Id. at 339, where the letter is reprinted.

6 *Aurora*, Nov. 1, 1798, at 4; "Regular Government," id., Nov. 9, 1798, at 1–2.

7 Wharton, *State Trials*, supra note 2, at 342.

8 "To the Freemen of the Western District of Vermont," *Aurora*, Feb. 8, 1799, at 3.

9 Smith, *Freedom's Fetters*, supra note 1, at 241–46; *The Age of Federalism*, supra note 1, at 711.

10 5 *Cong. Debates* (*Annals of Congress*) 2954 (Feb. 1799).

11 Id. at 2960 (Bayard), 2963–64 (Nicholas).

12 Id. at 2972 (Gallatin), 2973 (the vote).

13 11 *DAB*, supra note 1, at 532–34 (1933); *The Age of Federalism*, supra note 1, at 706–11.

14 *Cong. Globe*, 26th cong., 1st Sess., 409 (1840).

15 "A Beacon for the Seditious," *Massachusetts Mercury*, Apr. 9, 1799, at 2; "Historical Facts," *Independent Chronicle* (Boston), Feb. 14–18, 1799, at 3.

16 Smith, *Freedoms Fetters*, supra note 1, at 253.

17 "Trial," *Independent Chronicle* (Boston), Apr. 8–11, 1799, at 1–2; "Trial," *Independent Chronicle* (Boston), Apr. 18–22, 1799, at 2; "Trial," *Independent Chronicle* (Boston), Apr. 25–29, 1799, at 1 (indicating that some discussion foreclosed by the court was included in the paper's account of the trial).

18 "Trial," *Independent Chronicle* (Boston), Apr. 11–15, 1799, at 1–2.

19 "Trial," *Independent Chronicle* (Boston), Apr. 15–18, 1799, at 1; id. Apr. 25–29, 1799, at 1.

20 "Trial," *Independent Chronicle* (Boston), Apr. 25–29, 1799, at 1.

21 See Smith, *Freedom's Fetters*, supra note 1, at 252–54; *Massachusetts Mercury*, Mar. 8, 1799, at 2. Thomas Cooley, *A Treatise on the Constitutional Limitations Which Rest upon the Legislative Power of the States of the American Union* 460 (Legal Classics Library 1987) (1868), citing Rex v. Woodfall, 20 State Trials 895. "The People's Ancient and Just Liberties Asserted in the Trial of William Penn and William Mead, 1670," in 1 *The Bill of Rights: A Documentary History* 152–58 (Bernard Schwartz ed., 1971).

22 "A Beacon for the Seditious," *Massachusetts Mercury*, April 9, 1799 at 2; "Trial," *Independent Chronicle*, Apr. 25–29, 1799, at 1; "Summary," *Independent Chronicle* (Boston) Apr. 22–25, 1799, at 1; "Trial," *Independent Chronicle* (Boston) Apr. 29–May 2, 1799, at 1.

23 Smith, *Freedom's Fetters*, supra note 1, at 258–63.

24 "Brown," *Massachusetts Mercury*, June, 21, 1799, at 1.

25 Smith, *Freedom's Fetters*, supra note 1, at 264–69.

26 "Thomas Cooper," 4 *DAB*, supra note 1, at 414–15 (1930).

27 United States v. Cooper, 25 Fed. Cas. 631, 632 (C.C.D. Pa. 1800).

28 Id. at 635.

29 Id. at 634, 636.

30 Id. at 635.

31 Id at 637, 639.

32 *United States v. Cooper* at 640.

33 Id. at 641, 642, 640.

34 Id. at 641–42.

35 Ruth Wedgewood, "The Revolutionary Martyrdom of Jonathan Robbins," 100 *Yale L.J.* 229, 310–11 (1990).

36 United States v. Cooper 645; "Thomas Cooper," 4 *DAB*, supra note 1, at 414–15.

37 4 *DAB*, supra note 1, at 415; Dumas Malone, *The Public Life of Thomas Cooper, 1783–1839,* at 20–21, 288–89, 387–88, 290, 310–11, 305 (Univ. of South Carolina Press, 1961) (1926).

38 Thomas Cooper, *The Right of Free Discussion* 4 (1840).

39 Id. at 8–9.

40 Cooper to Hammond, Jan. 8, 1836, James Hammond papers, Library of Congress.

41 Thomas Cooper, *The Right of Free Discussion* 4 (1840).

42 Smith, *Freedom's Fetters,* supra note 1, at 185–86, 255.

43 Id. at 185–86.

44 Id., at 279–83; Richard N. Rosenfeld, *American Aurora: A Democratic Republican Returns* 588, 592–95 (1997) [hereafter Rosenfeld, *American Aurora*].

45 Smith, *Freedom's Fetters,* supra note 1, at 282–89, 289–300; Rosenfeld, *American Aurora,* supra note 44, at 707.

46 Throop Wilder, *New York History* 296–98 (1941); *The Age of Federalism,* supra note 1, at 705–06; 1 DeAlva Stanwood Alexander, *A Political History of New York* 89 (1906).

47 *The Age of Federalism,* supra note 1, at 731–32; Dumas Malone, *Jefferson and the Ordeal of Liberty* 437–41, 487–89; Rosenfeld, *American Aurora,* supra note 44, at 787. On Hamilton and Adams, see Adrienne Koch, "Hamilton, Adams, and the Pursuit of Power," 16 *Rev. of Politics* 37 (1954).

48 James Madison, *The Virginia Report of 1799–1800* [hereafter Madison, *Report*], in *Freedom of the Press from Zenger to Jefferson* [hereafter Levy, *Zenger to Jefferson*] 198–200, 209–12 (Leonard Levy ed., 1966).

49 Id. at 213.

50 Id. at 213–14.

51 Id. at 215.

52 Id. at 215–16.

53 See, Leonard Levy, "The Legacy Reexamined," 37 *Stan. L. Rev.* 767, 768 (1985); Jensen, Book Review, 75 *Harv. L. Rev.* 456 (1961); David Anderson, "The Origins of the Press Clause," 30 *U.C.L.A. L. Rev.* 455, 510–15 (1983).

54 Madison, *Report,* supra note 48, at 216.

55 Id. at 221–22.

56 Id. at 224.

57 Id. at 225.

58 Gregg Costa, "John Marshall, the Sedition Act, and Free Speech in the Early Republic," 77 *Tex. L. Rev.* 1011, 1032–33 (1999).

59 Tunis Wortman, *A Treatise Concerning Political Enquiry and the Liberty of the Press* 28–29, 116 (New York, George Forman, 1800).

60 Id. at 33.

61 Id. at 63–64, 130.

62 Id. at 146.

63 Id. at 150–51.

64 Id. at 168.

65 Id. at 159.

66 Id. at 177.

67 Id. at 249.

68 Id. at 174.

69 Id. at 172–73.

70 Id. at 163.

71 John Thomson, *An Enquiry Concerning the Liberty, and Licentiousness of the Press, and the Uncontroulable Nature of the Human Mind* 76–77 (New York, Johnson and Stryker, 1801).

72 Id. at 19–20.

73 Id. at 7.

74 Id. at 77.

75 Id. at 83–84.

76 Thomas Jefferson, "First Inaugural Address, March 4, 1801," in Levy, *Zenger to Jefferson*, supra note 48, at 358.

77 Jefferson to Madison, August 28, 1789, in Levy, *Zenger to Jefferson*, supra note 48, at 340 (see also letter of July 31, 1788, id. at 337).

78 Jefferson to Thomas McKean, Feb. 19, 1803, in Levy, *Zenger to Jefferson*, supra note 48, at 164.

79 Jefferson to Abigail Adams, Sept. 11, 1804, and Jefferson to John Norvell, June 11, 1807, in Levy, *Zenger to Jefferson*, supra note 48, at 367, 372.

80 Jefferson to N. G. Dufief, April 19, 1814, and Jefferson to Adamantious Coray, Oct. 31, 1823, in Levy, *Zenger to Jefferson*, supra note 48, at 374, 376.

81 St. George Tucker, *A Dissertation on Slavery, with a Proposal for the Gradual Abolition of it in the State of Virginia* 8 (Negro Univ. Press, 1970) (1796).

82 2 St. George Tucker, *Tucker's Blackstone* app. at 29–30 (Law Book Exchange, 1996) (1803).

83 Id. at 11.

84 Id. at 30.

85 Joseph Story, "Commentaries on Constitution, sec. 1878," in 5 Phillip Kurland and Ralph Lerner, eds., *The Founders Constitution* 183 (1987).

86 Id. at 184, secs. 1881, 1882.

87 Id. at 184–85, secs. 1883, 1885.

4   SEDITION: REFLECTIONS AND TRANSITIONS

1 Walter Berns, "Freedom of the Press and the Alien and Sedition Laws: A Reappraisal," 1970 *S. Ct. Rev.* 109,129 [hereafter Berns, "Sedition Laws"]; for an article that sees the First Amendment as a jurisdictional denial of power to the national government over religion, speech, and press, and that reads the Republican position on the Sedition Act as a jurisdictional complaint, see Jay S. Bybee, "Taking

Liberties with the First Amendment," 48 *Vand. L. Rev.* 1539, 1567–76 (1995); see also Dale A. Herbeck, "*New York Times v. Sullivan*: Justice Brennan's Beautiful Lie," 28 *Free Speech Yearbook* 37 (1990).

2   Berns, "Sedition Laws," supra note 1, at 142.

3   Id. at 111.

4   Id. at 121–22.

5   See, e.g., Clement Eaton, *The Freedom of Thought Struggle in the Old South*, ch. 1 (1964); Robert M. Cover, *Justice Accused* 67–75 (1975); St. George Tucker, *A Dissertation on Slavery, with a Proposal for the Gradual Abolition of It in the State of Virginia* (Negro Univ. Press 1970) (1796) [hereafter Tucker, *Dissertation on Slavery*].

6   7 *Dictionary of American Biography* 103–06 (1931) [hereafter *DAB*]; Tucker, *Dissertation on Slavery*, supra note 5, at 8; John Keane, *Tom Paine: A Political Life* 194, 508 (1995).

7   *Aurora*, Sept. 24, 1800, in Richard Rosenfeld, *American Aurora, A Democratic Republican Returns* 854 (1997) [hereafter Rosenfeld, *American Aurora*]; but see later statements by Duane (the editor of the *Aurora*) cited in Michael Durey, *Transatlantic Radicals and the Early American Republic* 285 (1997).

8   Berns, "Sedition Laws," supra note 1, at 148–49.

9   *Aurora*, Sept. 24, 1800, in Rosenfeld, *American Aurora*, supra note 7, at 854; *Gazette of the United States*, Sept. 25, 1800, in Rosenfeld, *American Aurora*, supra note 7, at 855.

10 6 *Annals of Cong.* 229 (1800).

11 Id. at 230.

12 Id. at 231–32.

13 Id. at 233–34.

14 Id. at 234.

15 Id. at 245.

16 Speech of Harrison Gray Otis, *Niles' Wkly. Reg.*, Sept. 5, 1835, at 10.

17 Id. at 12.

18 Id. at 11.

19 Id. at 12. Later, as mayor of Boston, Otis refused to take legal action against abolitionists.

20 *Wash. Globe*, Sept. 1, 1835, at 2; see also 2 James Kent, *Commentaries on American Law* 245 (Lecture 32) (New York, E. B. Clayton, James Van Norden, 1836) and id. (1827 ed.) at 201.

21 "Great Meeting in the Park," *Wash. Globe*, Aug. 24, 1835, at 2–3, reporting the Aug. 15 resolutions of "the citizens of Portland."

22 Norman L. Rosenberg, *Protecting the Best Men: An Interpretative History of the Law of Libel* 72, 110–11 (1986) [hereafter, Rosenberg, *Best Men*]; James Morton Smith, *Freedom's Fetters: The Alien and Sedition Laws and American Civil Liberties* 153–54 (1956) [hereafter Smith, *Freedom's Fetters*].

23 "James Kent," 10 *DAB*, supra note 6, at 344–47 (1933).

24 3 Johns. Cas. 337 (N.Y. Sup. Ct. 1804).

25 John Theodore Horton, *James Kent: A Study in Conservatism* 176–77 (1969) [hereafter Horton, *Kent*]; Norman L. Rosenberg, *Best Men*, supra note 22, at 260.

26 People v. Croswell, 3 Johns. Cas. 359–60.

27 Id. at 362–63.

28 Id. at 362.

29 2 John Trenchard and Thomas Gordon, *Cato's Letters* 304 (Letter 101) (Da Capo Press 1971) (1755).

30 Horton, *Kent*, supra note 25, at 177.

31 Id. at 184–85.

32 United States v. Hudson and Goodwin, 11 U.S. 32 (1812). For a discussion of the case, see Gary Rowe, "The Sounds of Silence: *United States v. Hudson and Goodwin*, the Jeffersonian Ascendancy, and the Abolition of Federal Common Law Crimes," 101 *Yale L.J.* 919 (1992).

33 Smith, *Freedom's Fetters*, supra note 22, at 431–32 n. 32.

34 Harry Kalven, "The *New York Times* Case: A Note on 'The Central Meaning of the First Amendment," 1964 *Sup. Ct. Rev.* 191.

35 Rosenberg, *Best Men*, supra note 22, at 140–45; "The Press," in 2 William H. Seward, *The Works of William H. Seward*, 35–38 (1853).

5   THE DECLARATION, THE CONSTITUTION, SLAVERY, AND ABOLITION

1 See Zechariah Chafee Jr., *Free Speech in the United States* 21, 499, 501, 522 (1954); Michael K. Curtis, "In Pursuit of Liberty: The Levellers and the American Bill of Rights," 8 *Const. Commentary* 359 (1991).

2 The Declaration of Independence, in 1 *The Bill of Rights: A Documentary History* 252 (Bernard Schwartz ed., 1971).

3 Aldridge v. Commonwealth, 4 VA, 2 Va. Cas. 447 (1824). The Supreme Court later deprived even free blacks of the protections of the Federal Constitution in Dred Scott v. Sanford, 60 U.S. 393 (1856).

4 See generally, e.g., R. Alvan Stewart, *Writing and Speeches of Alvan Stewart on Slavery* (Luther Marsh ed., Haskell House 1969) (1860).

5 St. George Tucker, *A Dissertation on Slavery, with a Proposal for the Gradual Abolition of It in the State of Virginia* 7–8 (Negro Univ. Press 1970) (1796).

6 U.S. Const., art. I, secs. 9 (bill of attainder, ex post facto laws, habeas corpus) and 10 (bill of attainder, ex post facto laws).

7 Id., art. III, sec. 3, cl. 1.

8 See, e.g., id. art. I, sec. 2, cl. 3; sec. 9, cl. 1; art. IV, sec. 2, cl. 3 (fugitive slave clause); sec. 4 (protection of states against domestic violence).

9 Id., art. I, sec. 2, cl. 3 (three-fifths clause); id., art. II, sec. 1, cl. 3 (electoral college); id., art. I, sec. 9, cl. 1 (slave importation); id., art. IV, sec. 2, cl. 3 (fugitive slave clause); id., art. IV, sec. 4 (domestic violence).

10 U.S. Const., pmbl.

11 Id., amend. I (free speech, press, religion, petition).

12 Id., art. III, sec. 3 (treason clause); id., art. I, sec. 6, cl. 1 (speech and debate); id., amend. IV (protecting against unreasonable search and seizure); id., amend. V (protecting against double jeopardy, self-incrimination, and the violation of due process); id., amend. VI (providing for a right to a speedy trial and the right to

confront witnesses); id., amend. VIII (prohibiting cruel and unusual punishment); id., art. IV, sec. 4 (republican government); id., art. I, sec. 8, cls. 3, 7 (commerce, post roads); id., art. IV (supremacy clause); id., art. I, sec. 8, cl. 17 (federal enclaves); id., art. IV, sec. 3, cl. 2 (territory clause). See also Barron v. Baltimore, 32 U.S. (7 Pet.) 243 (1833).

13   1 *Documents of American Constitutional and Legal History* 86–89 (Melvin Urofsky ed., 1989).

14   William W. Freehling, *The Road to Disunion: Secessionists at Bay, 1776–1854*, at 144–48, 149, 153 (1990) [hereafter Freehling, *Road to Disunion*].

15   Letter from Thomas Jefferson to John Holmes, Apr. 22, 1820, in Thomas Jefferson, *Writings* 1434 (Library of America ed., 1984); Freehling, *Road to Disunion*, supra note 14, at 155.

16   Id. See also John Chester Miller, *The Wolf by the Ears: Thomas Jefferson and Slavery* 243–52 (1977).

17   Leonard L. Richards, *The Life and Times of Congressman John Quincy Adams* 90–91 (1986).

18   *Cong. Globe*, 36th Cong., 1st Sess. 285 (1859) (Rep. Pryor).

19   Freehling, *Road to Disunion*, supra note 14, at 79. "Denmark Vesey," 19 *Dictionary of American Biography* 58–59 (1936) [hereafter *DAB*].

20   19 *DAB*, supra note 19, at 340 (1936); Clement Eaton, *The Freedom of Thought Struggle in the Old South* 89–117 (1964) [hereafter Eaton, *Freedom of Thought*].

21   Jeffrey Rogers Hummel, *Emancipating Slaves, Enslaving Free Men: A History of the American Civil War* 56 (1996).

22   Eaton, *Freedom of Thought*, supra note 20, at 92.

23   W. Sherman Savage, *The Controversy over the Distribution of Abolition Literature, 1830–1860*, at 3–4 (photo. reprint 1968) (1938).

24   Charles S. Sydnor, *The Development of Southern Sectionalism, 1819–1848*, at 228 (1962) [hereafter Sydnor, *Southern Sectionalism*]. For a fine brief modern account of events in Virginia and later efforts at emancipation in Delaware and Maryland, see Freehling, *Road to Disunion*, supra note 14, at 162–210 (1990). For a detailed modern study, see Alison G. Freehling, *Drift Towards Dissolution: The Virginia Slavery Debate of 1831–1832*, e.g., at 78, 228, 239 (1982) [hereafter Freehling, *Drift Towards Dissolution*].

25   Sydnor, *Southern Sectionalism*, supra note 24, at 228. Some Southern states based representation in part on "federal population," incorporating the three-fifths clause by reference. Such provisions swelled the representation of slaveholders. E.g., Amendments to the Constitution, 1836 *Proceedings and Debates of the Convention of North-Carolina, Called to Amend the Constitution of the State* app. at 419 (representation in the House of Commons to be based on "federal population").

26   Charles Jas. Faulkner (of Berkeley), "Speech in House of Delegates of Virginia, on the Policy of the State with Respect to Her Slave Population" 9 (Jan. 20, 1832) (copy on file with author) [hereafter Faulkner].

27   E.g., id. at 9–14; Philip A. Bolling (of Buckingham), "Speech in the House of Delegates of Virginia, on the Policy of the State in Relation to Her Colored Population"

13 (2d ed. Jan. 25, 1832) [hereafter Bolling] in *Slavery Source Material and Critical Literature* (Louisville, Ky., Lost Cause Press; Microfiche Reprint SLA 185 (1971) [hereafter *Source Material*]; John A. Chandler (of Norfolk County), "Speech in the House of Delegates of Virginia, on the Policy of the State with Respect to Her Slave Population" 6–7 (Jan. 17, 1832) in Collection of Anti-Slavery Propaganda in Oberlin College Library (Louisville, Ky., Lost Cause Press; Microfiche Reprint SLB 826 (1964)) [hereafter Chandler]; Thomas J. Randolph (of Albemarle), "Speech in the House of Delegates of Virginia, on the Abolition of Slavery" 7 (2d ed. Jan. 21, 1832) (copy on file with author) [hereafter Randolph].

28 See Chandler, supra note 27, at 6; Randolph, supra note 27, at 7.

29 James M'Dowell, Jr. (of Rockbridge), "Speech in the House of Delegates of Virginia, on the Slave Question" 29, 21 (Jan. 21, 1832) (copy on file with the author).

30 Id. at 5.

31 Faulkner, supra note 26, at 18.

32 *Cong. Globe*, 36th Cong., 1st Sess. 60 (Sen. Trumbull) (favoring "deportation" of free blacks).

33 Sydnor, *Southern Sectionalism*, supra note 24, at 227; Freehling, *Road to Disunion*, supra note 14, at 185.

34 Faulkner, supra note 26, at 15.

35 Chandler, supra note 27, at 8–9 (emphasis omitted).

36 "The Letter of Appomattox to the People of Virginia" 18 (1832) in *Source Material*, supra note 27 (Microfiche Reprint SLA 1084 (1971)). This letter is also published in the *Richmond Enquirer*, Feb. 4, 1832.

37 Id. at 21.

38 Id. at 29–30.

39 Faulkner, supra note 26, at 2.

40 Eaton, *Freedom of Thought*, supra note 20, at 171; Freehling, *Drift Towards Dissolution*, supra note 24, at 198–99.

41 Bolling, supra note 27, at 8, 14.

42 Sydnor, *Southern Sectionalism*, supra note 24, at 228. For a discussion of the Maryland and Delaware emancipation debates, see Freehling, *Road to Disunion*, supra note 14, at 202–10.

43 Act to Prevent Circulation of Seditious Publications, ch. 5, 1830 N.C. Sess. Laws 10 (codified at 1837 N.C. Rev. Stat. ch. 34, sec. 517).

44 Revised Code of North Carolina Enacted by the General Assembly at the Session of 1854, RS. C. 34, s. 17 (1855).

45 Acts Passed by the General Assembly of North Carolina, ch. 30, 1831 N.C. Sess. Laws 29.

46 Charles Warren, 1 *The Supreme Court in United States History, 1789–1835*, at 626 (1926). But see Justice Johnson's more active approach to the problem in Elkison v. Deliesseline, 8 F. Cas. 493 (C.C.D. S.C. 1823). See Paul Finkelman, "States Rights North and South in Antebellum America," in *An Uncertain Tradition, Constitutionalism and the History of the South* (Kermit Hall and James W. Ely Jr. eds., 1989).

47 Barron v. Baltimore, 32 U.S. (7 Pet.) 243, 248 (1833).

48   "Declaration of the Anti-Slavery Convention," *U.S. Telegraph*, Dec. 21, 1833, at 69.

49   *National Party Platforms, 1840–1964*, at 32 (Kirk Porter and Donald Johnson eds., 1956).

50   For an example of equivocation, see Letter of J. A. Thome and J. W. Alford to Theodore Weld, Feb. 9, 1836, in 1 *Letters of Theodore Dwight Weld, Angelina Grimké, and Sarah Grimké* 257 (Gilbert H. Barnes and Dwight L. Dumond eds., 1965) [hereafter 1 *Weld-Grimké Letters*].

51   Gilbert H. Barnes, *The Anti-Slavery Impulse, 1830–1844*, at 3–28, 100–08 (1933); Sydnor, *Southern Sectionalism*, supra note 24, at 238–42.

52   "Declaration of the Anti-Slavery Convention," *U.S. Telegraph*, Dec. 21, 1833, at 69.

53   See, e.g., Leonard L. Richards, *"Gentlemen of Property and Standing": Anti-Abolition Mobs in Jacksonian America* 47–49, 55–59, 158–59 (1970) [hereafter Richards, *Gentlemen of Property and Standing*].

54   *Cong. Globe*, 24th Cong., 1st Sess. 93 (1836) (Rep. Bouldin, urging all, north and south, to "leave this subject—too mysterious, deep, and dangerous for man's management, (or that of woman either)—to the operation of . . . the providence of God").

55   William Jay, *Miscellaneous Writings on Slavery* 12–13, 124 (Negro Univ. Press 1968) (1853).

56   Richards, *Gentlemen of Property and Standing*, supra note 53, at 64; Russell B. Nye, *Fettered Freedom: Civil Liberties and the Slavery Controversy, 1830–1860* (1972), at 161–62 [hereafter Nye, *Fettered Freedom*].

57   "Mob in New York—Slavery," *U.S. Telegraph*, June 14, 1834, at 817. Letter from Lewis Tappan to Theodore Weld, July 10, 1834, in 1 *Weld-Grimké Letters*, supra note 50, at 155.

58   Quoted in "Anti-Slavery Riots," *U.S. Telegraph*, July 24, 1834, at 853.

59   See Richards, *Gentlemen of Property and Standing*, supra note 53, at 131–54, 15; Nye, *Fettered Freedom*, supra note 56, at 194.

60   *Wash. Globe*, Aug. 6, 1835, at 3.

61   "The Richmond Meeting—Southern Pretensions," *Evening Post* (N.Y.), Aug. 17, 1835, at 3; *Wash. Globe*, Oct. 5, 1835, at 3; Governor Swain, *Niles' Wkly. Reg.*, Dec. 5, 1835, at 228.

62   "Mr. Van Buren—No Abolitionist," *Wash. Globe*, Mar. 19, 1836, at 2.

63   "The Slave Question," *Wash. Globe*, Aug. 1, 1835, at 2; *Wash. Globe*, from the *Albany Argus*, Aug. 14, 1835, at 3; *Evening Post* (N.Y.), Feb. 10, 1835, at 3.

64   "The Geographical Party," *Wash. Globe*, Aug. 2, 1836, at 2.

6   SHALL ABOLITIONISTS BE SILENCED?

1   See, e.g., T. R. Sullivan, *Letters Against the Immediate Abolition of Slavery Addressed to the Free Blacks of the Non-Slave-Holding States, Comprising a Legal Opinion on the Power of Legislature in Non-Slave-Holding States to Prevent Measures Tending to Immediate and General Emancipation, in a Letter to the Author from William Sullivan, L.L.D.* 42 (Boston, Hilliard, Gray, and Co. 1835) (setting forth letters originally printed in the *Boston Courier*). *The Trial of Reuben Crandall,*

M.D. Charged with Publishing and Circulating Seditious and Incendiary Papers &c. in the District of Columbia, with the Intent of Exciting Servile Insurrection (Washington 1836), reprinted in *Slave Rebels, Abolitionists, and Southern Courts: The Pamphlet Literature* 364 (Paul Finkelman ed., 1988).

2   See 24 Cong. Deb. 1152 (1836) (Sen. Davis); id. at 1721 (1836) (Sen. Webster); id. at 1723–24 (1836) (Sen. Buchanan). But see 2 James Kent, *Commentaries on American Law*, 21, 23–24 (New York, E. B. Clayton, James Van Norden 1836) [hereafter *Kent's Commentaries*].

3   For an example of recondite doctrine, see R.A.V. v. City of St. Paul, 112 S. Ct. 2538 (1992).

4   See Brandenburg v. Ohio, 395 U.S. 444 (1969); Bond v. Floyd, 385 U.S. 116 (1966); and Herndon v. Lowry, 301 U.S. 242, 259–61 (1937); but see Dennis v. United States, 341 U.S. 494 (1951).

5   W. Sherman Savage, *The Controversy over the Distribution of Abolition Literature, 1830–1860*, at 3–4 (1968).

6   *Journals of the Senate and House of Commons of the General Assembly of the State of North Carolina, 1830–31*, at 161; Clement Eaton, *The Freedom of Thought Struggle in the Old South* 124 (1964).

7   1 Henry Wilson, *The Rise and Fall of the Slave Power in America* 186 (Negro Universities Press 1969) (1872) [hereafter Wilson, *Slave Power*].

8   2 *Kent's Commentaries*, supra note 2, at 254.

9   *Wash. Globe*, Aug. 24, 1835, at 2.

10 "Speech of Harrison Gray Otis," *Niles' Wkly. Reg.*, Sept. 5, 1835, at 11 [hereafter "Speech of Otis"].

11 See 9 John Quincy Adams, *Memoirs of John Quincy Adams* 254 (1877); see also Leonard L. Richards, *The Life and Times of Congressman John Quincy Adams* 111 (1986).

12 "To the Editors of the Evening Post," *Evening Post* (N.Y.), Sept. 10, 1835, at 2.

13 Id.

14 See William Freehling, *Prelude to Civil War: The Nullification Controversy in South Carolina, 1816–36*, at 333–39 (1966).

15 "Speech of Otis," supra note 10, at 21.

16 "The Slave Question," *U.S. Telegraph*, June 22, 1834, at 843.

17 "Southern Sentiment," *Wash. Globe*, Sept. 26, 1835, at 2.

18 Act to Prevent the Circulation of Seditious Publications, ch. 5, 1830 N.C. Sess. Laws 10 (codified at 1837 N.C. Rev. Stat. ch. 34, sec. 17).

19 Acts Passed at the Thirteenth Annual Session of the General Assembly of the State of Alabama, Begun and Held in the Town of Tuscaloosa, on the Third Monday in November, One Thousand Eight-Hundred and Thirty-One, sec. 13 116–17 (1832).

20 An Act to Suppress the Circulation of Incendiary Publications, 1836 Va. Acts 44, 45.

21 "Legislature of New York: Requisition of the Governour of Alabama," *Evening Post* (N.Y.), Jan. 11, 1836, at 2 (reprinting Alabama indictment and requisition of the governor of Alabama for extradition).

22 "Incendiaries," *Niles' Wkly. Reg.*, Oct. 3, 1835, at 65.

23 "Important Public Meeting," *Niles' Wkly. Reg.*, Aug. 22, 1835, at 446.

24   "Town Meeting in Philadelphia," *Wash. Globe*, Aug. 29, 1835, at 2.

25   "Report of the Postmaster General," *Cong. Globe*, 24th Cong., 1st Sess. app. 9 (1835).

26   See, e.g., *Cong. Globe*, 24th Cong., 1st Sess. 1108 (1836) (Sen. Davis); *Cong. Globe*, 24th Cong., 1st Sess. 1728 (1836) (Sen. Henry Clay).

27   See, e.g., 1 *Journal of the Senate of the Commonwealth of Pennsylvania* 422, 423 (attaching the report of the New York Joint Legislative Committee) (1835–36). But cf. "Great Meeting," *Wash. Globe*, Sept. 28, 1835, at 2.

28   "Anti-Abolition Meeting," *Wash. Globe*, Oct. 3, 1835, at 3; "Great Meeting at Bath, Maine," *Wash. Globe*, Sept. 3, 1835, at 2; "Great Meeting in the Park," *Wash. Globe*, Sept. 1, 1835, at 2; "Public Meeting," *Wash. Globe*, Sept. 7, 1835, at 2.

29   "Town Meeting in Philadelphia," *Wash. Globe*, Aug. 29, 1835, at 2.

30   "Meeting of the Citizens of Albany," *Wash. Globe*, Sept. 10, 1835, at 2.

31   See supra note 28 and accompanying text; "Southern Sentiment," *Wash. Globe*, Sept. 26, 1835, at 2.

32   *Wash. Globe*, Sept. 13, 1836, at 2; "The Geographical Party," *Wash. Globe*, Sept. 2, 1836, at 2.

33   See, e.g., "More of the Incendiaries," *Wash. Globe*, Oct. 8, 1835, at 2; "Anti-Abolition Meeting," *Wash. Globe*, Oct. 8, 1835, at 2; "Meeting of the Citizens of Albany," *Wash. Globe*, Sept. 10, 1835, at 2.

34   See, e.g., "Protest of the American Anti-Slavery Society," *Evening Post* (N.Y.), Jan. 28, 1836, at 2.

35   See Leonard L. Richards, *"Gentlemen of Property and Standing": Anti-Abolition Mobs in Jacksonian America* 62 (1970) [hereafter Richards, *Gentlemen of Property and Standing*].

36   *Niles' Wkly. Reg.*, Oct. 31, 1835, at 146.

37   "Abolition Meeting Abolished," *Wash. Globe*, Oct. 27, 1835, at 3.

38   "Abolitionists," *Wash. Globe*, Oct. 26, 1835, at 2; Letter from Secretary of State Forsyth to President Martin Van Buren (Aug. 5, 1835), in William A. Butler, *A Retrospect of Forty Years, 1825–1865, at 78–79 (1911)*. The Forsyth letter was discovered by Richard John. See Richard R. John, *Spreading the News: The American Postal System from Franklin to Morse* (1995).

39   Quoted in *Niles' Wkly. Reg.*, Oct. 31, 1835, at 148.

40   "Abolitionists," *Wash. Globe*, Oct. 26, 1835, at 2.

41   See generally Richards, *Gentlemen of Property and Standing*, supra note 35, at 69, 93–95 (describing how a Philadelphia mob of 1835 seized abolitionist pamphlets and threw them in the Delaware River); 1 Wilson, *Slave Power*, supra note 7, at 274–98.

42   *Cong. Globe*, 24th Cong., 1st Sess. 78 (1836).

43   Id. at 121.

44   Alvan Stewart, Speech before the New York Antislavery Convention (Utica, Oct. 21, 1835), and before the New York Antislavery State Society (Petersboro, Oct. 22, 1835), in *Proceedings of the New York Anti-Slavery Convention at Utica, October 21, and New York Anti-Slavery State Society Held at Petersboro, October 22, 1835*, at 4–5 (1835).

45 "Philadelphia Mass Meeting," *Wash. Globe*, Aug. 29, 1835, at 2; "Great Meeting in the Park," *Wash. Globe*, Sept. 1, 1835, at 2; "Great Meeting at Bath, Maine," *Wash. Globe*, Sept. 3, 1835, at 2.

46 Id.

47 *Wash. Globe*, Aug. 4, 1835, at 3.

48 *Evening Post* (N.Y.), July 18, 1835, at 2.

49 See Letter from James Birney to Theodore Weld (July 26, 1834), in 1 *Letters of Theodore Dwight Weld, Angelina Grimké, and Sarah Grimké* 162 (Gilbert H. Barnes and Dwight L. Dumond eds., 1965) [hereafter 1 *Weld-Grimké Letters*]; see also, Letter from William Ellery Channing to James Birney (Nov. 1, 1836), in *Freedom of the Press from Hamilton to the Warren Court* 195 (Harold L. Nelson ed., 1967) ("The abolitionists then not only appear in the character of champions of the colored race. . . . They are sufferers for the liberty of thought, speech, and the press.").

50 The account of Weld's life is taken from the entry in the *Dictionary of American Biography* written by Gilbert Barnes. "Theodore Dwight Weld," 19 *Dictionary of American Biography* 625–27 (1936) [hereafter *DAB*]; for the account of Weld's abolition crusade, see Letter from Theodore Weld to E. Wright Jr. (Mar. 2, 1835), in 1 *Weld-Grimké Letters*, supra note 49, at 206.

51 Id. at 236–39, 238 n.4.

52 Letter from John Green to James Birney (Nov. 2, 1836), in 1 *Letters of James Gillespie Birney, 1831–1857*, at 370–71 (Dwight L. Dumond ed., 1966) [hereafter *Birney Letters*].

53 "Mob in New York—Slavery," *U.S. Telegraph*, June 14, 1834, at 817.

54 "The North and the South—Fanaticism—And Syren Songs," *U.S. Telegraph*, Aug. 14, 1835, at 2; "Legislative Measures Against the Incendiary Tracts," *U.S. Telegraph*, Sept. 11, 1835, at 2; "Arbitrary Proposition—Abolitionists," *U.S. Telegraph*, Oct. 23, 1835, at 2; "Abolition—The Norwalk Gazette," *U.S. Telegraph*, Jan. 5, 1836, at 94.

55 *The Universal Almanac* 91 (John W. Wright ed., 1997).

56 Id.

57 Birney, "James Gillespie," in 2 *DAB*, supra note 50, at 291–94 (1929).

58 Id. at 292.

59 Executive Comm. of the Ohio Anti-Slavery Soc'y, *Narrative of the Late Riotous Proceedings Against the Liberty of the Press, in Cincinnati* (1836) [hereafter *Narrative of Cincinnati Riots*].

60 See Richards, *Gentlemen of Property and Standing*, supra note 35, at 92–101 (providing a detailed account).

61 *Narrative of Cincinnati Riots*, supra note 59, at 9.

62 Id. at 9–10 (emphasis omitted); see Richards, *Gentlemen of Property and Standing*, supra note 35, at 94.

63 *Narrative of Cincinnati Riots*, supra note 59, at 11; Richards, *Gentlemen of Property and Standing*, supra note 35, at 94.

64 Letters from James Gillespie Birney to Lewis Tappan (Mar. 17, 1836) in *Birney Letters*, supra note 52, at 311.

65 *Narrative of Cincinnati Riots*, supra note 59, at 12, 14; Richards, *Gentlemen of Property and Standing*, supra note 35, at 95–96.

66 *Narrative of Cincinnati Riots*, supra note 59, at 15.

67 Id. at 18.

68 Quoted in id. at 19–20; see Richards, *Gentlemen of Property and Standing*, supra note 35, at 97.

69 Quoted in *Narrative of Cincinnati Riots*, supra note 59, at 21; Richards, *Gentlemen of Property and Standing*, supra note 35, at 97.

70 Quoted in *Narrative of Cincinnati Riots*, supra note 59, at 22.

71 *Narrative of Cincinnati Riots* at 24; see Richards, *Gentlemen of Property and Standing*, supra note 35, at 97.

72 *Narrative of Cincinnati Riots*, supra note 59, at 25; Richards, *Gentlemen of Property and Standing*, supra note 35, at 98.

73 Quoted in *Narrative of Cincinnati Riots*, supra note 59, at 28.

74 Quoted in id. at 28–29.

75 Richards, *Gentlemen of Property and Standing*, supra note 35, at 98.

76 *Narrative of Cincinnati Riots*, supra note 59, at 35–37.

77 Id. at 40; see Richards, *Gentlemen of Property and Standing*, supra note 35, at 99.

78 Richards, *Gentlemen of Property and Standing*, supra note 35, at 100; *Narrative of Cincinnati Riots*, supra note 59, at 42.

79 *Narrative of Cincinnati Riots*, supra note 59, at 44; Richards, *Gentlemen of Property and Standing*, supra note 35, at 100.

80 Richards, *Gentlemen of Property and Standing*, supra note 35, at 93.

81 Letter from William T. Allan et al. to Theodore Dwight Weld (Aug. 9, 1836), in 1 *Weld-Grimké Letters*, supra note 49, at 324.

82 Letter from James Gillespie Birney to Gerrit Smith (Aug. 13, 1835), in *Birney Letters*, supra note 52, at 243.

83 *Niles' Wkly. Reg.*, Aug. 22, 1835, at 445, 446 (setting forth the reports of public meetings in Richmond, Virginia, and Charleston, South Carolina).

84 Id. at 446.

85 "Great Meeting in New York," *Wash. Globe*, Sept. 1, 1835, at 2; "Great Meeting at Bath, Maine," *Wash. Globe*, Sept. 3, 1835, at 2; "Great Meeting," *Wash. Globe*, Sept. 7, 1835, at 3; "Great Meeting," *Wash. Globe*, at Sept. 28, 1835, at 2; "New Jersey," *Wash. Globe*, Nov. 10, 1835, at 2.

86 "Town Meeting in Philadelphia," *Wash. Globe*, Aug. 29, 1835, at 2; "Anti-Abolitionist Meeting in Jefferson Hall—Portsmouth," *Wash. Globe*, Sept. 18, 1835, at 2; "Incendiaries," *Wash. Globe*, Oct. 7, 1835, at 1–2.

87 "Meeting of the Citizens of Albany," *Wash. Globe*, Sept. 10, 1835, at 2.

88 Id.

89 "Incendiary Tracts," *Wash. Telegraph*, Aug. 17, 1835, at 2. For a Northern view of the danger of political success by abolitionists in the North, see "Speech of Otis," supra note 10, at 11.

90 Resolutions of South Carolina, in *State Documents on Federal Relations: The States and the United States* 24 (Herman Ames ed., 1906).

91 "The Northern Fanatics," *Wash. Globe*, Sept. 22, 1835, at 2, quoting the *Wilmington, Delaware Watchman*.

92 "Committee of Vigilance," *Wash. Globe*, Oct. 2, 1835, at 2–3.

7 Congress Confronts the Abolitionists

1 Leonard L. Richards, *"Gentlemen of Property and Standing": Anti-Abolition Mobs in Jacksonian America* 54 (1970) [hereafter Richards, *Gentlemen of Property and Standing*].

2 Letter from Postmaster General Kendall to President Andrew Jackson (Aug. 7, 1835), in 5 *The Correspondence of Andrew Jackson*, 359–60 (John S. Bassett ed., 1931) [hereafter 5 *Correspondence of Andrew Jackson*].

3 "The Postmaster General and the Incendiaries," *Wash. Globe*, Aug. 12, 1835, at 2.

4 "Post Office Correspondence," *Wash. Globe*, Aug. 17, 1835, at 2.

5 Richards, *Gentlemen of Property and Standing*, supra note 1, at 74.

6 5 *Correspondence of Andrew Jackson*, supra note 2, at 361. Much more recently, Congress adopted a somewhat similar scheme to the one President Jackson advocated, with respect to "communist political propaganda." However, it was struck down in Lamont v. Postmaster Gen., 381 U.S. 301 (1965).

7 "Letters from Mr. Kendall, P.M.G.," *Niles' Wkly. Reg.*, Sept. 5, 1835, at 8.

8 "Great Meeting in the Park," *Wash. Globe*, Sept. 1, 1835, at 2; see also 1 Henry Wilson, *The Rise and Fall of the Slave Power in America* 186 (Negro Univ. Press 1969) (1872); *Niles' Wkly. Reg.*, Aug. 22, 1835, at 445, 446 (setting forth the reports of public meetings in Richmond, Virginia, and Charleston, South Carolina).

9 *Wash. Globe*, Sept. 11, 1835, at 2.

10 "From the Charleston Courier," *Wash. Globe*, Sept. 24, 1835, at 2.

11 Id.

12 Id.

13 *Niles' Wkly. Reg.*, Oct. 3, 1836, at 65.

14 *Evening Post* (N.Y.), Aug. 12, 1835, at 2.

15 *Evening Post* (N.Y.), Aug. 8, 1835, at 2.

16 *Cong. Globe*, 24th Cong., 1st Sess. app. 9 (1835).

17 Andrew Jackson, Seventh Annual Message to Congress, in 3 *A Compilation of the Messages and Papers of the Presidents, 1789–1897*, at 175–76 (James Richardson ed., 1896).

18 "Protest of the American Anti-Slavery Society," *Evening Post* (N.Y.), Jan. 28, 1836, at 2. The complaint followed a strategy Jackson had used in response to a Senate resolution condemning him.

19 "Protest of the American Anti-Slavery Society," id., Jan. 28, 1836, at 2. For a critical view of the idea that Jefferson was truly an opponent of slavery, see Paul Finkelman, "Jefferson and Slavery: 'Treason Against the Hopes of the World,'" in *Jeffersonian Legacies* (Peter S. Onuf ed., 1993).

20 "Protest of the American Anti-Slavery Society," *Evening Post* (N.Y.), Jan. 28, 1836, at 2.

21 Id.

22 Id.

23 "William Jay," 10 *Dictionary of American Biography* 11–12 (1933) [hereafter *DAB*]; William Jay, *Miscellaneous Writings on Slavery* 151 (Negro Univ. Press 1968) (1853) [hereafter Jay, *Writings on Slavery*].

24 Jay, *Writings on Slavery*, supra note 23, at 345.

25 Id. See "Legislature of New York, Requisition of the Governour of Alabama," *Evening Post* (N.Y.), Jan. 11, 1836, at 2.

26 For the composition of the committee, see *Cong. Globe*, 24th Cong., 1st Sess. 36 (1835); *Niles' Wkly. Reg.*, Dec. 26, 1835, at 285. For Calhoun's biography see 3 *DAB*, supra note 23, at 411–19 (1929); Richard Hofstadter, "John C. Calhoun—the Marx of the Master Class," in Richard Hofstadter, *The American Political Tradition and the Men Who Made It* 80–83 (1957) [hereafter Hofstadter, "Calhoun"].

27 Hofstadter, "Calhoun," supra note 26, at 90; Clement Eaton, *The Freedom of Thought Struggle in the Old South* 203–04 (1964).

28 12 *Cong. Deb.* 27 (1835).

29 Id. at 29.

30 Id. at 33.

31 *Cong. Globe*, 24th Cong., 1st Sess. 165 (1836).

32 John C. Calhoun, *Speeches of John C. Calhoun* 189–90 (1843).

33 Id. at 190.

34 Id. at 191.

35 Id. at 192.

36 Id. at 193, 197.

37 *Cong. Globe*, 24th Cong., 1st Sess. 291 (1836).

38 "Incendiary Publications," *Nat'l Intelligencer*, Mar. 26, 1836, at 3.

39 "Proposed Report by Mr. Hall (of Vt.), on Incendiary Publications," *Nat'l Intelligencer*, Apr. 8, 1836, at 2. The report also appears as "Report of the Minority of Committee on Post Offices and Post Roads on the President's Message," Hiland Hall Papers (Burlington, Vt., Park McCulloch House 1836). Richard John of the Department of History at the University of Illinois at Chicago is the first scholar I know of to have located this report. He generously furnished a copy to me, and he has since published it. Richard John, Highland Hall's "Report on Incendiary Publications," A Forgotten Nineteenth-Century Defense of the Freedom of the Press, 41 *Am. J. Legal Hist.* 94 (1997).

40 See "Proposed Report by Mr. Hall (of Vt.), On Incendiary Publications," *Nat'l Intelligencer*, Apr. 8, 1936, at 2.; see also "Report of Minority of Committee of Post Offices and Post Roads on the President's Message," Hiland Hall Papers (Burlington, Vt., Park McCulloch House 1836) [hereafter Hall, "Report"].

41 "Proposed Report by Mr. Hall (of Vt.), On Incendiary Publications," *Nat'l Intelligencer*, Apr. 8, 1836, at 1.

42 Hall, "Report," Hall papers, supra note 40, at 6.

43 Id.

44 Id. at 8.

45 "Mr. Calhoun's Constitutional Scruples," *Wash. Globe*, Feb. 26, 1836, at 2.

46 Id.

47 Id.

48 Id.

49 Cincinnatus, *Freedom's Defense or a Candid Examination of Mr. Calhoun's Report on Freedom of the Press* 6 (Worcester, Dorr, Howland and Co. 1836).

50 Id. at 8.

51 Id. at 9.

52 Id. at 14.

53 Id. at 20, 22.

54 12 *Cong. Deb.* 1103–04 (1836); "John Davis," 5 *DAB*, supra note 23, at 133–34 (1930).

55 12 *Cong. Deb.* 1003–04.

56 Id. at 1105. See Commonwealth v. Aves, 35 Mass. 193 (1836).

57 12 *Cong. Deb.* 1105.

58 See chapter 12; Michael Kent Curtis, "The 1859 Crisis over Hinton Helper's Book, *The Impending Crisis*: Free Speech, Slavery, and Some Light on the Meaning of the First Section of the Fourteenth Amendment," 68 *Chi.-Kent L. Rev.* 1113, 1153, 1162, 1162 nn.280 and n.281 (1993).

59 12 *Cong. Deb.* 1106 (1836).

60 Id.

61 Id. at 1107.

62 Id. at 1108.

63 Id. at 1151–52.

64 Id. at 1152.

65 Id. at 1152–53.

66 Id. at 1153.

67 Id. at 1721; "Daniel Webster," 19 *DAB*, supra note 23, at 585–89 (1936).

68 12 *Cong. Deb.* at 1722.

69 Id. at 1731.

70 Id. at 1728.

71 Id. at 1167.

72 Id. at 1168.

73 Id. at 1171.

74 Id. at 1153 (Sen. Davis); id. at 1729 (Sen. Clay).

75 Id. at 1158 (Sen. Niles).

76 Id. at 1157.

77 Id. at 1723.

78 Id. at 1128.

79 Id.

80 These included Senators Niles, Benton, and Morris.

81 12 *Cong. Deb.* 1155 (1836).

82 Id. at 1156.

83 Id. at 1721.

84 Id. at 1723.

85 Id. at 1727.

86 Id. at 1161.

87 Act of July 2, 1836, ch. 270, 5 Stat. 80, 87. The full title to this act was "An Act to Change the Organization of the Post Office Department, and to Provide Effectually for the Settlement of the Accounts Thereof." "Post Office Law," *Wash. Globe*, July 13, 1836, at 3.

88 Yazoo City Post Office Case, 8 Op. Att'y Gen. 489, 494 (1858).

89   *Cong. Globe*, 24th Cong., 1st Sess. 291 (1836) (Sen. Morris, Ohio).

90   See id. at 40, 75–77 (statements of Sen. Bouldin, Sen. Calhoun, Sen. Preston, and Sen. Benton). For discussions of the right to petition, see, e.g., David C. Frederick, "John Quincy Adams, Slavery, and the Disappearance of the Right of Petition," 9 *Law and Hist. Rev.* 113 (1991); Eric Schnapper, "'Libelous' Petitions for Redress of Grievances—Bad Historiography Makes Worse Law," 74 *Iowa L. Rev.* 303 (1989); Norman B. Smith, "'Shall Make No Law Abridging . . .': An Analysis of the Neglected but Nearly Absolute, Right of Petition," 54 *U. Cin. L. Rev.* 1153 (1986). Two classic studies are William Lee Miller, *Arguing About Slavery: The Great Battle in the United States Congress* (1996) [hereafter Miller, *Arguing About Slavery*] and Gilbert H. Barnes, *The Anti-Slavery Impulse, 1830–1844* (1964).

91   *Cong. Globe*, 24th Cong., 1st Sess. 75 (1836).

92   Id. at 75–76.

93   Id. at 83.

94   Id. at 120. E.g., Miller, *Arguing About Slavery*, supra note 90, at 95.

95   U.S. Const., amend. I. The contention was that the gag rule violated at least the spirit of this guarantee.

96   U.S. Const., art. I, sec. 6, cl. 1.

97   *Cong. Globe*, 24th Cong., 1st Sess. 75 (1836) (Sen. Morris).

98   Id. at 121.

99   Id. at 137.

100   Abolition Report, reprinted in 12 *Cong. Deb.* 4052–53 (1836).

101   Id. at 4053.

102   Miller, *Arguing About Slavery*, supra note 90, at 303–04.

103   Id. at 230–39.

104   Id. at 247.

105   Quoted in id. at 251–52.

106   Id. at 270; see also 262–67.

107   Id. at 477, quoting the *New York Tribune*, Dec. 5, 1844.

108   See *Cong. Globe*, 24th Cong., 1st Sess. 187 (1836).

109   Bacon v. Commonwealth, 48 Va. (7 Gratt.) 602, 602–03 (1850).

8   THE DEMAND FOR NORTHERN LEGAL ACTION
AGAINST ABOLITIONISTS

1   Quoted in *Wash. Globe*, Aug. 29, 1835, at 2.

2   2 James Kent, *Commentaries on American Law* (New York, Clayton, Van Norden, 1836) 254 (lecture 32) [hereafter 2 *Kent's Commentaries*].

3   2 *Journal of the Senate of the Commonwealth of Pennsylvania Which Commenced at Harrisburg on the First Day of December* 364 (1835) (reprinting the Virginia Resolutions).

4   *Acts Passed by the General Assembly of the State of North Carolina at the Session of 1835*, at 121 (1836).

5   *Acts Passed at the Annual Session of the General Assembly of the State of Alabama*

Begun and Held in the Town of Tuscaloosa, on the Third Monday in November, One Thousand Eight Hundred and Thirty-Five, at 175 (1836).

6   Id. at 364.

7   2 *Journal of the Senate of the Commonwealth of Pennsylvania* 137 (1836) [hereafter 2 *Pennsylvania Senate Journal*] (reprinting the Report of the Joint Committee of Federal Relations, in the Legislature of South Carolina). For other Southern resolutions, often shorter and sometimes lacking explicit demands for Northern legislation suppressing abolition societies in the North, see e.g., *Acts Passed at the First Session of the Forty-Fourth General Assembly of the Commonwealth of Kentucky* 683–87 (1836); *Acts Passed at the First Session of the Thirteenth Legislature of the State of Louisiana* 18–19 (1837); *Laws of the State of Missouri Passed at the First Session of the Tenth General Assembly* 337–38 (1838); *Acts of the General Assembly of the State of Georgia Passed in November and December 1835*, at 297–300 (1836); *Acts of the General Assembly of Virginia, Passed at the Session of 1835–36*, at 395–97 (1836); *Laws of the State of Mississippi Passed in January and February 1836*, at 101–03 (1836).

8   2 *Pennsylvania Senate Journal*, supra note 7, at 141 (reprinting the North Carolina Report).

9   Id. at 271.

10   Id. at 136 (Reprinting the South Carolina Report).

11   "Gov. Marcy's Message—Abolition," *Wash. Globe*, Jan. 11, 1836, at 3.

12   Id.

13   Alvan Stewart, *Writings and Speeches of Alvan Stewart on Slavery* 59, 65 (Luther Marsh ed., 1860).

14   Id. at 66.

15   Id. at 84.

16   See, e.g., *Cong. Globe*, 36th Cong., 1st Sess. 1837 (1859–60) (Senator Clingman); *Cong. Globe*, 36th Cong., 1st Sess. 1618 (1859–60) (Senator Chesnut); *Cong. Globe*, 36th Cong., 1st Sess. 436 (1859–60) (Rep. Smith, who repudiated many statements by men of the revolutionary generation as "false in philosophy and unsound in fact"); see also *Cong. Globe*, 36th Cong., 1st Sess. 1049 (1859–60) (Senator Collamer, quoting Senator Calhoun).

17   *U.S. Telegraph*, Jan. 19, 1836, at 442. The *Telegraph* insisted that nullification was the way to protect the South against the dangers posed by opponents of slavery.

18   "Governor Marcy's Message," *U.S. Telegraph*, Jan. 15, 1836, at 131.

19   *U.S. Telegraph*, Jan. 19, 1836, at 442.

20   12 *Cong. Deb.* 1147 (1836).

21   *Acts Passed at the First Session of the Forty-Fourth General Assembly of the Commonwealth of Kentucky* 685 (1836).

22   *Niles' Wkly. Reg.*, Oct 3, 1835, at 1.

23   "Freedom of Speech and of the Press," *Niles' Wkly. Reg.*, Dec. 5, 1835, at 236.

24   "Great Meeting," *Wash. Globe*, Sept. 28, 1835, at 2.

25   *Niles' Wkly. Reg.*, Oct. 3, 1835, at 65.

26   "Slavery—Abolition—No. 1," *Wash. Globe*, Oct. 5, 1835, at 3.

27 See "The New York Report on Slavery," reprinted in 2 *Pennsylvania Senate Journal*, supra note 7, at 423 (1836). The reprint also contains the resolutions and reports from a number of states.

28 Id.

29 Id. at 424, 425.

30 Edward Everett, *Address of His Excellency Edward Everett to the Two Branches of the Legislature* 30 (Boston, Dutton and Wentworth 1836).

31 Letter from Elizur Wright Jr. to Theodore Weld (Mar. 24, 1836), in 1 *Letters of Theodore Dwight Weld, Angelina Grimké and Sarah Grimké*, 281 (Gilbert H. Barnes and Dwight L. Dumond eds. 1965).

32 George Wolf, "Annual Message to the Assembly—1835," in IV *Pennsylvania Archives, Papers of the Governors* 243 (1901).

33 Id. at 291–92 (Message of Governor Ritner).

34 *Report Relative to Abolition Societies and Incendiary Publications on March 30, 1836*, in 1835–36 *Journal of the House of Representatives* (Pennsylvania) 250 (1836).

35 "The Ball Rolling," *Wash. Globe*, Dec. 2, 1836, at 3; William M. Wiecek, *The Sources of Antislavery Constitutionalism in America, 1760–1848* 181–82 (1977).

36 "Ohio Report on Slavery," in 2 *Pennsylvania Senate Journal*, supra note 7, at 417–18 (1836).

37 "Abolition Movements," *U.S. Telegraph*, Sept. 2, 1835, at 2.

38 12 *Cong. Deb.* 1732 (1836).

39 See, e.g., Leonard W. Levy, *The Emergence of a Free Press* 251, 307 (1985).

40 See, e.g., *Wash. Globe*, Aug. 28, 1835, at 2 (appearing under letters to the editor).

41 *Evening Post* (N.Y.), July 14, 1836, at 2.

42 Letter from Francis Lieber to John C. Calhoun, in *Freedom of the Press from Hamilton to the Warren Court* 179 (Harold L. Nelson ed., 1967); see also, William W. Freehling, *The Road to Disunion*, vol. 1, *Secessionists at Bay, 1776–1854*, at 301–04 (1990).

9 LEGAL THEORIES OF SUPPRESSION AND THE DEFENSE OF FREE SPEECH

1 U.S. Const. art III, sec. 3; William Mayton, "Seditious Libel and the Lost Guarantee of a Freedom of Expression," 84 *Colum. L. Rev.* 91 (1984); *The Federalist* No. 84, at 435 (Alexander Hamilton) (Bantam Books 1982) (citing the treason clause as a guarantee of liberty) [hereafter *The Federalist* No. 84].

2 *The Federalist* No. 84, supra note 1, at 435.

3 Id.; U.S. Const. art. III, sec. 3.

4 See *A Full Statement of the Reasons Which Were in Part Offered to the Committee of the Legislature of Massachusetts on the Fourth and Eighth of March Showing Why There Should Be No Penal Laws Enacted, and No Condemnatory Resolutions Passed by the Legislature Respecting Abolitionists and Anti-Slavery Societies*, 11 (Boston, Anti-Slavery Society 1836) [hereafter *Full Statement*]. The treason clause provision was also cited by Congressman John Quincy Adams in defending himself against similar charges. See John Quincy Adams, *Letters from John Quincy Adams to His*

Constituents of the Twelfth Congressional District in Massachusetts 24 (Boston, Mass.: Issac Knapp, 1837). For examples in which abolitionists were accused of treason, see William Jay, *Miscellaneous Writings on Slavery* 141, 148 (Negro Univ. Press 1968) (1853) [hereafter Jay, *Writings on Slavery*].

5 1 Joel Prentiss Bishop, *Commentaries on the Criminal Law*, 312, sec. 357 (1856).

6 Leonard L. Richards, *The Life and Times of Congressman John Quincy Adams* 128, 142 (1986); "House Report on the Censure of Mr. Adams," in 13 *Cong. Deb.* 1638 (1837).

7 See, e.g., 12 *Cong. Deb.* 1728 (1836) (Sen. Clay of Kentucky); 12 *Cong. Deb.* 1721–22 (1836) (Sen. Webster of Massachusetts). See also John C. Calhoun, *Speeches of John C. Calhoun* 190 (Harper and Brothers 1843).

8 James Madison, "Report of the Committee to Whom Were Referred the Communications of Various States, Relative to the Resolutions of the Last General Assembly of this State Concerning the Alien and Sedition Laws," in VI *The Writings of James Madison* 395–98 (Gaillard Hunt ed., 1906).

9 Donna L. Dickerson, *The Course of Tolerance: Freedom of the Press in Nineteenth-Century America* at 6–7 (1990).

10 Id. at 22–34. For a discussion of nineteenth-century libel law in New York, see Donald Roper, "James Kent and the Emergence of New York's Libel Law," 17 *Am. J.L. Hist.* 223 (1973). Ultimately, Roper concludes that Kent's role as a protector of free speech has been exaggerated.

11 2 James Kent, *Commentaries on American Law* at 21, 23 (lecture 24) (3d ed. New York, E. B. Clayton, James Van Norden 1836).

12 See generally Leonard Levy, *The Emergence of a Free Press* 338–49 (1985).

13 2 Joel P. Bishop, *Commentaries on the Criminal Law* 516, sec. 784; 517, sec. 789; 518, sec. 791; see also id. at 518 n. 2 (Boston, Little, Brown and Co. 1858) [hereafter Bishop, *Commentaries*].

14 T. R. Sullivan, *Letters Against Immediate Abolition of Slavery Addressed to the Free Blacks of the Non-Slave-Holding States, Comprising a Legal Opinion on the Power of Legislature in Non-Slave-Holding States to Prevent Measures Tending to Immediate and General Emancipation, in a Letter to the Author from William Sullivan, L.L.D.* at 42 (Boston, Hilliard, Gray and Co. 1835) (setting forth letters originally printed in the *Boston Courier*).

15 Id. at 43, 44.

16 "The Law of Libel and the Abolitionists," *Evening Post* (N.Y.), Aug. 31, 1835, at 2.

17 Id.

18 "The Richmond Meeting—Southern Pretensions," *Evening Post* (N.Y.), Aug. 17, 1835, at 2.

19 Id.

20 Id.

21 "The Law of Libel and the Abolitionists," *Evening Post* (N.Y.), Sept. 14, 1835, at 2.

22 Id. Veto did admit that the tendency of the writing could be evidence of intent.

23 People v. Croswell, 3 Johns. Cas. 337 (N.Y. 1804). Although a divided court in *Croswell* did not establish the more libertarian standard of truth published for good motives and justifiable ends, that standard, together with a broad role for the jury,

was established in An Act Concerning Libels, Laws of the State of New York (Albany, 1805), reprinted in *Freedom of the Press from Hamilton to the Warren Court* 40–42 (Harold L. Nelson ed., 1967) [hereafter Nelson, *Freedom of the Press*].

24 "The Law of Libel and the Abolitionists," *Evening Post* (N.Y.), Sept. 14, 1835, at 2.

25 See, e.g., Cincinnatus, *Freedom's Defence*, 17–20 (Worcester, Dorr, Howland, and Co. 1836).

26 *The Trial of Reuben Crandall, M.D., Charged with Publishing and Circulating Seditious and Incendiary Papers, etc. in the District of Columbia, with the Intent of Exciting Servile Insurrection* (1836), reprinted in *Slave Rebels, Abolitionists, and the Southern Courts* 8 (Paul Finkelman ed., Garland Pub. 1988).

27 Id. at 46.

28 See, e.g., *Cong. Globe*, 24th Cong., 1st Sess. 119–22 (1836); *Cong. Globe*, 24th Cong., 1st Sess. 83 (1836) (Senator Calhoun).

29 Id. at 158.

30 2 Bishop, *Commentaries*, supra note 13, at 519.

31 Beauharnais v. Illinois, 343 U.S. 250, 271–72 (1952) (Black, J., dissenting). But see id. at 258 and n. 7 (wherein the Court refers to "authority, however dubious" that group libel utterances were crimes at common law).

32 *A Brief Sketch of the Trial of William Lloyd Garrison for an Alleged Libel on Francis Todd, of Massachusetts* (1830), reprinted in 1 *Slave Rebels, Abolitionists, and Southern Courts: The Pamphlet Literature* 197 (Paul Finkelman, ed., Garland Pub. 1988) [hereafter *Garrison Trial* (1830)].

33 Id. at 194–95. See also Appendix to *A Brief Sketch of the Trial of William Lloyd Garrison for an Alleged Libel on Francis Todd, of Massachusetts* (1834) reprinted in 1 *Slave Rebels, Abolitionists, and Southern Courts: The Pamphlet Literature* 218–19 (Paul Finkelman ed., Garland Pub. 1988) [hereafter *Garrison Trial* (1834)].

34 Id. at 222.

35 Henry Mayer, *All on Fire: William Lloyd Garrison and the Abolition of Slavery* 91–93 (1998) [hereafter Mayer, *All on Fire*]; see also id. at 84–94; *Garrison Trial* (1834), supra note 33, at 203.

36 *Garrison Trial* (1830), supra note 32, at 193 and 200.

37 *Garrison Trial* (1834), supra note 33 at 220.

38 Id. at 222–23.

39 Mayer, *All on Fire*, supra note 35, at 84–85, 149 (later attack by another libel action), 162, 172.

40 *Garrison Trial* (1830), supra note 32 at 193.

41 William Seward, *Notes on New York*, in 2 *The Works of William H. Seward* 37–38 (George Baker ed., 1853).

42 Mass. House Doc. No. 6, *Address of His Excellency Edward Everett to the Two Branches of the Legislature, on the Organization of the Government, for the Political Year Commencing January 6, 1836*, at 29–30 (Boston, Mass. 1836).

43 Id. at 30.

44 Id.

45 "History of Calhoun's Sedition Law," *Evening Post* (N.Y.), June 18, 1836, at 2.

46 "A Grand Jury Presentment," *Wash. Globe*, Sept. 29, 1835, at 2.

47 Jay, *Writings on Slavery*, supra note 4, at 345.

48 *Cong. Globe*, 24th Cong., 1st Sess. 123–24 (1836).

49 U.S. Const. art. IV, sec. 2, cl. 2.

50 "Fugitives from Justice," *Evening Post* (N.Y.), Oct. 14, 1835, at 2.

51 Id.

52 "Legislature of New York: Requisition of the Governour of Alabama," *Evening Post* (N.Y.), Jan. 11, 1836, at 2.

53 Id.

54 *Niles' Wkly. Reg.*, Oct 3, 1835, at 65.

55 Id.

56 *Evening Post* (N.Y.), Nov. 13, 1835, at 2.

57 Id.

58 *Evening Post* (N.Y.), Aug. 8, 1835, at 2.

59 William Ellery Channing, *Slavery* 4 (Boston, James Munroe 1835) [hereafter Channing, *Slavery*]. See also William E. Channing, *Slavery* (1835), in *Slavery and Emancipation* 4 (3d ed., Negro Univ. Press, 1968) (1836).

60 Channing, *Slavery* supra note 59, at 163.

61 "Letter of Dr. W. E. Channing to James G. Birney, Boston, Nov. 1st, 1836," in *Philanthropist*, Dec. 9, 1836, at 2; also reprinted in 2 William Ellery Channing, *The Works of William E. Channing*, 156, 161 (1980) [hereafter Channing's Letter].

62 Id. at 163–64. Birney published Channing's letter, supra note 61. For another rejection of the bad-tendency rationale cf., e.g., Cincinnatus, *Freedom's Defence, or, A Candid Examination of Mr. Calhoun's Report on Freedom of the Press* 22 (Worcester, Dorr, Howland and Co. 1836).

63 In the South, Congressman John Quincy Adams said, "the doctrine of the Declaration of Independence … is … held as incendiary doctrine, and deserves lynching." 2 *Emancipator* 47, July 19, 1838.

64 Letter from James G. Birney to Gerrit Smith (Sept. 13, 1835), in 1 *Letters of James Gillespie Birney, 1831–1857*, at 243 (Dwight Dumond ed., 1966).

65 Id.

66 *Proceedings of the New York Anti-Slavery Convention Held at Utica, October 21, and New York Anti-Slavery State Society Held at Peterboro, 22 October 1835* at 3 (Utica Standard and Democrat, 1835).

67 Id. at 12.

68 Id. at 12, 13, 16.

69 Id. at 19, 16.

70 "To the People of the United States, or, To Such Americans as Value Their Rights, and Dare to Maintain Them," *Evening Post* (N.Y.), Aug. 2, 1836, at 2.

71 *Full Statement*, supra note 4, at 10.

72 Id. at 17.

73 Id at 10.

74 Tunis Wortman, *A Treatise Concerning Political Enquiry and the Liberty of the Press* 174 (New York, George Forman, 1800).

75 Id. at 10–11. See also Letter from William Ellery Channing to James G. Birney (Nov. 1, 1836), reprinted in Nelson, *Freedom of the Press*; supra note 23, at 199 stat-

ing: "Almost all men see ruinous tendencies in whatever opposes their particular interests or views. . . . So infinite are the connections and consequences of human affairs, that nothing can be done in which some dangerous tendency may not be detected."

76 *Full Statement*, supra note 4, at 34.

77 Id. at 36.

78 *An Account of the Interviews Which Took Place on the Fourth and Eighth of March between a Committee of the Massachusetts Anti-Slavery Society and the Committee of the Legislature* 15–16 (Boston, Mass., n.p., 1836).

79 William Lee Miller, *Arguing About Slavery: The Great Battle in the United States Congress* 317, 315–19 (1996) [hereafter Miller, *Arguing About Slavery*].

80 Angelina Emily Grimké, *Letters to Catherine E. Beecher* 71–72, 81, 27, 69 (Black Heritage Library 1971) (1838).

81 Id. at 95, 102.

82 Id. at 104.

83 Id. at 112.

84 Miller, *Arguing About Slavery*, supra note 79, at 319–20.

85 Id. at 322.

86 1 *Letters of Theodore Dwight Weld, Angelina Grimké and Sarah Grimké* 426–30, 433 (Gilbert H. Barnes and Dwight L. Dumond eds., 1965); Akhil Reed Amar, "The Bill of Rights and the Fourteenth Amendment," 101 *Yale L.J.* 1193, at 1279–84 (1992).

10 ELIJAH LOVEJOY

1 Leonard Richards, *Gentlemen of Property and Standing: Anti-Abolition Mobs in Jacksonian America* 105 (1970) [hereafter Richards, *Gentlemen of Property and Standing*]. There are a number of historical accounts of the Lovejoy affair. See, e.g., John Gill, *Tide Without Turning: Elijah P. Lovejoy and Freedom of the Press* (1958) [hereafter Gill, *Tide Without Turning*]; Merton L. Dillon, *Elijah P. Lovejoy, Abolitionist Editor* (1961) [hereafter Dillon, *Lovejoy*]; Paul Simon, *Freedom's Champion: Elijah Lovejoy* (1994).

2 Dillon, *Lovejoy*, supra note 1, at 161.

3 "Owen Lovejoy," 2 *Emancipator* 134 (Dec. 28, 1837).

4 See Dillon, *Lovejoy*, supra note 1, at 167 n. 27; Gill, *Tide Without Turning*, supra note 1, at 194–95 (asserting that the mob fired first); Edward Magdol, *Owen Lovejoy: Abolitionist in Congress* 21 (1967). But cf. Richards, *Gentlemen of Property and Standing*, supra note 1, at 109 (noting the uncertainty regarding who fired the first shot).

5 Richards, *Gentlemen of Property and Standing*, supra note 1, at 110.

6 James Madison, Amendments to the Constitution June 8, 1789, in 2 *The Bill of Rights: A Documentary History* 1030 (Bernard Schwartz ed., 1971); see also Paul Finkelman, "James Madison and the Bill of Rights: A Reluctant Paternity," 1990 *Sup. Ct. Rev.* 301.

7 See generally, Eric Foner, *Reconstruction: America's Unfinished Revolution, 1863–1877* (1989); Robert J. Kaczorowski, *The Politics of Judicial Interpretation: The Fed-*

eral Courts, Department of Justice and Civil Rights, 1866–1876 (1985); Vernon L. Wharton, *The Negro in Mississippi, 1865–1890* (1947).

8 Compare United States v. Cruikshank, 92 U.S. 542 (1876) with The Civil Rights Cases, 109 U.S. 3 (1883) and United States v. Harris, 106 U.S. 629 (1882). By contrast federal rights conferred on the citizen could be protected—such as the right to vote in a federal election or the right to assemble to discuss *national* matters and to petition the *federal* government. *Ex parte* Yarborough, 110 U.S. 651, 658, 666 (1884); *Cruikshank*, 92 U.S. at 552–53.

9 See, e.g., United States v. Lopez, 115 S. Ct. 1624 (1995); United Bhd. of Carpenters Local 610 v. Scott, 463 U.S. 825 (1983); Perez v. United States, 402 U.S. 146 (1971); Katzenbach v. Morgan, 384 U.S. 641 (1966); *Harris*, 106 U.S. at 629; *Cruikshank*, 92 U.S. at 542.

10 Compare, e.g., United States v. Price, 383 U.S. 787 (1966); United States v. Guest, 383 U.S. 745 (1966); and Adickes v. S. H. Kress & Co., 398 U.S. 144 (1970) with Griffin v. Breckenridge, 403 U.S. 88 (1971) and *Scott*, 463 U.S. at 825.

11 Stephen Labaton, "Reno Orders U.S. Mediation in Lesbian Harrassment Case," *N.Y. Times*, Feb. 19, 1994, at 1.

12 See Richard Cohen, "Sheldon Hackney's Dangerous Balance," *Wash. Post*, July 6, 1993, at A15; Mary Jordan, "Students Who Set Off Penn Newspaper Censorship Uproar Won't Be Punished," *Wash. Post*, Sept. 15, 1993, at A2 (discussing the University of Pennsylvania incident); see also Howard Kurtz, "A Trash Course In Free Speech; College Newspapers Pitched in Protests," *Wash. Post*, July 29, 1993, at C1 (discussing similar incidents on other college campuses).

13 "Gilbert H. Barnes," "Elijah Parish Lovejoy," in 6 *Dictionary of American Biography* 434–35 (Dumas Malone ed., 1961).

14 "E. P. Lovejoy," *St. Louis Observer*, Aug. 27, 1835, reprinted in *Memoir of the Rev. Elijah P. Lovejoy* 113–14 (Joseph C. Lovejoy and Owen Lovejoy eds., Arno Press, 1969) (1838) [hereafter *Lovejoy Memoir*].

15 Elijah P. Lovejoy, "Slavery," *St. Louis Observer*, June 1834, reprinted in *Lovejoy Memoir*, supra note 14, at 120.

16 Dillon, *Lovejoy*, supra note 1, at 54 (citing the *St. Louis Observer*, Apr. 16, 1835); Elijah P. Lovejoy, "Slavery," *St. Louis Observer*, Apr. 16, 1835, reprinted in *Lovejoy Memoir*, supra note 14, at 123.

17 *Lovejoy Memoir*, supra note 14, at 123.

18 Dillon, *Lovejoy*, supra note 1, at 54–55; Elijah P. Lovejoy, "Letter from the Editor," *St. Louis Observer*, May 21, 1835, reprinted in *Lovejoy Memoir*, supra note 14, at 131.

19 Dillon, *Lovejoy*, supra note 1, at 58, 60, 62, 66–67; Archibald Gamble et al., "To the Rev. E. P. Lovejoy, Editor of the *Observer*," *St. Louis Observer*, Oct. 5, 1835 [hereafter Gamble et al. to Lovejoy], reprinted in *Lovejoy Memoir*, supra note 14, at 138–39 [hereafter Gamble et al. to Lovejoy].

20 Gamble et al. to Lovejoy, supra note 19, at 139–40.

21 Elijah P. Lovejoy, "To My Fellow Citizens," *St. Louis Observer*, Nov. 5, 1835, reprinted in *Lovejoy Memoir*, supra note 14, at 141.

22 Id. at 143.

23 Id. 143–44.

24 Id. at 147, 149.

25 Id. at 153.

26 See, e.g., Richards, *Gentlemen of Property and Standing*, supra note 1, at 101.

27 Elijah P. Lovejoy, "Awful Murder and Savage Barbarity," *St. Louis Observer*, May 5, 1835, reprinted in *Lovejoy Memoir*, supra note 14, at 172–73.

28 Elijah P. Lovejoy, "The Charge of Judge Lawless," *St. Louis Observer*, July 21, 1836, reprinted in *Lovejoy Memoir*, supra note 14, at 175.

29 Dillon, *Lovejoy*, supra note 1, at 83–85.

30 *Lovejoy Memoir*, supra note 14, at 105.

31 Id. at 176–77.

32 Dillon, *Lovejoy*, supra note 1, at 88.

33 Id.; Richards, *Gentlemen of Property and Standing*, supra note 1, at 101.

34 "The Bubble Burst," *Alton Observer*, May 25, 1837, reprinted in *Lovejoy Memoir*, supra note 14, at 189–90.

35 "Illinois State Anti-Slavery Society," *Alton Observer*, July 6, 1837, reprinted in *Lovejoy Memoir*, supra note 14, at 214; Richards, *Gentlemen of Property and Standing*, supra note 1, at 102.

36 "Illinois State Anti-Slavery Society," in *Lovejoy Memoir*, supra note 14, at 217; Richards, *Gentlemen of Property and Standing*, supra note 1, at 102–03.

37 "Illinois State Anti-Slavery Society," in *Lovejoy Memoir*, supra note 14, at 218–19.

38 "Anti-Slavery Principles," *Alton Observer*, July 27, 1837, reprinted in *Emancipator Extra*, Feb. 12, 1838, at 1; in *Lovejoy Memoir*, supra note 14, at 235–39.

39 Letter from Elijah P. Lovejoy to B. K. Hart et al. (July 26, 1837), reprinted in *Lovejoy Memoir*, supra note 14, at 228.

40 Richards, *Gentlemen of Property and Standing*, supra note 1, at 104–05.

41 *Lovejoy Memoir*, supra note 14, at 269–70 (quoting proposed Resolutions from the City of Alton Public Meeting (Nov. 2, 1837)).

42 Id. at 274.

43 Id. at 279–80 (quoting the Remarks of Elijah P. Lovejoy Before the City of Alton Public Meeting (Nov. 3, 1837)) (internal quotation marks omitted).

44 "The Southern Agitators," *Wash. Globe*, May 18, 1835, at 2.

45 "The Impression That Is Making in the Slave States," 2 *Emancipator* 131 (Dec. 21, 1837) (quoting the *Louisville Journal*, Dec. 6, 1837).

46 "Testimonies of a Free Press," *Emancipator Extra*, Feb. 12, 1838, at 2 [hereafter "Testimonies of a Free Press"].

47 John Quincy Adams, Introduction to *Lovejoy Memoir*, supra note 14, at 12 [hereafter Adams, Introduction].

48 "Sentiments of the Press," 2 *Emancipator* 130 (Dec. 21, 1837) (quoting the *Easton Pennsylvania Whig*); id. (quoting the *Boston Times*); id. (quoting the *Providence Courier*).

49 "Some Particulars of the Abolition Riot and Deaths at Alton, from the *Cincinnati Whig*," Nov. 14, *Daily Albany Argus*, Wed. Nov. 22, 1837, at 2.

50 "Lynch Law," 2 *Emancipator* 141 (Jan. 11, 1838) [hereafter "Lynch Law"].

51 See *Emancipator Extra*, Feb. 12, 1838, at 1–4.

52 "Testimonies of the Spirit of Liberty," 2 *Emancipator* 129–30 (Dec. 21, 1837) (quoting the *Lutheran Observer*).

53 *Evening Post* (N.Y.), July 14, 1836, at 2; From the *Cleveland Whig*, quoted in *Philanthropist*, March 11, 1836 at 4; "The Voice of the Public Press," 2 *Emancipator* 120 (Nov. 30, 1837) (quoting the *Louisville Herald*) [hereafter "Voice of the Public Press"]; Id. (quoting the *New York Daily News*); "Testimonies of a Free Press," supra note 46, at 2 (quoting the *New Hampshire Courier*); *Emancipator Extra*, Feb. 12, 1838, at 3 (quoting the *Brooklyn Gazette* (Conn.)); "Supremacy of Laws—Meeting in Weymouth," *Boston Daily Advocate*, Dec. 19, 1837, at 2.

54 "Meeting of Young Men in New York," 2 *Emancipator* 154 (Feb. 1, 1838).

55 Id.

56 "Voice of the Public Press," supra note 53 (quoting the *Newark Daily Advertiser*); "Testimonies of a Free Press," supra note 46, at 3 (quoting the *Berkshire Courier*); "The Impartial Verdict of Free Citizens, Concord, N.H.," 2 *Emancipator* 168 (Feb. 22, 1838) [hereafter "Impartial Verdict, Concord, N.H."]; "The Impartial Verdict of Free Citizens, Susquehanna, Pa. County," 2 *Emancipator* 168 (Feb. 22, 1838).

57 "Appeal to Alton," 2 *Emancipator* 161 (Feb. 15, 1838).

58 "The Impartial Verdict of Free Citizens, Belfast Maine," 2 *Emancipator* 169 (Feb. 22, 1838) [hereafter "Impartial Verdict, Belfast, Maine"].

59 "Mobocracy and the Press," 2 *Emancipator* 133 (Dec. 28, 1837) (quoting the *Nashua Courier* (N.H.)).

60 Edward Beecher, *Narrative of Riots at Alton in Connection with the Death of Rev. Elijah P. Lovejoy* 5 (Alton, George Holton 1838) [hereafter Beecher, *Narrative*].

61 "The Alton Murder," 2 *Emancipator* 120 (Nov. 30, 1837) (quoting the *New York Evangelist*).

62 "Testimonies of a Free Press," supra note 46, at 3 (quoting the *Greenfield Gazette*).

63 "Murder!" 2 *Emancipator* 120 (Nov. 30, 1837) (quoting the *Philadelphia Commercial Herald*).

64 "The Voice of a Slaveholder to the Citizens of Alton," 2 *Emancipator* 127 (Dec. 14, 1837) (quoting the *Peoria Register* (Ill.)). The Illinois press was far less critical than papers in states farther north.

65 "The Impartial Verdict of Free Citizens, Washington County, N.Y.," 2 *Emancipator* 168 (Feb. 22, 1838).

66 "The Impartial Verdict of Free Citizens, Lawrence, Pa.," 2 *Emancipator* 169 (Feb. 22, 1838).

67 "Impartial Verdict of Belfast Maine," supra note 58, at 168.

68 "Freedom of Discussion," *Boston Daily Advocate*, Jan. 3, 1838, at 2.

69 Id. A line has been dropped in the copy of the paper I have examined; however, I think this is the intended meaning.

70 Id.

71 "Meeting at Faneuil Hall," *Emancipator Extra*, Feb. 12, 1838, at 1 (quoting the *Boston Daily Advertiser*).

72 "The Impartial Verdict of Free Citizens, Public Meeting at Rochester," 2 *Emancipator* 168 (Feb. 12, 1838) (quoting the *Rochester Democrat* (N.Y.)).

73 "The Alton Riot," 2 *Emancipator* 129 (Dec. 21, 1837) (quoting the *Boston Christian Watchman*).

74 The Massachusetts legislature and Governor Edward Everett assailed the congressional gag rule as a violation of the right to petition: "[I]t tends essentially to impair those fundamental principles of natural justice and natural law, which are antecedent to any written constitutions of government," the legislature asserted. Letter from Edward Everett, Governor of Mass., to Winthrop Atwill (Oct. 28, 1838), reprinted in 2 *Emancipator* 115 (Nov. 23, 1837).

75 "The Impartial Verdict, Concord, N.H.," supra note 56; "The Impartial Verdict of Free Citizens, Prospect, Maine," 2 *Emancipator* 168 (Feb. 22, 1838); Letter from Marcus Morton, Judge (Sept. 28, 1837), reprinted in 2 *Emancipator* 115 (Nov. 23, 1837) [hereafter Morton's Letter]; *Emancipator Extra*, Feb. 12, 1838, at 3 (quoting the *Brooklyn Gazette* (Conn.)); "The Impartial Verdict of Free Citizens, Public Meetings in Worcester County," 2 *Emancipator* 168 (Feb. 22, 1838) (referring to the Marlboro meeting on Dec. 19).

76 "From the *Lynn Record*, Great and Solemn Meeting," *Boston Daily Advocate*, Nov. 24, 1837, at 2.

77 E.g., Adams, Introduction, supra note 47, at 8; "Lynch Law," supra note 50; Morton's Letter, supra note 75.

78 "Horrible Outrage Against Constitution and Laws," *Phila. Public Ledger and Daily Transcript*, Nov. 20, 1837, at 4.

79 Id.

80 See "The Law of Libel and the Abolitionists," *Evening Post* (N.Y.), Aug. 31, 1835, at 2; "The Northern Fanatics," *Wash. Globe*, Sept. 22, 1833, at 2 (quoting the *Wilmington Watchman*); Letter from S. G. Goodrich to Elias Richards (Oct. 30, 1837), reprinted in 2 *Emancipator* 115 (Nov. 23, 1837).

81 "Sentiments of the Public Press," 2 *Emancipator* 117 (Nov. 23, 1837) (quoting the *New York Evening Post*).

82 Id.

83 "Mob in Alton, Ill.," 2 *Emancipator* 128 (Dec. 14, 1837) (quoting the *Magazine and Advocate* (Utica, N.Y.), in turn quoting Thomas Jefferson, "First Inaugural Address" [hereinafter "Mob in Alton"].

84 "Impartial Verdict, Concord, N.H.," supra note 56; see also "Freedom of Discussion," *Boston Daily Advocate*, Jan. 3, 1838, at 2.

85 "Impartial Verdict, Concord, N.H.," supra note 56.

86 "Mob in Alton," supra note 83.

87 "The Alton Riot," 2 *Emancipator* 133 (Dec. 28, 1837) (quoting the *Elmira Republican* (N.Y.)); see "The Contrast," *Boston Daily Advocate*, Dec. 2, 1837, at 2.

88 See, e.g., Letter of Reverend Thomas Brainerd to the Editor of the *Emancipator* (Dec. 12, 1837), reprinted in 2 *Emancipator* 152 (Jan. 25, 1838).

89 "Sound the Alarm," 2 *Emancipator* 133 (Dec. 28, 1837) (quoting the *Herald of Freedom*).

90 *Lovejoy Memoir*, supra note 14, at 279–80 (quoting the remarks of Elijah P. Lovejoy before the City of Alton public meeting (Nov. 3, 1837)).

91 Id. See also Elijah P. Lovejoy, "Europe," St. Louis *Observer*, Mar. 27, 1834, reprinted in *Lovejoy Memoir*, supra note 14, at 86.

92 Beecher, *Narrative*, supra note 60, at 83.

93 "The Impartial Verdict of Free Citizens, Cleveland, Ohio," 2 *Emancipator* 168 (Feb. 22, 1838).

94 *Lovejoy Memoir*, supra note 14, at 300.

11 AFTER LOVEJOY

1 Horace Greeley, *Recollections of a Busy Life* 287 (1868).

2 *The Diary of John Quincy Adams, 1794–1845*, at 489 (Allan Nevins ed., 1929).

3 Ralph Waldo Emerson, *The Heart of Emerson's Journals*, 119 (Bliss Perry ed., 1926). See generally Len Gougeon, "Abolition, The Emersons, and 1837," 54 *New Eng. Q.* 345 (1981) [hereafter Gougeon, "Abolition"].

4 Richard Hofstadter, *The American Political Tradition and the Men Who Made It* 139 (1959).

5 Letter from Isabella Beecher to the Beecher Family (Jan. 22, 1838), quoted in Joan D. Hedrick, *Harriet Beecher Stowe, A Life* 109 (1994).

6 Isaac N. Arnold, *The Life of Abraham Lincoln* 169–170 (1885).

7 See Abraham Lincoln, "Address to the Young Men's Lyceum of Springfield, Illinois: The Perpetuation of our Political Institutions," in *Abraham Lincoln: Speeches and Writings, 1832–1858*, at 28–36 (Don Fehrenbacher ed., 1989); see also Benjamin P. Thomas, *Abraham Lincoln: A Biography* 72 (First Modern Library ed. 1968) (1952).

8 Letter from Theodore Dwight Weld to Louis Tappan (Dec. 14, 1841), in 2 *Letters of Theodore Dwight Weld, Angelina Grimké Weld, and Sarah Grimké, 1822–1844*, at 881 (Gilbert H. Barnes and Dwight L. Dumond eds., 1965).

9 "Anti-Slavery Publication Office, at Washington," 3 *Emancipator* 55 (August 2, 1838).

10 "A Memoir of the Reverend Elijah P. Lovejoy," *Evening Post* (N.Y.), Mar. 27, 1838, at 2.

11 See Gougeon, "Abolition," supra note 3, at 358–59 (quoting Daniel Walker Howe, *The Unitarian Conscience* (1988)).

12 William Ellery Channing, *Tribute of William Ellery Channing to the American Abolitionists for their Vindication of Freedom of Speech* 9 (New York, American Anti-Slavery Society 1861) (1836).

13 Id. at 11.

14 From the "New York Sunday Morning News, Southern Sentiment," *Wash. Globe*, Sept. 26, 1835, at 2.

15 See "The Alton Meeting," *Mo. Republican*, July 17, 1837, reprinted in *Memoir of the Rev. Elijah P. Lovejoy* 229–30 (Joseph C. Lovejoy and Owen Lovejoy eds., Arno Press 1969) (1838) [hereafter *Lovejoy Memoir*]; "Abolition," *Mo. Republican*, Aug. 17, 1837, reprinted in *Lovejoy Memoir* at 230; see also Merton L. Dillon, *Elijah P. Lovejoy, Abolitionist Editor* 112 (1961).

16 "Sentiments of the Press," 2 *Emancipator* 130 (Dec. 21, 1837) (quoting the *Fall River Patriot* (Mass.)).

17 "Faneuil Hall Refused," 2 *Emancipator* 124 (Dec. 7, 1837) (quoting the *Salem Gazette*, in turn quoting Order of Boston Mayor and Aldermen, Nov. 29, 1837).

18 Id.

19 See id. (quoting Letter from William E. Channing to the Citizens of Boston (Nov. 27, 1837)).

20 Id.

21 See "Opinion of the Press," *Boston Daily Advocate*, Dec. 4, 1837, at 2; "Public Opinion in Defence of the Liberty of the Press," *Boston Daily Advocate*, Dec. 4, 1837, at 2. Several papers were unsympathetic to granting the hall. See "Faneuil Hall Granted," *Boston Daily Advocate*, Dec. 7, 1837, at 2.

22 "Meeting at Faneuil Hall," *Emancipator Extra*, Feb. 12, 1838, at 1 (quoting the *Boston Daily Advertiser*) [hereafter "Meeting at Faneuil Hall"].

23 "The Denial of Faneuil Hall," *Boston Daily Advocate*, Dec. 4, 1837, at 2.

24 "Meeting at Faneuil Hall," supra note 22.

25 "Mr. Austin's Speech, Delivered at Faneuil Hall, Dec. 8, 1837," *Boston Daily Atlas*, Dec. 12, 1837, at 2.

26 Id. For the argument that the analogy of Alton to the Boston Tea Party was false because the tax on tea was a law made without the consent of the colonists while the laws violated in destroying Lovejoy's presses had been consented to by the voters, see "The Destruction of the Tea," *Boston Daily Advocate*, Dec. 12, 1837, at 2.

27 See Wendell Phillips, "The Murder of Lovejoy," in *Speeches, Lectures, and Letters* 1–10 (Boston, James Redpath 1863). The *Boston Daily Advocate* published the speech on Dec. 12, 1837. "Speeches in Faneuil Hall," *Boston Daily Advocate*, Dec. 12, 1837, at 2.

28 "Speeches in Faneuil Hall, Remarks of Wendell Phillips, Esq.," *Boston Daily Advocate*, Dec. 12, 1837, at 2.

29 "Faneuil Hall Has Spoken for Liberty," 2 *Emancipator* 129 (Dec. 14, 1837). To the same effect, see "Great Meeting in Faneuil Hall," *Boston Daily Advocate*, Dec. 9, 1937, at 2.

30 See "A Great Meeting at Boston," *Evening Post* (N.Y.), Dec. 11, 1837, at 2 (citing the *Boston Daily Advocate*).

31 "Meeting in Boston," *Richmond Whig and Pub. Advertiser*, Dec. 15, 1837, at 1.

32 "The Meeting at Faneuil Hall," *Boston Daily Evening Transcript*, Dec. 8, 1837, at 2.

33 Letter from John Quincy Adams to Samuel Webb and William H. Scott, reprinted in 3 *Emancipator* 15 (May 24, 1838).

34 Letter from Senator Thomas Morris on the Occasion of the Opening of the Pennsylvania Hall, reprinted in 3 *Emancipator* 21 (June 7, 1838).

35 Id.

36 See, e.g., "The Philadelphia Arson," 3 *Emancipator* 18 (May 31, 1838) (quoting the *Commercial Advertiser* which suggested that promenading incited the riot); "For the Evening Post," *Evening Post* (N.Y.), May 30, 1838, at 2 (reporting that no promenading took place); "Causes," 3 *Emancipator* 29 (June 21, 1838) (quoting the *Mon-*

trose Spectator (Pa) in reporting that blacks and whites were hired to promenade and incite a riot).

37 *Richmond Whig and Pub. Advertiser*, May 22, 1838, at 2.

38 "A Proclamation," 3 *Emancipator* 19 (May 31, 1838).

39 "Another Outrage," 3 *Emancipator* 29 (June 21, 1838) (quoting the *Massachusetts Spy*). Henry Mayer, *All on Fire: William Lloyd Garrison and the Abolition of Slavery* 402 (1998).

40 *Cong. Globe*, 25th Cong., 2nd Sess. app. at 22 (1838).

41 See "Twenty-Fifth Congress, Second Session, Tuesday, January 10," *Evening Post* (N.Y.), Jan. 11, 1838, at 2.

42 *Cong. Globe*, 25th Cong., 2d Sess. 73 (1838).

43 Id. app. at 24.

44 Id. app. at 25.

45 Id. See also "Twenty-Fifth Congress, Second Session," *Daily Nat'l Intelligencer*, Jan. 1, 1838, at 1.

46 "Washington, Friday Jan. 5th," *Boston Daily Advocate*, Jan. 10, 1838, at 2.

47 *Cong. Globe*, 25th Cong., 2d Sess. app. at 26 (1838).

48 Id. app. at 23.

49 Id. at 583.

50 Id. at 585.

51 Id. at 585–86.

52 "Mr. Calhoun's Policy," *Boston Daily Atlas*, Feb. 1, 1838, at 2.

53 *Cong. Globe*, 36th Cong., 1st Sess. 2321 (1860).

54 Seymour B. Treadwell, *American Liberties and American Slavery: Morally and Politically Illustrated* (Negro Univ. Press 1969) (1838) [hereafter Treadwell, *American Liberties*].

55 Id. at xxxv.

56 Id. at xxxvii.

57 Id. at xiii–xiv.

58 The resolution in favor of suppressing Birney's press said protections for speech and press were "controlled by the same rules which govern other rights, viz: to be used in such a manner as not to injure the acknowledged rights of others." "Public Meeting," *Philanthropist*, Jan. 29, 1836, at 2. Birney's view was unlike most public statements that supported free speech: "[A]ny *previous* restraint amounts to a censorship destructive of the right, whilst punishment for its *abuse*, is its life and means of perpetuating its vigor and usefulness." "The Cincinnati Preamble and Resolutions, Number II," *Philanthropist*, Feb. 26, 1836, at 2. Birney saw the public meeting demanding cessation of his paper as a prior restraint, and he did not elaborate fully on the distinction between protected speech and abuse. True statements on matters of public concern, he insisted, were protected. He suggested that free speech was limited by the rights of others but denied slaveholders had any right to hold slaves. Id.

59 See. e.g., "Extract from Governor M'Duffie's Message," *Philanthropist*, Jan. 1, 1836, at 1; Henry Mayer, *All on Fire: William Lloyd Garrison and the Abolition of Slavery* 422 (1998).

60   13 *The Papers of John C. Calhoun, 1835–1837*, at 625–26 (Clyde N. Wilson ed., 1980). (editorial remarks omitted). The editor comments that if Calhoun got the letter, he did not respond.

61   S.A., "Mobs," 3 *Emancipator* 15 (May 24, 1838).

62   See *Lovejoy Memoir*, supra note 15, at 279–80 (quoting the remarks of Elijah P. Lovejoy before the City of Alton public meeting (Nov. 3, 1837)); Leonard L. Richards, *Gentlemen of Property and Standing: Anti-Abolition Mobs in Jacksonian America* 94 (1970).

63   "Lovejoy's Sentiments," 2 *Emancipator* 155 (Feb. 1, 1838).

64   "Letter of Dr. W. E. Channing to James G. Birney, Boston, November 1st, 1836," *Philanthropist*, Dec. 9, 1836, at 2, reprinted in 2 William Ellery Channing, *The Works of William E. Channing* 750–51 (1980).

65   "The Alton Murder," 2 *Emancipator* 124 (Dec. 7, 1837) (quoting the *Portland Daily Courier* (Me.)).

66   "Additional Resolutions," 2 *Emancipator* 125 (Dec. 7, 1837) (listing resolutions passed by the Executive Committee of the American Anti-Slavery Society on Dec. 4, 1837).

67   Act of March 23, 1836, ch. 66, 1836 Va. Acts 44–45.

68   Clement Eaton, *The Freedom-of-Thought Struggle in the Old South* 211–12 (1964).

69   Act of March 23, 1836, ch. 66, at sec. 3.

70   *Letter of Appomattox to the People of Virginia*, in *Slavery Source Material and Critical Literature*, Microfiche Reprint *SLA* 1084 (Lost Cause Press 1971) (1832).

71   9 Leigh 665 (1839). The right to petition Congress might well have been held protected under the federal Constitution, even though the guarantees of the First Amendment apparently did not limit states. Compare Barron v. Baltimore, 32 U.S. (7 Pet.) 243 (1833) with United States v. Cruikshank, 92 U.S. (2 Otto) 542, (1876) (dicta).

72   Act of Virginia, ch. 10. sec. 25 (1848).

73   Bacon v. Commonwealth, 7 Gratton 602, 603–07 (Va. 1850).

74   Id. at 612.

75   "Crooks and McBride," *Raleigh Register*, Oct. 23, 1850, at 3. Act of 1830, N.C. Rev. Stat. ch. 34, sec. 17 (1837).

76   Const. of N.C., Declaration of Rights, secs. 15 and 19 (as amended 1835).

77   "Crooks and McBride," *Raleigh Register*, Oct. 23, 1850, at 3. For a fine account see, Clifton H. Johnson, "Abolitionist Missionary Activities in North Carolina," 40 N.C. *Hist. Rev.* 295, 295–301 (1963).

78   William Ellery Channing, "Dr. Channing on Texas," 2 *Emancipator* 87 (Oct. 5, 1837).

79   Id.

80   Don E. Fehrenbacher, *The Dred Scott Case*, 74–113, 184–88, 192 (1978); Dred Scott v. Sandford, 60 U.S. 393 (1857).

81   Paul Finkelman, *An Imperfect Union: Slavery, Federalism and Comity*, 285–338 (1981); *Cong. Globe*, 36th Cong., 1st Sess. 2595 (1860) (Sen. Sumner); *Cong. Globe*, 39th Cong., 1st Sess. 1013 (1866) (Rep. Plants).

82   2 Abraham Lincoln, *Speeches and Writings*, 53, 57–58 (Don Fehrenbacher ed.,

1989); James McPherson, *Battle Cry of Freedom: The Civil War Era*, 78–188 (1988) [hereafter McPherson, *Battle Cry of Freedom*].

83 E.g., Bacon v. Commonwealth, 48 Va. (7 Gratt.) 602 (1850). For other prosecutions see State v. Read, 6 La. Ann. 227 (1851); State v. McDonald, 4 Port. 449 (Ala. 1837).

84 Michael Kent Curtis, *No State Shall Abridge: The Fourteenth Amendment and the Bill of Rights* 42–44 (1986) [hereafter Curtis, *No State Shall Abridge*].

85 Phillip S. Paludan, *A Covenant with Death: The Constitution, Law, and Equality in the Civil War Era* 3 (1975).

86 William M. Wiecek, *The Sources of Anti-Slavery Constitutionalism in America*, 239 (1977). W. Phillips, *The Constitution, A Pro-Slavery Compact* 96–97 (photo. reprint 1969) (1844). For an analysis of one abolitionist theory, see Randy E. Barnette, "Was Slavery Unconstitutional Before the Thirteenth Amendment?" 28 *Pac. L.J.* 977 (1997); the *Pacific Law Journal* reprints much of Spooner's book, id. at 1015–14.

87 Treadwell, *American Liberties*, supra note 54.

88 Id. at 57.

89 Id. at 177–78.

90 Joel Tiffany, *A Treatise on the Unconstitutionality of American Slavery* (photo. reprint 1969) (1849) [hereafter Tiffany, *Treatise*].

91 Curtis, *No State Shall Abridge*, supra note 84, at 24–25, 46–56; Akhil Reed Amar, "The Bill of Rights and the Fourteenth Amendment," 101 *Yale L.J.* 1193, 1205–14 (1992).

92 Tiffany, *Treatise*, supra note 85, at 97.

93 Id.

94 Id. at 56–57, 84–89, 99.

95 Id. at 57–58.

96 Id. at 93–94.

97 McPherson, *Battle Cry of Freedom*, supra note 82, at 147.

98 *Cong. Globe*, 34th Cong., 1st Sess. 124 (1856).

99 E.g., N.C. Rev. Code ch. 34, sec. 16 (1855) referring to circulation of matter "the evident tendency whereof is to cause slaves to become discontented"; State v. Worth, 52 N.C. 488 (1860).

100 Barron v. Baltimore, 32 U.S. 243 (1832); Michael Kent Curtis, *No State Shall Abridge*, supra note 84, at 22–56; Nunn v. Georgia, 1 Ga. 243 (1846); Cochrun v. State, 24 Tex. 394 (1859); Rinehart v. Schuler, 7 Ill. 473, 522 (1846). Most state courts followed *Barron*.

101 U.S. Const. art. IV, sec. 2, cl. 1.

102 *Cong. Globe*, 35th Cong., 2d Sess. 984 (1859).

103 For Bingham's views in 1859, see id. at 983–84; Curtis, *No State Shall Abridge*, supra note 79, at 60–63. "Privilege . . . 1. a right, immunity or benefit enjoyed by a particular person or a restricted group of persons . . . 5. any of the rights common to all citizens under a modern constitutional government," *Random House Webster's College Dictionary* 1074 (1991). An 1851 law dictionary included among other definitions, "a right peculiar to some individual or body," 2 *A New Law Dictionary and Glossary* 828 (New York, J. S. Voorhies 1851). In *Dred Scott*, as William Crosskey

noted, the Chief Justice said that all rights and privileges under the Constitution belonged only to American citizens; blacks could not be citizens and so had no rights under the Constitution. 60 U.S. (19 How.) 393, 404, 449; William Winslow Crosskey, "Charles Fairman, 'Legislative History,' and the Constitutional Limitations on State Authority," 22 *U. Chi. L. Rev.* 1, 5 (1954).

104 Curtis, *No State Shall Abridge*, supra note 84, at 64–65, 67, 75–76 (Blackstone describing English liberties as "privileges" and "immunities"). For the mixed heritage of the words, see id. at 67–68. For Madison's use of the word "privilege" to describe Bill of Rights liberties, see 2 *The Bill of Rights: A Documentary History* 1030, 1096, 1033 (Bernard Schwartz ed., 1971) (Madison in the first Congress) [hereafter *Documentary History*].

105 See Kentucky v. Dennison, 65 U.S. (24 How.) 66 (1860); Prigg v. Pennsylvania, 41 U.S. (7 Pet.) 539 (1842). Curtis, *No State Shall Abridge*, supra note 79, at 63–64.

106 *Documentary History*, supra note 105, at 1030.

107 Curtis, *No State Shall Abridge*, supra note 84, at 27–28, 46–47.

12 THE FREE SPEECH BATTLE OVER HELPER'S *IMPENDING CRISIS*

1 John S. Bassett, *Anti-Slavery Leaders of North Carolina* 11–12 (Johnson Reprint Corp. 1973) (1898) [hereafter Bassett, *Anti-Slavery Leaders*].

2 Hinton Rowan Helper, *The Impending Crisis of the South: How to Meet It* 155–56 (George M. Fredrickson ed., Harvard University Press 1968) (1857) [hereafter Helper, *Impending Crisis*]; Bassett, *Anti-Slavery Leaders*, supra note 1, at 23.

3 E.g., Helper, *Impending Crisis*, supra note 2, at 35–39, 62–66, 175–79.

4 Id. at 116. Unlike most Northern abolitionists, Helper advocated colonization as one alternative for the South's black population.

5 Id. at 409.

6 Id. at 149; Bassett, *Anti-Slavery Leaders*, supra note 1, at 23.

7 Helper, *Impending Crisis*, supra note 2, at 149, quoted in "A False and Genuine Helper," *Richmond Whig*, Jan. 8, 1860, at 4.

8 Helper, *Impending Crisis*, supra note 2, at 151.

9 David M. Potter, *The Impending Crisis, 1848–1861*, at 387 (1976).

10 "Revolutionary Designs of the Abolitionists—New York Names Endorsing Treason," *N.Y. Herald*, Nov. 26, 1859, at 4.

11 *N.Y. Herald*, Oct. 18, 1859, at 1.

12 "The 'Irrepressible Conflict,' Wm. Seward's Brutal and Bloody Manifesto," *N.Y. Herald*, Oct. 19, 1859, at 2 [hereafter "Irrepressible Conflict"].

13 Speech by Gov. Seward, (Oct. 25, 1858) in Collection of Anti-Slavery Propaganda in the Oberlin College Library (Louisville, Ky., Lost Cause Press 1964) (Microfiche Reprint SLB 1255 (1964)) [hereafter Speech by Gov. Seward].

14 "Irrepressible Conflict," supra note 12, at 2.

15 "The Text Book of Revolution," *N.Y. Herald*, Nov. 28, 1859, at 1 [hereafter *Text Book of Revolution*].

16 *N.Y. Wkly. Tribune*, Dec. 24, 31, 1859, cited in Earl S. Miers, Introduction to Helper, *Impending Crisis* 13 (Collier Books 1963) (1857).

17 Henry Mayer, *All on Fire: William Lloyd Garrison and the Abolition of Slavery* 320, 448 (1998) [hereafter Mayer, *All on Fire*].

18 See generally Edward J. Renehan Jr., *The Secret Six: The True Tale of the Men Who Conspired with John Brown* 147, 173–75, 182 (1995); Garry Wills, *Lincoln at Gettysburg* 104–120 (1992); Stephen B. Oates, *The Approaching Fury: Voices of the Storm, 1820–1861*, at 292 (Douglass) (1997); *All on Fire*, supra note 17, at 485–87 (Herndon and Garrison), 497 (Phillips), and 498 (Douglass) (1998).

19 E.g., *Cong. Globe*, 36th Cong., 1st Sess. 17 (1859–60) (Rep. Clark); id. at 21 (Rep. Millison); id. at 24 (Rep. Keitt); id. at 28 (Sen. Mallory); id. at 29–30 (Sen. Iverson); id. at 45 (Rep. Lamar); id. at 49 (Rep. Pryor); 61–62 (Rep. Davis); 95–96 (Rep. Curry); id. at 110–11 (Rep. Stewart); id. at 121 (Sen. Clay); id. at 281–82 (Rep. Pryor).

20 Id. at 94 (Rep. Curry); id. at 121 (Sen. Clay).

21 Id. at 3; Ollinger Crenshaw, "The Speakership Contest of 1859–60," 29 *Miss. Valley Hist. Rev.* 323, 323–24 (1942) [hereafter Crenshaw, "Speakership Contest"].

22 *Cong. Globe*, 36th Cong., 1st Sess. 14.

23 Id. at 281.

24 Id at 17.

25 Id at 30. See also id. at 43 (Rep. Garnett); id. at 62–63 (Rep. Davis); id. at 71 (Rep. Moore); id. at 94 (Rep. Curry); id. at 104–05 (Sen. Johnson) (claiming that Harper's Ferry was the result of Republican teaching).

26 Id at 62.

27 Id. at 69.

28 Id. at 524.

29 Crenshaw, "Speakership Contest," supra note 21, at 332–37; *Cong. Globe*, 36th Cong., 1st Sess. 819 (Rep. Anderson); see also id. at 841 (collection by Rep. Clark).

30 *Cong. Globe*, 36th Cong., 1st Sess. 346 (Rep. Wells).

31 E.g., id. at 21 (Rep. Sherman); id. at 74 (Rep. Stanton); Crenshaw, "Speakership Contest," supra note 21, at 325.

32 *Cong. Globe*, 36th Cong., 1st Sess. at 4 (Rep. Kilgore); id. at 40 (Rep. Kellogg); id. at 394 (Rep. Morris).

33 Id. at 45.

34 E.g., id. at 826 (Rep. Fenton); id. at 930–31 (Rep. Edgerton); id. at 1887–88 (Rep. Alley).

35 Id. at 40 (Rep. Kellogg) (quoting from *N.Y. Wkly. Tribune*, Dec. 6, 1859).

36 Richard H. Sewell, *Ballots for Freedom: AntiSlavery Politics in the United States, 1837–1860*, 357 (1976) [hereafter Sewell, *Ballots for Freedom*].

37 Speech by Gov. Seward, supra note 13.

38 The Southern "bad tendency" approach was later followed in Massachusetts and in the United States Supreme Court. Commonwealth v. Karvonen, 106 N. E. 556, 557 (Mass. 1914); Debs v. United States, 249 U.S. 211 (1919).

39 *Cong. Globe*, 36th Cong., 1st Sess. 63.

40 E.g., "Revolutionary Designs of the Abolitionists," *N.Y. Herald*, Nov. 26, 1859, at 4; "Text Book of Revolution," supra note 15, at 1; "Incitement to Treason and Civil War," *Raleigh Wkly. Standard*, Dec. 7, 1859, at 1.

41 *Cong. Globe*, 36th Cong., 1st Sess. at 141; see also id. at 58 (Sen. Trumbull).

42   Joaquin J. Cardoso, "Lincoln Abolitionism, and Patronage: The Case of Hinton Rowan Helper," 53 *J. Negro Hist.* 144, 147 (1968).

43   "Helper's Crisis," *N.Y. Trib.*, Dec. 27, 1859, at 4.

44   *Cong. Globe*, 36th Cong., 1st Sess. 7.

45   3 Abraham Lincoln, *The Collected Works of Abraham Lincoln* 541 (Roy Basler ed., 1953).

46   *Cong. Globe*, 36th Cong., 1st Sess. 1861.

47   2 Abraham Lincoln, *The Collected Works of Abraham Lincoln* 406 (Roy Basler ed., 1953); 2 Abraham Lincoln, *Speeches, Letters, Miscellaneous Writings (1859–1865)*, at 134–35 (Don E. Fehrenbacher comp., Library of America 1989).

48   *Cong. Globe*, 36th Cong., 1st Sess. 240–41 (Rep. Smith, Va.).

49   Id. at 407 (Rep. Pugh).

50   Eric Foner, *Free Soil, Free Labor, Free Men: The Ideology of the Republican Party Before the Civil War* 122, 207 (1970); *Cong. Globe*, 36th Cong., 1st Sess. 240 (Rep. Smith, Va.); id. at 282 (Rep. Pryor, Va.); id. at 462 (Rep. Underwood); id. at 95 (Rep. Curry); id. at 912 (Sen. Seward) (asserting that freedom of speech and ballot would produce a large Republican party in the South); id. at 125 (Rep. Gwin); id. at 407 (Sen. Pugh).

51   *Cong. Globe*, 24th Cong., 1st Sess. app. at 9 (1835) (report of Postmaster General Kendall).

52   E.g., United States v. Cruikshank, 92 U.S. 542, 552 (1875); Charles L. Black Jr., *Structure and Relationship in Constitutional Law* 33–50 (1969).

53   *Cong. Globe*, 36th Cong., 1st Sess. 54 (Sen. Trumbull); id. at 66 (Rep. Leach); Abraham Lincoln, *Speeches and Writings, 1859–1865*, at 61 (Library of America, Don E. Fehrenbacher ed., 1989) [hereafter *Lincoln's Speeches, 1859–1865*].

54   See infra notes 60, 61, 66, 67, 70–79, 81–85.

55   Sewell, *Ballots for Freedom*, supra note 36, at 284.

56   For a discussion of the two approaches to the free speech issue, see Hugo L. Black, "The Bill of Rights," 35 *N.Y.U. L. Rev.* 865, 867 (1960); Laurent B. Frantz, "The First Amendment in the Balance," 71 *Yale L.J.* 1424, 1430–32 (1962).

57   *Cong. Globe*, 36th Cong., 1st Sess. 12.

58   Id.

59   Id. at 31.

60   Id. at 57.

61   *Created Equal? The Complete Lincoln Douglas Debates of 1858*, at 290–91, 300 (Paul Angle ed., 1958).

62   *Cong. Globe*, 36th Cong., 1st Sess. 128.

63   Id. at 64.

64   Id.

65   Id. at 64–65.

66   Id. at 63–64.

67   Id at 144.

68   Id. at 913.

69   Id at 930.

70   Id. at 930–31.

71 Id. at 931.

72 Id. at 1872.

73 Id. at 1031–32 (Rep. Van Wyck); id. at 1039–40 (Rep. Perry) (appealing also to a somewhat more conventional reading of the interstate privileges-or-immunities clause to bolster his complaint of lack of protection for visitors from the North); id. at 1585 (Rep. Wells); id. at 1861–62 (Rep. Bingham).

74 Id. at 1861.

75 Id. at 1857.

76 Id. at 133 (Rep. Sickles); id. at 44 (Rep. Garnett).

77 *Lincoln's Speeches, 1859–1865*, supra note 53, at 128 (Address at Cooper Institute); id. at 149 (Address at New Haven).

78 *Cong. Globe*, 36th Cong., 1st Sess. at 2321 (emphasis added).

79 Id. (emphasis added).

80 Id.

81 For a similar use of the word *domestic* by Stephen A. Douglas, see Stephen B. Oates, *The Approaching Fury: Voices of the Storm, 1820–1861* at 239 (1997).

82 *Cong. Globe*, 36th Cong., 1st Sess. app. at 202.

83 Id. at 205.

84 Id.

85 Id. at 207.

13   DANIEL WORTH

1 *Cong. Globe*, 36th Cong., 1st Sess. app. at 205 (1860).

2 "Case of Rev. Daniel Worth," *N.Y. Times*, Apr. 5, 1860, at 5; see also "Case of Rev. Daniel Worth," *N.Y. Times*, Apr. 6, 1860, at 6.

3 "Case of Rev. Daniel Worth," *N.Y. Times*, Apr. 6, 1860, at 6.

4 "Freedom of Speech in the South," *Nat'l Era*, Jan. 12, 1860, at 6.

5 Noble J. Tolbert, "Daniel Worth: Tar Heel Abolitionist," 39 *N.C. Hist. Rev.* 284, 284–90 (1962) [hereafter Tolbert, "Daniel Worth"]. Clifton H. Johnson, "Abolitionist Missionary Activities in North Carolina," 40 *N.C. Hist. Rev.* 295–301 (1963) [hereafter Johnson, "Missionary Activities"]. I am indebted to these very fine, powerfully researched accounts.

6 Letter from Daniel Worth to Aaron Worth (Apr. 30, 1858), in Tolbert, "Daniel Worth," supra note 5, at 290.

7 Id.

8 "Mr. Hedrick, Once More," *Raleigh Wkly. Standard*, Nov. 5, 1856, at 1. For other articles in the same paper, see "Professor Hedrick's Defence," *Raleigh Wkly. Standard*, Oct. 8, 1856, at 4; "Prof. Hedrick, of the University," *Raleigh Wkly. Standard*, Oct. 8, 1856, at 1. See also John S. Bassett, *Anti-Slavery Leaders of North Carolina* 29–47 (Johnson Reprint Corp. 1973) (1898).

9 Letter from Daniel Worth to Aaron Worth (Apr. 30, 1858), in Tolbert, "Daniel Worth," supra note 5, at 291.

10 "An Abolition Emissary," *Raleigh Weekly Standard*, Dec. 14, 1959, at 1, in Tolbert, "Daniel Worth," supra note 5, at 291.

11 "The Abolition Emissary," *N.C. Presbyterian*, Dec. 17, 1859, at 1.

12 "The Council of State," *Raleigh Wkly. Standard*, Dec. 14, 1859, at 1.

13 Letter from Daniel Worth to American Missionary Association (Dec. 21, 1859), in Johnson, "Missionary Activities," supra note 5, at 312.

14 "Hinton R. Helper's Infamous Book—What the Sixty-Eight Demand," *Wkly. Raleigh Reg.*, Dec. 14, 1859, at 1.

15 "Arrest of Rev. Daniel Worth," *Raleigh Wkly. Standard*, Dec. 28, 1859, at 3; "Arrest of Rev. Daniel Worth," *Wkly. Raleigh Reg.*, Jan. 4, 1860, at 1; "Arrest and Trial of Rev. Daniel Worth," *Greensboro Patriot*, Jan. 6, 1860, at 3 [hereafter "Arrest and Trial of Worth"].

16 "Arrest and Trial of Worth," supra note 15, at 3.

17 See, e.g., *Cong. Globe* 36th Cong., 1st Sess. 124, 188 (1859–60) (Rep. Gilmer); "Helper's Book," *Greensboro Patriot*, Aug. 12, 1859, at 2.

18 "Incendiary Documents," *Raleigh Wkly. Standard*, Jan. 4, 1860, at 1.

19 John T. Harriss to John W. Ellis (Dec. 30, 1859), in 1 *Papers of John W. Ellis* 340 (1964).

20 Id. at 342–43.

21 Id. at 343–45. Throughout this account of Daniel Worth I am indebted to the very fine historical work by Noble J. Tolbert and Clifton H. Johnson, whose detailed accounts led me to many primary sources cited here. See Tolbert, "Daniel Worth," and Johnson, "Missionary Activities," supra note 5.

22 "The Abolitionist George W. Vestal," *Daily Progress*, Jan. 3, 1860, at 2; "The Abolitionists Worth and Turner," *Daily Progress*, Jan. 3, 1860, at 2; "Abolitionists Worth and Turner," *Raleigh Wkly. Standard*, Jan. 4, 1860, at 1; "Arrest of a Suspicious Character," *Wkly. Raleigh Reg.*, Jan. 4, 1860, at 1.

23 Benjamin S. Hedrick to Thomas Ruffin (Jan. 16, 1860), in 3 *Papers of Thomas Ruffin* 64 (J. G. de Roulhac Hamilton ed., 1920) [hereafter *Papers of Thomas Ruffin*].

24 Id. at 65. For the antislavery pamphlet, see *Address to the People of North Carolina on the Evils of Slavery*, Manumission Society of North Carolina 5, 9, 13, 15 (William Swain 1860) (1830).

25 Tolbert, "Daniel Worth," supra note 5, at 298.

26 George McNeill Jr. to Thomas Ruffin (Mar. 12, 1860), in 1 *Papers of Thomas Ruffin*, supra note 23, at 73.

27 From Jonathan Worth to George McNeill Jr. (Mar. 10, 1860), in 1 *Papers of Thomas Ruffin*, supra note 23, at 74.

28 Id.

29 Act to Prevent Circulation of Seditious Publications, N.C. Rev. Code ch. 34, sec. 16 (1854) (revising 1830 N.C. Sess. Laws ch. 5, at 10–11).

30 "Arrest and Trial of Worth," supra note 15, at 3. The following account of Worth's trial comes from fragmentary press accounts and from the few surviving appellate papers. These do not include the defendant's brief.

31 Johnson, "Missionary Activities," supra note 5, at 315.

32 Indictment, *State v. Worth*, Guilford County, North Carolina Department of Archives and History, 1–6 (1860).

33 Id. at 7–8.

34   See Johnson, "Missionary Activities," supra note 5, at 317; "Randolph Superior Court," *Greensboro Patriot*, Apr. 6, 1860, at 2.

35   "Randolph Superior Court," *Greensboro Times*, Apr. 7, 1860, at 6.

36   Id.; "Randolph Superior Court," *Greensboro Patriot*, Apr. 6, 1860, at 2.

37   "Trial of Rev. Daniel Worth," *Greensboro Times*, May 5, 1860, at 6.

38   "Daniel Worth in New York," *Greensboro Times*, May 19, 1860, at 2.

39   Id. at 2–3. "A Christian Minister in The South: The Story of Rev. Daniel Worth," *N.Y. Trib.*, May 8, 1860, at 5. See also "Church Anti-Slavery Society," *N.Y. Times*, May 7, 1860, at 8.

40   State v. Worth, 52 N.C. 488 (1860).

41   Id. at 492.

42   Id. at 490.

43   Id. at 493.

44   N.C. Const., Declaration of Rights, sec. 15, quoted in 1836 *Proceedings and Debates of the Convention of North-Carolina Called to Amend the Constitution of the State* 410.

45   1860 N.C. Sess. Laws ch. 23, at 39 (1860).

46   James M. McPherson, *Abraham Lincoln and the Second American Revolution* 23–42, 131–52 (1991). The extent to which the second American Revolution envisioned consolidation of power in the federal government is subject to dispute, and any theory of full consolidation is hard to square with the evidence.

47   E.g., *Cong. Globe* 36th Cong., 1st Sess. 1617 (Sen. Chestnut).

48   Id. at 1619.

49   Id. at 1617.

50   Id.

51   Id. at 1618.

52   E.g., id. at 822–26 (Rep. Fenton).

53   Id. at 823.

54   Abraham Lincoln, *Speeches and Writings, 1859–1865*, at 129–30 (Don E. Fehrenbacher comp., Library of America 1989); *Cong. Globe*, 36th Cong., 1st Sess. 912–13 (Sen. Seward).

55   *Cong. Globe*, 36th Cong., 1st Sess. 125 (Sen. Gwin); id. at 455 (Sen. Clingman).

56   *Cong. Globe*, 39th Cong., 1st Sess. 728 (Rep. Welker) (1866); id. at 586 (Rep. Donnelly); id. at 632 (Rep. Kelley); id. at 1088 (Rep. Woodbridge) (on need to keep states within their orbits); id. at 1088 (Rep. Bingham); id. at 1183 (Rep. Pomeroy); id. at 1152 (Rep. Thayer); id. at 1263 (Rep. Broomall); id. at 1629 (Rep. Hart); id. at 1832–33 (Rep. Lawrence); id. at 2542 (Rep. Bingham); id. at 1072 (Sen. Nye); id. app. 67 (Garfield); id. at 256 (Rep. Baker); Curtis, *No State Shall Abridge: The Fourteenth Amendment and the Bill of Rights* 49–56, 59, 63–91 (1986) [hereafter Curtis, *No State Shall Abridge*].

57   E.g., *Cong. Globe*, 39th Cong., 1st Sess. 1313 (Sen. Trumbull); id. at 1439 (Sen. Harlan); id. at 2615 (Rep. Morris); id. at 1013 (Rep. Clarke); id. at 1263 (Rep. Bromall); id. at 1072 (Sen. Nye). Cf. *Cong. Globe*, 38th Cong., 1st Sess. 114 (1864) (Rep. Arnold); id. at 1202 (Rep. Wilson); id. at 1971–72 (Rep. Scofield); *Cong. Globe*, 38th Cong., 2d Sess. 138 (Rep. Ashley); id. at 193 (Rep. Kasson); *Cong. Globe*, 39th Cong.,

1st Sess. 157–58 (1866) (Rep. Bingham); id. at 1617 (Rep. Moulton); id. at 1627 (Rep. Buckland); id. at 1627–29 (Rep. Hart); id. app. at 255–56 (Rep. Baker). See also Curtis, *No State Shall Abridge*, supra note 56, at 27–59, 131–53.

58 *Cong. Globe*, 38th Cong., 1st Sess. 1202 (1864) (Rep. Wilson).

59 See George W. Paschal, *The Constitution of the United States Defined and Carefully Annotated* 256 (Washington, D.C., W. H. and O. H. Morrison 1868). Joseph Story seems both to embrace Blackstone's analysis of prior restraint and to justify suppression of items adjudged at trial to have a "pernicious tendency." Joseph Story, *Commentaries on the Constitution of the United States* 703–07 (Carolina Academic Press 1987) (1833). For a more libertarian approach to the subject and a rejection of the idea of freedom of expression limited to protection against prior restraint, see Cooley, *Constitutional Limitations* 414–30 (Legal Classics Library, 1987) (1868).

60 *Cong. Globe*, 36th Cong., 1st Sess. 763 (1859–60) (Sen. Hale).

61 Harry Kalven, *The Negro and the First Amendment* 15–16, 63–64 (1965).

62 Akhil Reed Amar, "The Case of the Missing Amendments: *R.A.V. v. City of St. Paul*," 106 *Harv. L. Rev.* 124, 140–42 (1992). See Curtis, *No State Shall Abridge*, supra note 56. For the retrospective views of Republicans who mentioned Worth's case see George W. Julian, *Political Recollections, 1840 to 1872* 171–73 (Mnemosyne Pub. 1969) (1883); 2 Henry Wilson, *History of the Rise and Fall of the Slave Power in America* 668 (Negro Universities Press 1969) (1872).

14 THE STRUGGLE FOR FREE SPEECH IN THE CIVIL WAR

1 "The Circumstances of the Arrest of C. L. Vallandigham," *Cincinnati Commercial*, May 6, 1863, at 2; Frank L. Klement, "Clement L. Vallandigham," [hereafter, Klement, "Vallandigham"] in *For the Union: Ohio Leaders in the Civil War* 38–39 (1966) [hereafter Klement, *For the Union*]. For other discussions of Vallandigham and the arrest, see, e.g., William H. Rhenquist, *All the Laws but One: Civil Liberties in Wartime*, ch. 5 (1998); Frank Klement, *The Limits of Dissent: Clement L. Vallandigham and the Civil War* 157–58 (1970) [hereafter Klement, *Limits of Dissent*]. Klement, relying partly on accounts many years later and partly on circumstantial evidence, suggested that Vallandigham courted martyrdom as a means of gaining the Democratic nomination for governor. Id. at 150–53. See also, Erving E. Beauregard, "The Bingham-Vallandigham Feud," 15 *Biography*, 29 (1992). For an account of the events reported here that is more sympathetic to the position taken by Lincoln, see, e.g., Robert S. Harper, *Lincoln and the Press* 239–51 (1951). See also Harold Hyman's classic work, *A More Perfect Union: The Impact of the Civil War and Reconstruction on the Constitution* 124–40 (1975). For an analysis that is critical of Republicans, see Jeffrey Rogers Hummel, *Emancipating Slaves, Enslaving Free Men: A History of the American Civil War*, chs. 8 and 10 (1996). For an analysis less critical of the suppression of free speech in the Vallandigham case, see Craig Davidson Tenney, "Major General A. E. Burnside and the First Amendment: A Case Study of Civil War Freedom of Expression" (1977) (Ph.D. dissertation, Indiana Univ., reprint UMI Dissertation Service) [hereafter Tenney, "Burnside"].

2 E.g., "Mob at Dayton," *Detroit Free Press*, May 7, 1863, at 1.

3   *Cong. Globe*, 36th Cong., 1st Sess., app. 205.

4   *Cong. Globe*, 36th Cong., 1st Sess., 2321.

5   See generally, Michael Kent Curtis, "The 1859 Crisis over Hinton Helper's Book *The Impending Crisis*: Free Speech, Slavery, and Some Light on the Meaning of the First Section of the Fourteenth Amendment," 68 *Chi. Kent L. Rev.* 1113, 1174–77 (1993).

6   Richard Sewell, *Ballots for Freedom* 284 (1976).

7   See generally the splendid accounts in William Lee Miller, *Arguing About Slavery: The Great Battle in the United States Congress* (1996); Leonard L. Richards, *The Life and Times of Congressman John Quincy Adams* (1986); and Gilbert Hobbs Barnes, *The Antislavery Impulse, 1830–1844* 109–45 (1933).

8   See generally Don E. Fehrenbacher, *The Dred Scott Case* 188–92 (1978).

9   C. L. Vallandigham, *History of the Abolition Movement: The Record of Hon. C. L. Vallandigham on Abolition, the Union, and the Civil War* at 38 (Cincinnati, J. Walter 1863) [hereafter Vallandigham, *Record*].

10   Id. at 22.

11   Id.

12   Id. at 26.

13   Id. at 236.

14   E.g., Michael Kent Curtis, *No State Shall Abridge: The Fourteenth Amendment and the Bill of Rights* 81 (1986).

15   Klement, "Vallandigham," supra note 1, at 38.

16   Id. at 24.

17   "The Great Civil War in America," in Vallandigham, *Record*, supra note 10, at 183.

18   Id. at 189.

19   Robert S. Harper, *Lincoln and the Press* 195 (1951).

20   Klement, "Vallandigham," supra note 1, at 8.

21   Id. at 29.

22   "The Great Civil War in America," in Vallandigham, *Record*, supra note 10, at 189.

23   "The State of the Country," Speech Delivered at Dayton, August 2, 1862, in Vallandigham *Record*, supra note 10, at 148.

24   Id. at 137.

25   Klement, *For the Union*, supra note 1, at 16.

26   4 Roy Basler, ed. *The Collected Works of Abraham Lincoln* 429–32 (1956) [hereafter Lincoln, *Collected Works*].

27   David Herbert Donald, *Lincoln* 441 (1995).

28   See generally Harold M. Hyman, *A More Perfect Union: The Impact of the Civil War and Reconstruction on the Constitution* ch. 8 (1975) [hereafter Hyman, *A More Perfect Union*].

29   48 U.S. 1, 45–46 (1849)

30   George M. Dennison, "Martial Law: The Development of a Theory of Emergency Powers, 1775–1861," 18 *Am. J. Leg. Hist.* 58, 78 (1974).

31   5 Lincoln, *Collected Works*, supra note 25, at 436–37.

32   An Act Relating to Habeas Corpus, and Regulating Judicial Proceedings in Certain Cases, March 3, 1863, ch. 81, sec. 2, 12 Stat. 755 (1863). For discussions of the act, see

Hyman, *A More Perfect Union*, supra note 28 at ch. 15, especially 252–54 (1973); James Randall, *Constitutional Problems Under Lincoln*, 163–68 (1951).

33 § 2, 12 Stat. 755 (1863).

34 Klement, "Vallandigham," supra note 1, at 35.

35 *The Trial of Clement L. Vallandigham by a Military Commission* 7 (Cincinnati, Rickey and Carroll 1863) [hereafter *Vallandigham Trial*].

36 "Court-Martial—Order No. 38—Warning," *Cincinnati Commercial*, Apr. 29, 1863, at 1.

37 "Union Mass Meeting," *Cincinnati Commercial*, Apr. 21, 1863, at 2.

38 "Kentucky Politics," *Cincinnati Commercial*, Apr. 23, 1863, at 1

39 "General Hascall on Order No. 9," *Cincinnati Commercial*, May 8, 1863, at 1. For a short discussion of General Hascall and his order, see Robert S. Hunter, *Lincoln and the Press* 251–54 (1951).

40 See, e.g., Klement, *Limits of Dissent*, supra note 1, at 108–09.

41 Tenney, "Burnside" 186–87.

42 Id. at 188.

43 "What Do They Mean?" *Detroit Free Press*, Apr. 14, 1863 at 2.

44 Klement, *The Limits of Dissent*, supra note 1, at 166.

45 *Vallandigham Trial*, supra note 35, at 11.

46 Id. at 11–12. On the peace question, see William Harlan Hale, *Horace Greeley, Voice of the People* 267–71 (1950).

47 See Abraham Lincoln, "To Erastus Corning and Others," in Abraham Lincoln, *Speeches and Writings, 1859–1865*, at 462 (Don E. Fehrenbacher comp., Library of America 1989) [hereafter *Lincoln Speeches*].

48 Craig D. Tenney, "To Suppress or Not to Suppress: Abraham Lincoln and the *Chicago Times*," 29 *Civ. War Hist.* 249, 250 at n. 11 (1981) [hereafter Tenney, "*Chicago Times*"]. See also Tenney, *Burnside*, supra note 1.

49 *Vallandigham Trial*, supra note 35, at 263–64.

50 Id. at 270.

51 Klement, *Limits of Dissent*, supra note 1, at 153–54.

52 *Vallandigham Trial*, supra note 35, at 14–15.

53 Id. at 21 (testimony of Captain John A. Means).

54 Id. at 24.

55 Id. at 22–23.

56 "Vallandigham's Followers . . . ," *Cincinnati Commercial*, May 6, 1863, at 1.

57 *Vallandigham Trial*, supra note 35, at 27.

58 Id. at 29–30.

59 Id. at 30.

60 Id. at 262–70, where the decision in the habeas case is reported. *Ex parte Vallandigham*, 68 U.S. 243 (1864) (Supreme Court denial of review of the order of the military commission). If Vallandigham had sought review from denial of his habeas petition, he might have fared better—at least if the matter had not reached the Court until after the war. See *Ex parte Milligan*, 71 U.S. 2 (1866). "Until 1983 Congress had never granted the Supreme Court 'appellate jurisdiction to super-

vise the administration of criminal justice in the military.'" Laurence H. Tribe, *American Constitutional Law* 59 (2d ed. 1988).

61 *Lincoln Speeches* (1859–1865), supra note 47, at 451. For a sampling of some protests, see "The Vallandigham Outrage: The Voice of the People," *Albany Argus,* May 26, 1863, at 2.

62 E.g., "From Columbus," *Cincinnati Commercial,* May 17, 1863 at 3; "Newport," id., May 12, 1863, at 2; "Covington," id., June 12, 1863, at 3; "Arrests for Using Disloyal Language," id., June 15, 1863, at 2; 6 Lincoln, *Collected Works,* supra note 26, at 326.

63 E.g., "Suppression of Newspapers," *National Intelligencer,* May 13, 1863, at 3.

64 The description here is abbreviated. For a detailed and very fine account, see Tenney, The "*Chicago Times,*" supra note 48, at 248. See also, Robert S. Harper, *Lincoln and the Press* 257–64 (1951). The quotations from Storey come from Garry Wills, Book Review, "The Colonel: The Life and Legend of Robert McCormick," *N.Y. Rev. of Books,* Sept. 25, 1997, at 32.

65 *Chicago Times,* May 29, 1863, quoted in Tenney, *Burnside,* supra note 1, at 168.

66 "The *Chicago Times* Establishment Taken Possession of by the Military Authorities," *Chicago Tribune,* June 4, 1863, at 4.

67 "*Chicago Times* Demonstration," *Cincinnati Commercial,* June 4, 1863, at 3.

68 "Suppression of the *Chicago Times*: The Military Authorities Disregard the Writ of the Court," *N.Y. Daily Tribune,* June 4, 1863, at 1.

69 "General Burnside's Orders," *Cincinnati Commercial,* June 5, 1863, at 1.

70 1 Gideon Welles, *Diary of Gideon Welles,* 321–22 (1911). Republicans at the time thought Vallandigham was secretly involved with pro-Confederate societies that were conspiring with rebel agents. James McPherson concludes that while a lunatic fringe existed that was engaged in such activities, Vallandigham and other prominent Democrats probably took no active part. James McPherson, *The Battle Cry to Freedom: The Civil War Era* 783 (1988).

71 Tenney, "Chicago Times," supra note 48, at 248, 254–55.

72 "Action of the Illinois Legislature on General Burnside's Recent Order" [byline Springfield, Ill., June 3], *Cincinnati Commercial,* June 4, 1863, at 3. See also "Copperheadiana," *Chicago Tribune,* June 4, 1863, at 2; "From Illinois," *Detroit Free Press,* June 4, 1863, at 1; "From Chicago," *Detroit Free Press,* June 5, 1863, at 4; "Revocation," *Chicago Tribune,* June 5, 1863, at 1.

73 Tenney, "*Chicago Times,*" supra note 48, at 248, 254–55.

74 "Revocation," *Chicago Tribune,* June 5, 1863, at 1.

75 Tenney, "*Chicago Times,*" supra note 48, at 248, 255–56.

76 "The Attempted Suppression of the Chicago Times: And Its Defeat," *Albany Argus,* June 13, 1863, at 2.

77 "Free Speech—Free Press," *Detroit Free Press* (quoting the *Chicago Times*), June 6, 1863, at 1 [emphasis added]. The words "privileges" and "immunities" are used regularly by both supporters and critics of suppression of antiwar speech to describe the rights of free speech, free press, and assembly.

78 E.g., Joseph Story, 3 *Commentaries on the Constitution,* sec. 1881 ("free, but not licentious, discussion must be encouraged") (1833), reprinted in 5 *The Founder's*

Constitution 184 (Philip B. Kurland and Ralph Lerner eds., 1987) [hereafter *Founder's Constitution*]. Story reserved judgment on whether the national government had the power of "not restraining the liberty of the press, but punishing the licentiousness of the press." Id. at 185. Cf. People v. Croswell, 3 Johns. Cas. 337 (1804), reprinted in 5 *Founders Constitution*, supra at 158, 169 ("The founders of our government were too wise and too just, ever to have intended, by freedom of the press, a right to circulate falsehood as well as truth, or that the press should be the lawful vehicle of malicious defamation, or an engine for evil and designing men, to cherish, for mischievous purposes, sedition, irreligion, and impurity"). Cf. also Updegraph v. Commonwealth, 11 Serg. and Rawle 394 (Pa. 1824)—a blasphemy prosecution. But see e.g., 3 James Burgh, *Political Disquisitions* 254 (1775) ("No man ought to be hindered saying or writing what he please on the conduct of those who undertake the management of national affairs, in which all are concerned, and therefore have a right to inquire, and to publish their suspicions concerning them. For if you punish the slanderer, you deter the fair inquirer."). Cf. also St. George Tucker, 1 *Blackstone's Commentaries*, app. at 298–99; 2 *Blackstone's Commentaries* app. at 12–25, 27–30 (1803), in 5 *Founder's Constitution* 152–58.

15 THE FREE SPEECH TRADITION CONFRONTS THE WAR POWER

1   "The Case of C. L. Vallandigham," *Cincinnati Commercial*, May 6, 1863, at 2.

2   "Order Thirty-Eight," *Cincinnati Commercial*, May 15, 1863, at 2.

3   Frank Klement, *The Limits of Dissent: Clement L. Vallandigham and the Civil War* 157–58, at 164 (1970) [hereafter Klement, *Limits of Dissent*].

4   "The Dayton Empire," *Cincinnati Commercial*, May 7, 1863, at 2.

5   "The Arrest of Vallandigham," *Albany Argus*, May 8, 1863, at 2.

6   "The Arrest of Vallandigham," *Detroit Free Press*, May 8, 1863, at 2.

7   "A Public Meeting," *Detroit Free Press*, May 21, 1863, at 2.

8   "The Arrest of Vallandigham," *Detroit Free Press*, May 8, 1863, at 2.

9   "Mr. Vallandigham and Free Speech," *Detroit Free Press*, May 15, 1863, at 2.

10   "Vallandigham—Meeting in Albany: Letter from Governor Seymour," *Detroit Free Press*, May 20, 1863, at 1.

11   Klement, *The Limits of Dissent*, supra note 3, at 163.

12   "Francis Kernan," 5 *Dictionary of American Biography* 356 (1933) [hereafter *DAB*].

13   "The Vallandigham Outrage: Immense Meeting at the Capital—Speech by Francis Kernan," *Albany Argus*, May 18, 1863, at 2. See also "Hon. C. L. Vallandigham," *Cincinnati Enquirer*, May 19, 1863, at 2, and "Speech of Judge Parker at the Brooklyn Meeting," *Albany Argus*, June 15, 1863, at 2.

14   Klement, *The Limits of Dissent*, supra note 3, at 179–80, reports that nearly every Northern city had a protest meeting.

15   "George Van Ness, Lothrop," 6 *DAB*, supra note 12, at 424 (1935–36); "Speech of Hon. Geo. V. N. Lothrop," *Detroit Free Press*, June 7, 1863, at 2.

16   "Speech of Hon. Geo. V. N. Lothrop," *Detroit Free Press*, June 7, 1863, at 2. On the democratic government point, see also "Speech of Judge Parker at the Brooklyn Meeting," *Albany Argus*, June 15, 1863, at 2. On the political fiction that the people

rule and the sense in which it is true and the sense in which it is false, see Steven D. Smith, "Radically Subversive Speech and the Authority of Law," 94 *Mich. L. Rev.* 348, 351–52, 360, 362, 365–67, 369 (1995). In addition to Smith's insightful essay, see, Michael Kent Curtis, "Resurrecting the Privileges or Immunities Clause and Revising the Slaughter-House Cases Without Exhuming *Lochner*: Individual Rights and the Fourteenth Amendment," 38 *Bt. Cl. L. Rev.*, 1, 9–10 (1996), and Edmund S. Morgan, *Inventing the People: The Rise of Popular Sovereignty in England and America* 282–84 (1988).

17   "Speech of Hon. Geo. V. N. Lothrop," *Detroit Free Press*, June 7, 1863, at 2.

18   Id.

19   Id.

20   Id.

21   "The Voice of Reason" *National Intelligencer*, May 16, 1863, at 3 (reprinted from the *N.Y. Evening Post*)

22   "The Vallandigham Outrage: Immense Meeting at the Capitol—Resolutions," *Albany Argus*, May 18, 1863, at 2.

23   "Will The People Be Allowed To Vote?" *Detroit Free Press*, June 5, 1863, at 2. On the relation of free speech to popular government, see also "Hon. Geo. E. Pugh's Speech," *Cincinnati Enquirer*, Aug. 7, 1863, at 2.

24   "The Military Discretion," *Detroit Free Press*, June 10, 1863, at 2.

25   "Vallandigham Nominated for Governor: George E. Pugh's Speech," *Cincinnati Commercial*, June 12, 1863, at 2.

26   Id.

27   Id. See also "Maine Democratic State Convention," *Albany Argus*, Aug. 12, 1863, at 2.

28   "Loyalty—Disloyalty," *Detroit Free Press*, June 26, 1863, at 2. See also with reference to governmental officials as agents, "Speech of Judge Parker at the Brooklyn Meeting," *Albany Argus*, June 15, 1863, at 2.

29   "Persecution of Democrats," *Detroit Free Press*, Aug. 27, 1863, at 2 (from the *Empire* (Dayton, Ohio)).

30   "Speech of Daniel W. Voorhees," *Cincinnati Commercial*, Sept. 17, 1863, at 1. On its face, at least, the Sedition Act reached only malicious falsehoods, while the action against Vallandigham reached opinions. As it was used, the Sedition Act reached and punished political opinions, and perhaps for that reason Voorhees did not point out that falsity was required by the Sedition Act. See, e.g., 1 Stat. 596, sec. 3 (July 14, 1798); United States v. Cooper, 25 Fed. Cas. 631 (1800); United States v. Lyon, 15 Fed. Cas. 1183 (1798).

31   "The Arrest of Vallandigham," *Harper's Weekly*, May 30, 1863, at 338.

32   "Arbitrary Arrests: Meeting in Troy," *Albany Argus*, May 28, 1863, at 4. U.S. Const., art. III, sec. 3, provides: "Treason against the United States, shall consist only in levying War against them, or in adhering to their Enemies, giving them Aid and Comfort. No person shall be convicted of Treason unless on the Testimony of two Witnesses to the same overt Act, or on Confession in open Court." On the treason clause as a free speech guarantee, see William T. Mayton, "Seditious Libel and the Lost Guarantee of a Freedom of Expression," 84 *Colum. L. Rev.* 91 (1984); for a dis-

cussion of treason at English law and the background of American guarantees, see Alexander H. Shapiro, "Political Theory and the Growth of Defensive Safeguards in Criminal Procedure: The Origins of the Treason Trials Act of 1696," 11 *Law and Hist. Rev.* 215 (1993).

33 "The Voice of Reason," *National Intelligencer*, May 16, 1863, at 3 (reprinted from the *N.Y. Evening Post*).

34 Id. See also "The Vallandigham Case" (Speech of former Governor Washington Hunt), *Albany Argus*, May 22, 1863, at 2.

35 "Vallandigham," *N.Y. Daily Tribune*, May 15, 1863, at 4.

36 "Gov. Seymour on Vallandigham's Arrest," *N.Y. Daily Tribune*, May 18, 1863, at 4. Curiously, the *N.Y. Tribune* rejected the claim that Vallandigham could not be amenable to military authority. Id.

37 " 'The Traitor Vallandigham,' from the *Boston Pioneer* (German Abolition Paper)," *Detroit Free Press*, May 27, 1863, at 2.

38 "From the *Bedford (Rep.) Standard*," *Detroit Free Press*, May 27, 1863, at 2.

39 "Alexander Samuel Diven," 3 *DAB*, supra note 12, at 322 (1931).

40 "Remarks of Col. A. S. Diven, at the Republican Meeting at the Capitol, May 20, 1863," *Albany Argus*, May 22, 1863, at 2.

41 "The Vindication of the Right of Free Speech," *Detroit Free Press*, May 28, 1863, at 2.

42 David Rabban, *Free Speech in Its Forgotten Years* 32–33 (1997), citing Martin Henry Blatt, *Free Love and Anarchism: The biography of Ezra Heywood* 29–31 (1989).

43 "Wanted: Free Speech!" *Albany Argus*, May 20, 1863, at 2.

44 "The Mask Off," *Chicago Tribune*, May 30, 1863, at 2.

45 "The *Chicago Times*, That Crowd," *Cincinnati Commercial*, June 5, 1863, at 2 (from the *Chicago Tribune*).

46 "The Limitations of Criticism," *National Intelligencer*, June 10, 1863, at 3; "Senator Trumbull's Chicago Speech," *Cincinnati Commercial*, June 11, 1863, at 2.

47 "Senator Trumbull's Chicago Speech," *Cincinnati Commercial*, June 11, 1863, at 2.

48 Id.

49 "Speech of Hon. Geo. V. N. Lothrop," *Detroit Free Press*, June 7, 1863, at 2.

50 "From the *Bedford (Rep.) Standard*," *Detroit Free Press*, May 27, 1863, at 2.

51 "Arbitrary Arrests: Meeting in Troy," *Albany Argus*, May 28, 1863, at 4.

52 "Mass Meeting of the Citizens of Erie County," *Albany Argus*, June 5, 1863, at 2; Francis Bergan, *The History of the New York Court of Appeals, 1847–1932*, at 112–13 (1985).

53 "The Vindication of the Right of Free Speech," *Detroit Free Press*, May 28, 1863, at 2. To the same effect, see "Arbitrary Arrests: Meeting in Troy," *Albany Argus*, May 28, 1863, at 4.

54 "Wirt Dexter," 3 *DAB* 283–83 (1958–59).

55 "Free Speech—Free Press: Immense Meeting at Chicago," *Detroit Free Press*, June 6, 1863, at 1.

56 "Senator Trumbull's Chicago Speech," *Cincinnati Commercial*, June 11, 1863, at 2.

57 "Free Speech," *Detroit Free Press*, May 26, 1863, at 2 (quoting the *N.Y. J. of Commerce*).

58 "'The Traitor Vallandigham,' from the *Boston Pioneer* (German abolition paper)," *Detroit Free Press*, May 27, 1863, at 2.

59 "Declaring Disloyal Sentiments," *National Intelligencer*, May 14, 1863, at 3. See also "An Irrepressible in Freedom of Speech," *Cincinnati Enquirer*, June 4, 1863, at 2.

60 "Argument of James F. Joy," *Detroit Free Press*, June 9, 1863, at 2.

61 E.g., Akhil Reed Amar, *The Bill of Rights: Creation and Reconstruction* 36 (1998) (views of the framers and ratifiers of the original Constitution); Michael Kent Curtis, "The Curious History of Attempts to Suppress Antislavery Speech in 1835–37," *Nw. U. L. Rev.* 785, at 794–96, 817–36 (1995); chapters 2, 3, and 6–11 in this volume.

62 "Argument of James F. Joy," *Detroit Free Press*, June 9, 1863, at 2.
   "The right [of free speech] contended for by us is as clear now in the loyal States as in times of peace," said Mr. Ganson, a speaker at a protest meeting in Erie County New York. If it is abused, the offender can be punished under the civil laws." "Where is our boasted right of free speech," said Sandford Church, another speaker at the meeting, "if it is left to any man as to say what may and what may not be spoken?" "Mass Meeting of the Citizens of Erie County," *Albany Argus*, June 5, 1863, at 2.

63 "The Limitations of Criticism," *National Intelligencer*, June 10, 1863, at 3.

64 "Free Speech," *Chicago Tribune*, June 1, 1863, at 2 (emphasis added).

65 Id.

66 "Immense Union Mass-Meeting in Fifth Street Market-Space, Last Night: Great Speech of the Hon. John Brough," *Cincinnati Commercial*, July 28, 1863, at 2.

67 "Free Speech," *N.Y. Daily Tribune*, May 20, 1863, at 4.

68 Id.

69 Id. "Free Speech," *N.Y. Daily Tribune*, May 20, 1863, at 4.

70 "Respect for Law," *National Intelligencer*, May 27, 1863, at 3.

71 "Headquarters Department of the Ohio, Cincinnati, Ohio, May 11, 1863," *Detroit Free Press*, May 14, 1863, at 2.

72 "Military and Civil Law," *Chicago Tribune*, June 12, 1863, at 2. The *Tribune* published two additional and lengthy installments supporting the actions of the administration. "Military and Civil Law No. 2," *Chicago Tribune*, June 13, 1863, at 2 and "Military and Civil Law—No. 3," id. at 3.

73 "Extracts from the Speech of Jehu Baker," *Chicago Tribune*, June 19, 1863, at 3.

74 David Herbert Donald, *Lincoln* 285–86 (1995); "To Erastus Corning and Others," in Abraham Lincoln, *Speeches and Writings, 1859–65*, at 462 [hereafter *Lincoln Speeches*].

75 William G. Carleton, "Civil War Dissidence in the North: The Perspective of a Century," 65 *S. Atlantic Q.* 390, 400–01 (1966).

76 "What Will He Do With It?" *Detroit Free Press*, June 9, 1863, at 2. Craig D. Tenney in his very fine account of the case also concludes the political press was the main determinant of Lincoln's change of course. Craig D. Tenney, "To Suppress or Not to Suppress: Abraham Lincoln and the *Chicago Times*," 29 *Civ. War Hist.* 248, 259 (1981).

77 6 Roy Basler, ed. *The Collected Works of Abraham Lincoln* 326 (1956) [hereafter Lincoln, *Collected Works*].

78 Mark E. Neely Jr., *The Fate of Liberty, Abraham Lincoln and Civil Liberties*, 46 (1991) (quoting Lincoln's letter).

79 James G. Randall, *Constitutional Problems Under Lincoln* 167 at 495 (rev. ed. 1951) [hereafter Randall, *Constitutional Problems*].

80 "Military and Civil Law," *Chicago Tribune*, June 12, 1862, at 2; "Military and Civil Law—No. 3," *Chicago Tribune*, June 18, 1863, at 3.

81 William Whiting, *War Powers Under the Constitution of the United States* 168–69 (Boston, Lee and Shepard 1871) [hereafter Whiting, *War Powers*]. See also Harold Hyman's classic work, *A More Perfect Union: The Impact of the Civil War and Reconstruction on the Constitution* 124–40, at 132 (1975).

82 Whiting, *War Powers*, supra note 81, at 188.

83 Craig Davidson Tenney, "Major General A. E. Burnside and the First Amendment: A Case Study of Civil War Freedom of Expression" (1977, UMI Dissertation Services), quoting Whiting, *War Powers*, supra note 81, at 162.

84 Lorraine A. Williams, "Northern Intellectual Reaction to Military Rule During the Civil War," *The Historian* 334, 347 (1965), citing 7 *Harper's Weekly* 163 (1863) [hereafter Williams, "Northern Intellectuals"].

85 Williams, "Northern Intellectuals," supra note 84, at 334, 346–47, citing Ralph Waldo Emerson, "American Civilization," 9 *Atlantic Monthly* 508–09 (1862).

86 2 *Letter of the Committee, Union Pamphlets of the Civil War* 741–42 (Frank Freidel ed., 1967).

87 "Senator Trumbull's Chicago Speech," *Cincinnati Commercial*, June 11, 1863, at 2.

88 "The Voice of Reason" (reprinted from the *N.Y. Evening Post*) *National Intelligencer*, May 16, 1863, at 3.

89 "The Law in the Case" (reprinted from the *National Intelligencer*) *Albany Argus*, May 23, 1863, at 2. See also, e.g., "Speech of Hon. Geo. V. N. Lothrop," *Detroit Free Press*, June 7, 1863, at 2. See also "Remarks of Col. A. S. Diven, at the Republican Meeting at the Capitol, May 20, 1863," *Albany Argus*, May 22, 1863, at 2.

90 Randall, *Constitutional Problems*, supra note 79, at 164–65.

91 Id. at 167.

92 Lincoln, *Speeches*, supra note 74, at 458.

93 Id.

94 Id. at 459.

95 Id.

96 Abraham Lincoln, "Reply to Ohio Democrats," in *Lincoln Speeches*, supra note 74, at 468.

97 Id. at 469.

98 Id. at 460.

99 Id.

100 "The President's Claim of Power," *Detroit Free Press*, June 16, 1863, at 2.

101 Id.

102 "President Lincoln Answered," *Detroit Free Press*, July 7, 1863, at 2.

103 Id.

104 Id.

105 Id.

106 *Cong. Globe*, 38th Cong., 1st Sess. 1506 (1864).

107 Id. at 1546.

108 Id. at 1547.

109 Id. at 1581.

110 Id. at 879. The vote was forty-seven yeas and seventy-six nays, with Democrats voting yea and Republicans and all but one Unionist voting nay.

111 Id. at 1621.

112 Id. at 1577.

113 Id. at 1549.

114 Id.

115 Id. at 1619.

116 Id.

117 Id. at 1552, 1554.

118 Id. at 1577.

119 Id. at 1585.

120 Id.

121 Id. at 1585, 1586.

122 Id. at 1593.

123 Id. at 1634.

124 Id. at 1593 (Rep. Broomall).

125 "The Parliamentary Issue," *National Intelligencer*, Apr. 14, 1864, at 3.

126 "Republican Opinion" (reprinted from the *N.Y. Evening Post* of Apr. 11), *National Intelligencer*, Apr. 14, 1864, at 3.

127 "From the *N.Y. Evening Post* of April 12th," *National Intelligencer*, April 14, 1864, at 3.

128 U.S. Const. art. I, sec. 6(1): "[F]or any speech or debate in either House, they shall not be questioned in any other place." For the power to expel by a two-thirds vote, see Article I, Section 5, Clause 1.

129 "From the *New York Times* of April 12th," *National Intelligencer*, Apr. 14, 1864, at 3.

130 Id.

131 "From the *New York Times* of April 13th," *National Intelligencer*, Apr. 14, 1864, at 3.

132 E.g., "From the *New York Commercial Advertiser* of April 12th; Freedom of Debate," *National Intelligencer*, Apr. 14, 1864, at 3.

133 See, e.g., Brandenburg v. Ohio, 395 U.S. 444, 448, (1969) citing Bond v. Floyd, 385 U.S. 116 (1966); West Virginia Board of Education v. Barnette, 319 U.S. 624, 642 (1943).

134 See *Ex parte* Milligan, 71 U.S. 2, 136 (1866); Korematsu v. United States, 323 U.S. 214 (1944).

135 Friedrich A. von Hayek, *The Constitution of Liberty* 109 (1960). See also American Booksellers v. Hudnut, 771 F.2d 323, 332 (7th Cir. 1985): "Free speech has been on balance an ally of those seeking change."

136 "Speech of Daniel W. Voorhees," *Cincinnati Commercial*, Sept. 17, 1863, at 1.

137 Lincoln, *Speeches*, supra note 74, at 460–61.

138 For a comparison of World War I and Civil War "disloyalty" issues, written in 1919 by conservative historian William A. Dunning, see "Disloyalty in Two Wars," 24 *Am. Hist. Rev.* 625 (1919).

139 "Response to Serenade, Washington, D.C., October 19, 1864," Lincoln, *Speeches*, supra note 74, at 635–36.

140 8 Lincoln, *Collected Works*, supra note 77, at 100–01.

141 "Address of the Mayor to the Police," *Cincinnati Commercial*, Aug. 20, 1863, at 2.

142 "What Will He Do with It?" *Detroit Free Press*, June 9, 1863, at 2.

143 "Our Washington Correspondent," *National Anti-Slavery Standard*, June 13, 1863, at 3. The correspondent suggested that there should be no interference with the press except by law and through the courts.

144 "Free Speech, Free Press," *Detroit Free Press*, June 6, 1863, at 1.

145 "The *Chicago Times* Case," *N.Y. Daily Tribune*, June 16, 1863, at 4.

146 Stanley Fish, *There's No Such Thing As Free Speech and It's a Good Thing Too* 102 (1994).

147 Id. at 114.

148 "Respect for Law," *National Intelligencer*, May 27, 1863, at 3.

149 E.g., Michael Kent Curtis, "The Curious History," 89 *Nw. U. L. Rev.* 785, 817–36 (1995); chapters 6–11 in this volume.

150 "Free Speech—Free Press," *Detroit Free Press*, June 6, 1863, at 1.

151 Paul Finkelman, "Civil Liberties and the Civil War: The Great Emancipator as Civil Libertarian," 91 *Mich. L. Rev.* 1353, 1356 (1993).

152 Stuart Sutherland, *Irrationality: The Enemy Within* 28 (1992).

153 The Prize Cases, 67 U.S. 636 (1863). The Justices who dissented from the decision, holding that Lincoln (rather than Congress) had the power to blockade Southern ports, said that the laws of war (including civil wars) "convert every citizen of a hostile state into a public enemy." Id. at 693.

154 See *Cong. Globe*, 26th Cong., 1st Sess. 410–14, 478 (1840) reporting that Congress voted to refund Matthew Lyon's Sedition Act fine because the Sedition Act was unconstitutional.

155 Civil Liberties Act of 1988, P. L. 100–383, 102 Stat. 904.

16 A NEW BIRTH OF FREEDOM?

1 James McPherson, *Abraham Lincoln and the Second American Revolution* 23–42, 131–52 (1991).

2 The metaphor comes from Randy E. Barnett, "Reconceiving the Ninth Amendment," 74 *Cornell L. Rev.* 1, 23–25 (1988).

3 See, e.g., *Cong. Globe*, 38th Cong., 1st Sess. 2979 (1864) (comments of Rep. Farnsworth); id. at 1202 (Rep. Wilson); *Cong. Globe*, 38th Cong., 2d Sess. 193 (1865) (Rep. Kasson).

4 E.g., "Proposed Report of Mr. Hall (of Vt.) On Incendiary Publications," *Daily Nat'l Intelligencer*, Apr. 8, 1836, at 2.

5 1 *Documentary History of Reconstruction* 279–81 (Walter L. Fleming ed., 1906). Petitions presented by lawmakers from citizens demanded protection for rights of

speech, press, assembly, and the right to bear arms. *Cong. Globe*, 39th Cong., 1st Sess. 337 (1866) (Sen. Sumner); id. at 494 (Sen. Howard); see also id. at 462 (Rep. Baker) ("[T]he American citizen shall no more be degraded . . . by being required to surrender his conscience as a peace-offering to . . . an . . . aristocracy of class"); id. at 1617 (Rep. Moulton) (complaining of outrages against Union men and freedmen; "There is neither freedom of speech, of the press, or protection to life, liberty, or property"); id. at 1629 (Rep. Hart) (insisting on the need to ensure that rebel states have a government that respects guarantees in the Bill of Rights); id. at 1837 (Rep. Clarke) (need for "irreversible guarantees" of civil liberty, including for rights recognized and secured by the Constitution). For a fuller review, see Michael Kent Curtis, *No State Shall Abridge: The Fourteenth Amendment and the Bill of Rights* 34–91 (1986) [hereafter Curtis, *No State Shall Abridge*].

6   *Cong. Globe*, 39th Cong., 1st Sess. 432 (1866).

7   Id. at 1294 (Rep. James Wilson) and 1153, 1270 (Rep. Thayer).

8   Joseph B. James, *The Ratification of the Fourteenth Amendment* 1–10 (1984); Eric L. McKitrick, *Andrew Johnson and Reconstruction* 359–61, 448–85 (1960).

9   Lincoln, *Speeches and Writings, 1859–1865*, at 130, 150 (Don E. Fehrenbacher ed. 1989).

10   Henry Mayer, *All on Fire: William Lloyd Garrison and the Abolition of Slavery* 559–60, 568, 577 (1998).

11   Schuyler Colfax was Speaker of the House. Ellihu B. Washburne, Justin S. Morrill, and John A. Bingham were members of the Joint Committee who had endorsed the compendium. *Report of the Joint Committee on Reconstruction at the First Session, Thirty-Ninth Congress* at iii (Negro Universities Press 1969) (1866). For a list of congressional endorsers, see, e.g., "Hinton Helper's Infamous Book—What the Sixty-Eight Demand," *Raleigh Register*, Dec. 14, 1859, at 1.

12   E.g., *Cong. Globe*, 39th Cong., 1st Sess. 2765–66 (Sen. Howard); id. at 157–58, 1090, 2542–43 (Rep. Bingham); *Cong. Globe*, 42d Cong., 1st Sess. app. at 84 (1871) (Rep. Bingham).

13   Curtis, *No State Shall Abridge*, supra note 5, at 48–49, 53, 90.

14   Adamson v. California, 332 U.S. 46, 74 (1947) (Black, J., dissenting).

15   Raoul Berger, *Government by Judiciary: The Transformation of the Fourteenth Amendment* 145–46 (1977); 6 Charles Fairman, *History of the Supreme Court of the United States: Reconstruction and Reunion* 462, 1289 (1971). For a defense of Bingham from the ad hominem attacks of his critics, see Richard L. Aynes, "On Misreading John Bingham and the Fourteenth Amendment," 103 *Yale L.J.* 57 (1993). For a careful analysis of the post–Civil War constitutional amendments in light of the original Constitution and federalism, see Michael P. Zuckert, "Completing the Constitution: The Fourteenth Amendment and Constitutional Rights," 22 *Publius* 69 (spring 1992); see also Michael P. Zuckert, "Congressional Power Under the Fourteenth Amendment—The Original Understanding of Section Five," 3 *Const. Commentary* 123 (1986) and Michael Perry, *The Fourteenth Amendment and the Supreme Court* (1999).

16   2 *The Bill of Rights: A Documentary History* 1027 (Bernard Schwartz ed., 1971) [hereafter Schwartz, *Documentary History*] ("No state shall violate the equal

rights of conscience, or the freedom of the press, or the trial by jury in criminal cases.").

17   *Cong. Globe*, 39th Cong., 1st Sess. 2542 (1866). See *Cong. Globe*, 39th Cong., 2d Sess. 810–11 (Reps. Kasson and Bingham). Stephen P. Halbrook, *The Freedmen, The Fourteenth Amendment, and the Right to Bear Arms, 1866–1876*, at 62–64 (1998) [hereafter Halbrook, *Freedmen*].

18   *Cong. Globe*, 39th Cong., 1st Sess. 2765–66 (1866).

19   Curtis, *No State Shall Abridge*, supra note 5, at 89–91, 131–53. But see, e.g., *Cong. Globe*, 39th Cong., 1st Sess. app. 219 (1866) (Sen. Howe) (referring in connection with privileges and immunities to the protection of equal laws and citing the rights of citizenship as including the right to testify, hold property, and to bring court actions).

20   Curtis, *No State Shall Abridge*, supra note 5, ch. 5.

21   *N.Y. Daily Tribune*, Sept. 4, 1866, at 1, col. 4.

22   *Philadelphia Inquirer*, Aug. 25, 1866, at 2, cols. 1–2.

23   *Newark Daily Advertiser*, Sept. 7, 1866, at 1, col. 7.

24   *N.Y. Daily Tribune*, Sept. 11, 1866, at 5, cols. 1–2.

25   Curtis, *No State Shall Abridge*, supra note 5, ch. 5.

26   *Cong. Globe*, 42d Cong., 1st Sess. app. at 84 (1871).

27   Curtis, *No State Shall Abridge*, supra note 5, at 161; *Cong. Globe*, 42d Cong., 1st Sess. app. at 84 (1871).

28   *Cong. Globe*, 42d Cong., 1st Sess. 334 (Rep. Hoar) (1871); id. at 475–76 (Rep. Dawes); id. at 370 (Rep. Monroe); see id. at 382 (Rep. Hawley) and 414 (Rep. Roberts) (referring to freedom of speech); *Cong. Globe*, 41st Cong., 3d Sess. 1245 (1871) (Rep. Lawrence) (referring to civil jury trial). See also *Cong. Globe* 41st Cong., 2d Sess. 515 (1870) (Sen. Fowler) and app. 310 (1871) (Maynard); *Cong. Globe*, 42d Cong., 2d Sess. 843–44 (1872) (Sen. Sherman). See also 2 *Cong. Rec.* 384–85 (Rep. Mills), and id. at app. 241–42 (Sen. Norwood) (1874). But cf., e.g., *Cong. Globe*, 42d Cong., 1st Sess. app. 113–17 (1871) (Rep. Farnsworth) and id. 149–54 (Rep. Garfield). See generally, Curtis, *No State Shall Abridge*, supra note 5, ch 6.

29   *Cong. Globe*, 39th Cong., 1st Sess. app. 133 (1866) (Rep. Rogers); id. at 1270 (Rep. Kerr).

30   Id. at 1290–91.

31   2 *Cong. Rec.* 384–85 (1874) (Rep. Mills); id. at app. 241–42 (Sen. Norwood); Curtis, *No State Shall Abridge*, supra note 5, at 166–68.

32   Timothy Farrar, *Manual of the Constitution of the United States of America* (Boston, Little, Brown 1867). In the 1872 edition of his work, Farrar acknowledged decisions that held that states were not bound by the guarantees of the federal Bill of Rights. He concluded that all those decisions were "entirely swept away" by the Fourteenth Amendment. See also, George W. Paschal, *The Constitution of the United States Defined and Carefully Annotated* 290 (Washington, D.C., W. H. and O. H. Morrison 1868) and John Norton Pomeroy, An *Introduction to the Constitutional Law of the United States* 147–53 (New York, Hurd and Houghton 1886) (1868). See also Curtis, *No State Shall Abridge*, supra note 5, at 173. See Richard L.

Aynes, "On Misreading John Bingham and the Fourteenth Amendment," 103 *Yale L.J.* 57, 83–92 (1993). On Cooley, see, Everett S. Brown, "The Contribution of Thomas M. Cooley to Bryce's *American Commonwealth*," 31 *Mich. L. Rev.* 346, 352 (1933). Thomas Cooley's 1868 *Constitutional Limitations* seems not to have addressed the meaning of Section 1. Thomas Cooley, *Constitutional Limitations* (Legal Classics Library 1987) (1868). But see 2 Joseph Story, *Commentaries on the Constitution of the United States* sec. 1937 (Thomas Cooley ed., Boston, Little, Brown 1873) which is consistent with the analysis in *Slaughter-House*.

33 2 Schwartz, *Documentary History*, supra note 16, at 1028 (emphasis added). For support for reading the privileges of the Fourteenth Amendment as including free speech and press, among others, see, e.g., Akhil Reed Amar, *The Bill of Rights: Creation and Reconstruction* 163–80, 181–214 (1998); Michael Kent Curtis, "Historic Linguistics, Inkblots, and Life After Death: The Privileges or Immunities of Citizens of the United States," 78 *N.C. Law Rev.* 1071 (2000); Curtis, *No State Shall Abridge*, supra note 5, at 24–25, 43–44, 49, 53–54, 64–65, 74–76, 88, 161–62 (1986); for an elegant textual argument that the Fourteenth Amendment applies the privileges of American citizens in the Bill of Rights to the states, see Amar, *The Bill of Rights*, supra at 163–180.

34 2 Schwartz, *Documentary History*, supra note 16, at 1033 (emphasis added).

35 "Spirit of the Times, Kentucky," *Independent Chronicle* (Boston), Sept. 24–27, 1798, at 1; "Spirit of the Times, Kentucky," *Independent Chronicle* (Boston) Oct. 1–4, 1798, at 1. See "Kentucky," *Independent Chronicle* (Boston), Oct. 18–22, 1798, at 1; "Virginia," *Independent Chronicle* (Boston), Oct. 8–11, 1798, at 1; "Spirit of the Times, Knoxville," *Independent Chronicle* (Boston), Nov. 15–19, 1798, at 1; "Spirit of the Times, Albany," *Independent Chronicle* (Boston), Dec. 6–10, 1798, at 1. 5 *Annals of Cong.* 2151 (1798) (Otis); "No. III, On the Election of the President of the United States," *Aurora*, Oct. 21, 1800, at 3. For the usage in connection with the Lovejoy tragedy, see chapter 10 of this book.

36 *Cong. Globe*, 36th Cong., 1st Sess. app. 202, 205, 207.

37 *Cong. Globe*, 38th Cong., 1st Sess. 1202 (1864).

38 "Free Speech—Free Press," *Detroit Free Press*, June 6, 1863, at 1 (quoting the *Chicago Times*) (emphasis added).

39 For alternative understandings of the privileges or immunities clause of Section 1, cf., e.g., Raoul Berger, *Government by Judiciary*, ch. 8 (1977); John Harrison, "Reconstructing the Privileges or Immunities Clause," 101 *Yale L.J.* 1385 (1992); David Currie, *The Constitution in the Supreme Court: The First Hundred Years* 342–51 (1985); James E. Bond, *No Easy Walk to Freedom: Reconstruction and Ratification of the Fourteenth Amendment* (1997).

40 For support for an antidiscrimination reading see, e.g., William E. Nelson, *The Fourteenth Amendment: From Political Principle to Judicial Doctrine*, ch. 6 (1988).

41 See, e.g., *Cong. Globe*, 39th Cong., 1st Sess. 2511 (Rep. Elliot) (1866); id. at app. 219 (Sen. Howe) (referring, in connection with privileges and immunities, to the protection of equal laws and citing the rights of citizenship as including the right to testify, hold property, and to bring court actions).

42 Cf., id. at 1835 (Rep. Lawrence); id. at 1117–18 (Rep. Wilson).

43 Jay S. Bybee, "Taking Liberties with the First Amendment: Congress, Section 5, and the Religious Freedom Restoration Act," 48 *Vand. L. Rev.* 1539, 1555 (1995).

44 E.g., *Cong. Globe*, 39th Cong., 1st Sess. 2883 (1866) (Rep. Latham).

45 On the significance of this language, see Aviam Soifer, "Protecting Civil Rights: A Critique of Raoul Berger's History," 54 *N.Y.U. L. Rev.* 651, 683–84 (1979).

46 Dred Scott v. Sandford, 60 U.S. at 449–50 (1856); Curtis, *No State Shall Abridge*, supra note 5, at 72. Robert Kaczorowski, "Revolutionary Constitutionalism in the Era of the Civil War and Reconstruction," 61 *N.Y.U. L. Rev.* 863, 923, 932 (1986). James Kent, "Of the Absolute Rights of Persons," in 2 *Commentaries on American Law* 9–11 (New York, O. Halsted 1827); *Cong. Globe*, 39th Congress, 1st Sess. 1117 (Rep. Wilson) and 1757 (Sen. Trumbull) both citing Chancellor Kent. James Kent, "Lecture 24," in 1 *Commentaries on American Law* 599–648 (New York: William Kent, 1854).

47 See generally, Curtis, *No State Shall Abridge*, supra note 5, at 41–56.

48 *Cong. Globe*, 39th Cong., 1st Sess. 2332 (1866) (Sen. Dixon); cf. also id. at 2465 (Rep. Thayer); 2468 (Rep. Kelly), suggesting that the provisions of Section 1—which include requiring states to accord due process—may already be in the Constitution); 2539 (Rep. Farnsworth—all provisions in Section 1 are in the Constitution already—which would include the due process clause as a limit on the states—except for equal protection).

49 Horace E. Flack, *The Adoption of the Fourteenth Amendment* 42 (1908); Akhil Reed Amar, *The Bill of Rights: Creation and Reconstruction* 245 (1998); see also *Cong. Globe*, 39th Cong., 2d Sess. 115–16 (1866) (Rep. Ward); Halbrook, *Freedmen*, supra note 17, at 31 and at 60 (citing "The Civil Rights Bill in the Senate," *N.Y. Evening Post*, Apr. 7, 1855, at 2, and remarks of Rep. Ward).

50 E.g., *Cong. Globe*, 36th Cong., 1st Sess. 931 (Rep. Edgerton) (1860); id. at 1872 (Rep. Waldron); id. at app. 205 (Rep. Lovejoy); *Cong. Globe*, 38th Cong., 1st Sess. 1202 (1864) (Rep. Wilson); id. at 114–15, 1197 (Rep. Arnold); *Cong. Globe*, 39th Cong., 1st Sess. 1072 (Sen. Nye).

51 Eric Foner, "Reconstruction," in *The Reader's Companion to American History* 917, 920 (Eric Foner and John Garraty eds., 1991).

52 Robert C. Kaczorowski, *The Politics of Judicial Interpretation: The Federal Courts, Department of Justice, and Civil Rights, 1866–1876*, at 50–134 (1985) [hereafter Kaczorowski, *Politics*].

53 26 F. Cas. 79, 81–82 (C.C.S.D. Ala. 1871) (No. 15, 282).

54 Act of May 31, 1870, 16 Stat. 140, sec. 6.

55 Kaczorowski, *Politics*, supra note 52, at 143.

56 A major recent reevaluation of the *Slaughter-House Cases* appears in Richard L. Aynes, "Constricting the Law of Freedom: Justice Miller, the Fourteenth Amendment, and the *Slaughter-House Cases*," 70 *Chi.-Kent. L. Rev.* 627 (1994). The most novel and powerful aspect of Aynes's important analysis is his historical attempt to explain why the majority reached the conclusion it did. A full discussion of the Court's transformation of the Fourteenth Amendment including a fine discussion

of the *Slaughter-House Cases* appears in W. W. Crosskey, *Politics and the Constitu- tion* 1119–58 (1953). For a novel, but I think ultimately unpersuasive, suggestion that Miller in *Slaughter-House* did read the Fourteenth Amendment as incorpo- rating the Bill of Rights, see Robert C. Palmer, "The Parameters of Constitutional Reconstruction: *Slaughter-House*, Cruikshank, and The Fourteenth Amend- ment," 1984 *U. Ill. L. Rev.* 739 (1984).

57 *Slaughter-House*, 83 U.S. 36, 67 (1872).

58 Id. at 71–72.

59 Id. at 70.

60 Richard Sewell, *Ballots for Freedom* 284 (1976).

61 83 U.S. at 123 (Bradley, J., dissenting).

62 83 U.S. at 74.

63 83 U.S. at 77.

64 Id.

65 *Slaughter-House*, 83 U.S. at 79.

66 *Cong. Globe*, 39th Cong., 1st Sess. 1115 (1866) (Rep. James Wilson).

67 83 U.S. at 129 (Swayne, J., dissenting).

68 Id. at 82.

69 "*Slaughter-House Cases* Brief for Defendants," in 6 *Landmark Briefs* 587–601; Lochner v. New York, 198 U.S. 45 (1905).

70 92 U.S. 542 (1876).

71 Id. at 550–51.

72 32 U.S. 243 (1833).

73 United States v. Cruikshank, 92 U.S. at 552.

74 Id. at 553.

75 Id.

76 *Cruikshank*, 92 U.S. at 552–53: "The right of the people peaceably to assemble for the purpose of petitioning Congress for a redress of grievances, or for anything else connected with the powers or the duties of the National Government, is an attribute of national citizenship, and, as such, under the protection of, and guar- antied by, the United States. The very idea of a government, republican in form, implies a right on the part of its citizens to meet peaceably for consultation in re- spect to public affairs and to petition for a redress of grievances. If it had been al- leged in these counts that the object of the defendants was to prevent a meeting for such a purpose, the case would have been within the statute, and within the scope of the sovereignty of the United States."

77 U.S. Const. art. IV, sec. 4.

78 *Cruikshank*, 92 U.S. at 553–54.

79 Of the prototype, Representative Hale said: "I submit it is in effect a provision un- der which all State legislation, in its codes of civil and criminal jurisprudence and procedure, affecting the individual citizen, may be overridden and the law of Con- gress established instead." Hale was not upset with a plan to require states to obey the Bill of Rights, because he thought (mistakenly) that existing law already made the Bill of Rights a limit on the states. *Cong. Globe*, 39th Cong. 1st Sess. 1063–64

(1866). On Hale's concern for federalism, see id. at 1065. For Giles Hotchkiss's two objections to the prototype, id. at 1095; Senator Steward suggested that the prototype would "obviate the necessity of . . . any more State Legislatures." Id. at 1082.

80 The state action question is complex, and the discussion here is incomplete. Of course, the Fourteenth Amendment debates highlight Republican concern with preserving Federalism. Advocates of a strong state action limit point to the change in the form of the Fourteenth Amendment from one giving Congress power to legislate generally to secure equal protection, etc. to one establishing citizenship, putting limits on states, and providing power to enforce these provisions. Even advocates of a stronger state action limit might concede that state inaction—failure to protect—might trigger congressional power.

Abolitionist legal theorist Joel Tiffany in his 1849 *Treatise on the Unconstitutionality of Slavery* (Mnemosyne Pub. Co. 1969) (1849) argued (before the Fourteenth Amendment) that the provisions of the Bill of Rights limited the states and that Congress had power to enforce the guarantees, if states by positive enactments had authorized a violation of basic rights. Id. at 55–57, 85.

81 Act of May 31, 1870, 16 Stat. 140, sec. 6 (emphasis added).

82 Act of April 20 1871, 17 Stat. 13 (emphasis added).

83 E.g., *Cruikshank*, 92 U.S. at 552–54.

84 See, e.g., Near v. Minnesota, 283 U.S. 697 (1931); Duncan v. Louisiana, 391 U.S. 145 (1968).

17 Where Are They Now?

1 See generally, Edward J. Bloustein, "The First Amendment 'Bad Tendency' of Speech Doctrine," 43 *Rutgers L. Rev.* 507, 510–11 (1991); see also, Zechariah Chafee Jr., *Freedom of Speech* 24–34, 55–56 (1920).

2 Abraham Lincoln, "Reply to the Ohio Democratic Convention," in *Speeches and Writings, 1859–1865*, at 468–69 (Library of America, Don E. Fehrenbacher ed., 1989).

3 Id. at 460.

4 This account is taken from Lucas A. Powe Jr., *The Fourth Estate and the Constitution: Freedom of the Press in America* (1991).

5 Id. at 2–6.

6 Id. at 1, 15.

7 Patterson v. Colorado, 205 U.S. 454, 462–63 (1906) (emphasis added).

8 Id.

9 2 Sir James Stephen, *A History of the Criminal Law of England* 299–300 (1883). See Zechariah Chafee Jr., *Free Speech in the United States* 22 (1941) [hereafter Chafee, *Free Speech*]; Thomas M. Cooley, *A Treatise on the Constitutional Limitations Which Rest upon the Legislative Power of the States of the American Union* 420–21, 426–40 (Legal Classics Library 1987) (1868).

10 E.g., Sheppard v. Maxwell, 384 U.S. 333 (1966).

11 Marshall v. Gordon, 243 U.S. 521 (1917).

12 Gandia v. Pettingill, 222 U.S. 452, 457 (1912); Michael Gibson, "The Supreme Court and Freedom of Expression from 1791 to 1917," 55 *Fordham L. Rev.* 263, 283 (1986). See also United States v. Smith, 173 F. 227 (1909); United States v. Press Publishing Co., 219 U.S. 1 (1911).

13 Commonwealth v. Karvonen, 219 Mass. 30, 106 N.E. 556, 557 (1914).

14 David Rabban, *Free Speech in Its Forgotten Years,* ch. 3 (1998) [hereafter Rabban, *Free Speech*].

15 Act of June 15, 1917, ch. 30, title I, sec. 3.

16 40 Stat. 553 (1918); Chafee, *Free Speech*, supra note 9, at 39–41 (1941).

17 Chafee, *Free Speech*, supra note 9, at 50.

18 Id. at 51–56, citing among other cases, State v. Freersk, 140 Minn. 349 (1918); Friana v. United States, 255 Fed. 28 (2d Cir. 1918); Goldstein v. United States, 258 Fed. 908 (9th Cir. 1919); Doe v. United States, 253 Fed. 903 (8th Cir. 1918).

19 See *Ex parte* Starr, 263 F. 145 (D. Mont. 1920).

20 Schenck v. United States, 249 U.S. 47, 51 (1919). For accounts of the Progressive view of free speech, the World War I era, and the transformation of the thought of Justices Holmes and Brandeis, see Rabban, *Free Speech*, supra note 9, at 211–393 (1997) and Mark A. Graber, *Transforming Free Speech: The Ambiguous Legacy of Civil Libertarianism*, ch. 3 (1991) [hereafter Graber, *Transforming Free Speech*].

21 249 U.S. at 52.

22 249 U.S. 211 (1919).

23 Id. at 214.

24 Harry Kalven, "Ernst Freund and the First Amendment Tradition," 40 *U. Chi. L. Rev.* 235, 237 (1973).

25 For a full discussion of the World War I cases, scholarly criticism of them, Professor Chafee's role in revising the clear and present danger test, and the growth of the modern civil liberties movement see Rabban, *Free Speech*, supra note 14, chs. 6 and 7 (1998).

26 Ernst Freund, "The *Debs Case* and Freedom of Speech," *New Republic*, May 3, 1919, at 13, reprinted in 40 *U. Chi. L. Rev.* 235, 239–42 (1973).

27 Walter Nelles, "*Espionage Act Cases*" 77–78, 80 (1918) in William Lockhart et. al, *Constitutional Rights and Liberties: Cases and Materials* 358–59 (3d ed. 1970).

28 Graber, *Transforming Free Speech*, supra note 20, at 38–39 (1991).

29 Masses Publishing Co. v. Patten, 244 F. 535 (S.D.N.Y. 1917), rev. 246 Fed. 24 (2d Cir. 1917); Gerald Gunther, Document 4, "Hand to Holmes, March 1919" in "Learned Hand and the Origins of Modern First Amendment Doctrine: Some Fragments of History," 27 *Stan. L. Rev.* 719, 758 (1975).

30 Zechariah Chafee Jr., *Freedom of Speech*, 8–9 and n.12 (1920) [hereafter Chafee, *Freedom of Speech*] (citing *Patterson v. Colorado*); id. at 188 and n.36 (citing *Fox v. Washington*); id. at 90, criticizing the decision in *Debs v. United States*; 187 and n.32, citing *Comm. v. Karvonen*; cf. id. at 199.

31 Id. at 88–89, 15–16. Chafee's book benefited from criticisms of his earlier article, "Freedom of Speech in Wartime," 32 *Harv. L. Rev.* 932 (1919) and corrected some of its shortcomings. See Rabban, *Free Speech*, supra note 14, at 323–32.

32 Chafee, *Freedom of Speech*, supra note 30, at 16–27, 88–89, 213–14, 40–109, 294–365; Graber, *Transforming Free Speech*, supra note 20, at 84–85; Rabban, *Free Speech*, supra note 14, at chs. 5 and 9.

33 Cf. Chafee, *Freedom of Speech*, supra note 30, at 171 (discussing speech about sexual matters).

34 Rabban, *Free Speech*, supra note 14, at 4–8, 303, 316–35; Graber, *Transforming Free Speech*, supra note 20, chapter 4; Bridges v. California, 314 U.S. 252 (1941); Brandenburg v. Ohio, 395 U.S. 444, 449 (1969) (Black and Douglas, JJ., concurring); Hans A. Linde, "'Clear and Present Danger' Reexamined: Dissonance in the Brandenburg Concerto," 22 *Stan. L. Rev.* 1163 (1970); David R. Dow, "The Moral Failure of the Clear and Present Danger Test," 6 *Wm. & Mary Bill of Rts. J.* 733 (1998). On Holmes, see Gilbert v. Minnesota, 254 U.S. 325, 334 (1920); Graber, *Transforming Free Speech*, supra note 20, at 111.

35 Note 30, supra; Rabban, *Free Speech*, supra note 14, at 4–8, 316–36.

36 Whitney v. California, 274 U.S. 357, 371 (1927) (Brandeis, J., concurring); Rabban, *Free Speech*, supra note 14, at 356, 362, 369.

37 250 U.S. 616, 630 (1919) (Holmes, J., dissenting).

38 Id. at 630.

39 Id.

40 William Van Alstyne, *First Amendment, Cases and Materials* 189 n. 83 (2d ed. 1995).

41 268 U.S. 652 (1925).

42 Whitney v. California, 274 U.S. 357, at 375–77 (1927) (Brandeis, J., concurring).

43 Id. at 378, 376.

44 Id. at 371.

45 Gitlow v. New York, 268 U.S. 652, 669 (1925).

46 E.g., Herndon v. Lowry, 301 U.S. 242, 262 (1937); Stromberg v. California, 283 U.S. 359 (1931); De Jonge v. Oregon, 299 U.S. 353 (1937); Hague v. CIO, 307 U.S. 496 (1939); Schneider v. New Jersey, 308 U.S. 147 (1939).

47 Herndon v. Lowry, 301 U.S. 242, 262 (1937); Rabban, *Free Speech*, supra note 14, at 375 (1997).

48 301 U.S. 242, 262 (1937).

49 Bridges v. California, 314 U.S. 252, 263 (1941).

50 Dennis v. United States, 341 U.S. 494, 510 (1951)(opinion of Vinson, J.).

51 Id. at 545 (Frankfurter, J., concurring).

52 Id. at 549.

53 Memoirs v. Massachusetts, 383 U.S. 413 (1966); New York Times Co. v. Sullivan, 376 U.S. 254 (1964).

54 Bond v. Floyd, 385 U.S. 116, 120–25 (1966).

55 Id. at 134.

56 Brandenburg v. Ohio, 395 U.S. 444, 447 (1969); Texas v. Johnson, 491 U.S. 397, 409 (1989); NAACP v. Claiborne Hardware Co., 458 U.S. 886, 928 (1982). But the clear-and-present-danger principle did not hold up well when the threat of communism seemed great: see, Bridges v. California, 314 U.S. 252 (1941) (applying a strong version of the test to convictions for contempt of court for criticism directed at judicial action) and Dennis v. United States, 341 U.S. 494 (1951) (redefining the

clear-and-present-danger principle, for the purpose of prosecuting leaders of the Communist Party, to one where the improbability of an evil was discounted if the evil was very grave).

57 See Brandenburg v. Ohio, 395 U.S. 444, 447 (1969); Bond v. Floyd, 385 U.S. 116 (1966); Texas v. Johnson, 491 U.S. 397, 409 (1989) (statute forbidding flag burning deemed unconstitutional, it being a form of symbolic political expression); Cohen v. California, 403 U.S. 15, 24–26 (1971) (slogan "Fuck the Draft" on a jacket held protected in circumstances of that case); but see Dennis v. United States, 341 U.S. 494 (1951) (punishment for advocacy of revolution justifiable when evil is so grave that its improbability must be discounted, which is bad tendency slightly modified) and Korematsu v. United States, 323 U.S. 81 (1943) (executive order for incarceration of West Coast Japanese Americans upheld). For antecedents of the current approach, see Whitney v. California, 274 U.S. 357, 378 (1927) (Brandeis, J., concurring); cf. Masses Pub. Co. v. Patten, 244 F. 535 (1917).

58 Brandenburg v. Ohio, 395 U.S. 444, 446 (1969).

59 Id. at 447.

60 Dennis v. United States, 341 U.S. 494, 510 (1951) (opinion of Vinson, J.).

61 See Butler v. Michigan, 352 U.S. 280 (1957); Ginzberg v. New York, 390 U.S. 629, 638 (1968); Reno v. ACLU, 521 U.S. 844, 117 S.Ct. at 2346 (1997). See also Bolger v. Youngs Drug Products Corp., 463 U.S. 60, 74–75 (1983): "[R]egardless of the strength of the government's interest" in protecting children, "[t]he level of discourse reaching a mailbox simply cannot be limited to that which would be suitable for a sandbox."

62 403 U.S. 15 (1971).

63 Id. at 16.

64 Id.

65 Texas v. Johnson, 491 U.S. 397 (1989).

66 Id.; James M. McPherson, *Battle Cry of Freedom: The Civil War Era* 119–20; Phillip S. Paludan, *A Covenant with Death: The Constitution, Law, and Equality in the Civil War Era* 2–3 (1975).

67 Cantwell v. Conn., 310 U.S. 296, 310 (1940).

68 R. A. V. v. City of St. Paul, 505 U.S. 377, 414 (1992) (White, J., concurring). Justice White cited Texas v. Johnson, 491 U.S. 397, 409, 414 (1989); Hustler Magazine v. Falwell, 485 U.S. 46, 55–56 (1988) and Cohen v. California, 403 U.S. 15, 20 (1971).

69 Hustler v. Falwell, 485 U.S. at 55. For the paradoxical nature of rules need to protect public discourse, see Robert C. Post, "The Constitutional Concept of Public Discourse: Outrageous Opinion, Democratic Deliberation, and *Hustler Magazine v. Falwell*," 103 *Harv. L. Rev.* 601 (1990).

70 Compare, e.g., Pickering v. Board of Edu., 391 U.S. 563 (1968), with Harris v. Forklift Systems, Inc. 510 U.S. 17 (1993). See also, NLRB v. Gissel Packing Co., 395 U.S. 575 (1969).

71 West Virginia Bd. of Education v. Barnette, 319 U.S. 624, 638 (1943), overruling Minersville School District v. Gobitis, 310 U.S. 586 (1940).

72 319 U.S. at 639, 640.

73 Id. at 642.

74 "Proposed Report by Mr. Hall (of Vt.), on Incendiary Publications," *Daily Nat'l Intelligencer*, Apr. 8, 1836, at 2; *N.Y. Evening Post*, Aug. 8, 1835, at 2.

75 Edwards v. South Carolina, 372 U.S. at 238 (1963) and Bond v. Floyd, 385 U.S. at 134 (1966), citing Terminiello v. Chicago, 337 U.S. 1 (1949).

76 Brandenburg, v. Ohio, 395 U.S. 444 (1969), citing Bond v. Floyd, 385 U.S. 116 (1966); Texas v. Johnson, 491 U.S. 397, 409 (1989), citing *Brandenburg*.

77 5 *Correspondence of Andrew Jackson* 361 (John S. Bassett ed., 1931).

78 12 *Cong. Deb.* 1152 (Sen. Davis); id. at 1723 (Sen. Buchanan).

79 Lamont v. Postmaster General, 381 U.S. 301, 305, 306 (1965).

80 Cf., W. Page Keeton, Dan B. Dobbs, Robert E. Keeton, David G. Owen, *Prosser and Keeton on the Law of Torts* 784–85 (typically, no private civil action for group defamation) (1984).

81 Beauharnais v. Illinois, 343 U.S. 250, 252 (1952). Beauharnais was asking the city counsel to do something that was beyond its constitutional power. In 1917 the Supreme Court held municipal segregation of neighborhoods by race violated the Fourteenth Amendment. Buchanan v. Warley, 245 U.S. 60 (1917). See also the Civil Rights Act of 1866, now 42 U.S.C. 1981 and 1982, and Jones v. Alfred H. Mayer Co., 392 U.S. 409 (1968).

82 343 U.S. 250, 251.

83 Id. at 258.

84 Id. at 266, 263.

85 Id. at 265.

86 Philadelphia Newspapers v. Hepps, 475 U.S. 767 (1986).

87 343 U.S. 250 at 272.

88 376 U.S. 254, 270 (1964).

89 R.A.V. v. St. Paul, 505 U.S. 377 (1992).

90 376 U.S. 254 (1964).

91 376 U.S. 254, 269–71 (1964) (citation omitted).

92 Id.

93 Id. at 273.

94 98 P. 281, 289 (Kan. 1908).

95 Id. at 284 (citing Thomas Cooley, *Constitutional Limitations* 603, 604 (7th ed. 1903)).

96 376 U.S. at 280 and n.20.

97 Id. at 294, 295 (Black and Douglas, JJ., concurring). For a full discussion of the case and its history see Anthony Lewis, *Make No Law: The Sullivan Case and the First Amendment* (1991).

98 Akhil Reed Amar, *The Bill of Rights: Creation and Reconstruction* 307 (1998).

99 NAACP v. Button, 371 U.S. 415 (1963).

100 NAACP v. Alabama, 357 U.S. 449 (1958).

101 E.g., Edwards v. South Carolina, 372 U.S. 229 (1963); but see Adderley v. Florida, 385 U.S. 39 (1966).

CONCLUSION

1   Catharine A. MacKinnon, *Only Words* 74–77 (1993).

2   Robert Dahl, *Democracy and Its Critics* 112 (1989).

3   Id. at 114–15.

4   Some Southern courts did find for defendants charged under incendiary literature statutes, either because the statements did not violate the statute or for technical reasons. For cases from Southern courts, see State v. Worth, 52 N.C. 488 (1860); Commonwealth v. Barrett, 9 Leigh 665 (Va. 1839); Bacon v. Commonwealth, 7 Grat. 602 (Va. 1850); State v. McDonald, 4 Port. 449 (Ala. 1837); State v. Read, 6 La. Ann. 227 (1851).

5   E.g., Vernon L. Wharton, *The Negro in Mississippi, 1865–1890*, at 181–215 (1947); Eric Foner, *Reconstruction: America's Unfinished Revolution, 1863–1877*, at 412–60, 553–63 (1988); *Democracy Betrayed: The Wilmington Race Riot of 1898 and Its Legacy*, 15–38, 94–110 (David S. Cecelski and Timothy B. Tyson eds., 1998); Albion Tourgee, *The Invisible Empire* (Louisiana State Univ. Press 1989) (1880).

6   E.g., "Address to the Inhabitants of Quebec," in 1 *The Bill of Rights: A Documentary History* 223 (Bernard Schwartz ed., 1971); Tunis Wortman, *A Treatise Concerning Political Enquiry, and the Liberty of the Press* 146 (New York, George Forman 1800); "Sound the Alarm," 2 *Emancipator* 133 (Dec. 28, 1837) (quoting the *Herald of Freedom*); *Memoir of the Rev. Elijah P. Lovejoy* 300 (Joseph C. Lovejoy and Owen Lovejoy eds., Arno Press 1969) (1838); Seymour B. Treadwell, *American Liberties and American Slavery: Morally and Politically Illustrated* at xxxvii (Negro Univ. Press 1969) (1838); 2 St. George Tucker, *Tucker's Blackstone*, app. 11 (Law Book Exchange 1996) (1803).

7   "Vallandigham," *N.Y. Daily Tribune*, May 15, 1863, at 4.

8   Id.

9   Henry Mayer, *All on Fire: William Lloyd Garrison and the Abolition of Slavery* 120 (1998).

10   For a powerful explication of this idea, see Steven J. Heyman, "Righting the Balance: An Inquiry into the Foundations and Limits of Freedom of Expression," 78 *B.U. L. Rev.* 1275 (1998).

11   Schenck v. United States, 249 U.S. 47 (1919); Debs v. United States, 249 U.S. 211 (1919); *Ex parte* Starr, 263 F. 145 (D. Mont. 1920); Minersville School District v. Gobitis, 310 U.S. 586 (1939); Dennis v. United States, 341 U.S. 494 (1951).

12   For an example of the Southern claim see *Cong. Globe*, 24th Cong., 1st Sess. 120 (1836) (John C. Calhoun).

13   Robert Post, "Meiklejohn's Mistake: Individual Autonomy and the Reform of Public Discourse," 64 *Colo. L. Rev.* 1109, 1118 (1993); Robert A. Dahl, *Democracy and Its Critics* 109 (1989).

14   Elijah P. Lovejoy, "To My Fellow Citizens," *St. Louis Observer*, Nov. 5, 1835, reprinted in *Memoir of the Rev. Elijah P. Lovejoy* 143–44 (Joseph C. Lovejoy and Owen Lovejoy eds., Arno Press 1969) (1838). See also Mark A. Graber, "Old Wine in New Bottles: The Constitutional Status of Unconstitutional Speech," 48 *Vand. L. Rev.* 349 (1995); Eugene Volokh, "Freedom of Speech and the Constitutional

Tension Method," 3 *U. Chi. L. Sch. Roundtable* 223 ff. (1996); Michael Kent Curtis, "Critics of 'Free Speech' and the Uses of the Past," 12 *Const. Comm.* 29 (1995).

15 See Godcharles v. Wiegman, 6 A. 354 (1886) (striking down a law requiring manufacturing and mining companies to pay in cash rather than in vouchers redeemable only at the company store); Lochner v. New York, 198 U.S. 45 (1905) (striking down a sixty-hour week for bakers); Howard Gillman, *The Constitution Besieged: The Rise and Demise of Lochner Era Police Powers Jurisprudence* (1993); James Weaver, *Call to Action*, quoted in Norman Pollack, *The Just Polity* 63 (1987); Paul Kors, *Lochner v. New York: Economic Regulation on Trial* (1998).

16 Otto Olsen, *Carpetbagger's Crusade: The Life of Albion Winegar Tourgee* 285–86 (1965).

17 James Weaver, *Call to Action*, quoted in Norman Pollack, *The Just Polity* 63 (1987).

18 Theodore Roosevelt, "Address at San Francisco, Sept. 14, 1912," quoted in Howard Gilman, *The Constitution Besieged: The Rise and Demise of Lochner-Era Police Powers Jurisprudence* 151 (1993).

19 2 Karl Popper, *The Open Society and Its Enemies* 124–25 (1966).

20 Mark A. Graber, *Transforming Free Speech: The Ambiguous Legacy of Civil Libertarianism*, ch. 3 (1991); David M. Rabban, *Free Speech in Its Forgotten Years*, ch. 5 (1997).

21 See, e.g., Catharine A. MacKinnon, *Only Words* 104, 80–86 (1993) [hereafter MacKinnon, *Only Words*]; Robert Bork, "Neutral Principles and Some First Amendment Problems," 47 *Ind. L.J.* 1, 23–25 (1971).

22 E.g., Bill Moyers, *Free Speech for Sale*, documentary aired on PBS on June 8, 1999. See also, Dean Alger, *Megamedia: How Giant Corporations Dominate Mass Media, Distort Competition, and Endanger Democracy* (1998). On the importance of information to democracy see Robert A. Dahl, *Democracy and Its Critics* 112 (1989). On the problem of control of the flow of information for purposes of corporate profit, see, e.g., "Murdoch's Beijing Love-Fest," *Guardian* (London), Dec. 12, 1998, at 14. Seth Faison, "Dalai Lama Movie Imperils Disney Future in China," *N.Y. Times*, Nov. 26, 1996, at A1; see Kevin Sack, "Gingrich Attacks Media as Out of Touch," *N.Y. Times*, April 23, 1997, at D 21. Gingrich suggested that corporations use their economic power to try to improve news coverage; he noted that if the electric light were invented today, the media would cite Ralph Nader on the dangers of electrocution and another source on the threat to the jobs in the candle industry. "Is It a Crime to Criticize Food?" *Consumer Reports*, Sept. 1996, at 7; Geraldine Fabrikant, "Fox Drops Drama Based on Charge Against Thomas," *N.Y. Times*, Sept. 14, 1998, at C-1; Cf., G. Bruce Knecht, "Magazine Advertisers Demand Prior Notice of 'Offensive' Articles," *Wall St. J.*, Apr. 30, 1997, at 1; Michael Kent Curtis, "Monkey Trials: Science, Defamation, and the Suppression of Dissent," 4 *Wm. and Mary Bill of Rights J.* 507, 530–44, 557–65 (1995). See generally Tom Goldstein, "Does Big Mean Bad?" *Col. J. Rev.*, Sept./Oct. 1998, at 52. For poll results showing many Americans believe we have a democracy in name only, see E. Joshua Rosenkranz, *Buckley Stops Here: Loosening the Judicial Stranglehold on Campaign Finance Reform* 15–17 (1998). For similar poll results, see "What Americans Think," *Washington Post Wkly.*, May 17, 1999, at 34. On campaign finance see, e.g.,

Federal Election Commission v. National Conservative Political Action Committee, 470 U.S. 480, 517 (1985) (White, J., dissenting); Robert Kuttner, *Everything for Sale: The Virtues and Limits of Markets* 347 (1997); Robert B. Reich, "Party Favors," 73 *New Yorker* 11–12 (Oct. 13, 1997). See also Robert A. Dahl, *Democracy and Its Critics* 109 (1989).

23 1 Alexis de Tocqueville, *Democracy in America Chapter* 3, at 50 (Vintage Books, Random House 1945).

24 Stanley Elkins and Eric McKitrick, *The Age of Federalism* 267 (1993).

25 E.g., "Free Discussion," *Boston Daily Advocate*, Jan. 3, 1838, at 2; Cincinnatus, *Freedom's Defense* 14 (1936).

26 2 Abraham Lincoln, *The Collected Works of Abraham Lincoln* 406 (Roy Basler ed., 1953); 2 Abraham Lincoln, *Speeches, Letters, Miscellaneous Writings, 1859–1865* 134–35 (Don Fehrenbacher Comp., Library of America 1989).

27 Brandenburg v. Ohio, 595 U.S. 444 (1969). The *Brandenburg* principle seems not to apply when people teach the techniques of terror or killing and advocate their use. Cf., Scales v. United States, 367 U.S. 203 (1961); Rice v. Paladin Enterprises, 128 F. 3d 233 (4th Cir. 1997), cert. denied, 523 U.S. 1074 (1998).

28 State v. Worth, 52 N.C. 488 (1860); U.S. v. Cooper, 25 F. Cas. 631 (G.C. D. Pa. 1800).

29 6 *Cong. Debates* (*Annals of Cong.*) 1, at 93–96 (1800); *Gilbert v. Minnesota*, 254 U.S. 325 (1920).

30 Carol E. Jensen, "Agrarian Reforms and the Politics of Loyalty," in John W. Johnson, ed., *Historic U.S. Court Cases, 1690–1990: An Encyclopedia* 498 (1992).

31 "Letter of Dr. W. E. Channing to James G. Birney, Boston, Nov. 1st, 1836," *Philanthropist*, Dec. 9, 1836, at 2, reprinted in 2 William Ellery Channing, *The Works of William E. Channing*, 156, 162–63 (1980); W. Sherman Savage, *The Controversy over the Distribution of Abolition Literature, 1830–1860*, at 3–4 (1968).

32 Masses Publishing Co. v. Patten, 244 F. 535, 538 (S.D.N.Y. 1917), rev. 246 Fed. 24 (2d Cir. 1917).

33 Otto H. Olsen, *Carpetbagger's Crusade: The Life of Albion Winegar Tourgee* 114, 145 (1965); Albion Tourgee, *A Fool's Errand, by One of the Fools* 155–57, 166 (Ford, Howard, and Hulbert 1880) [hereafter Tourgee, *Fool's Errand*]; Michael Kent Curtis, "Albion Tourgee," 13 *Const. Comm.* 187, 195 (1996).

34 Tourgee, *Fool's Errand*, supra note 33, at 286–96, 339.

35 Cf., e.g., MacKinnon, *Only Words*, supra note 21, at 80–86; Mari J. Matsuda, "Public Response to Racist Speech: Considering the Victim's Story," 87 *Mich. L. Rev.* 2320, 2358–59 (1989). For critical appraisals, see Nadine Strossen, *Defending Pornography: Free Speech, Sex, and the Fight for Women's Rights* (1995); John M. Blim, "Undoing Ourselves: The Error of Sacrificing Speech in the Quest for Equality," 56 *Ohio St. L.J.* 427 (1995). See also Melvin I. Urofsky, Book Review, "Defending Pornography: Free Speech, Sex, and the Fight for Women's Rights," 29 *U. Rich. L. Rev.* 401 (1995). For a recent account, see James Weinstein, *Hate Speech, Pornography, and the Radical Attack on Free Speech Doctrine* (1999).

36 See chapters 8 and 9 of this book.

37 John M. Blim, "Undoing Ourselves: The Error of Sacrificing Speech in the Quest for Equality," 56 *Ohio St. L.J.* 427, 433 (1995). See also Mark A. Graber, "Old Wine

in New Bottles: The Constitutional Status of Unconstitutional Speech," 48 *Vand. L. Rev.* 349 (1995); C. Edwin Baker, "Of Course More Than Words," 61 *U. Chi. L. Rev.* 1181 (1994).

38 Seneca Falls Declaration of Sentiments and Resolutions (1848) in *Law and Jurisprudence in American History* 546 (Stephen Presser and Jamil Zainaldin eds., 1995).

39 In addition to this book, see also e.g., Clement Eaton, *The Freedom of Thought Struggle in the Old South* 124 (Harper and Row 1964) (1940); Zechariah Chafee Jr., *Free Speech in the United States* (1941). Vincent Blasi, "The Checking Value in First Amendment Theory," 1977 *A.B.F. Res. J.*, 521, and "The Pathological Perspective and the First Amendment," 85 *Col. L. Rev.* 449 (1985); "Steven Shiffrin, The Politics of the Mass Media and the Free Speech Principle," 69 *Ind. L.J.* 689 (1994); David M. Rabban, *Free Speech In Its Forgotten Years* (1998).

40 Renton Theatres, Inc. v. City of Renton, 475 U.S. 41 (1986); Alexander v. United States, 113 S.Ct. 2766 (1993).

41 Chapters 6–9 of this book.

42 See Robert Dahl, *Democracy and Its Critics* 305 (1989).

43 Nat Hentoff, "The Boy With a Confederate Flag on His Back," *Village Voice*, July 5, 1988, at 31. I appeared as counsel for students wearing the Confederate flag patch and played a part in crafting settlements that emphasized use of dialogue and techniques like mediation. The Confederate flag had very different meanings to some of the students wearing it and to black students.

INDEX

Michael Kent Curtis is Professor of Law at Wake Forest
University, where he teaches free speech, constitutional
law, and American constitutional and legal history.
He is the author of *No State Shall Abridge: The Fourteenth Amendment and the Bill of Rights*, which was
published by Duke University Press in 1986, and the
editor of *The Constitution and the Flag* (1993).

Library of Congress Cataloging-in-Publication Data
Curtis, Michael Kent
Free speech, "the people's darling privilege" :
struggles for freedom of expression in American
history / Michael Kent Curtis.
p. cm. — (Constitutional conflicts)
Includes bibliographical references and index.
ISBN 0-8223-2529-2 (cloth : alk. paper)
1. Freedom of speech—United States—History.
I. Title. II. Series.
KF4772 .C87 2000 342.73'0853—dc21 00-029394